THE SHAMAMA CASE

The Shamama Case

CONTESTING CITIZENSHIP ACROSS THE MODERN MEDITERRANEAN

JESSICA M. MARGLIN

PRINCETON UNIVERSITY PRESS
PRINCETON & OXFORD

Published by Princeton University Press
41 William Street, Princeton, New Jersey 08540
99 Banbury Road, Oxford OX2 6JX

press.princeton.edu

First paperback printing, 2025
Paper ISBN 9780691237138
Cloth ISBN 9780691235875
ISBN (e-book) 9780691235882
LCCN: 2021059946

British Library Cataloging-in-Publication Data is available

Editorial: Fred Appel and James Collier
Production Editorial: Jaden Young and Ali Parrington
Jacket/Cover Design: Chris Ferrante
Production: Erin Suydam
Publicity: Kate Hensley and Charlotte Coyne
Copyeditor: Cindy Milstein

Jacket/Cover Credit: David Rumsey Map Collection, David Rumsey Map Center, Stanford Libraries.

This book has been composed in Arno

For my parents

CONTENTS

Prologue: Death in Livorno xiii

Introduction: Legal Belonging across the Mediterranean 1

PART I. NISSIM SHAMAMA 11

1 Tunis (1805–59) 13

2 Financial Trouble (1859–64) 37

3 Tunis to Paris (1864–68) 58

4 Paris to Livorno (1868–73) 78

PART II. *SHAMAMA V. SHAMAMA* 93

5 Heirs Apparent (1873) 95

6 Conte Shamama the Italian 119

7 Qā'id Nissim the Tunisian 137

8 Rav Nissim the Jew 158

9 Lucca to Florence (1880–83) 178

PART III. AFTERLIVES 201

10 Descendants (1883–1945) 203

Epilogue: Legal Belonging, Past and Present 225

Afterword: Writing Nissim Shamama 233
Cast of Characters 239
Acknowledgments 245
Notes 249
Bibliography 325
Index 355

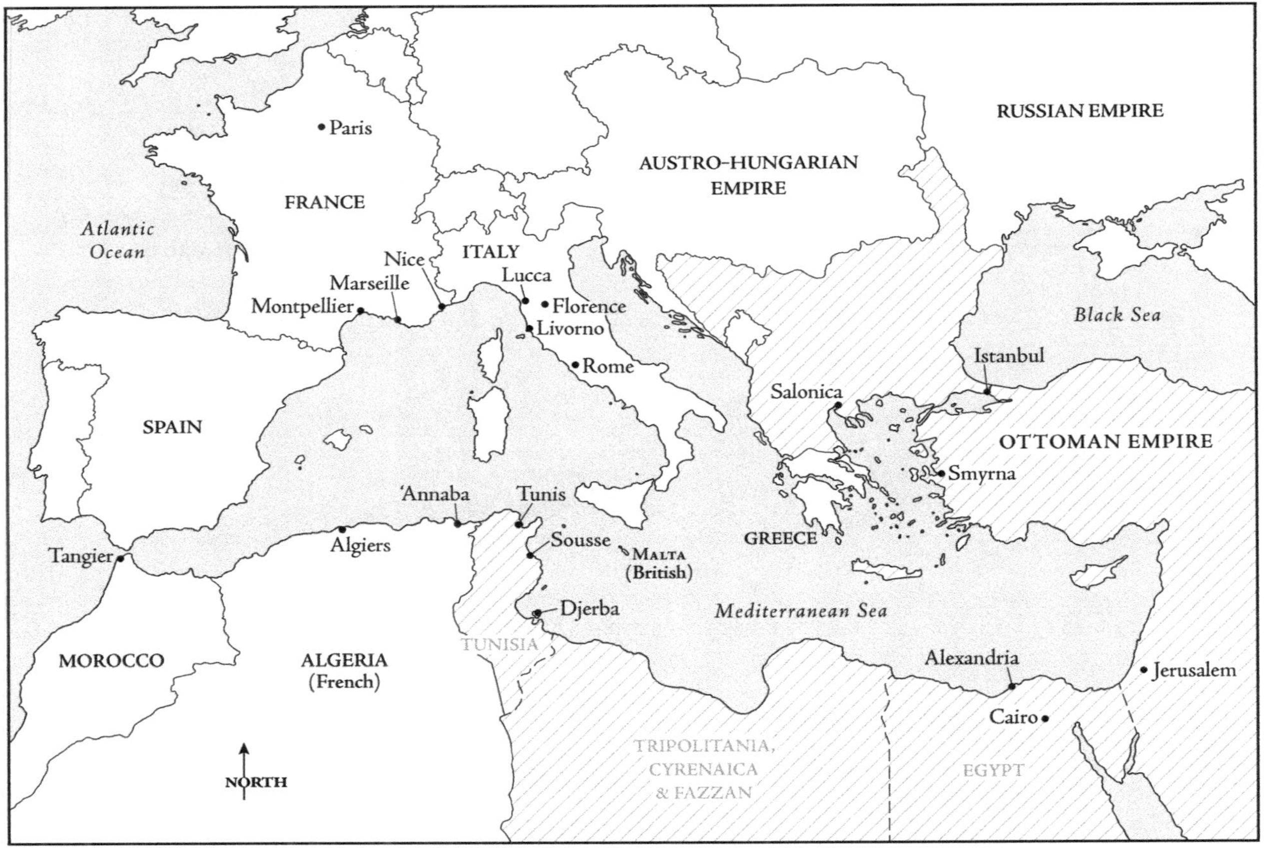

FIGURE 0.1. Map of the Mediterranean, circa 1873

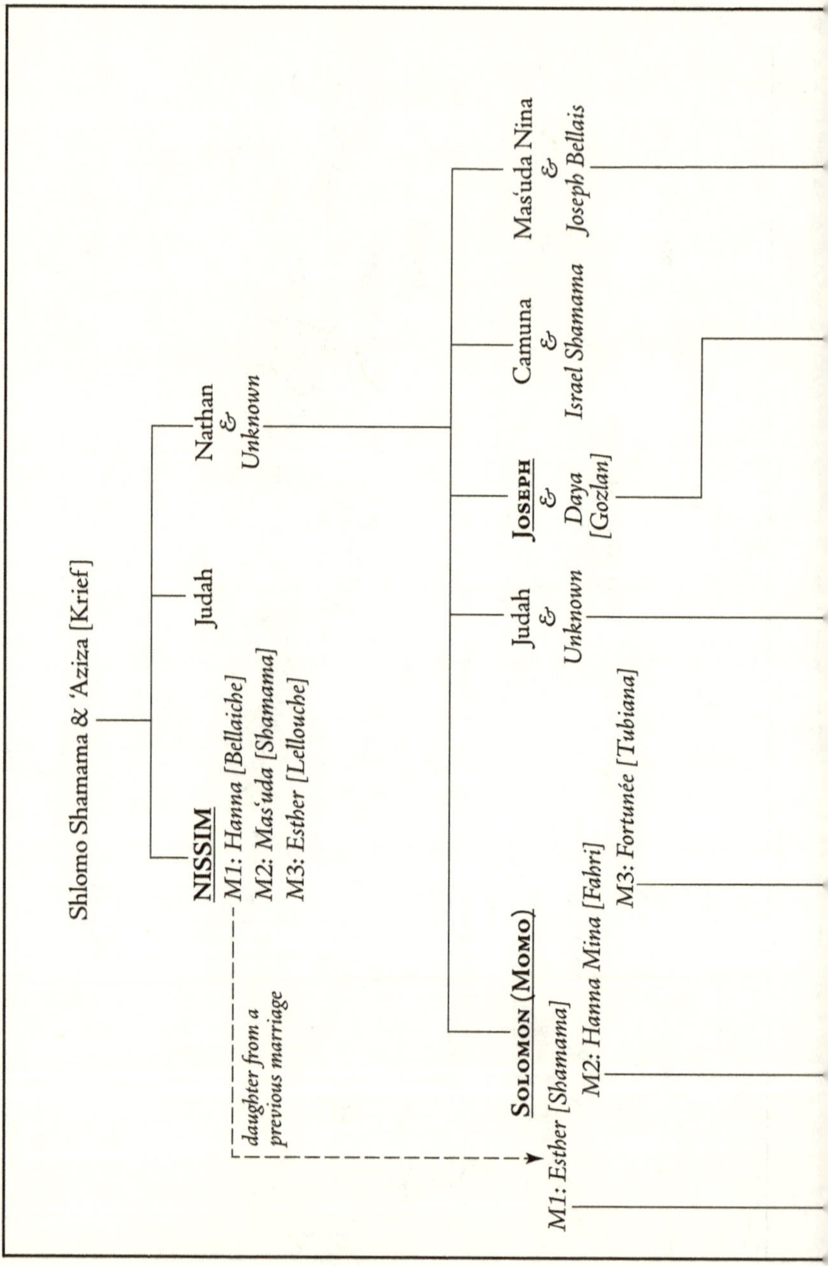

FIGURE 0.2. Shamama Family Tree

- **‘Aziza** & *Moses Shamama*
  - **Nissim Jr.**
    M1: Emilie Scemama de Gialluly
    M2: Rose Itier

- Rachel
- Albert Abraham
- Isaac

- Rebecca Renée
- Isaac Jacques & *Jeanne [Bloch]*
- Alexandrine
- Emilie
- Amélie Maya Esther
- Nathan Donat

- **Nathan** & *Corinna [Salmon]*
  - Emily
  - Inès
  - Leonetto
- Esther & *Nissim Attal*

- Eugenia
- Emilia
- Abraham/Abramo Alberto
  - Daya & *Alfonso Fiorentini*
    - Leone
    - Giuliana
  - Albertina
- Nathan
- Nissim
- Salvatore
- Umberto
- Elia & *Anita [Montelativi]*
  - Giuseppe
  - Annamaria
  - Iolanda
  - Maria Giovanna
- Carlo

- Hai Aaron
- Mordekhai & *Vittoria Ida [Stracca]*

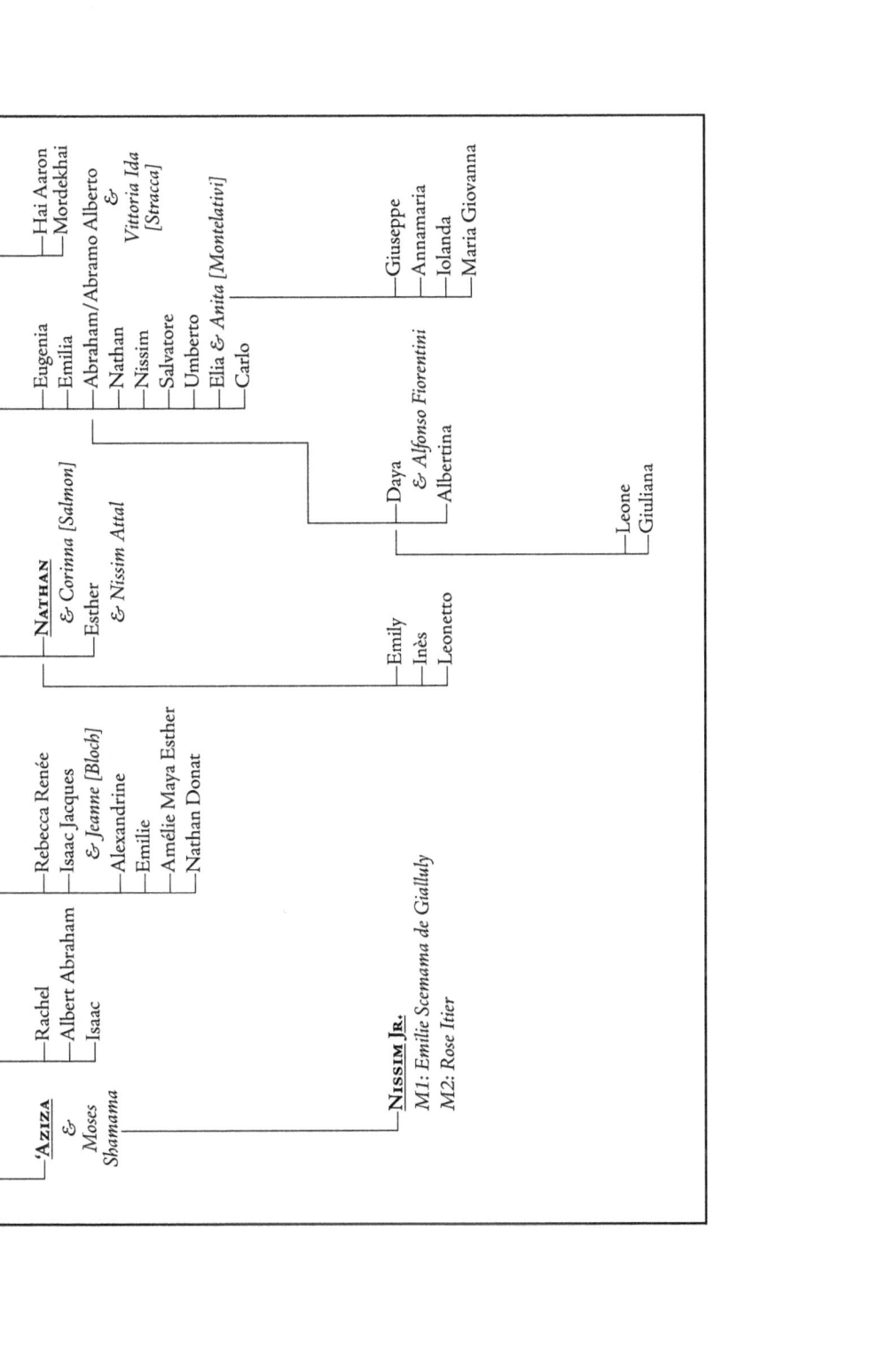

PROLOGUE

Death in Livorno

NISSIM SHAMAMA did not take long to die. He awoke in the early morning hours on Friday, January 24, 1873, with an acute case of enteritis, an inflammation of the small intestine. The pain was severe; Nissim could barely get out of bed. Two local doctors arrived at his palazzo in Livorno, Tuscany's port city. At 9:00 a.m., they pronounced him dead.[1]

Nissim was sixty-eight years old when he succumbed to his sudden illness; he was not a young man, yet no one expected him to die so suddenly. His entire household was in a state of shock—servants, secretaries, rabbis, and especially his favorite great-niece, 'Aziza. She was born in Tunis, like Nissim himself. In 1864, 'Aziza left her homeland to accompany Nissim to Paris, along with her husband, Moses, and their three-day-old son. When Nissim moved to Italy, she followed again. 'Aziza was like the child Nissim never had, despite three marriages. But in the eyes of the law, these bonds of affection were just that: fictive kinship without legal weight. 'Aziza, her husband, and her child—also named Nissim, in honor of her uncle—had lived off the elder Nissim's largesse for a decade. Now that he was dead, what would become of them?

'Aziza was not the only one wondering about the future. Nissim died an extremely wealthy man. No one actually knew just how wealthy; he kept his accounts secret, and not even his private secretary could say how much the man was worth. Yet there was no doubt he was rich. In Tunis, Nissim had been the receiver general, in charge of collecting taxes for the entire country; the director of finances; and head of the Jewish community. In Paris, he installed himself in an elegant town house in the upscale sixteenth arrondissement and bought a second one next door for 'Aziza and her family. The king of Italy made him a count and conferred on him a royal decree of naturalization as a citizen of the newly minted state. When Nissim moved to Livorno, he built himself another palace, grander still. Rumors estimated his fortune at tens of millions of francs—on the order of banking giants like Baron James de Rothschild.[2]

The police arrived not long after Nissim's death. Their first order of business was to find out whether the deceased had left a will. Nobody knew for sure—not even his beloved 'Aziza. Nissim's secretary had a hunch that perhaps his master had written a will when he was living in Paris. If so, it would be in his study. Without delay the police pried the only key from Nissim's cold bosom. They opened the door and there, on the desk, were four sealed envelopes, with four identical copies of a will.[3]

News of Nissim's death flew across the city. Adriano Bargellini, the Tunisian agent in Livorno, heard shortly after Nissim was pronounced dead. He rushed to the telegraph office and dashed off a breathless message to the Tunisian prime minister, Mustafa Khaznadar: "I announce the death of the General Qā'id Nissim Shamama and request instructions."[4] Then he ran to the Shamama palazzo to see what he could learn.

When Bargellini arrived, the police were busy applying seals to secure the late Nissim's possessions. Bargellini tried to assert himself in his capacity as the official representative of Tunisia. It was standard practice for consuls to take charge of applying seals to the possessions of deceased foreigners or those leaving behind foreign heirs.[5] At this point, everyone believed that Nissim was an Italian citizen; the Tunisian agent did not expect to have the privilege of applying the seals himself. Nonetheless, Bargellini was peeved that he had not been contacted officially. He confronted Isacco Rignano, a Livornese Jewish lawyer whom 'Aziza and her husband, Moses, had summoned: "Seeing that there might be heirs who are Tunisian subjects" still in Tunisia, Bargellini said testily, the lawyer "might have invited me to be present during the formality" of applying the seals. Rignano responded crisply, "If after the will was read, it appears that there are Tunisian heirs," he would invite Bargellini to "attend the lifting of the seals and the compilation of the inventory" of the estate.[6] Until then, no promises would be made.

Bargellini went home and wrote his weekly update to Prime Minister Khaznadar. He began with an apology for not having sent the elephant tusks that Khaznadar had ordered. Then he described everything he had learned thus far about the death of Qā'id Nissim. Since Nissim was "an Italian subject," Bargellini explained, the lawyer Rignano had demanded that the Italian authorities apply the seals. He ended his letter as he had his telegram: "I now await Your Excellency's instructions."[7]

Jewish tradition calls for burial as soon as possible following death. Because Nissim died on a Friday, his funeral had to wait until Sunday since Jews do not bury their dead on the Sabbath. On January 26, Livorno's Jewish notables accompanied Nissim's body to the new Jewish cemetery, east of the city center. Two members of Tunisia's Italian Jewish community served as pallbearers: Abraham Lumbroso, personal doctor to the bey of Tunis, and Pinchas Ererra.[8] To honor the memory of their deceased uncle, 'Aziza and Moses made generous donations to the Jewish community: a lump sum of 2,500 lire—enough to feed 150 people for a week—as well as 2 pounds of bread and 1 lira for each person registered as a recipient of communal alms.[9] They also offered donations to Livorno's Catholic charities, including the orphanage, hospital, poorhouse, and Catholic schools—totaling a hefty 6,000 francs. In giving so generously to Jewish and Catholic charitable causes, the couple both honored Nissim's memory and proclaimed their devotion to Livorno, their new home.[10]

The funeral proceedings had only just wrapped up when the solemnity of the occasion was interrupted by news from Tunisia. Rignano, 'Aziza's lawyer, announced that he had received a power of attorney by telegraph from Sousse, a city on the coast about 150 kilometers south of Tunis. The telegram came from Mas'uda Shamama, Nissim's estranged widow. Unlike 'Aziza, Mas'uda had remained behind in Tunisia when Nissim left for Europe. Having learned of her husband's death, she empowered Rignano to protect her interests in her late husband's estate. She also convinced the Italian consul in Sousse to write on her behalf. Although Mas'uda had never once set foot in Italy, her late husband's naturalization as an Italian gave her access to the consulate's services. Since wives followed their husband's state membership, Nissim's royal decree automatically conferred Italian nationality on Mas'uda as well. Nissim's widow worked at lightning speed to secure her share of her late husband's fortune; the miracle of telegraphic communication meant that less than forty-eight hours after Nissim's death, she had engaged legal counsel on the other side of the Mediterranean.[11]

The next day, Livornese officials organized a public reading of the will. Someone translated from the original Judeo-Arabic into Italian so that locals could understand. When the envelopes were opened, those present learned that Nissim had written the will five years earlier—in 1868—when he was still living in Paris. The will began:

> In the name of God, may God who realizes my desires be praised. Here are the conditions of my last wishes, which I write by my own hand in my home, Rue du Faubourg Saint-Honoré number 47, while I am in good health and in possession of all my faculties—knowing that all is in the hands of the Holy One blessed be He, who directs and governs our life.[12]

Nissim proceeded to divide his fortune into four equal parts. The first two—half of his estate—went to 'Aziza and her son Nissim Jr. The third quarter went to Joseph Shamama, Nissim's nephew. Nissim gave the final quarter to his great nephew Nathan Shamama. To other relatives, friends, and loyal servants, he gave smaller sums. Mas'uda, his widow, got a hundred thousand francs. 'Aziza's estranged father, Nissim's nephew Solomon—known to everyone as Momo—was given twenty-five thousand.[13]

Nissim ended his will with a warning, forbidding his heirs from pursuing "a greater share than what I have given them."[14] The great man must have suspected that the estate would do more to divide the Shamamas than to unite them. He had reason to worry; battles over a large inheritance are almost as certain as death itself.

After the will had been read, only 'Aziza and Moses breathed sighs of relief; their uncle had provided handsomely for them. But the rest of the Shamama family expected that Nissim would apportion his fortune among his closest male relatives, as stipulated in the biblical laws of inheritance. Three nephews had the strongest blood ties to Nissim: Joseph and Nathan—each of whom had gotten a quarter of the estate in the will—and 'Aziza's father, Momo. Joseph, Nathan, and Momo had long ago calculated that they stood in line to split their childless uncle's millions. But the will threatened to alter their calculus: Nissim reduced each of Joseph and Nathan's portions from a third to a fourth, which amounted to a significant sum in such a large estate; this allowed him to provide more generously for his beloved 'Aziza and little Nissim Jr. As for Momo, Nissim cut him out almost entirely following bitter fights over money; Nissim's will allotted his eldest nephew only twenty-five thousand instead of the millions he had been expecting. 'Aziza knew her father; Momo would not take this news lying down.

Momo, Joseph, and Nathan were not the only ones in Tunis concerned about Nissim's estate. The Tunisian government claimed Nissim had died owing enormous sums to the treasury. On top of Nissim's debts, Momo was also heavily indebted to the government—and the prime minister had been counting on Nissim's inheritance to ensure that Momo paid. The secret will was a blow to the Tunisian officials, but Khaznadar was hardly ready to give up on the treasury's claims on the estate. He instructed Bargellini to inquire into how Italian courts would determine the distribution of Nissim's fortune.

On Monday, February 17, the Tunisian agent boarded a train to Florence, where he met with Leopoldo Galeotti, one of Tuscany's best-known lawyers and a prominent politician.[15] Bargellini asked Galeotti a series of questions about how the Italian courts would handle Nissim's estate. The bottom line, Galeotti explained, was that inheritance must be adjudicated according to the national law of the deceased. In other words, since Nissim had died an Italian national—as everyone presumed—then Italian law would apply to his estate. And according to Italian law, the will would certainly be deemed valid.[16]

But Bargellini had a hunch that Nissim's nationality might not be so clear-cut. It was possible, he thought, that "the late Mr. Shamama had not fulfilled the requirement to register his royal decree of naturalization at the Italian legation in Paris—a registration that must be done within six months of the decree."[17] Bargellini sent a telegraph to his colleague Jules de Lesseps, the Tunisian agent in Paris. De Lesseps did some digging at the Italian embassy and came up with nothing—excellent news for the Tunisian government. Nissim had indeed failed to register his decree of naturalization with the Italian authorities.

If Nissim never became Italian—and thus had died a Tunisian national—then the Italian courts would apply Tunisian law to his estate. Jews in Tunisia were under the jurisdiction of Jewish law for personal matters like bequests; if Tunisian law were applied, then the will would have to meet Jewish legal standards for a valid testament. This seemed unlikely at best, as the will was missing various elements required in the rabbinic tradition. If Jewish law deemed the will invalid, then the biblical laws of inheritance would apply. Momo would inherit his millions, and 'Aziza and Nissim Jr. would get nothing. There was hope for Momo and hence the Tunisian treasury. Bargellini sent another breathless telegraph to Tunis: "Lawyers say that without having completed formalities, naturalization decree becomes null."[18]

What had seemed certain when Nissim died was now suddenly thrown into doubt. Was Nissim an Italian national, as everyone thought? Or did he pass away a Tunisian subject? Bargellini's discovery marked the beginning of a legal saga that would eat up vast quantities of time and treasure. The lawsuit over the estate pitted the heirs who hoped to have the will upheld—'Aziza and Mas'uda—against those who hoped to have it thrown out—Momo, Joseph, and Nathan, all backed by the Tunisian government. Shamama heirs flocked to Livorno, hoping to claim a part of Nissim's legacy. Khaznadar sent one of the government's most trusted officials, General Husayn ibn 'Abdallah, to oversee the Tunisian government's interests in the case. Husayn, in turn, hired an Algerian Jewish fixer named Léon Elmilik. And each side engaged some of the most renowned scholars of international law in Italy, indeed in all of Europe. Before the case was finally decided—over a decade after Nissim's death—both sides had produced thousands of pages of legal briefs in Italian, Arabic, French, and Hebrew—all trying to answer one question: To which state did Nissim belong?

INTRODUCTION

Legal Belonging across the Mediterranean

THE QUESTION at the heart of the Shamama case seems, on its face, a simple matter of citizenship. Had Nissim successfully naturalized as an Italian national, in which case Italian law would apply to the estate? Or did he remain a subject of the bey of Tunis, forcing the courts to adjudicate according to Tunisian law? These alternatives are certainly beguiling. But reducing the fight over Nissim's inheritance to a straightforward application of nationality law would do a great disservice to the past. The puzzle at the heart of the lawsuit requires a different approach to belonging—one that changes our understanding of citizenship on both sides of the Mediterranean.

The Shamama case, in all of its messy glory, should be worth unearthing simply as a good story for the historically minded. For those invested in debates around the law of belonging, the Shamama lawsuit does more: it points to the imbalances and gaps in the way historians have approached citizenship itself. In trying to make sense of the battle over Shamama's estate, the very category of citizenship proves unequal to the task.

In place of citizenship—and near cognates like nationality and subjecthood—I view the Shamama case in light of a broader, even more abstract category. I call this "legal belonging." Belonging, because it involves both the formal bonds that tie people to a state, as well as forms of membership that stray beyond the strict boundaries imposed by words like "citizen" and "national." Legal, because it nonetheless concerns ligatures that produce some formal obligation on the part of a state—as opposed to, say, the kinds of belonging that are purely a matter of self-identification (such as soccer fans or intellectuals) or that transcend the state (religion or ethnicity). The state-based dimension of legal belonging is what makes this abstract concept an attribute of sovereignty.[1] The belonging I am after accords rights—both to the individual, such as the right to vote, marry, and claim protection; and to the state, including the right to tax, conscript, and exercise jurisdiction. Just as sovereignty varied across time and space, so did the nature of the bonds of belonging. Some enjoyed the state's tight embrace—one that accorded all the political and civil rights of full citizenship. (In nineteenth-century Europe and North America, this was mostly Christian men of European descent.) Many others, however—especially women, religious others, and colonial subjects—found that the state kept them at arm's length.[2]

The neutral category of legal belonging frees us from the baggage of more familiar terms like citizenship and nationality. It allows us to observe the ways in which the furnace of nationalist fervor forged new molds of inclusion and exclusion, especially for Jews. And it permits us to view the modernization of state membership in both North Africa and Europe as an entangled process of legal change that played out across the Mediterranean—rather than an example of a Western invention exported abroad. The sprawling legal battle over the estate of a Tunisian Jew who died in Italy challenges old assumptions—about citizenship, Jews, and the Islamic world. It also offers new ways to think about what it means to legally belong.

In the course of the lawsuit, lawyers threw doubt on almost every aspect of Nissim's life, with perhaps one exception: that he was Jewish. Yet even this undeniable fact generated extensive disagreement. Nissim's membership in the Jewish people produced more questions than answers when it came to his legal belonging. As religious others in both Europe and the Middle East, Jews had always occupied an outsized role in debates about belonging, equality, and rights. But as nationalism came of age in the nineteenth century, the powerful new ideology offered novel ways to exclude Jews—from the legal belonging they were accorded in polities on both shores of the Middle Sea, and from the shared narratives that bound people together in a normative world.[3]

Jews in medieval and early modern Europe had always been considered subjects of the local sovereign, even as the vast majority lacked full citizenship. Often the relationship between Jews and their ruler was a privileged one: the king, queen, or prince was seen as the ultimate protector of Jews.[4] But nationalist ideals of homogeneous nation-states gave new meaning to Jewish difference. According to the logic of nationalism, Jews were often considered inherently foreign and thus unassimilable to the nation. If Judaism was its own nationality, then how could Jews be fully Italian (or French, German, etc.)? Among the most committed antisemites, one solution to Jews' inherent otherness was quite simple: deprive them of membership in the state through expulsion.[5] Even liberals accused Jews of constituting a "state within a state" and possessing "dual nationality"—as members of the Jewish nation and the nation-states in which they lived.[6] Nationalism required homogeneity; hence the slippage between nationality as a legal bond between individuals and states, and nationality as an ethnocultural form of affiliation.[7] Nor did Jews ever quite fit the image of sameness presumed by slogans like *fraternité* and *égalité*.

The lawyers arguing the Shamama case came up with a rather unusual twist on Jews' uneasy fit with nationalist-inflected legal belonging. As we have seen, the two most obvious answers to the question of Nissim's belonging placed him as a member of Italy or Tunisia; either he had become Italian or he had remained Tunisian. But as the case grew in complexity, a third possibility emerged: that Nissim's national law was neither Italian nor Tunisian but instead Jewish—and thus that his nationality *was* his Jewishness. Jews were frequently designated a "nation" in early modern Europe. In arguing over whether Jews constituted a nationality, both sides found themselves faced with basic questions about how nationalist ideas intersected with older versions of belonging.[8]

When applied to North Africa, the homogenizing impulse of nationalism became an accusation: Europeans found fault with Islamic states for privileging Muslims over Christians and Jews.[9] In the course of the Shamama case, Italian jurists questioned whether a Jew like Nissim could even possess Tunisian nationality. As dhimmīs (protected non-Muslim monotheists), these jurists maintained, Jews were not the equals of Muslims—and were thus excluded from the nation. The Muslim and Jewish North Africans working on the case disagreed: they refused the nationalist impulse to exclude Jews on the basis of religious difference. They also rejected the assumption that state membership required absolute equality. Instead, they asserted that Jews were full members of the Tunisian state, despite being legally distinct from Muslims. Tunisians' insistence on including Jews in the definition of who belonged would not last forever. Yet the story of nationalist calls for religious and ethnic homogeneity in the Middle East belongs almost entirely to the twentieth century, not the nineteenth.[10]

Nissim's Jewishness stood at the center of the lawsuit because it raised questions about the nature of equality and difference in an age of nationalism. The Shamama case offers an opportunity to think at the margins, as feminist critics have been urging us to do for decades: to view the history of legal belonging through the lens of those whose very existence challenged emerging conceptions of modern citizenship.[11]

Thinking at the margins similarly pushes us to reconsider the history of law in the modern Middle East. As with so much about the non-West, citizenship in the Islamic world has largely been described as an import from Europe. But seen through the lens of the Shamama case, modern belonging emerges from an entangled process of legal change across the Mediterranean.[12]

Historians have generally told the story of modern Middle Eastern citizenship in the mode of an older approach to modernization. In this narrative, modernity is a set of ideas, forces, and relations invented in Europe that radiated outward to the rest of the world.[13] At the same time, scholars imagined protocitizenship in the Islamic world as entirely dependent on religious status: whether one was a Muslim or dhimmī. Only Muslims had full rights, as close to full citizenship as one got under Islamic rule.[14] But these rights did not amount to state-based citizenship; rather, Muslims' rights derived from their membership in the *umma*, the community of Muslims worldwide—a group that transcended political boundaries.[15] Jews' status similarly depended on their religion; as dhimmīs, they had largely the same rights across the Islamic world. The only relevant law—*shari'a* for Muslims and *halakhah* for Jews—existed wherever an individual might travel; territorially based belonging supposedly had little impact on people's legal lives.[16] Because rights were presumably located in religious identity, scholars conclude that true, state-based citizenship could only emerge once states stopped defining personal status based on religion—a form of secularization imported from Europe.[17] In short, according to this approach, Middle Eastern citizenship required modernization and was necessarily a product of Westernization.[18]

But this narrative fails us when it comes to the Shamama case, particularly in grasping how Tunisian officials understood what it meant to belong to their state. If we view legal belonging as a dimension of sovereignty—an aspect of the authority exercised by a government over people under its jurisdiction—then there is no need to locate a moment of invention or importation. Husayn, the civil servant charged with overseeing the government's interests in the lawsuit, grounded his assertion that Shamama was Tunisian in classical Islamic law. For him, the 1861 laws outlining the duties and rights of Tunisian nationals—usually viewed by Europeans as the beginning of Tunisian nationality—were an articulation of belonging already outlined in Islamic jurisprudence. Husayn's case for why Nissim died a subject of the bey was not grafted onto a rootstock of European ideology; it grew from Islamic soil.[19] If we are to take Husayn's conception of Tunisian nationality seriously, we must recognize that legal belonging in Tunisia existed well before the modernizing reforms of the mid-nineteenth century.

Following Husayn's lead, the framework of legal belonging frees us from the twinned teleologies of Westernization and secularization.[20] Put most simply, Jews and Muslims in Tunisia legally belonged to the bey because they were under his sovereignty. Even if they used Jewish or Islamic courts, both these institutions were under the bey's authority. Nor did these explicitly religious courts have a monopoly on the resolution of conflict: governors presided over their own tribunals, where they adjudicated in the name of the bey. While describing these governors' courts as secular would be anachronistic, they were nonetheless undeniably linked to the sovereignty of the state. And all subjects had the right to appeal to the bey as the ultimate arbiter of justice in the land.[21] The presumption that only religious courts mattered—and thus that religious identity was the only marker of belonging—simply ignores the reality of sovereignty in Tunisia and throughout the Middle East. Legal belonging may have looked different in premodern Tunisia, but it nevertheless existed.

Moving away from a centrifugal model of legal modernization does not require ignoring the power imbalance that overshadowed the modern Mediterranean. In this period, Muslim rulers undertook major centralizing reforms, which were mainly designed to stave off European threats to their sovereignty; the history of nationality law in the Middle East is undeniably bound up with these efforts. Beginning in the late eighteenth century, the Ottoman Empire experienced a series of devastating military defeats to Russia. In 1829, Greece declared its independence, backed by a concert of European states. And in 1830, France invaded Algeria, the Empire's westernmost province. Western states also used the painfully obvious dominance of their militaries to impose free trade, flooding local markets with imports and tipping the scales of economic power.[22] But the reality of European imperialism need not lull us into a diffusionist understanding of modernity.[23]

Putting Europe and the Middle East into a single analytic frame also forces us to rethink our assumptions about citizenship in the West. A Whiggish narrative of Western modernity relegates the fragmentation of legal belonging along religious lines to an evolutionary stage. Belonging based on religion is considered a holdover from a premodern era when entire categories of people were regularly and unabashedly excluded from citizenship; in Europe, this was true of Jews, women, and the poor.[24] The promise of the age of revolutions was to transform society from a series of rigid social hierarchies to a flat, equal mass. Yet in the nineteenth-century Western world, this equality mostly remained limited to free men of European descent.[25] Society—and with it, legal belonging—remained hierarchical and fractured. Various groups continued to possess differentiated rights and distinct duties: enslaved Africans, Indigenous peoples, women, felons, colonial subjects, and in many places, Jews.[26] Even today, the spectrum of ways people might legally belong does not match the ideal of absolute equality. In the United States, Puerto Ricans are citizens, yet remain unrepresented in federal elections; American Samoans are nationals, but not citizens.[27] And of course the ideal type of equal citizenship conceals the profound fragmentation of society; there are many who on paper are full citizens, but whose race, ethnicity, sexual orientation, religion, class, and so on, prevent them from accessing the full promise of their citizenship. We have yet to recognize how the imagined boundary between "citizen" and "foreigner" obscures the range of ways one can legally belong to a state—in the past as well as the present.

Nissim was a fabulously wealthy man; this, of course, is why his life—and even more so his death—spawned such an enormous paper trail. But the question of belonging at the center of the Shamama lawsuit was one asked over and over again across the Mediterranean. Shifting our gaze toward the indeterminacy of legal belonging frees us from attention to the political and civil rights that have largely preoccupied historians. Scholars interested in citizenship have usefully suggested moving beyond formal membership in a state, looking instead at the multiple ways in which individuals claim rights and duties vis-à-vis a range of state and nonstate actors.[28] Yet for all of this broadening, the focus remains on substantive citizenship.[29] These questions fail to capture the beating heart of the Shamama case—or dozens of similar cases that played out in both Europe and the Middle East.

A seemingly simple query—to which state did an individual belong?—frequently proved arduous to answer, even well into the twentieth century. Today we have paperwork to determine whether individuals are entitled to the citizenship they claim, such as birth certificates and various forms of state-issued identification (passports, drivers licenses, social security cards, etc.).[30] But Western states did not even attempt universal regimes of identification until after World War I.[31] Even though nationality law in nineteenth-century Europe often presumed the existence of this documentation, everyone knew this was the theory, not the reality. Archives recording births, deaths, and marriages were incomplete at best, and more often than not completely absent.[32]

Little wonder, then, that Nissim was hardly alone in provoking basic questions about legal belonging. On both sides of the Mediterranean, countless individuals found that their status as a national, citizen, or subject was radically uncertain. Questions about legal belonging almost always arose in moments of transition or crisis; marriage or divorce frequently forced the issue, as did the arrival of a draft summons. Before they could tie the knot, Italians in France found themselves in need of documentation proving their birth and thus their citizenship.[33] Young men in Italy, fearing that life's pleasures and possibilities might be cut short by a bullet, claimed they were not Italian citizens and hence were exempt from military service; some invoked parents from Switzerland, others the jurisdiction of the Papal States, and still others their French origins. But it often took multiple rounds of appeal before courts could determine to which state these unwilling soldiers belonged.[34] The same thing happened further east; Jews and Christians in Romania wrote to the local Ottoman consulate in hopes of proving their status as subjects of the sultan, thereby exempting them from serving in the dreaded Romanian army. Youths throughout the Ottoman Empire attempted to avoid the equally unappealing Ottoman military by claiming foreign citizenship. Ottoman bureaucrats in the Nationality Bureau (*tabiiyet kalemi*) had their hands full trying to verify competing claims of belonging; as in the Italian courts, this was rarely a straightforward process.[35]

The most labyrinthine cases of indeterminate belonging frequently began with the death of a wealthy person. Antun Yussuf 'Abd al-Massih, a financially successful Iraqi Christian, died in Egypt in 1885; it took years to determine whether his estate was under Ottoman jurisdiction or that of the British consulate. These problems persisted into the twentieth century; the fortune of Silas Aaron Hardoon, a Jew who died in Shanghai in 1931, forced courts to decide whether the late millionaire had been an Iraqi citizen or British subject.[36] In this sense, the Shamama lawsuit was typical of a somewhat exceptional phenomenon; as in the cases of al-Massih and Hardoon, the fight over

Shamama's enormous inheritance opened a floodgate of contested claims about belonging, all pushed along by the promise of a hefty inheritance. The questions raised in these lawsuits, however, were simply better-funded versions of the ones asked in hundreds of more ordinary cases—in which young men trying to avoid the draft or lovers hoping to marry found that they first had to prove to which state they belonged.[37]

Many people lived their entire life without ever having to establish their belonging. Even those who moved across political borders rarely found their mobility inhibited by questions of state membership. In the world Nissim inhabited, the right to enter the territory of a state—a privilege most closely associated with state membership today—was largely decoupled from citizenship.[38] But the existence of mostly open borders hardly made belonging irrelevant. Across the Mediterranean, countless people had their lives put on hold because it proved difficult to answer this basic question: Under whose sovereignty are you? Turning our attention to the history of legal belonging exposes the urgency of this query and the deception of its simplicity.

———

For historians invested in scholarly debates about law and citizenship, the human interest of Nissim's life and death may seem of secondary concern. Yet it is this story that forms the heart of the book: the tale of a man who rose to power only to die in self-imposed exile; a decade-long battle over his estate, in which courtrooms served as the front lines, legal memos as artillery, and famous jurists as generals commanding small armies of lawyers; and a cast of characters as varied as the Victorian novels depicting inheritance disputes. As Charles Dickens and Anthony Trollope discerned, there is nothing like a good fight over an estate to frame a slice of humanity.[39]

But telling this history as a story, with a beginning, middle, and end (of sorts), is not merely a stylistic choice. The arc of the book reflects a key insight into the way legal belonging was proved—not only in the Shamama lawsuit, but in countless cases both before and since: as a narrative. Legal belonging was not a fact to be discovered but rather a series of competing, overlapping, and intersecting tales, all attempting to make meaning of a life. Legal theorists have argued for decades that law is animated by storytelling. In Robert Cover's words, "The very imposition of a normative force upon a state of affairs, real or imagined, is the act of creating narrative."[40] The power of narration in law runs through the thousands of pages of legal briefs written for the Shamama case. The task of the jurists, first and foremost, was to offer an interpretation of Nissim's life that would prove his belonging—whether to Italy, Tunisia, or the Jewish nation.

Understanding the centrality of narration to legal belonging requires (once again) shedding our twenty-first-century presumptions: today, the ubiquity of paperwork suggests that verifying citizenship is as easy as producing a birth certificate or passport.[41] But the Shamama case indicates that proving legal belonging was not so simple. For those arguing that Nissim died an Italian citizen, the failure to register his naturalization decree was a minor detail; it could not erase Nissim's claim of Livornese heritage, his good faith belief that he had become Italian, and the general consensus among others that he was a citizen of Italy. For those contending that Nissim died a subject of the bey, the continued use of his bureaucratic titles—receiver general and director of finances—proved that he considered himself a Tunisian government official, and thus a Tunisian, until the day he died.[42] The idea that one had to tell a plausible story in order to establish legal status is familiar to other fields, including scholars of citizenship in premodern contexts as well as historians of race and slavery.[43] Yet the glare of nationality legislation has prevented modernists from seeing the continued power of narrative in the quest to prove belonging.[44] Putting narration in the spotlight illuminates a more accurate—and far more intriguing—view of citizenship's past.

The Shamama case offers a way to peel back the siding from the machinery of legal belonging in both Europe and the Middle East, allowing us to observe the functioning of the gears inside.[45] The boundaries of the story are traced by the sources—legal briefs, rulings, and correspondence in Arabic, French, Hebrew, Italian, Judeo-Arabic, and Ottoman—gathered from archives and libraries in Tunisia, Italy, Turkey, Israel, and France. These sources largely ignore questions that would have interested me quite a bit. The possibility that Nissim died an Ottoman national is barely mentioned throughout the lawsuit. Tunisia was a semiautonomous province of the Ottoman Empire; it seems only natural that someone would have argued for Nissim's Ottoman nationality. Yet no one took this idea seriously.[46] In any case, it is the stories mobilized by those who sought to construct different versions of Nissim's life that most interest me. And it is the wonderfully twisting trail of evidence they left behind that I have largely followed—a path with the power to change how we think about belonging, across the Mediterranean and beyond.

PART I

Nissim Shamama

1

Tunis (1805–59)

SHORTLY BEFORE Nissim left Tunis for Europe, Armand de Flaux, a French Orientalist, arrived for a tour of Tunisia. De Flaux came on a "scientific" mission commissioned by the French government—a form of "peaceful penetration" into regions coveted by the expanding empire. He published a book about his travels in which he confirmed widespread perceptions of Muslims as fanatic and lazy, and Jews as fanatic and rapacious—all in amusing, flowery prose. Although it is unlikely that de Flaux actually met Nissim, this did not stop him from offering a description of one of the most powerful figures in the country. According to de Flaux, Nissim was even more opulent than the bey himself: he "wears a *shāshīya* [a typically Tunisian hat resembling a fez] with samples of all the kinds of coins that are used in Tunisia."[1] Explaining how a Jew like Nissim might have acquired such a "gigantic" fortune, de Flaux reports that since the reforms that provided Tunisian Jews with security, they have used their "innate mercantile qualities" to "monopolize" all the business opportunities in the country.[2]

His antisemitic overtones aside, de Flaux managed to capture some of the spirit of Nissim's persona. We may not trust de Flaux's claim that Nissim walked around with his wealth displayed on his headgear, yet Nissim was hardly one for modesty. He rose to power in the 1840s and 1850s, a period of rapid transformation in Tunisia and the rest of the Ottoman Empire. The turbulence of these decades also produced shifts in the nature of legal belonging. Like sovereignty, legal belonging was shared between Tunis and Istanbul; in the age of centralization, the division of power became increasingly contested.

De Flaux's pronouncements on Jews' newfound security should be approached with the same wariness with which we read his opinion of their avarice. Still, de Flaux was onto something: Jews played a starring role in debates about reform in the years preceding the Orientalist's visit. And de Flaux's assertions hit on some of the most radical changes in Tunisian politics: the gradual abolition of Jews' status as dhimmīs through the reforms initiated in 1857. Tracing Nissim's ascension through the ranks of power offers a chance to rewrite the history of citizenship in nineteenth-century Tunisia—not as a story of creation ex nihilo, nor as another example of how modern forms of law pierced the imagined boundary between West and East, but as an account of legal belonging as it emerged in its North African context.

Almost every fact about Nissim's life was contested in the course of the decade-long lawsuit over his estate. But on the city of his birth, all could agree: Nissim was born in Tunis in 1805. Since the glory days of its ancient predecessor, Carthage, Tunis has lived and breathed with the sea. Nicknamed *al-maḥrūsa* (the well protected), the city sits perched on the inland side of a natural lagoon known as the Lake of Tunis, or simply *the* lake in Arabic (*al-buḥayra*). The walls surrounding the city offered a second layer of protection, punctuated by imposing, magisterial gates: the Bab al-Bahr (the gate of the sea) faces toward the lagoon, and beyond, to La Goulette (Halq al-Wadi in Arabic), Tunis's port.

Like all Jews, Nissim's family lived in the *ḥāra,* the Jewish quarter tucked just inside the walls of the city, near the Bab al-Qartajina (the Carthage Gate, which led to the ruins of the ancient city on the north side of the lagoon). Ḥāra simply means "neighborhood" in Arabic, but in Tunisia and parts of Algeria, the word came to denote the section of the city reserved for Jews. (Across North Africa, indigenous Christians had either converted or fled by the late medieval period so Jews were the only local non-Muslim population.) According to legend, Tunis's ḥāra dates to the tenth century, when Sidi Mahriz, one of the city's leading scholars, designated a section of the town for Jews. He did this by standing on the minaret of the mosque now bearing his name and throwing his staff; Jews could live in those areas within striking distance to ensure that they remained under his personal protection.[3]

The mythical origin of Tunis's ḥāra says something about the nature of Jews' belonging in Tunisia. The legend of the ḥāra is almost certainly no more than that, given the scant evidence that Sidi Mahriz had any authority to delineate a Jewish quarter. As with all good myths, however, the story about Sidi Mahriz's staff hints at a deeper truth—in this case, by underscoring the relationship between government and non-Muslims in the Islamic world. Jews in Tunisia were considered *ahl al-dhimma*; dhimma means "protection," referring to the protection that Muslim sovereigns guaranteed their non-Muslim subjects. These were known as dhimmīs, literally "the protected." In the same way that the legend of Sidi Mahriz has him guaranteeing his personal protection to Jews, so did Muslim rulers consider themselves bound to protect dhimmīs under their sovereignty. Of course, Muslim sovereigns owed all of their subjects protection; this was part of the circle of justice by which rulers throughout Islamic history ensured peace and prosperity as well as justified their reign.[4] But as vulnerable members of society who were not expected to defend themselves, dhimmīs merited special protection.

In exchange for this protection, dhimmīs agreed to certain restrictions designed to ensure their lower place on the social hierarchy—constraints that varied considerably from place to place and across time.[5] Jews were often expected to wear distinctive clothing. In Tunisia this meant black shoes and a black skullcap, around which most wound a black or dark blue turban; the red *shāshīya* (or *chechia* in its Francophone form) was reserved for Muslims.[6] And dhimmīs paid distinct taxes from Muslims; throughout the Islamic world, non-Muslim subjects paid the *jizya*, a capitation tax referred to in the Quran.[7] A particularly harsh restriction levied on dhimmīs in Tunisia was the prohibition against owning real estate, instituted by Hammuda Pasha in the late eighteenth century. Yet even this rule was frequently circumvented by both Jewish and Islamic forms of usufruct rights that permitted Jews to effectively own buildings despite the strict letter of the law.[8]

In Tunisia, the sovereign to whom Jews like the Shamamas could turn for protection was effectively the bey of Tunis. Though technically Ottoman functionaries, the beys of Tunis had been granted authority over almost all state functions since in the early eighteenth century. The bey appointed governors (s. *qā'id*, pl. *quwwād*) over about sixty provinces (*qiyāda*) who acted as the bey's representatives. These governors were responsible for overseeing the collection of most taxes, including the jizya; they generally delegated the actual work of collecting taxes to tax farmers. Starting in the eighteenth century, many of those charged with collecting taxes in Tunisia were Jews.[9] The bey also administered justice. His governors oversaw the qadis (judges) of the shari'a courts applying Islamic law, and held their own tribunals in which they adjudicated a range of civil and criminal matters.[10] When the bey's subjects felt they could not obtain justice at the local level, they had the option of appealing directly to the bey. One of the bey's duties was to administer a court that served as a kind of supreme court of appeals. This tribunal convened in a large hall dedicated to this purpose in the Bardo, the bey's sprawling palace about four kilometers inland from the walled city of Tunis.[11] In mountainous regions, where tribes lived outside the jurisdiction of the governors, the bey's sovereignty was largely limited to collecting taxes. This was done by sending a biannual military expedition (*maḥalla*), which doubled as a way to display the government's power. The bey personally oversaw the collection of certain taxes that fell outside the purview of the governors, such as customs. He, too, farmed these out to elites who made bids for the privilege, betting that the taxes they collected would exceed their bid and they could keep the profits.[12]

Although dhimmīs claimed a distinct set of rights from Muslims, they were nonetheless subject to the bey's sovereignty just like their Muslim neighbors. Jews had to answer to the authority of local governors and could appeal to their courts when they had a legal dispute. They could also submit cases to the shari'a courts as well as the rabbinic courts that applied Jewish law (*batei din*).[13] And when Jews believed that justice had been miscarried at the local level, they appealed directly to the bey in his court at the Bardo.[14]

While the bey of Tunis exercised a considerable degree of authority over the inhabitants of Tunisia, he did so in the name of the Ottoman sultan. When Tunisia became part of the Ottoman Empire in the sixteenth century, it did not take long for the small coterie of Ottoman officers stationed in the new province to resist the sultan's efforts to appoint governors directly from Istanbul. In the early eighteenth century, Husayn b. 'Ali founded a dynasty of beys known as the Husaynīs, which ruled until Tunisian independence in 1956. On the one hand, the beys of Tunis governed quite independently of the sultan and his ministers in the Sublime Porte. They had their own armed forces and concluded their own treaties with foreign powers. Yet the sultan remained the supreme ruler. On Fridays, prayers were said in the sultan's name. Coins bore only his calligraphic monogram (*tuğra*). Each new bey sent a delegation to Istanbul to request an investiture from the sultan, just as each new sultan sent confirmations to all of his provincial governors—including the beys of Tunis.[15] The Husaynī beys belonged to an Ottoman-identified ruling class, though by the nineteenth century their administration was conducted entirely in Arabic and the beys themselves had only a shaky command of Ottoman. In short, sovereignty in Tunisia was layered—divided between the local and imperial governments.[16]

When Nissim was born in 1805, the authorities in both Tunis and Istanbul were relatively content with the distribution of power. But this status quo would not last for long. The French invasion of Algeria in 1830 dealt a jarring blow to the way sovereignty had been shared between Istanbul and Tunis. Partly in response to the threat of European imperialism, the Sublime Porte sought to consolidate its authority and centralize the administration of the empire. This is precisely what happened in Tripolitania (present-day Libya), which had been a largely autonomous province much on the model of Tunisia, but that the Sublime Porte folded into the direct administration of the empire in 1835. The beys of Tunis feared that a similar fate awaited them and tried to maintain their autonomy as best they could. Sometimes doing so meant cultivating the protection of France—the very state that had already torn the Ottoman Empire apart.[17]

At the same time, the beys of Tunis attempted to strengthen their ability to manage their own international relations. Yet in the nineteenth century, the beys' ability to engage in direct diplomacy became a matter of contention between Tunis and Istanbul. Part of the trouble centered on Tunisian representatives in Europe. Since the eighteenth century, Ottoman sultans had recognized Tunisian representatives (s. *wakīl*, pl. *wukalā'*) in various commercial centers of the Ottoman Empire, including Istanbul, Alexandria, and Smyrna (present-day Izmir). These representatives acted as liaisons between Ottoman authorities, the local community of Tunisians, and the bey back in Tunis. The beys had even appointed representatives in the southern European cities where many Tunisians engaged in trade.[18] Starting in the early nineteenth century, however, successive beys made concerted efforts to have their representatives in Europe recognized as full-fledged consuls. The first consul in Livorno, a Sardinian man named Giuseppe Tausch, called himself the "Consul of His Highness the Pasha Bey of Tunis" beginning in 1821.[19] In 1846, Ahmad Bey named Jules de Lesseps as Tunisian agent in Paris (though he was never officially recognized as a consul by the French government). De Lesseps was the son of the French consul in Tunis and fluent in Arabic; his brother Ferdinand was the principal force behind the construction of the Suez Canal. De Lesseps would later become one of Nissim's closest colleagues in Paris.[20]

Starting in the 1850s, the Ottoman central government came to perceive the beys' growing diplomatic ranks in Europe as a direct threat to the sultan's sovereignty over Tunisia. A decade after Ahmad Bey named de Lesseps his agent in Paris, the Sublime Porte asked the French ambassador in Istanbul to ensure that the Tunisian representative was denied official diplomatic recognition. Admitting that an Ottoman province could appoint its own consul in Paris, the Porte explained, would be "contrary to the principles of international relations."[21] After Italian unification, the Ottomans joined forces with the French

Ministry of Foreign Affairs to convince the new Italian state to refuse official recognition to Tunisian consuls. Adriano Bargellini—who succeeded Pietro Tausch as Tunisian consul in Livorno—was recognized by the dukes of Tuscany and listed in the official diplomatic almanac. But in 1861, the unified Italian state downgraded Bargellini to a mere unofficial representative.[22] The conflict between Tunis and Istanbul over the contours of sovereignty simmered right up until the Treaty of Bardo established the French protectorate in 1881.

Nonetheless, in the daily lives of most Tunisians, the influence of Istanbul was distant indeed. The exceptions were two groups with roots in the Ottoman heartlands: *kulughlis* were members of the Ottoman-speaking ruling class—descendants of those who had immigrated to Tunisia to join the army since it first became part of the Ottoman Empire in the sixteenth century. *Kulughlis* often retained ties to Istanbul and other parts of the empire. So did some mamluks (s. *mamlūk*, pl. *mamālīk*), who were educated slaves converted at a young age from Christianity, trained as soldiers in Istanbul, and then sold or given to the bey and other members of the governing elite in Tunis.[23] It was from these two groups that the bey chose representatives to send to Istanbul to receive an imperial decree of investiture from the sultan, offer gifts, and formally reaffirm the relationship between Tunisia and the Sublime Porte. But for the vast majority of Tunisia's inhabitants—the Arabic-speaking elites prominent in government and religious institutions, urban merchants and artisans, rural peasants, nomadic and seminomadic peoples in mountainous regions—the Ottoman sultan was more a symbol than an active sovereign. This was especially true for Tunisia's Jews, who invested little metaphysical significance in the sultan's role as spiritual head of the world's largest Islamic empire.

The overlapping sovereignty between Tunis and Istanbul translated into an equally layered approach to legal belonging. For all intents and purposes, the inhabitants of Tunisia owed their allegiance to the bey, to whom they paid taxes and looked to ensure justice. The bey, in turn, exercised sovereignty by collecting taxes, overseeing the administration of justice, and controlling the military. Yet when these subjects of the bey went to other parts of the Ottoman Empire—such as Tripolitania and Istanbul, where small but visible communities of Tunisian merchants and artisans lived—they were almost always considered to be subjects of the sultan.[24] That is, a Tunisian could legally belong to Tunisia within the province as well as to the Ottoman sultan in other parts of the empire. Legal belonging, like sovereignty itself, was divided between Tunis and Istanbul. And for the most part, nobody minded.

As a child of the ḥāra, Nissim lived in a very Tunisian, very Jewish space. Dozens of small synagogues dotted the narrow streets, most occupying the ground floors of the wealthiest Jews' houses. Butchers in the ḥāra slaughtered meat according to halakhah, Jewish law. Wine and *boukha,* the local spirit made from figs, were sold openly. But Tunis's Jewish quarter should not be mistaken for a ghetto along the lines of those in Venice or Rome. No walls definitively marked the end or beginning of the ḥāra. And plenty of Muslims came to the Jewish quarter to do business, indulge in booze and other illicit activities, and sometimes, even live. When Jews like the Shamamas conversed with the Muslim residents of Tunis, they did so in a common dialect of Arabic. Their houses, like those in the rest of the city, were built around central courtyards in which much of life was lived—cooking, washing, cleaning, and socializing.[25]

The Shamamas were a large, influential family; one branch produced learned scholars, suggesting that they belonged at the very least to the middling class of Jews with extra income to support the study of sacred texts. Nissim's father, Shlomo Shamama, wrote various books; his *Shoresh Yishai,* a commentary on the Talmud, appeared posthumously thanks to the generosity of his brother, Isaac Hai Shamama.[26] (We know nothing about Nissim's mother, 'Aziza née Khrief.) Shlomo died in 1806, when Nissim was still an infant.[27]

But Nissim did not follow in his father's footsteps. He received enough of an education to read Hebrew—the minimum for participation in Jewish ritual life and the cornerstone of Jewish schooling. He also knew how to write in Tunisian Judeo-Arabic, the local Arabic dialect written in Hebrew letters. In this Nissim was entirely typical of Jews in the Arabic-speaking Middle East—indeed, of Jews across the globe, many of whom used the Hebrew alphabet to write the local tongue.[28] Although the only language Nissim spoke fluently was Tunisian Arabic, he never learned to read or write standard Arabic. Like most elite Jews, he contented himself with the services of secretaries, members of the small but growing group of Jews who acquired a knowledge of written Arabic, often as part of their work as translators for European consulates in the Islamic Mediterranean.[29] The few documents we have that Nissim wrote himself—including the troublesome will—are all in Judeo-Arabic.

Nissim's inclination was not to books. It was power that attracted him. Like many prominent Jews in Tunisia, Nissim sought his fortune serving the government.[30] He began under the patronage of one of the most famous of the local elites, Mahmud Ibn ʿAyyad. The Ibn ʿAyyads were a wealthy family from Djerba, an island off Tunisia's southern coast; for many decades, the Ibn ʿAyyads served as *qāʾids* of their native region. Mahmud's father, Muhammad Ibn ʿAyyad, became particularly powerful under the reign of Ahmad Bey (1837–55). Muhammad lent Ahmad Bey the money he needed to modernize his army; in exchange, he was given a huge number of tax farms. When Mahmud came of age, he followed his father's path: he first became governor of Djerba, then Sousse, a major port city in the south, and finally Cap Bon, the peninsula just to the west of the capital. Together, Mahmud and Muhammad obtained tax farms and monopolies on the export of various commodities. More and more of the finances of the Tunisian state fell into their hands. Starting in 1846, when a *mamlūk* named Mustafa took over as minister of finance—which came with the title Khaznadar, as he was known thereafter—the Ibn ʿAyyads managed to increase the treasury's revenues steadily.[31]

The origins of Nissim's relationship with Mahmud Ibn ʿAyyad remain obscure.[32] In bringing a wealthy Jew into his inner circle, however, Ibn ʿAyyad was following the precedent of dozens of officials before him in Tunisia and across the Middle East. Jews had occupied prominent positions in Tunisian finances since the beginning of the Husaynid dynasty, primarily as tax farmers. Nissim was the first among the Shamamas to secure a tax farm. But many other prominent Jewish families had done so for decades; Cohens, Bismuths, Natafs, ʿAttals, Hayyats, and Bellaichs paid hefty sums for the right to collect taxes. In the eighteenth century, Jewish tax farmers concentrated in silver and leather as well as the collection of the jizya, levied only on Jews. By the nineteenth century, they started to branch out into taxes on tallow, silk, and customs duties.[33]

In 1837, Nissim was appointed to his first government position: a tax farmer for the Aʿrād region (*qābiḍ al-aʿrāḍ*), the southeastern corner of Tunisia bordering on Tripolitania, which encompassed Ibn ʿAyyad's familial home of Djerba. This was the same year Ahmad Bey made Ibn ʿAyyad the governor of Cap Bon, the peninsula just to the east of Tunis.[34] Nissim proved himself an able administrator—which essentially meant he was able to bleed the peasants of the Aʿrāḍ dry enough to meet his yearly tax quotas and still have enough left over to enrich himself. He purchased more tax farms: almonds, iron, and medicine in 1846, and custom duties on merchandise in 1848.[35] That same year, Nissim received public recognition for his aptitude: Ahmad Bey decorated him with the third rank of the Nīshān al-Iftikhār (mark of distinction), Tunisia's first honorary order, modeled after the Ottoman decoration of the same

FIGURE 1.1. Mahmud Ibn ʿAyyad, n.d., attributed to Charles Gleyres

name. Nissim received a medal made of gold—a teardrop emblem with Ahmad's name set in diamonds, framed by more diamonds hanging from a diamond-encrusted crescent and star.[36] The following year, Ahmad Bey promoted Nissim to head tax collector for the entire country (*qābiḍ amwāl al-dawla*).[37]

———

The early years of Nissim's rise to power accompanied a period of heady reform in Tunisia. After succeeding to the throne, Ahmad Bey embarked on an ambitious project to completely restructure the Tunisian army. Much like the Ottoman sultan and the semi-independent governor of Egypt Mehmet 'Ali (or Muhammad 'Ali in Arabic), Ahmad Bey was determined to create a military force that could withstand European encroachment into the empire. Starting in the late eighteenth century, Russian forces had lopped off sizable chunks of territory. In 1798, Napoléon invaded Egypt; his ouster was followed by the rise of Mehmet 'Ali, who instituted a largely independent dynasty of khedives. And in the 1820s, Russia backed Greek-speaking Orthodox rebels who demanded independence from the Ottoman Empire; the Greek cause was actively supported by all the major European powers, and Greece became an independent state in 1830.

Most troubling for the beys of Tunis, France had occupied the Ottoman province of Algeria in 1830—making their eastern border a frontier with the mighty French Empire. The conquest confirmed that the nature of war had changed dramatically; the French easily dominated Ottoman forces.[38] Husayn Bey, Ahmad's uncle, ruled Tunisia when Algiers fell to the French. Eyeing his new neighbor to the west, Husayn Bey followed in the footsteps of Sultan Mahmud II and set out on the path of revitalizing the army. Four years earlier, Mahmud II had abolished the janissary corps, which served as the Ottoman professional military force for centuries. In its place, Mahmud II instituted a conscript-based army known as the *nizam-i cedid*, meaning the "new order." Mehmet 'Ali in Egypt similarly reorganized his army and implemented a draconian regime of conscription, recruiting Europeans to train the new troops in the most advanced military tactics. In 1831, Husayn Bey followed suit by creating a *niẓāmī* unit of the Tunisian army. Instead of professional soldiers, this new unit was made up of sons of the Ottoman military class as well as locals (*min awlādi al-bilād*).[39]

But Husayn Bey's ambitions for his military threatened to destabilize his relationship with Sultan Mahmud II. The new unit was initially trained by two

French officers, following negotiations with a French general to put two of Husayn Bey's relatives in charge of Constantine and Oran, two provincial capitals in Algeria. When the sultan heard about the bey's secret dealings with the French, he was furious; Husayn Bey quickly dispatched two of his most trusted officials to Istanbul, tasked with both allaying Mahmud's fears about the now-abandoned idea of collaborating with France and requesting permission to establish a *niẓāmī* army. The sultan agreed. Perhaps he was unaware that the bey had already begun training his new forces, or perhaps he was happy to shut his eyes in the interest of preserving the delicate division of sovereignty.[40]

Either way, Mahmud II's tolerance of Husayn Bey's military tactics hardly resolved tensions between Istanbul and Tunis. Four years later, Mahmud II's establishment of direct Ottoman rule in Tripolitania presented a serious threat to Tunis's autonomy. Correspondence from Istanbul made it known that the sultan could end the Husaynid dynasty, just as he had ended that of the Qaramanlis—the hereditary dynasty of governors in Tripoli from 1711 to 1835. Successive sultans attempted to extract an annual tribute from Tunis; impose legal and administrative legislation on the province; and dictate local fiscal and military reforms. Looking east, the beys saw the threat of direct rule from Istanbul. Looking west, the beys feared that the French would annex Tunisia to their growing empire.[41]

When Ahmad Bey took the throne in 1837, it appeared all the more urgent to finish the work his predecessor had started. Only a strong military could preserve the degree of autonomy his predecessors had taken for granted. The new bey was eager to expand the small *niẓāmī* unit to include the entire army. He focused on enlarging the infantry by expanding conscription, which reflected the latest European military tactics. Before the 1830s, the Tunisian army had been exclusively staffed by members of the Ottoman military class; the new conscription system thus imposed novel duties on the bey's subjects. As in the Ottoman Empire, Egypt, and Europe, thousands of Tunisian men now found themselves subject to grueling years of obligatory military service. The luckier conscripts could shift to reserve duty after some years; the more unfortunate performed active service for the rest of their lives. Jews, however, were spared this bleak prospect; as in the Ottoman Empire, Ahmad Bey's new army recruited only Muslims. The *niẓāmī* army introduced a new distinction between Muslims and non-Muslims in their relationship to the state.[42] Ahmad Bey's military innovations thus produced major shifts in the nature of belonging in Tunisia.

Ahmad Bey's *niẓāmī* army did not come cheap; new uniforms, a new military school, new weapons, foreign military advisers, and state-run factories to furnish the military's needs—all of these investments cost enormous sums. Already in 1846, Ahmad Bey began to explore the possibility of obtaining a state loan in Europe. This was the model being used by more and more countries seeking to modernize their infrastructure; bankers in the world's financial capitals—London, Paris, and Frankfurt—were making larger and more frequent loans to states across the globe.[43] Ahmad Bey initially sought a loan of thirty million francs from banks in Paris. But the bankers were skittish, in part because of the Sublime Porte's firm opposition to the idea that one of its governors could take out a loan as if he were the ruler of a sovereign state. The Ottoman ambassador in Paris warned the bankers—including Count Salomon Henri d'Avigdor, a Jew from the southwest of France—that the bey of Tunis had no authority to contract a loan on his own.[44] The Sublime Porte's intimidation tactics worked; no banker in Paris would consent to lend Ahmad Bey money.

For some years, Ibn 'Ayyad's success in fleecing the taxpayers paid for Ahmad Bey's innovations and staved off financial ruin. In the Islamic year 1267 (1850–51), however, revenue dropped considerably—to 9.1 million piastres, from a high of nearly 17 million piastres a few years earlier. The following year, 1268 (1851–52), was even worse, with only 6.3 million piastres in revenue.[45] Everyone knew that the only way to confront the looming fiscal crisis was to decrease expenditures, particularly by cutting back on military expenses. But Ahmad Bey flatly refused; the *niẓāmī* army was his greatest accomplishment and only hope of avoiding the fates of his neighbors.[46]

Ibn 'Ayyad was no fool; as the most powerful man in the country after the bey himself, he knew he would be blamed for the impending disaster. Quietly, he transferred his wealth out of the country—along with large sums skimmed from the treasury. Then in June 1852, Ibn 'Ayyad abruptly left Tunisia. He used his millions to install himself rather lavishly in Paris, buying a *hôtel particulier* on the Quai d'Orsay overlooking the Seine. He invested money in real estate, buying the fashionable Passage Saumon, which to this day is known as the Passage Benayed.[47]

Not three months after arriving in Paris, Ibn 'Ayyad took the prudent step of acquiring French nationality. On September 13, 1852, the French government approved a decree of *grande naturalisation* for "Mahmoud Ben Ayad."[48] Becoming a French citizen was not particularly hard, but the vast majority of individuals who naturalized did so through *petite naturalisation*, which gave them only limited political rights. Full (or "great") naturalization required the approval of both chambers of Parliament; it was normally reserved for those who had rendered exceptional services to the state.[49] Ibn ʿAyyad could only have secured such a privilege through his considerable connections and wealth.

Back in Tunis, Ahmad Bey was left with empty coffers and mounting debts. The next month, he suffered a stroke from which he never fully recovered. Mustafa Khaznadar, the minister of finance, stepped into the void that Ibn ʿAyyad left behind, becoming one of the bey's most trusted advisers. With his patron a persona non grata in the Bardo, Nissim demonstrated that his loyalties lay with the bey and Khaznadar, now the bey's prime minister. Khaznadar took Nissim under his wing. When the dust settled, it turned out that rather than sinking Nissim into oblivion, Ibn ʿAyyad's flight allowed Nissim's star to rise even higher.[50]

As Nissim's influence grew, so did his ability to enrich himself. Ibn ʿAyyad paved the way for a concentration of power and wealth, and Nissim hit the ground running. The bey granted his chief tax collector concession after concession, including monopolies on the export of some of Tunisia's most precious commodities, including wood, lime, salt, and charcoal. In the Islamic year 1271 (September 1854 to September 1855), Nissim acquired a monopoly on the exportation of all the country's olives—a privilege for which he paid over a million riyals. For years, Nissim bought the right to farm the customs taxes, which earned him about 150,000 piasters per year.[51] He was well on his way to becoming one of the wealthiest and most influential men in Tunisia.

By now Nissim was spending almost all of his time in the Bardo. At a remove from the dense urban fabric of Tunis, the Bardo's massive scale dominated the landscape. Inside, the palace was decorated in a bewildering mix of North African, Ottoman, and Italian influences: enormous Murano glass chandeliers hung from soaring ceilings, themselves carved with elaborate stucco reliefs; frescoes depicting boating parties and pleasure gardens adorned some rooms; in others, ornate tiles marched across the walls, their floral motifs echoing across the Mediterranean from Grenada to Iznik.

As Nissim rose in the ranks of government service, he did not forget his origins. He introduced family members to his patrons, helping them secure government positions of their own. When Nissim was promoted to head tax collector in 1849, he put forward his brother Nathan to replace him as the tax collector for the Aʿrād (*qābiḍ al-aʿrāḍ*). Nathan's son Solomon (Shlomo in Hebrew)—known by his nickname Momo—became the head of the mint (*qāʾid al-fiḍḍa*), an institution established between 1854 and 1855 as part of Tunisia's efforts to reform its finances and currency.[52] Thanks to Nissim, the

FIGURE 1.2. Mustafa Khaznadar and his son Muhammad, artist unknown, circa 1858–59 (Tunis, Institut National du Patrimoine, Collection Qsar es-Saïd)

Shamamas became a force in the Bardo—a new addition to the country's elite Jewish families with direct access to power.

Despite Ahmad Bey's energy, no amount of reform could stave off the European expansionism that threatened Ottoman integrity. In 1853, another war broke out between the Russian and Ottoman Empires; this time, however, the Ottomans could count on French and British troops to stop further Russian annexation of Ottoman territory. At the beginning of the Crimean War, Sultan Abdulmejid demanded that Tunisia send soldiers from Ahmad Bey's *niẓāmī* army to help with the war effort. Ahmad Bey eagerly complied; at a time of financial uncertainty, demonstrating his loyalty to the empire seemed wise. He sent thousands of infantrymen to join the sultan's army. But Ahmad Bey was denied the satisfaction of seeing his troops bring glory to Tunisia; most perished of disease before they had even seen combat.[53] Ahmad Bey himself passed away before the Treaty of Paris ended the Crimean War. In 1855, his cousin Muhammad succeeded him as bey of Tunis.

In February 1856, Ottoman, French, British, Austro-Hungarian, and Russian diplomats gathered in Paris to negotiate a peace treaty. The Ottomans wanted more than an end to the war; they were determined to be admitted to the community of nations that together made up the budding field of international law. The French and British diplomats involved made it clear that certain reforms would have to be made first, particularly the granting of equality to non-Muslims. This was a profound shift away from the structure of Ottoman society, which up to this point had been premised on a religious hierarchy that privileged Muslims above dhimmīs. The Ottomans could resist neither French and British pressure nor the promise that their sovereignty would at last be fully recognized. Yet while the new laws inaugurated some changes in the nature of legal belonging, the Sublime Porte stopped short of adopting a form of absolute equality like that introduced during the French Revolution.

Sultan Abdulmejid issued the Rescript of Reform (*hatt-i hümayun*), formally abolishing the social and legal hierarchy that had placed Muslims above dhimmīs: "Every distinction or designation tending to make any class whatever of the subjects of my Empire inferior to another class, on account of their religion, language, or race, shall be forever effaced from the Administrative Protocol."[54] The rescript specified a number of concrete ways in which distinctions between religions would cease to matter: from now on, all taxes would be levied equally, all subjects of the empire would be admitted to government schools, and mixed tribunals would be constituted to adjudicate commercial, correctional, and criminal affairs among Muslims and non-Muslims.[55] A month after the rescript was promulgated, the Treaty of Paris officially ended the Crimean War. This treaty technically admitted the Ottoman Empire to the "family of nations" with full sovereign rights under international law. The reality was otherwise, however, as Western states still refused to treat the Ottomans as equals.[56]

While the rescript formally abolished the status of dhimmī, Ottoman reformers had no desire to erase all distinctions between religious groups overnight. In practice, people of different faiths continued to be subject to their respective religious laws for personal matters such as marriage and divorce. For Jews, this meant that rabbinic courts (*batei din*) still had jurisdiction over much of their private life. The government also continued to distinguish between Muslims and non-Muslims in important ways. The rescript demanded that "equality of duties entails that of rights," implying that Christians and Jews would henceforth be subject to military conscription—from which they had previously been exempt.[57] But the government quickly moved to allow non-Muslims to pay an exemption tax instead of performing military service. This tax, called the *bedel-i askeri*, effectively replaced the jizya (*cizye* in Ottoman), the capitation tax formerly paid by dhimmīs. Although there had been some discussion of actually conscripting non-Muslims, military authorities feared it would demoralize troops. Islam was a major source of morale, and Ottoman soldiers traditionally cried "God is great!" (*Allāhu akbar*) when going into battle. From the non-Muslim side, too, there was overwhelming resistance to compulsory military service; Christian authorities categorically opposed conscription. No less consequentially, the jizya was the state's second-largest source of tax income; replacing it with the *bedel-i askeri* ensured that the empire's ever-inadequate revenue stream did not diminish even further.[58]

Nonetheless, the 1856 Rescript of Reform reconfigured the nature of belonging in the Ottoman Empire. The formal abolition of the dhimma may have done relatively little to change the everyday lives of non-Muslim Ottoman subjects. Jews and Christians in the Ottoman Empire still paid taxes to Ottoman-appointed tax collectors—though now instead of the jizya, they paid the *bedel-i askeri*. Jews and Christians were still under the jurisdiction of Ottoman courts, though now their cases with Muslims would go before the new mixed tribunals rather than the courts of governors and *kadis*. But the rescript was hugely important in offering a new basis on which non-Muslim subjects might claim their rights and assert their place in civil society. Some Jews even opted to serve in the military as an expression of patriotism.[59] In the history of Ottoman legal belonging, the 1856 rescript is best understood not as the creation ex nihilo of empire-wide citizenship but rather as a modification of the status quo.

Sultan Abdulmejid was quite clear: he expected Muhammad Bey to promulgate the 1856 Rescript of Reform in Tunisia. But Muhammad Bey, eager to preserve a degree of autonomy from Istanbul, was not keen on doing so. Before long, however, circumstances forced the bey's hand—as it happens, following the execution of a Jew who worked for Nissim. Now ensconced in the halls of power, Nissim played a supporting role in the drama that unfolded.

It all began when Nissim's coachman, Shmuel Sfāz (or Sfez, as Europeans rendered it)—better known by his nickname Bāṭū—was accused of insulting Islam and the Prophet Muḥammad. Some reports claimed that Sfez also ran over a Muslim child while driving Nissim's carriage, and that he was under the influence of alcohol. Calls for Sfez's death came swiftly and loudly. To appease the crowds, the *shaykh al-islām*, the highest Islamic authority in Tunisia, insisted that Sfez be tried according to the Mālikī school of law—which condemned blasphemers to death. The case had a high enough profile to warrant additional scrutiny, so the Mālikī judge's ruling was reviewed by a Hanafī qadi as well. Observers would later claim that the bey deliberately brought the case to a Mālikī court, whose laws regarding the punishment for blasphemy were more stringent than in the Ḥanafī school. Recent research, however, suggests that a death sentence for someone like Sfez was entirely within the norm of both schools of law—and that charges of anti-Jewish sentiment in the sentencing were overblown.

According to one account—quite likely apocryphal, though useful as a lens onto the importance of extraterritoriality in Tunis at the time—Nissim tried to intervene on Sfez's behalf by enlisting the help of the French consul. Ever ready to increase France's influence in Tunisia, the consul agreed to claim Sfez as a French protégé; this would presumably have constituted a form of informal protection with little basis other than his own sympathy for a Jew on death row. Were the bey to consent, then the sentence of the Mālikī qadi would be nullified; Sfez would be under the jurisdiction of the French consulate, and the shari'a court would have no say in the matter. The bey, however, refused the French consul's demands, fearing popular backlash should the blaspheming Jew go unpunished. Sfez was executed on July 24. Another story—again, almost certainly fabricated after the events themselves—recounts that Nissim's only successful intervention on behalf of his late coachman was to prevent an angry mob from throwing his body to the dogs. By tossing coins out of the window of the Bardo, Nissim distracted the crowd long enough for Sfez's corpse to be taken to a secret burial place.[60]

Although these kinds of elaborations on the Sfez story are of dubious accuracy, all agree on the fallout of the execution. Sfez's beheading caused outrage among Tunis's diplomatic community, which used the supposedly unjust punishment to advance its own agenda. The diplomats insisted that even had Sfez been guilty, Muhammad Bey might have had him tried in a Ḥanafī court, which they claimed would have been more lenient. The French and British consuls were particularly vociferous in demanding more protections for non-Muslims; they insisted that the bey enact reforms similar to the Ottoman rescript of the previous year. At first, Muhammad Bey dug in his heels: he had no desire to enforce the rescript in Tunisia. But when a French naval fleet arrived in La Goulette at the end of August, he realized he had little choice in the matter. Once again, gunboat diplomacy allowed European powers to impose their will. The bey convened his advisers, including the *shaykh al-islām* and Mustafa Khaznadar, to discuss the promulgation of the sultan's Rescript of Reform in Tunisia. Khaznadar argued in favor of reform, and the *shaykh al-islām* affirmed that the rescript did not violate the shari'a. On September 10, 1857, Muhammad Bey proclaimed the 'Ahd al-Amān (pact of security), dubbed the "Fundamental Pact" in European languages. Although not a direct translation of the Ottoman rescript, the 'Ahd al-Amān was very much in the spirit of its predecessor.[61]

The 'Ahd al-Amān laid the foundation for the formal abolition of dhimmī status, as in the Ottoman Empire. Yet the text of the new law was careful to adhere to Islamic legal precedents.[62] For instance, Article 3 declared that "the inhabitants of our province, both Muslims and non-Muslims, are equal regarding the pursuit of justice." The French translation, however, rendered this clause as "equal before the law."[63] Having equal rights to pursue justice and claiming an identical status before the law are two different things; it was part of the traditional interpretation of the protection (dhimma) accorded to non-Muslims that the sovereign was responsible for ensuring their just treatment—that is, guaranteeing their right to justice. A Muslim sovereign's duties required him to ensure justice for all of his subjects. The Arabic, in other words, is far less radical than the French and implies a different kind of equality.

This mistranslation may well have been deliberate—either on the part of the European diplomats who pressured Muhammad Bey into promulgating the ʿAhd al-Amān or that of the Tunisian government itself. The language of equality employed in the bey's decree gestured toward the expanded rights for Jews demanded by the French and British ambassadors, while avoiding making any proclamations that would go against Islamic law or political theology. Nor was Muhammad Bey alone in adopting this strategy; in 1864, the sultan of Morocco, Mawlay Hasan, similarly found himself under diplomatic pressure to abolish Jews' status as dhimmīs. Instead, he issued a decree that employed a new language of equal treatment, proclaiming that "all people are equal in justice."[64] The difference was not in kind but rather in interpretation: the Moroccan decree was never understood as having abolishing Jews' status as dhimmīs.

While the ʿAhd al-Amān proclaimed a certain kind of equality among Muslims and non-Muslims, it also continued to use the language of dhimma and refer to Jews as dhimmīs. The fourth article begins with the assurance that no "dhimmī from among our subjects will be forced to change his religion" nor will dhimmīs be prevented from fulfilling the duties of their religion. This is "because their dhimma [protection] requires that they have the same rights as us and the same duties as us."[65] This ambiguity is not apparent in the French version of the ʿAhd al-Amān, which translates dhimmīs as "our Jewish subjects" (*nos sujets israélites*). The ʿAhd al-Amān was similarly vague concerning the way in which Muslims and non-Muslims were to be "equal regarding the pursuit of justice"—far more so than its model, the Ottoman Rescript of Reform. Sultan Abdulmejid's decree prescribed equality among Muslims, Jews, and Christians, both in the administration and public sphere. But the ʿAhd al-Amān said nothing about abolishing hierarchies. Similarly, the Ottoman rescript loosened many of the restrictions on the "public exercise of religion" among non-Muslims.[66] Muhammad Bey's version, on the other hand, merely said that a dhimmī "would not be prevented from that which is required by his religion."[67]

The ambiguity of the ʿAhd al-Amān was not lost on Tunisian officials. Nearly two months after the ʿAhd al-Amān was promulgated, Khaznadar convened a council of Muslim notables and scholars to produce a commentary on the new decree. They were to meet every Wednesday and Thursday in the *qasba,* the bey's complex at the western edge of Tunis. The scholars, however, were uncomfortable with the sweeping nature of the reforms, particularly around the status of Jews. They could not accept absolute equality that abolished the hierarchy placing Muslims above Jews. And while they were happy to accord non-Muslims the right of religious freedom, they insisted that public religious displays, forbidden to dhimmīs in Islamic law, remain off-limits. The scholars knew they were fighting a losing battle in taking a strictly traditionalist approach to the dhimma and other matters; they requested that the bey permit them to step down from the council tasked with explicating the ʿAhd al-Amān.[68]

The administrative officials carried on their debates without the scholars. In a session in February 1858, the question of the term dhimmī arose. The governor of the Aʿrād, a man named Muhammad, objected: "We should not accept this word, since the people left the dhimma."[69] The minister of war, Mustafa Bash Agha, concurred. But as became clear in subsequent deliberations on the legal belonging of Tunisian Jews, the debate over the new status of dhimmīs hardly ended with this council.

Even if the ʿAhd al-Amān did not institute absolute and immediate equality between the bey's Jewish and Muslim subjects, it did usher in a number of changes in the rights that Jews could claim. The ʿAhd al-Amān demanded that any time a Jew was accused of a crime in a government court, the Jewish community could name a representative "who will defend against any injustice that they might commit against him."[70] (The decree was silent regarding whether Jews would serve in the military, and there is no indication that Jews were ever conscripted.) Following the promulgation of the ʿAhd al-Amān, Muhammad Bey specified that the proclamation of equality meant that Jews could now acquire real estate.[71] Jews were also permitted to wear the same clothing as Muslims—including the red *shāshīya* previously prohibited to them. Shortly thereafter, they were also allowed to live outside the ḥāra, where the demand for space had driven real estate prices impossibly high.[72] Together, the ʿAhd al-Amān and the decrees that followed made an important statement regarding the bey's commitment to ensuring justice for all of his subjects.

Nor was the ʿAhd al-Amān the only sign of change in Tunisia. Muhammad Bey embraced a number of reforms intended to improve living conditions in Tunis, including establishing a municipal council to improve the city's sanitation. The chair of the new city council was none other than Husayn b. ʿAbdallah, who would later play an outsized role in the Shamama case.[73] The bey also authorized the building of telegraph lines connecting the palaces and ministerial chambers of the Bardo to Tunis and then on to La Goulette. But he was not to live to see the fruits of his labor. On September 21, 1859, just four years after taking the throne, Muhammad Bey passed away.[74]

Muhammad III al-Sadiq succeeded his brother. Sadiq Bey, as he was known, had a handsome, commanding face and an imposing presence. The new bey

FIGURE 1.3. Sadiq Bey, by Auguste Moynier, 1861 (Tunis, Institut National du Patrimoine, Collection Qsar es-Saïd)

was an enthusiastic adopter of the reforms his predecessor had so tentatively ventured. As he prepared to occupy expanded and renovated quarters in the Bardo, he set the tone for a new chapter in Tunisia's history.[75]

Sadiq Bey was happy to give Nissim even more power. About a month after he took the throne, the bey appointed Nissim *qā'id al-yahūd*, head of the Jewish community.[76] In this position, Qā'id Nissim—as he was now known—stood at the intersection between the organized Jewish community and the bey. When Jews complained of abuses by government officials, it was Nissim's role to intervene with Khaznadar and even the bey himself. Some traces of this activity survive. In 1861, a Jewish woman was abducted by a Muslim in El Kef, a small town near the Algerian border. Nissim sent a letter to the suspected abductor, hoping the intervention would rescue his coreligionist.[77] As qā'id, Nissim also played a judicial role. The qā'id al-yahūd typically ran an informal court alongside the *beit din*, the rabbinic court headed by the chief rabbi in Tunis. Nissim might well have adjudicated a wide range of intra-Jewish civil disputes, such as unpaid debts, accusations of theft, violations of the Sabbath, and perhaps even some minor crimes.[78]

The following spring, Sadiq Bey named Nissim receiver general (*ra'īs al-qubbāḍ*) and director of finance (*mudīr al-mālīya*).[79] The appointment of a Jew to such a high position should not be mistaken for a result of modernizing reforms or a product of the administration's new commitment to equality. Jews had occupied senior positions in the country's treasury since the early modern period.[80] Nissim, however, was the first member of the Shamama family to climb to such a high post in Tunisia's government.

Head of the country's finances, head of its Jewish community, and intercessor par excellence—Nissim was indisputably the most powerful Jew in Tunisia. At the same time, he amassed more and more wealth through tax farms, concessions for the exportation of raw materials, and investments in real estate. Jewish newspapers in Europe reported that Nissim was on intimate terms with the bey himself—seeing him on a daily basis, and accompanying him to his summer residences and excursions to hot springs. The press even claimed that Nissim alone controlled the finances of the entire state—a report that smacks of internalized antisemitism.[81]

As Nissim's wealth increased, so did his philanthropy. He founded a yeshivah, a Jewish institution of higher learning where "scholars study and are fed every day."[82] He financed the publication of dozens of books, mainly in Livorno—a major center of Hebrew printing since the eighteenth century—as well as in Palestine.[83] The same year he became receiver general, he made an ostentatious gift to the main synagogue in Tunis. He engaged the renowned goldsmith Maurice Meyer in Paris to make an octagonal case (*tik*) for a Torah scroll, a crown to decorate the Torah, two finials (*rimonim*) to adorn the top of the scroll, and a pointer (*yad*)—all silver and gold ornaments "of exceptional artistic value."[84] Nissim worked hard to craft a reputation as someone who was "generous and feared God."[85]

Once the restrictions on Jews' ownership of real estate were lifted, Nissim set out to build a lavish palace—one that would rival those of other high officials like the Ibn 'Ayyads and Khaznadar himself. He bought a property at the edge of the ḥāra on an unnamed street later known as Qā'id Nissim Street (now Nahj al-Mishnaqa), a narrow road whose houses on the east side abutted the walls of the city.[86] Nissim's residence was massive; occupying nearly the entire block, its sheer size would have impressed any passerby. It must have seemed particularly out of place amid the modest residences of the ḥāra; unlike other parts of the city where moneyed families had lived for centuries, the ḥāra's streets were lined by small buildings with only a first or at most second floor. Nissim's palace rose three ostentatious stories high, with enormous windows on each floor.

Yet like most of the grand residences of Tunis, Nissim's palace kept its greatest splendors hidden. From the street, little other than the size of the palace was visible. Two small doors flanked the main entrance; one led to private apartments, and the other to a private synagogue on the second floor—what Yiddish speakers would call a *shtibl*—common in the houses of wealthy Jews across the Maghrib.[87] Two columns framed the oversized, imposing door of the porte cochere. But once one penetrated the carriage entrance, the full extent of Nissim's illustriousness came into view. On the ground floor, a grand hallway with a large marble staircase at the end gave way to a vast interior courtyard housing stables, kitchens, and storehouses. On the second floor, an interior patio led to elegant reception rooms. One long room parallel to the street held a series of safe boxes, some sealed to the wall. Here Qā'id Nissim stored the taxes he collected. The walls of these elegant rooms were covered in Italian tiles up to the ceiling, from which a Venetian chandelier was suspended—echoing the grand rooms in the Bardo. The third floor housed the family's private apartments. On clear days, Nissim was able to see across the city's rooftops to the lagoon and even the Mediterranean beyond.[88]

Yet no amount of wealth or luxury could mask the personal disappointment that haunted Nissim's worldly success. His first wife, Hanna Bellaiche—the widow of his cousin Moshe—could not give him any children.[89] As was common among wealthy Jews in the Middle East, Nissim took a second wife, Mas'uda Elmaya, his paternal cousin. But Mas'uda was also unable to produce an heir for Nissim. One imagines that the reproductive problem was his. Despite having two wives, the most powerful Jew in Tunis was without a child to carry on his legacy or to fulfill the commandment to be fruitful and multiply.

Nissim was not a man to wallow in self-pity, however. And though he was unable to have children of his own, he found an outlet for his paternal instincts. Nissim's first wife, Hanna, had been married previously—to another Shamama who died in 1840 and with whom she had a daughter named Esther. The desire to keep marriages in the family was strong enough that Esther married Nissim's nephew Momo. But Momo and Esther did not get along, and the marriage swiftly ended in divorce. Esther returned to live with her mother, Hanna—now married to Nissim. She had managed to get pregnant before divorcing, though; not long after leaving Momo, she gave birth to a baby girl, whom she named 'Aziza—who came to be known by the affectionate diminutive Zeza. Even after Esther remarried (to yet another Shamama), young 'Aziza remained in her great uncle Nissim's house. Although Jewish law does not allow for formal adoption, Nissim became 'Aziza's de facto father: "The qā'id loved 'Aziza, and she was like a daughter to him. . . . [H]e did everything for her, and fulfilled her every desire."[90] From this point on, 'Aziza provided the light that illuminated Nissim's life, the outlet for his affection, and the comfort he never found in his marriages. She would remain by his side until the day he died.

2

Financial Trouble (1859–64)

AMONG THE MANY properties that Nissim acquired was a large house with a vast interior courtyard in the port town of Halq al-wadi. Known as La Goulette in European languages, this sleepy village—perched on a narrow strip of land between the lagoon and the Mediterranean—remains Tunis's gateway to the world. Nissim was just a short walk away from the docks where ships lumbered into harbor. There he might have glimpsed weary migrants from across the Mediterranean arriving to try their luck in North Africa. Many came to work on the ambitious engineering projects commissioned by Sadiq Bey. Others planned to take advantage of an expanding economy. Almost all the immigrants were Christians from southern Europe, hoping to escape the desperate poverty they faced in their home countries.[1]

But even poor laborers arriving from Sicily in the 1860s found themselves in an advantageous legal position. Thanks to the capitulations—a series of privileges first granted by Ottoman sultans to European states in the medieval period—Europeans benefited from extraterritorial privileges in Tunisia. Thus a penniless Sicilian in Tunis lived almost entirely under the jurisdiction of the Italian consul.[2] Over the course of the nineteenth century, the capitulations came to define the status of not only Sicilians and other European migrants in Tunis but growing numbers of the bey's subjects as well. Increasingly, legal belonging in Tunis was inflected by the expansion of extraterritorial privileges.[3] The extraterritorial context of legal belonging became a major point of contention in the Shamama lawsuit.

Even as Tunis became a magnet for migrants from all over the Mediterranean, a devastating financial crisis was brewing. Short on cash, the bey's government contracted one international loan after another, none of which the treasury could afford. The disastrous effects of these policies included a violent civil war, bankruptcy, and eventually, colonization. As director of finances,

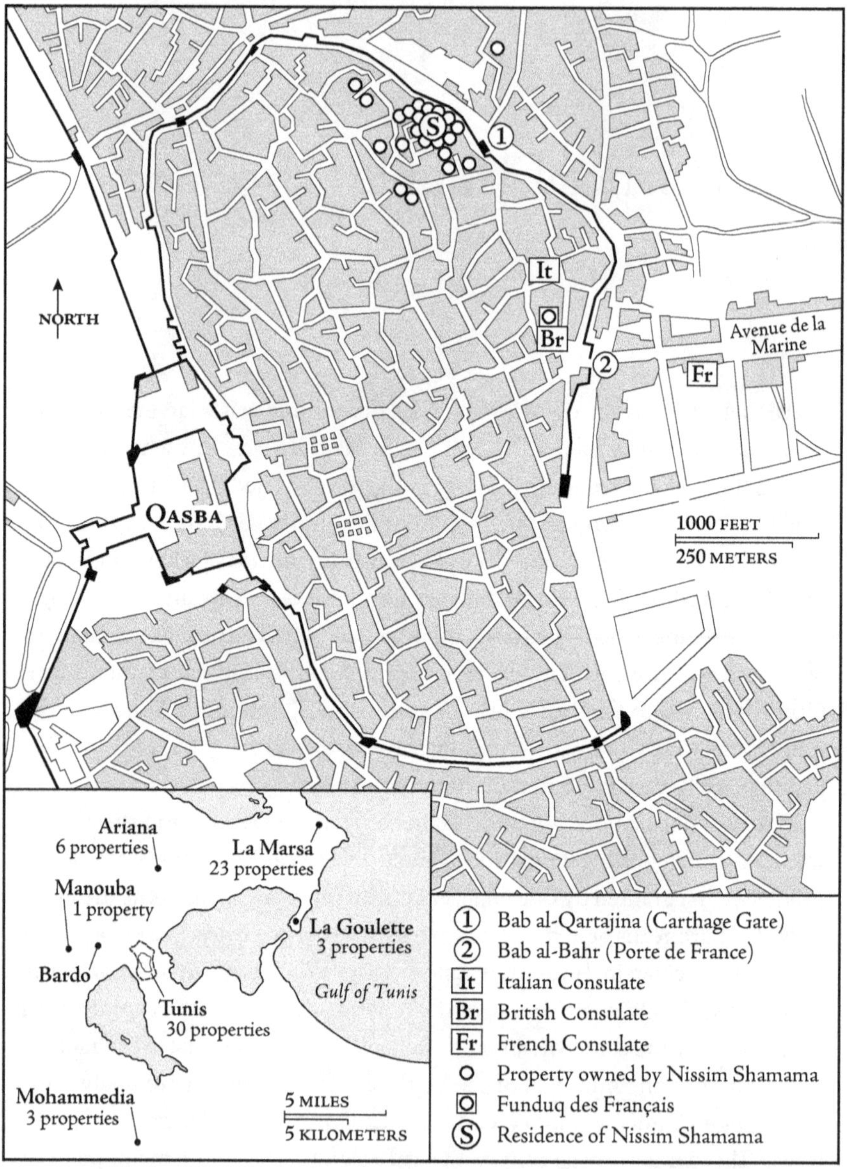

FIGURE 2.1. Tunis and its environs, with Nissim's sixty-six properties, circa 1873

Nissim played a major role in both the negotiations for loans and in the popular uprising; this confluence of events eventually pushed him to depart for Paris, leaving behind his homeland forever.

Tunis had been tightly connected to the northern shores of the Mediterranean for hundreds of years by commercial networks, and especially in the early modern period, an economy of captivity and ransom. Privateers from Italian city-states, the Spanish Empire, and the Knights of Malta raided ships from what was known as the Barbary Coast. In return, North African corsairs captured vessels from across Europe. Tunis was a center of this exchange; until the late eighteenth century, thousands of enslaved Christians lived as domestic slaves or languished in the bagnios (slave quarters) of the bey awaiting sale or ransom. In 1662, a missionary and consul of France named Jean le Vacher founded Saint-Croix, the first Catholic parish within the walls of Tunis.[4] And even during the height of Mediterranean privateering, a small number of free Christians also made their home in the Frankish quarter. The community was a mix of French, Britons, Genoese, Sicilians, and Austro-Hungarians. They were mostly merchants engaged in international trade, with a smattering of artisans serving these foreigners' needs. In 1757, only twenty-one French residents were counted by the consul—mostly merchants, in addition to a baker and tavern keeper. In 1816, the small French "nation" had grown to 161 individuals, including a consul, vice-consul, three employees, and "agents" in Bizerte, Porto Farino, and La Goulette.[5]

With the rise of mass migration in the nineteenth century, thousands more southern Europeans crossed the Mediterranean and settled in Tunis. During the earliest years of the Risorgimento, Italian nationalists—exiled from their respective peninsular states—found refuge from prosecution in Tunis. Giuseppe Garibaldi, who became the greatest military hero of Italian unification, stayed in Tunis for a few months. When Sadiq Bey began to hire Sicilian laborers for his various public works projects, thousands more migrants arrived from the island. They came to dredge the *buhayra* and expand Tunis in the direction of the lagoon. These Sicilians at first settled in the Frankish quarter in the old city, close to the Bab al-Bahr, the gate of the sea.[6] Another set of Christians streamed into Tunis from Malta, which the British had ruled since 1800. These Maltese left their stony island in large numbers looking for work. Though Catholic, they had the advantage of already speaking the local language—Maltese being a dialect of Arabic closely related to the Tunisian one. They settled just outside the Carthage Gate, not far from Nissim's new palace.[7] The Maltese gained something of a monopoly on the business of carriages for hire in Tunis, just as immigrants across the United States today drive taxis. Anyone who needed a horse-drawn carriage, but was not wealthy enough to own one himself—as Qā'id Nissim did—would flag down a Maltese carriage driver. By the time Nissim acquired his property in La Goulette, the sleepy port town was already full of European tavern keepers. These businesses supplied a steady stream of alcohol to the growing non-Muslim population (and probably some Muslims on the sly).[8]

The city expanded to accommodate its new arrivals. In building new neighborhoods, the bey embraced the neoclassical ideal of wide, straight avenues, like the ones Baron Georges-Eugène Haussmann was cutting through Paris. Engineers finished the Promenade de la Marine in the summer of 1861—a wide, tree-lined boulevard connecting the walled city from the Bab al-Bahr to the lagoon. It is hard to imagine Tunis without this grand boulevard, today called Avenue Bourguiba.[9] In the early 1860s, the Promenade de la Marine was revolutionary; whereas the walled city turned its back on the water, the new neighborhoods opened directly onto the lagoon and the Mediterranean beyond. Soon houses, cafés, and stores sprung up along the promenade. Ever-growing numbers of immigrants from the Italian Peninsula settled near the docks.[10] The first and grandest building was the French consulate, situated just a few hundred yards from the Bab al-Bahr and giving onto the promenade itself. A majestic, imposing neoclassical building, the consulate commanded the new neighborhoods of Tunis in a foreshadowing of French domination to come.[11]

Given the danger and frequent tragedy of migration across the Mediterranean from south to north today, it is hard to imagine the flow being reversed. But such was the nature of booming ports in the nineteenth century—places like Alexandria, Smyrna (now Izmir), Beirut, and of course Tunis, where people from all over the Mediterranean arrived to make their fortunes. And like the other port cities of the late Ottoman Empire, the new arrivals meant an explosion in the extraterritorial privileges that came to define legal belonging.

These privileges were outlined in the capitulations. Named after the chapters, or *capituli*, into which they were organized, the capitulations accorded foreign consulates relatively broad jurisdiction over members of their "nations." The

Ottoman Empire first extended these sorts of privileges to Italian city-states in the late fourteenth century.[12] In 1589, the capitulation granted by Sultan Selim II to France became a model that states such as Britain, the Habsburg Empire, and the Netherlands soon followed.[13] It ensured that disputes between French subjects would be decided by their consul; those between a French subject and an Ottoman subject would go before an Ottoman court, but only in the presence of an official French interpreter. And French residents in the Ottoman Empire would be exempt from local taxes.[14] In other words, the capitulations ensured that the community of French subjects in the empire—made up mainly of merchants—remained almost entirely under the jurisdiction of French officials.

The capitulations' reach into Tunisia became another matter over which successive sultans and beys jockeyed in tracing the delineations of their overlapping sovereignty. Ottoman sultans signed capitulations with foreign powers in which the province of Tunisia was included. Yet the beys of Tunis began signing their own treaties early on. The first treaty between Tunis and France was signed in 1604, just fifteen years after the sultan's capitulation. The first paragraph guaranteed that the bey of Tunis would "order that the capitulations and treaties made between the kings of France and the sultans, emperors of the Turks . . . would be kept, followed, and observed as they should be."[15]

As in the rest of the Ottoman Empire, the privileges accorded to foreign subjects in Tunisia were gradually expanded; in another peace treaty signed with France in 1665, disputes between the bey's subjects and those of France would only be heard by the bey himself—"not by the *divan* [presumably a governor's court] or the *qadi*."[16] The beys of Tunis signed similar treaties with other European powers—Britain, the Netherlands, Sweden, and various Italian city-states.[17] By the late eighteenth century, the capitulations were a well-established fact of life in Tunisia. And though always modeled on those capitulations signed by the Ottoman sultans, foreign diplomats in Tunisia continued to communicate directly with the bey of Tunis for all matters concerning the people under their protection.

By the mid-nineteenth century, the capitulations posed a serious challenge to the bey's sovereignty. The balance of power between the Ottoman Empire and European states had shifted decisively over the course of the second half of the eighteenth century. With greater and greater frequency, foreign diplomats in Tunisia called on their countries' warships to put pressure on the beys when their requests were denied. This gunboat diplomacy lurked in the background of all the privileges enjoyed by those under foreign protection.[18]

In this context of military inequality, the privileges granted to Europeans took on new meaning. Until the first decades of the nineteenth century, only small numbers of foreigners escaped the bey's sovereignty by invoking the capitulations; the entire European population of Tunisia usually hovered in the hundreds or low thousands. But with European states' increasing appetite for commercial expansion and their newfound military might, the privileges granted by the capitulations took on new meaning. First, there were more and more Europeans settling in Tunisia—from the working-class Sicilians and Maltese, to French and British merchants eager to make their fortune by expanding the region's international trade. Second, the French and British Empires now ruled over parts of the Mediterranean from which migrants spread out across North Africa. The thousands of Maltese driving carts for hire in Tunis were subjects of the British Empire, as Malta had been under British rule since 1816. These Maltese were thus under the authority of the British consulate in Tunis. Algerians also settled in Tunisia—some to escape colonial rule, and others simply for economic opportunities. Shortly after the occupation of Algiers, French authorities declared that Algerians in the Ottoman Empire—including in Tunisia—were under the jurisdiction of French consulates.[19]

At the same time, subjects of the bey increasingly joined the ranks of those benefiting from extraterritorial privileges. During the early modern period, foreign consulates had extended their "protection" to local employees—primarily translators, or dragomen, who served as intermediaries with Ottoman officials. But throughout the eighteenth century, few individuals benefited from consular protection (*ḥimāya* in Arabic, or a *berat* in Ottoman).[20] As European consuls gained more and more power—and as the advantages of extraterritorial privileges became clearer—increasing numbers of the bey's subjects sought foreign protection. These protégés technically remained under the bey's sovereignty, yet were entitled to most of the extraterritorial privileges accorded to foreign nationals. Other subjects of the bey sought naturalization abroad, only to return to Tunisia as French, Italian, Austro-Hungarian, Prussian, or British nationals.[21]

The acquisition of foreign protection by Muslims proved particularly controversial for legal authorities in Tunis and elsewhere in North Africa. Some jurists considered foreign protection a form of apostasy since it required Muslims to submit themselves to laws other than the shari'a. A legal dispute over this question arose in 1847, when Muhammad 'Annabi, *qadi* of Ra's al-Jabal (in the northeast of Tunisia), claimed that the *amīr* of Ghar al-Milh (Porto Farina, not far from Ra's al-Jabal) had kidnapped his two sons. Even after 'Annabi paid the ransom, the official refused to free his sons. 'Annabi then sought refuge and protection in a foreign consulate, though sources differ over whether it was British or French. If it was in the French consulate, and he was indeed from 'Annaba (Bône) in Algeria, as his name suggests, then 'Annabi would have been entitled to French protection as a subject of France abroad.[22] If it was British protection he obtained, then 'Annabi simply invoked the consulate's status as a sanctuary, within which anyone was entitled to security. When word of the consul's actions reached Ahmad Bey, he sent a request for a *fatwā* (*istiftā'*) to Ibrahim al-Riyahi, the chief mufti of Tunis, asking whether 'Annabi had contravened Islamic law in seeking foreign protection. Al-Riyahi defended 'Annabi's choice to seek protection, explaining that nothing in Islamic law prohibited such an action. A prominent jurist in Morocco, however, disagreed; in a response to al-Riyahi's fatwa, al-Mahdi al-Wazzani ruled that "seeking the protection of the infidels today means abandoning Islam."[23]

Doubt about the permissibility of foreign protection did little to stem the tide of Muslims pursuing protégé status. Even prominent government officials obtained foreign protection; Muhammad Ibn 'Ayyad, Mahmud's father, took refuge in the British consulate in 1847, when a rift with his son—at the time, Ahmad Bey's most trusted adviser—made Muhammad fear for his property and perhaps his life.[24] Even if seeking the protection of foreign powers was not unanimously considered to be against Islamic law, the practice undoubtedly chipped away at the bey's sovereignty. One of the bey's most important roles was to ensure justice, which he did by both overseeing the judicial system and personally adjudicating disputes. When his own subjects turned instead to consulates and consular courts, not only was the bey prevented from exercising jurisdiction over them; his *raison d'être* as a ruler ebbed away.

Jews were even more likely than Muslims to seek out foreign protection. Jewish religious authorities saw no problem with submitting to consular jurisdiction since Jewish courts had always existed alongside other legal orders. Many Jews acquired patents of protection through ordinary channels by serving as translators, intermediaries, or commercial representatives for foreign consulates and merchants.[25] The largest group of Tunisian Jews that acquired extraterritorial privileges did so not as protégés but rather as descendants of Sephardic Jewish migrants who had come to Tunisia from the Italian Peninsula. Known as the Grana, after the Arabic name of Livorno (al-Ghurna), these

Sephardim came to Tunisia starting in the seventeenth century. Their history became a central point of contention in the Shamama case. Two years after leaving Tunis, Nissim wrote to the king of Italy asking for naturalization as an Italian; he explained that his desire for Italian citizenship came from his Livornese heritage. In other words, Nissim claimed membership in Tunisia's Grana community—and made this the basis of his request for citizenship in the new Italian state. By the mid-nineteenth century, the Grana were harbingers of the growing importance of extraterritoriality in Tunisia; as such, they are central to the story of legal belonging.

Most Grana came to Tunis via Livorno, the Mediterranean's first free port.[26] By the eighteenth century, a handful of Sephardi families dominated large parts of Tunisia's international trade, especially with Tuscany. In 1720, the recent Sephardi arrivals formally split from the local Jewish community, known as the Twansa (Tunisian dialect for *Tūnisīyūn*, or "residents of Tunis"); each group maintained its own synagogues, butcheries, cemeteries, and finances. The Grana were set apart from the Twansa in other ways; most wore European-style dress—though in the early nineteenth century, this caused conflict with governmental authorities. They employed a combination of different languages, using Spanish in addition to Judeo-Arabic and Hebrew, to record important documents in their communal record books (*pinkasim*), such as communal ordinances (*takkanot*), marriage records, and contracts.[27] Many prominent Grana merchants strategically stationed members of the family all over the Mediterranean—certainly in Livorno, but also in Alexandria, Smyrna, and elsewhere.[28]

When Livorno fell on hard times in the nineteenth century, a new infusion of Sephardic Jews headed for Tunis—part of a wave of Livornese Jews seeking better fortunes on the other side of the Mediterranean. The Guttieres family were among the second wave of immigrants. They arrived sometime in the 1820s or early 1830s, bringing their sons Giacomo and Angelo, born in Livorno in 1823 and 1824, respectively. After arriving in Tunis, three more sons were born: Cesare, Abramo, and Guglielmo.[29] Giacomo would later play a central role in the Shamama lawsuit. A few Jews arrived in smaller numbers from other parts of the Italian Peninsula and joined the Grana community. In 1840, the first Italian school in Tunis was founded by a Jewish man named Morpurgo, whose family originally hailed from Trieste.[30] These families came speaking Italian (rather than Spanish) and often with a highly developed sense of their Europeanness.

The Grana were considered subjects of the bey until the mid-nineteenth century. When Tuscany signed its first peace treaty with Tunisia in 1748, none of the Grana settled in Tunis attempted to avail themselves of the privileges accorded to other subjects of the duke of Tuscany. In 1822, Mahmud Bey signed another peace treaty with Tuscany, following the resumption of corsairing during the revolutionary and Napoleonic wars; he insisted that "the Jews who have lived here [in Tunis] for a long time, or for some years, known as Grana or Livornese, shall be considered local subjects."[31] But as more and more Europeans arrived in Tunis and claimed extraterritorial privileges, members of Tunis's Grana community realized that they were missing out on significant advantages. Some traveled to Tuscany, obtained passports in Livorno, and then returned to Tunis—where for two years at least, they would be recognized as Tuscan subjects. Finally, in 1846, the Tuscan consul in Tunis convinced Ahmad Bey to renegotiate the 1822 treaty and recognize Livornese Jews as subjects of the duke of Tuscany who could retain their extraterritorial privileges for as long as they remained in Tunisia.[32] Technically, however, the Grana Jews who arrived before 1822 would still be considered subjects of the bey. Yet given the dense networks tying the Grana in Tunis to their coreligionists in Livorno, it was not difficult to procure documentation attesting to their status as Tuscan subjects; again, a voyage and brief stay in Livorno would do the trick.[33] (Nissim, on the other hand, seems not to have bothered; though he would later claim Livornese ancestry, he never invoked this status to acquire Tuscan subjecthood while living in Tunis.) With unification in 1861, Tuscan Jews in Tunisia automatically became Italian citizens. The advantages of their extraterritorial status allowed this community to become even more prominent in Tunisia's international trade.[34]

Italian and Maltese migrants, French and British merchants, Algerians, Livornese Jews, and locals with consular protection—all of these individuals with extraterritorial privileges lived like turtles carrying shells of foreign sovereignty on their backs. They avoided paying almost all taxes to the bey, escaped the jurisdiction of the local government, and could count on their consular officials' support whenever they got into trouble. Each time foreigners appealed to their consuls for protection, the growing diplomatic corps in Tunis found a new excuse to meddle in Tunisia's internal affairs. Unpaid debts owed by Tunisian subjects, theft real or imagined, and accusations of assault or even murder—almost any problem could be referred to the consul, who would duly write to the relevant Tunisian authorities to claim justice on behalf of his people. Just as Sadiq Bey began in earnest to centralize his administration and consolidate power, he found his authority increasingly riddled with extraterritorial holes.

The drumbeat of consuls demanding privileges for their protégés gave new meaning to legal belonging in Tunisia. There was little the bey could do about the capitulations; Ottoman authorities had tried for years to abolish them, without much success. The balance of power was such that European states could simply demand the continuation of extraterritorial privileges. Nor could the bey limit the numbers of migrants from Italy or Malta, or the Algerians who were protected by the French consulate; closing borders to foreigners was largely unheard of at this time.[35] The only thing left to do was to curb the numbers of locals who acquired extraterritorial privileges by attaching themselves to a foreign state.

The challenge of extraterritorial incursions on the bey's sovereignty shaped the new rules around legal belonging promulgated in 1861. That year, Sadiq Bey issued a decree called the *Qānūn al-Dawla* (law of the state). Known subsequently as the Constitution—and considered the first of its kind in the Islamic world—Sadiq Bey's Qānūn was in many ways a follow-up to the 'Ahd al-Amān; comprising 114 articles, it prescribed the responsibilities of the bey, the organization of the government, and the rights and duties of ordinary Tunisians. Expanding on a promise made in the 'Ahd al-Amān, the Qānūn set a "fixed term" of military service required of all male Muslims and set the age of eligibility at eighteen.[36] New courts were to be instituted, including commercial courts, a civil and criminal court, and an appeals court; all were to adjudicate "in accordance with the laws enacted for them."[37] The Qānūn also instituted a grand council (*majlis al-akbar*), made up of sixty Muslim men—twenty ministers and forty notables chosen by the bey and his advisers—which would act as "the guardian of the pacts and laws, and the defender of the rights of all the inhabitants."[38] The council was charged with guaranteeing equality before the law for all Tunisians, regardless of religious persuasion. Nonetheless, Jews were not allowed to be members of the council—a sign of the ways in which their differentiated status persisted.[39]

In addition to these centralizing reforms, the Qānūn attempted to curb the explosion of Tunisians claiming extraterritorial privileges. Given the imbalance of power, launching a frontal attack on the prerogatives of European diplomats was out of the question. The only way to limit the number of Tunisians with foreign protection was to regulate their ability to escape the allegiance they owed the bey. An article devoted to those who sought naturalization abroad proclaimed that "every Tunisian [*al-tūnisī*] who is expatriated—for whatever reason, whatever the length of his absence, and whether he is naturalized abroad or not—becomes a Tunisian subject again on reentering Tunisia."[40] Rather than recognize these Tunisians as foreign nationals, the bey insisted that in Tunisia, they would remain Tunisian subjects. The Qānūn further specified that "non-Muslims subjects of the bey who change their religion will remain under the protection of Tunisia and among its subjects."[41] This article was mainly directed at Jews who, under the tutelage of foreign missionaries, converted to Christianity and then claimed consular protection as a kind of bonus.[42]

The regulations concerning legal belonging in the Qānūn were not the beginning of Tunisian nationality or citizenship.[43] But they were a new attempt to more closely define the nature of legal belonging in Tunisia, just as Ottoman authorities would do eight years later by passing the Ottoman nationality law (*tabiiyet-i osmaniye kanunnamesi*). The 1869 Ottoman law similarly forbade voluntary expatriation; it warned Ottoman subjects that even if they naturalized abroad, the Ottoman authorities would still consider them subjects of the sultan. Like the Qānūn, the drafters of the Ottoman nationality law hoped to curb the growing number of people with extraterritorial privileges, each of whom compromised the sultan's sovereignty.[44]

But the regulations of the Qānūn did relatively little to limit the expansion of extraterritoriality in Tunisia. As a high-ranking government official, Nissim regularly faced the challenges of dealing with those who had acquired extraterritorial privileges. In October 1861, for instance, Nissim wrote to Mustafa Khaznadar concerning a debt of 115,000 piasters that the government owed to Shim'on Natan and Monsieur "Kulun" (Colonne?). Three weeks later, he wrote again saying that Shim'on and Kulun had not been paid, and were demanding their money—along with three other merchants. Nissim was concerned precisely because these merchants were foreign nationals and had threatened to ask for their consul's help in securing payment.[45] This was no empty menace; consuls spent much of their time ensuring that those under their jurisdiction were able to collect their debts. Like the bey, Nissim was hamstrung by the webs of extraterritorial privileges surrounding the Tunisian government.

The hazards of the capitulations aside, a mood of optimism prevailed among reform-minded Tunisians. Nissim enthusiastically championed the government's latest legislation, financing a translation of the 'Ahd al-Amān and the Qānūn into Judeo-Arabic. The project was spearheaded by three of his coreligionists: Mordekhai Tapia, the son of the Grana's chief rabbi; Eliyahu Elmilik, born in Bône in Algeria (and thus benefiting from French protection), who would later play a central role in the Shamama lawsuit; and Moshe Bishi b. Ya'akov Shamama, who was the lead author of the translation thanks to his fluency in Arabic.[46] The three titled their translation *Qānūn al-dawla al-tūnisīya* (law of the Tunisian state); it was among the first Hebrew alphabet books printed in Tunisia.[47] As they explained in the introduction, the Qānūn was "written in proper Arabic, which makes it difficult to understand."[48] Since most Jews did not read Arabic, and since Sadiq Bey had promulgated the Qānūn for everyone—both Jews and Muslims—Moshe Shamama decided to publish this version in "the Barbary Arabic language [Tunisian Judeo-Arabic] so that all Jews, may God preserve them, can understand and know these laws."[49] The introduction ended with a prayer for the longevity and health of "General Nissim Shamama, head of the Jews, who shelters me under his wing; may God keep and protect him with everlasting strength and eternal happiness, Amen."[50]

Political success aside, Nissim's domestic misfortune continued. His first wife, Hanna, died in 1859.[51] In the winter of 1861, his second wife, Mas'uda, fell gravely ill. Nissim was too consumed with his work in the Bardo to sit by her sickbed in their house in La Goulette, and the 1.5-hour trip between Tunis and the port prevented him from visiting on a daily basis. Instead, he demanded that her caretakers send him daily telegrams—made possible by the new telegraph line connecting the Bardo to the city's port.[52] The telegrams refer to her as "Semha" (Simḥa), which in Hebrew means "happy" or "joyful," a translation of the Arabic Mas'uda; presumably this is the nickname by which Nissim's wife was known among her intimates. Each missive offered a brief, poignant evaluation of Mas'uda's health; the first, from February 7, reported that "Semha is now coughing up blood." The next day, a telegram reported that "Semha is better today; we gave her donkey's milk"—not a kosher substance, but permitted to save a life. "The doctor made her take ice, which did her a lot of good, and we will do it again today."[53] Nearly two weeks later, Mas'uda was cheered by a visit from her sister Bekia.[54]

Mas'uda survived, but the marriage barely did; perhaps the couple had already become estranged before Mas'uda's illness. Or perhaps she could not forgive Nissim for failing to check on her in person; then, as now, electronic communication was no substitute for flesh and blood. By 1864, Mas'uda had returned to her native Sousse. She and Nissim never again lived together.

Not long after Mas'uda's illness, Nissim decided to marry a third time. Perhaps he still hoped for children of his own. Or perhaps he simply could not stand to be alone in his giant palace in the ḥāra. He wed Esther Lellouche, about whom we know almost nothing; it is likely she was the daughter of Haim Lellouche, who served as an agent of the Paris-based banker Emile d'Erlanger; d'Erlanger would soon play a starring role in Tunisia's financial debacle, perhaps in part due to the connection between Lellouche and Nissim. Haim lent Nissim money in 1863 (even the extremely wealthy could find themselves short of cash, it seems). Unsurprisingly, Esther—like Hanna and Mas'uda—failed to give Nissim heirs of his own.[55]

But Nissim was not completely bereft of domestic happiness, thanks to his beloved 'Aziza. In 1862, Nissim arranged a marriage for her—naturally with someone in the family; Moses Shamama was a distant cousin from Bône, Algeria.[56] The newlyweds continued to live with their generous uncle. It would have been nothing to Nissim to pay for a lavish new dwelling for the young couple, but he preferred to keep 'Aziza as close as possible.

Nissim was also busy investing his growing wealth in real estate in and around Tunis. Parking money in property was a storied tradition among elite Muslim families, though only recently available to affluent Jews.[57] In addition to his imposing palace in the ḥāra, Nissim bought up all the other properties on his street—five small houses and two narrow buildings with stores and storage rooms. He bought a number of other small houses in the ḥāra and one just outside the city's walls, on Zanqat Tranja al-Qadima (Impasse de la Vieille Tronja), the street on which the writer Albert Memmi was born decades later. Nissim also invested in a few grand properties, including the former French consulate known as the Funduq des Français. After France moved its consulate to the imposing new edifice on the Avenue de la Marine at the end of 1860, the funduq was returned to the bey, who sold it to Nissim. The large caravansary was built in the seventeenth century. Each of the four sides of its elegant, arched peristyle gave onto an open courtyard. And the location could not be better—steps away from the Bab al-Bahr and just behind the equally imposing British consulate.[58]

Nissim also invested in property outside the city. In the new section of La Goulette, just steps from the sea, Nissim bought an enormous building that occupied an entire city block. The ground floor housed stores, offices, and a synagogue; the second floor was made up of apartments.[59] In La Marsa, a stylish coastal enclave where Tunis's elites escaped the summer heat, he bought twenty-two plots of land, some with houses; in Ariana, now a residential suburb of Tunis, he bought a 250-hectare olive grove and various houses;

and in Mohammedia, just south of Tunis, he bought two enormous plots of good agricultural land (400 and 500 hectares, respectively). In addition to his position in the government and his leadership in the Jewish community, Nissim was among the largest Jewish property owners in all of Tunisia.[60]

From the heights of his imposing palace, Nissim must have felt almost invincible. He was one of the most powerful men in Tunisia; he had just married a young wife; and in ʿAziza, he had a daughter whom he truly loved. The country's mood matched his own; Sadiq Bey promulgated the Qānūn in a period of optimism. Unlike his predecessor Muhammad Bey—whose ʿAhd al-Amān had essentially been written at gunpoint—Sadiq Bey was eager to embrace reforms that would strengthen his state. He continued the improvements to the military begun by Ahmad Bey; built new infrastructure for sanitation and running water; oversaw the creation of the telegraph line connecting the Bardo, Tunis, and La Goulette; and drained parts of the lagoon to expand Tunis toward the sea.[61] The European migrants who settled in Tunis shared this sunny outlook, populating the new neighborhoods that Sadiq Bey's ambitious engineering projects created. Yet this buoyant atmosphere masked a fatal flaw.

From the beginning of his reign, Sadiq Bey ran up against the same trouble that had plagued Ahmad Bey's attempts to revamp the military: the treasury was perpetually short of funds. Some of this was not Sadiq Bey's fault; he inherited debts from his predecessor, Muhammad Bey, who contracted with a Frenchman to renovate the Roman canal of Zaghwan. A functioning canal would bring much-needed water to the capital. But the renovation proved enormously expensive.[62] When Sadiq Bey began his rule, the treasury was already indebted to the tune of twenty million piasters—all in the form of government bonds issued to local merchants and state officials.[63] Called *teskeres* (Ottoman from the Arabic *tadhkira,* a catchall for official documents delivered by the state), these bonds were issued at 12 percent annual interest. Sadiq Bey found himself signing more and more teskeres, until he was no longer able to pay last year's bonds before being forced to issue new ones.

As one of Tunisia's richest men, Nissim was in a position to grow his wealth by lending money to the treasury. High rates of interest—anywhere from 12 to 18 percent—meant that he pocketed hefty profits when his teskeres came due. In 1862, for instance, the government issued a new kind of bond known as "triennials," which were payable by thirds every three years. Like others with capital in Tunis, Nissim bought a number of these triennial bonds.[64]

But each loan amounted to a small bandage applied to a gaping wound; the treasury only sank deeper into the red. Sadiq Bey's optimism came up against a hard reality. Anything was possible, if one had enough money to pay for it. Tunisia was by no means the only state keen to develop its industrial and military powers; across the globe, governments from Mexico to Russia looked for ways to expand their infrastructure in imitation of France and Great Britain, the world's superpowers. Western states—even new ones like Italy and Greece—benefited from the low interest rates of a well-established world of banking. Countries took out extensive loans to pay for railroads, modern ports, and industrialization; rates of 4 to 5 percent annual interest were standard in Europe, and in places like Mexico and Peru, bankers could charge as much as 6 to 7 percent.[65] The banking centers of Paris, London, and Frankfurt dominated the market in foreign loans; bonds and public offerings provided much of the capital. Then as now, most national budgets included provisions for servicing hefty amounts of public debt, made possible by the vast networks of credit that covered the globe like a web.

In the middle of the century, European bankers were still relatively new to the finances of the Middle East. The risks were high; banking rested largely on risk aversion and personal networks of trust. A play-it-safe approach was difficult, if not impossible, in places where established banks had no contacts and no local knowledge; the risks of doing business in a country like Tunisia were largely unknown. Nonetheless, as the field of bankers became increasingly crowded, the potential benefits of investing in the Middle East seemed to outweigh the drawbacks. Where banks could only charge up to 7 percent interest in Europe and the Americas, local interest rates in the Middle East started at 12 percent. Many of the more adventurous banking houses—especially those newer to the profession—were more than willing to take the plunge.[66]

Early adopters among European investors in the Middle East did not lack for potential clients. The Ottoman Empire was desperate for the kind of cash flow that allowed states in Europe to build railroads, steamships, and telegraphs. The Crimean War proved a watershed for the Ottoman Empire's finances. In 1854, Sultan Abdulmejid contracted a loan for 3.3 million Ottoman liras from the bankers Dent Palmer in London and Goldschmidt in Paris.[67] During the summer of 1860, Sa'id Pasha, the khedive of Egypt, took out a loan for 28 million francs from the Comptoir d'Escompte and Charles Laffitte et Cie, two of Paris's most reputable banks. As vast as these sums seem, they were not nearly enough. Sa'id's loan yielded only 21 million francs after the bankers deducted their fees and commissions. And that 21 million was immediately eaten up by creditors who had been demanding payment for years—not to mention by the 100 million in bonds already outstanding.[68] In hindsight, these first steps down the road to national debt were ill-advised. Yet the world was operating on credit. Why should Egypt and the Ottoman Empire—or Tunisia for that matter—be any different?

Ahmad Bey had failed in his attempts to contract an international loan in the 1840s, largely thanks to the energetic opposition of the Sublime Porte.[69] When Sadiq Bey took the throne—at which point the strain on Tunisia's finances was far greater—Prime Minister Mustafa Khaznadar redoubled previous efforts to seek a banker willing to loan his government money. He met with more success than his predecessors; starting in 1860, bankers in Paris and London offered various loans to Tunisia. As receiver general and director of finances, Nissim played a central role in the negotiations; in 1861, he wrote to Khaznadar concerning the conditions for a loan of nearly fourteen million riyals. The offer was a terrible deal for Tunisia; the lender—unnamed in this correspondence—was offering 12 percent annual interest *and* 15 percent annual fees. Ultimately, Khaznadar rejected the conditions as too onerous.[70]

In 1862, the Ottoman ambassador in London got wind that the bey of Tunis was again attempting to take out an international loan. He spoke to the financiers involved and convinced them that the loan was a bad idea for the same reasons they had rejected such a loan in the 1840s: Tunisia was not an independent state but rather a province of the Ottoman Empire. And the sultan would refuse to authorize a loan contracted by the bey; such a loan would thus lack the backing of the Ottoman state.[71] Faced with such conditions, the London bankers refused to offer Sadiq Bey a contract.

For better or worse, Khaznadar's agents had better luck in Paris. Rushayd Dahdah, a Lebanese Maronite Christian and one of Khaznadar's most trusted allies in the administration, was appointed to negotiate a loan in France. At first Dahdah approached the biggest banking houses, including the Rothschilds.[72] But Tunisia proved too risky an investment for such established bankers. Undeterred, Dahdah tried some of Paris's less storied houses; he finally succeeded with the banker Frederick Emile d'Erlanger.

D'Erlanger was the scion of a Prussian banking family; his father, Raphael, established a bank in Frankfurt, where he converted his family from Judaism to Catholicism in 1829. D'Erlanger was baptized at birth, but like many other descendants of converts, everyone continued to think of him as a Jew.[73] Like the Rothschilds before them, the d'Erlangers sent a son to establish a branch of the family bank in Paris, which was rapidly overtaking Frankfurt as a center of global finance. Emile arrived in 1858; he set himself up at 21 Rue de la Chaussée-d'Antin. In these early days, d'Erlanger's dingy office on the fourth floor was only accessible by a service staircase at the end of an interior courtyard.[74] His was hardly the most established of the Parisian merchant banking houses, which specialized in large-scale financial operations abroad. But d'Erlanger had the audaciousness required to break free from a crowded field. His penetrating gaze and sensuous mouth betrayed the raw ambition that drove his tumultuous career.

By the time Dahdah came along, d'Erlanger had already made a promising beginning. In 1862, he entered into a syndicate with a number of bankers in Frankfurt to extend a loan for 40 million francs to the government of Egypt.[75] In January 1863, he signed a contract for a loan of 14.5 million dollars to the Confederate States of America. Despite failing to sell all the shares in the loan and seeing their price slide precipitously, d'Erlanger came away from the Confederate enterprise significantly richer. He later wed Marguerite Mathilde Slidell, daughter of the Confederate senator who had negotiated the loan.[76] Like the shady financier Augustus Melmotte in Trollope's *The Way We Live Now*, d'Erlanger built his wealth not on a foundation of capital but rather confidence—which he projected with irresistible ease.

On May 7, 1863, the Tunisian government signed a contract with d'Erlanger for a loan of 35 million francs. Because the Tunisian government was already heavily in debt, d'Erlanger was able to negotiate a particularly profitable deal. He charged 7 percent interest—far less than the 12 percent that the treasury was paying its local creditors. Nonetheless, between fees, commissions, and other expenses, d'Erlanger pocketed over 5 million francs.[77] The loan was guaranteed by the revenue from the capitation tax—*majba* in Arabic—which supposedly amounted to 5 million francs per year. Including interest and fees, the Tunisian government agreed to make twice yearly payments of 2.1 million francs for the next fifteen years.[78]

To fund the loan, d'Erlanger arranged a public sale of shares. He offered 78,692 shares worth 500 francs each, which he sold at 480 francs. Twenty million francs worth of shares were sold in Tunis in the weeks following the

FIGURE 2.2. Emile d'Erlanger, circa 1869 (courtesy of Paul Tenkotte)

signing of the contract. Advertisements in French newspapers announced that the rest of the shares would be offered for sale in Paris, Lyon, Marseille, and Tunis on May 28.[79] Nissim bought thousands of them; at his death, he owned 17,143 shares, valued at nearly 8 million francs.[80] The public offering was a success. Tunisia was new to the world of international finance, and it was not hard for d'Erlanger to generate excitement about what he advertised as an excellent investment opportunity. D'Erlanger sent the first million francs in payment to Tunis through his agent, who handed it over to Nissim.[81]

The Ottomans were furious about the loan, but by the time they found out, there was little to be done. The day d'Erlanger offered the shares of the

Tunisian loan for sale to the public, an Ottoman diplomat in Paris sent an urgent telegraph to Aali Pasha, the minister of foreign affairs in Istanbul.[82] Aali Pasha responded that the loan was null without the sultan's authorization, which Sadiq Bey had never even sought, and that the Ottoman Empire would never guarantee the payment of the loan. He instructed Djemal Pasha, the Ottoman ambassador in Paris, to warn the French minister of foreign affairs, Edouard Drouyn de Lhuys, lest the French public be duped into investing in an illegal loan.[83] Drouyn de Lhuys was unimpressed by Djemal Pasha's objections: "We cannot interfere with the traditions that France has followed regarding [Tunisia]"—meaning that France would continue to negotiate with the bey of Tunis independently of the Ottoman sultan. "It is thus impossible for us to withdraw the authorization given by the [French] government for this loan. The Tunisian administration has the same right to contract this loan as it does to make roads, canals, and other improvements."[84] It was in the French government's interests to treat Tunisia as an independent state—in large part because this facilitated France's imperial designs on the Ottoman province. Djemal Pasha could only reiterate that the Tunisian government "was dependent on a sovereign territory and thus obliged to ask for its authorization in order to take out a loan."[85] But Drouyn de Lhuys was not to be moved. Given his "peremptory" remarks, Djemal Pasha thought it best to cut his losses and accept defeat. Subsequent efforts to save face by forcing Sadiq Bey to retroactively ask the sultan for permission were equally unsuccessful.[86] The Tunisian loan was a fait accompli, whether the Sublime Porte liked it or not.

Any satisfaction Sadiq Bey may have taken in shrugging off Ottoman objections to the loan proved fleeting. The d'Erlanger contract was not the magical remedy that the Tunisian treasury so desperately needed. On the contrary, it only increased the government's debts. A huge chunk of the 35 million francs was eaten up by fees and commissions; d'Erlanger, moreover, managed to conceal the fact that the initial public offering (the 78,692 shares) amounted to a cool 2,772,160 francs more than the 35 million he had loaned Tunis; the Tunisian government never saw the extra 2.7 million. After having used the d'Erlanger loan to pay its debts, the government immediately issued new bonds to the same Tunisian merchants it had been struggling to pay previously.[87]

More seriously, Sadiq Bey soon realized the enormous difference between loans contracted with his own subjects and those with foreign banks. When he had been unable to pay back his local lenders on time, the bey simply issued more teskeres—which his subjects had little choice but to accept in lieu of cold, hard cash. But d'Erlanger demanded payment in full each semester. And behind him stood the influence of the French government, always looking for an excuse to meddle in Tunisian affairs. The bey had no choice but to cough up the money.[88]

Instead of putting the country's finances back into the black, the semiannual payments to the Parisian bank sank the government further into debt. Shortly after signing d'Erlanger's contract, the government dramatically increased the majba, the head tax whose revenue had guaranteed the loan—from 36 piasters per person to 72 piasters.[89] A number of influential ministers opposed raising the tax; one of the bey's most trusted advisers, the *mamlūk* Husayn b. ʿAbdallah, was firmly against the idea. Husayn compared the peasants—squeezed to the last penny by the tax collectors—to "a cow that one milks until the last drop, to the point of making it bleed, thereby endangering its calf."[90]

When news of the new tax spread over the winter, tribes throughout the country prepared for armed resistance. They had been overtaxed for years; they were not about to consent to yet another attempt to bleed them dry. The bey tried to calm tensions by making the tax progressive—charging between 36 and 108 piasters, depending on a person's wealth. But the sliding scale still ensured that revenues would not fall short of an average tax of 72 piasters per person.[91] When the bey's agents set out to collect the new majba in the spring of 1864, the countryside erupted in violent rebellion. By April, a man named ʿAli b. Ghadhahim became the leader of the rebels. One by one, notables throughout the country pledged loyalty to him. Sadiq Bey scrambled to confront the mounting insurgency, but he was hamstrung by his empty coffers. The ambassadors of Britain, Italy, and France convinced their superiors in Europe to send warships to the ports of southern Tunisia (Sousse, Sfax, Monastir, and Mahdia). The ships ostensibly arrived to protect the foreigners and protégés under foreign jurisdiction. In fact, everyone knew that the diplomats hoped to exploit the chaos to their advantage—possibly even using the unrest as an excuse to colonize the province.[92]

Many of the rebels explicitly turned to the Ottoman sultan as a bulwark against the injustices of their bey. In Sousse and Sfax, two major coastal cities in the south, the rebels flew the Ottoman flag. Their prayers were answered on May 11, when an imperial frigate arrived from Istanbul and dropped anchor near La Goulette. In fact, the Sultan's motivation in sending the frigate was not so much to support the rebels as to remind Britain, Italy, and France that Tunisia was an Ottoman province, should they attempt a military occupation. Eventually, Sadiq Bey was forced to swallow his pride and ask the sultan for funds to cover the expense of civil war.[93] The bey might have coveted his autonomy, but he knew he could not win the fight alone—and what good was autonomy if he was pushed out of the Bardo?

The chaos that engulfed Tunisia in the spring of 1864 upended Nissim's comfortable life. The entire country was in open rebellion save for Tunis itself, and armed rebels were camped just a few kilometers from the capital. Those with British, French, and Italian nationality—including some members of the Grana community—sought refuge aboard the ships of their respective sovereigns, hoping to shield themselves from violence against foreigners.[94] As director of finances, Nissim was inevitably associated with the catastrophic d'Erlanger loan and resulting tax increase. There is no record of whether Nissim supported raising the majba, but his personal opinion mattered little. Nissim was a natural target—as the receiver general and director of finances, and as a Jew, especially at a time when modernizing reforms had disrupted the social hierarchies ensuring Muslims' superiority.[95] As rebels swarmed into the countryside surrounding Tunis, a "mob of Zwawa [Berber-speaking tribespeople from the north] planned to attack [Nissim's] house, kill him, and take his wealth."[96] The most powerful Jew in Tunisia suddenly found himself in grave danger.

In another sign of Nissim's disastrous luck in the personal sphere, the greatest domestic happiness of his life arrived as the violence of the rebellion threatened to burst through the gates of his palace. On June 2, 1864, 'Aziza gave birth to a healthy baby boy. If 'Aziza was the child that Nissim had always wanted, then her infant was the grandson he dreamed of—with all the promise of continuing a legacy Nissim had worked so hard to build. 'Aziza bestowed the highest honor on her great-uncle: rather than naming her baby after his paternal grandfather—as Maghribi Jews customarily did—she named him Nissim. Perhaps she also felt that keeping Nissim Jr. safe in the midst of a revolt would require the help of miracles, *nisim* in Hebrew.[97]

But even a name as auspicious as Nissim was not enough to protect the infant from the mobs calling for his uncle's head. Nissim Jr. spent just three days in the country of his birth before he was whisked away to safer shores across the Mediterranean.

3

Tunis to Paris (1864–68)

ON JUNE 7, 1864, Nissim boarded a steamship at the port of La Goulette. He was accompanied by his third wife, Esther, his great-niece, ʿAziza, her husband, Moses, and their infant son, Nissim Jr., just three days old, as well as two loyal servants. His first wife, Masʿuda, remained in Tunisia; they would never see each other again.[1] Nissim carried with him a letter from Sadiq Bey, authorizing his voyage to the "land of the Christians" along with five members of his household.[2] The indigent Jews of Tunis reportedly wept at the departure of their community's most generous benefactor.[3]

But before the ship could raise anchor, Luigi Pinna, the Italian consul, tried to stop the small party from leaving port. Pinna accused Nissim of having a number of teskeres—essentially IOUs—that had not been paid. It was customary to prevent anyone with outstanding debts from leaving the country; the consul must have been acting at the request of an Italian who claimed he was owed money by Nissim. Pinna's real motives are hard to parse. Was he truly concerned about the unpaid debts? Or had he simply seized another opportunity to flex his diplomatic muscles, with extraterritoriality as a pretext? Either way, this time he failed. Nissim was still too powerful, even for the Italian consul; the qāʾid wrote directly to Sadiq Bey, who sent a letter to Pinna that same day. Sadiq Bey explained that it would surprise him if Nissim did indeed possess unpaid teskeres since "the one who pursues his work in the ministry normally pays his money."[4] Pinna did not have enough evidence against Nissim to defy the bey's order; the ship was permitted to depart.

Although Nissim would never set foot in Tunisia again, he at first remained in constant touch with his superiors in the Bardo. And everywhere he went, he was surrounded by others in the service of the bey—a motley cast of characters that included a member of the Grana community, a Levantine Christian, and a Frenchman serving as the Tunisian agent in Paris—not to mention his small family and the growing entourage of Tunisian Jews he summoned to Europe. But over time, Nissim was pushed out of the prime minister's inner circle; as he grew more alienated from Khaznadar, he began to look for ways of securing his future outside Tunisia, including acquiring foreign citizenship. Yet even after obtaining Italian nobility and a decree of naturalization, he did not give up his outward deference to the bey, nor did he fully shed his legal status as a Tunisian Jew. Nissim lived as both an Italian and a Tunisian; this caused no alarm during his lifetime, though it produced endless confusion after his death.

Nissim's precise reasons for leaving Tunis remain a matter of some controversy. According to contemporary observers, the rebels blamed Nissim and Khaznadar for the higher taxes, and Nissim feared for his life if he stayed. The Tunisian chronicler Ahmad Ibn Abi al-Diyaf, known as Ibn Diyaf, generally had a high opinion of Nissim, whom he described as an honest government official—literally, one "whose hand was white."[5] Nissim was one of those People of the Book referred to in the Quran; "even if you were to entrust a treasure of gold" to him, he would "return it to you."[6] According to Ibn Diyaf, Nissim had no choice but to leave Tunisia once his life was threatened. The Jewish official did not want to flee under cover of darkness; Ibn Diyaf reported that Nissim went to the bey, from whom he asked permission to go abroad: "I am your servant and the servant of your fathers, and the son of your servants; there is a mob of commoners against whom it is impossible to defend myself, and I fear the anxiety will kill me. I ask that you spare my life and allow me to depart."[7] Only after the bey gave his blessing did Nissim prepare to go.

Other sources suggest that Nissim left in a state of panic. A letter written two years later by one of Nissim's associates, a Tunisian Jew named Abraham Beïda, described the qā'id as "trembling for his life." Nissim asked his friend to take his possessions out of his house that very night and put them in a secure place, fearing his home would be sacked.[8] Contemporary accounts in the Hebrew press also reported that the rebels' fury was directed at Nissim; some announced that the bey fired Nissim to appease them.[9]

Years later, Tunisian and French officials offered a far more damning account of the qā'id's departure. This version of events surfaced in the early 1870s, after Tunisia declared bankruptcy and the International Financial Commission took over the treasury. The president of the commission, a Frenchman named Victor Villet, placed the weight of the blame for the fiscal catastrophe on Khaznadar's shoulders. He accused Nissim of serving as Khaznadar's main accomplice in the corruption of Tunisia's finances. According to Villet, Nissim could only have accumulated such a vast fortune by skimming from the treasury; Khaznadar studiously ignored the fraud in exchange for Nissim's complicity in his crimes.[10] Nissim fled Tunis in order to make off with his ill-gotten gains—a replica of Ibn 'Ayyad's hasty departure twelve years earlier. This is the version of the story told by Husayn when he became the Tunisian government's representative for the Shamama lawsuit.[11]

Nissim himself insisted that his relationship to the government had not changed. He had not been fired, nor had he run away like a thief. As Nissim explained to anyone who would listen, he was traveling to Paris on official government business—part of a team of advisers charged with contracting a new international loan. It was undoubtedly true that he spent the following months involved in intensive negotiations with various bankers in Paris and London, d'Erlanger foremost among them. And at least one prominent Tunisian official publicly backed Nissim's version of events. According to Ibn Diyaf, Nissim settled all of his accounts with the bey; if he never returned to Tunisia, it was not for "lack of patriotism" but rather because he feared the jealousy and rapacity of the bey's servants.[12]

Whatever his motives, Nissim clearly did not think he was leaving Tunisia for good when he boarded the steamship in June 1864. Ibn Diyaf wrote as much: "Nissim traveled to France safe from his pursuers in order to cleanse himself of the stain of disloyalty and return to his birthplace, the spot dearest to him."[13] While preparing his departure, Nissim attempted to recover the keys to the customhouse, for which he had been the tax farmer for years. Under normal circumstances, Nissim entrusted the administration of the customhouse to an underling. Now that he was preparing to depart, he wanted the keys back; he feared that without them, he would lose this lucrative position. Even after leaving Tunis, Nissim wrote repeatedly to Khaznadar—from the ship's brief stop in Cagliari; from Livorno; and from Paris—asking for help recovering the keys.[14] His efforts failed; a month later, the bey appointed someone else to administer the customhouse in La Goulette.[15] It was not only Nissim who abandoned Tunisia; the Bardo, it seems, had begun to ignore Nissim.

Some truth about Nissim's desertion of his native city can undoubtedly be found in each of these narratives. Nissim must have feared for his safety in the midst of a rebellion against higher taxes; such situations could easily turn against the government officials deemed responsible for the suffering of ordinary people. And Nissim's Jewishness made him doubly vulnerable. Jews had served as high-profile advisers to Muslim sovereigns for centuries, but over and over again, Jewish courtiers were the first to be blamed—partly because their position upset the hierarchy that placed Jews below Muslims.[16] Yet there is no question that Nissim had acquired significant wealth in Tunisia and would hardly be the first to have done so through corrupt means. The extent to which his gains were ill-gotten must remain something of an unanswered question; the evidence is too fragmentary and polarized to be conclusive either way.[17]

On June 10—three days after raising anchor in La Goulette—the steamship carrying Nissim, 'Aziza, Moses, and baby Nissim Jr. docked in Cagliari, on the island of Sardinia. During the brief call at port, Nissim managed to send the first of dozens of letters he wrote to Khaznadar during his time abroad—all penned in a beautiful Arabic hand by his secretary, since Nissim did not read or write Arabic.[18] Nissim took care to personally sign each letter, which he did in the Hebrew cursive typical of North Africa.[19] From Sardinia, the ship continued to Livorno, where Nissim and his entourage arrived on June 12.[20] The trip was relatively short by Mediterranean standards; in the winter, bad weather could make the crossing take much longer, even powered by steam. Nonetheless, Nissim wrote to Khaznadar that he had fallen ill during the voyage.[21] And even a mercifully brief trip must have caused 'Aziza and Moses considerable anxiety about their tiny son.

The group rested just a few days in Livorno, and then boarded another steamship bound for Marseille that was expected to arrive on the evening of June 15. The boat was delayed, however, and Nissim did not get there until midday on June 19. When he finally arrived, he and his family were exhausted. Nissim wrote to Khaznadar complaining that the food everywhere—in Marseille, Genoa, and Livorno—was so inedible that he had only been drinking water.[22]

Culinary vicissitudes notwithstanding, Nissim was hardly cast among a crowd of strangers. Throughout his journey and time abroad, he surrounded himself with people who, like him, served the bey. During his short stay in Marseille, he met with Giacomo "Coco" Lumbroso, a Jew from Tunisia who hailed from one of the country's most prominent Grana families. Coco's father, Isaac Vita, was the leader of the Grana community in Tunis, president of the Portuguese synagogue, and a judge (*dayyan*) in the rabbinic court.[23] Coco's brother Abraham served as the personal physician to Ahmad Bey, Muhammad Bey, and now Sadiq Bey; he would later be made a baron by the king of Italy, and in 1873 would accompany Nissim's body to the cemetery in Livorno. In 1850, Coco moved to Marseille, where he established himself as a prominent merchant. He also served as the local Tunisian agent.[24] As such, Coco threw himself behind Nissim's efforts to secure a new loan for the Tunisian treasury.

Nissim hoped to rest in Marseille for some days before continuing on to Paris; he probably stayed with his cousin Joseph Shamama, who also worked as a merchant there. This Joseph was more than just a cousin; he was the son of Nissim's first wife, Hanna, from a previous marriage. And Joseph's sister Esther was none other than 'Aziza's mother.[25] Everyone in Nissim's party must have breathed a sigh of relief at this reunion. But a letter from Khaznadar instructed Nissim not to tarry; he left on June 21, taking the overnight train to Paris. 'Aziza, Moses, and Nissim Jr. remained in Marseille.[26]

Nissim's traveling companion on the train to Paris was Jules de Lesseps, the Tunisian agent in Paris. De Lesseps was born in Pisa to Mathieu de Lesseps, a French diplomat who began his service in Morocco and ended his days at the consulate in Tunis. Father and son were both fluent in Arabic. Jules followed in his father's footsteps: he started his career in the French consulate in Tunis, eventually taking over as consul. In 1846, he reversed roles, entering Ahmad Bey's service as Tunisian agent in Paris.[27] The bey paid de Lesseps handsomely (twenty-five thousand francs a year—money the Tunisian treasury could not afford, and that de Lesseps no longer needed, having made a fortune working with his elder brother Ferdinand on the Suez Canal).[28] It was hardly strange for a French citizen like de Lesseps to serve as the bey's agent; in this period, states regularly appointed diplomatic representatives who were, technically speaking, foreigners.[29] For instance, d'Erlanger became the Greek consul while still living in Frankfurt and assumed the same position in Paris in 1868, although he claimed no ethnic or familial ties to Greece.[30] In fact, we can imagine that neither Nissim, de Lesseps, nor Lumbroso thought much about their status as Tunisians or foreigners; they were, quite simply, three competent men in the service of the bey.[31]

The disconnect between formal belonging and government service reminds us that citizenship was less of an identity than a tool. What mattered to the bey was not ethnicity or nationality but instead loyalty and competence. As for Nissim, he was presumably relieved to be among colleagues with whom he could converse in his native Arabic. Even if the food was terrible, the company, at least, was familiar.

Nissim arrived in Paris at 7:00 a.m. on June 22, with de Lesseps at his side to guide him through the bustling city.[32] When Nissim stepped out of the Gare de Lyon, he entered an endless construction zone; Haussmann was in the midst of cutting wide, straight avenues through the medieval tangle of streets. Teams of workers ripped up fields and villages that used to be outside the city center, replacing them with paved roads and wide sidewalks. Speculators bought up the tracts of land as soon as the new roads had been mapped out; they made fortunes erecting building after building, whose stone facades marched down the endless boulevards. The utopian fervor of the 1848 revolution had long receded as a wave of prosperity washed over the Second Empire. Under the firm leadership of Napoléon III, the whole country was "sleeping in late [*faisait la grasse matinée*]. . . . Society's main preoccupation was figuring out how best to amuse itself."[33]

Nissim did not immediately succumb to the temptations Paris had to offer; he instead went to work trying to secure a new loan for the Tunisian treasury. Nearly every day, he reported on his progress in letters to Khaznadar.[34] Shortly after his arrival in Paris, Nissim wrote to say that Rushayd Dahdah, who had been crucial to securing the initial loan from d'Erlanger the previous year, was back in town. Dahdah hailed from a Maronite Christian notable family with roots in the Ottoman province of Mount Lebanon. He moved to France in 1845, following his uncle who had established himself in Marseille. In Paris, he got his start as an international financier and installed himself in great luxury. In 1863, he became a French citizen—like Ibn 'Ayyad, through *grande naturalisation*, which required an act of Parliament. That same year Dahdah visited Tunis, where he earned the trust of Sadiq Bey; back in Paris, Dahdah became a kind of informal Tunisian agent and one of the bey's informants in Europe.[35]

Nissim's social world was still peopled by other advisers to the Tunisian government; he met regularly with Dahdah, de Lesseps, and Coco Lumbroso, who had arrived from Marseille shortly after Nissim. But no one seemed optimistic about the prospects for more credit. Lumbroso told Nissim it would be hard, if not impossible, to get another large loan right away. Lumbroso himself offered a smaller loan—of two million francs over the course of one and a half years.[36] Yet that amount would barely keep the treasury afloat, much less cover the state's mounting debts. As Nissim explained in a letter to Khaznadar, even taking out bills of exchange on the government's account was dubious; people in Paris were "afraid" and not particularly willing to loan money.[37]

Less than a week after arriving in Paris, de Lesseps engineered a meeting between Nissim and a high-ranking French official. Described only as "the vizier," this was probably none other than the foreign minister, Édouard Drouyn de Lhuys.[38] As Nissim was unable to speak French, de Lesseps served as interpreter. Nissim later recorded his (significantly adapted) version of the conversation in colloquial Tunisian Arabic in a letter to Khaznadar. According to Nissim, the minister began aggressively by asking his host about a loan that Khaznadar had just contracted in Paris.[39] Nissim deflected: "by my life," he knew nothing about this loan. Then he defended his patron, pointing out that Khaznadar had been the prime minister for eighteen years and the ruling bey "loved France very much." Somewhat placated, the minister asked why Nissim had come to Paris; he responded that his government had sent him to get a new loan. Would the minister grant Nissim permission to sign with French bankers? "Look," the minister answered, "how does France love Tunisia? In three ways: first, she wants Tunisia to be a friend of France; second, she wants Tunisia to be independent; and third, she wants Tunisia to be happy." He would gladly authorize the loan. The minister then turned to de Lesseps, with whom he spoke in French; about this part of the meeting, Nissim could only report that he did not understand a word.[40]

Any optimism Nissim might have felt about the interview with the minister was short-lived. Without any tax revenues, de Lesseps explained, nobody would give Tunisia a loan—not the Ottoman sultan, nor English bankers, nor even French financiers. The Tunisian state was "sick" inside and out. To make matters worse, the bey needed to pay the next installment on the d'Erlanger loan imminently—2.1 million francs that the treasury simply did not have.[41]

Under the circumstances, Nissim's decision to turn once more to d'Erlanger is entirely understandable. Nissim met with d'Erlanger shortly after arriving in Paris, but he was wary of discussing a new loan with the banker who had helped get Tunisia into its present financial mess.[42] Yet given the dim prospects of convincing anyone else to lend the bey money, Nissim succumbed. On July 5—just over two weeks after he arrived in Paris—he wrote to Khaznadar with a draft contract for a loan from d'Erlanger, for 15 million francs at 12 percent interest. That percentage was high for a loan originating in Europe; the previous loan to Tunisia charged 7 percent.[43] Nonetheless, Nissim warned Khaznadar that Tunisia would be hard-pressed to find anyone else willing to lend them money; he urged his patron to send permission to sign the contract.[44]

As difficult as it was to secure credit, no one else seemed convinced by the idea of getting another loan from d'Erlanger. Dahdah was against it. Lumbroso believed he could get a better deal from a banker friend of his in Paris. "I said to him, fine!" Nissim reported to Khaznadar, "But he didn't find anyone."[45] Khaznadar stalled, holding out for a more favorable deal.[46] Nissim waited and waited for an answer about the d'Erlanger loan; week after week, he wrote to Khaznadar begging for permission to sign the contract.[47] The silence from Tunis was a troubling sign, not just for the bey's finances, but for Nissim's relationship to his patrons at home.

While absorbed in seeking a new international loan, Nissim also had to find a home for his loved ones who had remained in Marseille. A week after arriving in Paris, Nissim signed a lease for an enormous apartment in a new building, number 47 Rue du Faubourg Saint Honoré.[48] He chose one of the city's toniest neighborhoods; his home stood less than a block from the mansion that would eventually become the Élysée Palace (number 55), and in the other direction, an enormous *hôtel particulier* that served as the embassy of Great Britain (number 39). Just a mile to the west, his colleague de Lesseps lived at number 22 Avenue de Montaigne.[49] Nissim rented the entire second floor—originally through Hai Lellouche, almost certainly another name for Haim Lellouche, d'Erlanger's agent and father of Nissim's newest wife, Esther.[50] The spacious apartment included two salons, two dining rooms, a balcony, a bathroom, multiple bedrooms, and various offices and powder rooms. Nissim rented three servants' quarters under the eaves and two stables for his carriages. All of this cost him eleven thousand francs per year—a small fortune for ordinary people, but a drop in the bucket for a millionaire.[51]

Even once he was lavishly settled in Paris, Nissim did not forget his coreligionists back home. Two months after departing North Africa, he gave word that he would continue his monthly contributions to the Jewish community's charitable fund, which distributed food and money to the poor Jews of Tunis. On holidays, he gave even more generously. Nissim also continued his patronage of Hebrew publishing, financing the printing of a book in Judeo-Arabic by Abraham b. Maimon, son of Maimonides.[52] He also acquired a rare copy of the *Kehillot Moshe*, an eighteenth-century printed edition of the Hebrew Bible with commentary and exquisite hand-painted illustrations in fourteen enormous volumes.[53] Never one for subtle displays of wealth, Nissim had the covers of each volume inscribed with his initials; a large gold "N. S." in the center, and at the top, a smaller inscription in Hebrew: "the Servant of God, Nissim

FIGURE 3.1. and 3.2 Edition of *Kehilot Moshe* owned by Nissim Shamama, cover and first page of Exodus (courtesy of Yeshiva University, Mendel Gottesman Library)

Shamama, may God protect and save him." Nissim was quite an addition to the Jewish community in Paris. The Tunisian correspondent for *Ha-Levanon*, a Hebrew-language newspaper published in Palestine, exclaimed, "Happy is the city of Paris, which shelters such a holy man!"[54]

But no amount of wealth or philanthropy could shore up Nissim's reputation in the Bardo. Khaznadar was beginning to lose his trust in his former protégé; he insinuated that Nissim might put his "hands on the money" that he was trying to secure for the treasury. Nissim swore "by God who is great" that such treachery was "impossible. . . . I haven't put my hand on one franc without your permission, and I have told you about everything." Nissim's emphatic denials—a far cry from the typically restrained and highly courteous style used in his correspondence—suggest a serious breach of trust between the prime minister and his Jewish associate. Nissim's repeated efforts to convince Khaznadar to sign the new d'Erlanger loan were doomed—not by d'Erlanger, but by virtue of Nissim's role in the negotiations. Resigned to failure, Nissim told Khaznadar that he should do "whatever seemed best" in his eyes.[55]

Meanwhile, other advisers in Paris took Nissim's place. At the end of September, Nissim learned that Carlo Marco Morpurgo, a Jew from Trieste, had made a loan to the Tunisian government some months ago.[56] Elias Mussalli, another adventurer turned adviser, arrived in Paris seeking to help the bey get a loan. Mussalli was a Melkite Greek Catholic from the Ottoman Empire who had moved to Tunis and climbed the ranks in the Foreign Ministry. In the fall of 1864, Morpurgo and Mussalli suggested forging a syndicate with Nissim in order to fund a loan to Tunisia. Nissim repeatedly asked Khaznadar for permission to enter into the syndicate with Mussalli and Morpurgo, but Khaznadar maintained his stony silence.[57] Back in Tunis, Nissim's elder brother Nathan took over his role as qā'id al-yahūd. And Qā'id Momo—'Aziza's biological father—replaced Nissim as receiver general. With the stoicism of a seasoned politician, Nissim wrote to congratulate Khaznadar on having found someone to fill this important role.[58]

On November 1, Khaznadar finally signed a contract for a loan with d'Erlanger for fifteen million francs—one whose terms were even less favorable than the loan Nissim had negotiated back in July.[59] Presumably, the deep red into which the treasury had sunk allowed d'Erlanger to make more demands. At first it looked like Nissim would be responsible for signing on the state's behalf. Not long afterward, however, Mussalli came to tell Nissim that everything was taken care of.[60] Nissim's services as an intermediary were no longer needed.

Khaznadar never broke with Nissim outright, and their relationship remained cordial. Nissim inquired about the denouement of the revolt that had driven him from his homeland, and Khaznadar reported on the bey's military excursions against the rebels.[61] In October, Nissim congratulated his superior on hearing that a high-ranking official had succeeded in collecting taxes in Sousse, an important coastal city (and home to Nissim's estranged wife, Mas'uda)—a sign that the rebellion was almost completely quashed.[62]

Nissim went from trusted adviser to ordinary informant. He reported on the prices at which shares of the Tunisian loans were selling on the Paris Bourse and occasionally about important local news.[63] The qā'id visited Khaznadar's sons Muhammad and al-Munji, who had been sent to study in Paris.[64] On December 25, Nissim gave a glowing report about the progress of Muhammad, at the time twenty-four years old: "I found Sidi Muhammad in front of all the pictures of the kings of France, and all the coins from the past until today, and he was holding books."[65] The relatively simple description of Muhammad's studies suggests that the young man's intellectual pursuits were somewhat beyond Nissim, who never had a Western education.

But these familial visits could not prevent a further chill in Nissim's relationship with his former patron. In the spring of 1866, the prime minister informed Nissim that Qā'id Momo was taking out bills of exchange against his uncle for 250,000 francs. This was the nineteenth-century equivalent of charging enormous purchases to Nissim's credit card—which Momo did with Khaznadar's approval. Nissim tried to protest, but there was little he could do.[66] Two months later, Khaznadar did it again: he took out bills of exchange against Nissim for Dahdah. Nissim again refused to pay, saying that he still had not been reimbursed for the bills of exchange that Momo had taken out against him. "I ask you not to take out [bills of exchange] against me," he pleaded feebly with Khaznadar.[67] A week later, Nissim wrote again to the prime minister, claiming he was owed 360,000 francs for the bills of exchange.[68] Nissim's repeated requests for reimbursement were met with more silence.[69]

As the possibility of going back to Tunis seemed less and less likely, Nissim made himself more comfortable in his adopted home. In 1865, he bought a stunning country house on the banks of the Seine in Sèvres, just outside Paris. The eighteenth-century building was situated on the grounds of the former Château de Bellevue, built by the Marquise de Pompadour, Louis XV's mistress; she had named the light-filled river house Brimborion.[70] Nissim also installed his family more lavishly in Paris. In 1866, he rented the apartment above his own for 'Aziza, Moses, and Nissim Jr., now two years old.[71]

FIGURE 3.3. Brimborion, Nissim Shamama's estate in Sèvres (from Paul Biver, *Histoire du Château de Bellevue*)

Nissim continued to prefer the company of familiar faces with whom he could converse in Arabic, the only language he spoke. As his stay in Paris appeared more and more permanent, he brought over a growing retinue of coreligionists from his native Tunis. In addition to his first secretary, Jacob Shamama—a distant cousin—he summoned Joseph Bessis to serve as his "second" secretary. Three more Tunisian Jews came to occupy the servants' quarters under the eaves of 47 Rue du Faubourg Saint Honoré: Shalom Zagdun, Shalom Fellous, and Meir Ashkenazi. Nissim even brought over a rabbi, Judah Sitruk; the members of Nissim's household alone almost made up a minyan, the quorum of ten men required for many Jewish prayers. And of course, Nissim hired local help. When Nissim traveled for pleasure, his entourage numbered no less than forty-three people.[72] Meanwhile, Nissim's palace in Tunis was "abandoned to the lizards and the dogs."[73]

Faced with undeniable evidence that he was no longer in favor at the Bardo, Nissim began to consider the disadvantages of being a subject of the bey.

During all of his years in Tunis, Nissim had resisted the trend among local elites to secure extraterritorial privileges. Members of the Grana community were recognized as subjects of the grand duke in 1846. Many more individual Jews pursued extraterritoriality, either through naturalization or by purchasing patents of protection. Falling under the jurisdiction of a foreign consulate was particularly attractive to those involved in trade; access to consular courts, lower tariffs, and the energetic support of diplomats were distinct advantages in the marketplace.[74]

Now that Nissim no longer lived in Tunisia, naturalization abroad would not afford him extraterritorial privileges like lower taxes or consular jurisdiction. But Nissim had other reasons for seeking to change his status. Wherever the capitulations were in effect, legal belonging became a matter of jurisdiction first and foremost. In Tunis, the court in which one could be sued depended on one's legal belonging; those who could prove French nationality were under the jurisdiction of the French consular court. Legal belonging was also relevant for Tunisians who fell out of the bey's good graces, as Nissim's former patron Ibn 'Ayyad knew well. Ibn 'Ayyad naturalized as a French citizen shortly after he left Tunis, in large part so that the bey's lawsuits against him would have to be adjudicated in French courts. Had Ibn 'Ayyad remained a Tunisian subject, the bey might have insisted that he stand trial in Tunisia.

As Nissim's conflict with Khaznadar continued to chill their relationship, he became increasingly nervous about jurisdiction. There is no indication that Nissim believed the Tunisian government wanted to sue him. No accusations against him had as yet been made publicly; even those who would later become his fiercest critics were more concerned with getting rid of Khaznadar himself.[75] But Nissim did not have only the Tunisian government to fear; Ibn 'Ayyad claimed that Nissim owed him vast sums of money. If Nissim remained a subject of the bey, Ibn 'Ayyad might sue him in a Tunisian court. Nissim preferred to avoid returning to Tunisia if at all possible; those who had called for his head in the spring of 1864 were likely to want it still. The only solution, it seemed, was to secure membership in his adopted country.

Nissim began proceedings to naturalize as a French citizen.[76] Like Ibn 'Ayyad, he had no choice but to pursue "great" naturalization; French nationality law required foreigners to reside in France for at least ten years before they were eligible for ordinary (*petite*) naturalization. Nissim, however, could not afford to wait so long; it was likely he might be called back to Tunis much sooner. The ten-year residency was no problem for most immigrants in France; indeed, for many, naturalization was a burden, not a benefit, as only French male citizens were required to perform military service.[77] Nissim was among the relatively small number of elites for whom "great" naturalization was attractive. Yet unlike his former patron Ibn 'Ayyad, Nissim could not muster the right connections; his attempt to fast-track French citizenship hit a dead end.

Undeterred, he set his sights across the Alps to the young Kingdom of Italy. The Italian nation was eager to extend its influence in the concert of Europe and thus more generous in its criteria of belonging. On June 1, 1866, Nissim's Italian lawyer wrote to King Vittorio Emanuele II to say that his client, "the General Commander Nissim, son of Solomon Shamama," humbly requested that the king grant him "Italian naturalization." The lawyer explained that Nissim was "a native of Tunis, but from a family that was originally Livornese." Nissim wanted to "return to live as a citizen in the land of his ancestors." He sweetened his request with a generous donation to the kingdom, offering fifty thousand Italian lire to be "disbursed in charitable works in whatever way Your Majesty thinks best." He asked only that he be rewarded with the noble title of count.[78]

Nissim's claim to Livornese origins might have come as a surprise to his family and friends back in Tunis—indeed, to the Jewish community in general, at whose head he stood for years as qā'id al-yahūd. In Tunisia, the Shamamas were generally known to be Twansa, members of the community of Jews indigenous to Tunisia; while some Shamamas later married Grana Jews, these were instances of the Livornese accepting outsiders into their fold through marital alliances.[79] But for the Italian Ministry of Interior, the precise contours of the Grana community in Tunisia were fuzzy at best. The king's secretaries might have been aware that some Jews in Tunisia traced their ancestry to Italy and were counted among the Italian citizens living abroad. It seems likely that no one thought to investigate whether or not Nissim really was of Livornese stock. Presumably, Nissim's lawyer counted on the fact that neither the king nor his ministers would thoroughly inspect his client's background, and that an assertion of Livornese ancestry—along with a generous donation—would be enough to convince the king.

Still, Nissim was not taking any chances. To ensure his success, Nissim contacted Giacomo del Castelnuovo, an Italian Jew who was one of Vittorio Emanuele II's court doctors. Castelnuovo was born in Florence; along with thousands of his coreligionists, he left Tuscany for better opportunities on the other side of the Mediterranean—first in Cairo and then in Tunis, where he became Ahmad Bey's personal physician in 1851. Castelnuovo remained in Tunisia until 1859, when he returned to Italy to join the Risorgimento and become physician to the new king. He went back and forth between Italy and Tunisia for the rest of his life.[80] Nissim and Castelnuovo must have met in the Bardo; perhaps they even forged a friendship, as fellow Jews in the service of the bey. Castelnuovo agreed to put in a good word for Nissim.

Nissim's strategy paid off; the king's personal secretary recommended him to the Ministry of Interior. The approval was astonishingly swift; on June 10, just a little over a week after sending his request, Nissim was made an Italian count.[81] In the royal decree, Vittorio Emanuele II noted that Nissim was "of Livornese origin" (*oriundo Livornese*).[82] Nissim had succeeded in reinventing himself as a member of the Sephardi diaspora from Livorno. Ironically, the king used much of Nissim's donation to build a parochial church for the village of San Salvatore Monferrato, in his native Piedmont.[83]

As an Italian nobleman, Nissim was entitled to a coat of arms. In his initial design, Nissim asked to incorporate an image of Moses "holding the tablets of the law . . . [with] a mountain in the background." The official in charge of heraldry objected: these symbols—"which undoubtedly allude to the Jewish religion that Count Shamama professes"—defied the rules and customs of heraldry. In other words, they were a bit too Jewish.[84] He proposed instead a more palatable reference to Nissim's faith: a shield topped by two stone tablets inscribed with the Hebrew words "I am the Lord your God" (*anokhi elohekha adonai*), above which floated a knight's helmet with a nine-pointed crown and laurel wreath. The new design was approved; in Italian, Nissim was now officially Conte Nissim Semama.[85]

Nissim's new title and his flashy coat of arms were impressive, but it was all a pretense for getting what he really wanted: Italian nationality. On August 25, 1866, Vittorio Emanuele II signed a decree that admitted Nissim "to the nationality of the Italian kingdom." The decree described Nissim as "a native of Tunisia, of Italian origin" (*oriundo italiano*). It also specified that Nissim's admission to Italian nationality was predicated on establishing his domicile in Italy and taking an "oath of fealty" to the king "according to Article 10 of the Civil Code."[86] As in France, foreigners typically had to wait until they had resided in the country for ten years before applying for naturalization. Those with royal decrees—like Nissim—could bypass the lengthy residency requirement.[87]

But Nissim did not move to Italy after receiving the naturalization decree. Nor did he take an oath of fealty to the king in the Italian consulate in Paris. Instead, he remained in France for another five years—well beyond the six-month deadline specified in the decree itself. Why Nissim failed to comply

FIGURE 3.4. Shamama coat of arms (Presidenza del consiglio dei ministri, consulta araldica, fascicoli nobiliari e araldici delle singole famiglie, Busta 9, Semama, Nissim e Moisè, ACS)

with the requirements of the decree remains something of a mystery. It seems unlikely that he simply neglected this detail given how much time and money he spent on naturalization in the first place. Perhaps Nissim and his legal advisers thought that such formalities were simply unnecessary. Would it really matter whether he dotted all of his i's and crossed all of his t's? Wouldn't everyone recognize him as an Italian count, registration or no?

Although his reasons for failing to register the decree remain murky, Nissim made sure to publicly proclaim his new status as an Italian count. He joined the Società di Beneficenza Italiana—a charitable organization composed primarily of Italians who, having emigrated, sought to consolidate their Italian identity through benevolence.[88] His title elevated him into a highly select group of Jewish nobles in Europe; it was still relatively rare for Jews to acquire noble titles.[89] Nissim, it seemed, was as Italian as he needed to be.

Although Nissim's grasp of Italian nationality law was a bit fuzzy, he knew exactly how his naturalization would be received in the halls of the Bardo. In all of his dozens of letters to Khaznadar and other Tunisian officials, Nissim did not once mention his new title or new nationality; these would be seen as an affront at best and treason at worst. Yet about far less consequential matters, Nissim was punctilious in asking for Khaznadar's permission. When the consul of Monaco offered Nissim a decoration as commander of the second rank, he asked for Khaznadar's permission before accepting the honor.[90] In the spring of 1867, de Lesseps was charged with organizing the Tunisian and Moroccan pavilions of the Universal Exposition in Paris; he invited Nissim to serve on the jury for the Moroccan pavilion. Nissim again asked for Khaznadar's permission.[91] Even as his responsibilities for the Tunisian government dwindled away, Nissim continued to act as if he were a state employee. Until the end of his life, he signed every letter "director of the treasury and receiver general."[92] Nissim's studied silence about his noble title and coat of arms suggest that he was hoping to have his cake and eat it too.

Still, no amount of noble titles, coats of arms, or naturalizations could prevent heartache. As mentioned earlier, Nissim had married a third time before leaving Tunis, hoping to have children of his own. His new wife, Esther—thirty-four years his junior—had failed to give him children. Before long, the couple had grown estranged. In the spring of 1866, Esther returned to her father's house.

Nissim could have remained married to Esther, as he had to Mas'uda, despite their separation. But Esther was much younger than he; she almost certainly wanted to remarry, and thus have another chance at children and domestic fulfillment. Nissim wrote to Le Roy, his lawyer in Paris, asking how a Jew like himself might go about getting a divorce in France. Le Roy explained that French law did not permit divorce, even for Jews; since Napoléon's Sanhedrin in 1807, rabbis in France had ceased to pronounce divorces according to Jewish law. Nor did Italian law allow for the dissolution of marriage. As a Tunisian Jew, however, Le Roy explained, Nissim had the right to be divorced by rabbinic authorities in Tunis. The lawyer's answer clearly presumed that Nissim was still Tunisian, despite the count's naturalization. Nor did Nissim seem concerned that a divorce might go against the laws of his new country. On January 30, 1868, Nissim gave Esther a *get*, a Jewish bill of divorce, prepared by rabbis in Paris.[93] It seems that in this instance, it was far more convenient to be Tunisian than Italian. Nissim proceeded as if his naturalization had never been.

In addition to his marital woes, Nissim found that a wealthy man like him was a magnet for lawsuits. When a Frenchman named Ramel sued Nissim for a debt of thirty-six thousand francs, he thought it wise to take no chances; Nissim engaged one of the best legal minds in Paris—none other than Adolphe Crémieux, who also happened to be the most famous Jew in France. During the short-lived Second Republic of 1848, Crémieux had served as minister of justice. In 1860, he became the first president of the Alliance Israélite Universelle, an organization dedicated to improving the lives of Jews across the world through political advocacy and education. Shortly after he began working for Nissim, Crémieux served another stint as minister of justice; it was during his term in 1870 that he pushed through the decree that later bore his name, by which Jews in Algeria were made into French citizens.[94] In his private life, however, Crémieux made his living representing wealthy people like Nissim.

In pleading the Ramel case, Crémieux made sure to capitalize on the mystique of his Tunisian client. He began by observing that "for these Orientals, a French court is justice itself." Continuing in this vein, Crémieux explained that "the qā'id has three wives"—at which the audience erupted in laughter.[95] Crémieux then revealed that Nissim had a distant relative of his first wife in Marseille, a certain Joseph Shamama (with whom Nissim had stayed briefly before arriving in Paris). To great dramatic effect, Crémieux produced a letter from Joseph, explaining that it was he—and not Nissim—who had borrowed money from Ramel.[96] Judge and audience alike were swayed, and Nissim was cleared of the alleged debt.[97]

Yet Ramel's suit proved only the start of Nissim's legal troubles. At the end of the year, his worst fears materialized: he received a summons from his former patron Ibn 'Ayyad, who was suing him in a Parisian court for unpaid debts. Ibn 'Ayyad had since moved to Istanbul, where he lived on an enormous estate on Çamlıca Hill in Üsküdar, on the Asian side of the city.[98] Tunuslu Mahmut Paşa, as he was known in the Ottoman Empire, had invested his immense wealth wisely and integrated into Istanbul's governing elite. In Paris, though, Ibn 'Ayyad was just a Frenchman suing an Italian count for millions of francs.

Ibn 'Ayyad's summons sent Nissim into a flurry of anxious activity. He immediately wrote to Crémieux, informing him of the case. Crémieux explained that Nissim would require documentation if he wanted to defend himself against Ibn 'Ayyad's claims. The problem was, Nissim's personal archives were woefully incomplete. He wrote a letter to Khaznadar, explaining that he needed documents from his time working for Ibn 'Ayyad in the 1840s and 1850s.[99] Nissim explained that he had made copies, "but now I can't find them. . . . I am still looking among my papers here . . . but it is possible that they got lost along the way, or that they are still in Tunis." He pleaded with Khaznadar to send along these documents, so crucial to proving his innocence.[100]

For six weeks, Khaznadar maintained his accustomed silence. Finally, a package arrived; inside were twelve letters from Ibn 'Ayyad to Nissim. But Nissim's relief soon turned to anger; the two critical documents he had requested were missing.[101] He was back at square one. Week after week, Nissim begged Khaznadar to send him the documents he needed: "I cry every night and every day."[102] His melodramatic flourishes failed. Khaznadar finally responded when the great lawyer Crémieux wrote, but he claimed he was unable to find the letters in question.[103] Six months later, Nissim's hopes soared again; Khaznadar had promised to send the papers at last. Yet again, the mail brought only disappointment. In a letter to Khaznadar, he explained that "when Crémieux looked at [the letters] he became angry at me, and got annoyed at you—because, he said, this copy would not do, as it is copied from a copy and not from the original."[104] When Nissim and Ibn 'Ayyad finally went to court, in May 1869, Khaznadar still had not sent the originals. As Crémieux had predicted, the judge refused to accept the copies as evidence.[105] In nearly every letter he wrote to Khaznadar in the remaining years of his life, Nissim doggedly asked for the originals of his correspondence with Ibn 'Ayyad.[106]

As Nissim despaired of ever getting the badly needed papers, he also went on the offensive, claiming that the Tunisian government owed him money. At first, the amounts he claimed were relatively minor: the salary of a certain

M. Afas, whom Khaznadar paid to send weekly dispatches with local intelligence; in 1869, Nissim asked to be reimbursed for 9,350.95 francs he had paid to Afas.[107] A year later, Nissim wrote to say that Khaznadar personally owed him 1.1 million riyals—for, among other things, bills of exchange Khaznadar and Qā'id Momo had taken out against him. Nissim also claimed the value of a house he owned in Tunis that Khaznadar had handed over to the German consul.[108] The prime minister tried to pass these debts off as being owed by the treasury, but Nissim insisted that Khaznadar was personally responsible. "All these accounts are owed by you," Nissim persisted; "I continue to ask you for a great deal of money, even if you are not able to pay it now."[109]

Perhaps more than the unpaid debts, Nissim railed against Khaznadar's silence: "Whom should I ask to settle the debts that I am owed by the state—since nobody I write to answers me? It is just like what happened with the documents I needed concerning Ibn 'Ayyad!"[110] But there was little he could do. The partnership between the Jewish financier and the prime minister had soured. Nissim was now truly on his own. It was time to plan accordingly.

4

Paris to Livorno (1868–73)

THE TIME between Rosh Hashanah, the Jewish new year, and Yom Kippur, the day of atonement, is known as the Ten Days of Repentance (*'aseret yemei teshuvah*). This period marks the last chance for Jews to take stock of their lives and to ask forgiveness from God and their fellow humans for the wrongs they committed, before the book of life is sealed for the year. During this week in 1868, Nissim sat down to write his last will and testament.

He wrote in Judeo-Arabic, the only language in which he was fully literate. He began as pious Jews did any document: by invoking God, who "consents to my intention." He then set out his "last will," explaining that he was writing in his house at 47 Rue du Faubourg Saint Honoré, being in "very good health." He took care to annul all previous testaments, for which he used a French term transliterated into Judeo-Arabic: *tiṣtāmān.*[1]

Nissim split his estate four ways; one-fourth he promised to his great-niece, 'Aziza, and one-fourth to her son, Nissim Jr. He divided the rest of his wealth between two of his closest male relatives: one-fourth went to his nephew Joseph (Yosef), son of his late brother Nathan, and the final fourth he gave to his great-nephew Nathan (Natan), son of his late nephew Judah. His third surviving nephew, Qā'id Momo—'Aziza's estranged father, and just as close a relation as Joseph and Nathan—was given only 25,000 francs. Undoubtedly Nissim had not forgiven Momo for having colluded with Khaznadar to charge him 360,000 francs in bills of exchange; by allotting Momo little more than a pittance of his enormous fortune, Nissim exacted the revenge he was powerless to realize during his lifetime.

Nissim specified gifts for other family members and loyal servants. He gave 100,000 francs to his estranged wife Mas'uda, who had remained in Sousse after Nissim's departure for France. He allotted various sums to more distant family members as well as the servants who had followed him from Tunisia and lived with him in Paris: his secretaries Jacob Shamama (25,000) and Joseph Bessis (25,000); Rabbi Judah Sitruk (4,000); Shalom Zagdun (3,000); Shalom Fellous (3,000); and Meir Ashkenazi (1,000).

Finally, Nissim did what wealthy people like him had done for generations, across cultures, in different languages and religious traditions: he set aside portions of his wealth for charitable donations. Nissim had been a philanthropist since he became wealthy. Writing his last will and testament was a chance to give even more spectacularly and leave his mark on the cities he held dear. He gave most generously to his coreligionists in Palestine, part of a tradition by which Jews across the diaspora supported scholars in the Land of Israel who dedicated their lives to sacred texts and pious acts.[2] Nissim allotted 25,000 francs each to the Jews of Hebron, Safed, and Tiberias. To the Jews of Jerusalem, he donated 200,000 francs—enough to build a yeshivah, where scholars could study full time with their basic needs provided for. He gave another 125,000 francs to build a yeshivah in Tunis as well as an additional 25,000 francs for the sages and poor Jews of Tunis. To the Jews of Paris, his adopted city, he bequeathed 25,000 francs.

Nissim dated his will according to the three calendars that marked the daily rhythm of his life: September 22, 1868; 6 Tishrei 5629 according to the Hebrew calendar; and 6 Jumādā II 1285 according to the Islamic one. He ended the document with a warning: "All of those who are given a portion of my inheritance may not pursue a greater share than what I have given them, nor may they pursue a share that is given to others."[3] Did he believe this admonition would stop his relatives from fighting over his estate? Or was this the resigned threat of a patriarch who knew he would be ignored by the next generation?

The need to write a will had been on Nissim's mind for some time. Two years earlier, Nissim had consulted with lawyers about how to dispose of his estate. Le Roy informed his client that foreigners had the right to make a holographic will—a private testament written, signed, and dated only by the testator, with no notarization or witnesses. Concerning Nissim's question about who might benefit from his estate after he passed, Le Roy explained that the content (not the form) of a foreigner's will in France depended on the requirements of his national law.[4]

When Nissim sat down to write his will, he had already considered himself an Italian citizen for over two years. Yet as we know, just nine months earlier, Nissim had divorced his third wife, Esther, according to Jewish law—that is, on the presumption that he was still a Tunisian subject. What, then, did Nissim think was his national law?

FIGURE 4.1. and 4.2 Nissim's properties on Rue de Chaillot, at the time #103 and #105 (VO11.537, #67 and #69 Rue de Chaillot, AP)

The will is hardly explicit on this point, but it does offer some clues. Nissim translated various formulations common in European testaments into his native Judeo-Arabic, such as specifying that these were his "last wishes" and he was fully in command of his faculties. And aspects of his will flew in the face of halakhic requirements for a valid testament, most notably the lack of a *kinyan*. The kinyan is a form of ritual acquisition, often through a symbolic act such as taking and then lifting an object of value. Its performance—whether in the context of the transfer of property or a marriage ceremony, in which the groom traditionally "acquires" the bride—enables the transfer of rights. Jewish law requires that most wills include a kinyan. This ritual act transfers the capital of the property to the heirs immediately, though the usufruct remains in the hands of the testator until his death.[5] Nissim's will, however, made no mention of a kinyan. Assuming that Nissim was following Le Roy's advice, it seems he was counting on Italian law applying to his estate—thus suggesting that in this instance at least, Nissim thought of himself as an Italian citizen.

Just how Nissim related to the various legal orders under whose shadow he lived remains obscure. Yet one thing became clear: the great man was increasingly convinced that he would never return to his native land. In the spring of 1869, Nissim bought two town houses in Paris, numbers 103 and 105 on the Rue de Chaillot. Both were new buildings made possible by Haussmann's dramatic urban transformation. The houses were nearly identical—each four stories, with a large porte cochere leading to a courtyard, and beyond a stable big enough for five horses and three carriages. Inside, enormous windows punctuated the generous rooms in classic Parisian style. Nissim himself moved into #105, and installed 'Aziza, Moses, and Nissim Jr. in #103. A week after buying the properties, he wrote to inform Khaznadar of his new address, which he had his secretary write out in French.[6] At the same time, Nissim ordered new stationery—elegant sheets in baby blue, embossed with his name in a gentle arc over his address.[7] Nissim's new home—like his letterhead—proclaimed his intention to remain in Paris for the foreseeable future.[8]

Shortly before the family moved to the Rue de Chaillot, Moses organized a soiree to which the entire "Tunisian colony" of Paris was invited; one wonders what "Tunisian" meant in this case, for presumably those like Dahdah and de Lesseps—both in the service of the bey, though neither of Tunisian origin—were invited too.[9] Moses also commissioned a family photograph, by this time a hallmark of bourgeois status. The resulting image, like the fete, reflect a family living between two worlds; 'Aziza, Moses, and Nissim Jr. had acquired all the trappings of a fully Parisian life, but they had shed neither their Tunisian social circles nor their Tunisian bearing.

As was customary, all three dressed up for the occasion. Moses wears a European suit, adorned with a vest, pocket watch, and striped tie, and sporting a mustache slightly upturned at the tips. He stares sternly into the camera, brow slightly furrowed, projecting gravitas or perhaps mild disapproval. 'Aziza stands behind him, her right arm resting on Moses's shoulder. Unlike her husband, she is not in European dress; her wide-sleeved blouse emerges from under an embroidered vest cinched at the waist. Her hair is tied back simply, severely even, but she herself is smiling slightly; she seems amused by the novelty of the photography studio. With her left arm, she holds little Nissim—four years old at the time—dressed in a velvet suit with a wide, starched collar, striped tie (much like his father's), and tall black boots. Nissim Jr.'s thick hair is parted and combed sideways in each direction, and he looks plaintively at the camera—perhaps betraying the loneliness of a childhood in exile, far from

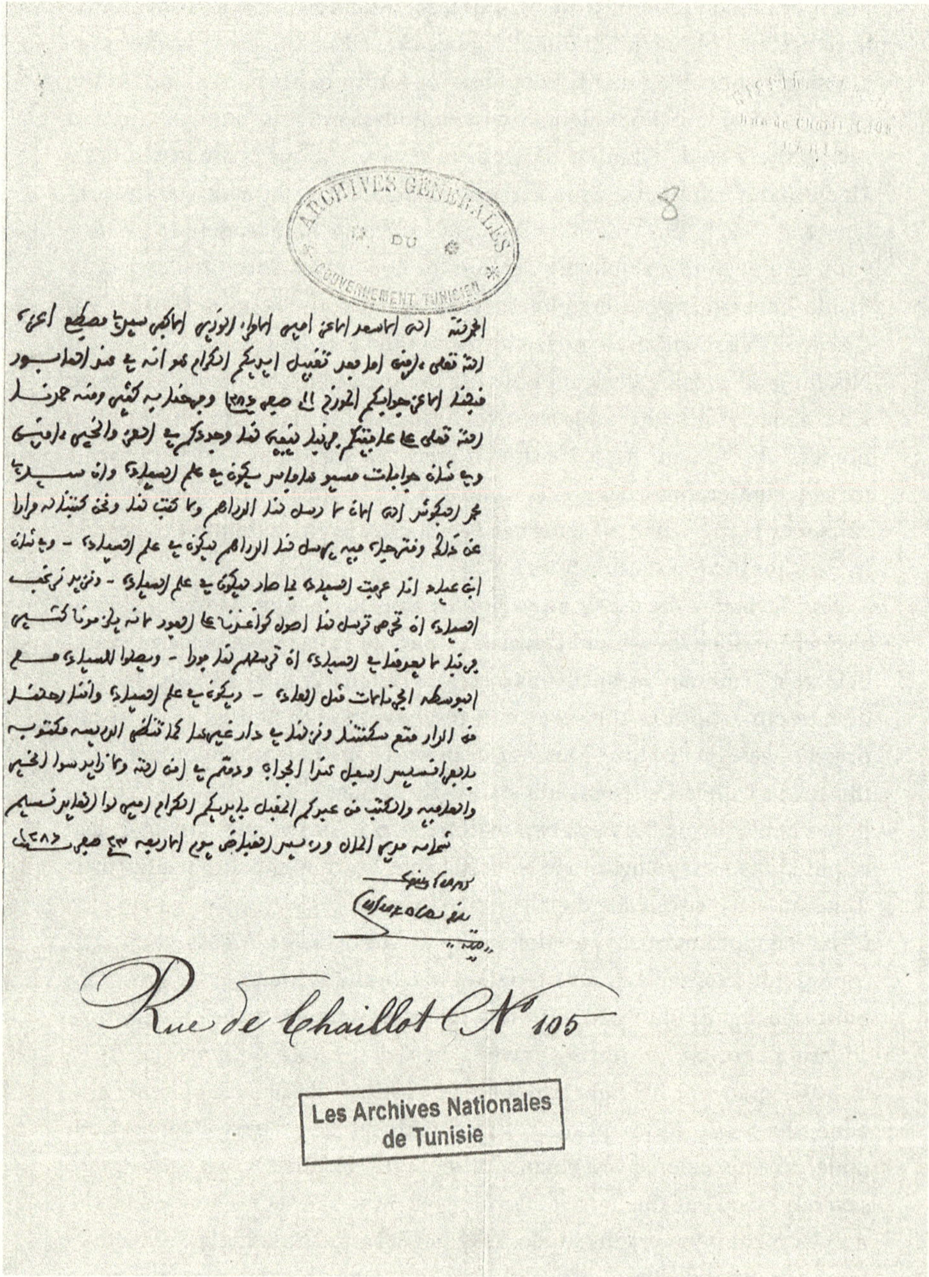

FIGURE 4.3. Letter from Nissim to Khaznadar on his new stationery, with his address given as "Rue de Chaillot, 105, Paris" (SH.C100.D221.8, ANT)

FIGURE 4.4. ʿAziza, Moshe, and Nissim Jr., 1868
(courtesy of Gilles Boulu)

cousins and neighbors who could share the same Tunisian Jewish language and culture.

———

Not long after the family photo and the move to the Rue de Chaillot, an eruption of violence once again upended Nissim's world. In September 1870, the Prussian army laid siege to Paris; the city was completely cut off until January 1871. As the trouble approached, Nissim sent ʿAziza and Nissim Jr. off to his cousin Joseph in Marseille. During the siege, he kept in constant touch with the family by means of carrier pigeons—improbably, the only reliable method of getting messages in and out of Paris. On the first of December, a tiny missive survived the flight from Marseille to Paris: Joseph wrote that he "received Moses's letter. Everyone is well. They receive your letters. Reassure yourself about them."[10] When the siege was finally over, Nissim's enthusiasm for France had dampened considerably. He traveled to Florence, from whence he wrote to his beloved ʿAziza. "I can't describe to you how cheered I am that I no longer love

Paris, but rather Italy."[11] The siege had darkened Nissim's view of the City of Lights; he was ready to return to the sunshine of the Mediterranean.

If Nissim had any qualms about leaving France, the chaos of that spring convinced him to depart immediately. Nissim was back in Paris when, on March 18, radical soldiers from the French National Guard captured dozens of cannons on Montmartre. Once socialist revolutionaries took control of the city and the red flag flew from the Hôtel-de-Ville, an exodus of the city's wealthy elite began. The following day, working-class people swarmed the elegant boulevards of the tony neighborhoods in which Nissim and his family lived. Barricades went up, shops stayed closed, and more and more wealthy Parisians headed for the provinces.[12] On March 22, a counterdemonstration in the Place Vendôme—just blocks away from Nissim's old apartment, in the heart of Paris's most elegant neighborhood—resulted in the death of twelve people. This was no place for a wealthy family like the Shamamas.

On March 24, a Friday—as the servants were preparing the dishes for Shabbat—Nissim made his way to the Italian embassy, located on the Rond-Point des Champs-Élysées, just a ten-minute walk from his home.[13] He requested a passport to travel to Italy and presented his naturalization decree as evidence of his Italian citizenship. The passport described Nissim as "the Count Semama, Nissim, General of the Cavalry, native of Tunis, originally from Livorno, naturalized Italian citizen: leaving from Paris, going to Italy." On the side of the passport, as was customary, the consular official penned in a brief description of Nissim: "Age: 64. Profession: privately wealthy. Last domicile: Paris." The Italian consul general, Louis Cerruti, signed the passport and stamped it with the consulate's seal.[14]

The passport that Nissim acquired in the Italian consulate had little to do with the passports people use today. Most international borders were open and did not require documentation to cross. Even in places that required passports—of which Italy was not one in the 1860s—it was generally simple to sidestep the regulations, especially for wealthy travelers like Nissim. Throughout the nineteenth century, passports functioned more like visas. They were not considered identity documents issued by the country to whom an individual formally belonged. Indeed, it was standard for those traveling abroad to obtain a passport from the authorities of their destination. In other words, Tunisian who wanted to travel to Italy would typically seek out passports from Italian officials—either at an Italian consulate or the Italian border.[15] Nissim's decision to obtain a passport from the Italian consulate in Paris probably had nothing to do with proving his Italian naturalization. Rather, since he was planning to settle in Livorno, he wanted to make sure that he had all the right documents for entering the country. Armed with official permission to travel to Italy, Nissim left the gray skies of Paris behind for good.

———

By Mediterranean standards, Livorno is a modern city. The Medicis built it in the sixteenth century to help Tuscany expand overseas trade, using the latest technologies of defense and urban planning. For two hundred years, Livorno flourished as one of the region's busiest harbors; it abandoned tariffs in order to attract commerce, thus becoming the first free port. For Jews, Livorno counted among the most famous havens in Christendom. In 1591, the grand duke of Tuscany issued a patent known as the Livornina, addressed primarily to Sephardic Jews; the Livornina not only gave the descendants of Jews from Iberia the right to settle in Livorno—something not to be taken for granted at a time when most of western Europe was closed to Jews—but also freedom of movement, the right to carry arms, and the right to practice any profession they chose. Livornese Jewish leaders even had the authority to grant formal citizenship to Jewish immigrants—a process called *ballotazione*. Jews were accompanied by other non-Catholics who flocked to the Tuscan tax haven: Protestants from England and the Netherlands, Orthodox Christians and Armenians from the Ottoman Empire, and even some Muslim merchants. Together these various "nations," as they were known, gave the city its reputation as a cosmopolitan hub. Still, it was Livorno's Jews whose outsized share of the city's international trade came to symbolize the profits and perils of toleration in early modern Europe.[16]

By the time Nissim arrived in 1871, however, Livorno's fortunes had declined steeply; as the geography of trade shifted to different shores and more ports became "free," Livorno was eclipsed as the Mediterranean's commercial jewel. Jews no longer flocked to Tuscany to make their fortunes; on the contrary, like other Livornese natives, they started leaving in droves. When Nissim arrived, he was swimming against a tide of Jewish emigration—mainly toward better opportunities on the southern shores of the Mediterranean. Livornese Jews settled in Algiers, Alexandria, Smyrna, and of course, Tunis—where an influx of Tuscan Jews in the mid-nineteenth century bolstered the local Grana community and lent it a distinctively Italian flavor.[17]

In 1861, Livorno became part of the fledgling Italian state. Municipal authorities rechristened streets and squares after the heroes of the Risorgimento. The city's main plaza was renamed Piazza Carlo Alberto, after unified Italy's first king. And though Livorno was no longer the major hub of international trade it had once been, new railroads connected the port to political centers—first to Florence, which served as united Italy's capitol from 1865 to 1870, and then to Rome, conquered by Italian troops in 1870. Livorno's harbor hardly stood empty; daily departures to destinations across the Mediterranean made the city a busy transit hub. And while Jews were leaving for better economic opportunities abroad, Livorno's reputation as a center of Hebrew printing followed its émigrés across the Mediterranean. By the nineteenth century, Livornese publishing houses dominated the market for Jewish communities in North Africa, the Middle East, and even as far as India.[18]

Nissim bought a large plot of land on the Via Ricasoli, another street renamed after a Risorgimento hero; Bettino Ricasoli was Italy's second prime minister and had personally signed Nissim's decree of naturalization back in 1866.[19] On this plot, Nissim set about building a splendid palazzo. Far larger than both his Parisian town houses combined, Nissim's new home appealed to Livorno's aesthetic of restrained elegance, with a few flourishes that announced the vast riches of the city's new resident. The neoclassical facade boasted sixteen generous windows on the second floor. Through the enormous carriage doors, a series of attached buildings led to ample grounds behind.[20] Various hallways and arcades connected to the courtyard, open to the mild Tuscan air. For a man accustomed to Tunisian sunshine, the palazzo embraced a welcome change from the overcast skies of Paris.

In the center of the facade, a coat of arms still rises just above the roof: a shield, undergirded with heavy floral garlands and topped with a knight's helmet nearly identical to the one on the Shamama coat of arms. On the shield are three symbols: a crescent moon, three five-pointed stars, and a circle enclosing a crescent and star. The palazzo's crowning touch announced Nissim's two public personas. The shield, floral garlands, and above all knight's helmet—lifted directly from his newly acquired armorial bearings—announced the abode of an Italian nobleman. The crescents and stars had featured on the Ottoman and Tunisian flags since the first decades of the nineteenth century; the celestial symbol's evoked Nissim's position as an official in the service of the bey of Tunis.

The arrival of a Jew as wealthy as Nissim was presumably welcomed by the Jewish community, whose members' fortunes had declined along with those of the city. Soon after settling in Livorno, Nissim donated five hundred lire to the Opera Pia Ospedale Israelitico, a Jewish charitable organization. He gave again the following winter, offering a lira and two pounds of bread to each person registered as a recipient of communal charity.[21] His reputation for grandeur long

FIGURE 4.5. The crest atop Nissim's palazzo in Livorno

outlasted him; decades after Nissim's death, Livornese Jews thought to be putting on airs were still chastised with the saying "You are not a Shamama!"[22]

Meanwhile, developments in Tunisia made Nissim more hesitant than ever to return home. The country's finances had never fully recovered after

Khaznadar's initial loan from d'Erlanger. After Khaznadar signed a contract for a new loan with the French banker in 1865, the treasury was no more successful in keeping up with the payments. In 1867, Khaznadar contracted yet a third loan, with d'Erlanger and a syndicate of banks in Frankfurt (including one owned by d'Erlanger's father, Raphael)—this time for the astronomical sum of a hundred million francs. Khaznadar guaranteed the loan with almost all the remaining state revenues, including tithes on grains, excise duties, and export taxes—"in short, all the taxes that are still unencumbered with claims from the loan of 1863."[23] In other words, the Tunisian government had agreed to mortgage all of its revenue to its European creditors. But the third loan never managed to attract enough subscribers to become a reality; after the nosedive in the price of the bonds issued on the Tunisian loan of 1863, no one was willing to take the risk d'Erlanger was offering. The syndicate had already advanced four million francs to the Tunisian government; when the loan failed completely on the stock market, d'Erlanger and his associates asked Prince Otto Eduard Leopoldo von Bismarck to intervene on their behalf to get the advance back.[24] The Parisian banker was still a citizen of Prussia; this was not the last time he would invoke his legal belonging to recover losses.

By 1868, the deterioration of Tunisia's finances had reached a crisis point. The bondholders of the first two loans were mostly French, Italian, and British nationals living in Tunis, and they proceeded to bombard their ambassadors with demands for payment. Ottoman diplomats in Paris and Malta sent regular updates to the Sublime Porte concerning Sadiq Bey's attempts to staunch the flood of red drowning Tunisia's accounts. But the sultan's officials were relatively powerless and had to content themselves with watching uneasily as the Ottoman province sank deeper into debt. In the spring of 1868, French, British, Italian, and Prussian diplomats began to discuss seizing control of Tunisia's finances.[25] There was not much Sadiq Bey could do; he sent two representatives to Paris to ask the French minister of foreign affairs for advice. The minister showed little pity for the bey's conundrum; he told the bey to stop addressing himself "to so-called bankers who have no credit in European markets and who can easily cause him difficulties"—a not-so-subtle dig at d'Erlanger's tainted reputation. Instead, the minister recommended that the bey set about improving his country's finances without a loan, declining, however, to specify how this might be done.[26] In the spring of 1869, Khaznadar made a final attempt to unify the Tunisian debt; this, too, failed spectacularly.[27]

On July 5, 1869, the bey succumbed to French, British, and Italian pressure; he signed a decree giving the International Financial Commission complete control over Tunisian finances. France successfully jockeyed for preeminence among European states seeking influence in Tunisia and secured the right to appoint the commission's president. It chose Victor Villet, a lifelong French bureaucrat who had completed a mission as a financial inspector in the Ottoman Empire. Villet's acerbic personality rapidly made him many enemies in Tunis. Compounding matters, Villet was extremely powerful; with the stroke of a pen, he could halve the worth of government bonds, leaving hundreds of frustrated investors to stew. Jealous of his power and resentful of his imperiousness, detractors soon dubbed him "the Bey Villet."[28]

Only one Tunisian official seems to have earned Villet's trust and admiration: Khayraddin, a mamlūk and government official. Like his rival (and father-in-law) Khaznadar, Khayraddin first rose to power under Ahmad Bey and remained in his successors' inner circles. But in 1862, disillusioned with the progress of administrative reform in Tunisia and having fallen out with Khaznadar, Khayraddin resigned from Sadiq Bey's service. For years he worked on his masterpiece, *The Surest Path to Knowledge regarding the Condition of Countries*—a political treatise calling for administrative reforms in Tunisia.[29] As Khaznadar's star was losing its luster, Sadiq Bey persuaded Khayraddin to return from his voluntary exile and head the Executive Committee of the International Financial Commission. Villet trusted Khayraddin, and together the two set about dredging the financial swamp into which Tunisia had sunk.

In addition to Villet and Khayraddin's Executive Committee, the International Financial Commission consisted of an Inspection Committee (Comité de Contrôle); this was composed of two French nationals, two British nationals, and two Italian nationals, all elected by the bondholders of the Tunisian debt.[30] The initial members of the Inspection Committee were not as foreign to Tunisia as the "International" in the commission's title might suggest. Two were members of the local Grana community. Moses Santillana was born in Tunis to a Grana family, as was his father. Santillana served as a dragoman for the British consulate general in Tunis; dragomen were technically interpreters, though also served as cultural brokers. In 1849, he was formally recognized as a British protégé.[31] Giacomo Guttieres, elected to represent Italy, was born in Livorno and moved to Tunis as a child. The second British representative, Moses Levy, was also born in Tunisia, as was his father; he was a British subject by virtue of his grandfather, Judah Levy, a native of Gibraltar—under British rule since 1704. The second Italian member of the commission, Gaetano Fedriani, was a Genoese who had exiled himself to Tunis with Garibaldi in 1834.[32] Only the French representatives were new to Tunisia; both worked for the banks that had lent Tunisia its disastrous loans.[33] The Inspection Committee mirrored the composition of Tunisia's European inhabitants, many of whom had lived in the country for generations and were foreigners mainly by virtue of their extraterritorial privileges.[34]

Over the course of years spent trying to sort out just how the treasury had reached such a crisis point, Villet amassed extensive evidence of mismanagement and corruption. In his eyes, the first offender was Khaznadar, who had served the beys of Tunis since the age of twenty and was still in power.[35] In a lengthy report written in May 1872, Villet blamed Khaznadar for "the series of profligate and senseless financial operations over the past ten to twelve years. . . . [A]s long as Sidi Mustafa [Khaznadar] held power, he had no other concern than the satisfaction of his cupidity, for which he never hesitated to sacrifice the country and the sovereign who adopted him."[36] The second villain was none other than d'Erlanger, whom Villet accused of fraud in his multiple loans to Tunisia. And the third was Nissim himself; Villet named Nissim as Khaznadar's right-hand man, who enabled the minister's corruption while enriching himself. According to Villet, the Jewish minister of finance double-dipped in the treasury, while Khaznadar "forgot" to ask him for accounts; when Nissim lent the government money, Khaznadar personally collected the commission on the loan and pocketed it.[37] In Villet's summation, it was in large part Nissim's embezzlement—enabled by Khaznadar's "self-interested tolerance"—that had forced Tunisia to seek a foreign loan in the first place.[38]

D'Erlanger was presumably accustomed to being vilified for the financial disasters he left in his wake. But he was not prepared to lose money in the process. As Villet worked to reduce Tunisia's debts, d'Erlanger put pressure on the French consul in Tunis. Although it was inevitable that Villet would reduce the remaining payments the treasury owed to d'Erlanger, the banker wanted to be paid as much as possible. As it became clear that the French consul was no longer on good terms with Villet, however, d'Erlanger realized he would get nowhere working through the French consulate. Instead, he turned to Prussia, the only state of which he was a citizen. As a native of Frankfurt, d'Erlanger had the right to ask Prussian officials to intervene on his behalf. And d'Erlanger must have known that Prussia was eager to assert its influence in Tunisia, largely as a way to combat French designs on the Ottoman province. As politicians discussed the installation of the International Financial Commission, Charles Tulin, the Prussian representative in Tunis, wrote to the Ministry of Foreign Affairs in Berlin to complain that Villet's proposals for cutting Tunisia's debt would cause harm to Prussian bankers like d'Erlanger.

Thanks in part to this threat, Tulin got himself appointed as the German consul in Tunisia.[39]

D'Erlanger's successful lobbying prompted Tulin to pay the bey a visit. The newly minted German consul demanded over 5 million gold francs in immediate payment to d'Erlanger. Desperate for a lifeline, the bey wrote to the Ottoman sultan, reporting on d'Erlanger's recourse to Germany and the German consul's demands. But the Sultan was not willing to bail out the bey; Ottoman officials had been against an international loan in the first place. Sadiq Bey was between a rock and a hard place. He could hardly afford to enrage Germany, nor could he leverage any pressure on the Sublime Porte. In 1872, the bey gave in to d'Erlanger's demands and paid the Franco-German banker 5,185,887 gold francs.[40] By nimbly deploying his citizenship, d'Erlanger managed to turn what threatened to be a huge loss into another financial success.

D'Erlanger was not the only one concerned about Bey Villet's extensive power; Nissim was keenly aware of the threat that Villet's accusations posed. More than ever, Nissim must have worried about being forced to return to Tunisia—by Ibn 'Ayyad's ongoing lawsuit, by Villet, or perhaps by the bey himself. Nissim was almost certainly concerned about jurisdiction above all else; if he could prove that he was domiciled in Italy, he could not legally be forced to appear in a Tunisian court. He had already acquired a royal decree of naturalization. His Italian passport, secured just days before his departure from Paris, described him as an Italian citizen. Now it was time to formally register his new domicile in Italy.

On November 9, 1871—a little over seven months after arriving in Livorno—Nissim requested the presence of a notary in his palazzo on the Via Ricasoli. When the notary had set out his writing paper and pen, Nissim formally renounced his domicile in Tunis and declared that he wished to establish his domicile in Livorno. He again noted that he was a naturalized Italian citizen according to the royal decree of August 25, 1866.[41] With this declaration of domicile, Nissim hoped, he could never again be sued in Tunisia.

After moving to Livorno, Nissim kept up an intermittent correspondence with his former colleagues at the Bardo, but his brief notes contained only platitudes and formulaic greetings. In September 1871, he wrote to Khaznadar to congratulate the prime minister on the marriage of his son Muhammad; the letter said nothing about the International Financial Commission, Nissim's relocation to Italy, or the debts he still claimed to be owed by Khaznadar.[42] Later that fall, Nissim wrote to say he had heard the reports about Khayraddin's trip to Istanbul. The mamlūk had been sent to collect a royal decree (*firman*) from the sultan affirming Tunisia's ties to the Ottoman Empire. Both Sadiq Bey and the Sublime Porte were eager to clarify that Tunisia was part of the empire, hoping to stave off the colonial ambitions of countries like France.[43] But Nissim did not breathe a word about politics; he merely congratulated Khaznadar on the rejoicing that accompanied the reading of the royal decree in Tunis—a public expression of anticolonial resistance before colonization had even begun.[44]

At the end of November 1872, Nissim wrote to Khaznadar to wish him a joyous ʿId al-fiṭr, the holiday that celebrates the end of Ramaḍān.[45] As always, he signed his letter "Brigadier General Qāʾid Nissim Shamama, Director of Finances and Receiver General." Nissim added his signature in Hebrew under the elegant Arabic script of his secretary. This would be his last letter to his erstwhile patron; by the time the next Muslim holiday came around, Nissim was dead.

PART II

Shamama v. Shamama

5

Heirs Apparent (1873)

THE SHOCK of Nissim's death came when Livorno's port stood largely silent; only a few steamboats continued to ply the Mediterranean during the most dangerous months for navigation. Despite all the technological innovations in the age of steam and rail, the poet Hesiod's advice from nearly three thousand years ago still stood: the winter was "no time to keep your ships on the wine-blue water."[1]

Just a few blocks from the sea, the Shamama palazzo was buzzing with activity. Nissim had fallen ill on the morning of January 24; he passed after just a few hours of agony. The sudden death of a man as important as Nissim meant not only shock and grief but endless logistics. It was up to 'Aziza and Moses to make appropriate arrangements to honor their deceased uncle. They made charitable donations in Nissim's memory to local hospitals and schools—both Jewish and Catholic. With the speed required by Jewish law, they hastily arranged a magnificent funeral. "An immense crowd" followed the coffin, including all the Jewish notables of the city in their splendid carriages.[2]

Nissim clearly had an impressive set of commemorations in mind when he wrote his will. He apportioned the enormous sum of twenty-five thousand francs to cover the expenses of the burial and tomb—a quarter of the value of his palazzo.[3] Moses and 'Aziza happily complied; both were eager to elevate their late uncle in the eyes of their adopted city. Doing so would also position the couple as successors to Nissim's legacy. They bought a plot in the Jewish community's newest cemetery, just outside the city walls, and set about having a monumental mausoleum designed. The structure they erected still dominates the cemetery—a riotous elegy to Nissim's embrace of Italy. Twelve fluted columns stand sentry around the periphery, drawing the eye up toward intricately carved capitals topped by enormous urns brimming with flowers. Between the base of each column, Nissim's coat of arms repeats on friezes

FIGURE 5.1. and 5.2 Nissim's tomb, Cimitero Ebraico di Livorno, viale Ippolito Nievo (photos by Roberto Zucchi)

decorating a low fence around the tomb itself. In the center, on an even taller pedestal, a towering sarcophagus announces the outsized personality of the man buried beneath.

Amid this explosion of neoclassical imagery, a single oversized fez atop the sarcophagus provides the sole hint of Nissim's origins. The fez's thick tassels brush the stone pillow on which it rests, quietly echoing the iconography of a small group of tombstones in the city's main cemetery just up the street. Known as the "Turks' Quadrant" (*quadrato dei turchi*), this small plot was reserved for the graves of Muslims who died in Livorno in the mid-nineteenth century. Some had inscriptions in Arabic, others in Italian. Many featured turbans, following the Ottoman style—such as the tomb of Hamet Neyal Turco, a merchant from Alexandria who died in Livorno in 1846. In the Ottoman Empire itself, it had since become fashionable to replace the tombstone's turban with a stone fez—once the signature red hats had replaced turbans among urban elites as a sign of modernity. Nissim wore the fez during his lifetime, thus aligning himself with reformists like his original patron, Ahmad Bey. The stone fez atop Nissim's tomb offered a quiet antiphony to the rest of the monument, which loudly trumpeted his *italianità*.

But completing Nissim's tomb hardly laid the matter of his estate to rest. In the months after Nissim's death, various heirs began preparations to claim their portion of the millionaire's estate. 'Aziza and Moses, along with Mas'uda, the estranged widow, developed plans to prove that Nissim had died an Italian, hoping to ensure that the will was upheld. Qā'id Momo, who had been cut out almost entirely in the will, joined forces with Joseph and Nathan, who stood to inherit more if the will was thrown out. The three nephews soon realized that having Jewish law applied to the estate was their only hope and set out to prove that Nissim had died a Tunisian. Before long, both sides recognized the importance of Jewish law to the case, and rabbinic authorities across the Mediterranean became involved. Meanwhile, Tunisian government officials put intense pressure on Joseph, Nathan, and Momo, Nissim's three nephews in Tunisia. The bey's advisers did everything in their power to convince the presumptive heirs to relinquish a percentage of their inheritance to the government—forcing the nephews to take dramatic measures to protect their claims on the estate.

Even as these battle lines were being drawn, nobody yet knew just how much Nissim had been worth; an Italian Jewish newspaper guessed that the count had left behind 12 million francs, while a French Jewish newspaper reported that his estate was estimated at 30 million.[4] It took nearly four years

FIGURE 5.3. Turks' Quadrant, Cimitero Comunale dei Lupi, Livorno

before an inventory of Nissim's possessions was completed; the inventory determined that Nissim had left behind the astonishing sum of 27,718,688 francs.[5]

It turned out that Nissim was not just wealthy but instead among the very richest people in all Europe. The average estate of the wealthiest 0.1 percent of the population in Paris in 1872 was 4.6 million francs. Only legends like the Rothschilds were significantly wealthier than this eccentric official from Tunisia.[6] To an ordinary person, Nissim's riches were unthinkable. The average daily wage for a laborer in Paris was somewhere between 3 and 4 francs, and such a worker would spend about 2.36 francs on three daily meals, each of which included wine—this was France, after all. In an entire year, the average French person spent 300 francs for food, lodging, and clothing. Nissim's wealth went even further in Italy, where the cost and standard of living was lower; the average worker there spent the equivalent of less than a franc on their daily fare, which only rarely included wine.[7] The vast sums in play not only raised the stakes on both sides but also funded a kind of legal arms race. Nissim's wealth intensified the fight over his inheritance—and thus over his nationality.

When news of Nissim's death reached Tunis, the entire Jewish community was reported to be in mourning.[8] In the Bardo, a buzz of speculation flew through the corridors. Khayraddin, now foreign minister, began a lively correspondence with Bargellini, the Tunisian agent in Livorno. Bargellini was the first to announce Nissim's death to the Bardo. Khayraddin's response explained his assessment of the situation: "Qā'id Momo, his brother [Joseph], and his nephew [Nathan]" were Nissim's heirs according to the biblical laws of succession. All three were "Twansa" and currently lived in Tunis.[9] In characterizing Nissim's nephews as Twansa, Khayraddin made it clear that Momo, Joseph, and Nathan were subjects of the bey. Unlike Grana Jews, most of whom had Italian citizenship, the Shamama heirs were under the jurisdiction of Tunisian law.

Khayraddin's knowledge about the Shamama family could only have come from Qā'id Momo. Momo had replaced Nissim as receiver general in 1864.[10] Since then, he had also amassed considerable debts to the government. Momo was well aware that he stood in line to inherit from his wealthy uncle according to Jewish law. It is easy to imagine that he deflected settling with the treasury by promising to pay in full when he got his inheritance from Nissim.[11]

But Momo could not ignore how furious Nissim had been with him in the years preceding his death. Nissim had never forgiven his nephew for the bills of exchange he drew in his name back in Paris. Even before anyone knew the contents of Nissim's will, Momo feared that his uncle might have cut him out entirely.

Ever the schemer, Momo set about doing his best to minimize the effects that his late uncle's anger might have on his inheritance prospects. The day after Nissim died, Momo summoned his brother Joseph and his nephew Nathan, son of his late brother Judah. Momo hoped to convince his relatives that they should agree to divide the estate equally in the event that Nissim had diminished the portion of one or another. "Even if my uncle did wrong by you," Momo crooned, "I will be your champion." But Joseph and Nathan knew that it was Momo who had infuriated Nissim, and thus Momo who risked being cut out of his inheritance. Seeing that his ploy had failed, Momo resorted to threats: "If I find that I have been excluded from the estate of my uncle—for which I have waited all my life—I will not rest and I will not desist; I will commit wicked deeds. If we do not inherit equally, then none of us will get anything: I will denounce you to the government and they will take everything!"[12] This was no idle threat; as receiver general, Momo had significant clout. Nonetheless, Nathan was brazen enough to leave. Joseph, however, caved and signed a contract agreeing to split the inheritance equally. As if by chance, two notaries emerged to ensure the document would carry legal weight.[13]

Momo's next move would be hard to believe if it was not documented in multiple sources; it seems more credible as a plot twist in Dickens's *Bleak House* than the stuff of history. After obtaining Joseph's signature on the dubious contract, Momo set out to secure another object of his desire: his niece Esther, Nathan's sister. Momo was already married, but he was determined to make Esther his second wife. Why, exactly, remains a mystery; perhaps he thought Esther would come with a handsome dowry. Or maybe he was simply in love with her.[14] But Esther had no interest in Momo, who was a full quarter-century her senior; she planned to marry her childhood sweetheart, a man named Nissim Attal.[15] Undaunted by his beloved's opposition, Momo brought Esther before two Jewish witnesses and performed *kiddushin*, the first of two steps required to marry under Jewish law. The witnesses signed a legal document attesting the marriage ceremony.[16] Desperate to escape the clutches of her uncle, Esther saw a glimmer of hope when one of the witnesses to the *kiddushin* reneged on his signature. The legal document might be invalid after all. Undaunted, Momo used his connections in the Bardo to convene a council of rabbis to review the situation. For what seemed like ages, the rabbis remained at a stalemate. Eventually Momo grew impatient and made his way home. Shortly after he left the room, the council concluded that the *kiddushin* was null and void. Momo got the bad news in a carriage on the way back to La Goulette.[17]

The skies darkened further for Momo once he learned about the contents of Nissim's will. His worst fears had been confirmed; rather than the millions he expected to inherit, Momo was allotted a paltry twenty-five thousand francs—which would not even make a dent in his debts. His only hope was to have the will thrown out and claim his third of the estate according to biblical law.

Compounding his own disappointment, Momo was under enormous pressure from his patrons in the Bardo. Given the desperate situation of the treasury, Khaznadar and Khayraddin could not afford to forgive Momo's debts to the government. Bargellini had given them hope that Nissim's will might be declared null; his inquiries with de Lesseps in Paris had revealed that Nissim never took the proper steps to register his naturalization decree and thus never became Italian. Nissim would have died a Tunisian, which meant that Jewish law would apply to the estate and the will would most likely be thrown out. In this scenario, Momo would inherit. And if that was the case, then Khaznadar and Khayraddin wanted to make sure that Momo paid what he owed. On Wednesday, February 26, the two officials called Momo to the Bardo. They presented him with a contract, by which he agreed to give a quarter of his inheritance to the government. The contract also stipulated that Momo would not attempt to claim any debts that the government might have owed Nissim and would hand over Nissim's properties in Tunisia as a security while the estate was being adjudicated. Momo had little choice. He signed his name in Hebrew: Shlomo de Natan Shamama, "may his end be good" (*sofo tov*).[18]

Momo's sole consolation was to double down on his determination to marry his niece, Esther. Just before signing away a quarter of his rights to the inheritance, he asked Khaznadar to convene another special council of rabbis to decide the question of his recent marriage. This time, one imagines, Momo would choose scholars willing to rule in his favor. Khaznadar agreed; presumably it mattered little to the prime minister whether Esther married her childhood sweetheart or her uncle.[19]

Next, Khayraddin and Khaznadar set out to convince Joseph and Nathan to endorse a similar contract to the one Momo had signed. By this point, Joseph and Nathan were already planning to travel to Livorno to pursue their share of the inheritance in person.[20] Khaznadar wrote to Domenico Spezzafumo, an Italian born in Tunis who worked as the bey's general counsel (*primo avvocato*). The prime minister wanted to know if he could legitimately prevent the two Shamama heirs from leaving. Spezzafumo responded in the negative: they had to be allowed to travel, according to the *firman* sent by the Ottoman sultan in 1871 requiring "the protection of individual liberty."[21] Khaznadar would have to act fast, before Joseph and Nathan decamped to Tuscany.

At 4:30 p.m. on Friday, February 28—two days after Momo signed away a quarter of his inheritance—a messenger showed up at Joseph and Nathan's home to summon them to the Bardo. Shabbat was about to begin, but Joseph and Nathan could hardly refuse. Once at the palace, they were whisked into a room where Khaznadar, Khayraddin, and other high-ranking government officials presented Joseph and Nathan with a contract whose terms were identical to the one Momo had signed. Neither of them could read the Arabic so someone read it aloud for them.[22]

Unlike Momo, Joseph and Nathan were not employees of the government; nor did they owe any money to the treasury. Despite being faced with an assembly of Tunisia's highest-ranking officials, Joseph and Nathan stood their ground; they asked for additional clauses in the contract, including a guarantee that they would be permitted to travel to Livorno. They also took Esther's side in the marriage debacle, insisting that she be permitted to marry Attal, whom they described as her "fiancé." The government officials balked at some of Joseph and Nathan's demands. The matter of Momo's marriage to Esther, they maintained, had nothing to do with the question of the inheritance. In any case, if Momo and Esther were indeed legally married, then Esther's engagement to Attal was "prohibited by religious law."[23] The two sides went back and forth; by the time they reached a compromise, it was late in the evening and Shabbat had already begun. Joseph and Nathan explained that Jewish law prevented them from signing anything until the Sabbath ended the next day. They promised to return first thing Sunday morning to sign the amended contract.[24]

Presumably neither Joseph nor Nathan ever intended to honor this pledge. The aspiring heirs did not return home that night. Instead they returned to Tunis (either a long walk or short carriage ride that would have required violating Shabbat) and fetched Esther. The three Shamamas headed toward the Bab al-Bahr; inside the city walls, they took the first right down the Rue des Glacières. At the corner of the Rue Zarkoun was the Italian consulate. Joseph, Nathan, and Esther somehow managed to enter the building, where they spent the night on the cold, hard floor.

Early the next morning, Saturday, March 1, Luigi Pinna, the Italian consul in Tunis, arrived at his office ready to attend to the endless correspondence demanded of diplomats. As he crossed the antechambers on his way to his desk, Pinna found two men and a young girl—all locals, from their dress—looking at him expectantly. After eight years in Tunis, Pinna was used to surprises.[25] Unphased, he ushered the trio into his office and settled in to hear their story.

Joseph got right to the point. He had come with his nephew and niece to seek the protection of the great nation of Italy. He and Nathan were being persecuted by the Tunisian authorities, who wanted them to sign a contract highly detrimental to their interests. And although they had resolved to travel to Livorno, Khaznadar and his associates were preventing them from leaving the country. Esther, meanwhile, was being compelled to marry the receiver general, her uncle Momo, despite being engaged to someone else. On behalf of the freedom that Italy stood for, they implored Pinna for "the help and the protection of the Italian flag to be liberated from the oppression of the local government."[26] To their great relief, Pinna immediately agreed.

Consulates in Tunisia served as sanctuaries—zones of asylum to which anyone could escape when they felt themselves victims of injustice.[27] As long as someone was physically in the consulate, he was immune from the bey's sovereignty. Moreover, Joseph and Nathan's account of their persecution fit the Orientalist stereotype of a despotic government trampling the rights of vulnerable non-Muslims. The Shamamas also banked on Pinna's eagerness to insert himself into internal Tunisian affairs on behalf of those deemed under his protection—a strategic assertion of authority used by consuls across the Mediterranean.[28] The Italian diplomat took up the Shamama heirs' case with his characteristic zeal, betting that there was glory to be gained for him and his country.

Pinna headed straight to the Bardo and requested an audience with Khaznadar. Once introduced, he asked why Joseph and Nathan had been prevented from leaving Tunis. Had they committed a crime? Did they owe the government any money? No, responded Khaznadar. So why were these good people refused "the permission to betake themselves to Livorno, where they are called to take care of their interests in the inheritance left to them by their uncle?"[29] At this Khaznadar became visibly angry and assumed a menacing tone; that very uncle had died owing considerable debts to the government, he explained. But Khaznadar knew that challenging the sanctuary of the Italian consulate would cause all kinds of problems for the bey. He had no interest in creating an international incident, to which the Italian government could always respond with more gunboats. Tersely, Khaznadar conceded that he did not personally object to the Shamama heirs' departure—though only the bey himself could provide final authorization.[30] Pinna returned to the consulate to bring Joseph, Nathan, and Esther the good news.

The next day, Sunday, a delegation of officials from the Bardo arrived at the Italian consulate. They asked Pinna's permission to speak to the Shamama heirs directly. From the safety of the consulate, Joseph, Nathan, and Esther were suddenly in a position of power—with all the ammunition and civilizational arrogance of Italy backing them. The nephews conceded nothing and refused to sign the contract they had spent so much time negotiating on Friday. The delegation left empty-handed, and shortly thereafter the bey gave permission for the Shamama heirs to depart on the next boat.[31]

Pinna described his intervention on the Shamamas' behalf in a long letter to his superiors in Rome. He explained that he had extended Italy's protection to the Shamama heirs in the name of "humanity."[32] This was a common trope among diplomats in the Islamic world. They invoked a notion of humanitarianism in justifying their intervention on behalf of those they believed to be oppressed, who were overwhelmingly non-Muslims.[33] Triumphantly, Pinna reported that his intervention on behalf of the Shamama heirs was "followed by the entire European colony [in Tunis], and with particular interest by the indigenous Jews; everyone, including my colleagues from France and England, have congratulated me, and continue to do so."[34] He ended the letter with a hastily written postscript: "I just heard this minute that Qā'id Shlomo Shamama [Momo], of whom I spoke various times in this letter, has himself taken refuge in the French consulate, though I cannot yet say what his motive is."[35]

Once Momo got word that his relatives had holed up in the Italian consulate, he began to worry. Not even the bey himself was willing to stand up to Pinna. Thanks to the cover of the Italian flag, Joseph, Nathan, and Esther would be off to Livorno—and who knew what new ways they might find to frustrate Momo's designs on the inheritance? He realized he had to change course; he got in a carriage and headed to the French consulate.

Inside the neoclassical building that dominated Tunis's new Promenade de la Marine, Momo pursued the same strategy that Joseph and Nathan had followed with Pinna. He explained to the French consul, Viscount Adolphe-François de Botmiliau, that he, too, had been wronged by the Tunisian government. On the face of it, such a claim might seem absurd; Momo was himself a government official and thoroughly at ease in the corridors of the Bardo. Yet he knew how to play the victim card. Through a translator, Momo recounted his version of all that had happened since Nissim died: his attempt to convince Joseph and Nathan to split the inheritance three ways, his marriage to Esther, and signing the contract giving away 25 percent of the inheritance. Finally, he added a new twist, claiming that on Friday—the same day Joseph and Nathan had been summoned to the Bardo—he too had been called to the palace. There Khaznadar insisted that Momo sign a second contract giving up another 5 percent of his inheritance. Momo had no choice but to comply.[36]

Having succeeded in painting himself as a casualty of the Tunisian government's Oriental despotism, Momo formally requested the protection of the French government. He asked de Botmiliau for help canceling the contract ceding an additional 5 percent of the inheritance. And he requested the consul's help in confirming his marriage to Esther; his new bride was, it seems, as important to him as the money he hoped to inherit. The dragoman translated Momo's statement into French and then read it back for his approval; as always, Momo signed his name in Hebrew letters.[37]

It is hard to say just how useful Momo's appeal to de Botmiliau turned out to be. No more mention was made of an extra 5 percent of his inheritance going to the government, perhaps because de Botmiliau successfully convinced Khaznadar to drop the matter. On the other hand, the French consul could not (or would not) insist on the validity of Esther's marriage to Momo. The bey had promised Pinna that he would let Esther go to Livorno, along with Joseph and Nathan.

Nonetheless, Momo successfully obtained French protection, just as Joseph, Nathan, and Esther had obtained Italian protection. Not one of these potential heirs had a formal bond connecting them to Italy or France; they were neither foreign nationals nor foreign protégés. The fact that the Shamama heirs nonetheless invoked the jurisdiction of Italy and France shows just how capacious legal belonging could be in Tunisia. Pinna extended Italy's protection to the Shamama heirs in the name of humanity. The structure of the capitulations offered a solid platform for Pinna's demands on their behalf, which he embellished with presumptions of civilizational superiority—all quietly reinforced by the threat of gunboat diplomacy. In the extraterritorial context of Tunisia, legal belonging—and the sovereignty to which it was tied—was an exceedingly flexible affair.

In early March, Joseph, Nathan, and Esther boarded a steamship at the port of La Goulette. Nathan, only twenty years old, was still a bachelor; he traveled alone. Joseph, more than ten years Nathan's senior, brought his sons Abraham, Nathan, and Nissim, and his wife, Daya (née Gozlan), six months pregnant with their fourth child.[38] Esther was accompanied by her fiancé, Attal. Once safely in Livorno and freed at last from Momo's grip, Esther married the man of her choosing. As a sign of gratitude for their adopted home, the newlyweds donated three hundred lire to the charitable fund of the Jewish community of Livorno.[39] Esther must have been the only Shamama for whom coming to Italy was an unmixed triumph. For everyone else, the promise of a share in Nissim's estate seemed to recede further out of reach with each passing day.

The palazzo on Via Ricasoli was fast filling up with potential heirs. Weeks before Joseph and Nathan arrived, Shlomo, the nephew of Mas'uda, Nissim's widow back in Sousse, came to pursue his aunt's share in the estate. Mas'uda had worked fast to secure her interests, which included the hundred thousand francs left to her in the will, and if Nissim were determined to have died an Italian citizen, a third of the usufruct on his wealth. Yet for reasons unknown to us, Mas'uda was not prepared to leave Sousse herself; she sent Shlomo in her stead, armed with a power of attorney. He arrived less than a month after Nissim died.[40] 'Aziza and Moses welcomed him to the palazzo.

But Joseph and Nathan received a cooler reception. Unlike Shlomo, Joseph and Nathan hoped to prove that Nissim had died a Tunisian subject; they preferred to inherit a third of the estate according to Jewish law rather than the fourth they were each allotted in the will. When Momo arrived in early April, he too installed himself in the palazzo. Not one of the Shamamas were happy to see him—least of all his estranged daughter. Despite their shared interest in having the will annulled, Joseph and Nathan were still furious at Momo for his outrageous behavior back in Tunis. At first, Bargellini must have been pleased to observe that "relations among the heirs are beginning to darken."[41] Family strife could only strengthen the Tunisian government's position. Eventually, even Bargellini lost patience with the Shamamas: "The heirs are always arguing with each other over the slightest thing; they lack all respectability, they are hypocrites, and they fight among themselves like little children!"[42]

In the midst of this animosity, the Shamama heirs struggled to understand the legal questions that would determine the fate of Nissim's estate. Italian courts unquestionably had jurisdiction over the lawsuit because Nissim died in Italy and had been legally domiciled there. But before the courts could adjudicate the validity of the will, they had to determine which law to apply to the estate. This question required knowing Nissim's nationality. The Italian Civil Code specified that the entire estate—"whatever the nature of the property, and wherever it may be situated"—must be "regulated by the national law" of the deceased.[43] Once the courts determined to which state Nissim belonged, they could begin the process of apportioning his wealth.

If Nissim had died a Tunisian national, then Jewish law would determine the fate of his estate. The validity of the will according to Jewish law was far from clear. But the alternative scenario meant applying Italian law, which would undoubtedly uphold the will. If the Italian courts applied Jewish law, there was an argument to be made that Nissim's testament was halakhically invalid. In that case, the biblical laws of inheritance would apply. Those who wished the will to be thrown out—Momo, Joseph, and Nathan—put all their resources into proving that Nissim had died a subject of the bey.

If, on the other hand, Nissim had died an Italian citizen, then Italian law would govern Nissim's inheritance. There was little question that the will would be upheld according to the testamentary requirements of the Italian Civil Code. Needless to say, 'Aziza and Moses quickly grasped that this was the safest path to securing their future. Shlomo, Mas'uda's nephew and legal agent, joined them in trying to prove that Nissim had died an Italian citizen.

Yet unlike their relatives on the other side of the lawsuit, 'Aziza and Moses had multiple options. While things would undoubtedly be simpler if the courts ruled that Nissim had died an Italian, it was also possible that Jewish law might work in their favor. After all, the validity of the will according to halakhah was a point to be debated, not a foregone conclusion. And 'Aziza and Moses had too much at stake to put all of their eggs in one basket; their future—and that of their young son—depended on the money Nissim had left them. If the courts declared that Nissim had died a Tunisian, they wanted to be ready; to this end, they sought out rabbinic opinions that would validate the will according to Jewish law.

It was not long before both sides understood that the question of Nissim's nationality had to be settled before anything else. But just *how* to do this remained a point of some confusion. In those tumultuous months immediately following Nissim's death, the heirs remained uncertain about who had jurisdiction to determine a case of questionable belonging. Figuring they had nothing to lose, both Bargellini and Moses sought to secure a favorable outcome by sidestepping the legal system altogether. Although both failed, their attempts suggest just how much uncertainty swirled around nationality in these early years of the Italian nation-state.

Bargellini convinced himself that the Tunisian government should be able to simply claim Nissim as a subject of the bey. Struggling with the terminology (and even more so with its orthography), Bargellini tried to convey to the government's lawyers "the concern that every government has—not material, but rather political—to decide the *subjecthood* [*sudditanza*] of a citizen [*cytoien*] that, having gone abroad, did not become a citizen [*cytoyen*] of the state in which he now resides."[44] But the consul's efforts went nowhere. Leopoldo Galeotti, the Florentine attorney advising the Tunisian government, patiently explained why Bargellini was mistaken: only the courts could decide whether Nissim had died an Italian or Tunisian. What seemed like a matter of sovereignty to Bargellini was, according to Italian law, a question of legal interpretation.

Moses got a bit further in his attempt to establish that Nissim had died an Italian citizen before the matter went to court. Moses had the chutzpah to write directly to the king of Italy; he asked Vittorio Emanuele II to issue a decree affirming that Nissim was an Italian citizen. In his shaky Italian, Moses summarized the history of Nissim's naturalization. Despite the royal decree Nissim received in 1866, "some pretenders want to place serious doubts concerning the Italianness of the late Count, General Shamama." These troublemakers claimed that Nissim did not "fulfill the formality demanded by the law to conserve the quality of Italianness granted to him." But, Moses objected, "it is impermissible to doubt his intention to benefit from a grace that he so favorously [*sic*] [*favorosamente*] implored." If Nissim had committed any omission, it was by no means intentional; the blame must be laid at the feet of the Italian embassy in Paris and the municipal authorities in Livorno, to whom Nissim "personally showed the royal decree."[45] Moses asked the king to simply confirm that Nissim had indeed died an Italian citizen.

The king's private secretary swiftly ascertained that such matters lay beyond the purview of a constitutional monarch bound by the rule of law. He nonetheless sent Moses's letter along to the Ministry of the Interior, but it found no more favorable of a reception in this corner of Italian bureaucracy. The interior minister responded that if Nissim had in fact failed to comply with the requirements of Article 10 of the Civil Code, then the naturalization decree "remained a dead letter." He even asked the Italian embassy in Paris and the prefect of Livorno to look into their archives to see if Nissim had registered his decree, but they answered in the negative. As everyone knew by now, Nissim had only registered his domicile in Livorno in November 1871, "five years after the end of the six months" during which he was required to establish his residency in

Italy.[46] The Ministry of Interior could not condone an executive confirmation of Nissim's Italian citizenship. He recommended that Moses's request be rejected.

Given this dead end, Moses was understandably even more anxious to cement his connection to Italy. As a Jew from Algeria, he already had the advantage of French citizenship, which he imparted to his wife and son. Presumably he felt no need to seek naturalization as an Italian; as a French citizen, Moses could not be summoned back to Tunis to answer for his uncle's alleged crimes. But if this small family of Maghribi Jews had learned anything during its exile, it was that legal belonging could be slippery—and hedging one's bets was always wise.[47]

Moses took advantage of his correspondence with the king to write a second letter explaining that he would like to donate twenty thousand lire to the treasury. Following in Nissim's footsteps, he subtly suggested that in return he might be honored with a noble title; in his case, Knight of the Equestrian Order of the Crown of Italy.[48] The king's secretary hesitated.[49] But Moses was determined not to fail again. He called on Castelnuovo, who had written in support of Nissim's ennoblement in 1866; Castelnuovo agreed to vouch for Moses. His letter explained that while he was suffering from "paralysis of the left side of his face," he nonetheless roused himself to ask for a favor on behalf of his friend Moisè, whose "honor—which I guarantee—is untouched by the civil lawsuit over the estate."[50] Castelnuovo's letter worked; Moses became a Cavaliere of the Ordine Equestre della Corona d'Italia. He received a handsome medal hung on a red and white ribbon, to be pinned proudly to his left breast—a marker not just of nobility but of his formal bond to Italy.

Moses, like Bargellini, had failed in his attempt to prove Nissim's citizenship by fiat. Yet this was hardly the only path that he and 'Aziza pursued; while both continued to hope that the courts would confirm Nissim's Italian citizenship, it seemed only prudent to prepare for all possible outcomes. If Jewish law were applied to the estate, they wanted to do everything they could to show that Nissim's will was valid according to halakhah.

Jewish law, however, was nothing like Italian law; no government backed the authority of legal institutions or policed the barriers of jurisprudential expertise. It was unclear who had the authority to determine whether Nissim's will was valid. In the absence of a state or formal religious hierarchy, 'Aziza and

Moses turned to the rabbis of Palestine, who held a special kind of cachet for Jews all over the world. Conveniently, the rabbis of the Holy Land also had a direct interest in the question of Nissim's estate. In his will, Nissim set aside generous donations for the scholarly Jewish community in Palestine's four holiest cities—twenty-five thousand francs each for the smaller towns of Hebron, Safed, and Tiberias, and two hundred thousand francs for Jerusalem. The rabbinical leadership in Palestine had already taken note of Nissim's will and was undoubtedly following the growing controversy over his estate.

A more or less constant flow of rabbinical emissaries from the Holy Land circulated throughout the Jewish Diaspora, soliciting donations to fund Palestine's community of Jews who dedicated their lives to scholarship.[51] After news of Nissim's will became public, two emissaries from Jerusalem arrived in Livorno, naively expecting to collect the promised funds. Their hopes were soon dashed; although the future of the Shamama estate remained uncertain, it was widely understood that Nissim's wealth would not be distributed any time soon. But Moses and 'Aziza saw an opportunity. They told the emissaries about the looming legal battle over the estate, and about Momo, Joseph, and Nathan's plan to have Jewish law applied and the will thrown out. The emissaries returned to Jerusalem with a copy of the will and a mission: find an eminent halakhic authority who would declare the will valid.[52]

In choosing a jurist, the emissaries prioritized political power over intellectual renown; they convinced the chief rabbi of Jerusalem (*rishon le-tzion*), a Sephardi from near Salonica named (confusingly) Abraham Ashkenazi, to write in support of Nissim's will. Ashkenazi had also recently been appointed *haham başı* by the Ottoman sultan—a relatively new position that gave him authority over Jews across Palestine.[53] In short order, Ashkenazi penned a *teshuvah*, a rabbinic responsum. In dense, technical Hebrew interspersed with Aramaic phrases from the Talmud, Ashkenazi built his case for why Nissim's will was valid according to Jewish law.

Ashkenazi had something of an uphill battle to fight. Jewish law provides for a default order of inheritance: estates were to be divided among the closest male relatives. This biblical law thus required that Momo, Joseph, and Nathan split the estate evenly. Halakhah also made provisions for writing a will that departed from the biblical order of inheritance. But there were a number of conditions required to make such a will kosher. Rules for wills written by a person on his or her deathbed (a *shekhiv me-ra'*) were relatively loose, yet wills made by a healthy person (*bari'*) required a kinyan, a ritual act of acquisition. After the kinyan, the heirs immediately became the owners of property—though the testator retained the use of the property while still living.[54] On the face of it, Nissim's will should have been classified as one written by a healthy person, thereby requiring a kinyan; he wrote the will in 1868 and died in 1873. In case the five-year gap between testating and death was not straightforward enough, Nissim stated at the beginning of the document that he was in "very good health."[55] Since no kinyan was mentioned, it seemed that Nissim's testament failed to meet the requirements for a kosher will.

Nonetheless, Ashkenazi argued that Nissim's will fulfilled the halakhic stipulations for a binding testament.[56] First, the rabbi found ways around the requirement of a kinyan; he contended that the will of a healthy person was valid as long as it specified that the document took effect "from this day and after my death" (*me-hayom u-le-aḥarei moti*).[57] Ashkenazi cited various instances of wills lacking a kinyan that were still upheld as legitimate because they had some version of this formula. Moreover, Ashkenazi pointed out that Nissim got up from his deathbed the day he died and put the will on his desk. Thus even though he did not write the will when he was ill, placing the will on his desk made it equivalent to one written by a sick person—meaning it did not require a kinyan.[58] Pivoting in another direction, Ashkenazi insisted that Jewish law followed local custom, and rabbis in both Italy and France had long upheld wills written according to the laws of the state. "It is known that all the jurists agree that in case of doubt concerning matters of money . . . including gifts and wills . . . it is important to follow the custom of the country, which is the custom of the merchants."[59] Even if one were to rule that Nissim's will was invalid according to halakhah, custom should overrule the strict letter of Jewish law.[60] Writing in Paris, Nissim was simply following the practice of the European Jews among whom he lived.

Ashkenazi ended his responsum ominously, threatening anyone who disputed his opinion with excommunication (*ḥerem*).[61] He signed and dated it the first third of Iyar 5663—corresponding to the first week of May 1873—a bit over three months after Nissim's death. Following standard practice in the printing of *teshuvot*, Ashkenazi sent a copy of his opinion to other rabbis, asking them to send back formal endorsements of his ruling (known as *haskamot*).[62] He sought these approbations first of all from colleagues in Jerusalem, including the chief rabbi of the Ashkenazi community, the judges of the rabbinic court, and the head of the Maghribi community; from rabbis in other parts of Palestine; from the highest rabbinic authorities of the Ottoman Empire, including the haham başı of Istanbul, the haham başı of Egypt, and the haham başı of Izmir; and even from rabbis in Russia. By the time Ashkenazi had the responsum printed in Jerusalem in the early months of 1874, he had collected twenty approbations from across the Ottoman and Russian Empires.[63] Ashkenazi's teshuvah might not guarantee 'Aziza and Moses success, but it certainly added an intimidating weapon to their legal arsenal.

While the Shamama heirs eyed each other uneasily across the courtyard of the palazzo, government officials in Tunis amassed ammunition in their pursuit of a share of Nissim's wealth. The first order of business was to muster evidence of the debts Nissim owed to the treasury when he died. Even these debts were contested, however; shortly after Nissim's death, 'Aziza and Moses publicly declared that the qā'id had left a "receipt," given to him by the bey on his departure from Tunis. This receipt supposedly attested that Nissim did not owe the treasury anything.[64] The government needed concrete proof if it wanted to mount a successful claim on the estate.

Khaznadar turned to Husayn b. 'Abdallah, a fellow mamluk of Greek origin.[65] Khaznadar had an uneasy relationship with Husayn, who had supported the reformist programs of Khayraddin, Khaznadar's longtime rival. Nevertheless, Husayn was loyal to the bey and cared deeply about extracting Tunisia from the financial mess into which the country had sunk. Khaznadar charged Husayn with drawing up a detailed account of all the money that Nissim owed the Tunisian treasury when he died.[66] At the same time, Khaznadar sent Spezzafumo, the bey's general counsel, to Livorno. He charged Spezzafumo with pursuing the debts owed to the government by Nissim's estate.[67] Bargellini and Spezzafumo eagerly awaited Husayn's reckoning of Nissim's accounts. Yet as so often happened with Khaznadar's correspondence, Bargellini's confidence turned to disappointment when he saw the woefully incomplete accounts. He wrote back to Khaznadar to say that the lawyers required more convincing documentation of the government's claims.[68] Bargellini's repeated requests never managed to produce the kind of authoritative accounting required by Italian courts.[69]

Whether Khaznadar was unable or unwilling to gather the evidence necessary to sue the estate remains unclear. He knew, however, that a thorough accounting of Nissim's debts was not the only path to securing a share of the estate. Momo had already signed a contract ceding 25 percent of his inheritance to the government. And while Khaznadar had failed in his attempts to force Joseph and Nathan to do the same, he had not given up hope that these heirs might also be persuaded to cede some of their rights. Khaznadar understood early on that it was in the government's interests to have Momo, Joseph, and Nathan inherit—which meant ensuring that the estate was adjudicated according to Jewish law.

By the time the Shamama heirs arrived in Tuscany in mid-March, Khaznadar was already considering the need for more permanent representation in Livorno. Bargellini and Spezzafumo had served the beys of Tunis for years, and both were presumably loyal. But the prime minister wanted someone from his own world to oversee what was quickly proving to be a highly complex lawsuit. Husayn was already familiar with Nissim's finances. In May, Khaznadar sent Husayn to Livorno, this time armed with a procuration appointing him as the representative of the Tunisian government in the Shamama case.[70]

Husayn's familiarity with the Tuscan legal system made him a particularly good candidate to represent the government's interests. Two years earlier, Khaznadar had charged Husayn with overseeing an ongoing lawsuit between the Tunisian government and Castelnuovo, the bey's former physician and friend to both Nissim and Moses. The lawsuit concerned Castelnuovo's estate in Djedeida, about thirty kilometers west of Tunis. When conflict erupted between Castelnuovo's son Guglielmo and local authorities, the Italian doctor sued the Tunisian government, claiming an astronomical sum in damages that far exceeded the value of the property itself. Castelnuovo had shrewdly based the company that owned the Djedeida estate in Florence, so the resulting lawsuit took place in Tuscan courts. Husayn managed the team of lawyers working on the Tunisian government's behalf, including many he would hire again to work on the Shamama case.[71]

But certain aspects of the Shamama lawsuit proved deeply unfamiliar to Husayn, especially the centrality of Jewish law. Unlike 'Aziza and Moses, neither Husayn nor any of the other officials working for the government had direct access to Jewish legal authorities. As early as March, Bargellini explained that it was necessary to "know with precision if, as a Tunisian abroad, Nissim could make a holographic will"—that is, an unnotarized will written by the testator himself—"and if this will would be considered valid according to Tunisian and Mosaic law."[72] Husayn did have close associations with Jews back in Tunis, including Momo himself, whom Husayn had assisted in his attempts to marry Esther. But when it came to questions of halakhah, the mamlūk was at a loss.[73] Husayn found himself in need of an expert. To his initial relief, a Jew named Léon Elmilik offered to assist Husayn in navigating this complicated world.

Elmilik managed to carve out a central role for himself in the Shamama affair; eventually, his caustic personality would alienate almost everyone involved.

Elmilik—Eliahu Almaliaḥ in Hebrew—was born in 1830 in ʿAnnaba (Bône), Algeria (also the birthplace of ʿAziza's husband, Moses).[74] By the early 1850s, Elmilik had settled in Tunis, where he worked as a translator, owned a stationary store (*librairie-papeterie*), and occasionally practiced as something of a self-taught lawyer.[75] Like many Algerian Jews, Elmilik might well have moved to Tunis in large part for the extraterritorial privileges afforded to French subjects like him.[76] Whatever his original motive for moving east, he made a name for himself as a champion of the extraterritorial rights of Algerian Jews in Tunisia. In the mid-1860s, Tunisian government officials attempted to limit the number of Jews registered as Algerians at the French consulate, contending that many of them were in fact Tunisians who were only passing as Algerians. In response, Elmilik mounted a campaign in French newspapers and with the Alliance Israélite Universelle in Paris. It was "well known," he argued, that the Algerian origins of the Jews in question "give them the right to French protection."[77]

Shortly after Nissim's death, Elmilik smelled opportunity.[78] His ambitions far outran his achievements thus far, and the looming lawsuit offered low-hanging fruit for a man of his talents. As a Jew educated in French, Arabic, and of course Hebrew, Elmilik possessed just the skills required to mediate between the world of rabbinic law and the Tunisian government. He approached Husayn and offered his services as an intermediary. Husayn knew about Ashkenazi's responsum; if he wanted to prove to Italian courts that the will was invalid according to Jewish law, he would need to produce rabbinic rulings making this case. Husayn agreed to hire Elmilik for "his knowledge of languages"; initially, it seems, Husayn saw Elmilik as more of a dragoman than a legal adviser.[79] In the summer of 1873, Elmilik and Husayn signed a contract. Elmilik would procure rabbinic rulings (*fatawāt* [*sic*]) countering Ashkenazi's teshuvah and proving that Nissim's will was invalid according to Jewish law. In return, Husayn agreed to pay Elmilik fifty thousand francs and promised that the Tunisian government would reimburse him for all living expenses he incurred while working on the case.[80] For months, Elmilik traveled back and forth between Tunis, where he solicited responsa invalidating Nissim's will from Tunisian rabbis, and Livorno, where he eventually settled.[81] At first he managed to hide his pugnacious nature enough to win over his new employer. Whatever trust he earned would not last.

While Husayn was busy in Livorno, the halls of the Bardo witnessed one of its most monumental political upsets in recent memory. Villet and Khayraddin finally succeeded in convincing the bey of Khaznadar's infamy. After serving in the innermost circles of three beys, Khaznadar was pushed out in October 1873; Khayraddin took over the position of prime minister.[82] Husayn wrote to Khayraddin on the second day of the holy month of Ramaḍān, congratulating him; the country, Husayn explained, "needs your good management."[83]

But the shake-up in Tunis changed relatively little for the Livorno mission, as the Maghribis working to secure the government's interests in the Shamama case came to be known. Husayn and Elmilik became progressively closer, eventually living together in rented lodgings in Livorno, along with Elmilik's wife and children.[84] As the two maneuvered to ensure that Nissim's will was thrown out, Elmilik convinced Husayn to give him direct responsibility for aspects of the Shamama case. With Husayn's approval, Elmilik became a party to the lawsuit; Husayn and Elmilik sought out Nissim's great-great-nephews who had been allotted relatively small sums in the will. They convinced a number of these Shamamas to join the government's fight to have the will thrown out. In exchange for sums greater than those allotted them in Nissim's testament, these distant relatives appointed Elmilik as their legal representative and gave him permission to seek the nullification of the will.[85] Before long, Elmilik would be writing his own legal briefs arguing why Jewish law should apply to the case.

Meanwhile, moments of joy barely penetrated the prevailing gloom in the Shamama palazzo. Joseph's wife, Daya, gave birth to two more sons: Salvatore, born just three months after the family arrived in Livorno; and Elia, born the following year.[86] But just two years later, the family lost Mas'uda, Nissim's widow, who passed away in Sousse.[87] Her nephew Shlomo mourned his aunt from afar. Now he was more determined than ever to collect Mas'uda's share in the estate since whatever she was allotted would devolve to him as her heir.[88] Needless to say, the births and deaths that punctuated life on the Via Ricasoli did little to mend relations among the potential heirs; their mutual enmity only grew as the months and years dragged on.

Everyone knew it would be a long slog through the various Italian courts of appeal before the lawsuit was over. Such an intricate case—with so much money at stake, and so many moving parts—would certainly be appealed multiple times. The tribunal of first instance was the civil court of Livorno; it would pronounce the initial ruling. However the Livornese court ruled, everyone counted on the losing side filing an appeal, which would send the case to the court of appeal in Lucca, a medieval city about forty kilometers northeast of Livorno. After Lucca, there was another stratum of courts in Florence, the provincial capital; the losing side in this round would undoubtedly appeal to the court of cassation, which could only reject or confirm the Luccan court's ruling (courts of cassation did not issue their own decisions). If the court of cassation chose to overturn the Luccan court's decision, the case would be heard by the court of appeal in Florence. The case could then be appealed to the highest court in the land, the supreme court in Rome—though as it happens, the court of appeal in Florence had the final say.[89]

It was not until the end of 1877 that the civil court of Livorno finally decided the case of *Samama v. Samama*.[90] To everyone's shock, the ruling explained that "Article 8 of the . . . Civil Code could not be applied for the simple reason that, being a foreigner in Italy, [Nissim] did not belong to any nation, and thus did not have—nor could he have—any national law."[91] In other words, Nissim had died neither Italian nor Tunisian, but stateless—a "cosmopolitan" (*cosmopolita*), as the court put it.[92] Italian law was relatively straightforward concerning stateless people who died on Italian soil; their estates were to be regulated by the law of their last domicile.[93] Nissim's estate therefore fell under the jurisdiction of Italian law, and the Livornese court declared his will valid.

Nobody expected the court to rule that Nissim had died stateless. In the field of international law, the presumption was that everyone should belong to a state. Statelessness—like dual nationality—was considered a juridical oddity, an extraordinary condition that was to be avoided if at all possible. Most jurists in the nineteenth century considered statelessness a feature of fiction and poetry, not of law.[94] Some grudgingly admitted that people might become stateless by falling through gaps between two sets of nationality law; for instance, in the eyes of French law, a French woman who married a British man acquired her husband's nationality, but British law did not automatically make her a British subject. These unfortunate exceptions aside, jurists considered it obvious that "no one should be without a nationality."[95]

Yet the Livornese court arrived at this surprising conclusion. The judges ruled that Nissim's actions after 1864 amounted to a tacit renunciation of his Tunisian nationality: his departure from Tunis without the "animus redeundi," the intention to return; his request for Italian citizenship; and the royal decree of naturalization issued by King Vittorio Emanuele II in 1866—all these amounted to evidence that Nissim no longer considered himself a Tunisian subject. Nissim's ability to renounce his nationality of birth rested on a natural right of expatriation.[96] Nonetheless, the act of requesting Italian citizenship and receiving a naturalization decree were legally meaningless without complying with the requirements of that decree—that is, swearing an oath of fealty to his new king and establishing residency in Italy.[97] Nissim died having lost his citizenship of birth, yet having failed to acquire a new one.

In deeming Nissim a "cosmopolitan"—a person who belonged to the world by virtue of lacking a state—the Livornese court echoed common tropes about European Jews in the age of nationalism. The specter of the wandering Jew was invoked by philosemites and antisemites alike: Jews were perpetually outsiders in the nations among which they lived. For ethnonationalists who saw Jews as a plague everywhere they went, Jews' cosmopolitanism made them dangerous enemies within. Those who defended Jews praised their ability to adapt, command of multiple languages, and far-flung networks that defied political boundaries—all evidence of their exceptional ability to thrive in an age of mobility.[98] One imagines that the Livornese judges were willing to declare Nissim stateless in no small part because he came from a people condemned to roam the face of the earth, never properly belonging anywhere.

With the stroke of a pen, the president of the civil court of Livorno erased Nissim's membership in the country of his birth and the nation-state of his adopted homeland. Legally speaking, Nissim floated somewhere above the Mediterranean.

6

Conte Shamama the Italian

THE LIVORNESE court's verdict caught both camps off guard. While 'Aziza and Moses certainly welcomed the decision in their favor, they were hardly triumphant. Everyone knew this was just the first round of a long fight. Now it was time to prepare for the more consequential battle, which would take place before the court of appeal of Lucca. And they understood that more powerful artillery was required.

Following the initial ruling in Livorno, each side hired some of the most famous scholars of international law in Italy—arguably *the* most famous. Pasquale Stanislao Mancini, father of the nationality principle that revolutionized private international law across the globe, agreed to represent 'Aziza and Nissim Jr. Augusto Pierantoni, Mancini's disciple and a rising star in his own right, joined the legal team working for Husayn and the Tunisian government.

Mancini set about proving that the will was valid. With the arrogance of a man at the top of his profession, Mancini ignored the lower court's ruling. Rather than agreeing that Nissim had died stateless—which would have ensured that the will was adjudicated according to Italian law—Mancini insisted that Nissim passed away as an Italian citizen. He argued this from two angles. First, because Nissim descended from Livornese Jews, the late count was subject to a distinct set of naturalization requirements. This approach relied on the increasing entanglement of legal belonging with ethnicity in the age of nationalism. Second, Mancini maintained that citizenship was not just a matter of paperwork; belonging could also be produced through good faith and reputation. In Mancini's deft hands, Nissim's belief that he had become Italian and his public performance of Italian citizenship became legally meaningful elements of his biography.

FIGURE 6.1. Leopoldo Galeotti, n.d.

Husayn announced the Livornese court's decision to Khayraddin in curt, matter-of-fact language that masked his disappointment: the judges had ruled that Nissim "was not Italian, but had lost his Tunisian nationality; he thus remained without a nationality, and was under the jurisdiction of Italian law." But Husayn was by no means ready to give up. "With the help of God, we will win in the court of appeal."[1]

Galeotti had served as the lead lawyer on the Shamama case since shortly after Nissim died; he was among Tuscany's most famous lawyers and knew Husayn from his time working on the Djedeida affair.[2] But now that the stakes were higher—now that the court of first instance had ruled against the Tunisian government—Galeotti's local reputation no longer sufficed. For the greatest legal minds Italy had to offer, Husayn had to look beyond Tuscany. He set his sights on an up-and-coming professor of international law, Augusto Francescopaolo Pierantoni.

Pierantoni was born in 1840 in the small city of Chieti in Abruzzo, then part of the Kingdom of the Two Sicilies. His father was a wealthy landowner, and the young Pierantoni was able to pursue his love of books while still finding time for horseback riding, fencing, and theater. Like so many of his peers,

FIGURE 6.2. Augusto Pierantoni, 1885

Pierantoni was enthralled by the revolutionary ideas of the Risorgimento. In 1860, he enlisted in the Garibaldian forces; when the Kingdom of the Two Sicilies joined unified Italy that same year, Pierantoni found himself on the right side of history. Shortly thereafter, he discovered his calling as a lawyer while studying law under Mancini.

Mancini, also a native of southern Italy, was the fledgling nation's greatest scholar of international law.[3] Mancini joined the first generation of activists working for a united Italy; as a young man, his outspoken journalism on behalf of the Risorgimento got him in trouble with the Bourbon monarchs of his native Naples. In 1849, he exiled himself to Turin, the center of efforts to unite the peninsula. Mancini's main contribution to the nationalist movement was to articulate a justification for the Risorgimento in the language of international law—what his detractors called legal propaganda.[4] His efforts were rewarded with Piedmont's first chair in international law.[5] Although jurists trace the law of nations to the ancient Greco-Roman world, the modern field of international law was only just forming when Mancini began his career; never one to hide from the limelight, he made sure he was at the center of efforts to articulate the new science.[6]

Mancini's legal philosophy was steeped in the nationalism that had shaped his generation.[7] With characteristic fervor, Mancini argued that nationality

FIGURE 6.3. Pasquale Stanislao Mancini, 1889

should be the "rational foundation of the law of nations."[8] But he was not particularly interested in nationality as legal belonging—at least not yet. His breakout book discussed nationality in the ethnocultural sense of the term, to describe the essence of a people that shared region, race, language, custom, history, law, and religion.[9] He argued that international law should be based not on states but instead on nations; he called this the "nationality principle" (though this initial version differed from the one eventually applied in the Italian Civil Code). Once Mancini's nationality principle was recognized as the basis for international law, "the respect and the independence of every nationality" would be guaranteed. States would match nations and empires would cease to run roughshod over nationalities—as, for instance, the Habsburgs were doing in the Italian-speaking provinces under their suzerainty.[10] In this sense, the nationality principle was a precursor to the principle of self-determination.[11] At its core, Mancini's ideas stemmed from a transposition of nationalism into international legal principles. His work on nationality immediately made him the judicial darling of the nascent Italian nation-state.

Pierantoni met Mancini in the 1860s, when the professor returned to Naples shortly after the Kingdom of the Two Sicilies joined the newly unified

Kingdom of Italy. At this point, Mancini was deeply involved in government affairs; he served in the Ministry of Justice and was called on to help draft the new Italian Civil Code. Pierantoni's passion for law and devotion to the Risorgimento made him a natural acolyte of Mancini. Perhaps it was overdetermined that he would fall in love with Mancini's eldest child, Grazia, an aspiring writer known as the most erudite of Mancini's four daughters.[12]

Under Mancini's guidance, Pierantoni dedicated himself to the study of the budding field of international law. In 1866, he published his doctoral thesis, *The Progress of Public and International Law.* Following in Mancini's footsteps, Pierantoni explained that "nationality, gentlemen, is not an abstract creation of the mind of man, but a true, objective, and necessary base for the secure order of the world."[13] Only "the implementation of the nationality principle in the fraternal communion of states will secure the new international jurisprudence on the basis of the indisputable and natural law of peoples, rather than on the malicious and unnatural law of princes."[14] Like Mancini before him, Pierantoni's timely ideas were rewarded with a university position.

Personal fulfillment soon followed; in 1868, he wed Grazia. Mancini came to think of Pierantoni as his own child, "son of my affection and of my scientific adoption."[15] Father and son-in-law both split their time between politics and private practice. When Mancini was not otherwise engaged by public service, he kept up a punishing schedule of travel, pleading case after case across newly unified Italy. Pierantoni joined his father-in-law on many of these cases; together they formed a formidable duo.[16] In September 1873, Europe's most prominent experts on international law gathered in Ghent, Belgium, to found the Institute of International Law; they elected Mancini president and invited Pierantoni to be among the ten founders of the institute.[17] In 1878, just before commencing work on the Shamama case, Mancini retired from his chair in international law at the University of Rome. None other than Pierantoni was chosen to succeed him.[18]

Pierantoni's reputation as a leading expert in international law made him an excellent candidate to head the legal team working for the Tunisian government. But his services did not come cheap; by 1878, Pierantoni was already in high demand. Husayn and Pierantoni met in the consulate of the Ottoman Empire in Florence, where Husayn explained that he needed Pierantoni to write studies and legal memos on the "doctrine of international law . . . the legal condition of Jews in the Orient, and the status of their customary law."[19] Husayn promised to pay him the astronomical fee of 150,000 lire—more than three times what he earned in an average year. Pierantoni accepted; they shook on it, apparently believing a contract unnecessary.[20]

The arms race of legal counsel had begun. 'Aziza and Moses must have feared that a name like Pierantoni would eclipse whatever prestige their local attorneys could marshal. Presumably it was the lawyers already working for them who advised seeking out a more prominent jurist to lead their cause. 'Aziza and Moses approached the only other lawyer in Italy whose fame outshone Pierantoni's: Mancini himself.[21]

When Pierantoni got word that his father-in-law would be working for the opposing side, he immediately contacted Husayn and offered his resignation; he preferred to "avoid the ethical dilemma of fighting against a person to whom I am bound by affection and reverence."[22] Husayn was determined not to let Pierantoni go—now more than ever, fearing Mancini's fame would doom the government's cause. He recruited the lawyer Pietro Muratori and the Ottoman consul Carlo Gallian to convince Pierantoni to remain on the Tunisian government's legal team. He also repeated his promise to pay Pierantoni 150,000 lire. Pierantoni relented; he would remain on the case.

Instead of working side by side, Mancini and Pierantoni now prepared to face each other across the courtroom. The personal and professional stakes were high. Pierantoni was arguing against his own father-in-law, who also happened to be one of Europe's greatest scholars of international law. For both lawyers, representing a high-profile case on nationality meant an occasion to put their ideas about international law into action. Each invoked notions of "progress" in their arguments; each claimed that "science" was on his side.[23] The Shamama case raised questions about legal belonging and sovereignty that had ramifications far beyond the estate of this particular Jew from Tunis.

In hiring Mancini, 'Aziza and Moses had struck gold. It was not just Mancini's fame; he was closer than anyone to the nationality principle that stood at the heart of the case. In fact, Mancini was almost solely responsible for writing the relevant section of the Italian Civil Code that constituted the basis of private international law in Italy.

Today the mention of international law tends to evoke questions of relations among states—the laws of war, occupation, and self-defense that make up public international law. Yet the public side of international law was only half the field in the nineteenth century. Private international law—also called conflict of laws in the Anglophone world—is concerned not with states but rather with individuals or things that cross national boundaries: people of different nationalities who do business together, marry each other, or inherit from one another. When Mancini and Pierantoni joined the illustrious group of jurists who founded the Institute of International Law, everyone understood their subject to include both the public and private dimensions of the field.[24]

Mancini began his career by proposing a new approach to public international law. His first book argued that nationality—rather than states—should serve as the building blocks of international relations; this was the original meaning of the nationality principle. It was in the field of *private* international law, however, that he made his name. Building on earlier jurists who embraced nationalism, Mancini maintained that nationality should serve as the bedrock of private international law.[25] This modified version of the nationality principle would ensure the application of a person's national law to matters of marriage, divorce, and inheritance—no matter in which state he might find himself. According to the nationality principle, a Frenchman who married in Italy should do so according to French law—just as he should divorce and bequeath his estate according to French law. Likewise, an Italian in France should have his family life regulated by Italian law.[26]

The nationality principle grew from the soil of nationalist ideology. Mancini held nationality to be sacred; for an Italian to be forced to marry, divorce, and bequeath his possessions according to French law was a violation of his "human rights" (*le droit des gens*).[27] In this, Mancini followed Montesquieu's proposition that each nation should have its own specific law, corresponding to its "spirit."[28] Mancini was convinced that all states should introduce the nationality principle in the form of binding laws; doing so would ensure the proper respect for national laws and customs as well as promote harmony among different nations.[29] Mancini eventually achieved considerable success in spreading his ideas: state after state in Europe and Latin America adopted his nationality principle to guide their approach to private international law. Only the Anglo-Saxon world—the United Kingdom and United States—insisted on regulating private matters according to domicile.[30]

While helping to draft Italy's new Civil Code, Mancini inserted his vision of the nationality principle into its first chapter. The Civil Code required that marriage, divorce, and inheritance would be "regulated by the national law of the person concerned."[31] It was thanks to Mancini that the future of Nissim's estate hinged on his nationality. Now it was Mancini's job to prove that Nissim had been an Italian national when he died.

Mancini was a charismatic man "who had seen much, loved much, and who appreciated good food and the simple pleasures of life."[32] Despite his grueling work schedule, he somehow found time to indulge his passion for literature, piano, and opera—he was especially fond of Gioachino Rossini. If anything, Mancini tended to overcommit; he never had the time or patience to write a systematic treatise expounding his ideas. Only his brilliance softened the pique caused by his tendency to overpromise; Mancini's colleagues at the Institute of International Law continued to appoint him to important committees, despite their annoyance at his chronic delays.[33]

His many commitments notwithstanding, Mancini attacked the Shamama case with his singular voracity. It helped that he saw it as a chance to make a point about his vision of Italian nationality law. The civil court of Livorno upheld Nissim's will—and thus ruled in favor of 'Aziza and Moses; Mancini could have made a relatively straightforward argument confirming the lower court's ruling. But the great lawyer had no interest in demonstrating that Shamama had died stateless. Instead, he set out to prove that Nissim had died an Italian citizen—and in so doing, further shape emerging ideas about legal belonging.[34]

Mancini constructed his first argument on a foundation of heredity.[35] He had always held that nationality was more than just a choice; it was something integral to a person, to her spirit, to her very being—a biological inheritance as hard to change as the features of her face. In Mancini's first book, he observed that the "two perpetual forms of human association"—both present since birth—are "family and nation." Nationality was so strong that it created "a particular intimacy of relations"—one that "is impossible to find among people of different nations."[36] This is precisely why Mancini insisted on the respect of an individual's national law wherever he may be; it is why he wrote the nationality principle into the Italian Civil Code.[37]

As descent was central to Mancini's conception of nationality, it is hardly surprising that he focused on Nissim's claim to Livornese roots. Mancini pointed to "valid and sufficient proof of Nissim's Italian origin." These included two acts of notoriety signed by rabbis and Jewish notaries in Tunisia. This type of legal document recorded the testimony of witnesses considered to possess knowledge about a certain subject. In the era before civil records became widespread, such acts of notoriety were frequently relied on as evidence of a person's origins.[38] Both acts of notoriety claimed that Nissim and his father were widely known to be of Italian descent.[39]

Mancini insisted on Nissim's Italian ancestry in part to sidestep the question of whether Nissim had properly registered the naturalization decree. Ever since Bargellini discovered that Nissim had failed to fulfill the requirements stipulated in the royal decree—outlined in Article 10 of the Civil Code—Nissim's Italian citizenship had been thrown into doubt. Mancini countered that these requirements had been mistakenly applied to Nissim's case. Italian nationality law distinguished between true foreigners, with no hereditary ties to Italy, and non-Italian citizens who nonetheless had Italian blood. Article 10 stipulated the need to register a royal decree of naturalization in the new citizen's domicile and take an oath of fealty. This law, though, only concerned the acquisition of citizenship by a "foreigner" (*straniero*). Had Nissim been a foreigner, he would indeed have been required to "register with the state officials in the place where he intended to fix his domicile," and "take an oath before these officials to be faithful to the king and observe the statutes and laws of the kingdom."[40]

"But," Mancini pointed out, "it mattered little" if Nissim had fulfilled these requirements, for Nissim was not a foreigner at all.[41] As a descendant of Livornese Jews, Shamama was an *oriundo italiano,* a "person of Italian extraction."[42] And an oriundo italiano was subject to a distinct set of laws regulating naturalization from those applied to foreigners. The citizenship of an oriundo italiano like Nissim was regulated not by Article 10, but by Article 6, which concerned a man born abroad to a former Italian citizen. If such a person wanted to recover his father's original citizenship, he "can elect to become a citizen by declaring [his residence in Italy before state officials], and fixing his domicile in the kingdom within a year of making this declaration."[43] In other words, Mancini argued, Nissim had never been a foreigner; he thus never needed to naturalize as an Italian. Instead, he "reacquired and recuperated" his Italian citizenship. To do so, he merely needed to "declare his desire to be readmitted to Italian nationality" and formally establish his domicile in Italy.[44] Everyone agreed that Nissim had done both: he had expressed his desire to become an Italian citizen by soliciting a decree of naturalization, and had formally registered his domicile in Livorno in the fall of 1871. In short, Nissim had more than fulfilled the requirements for an oriundo italiano to recover his Italian nationality.

In arguing that the rules for an oriundo italiano should apply to Nissim, Mancini elided the fact that no one agreed on the citizenship status of Nissim's father. Even if he could claim Livornese ancestors and membership in the Grana community, there was no guarantee that Nissim's father had been a Tuscan subject. But for Mancini, it was the *principle* of Italian heritage that mattered, more than the details of nationality paperwork.

Mancini anticipated another objection to his line of reasoning: if Nissim only had to state his intention to become Italian again, why had he bothered seeking a royal decree of naturalization—a decree for which, strictly speaking, he had no need? Mancini explained that Nissim had sought out the decree "to avoid the obligation and the difficulty of preparing copious documents and proofs of his original citizenship. . . . The naturalization decree was acquired out of an overabundance of caution, to remove any doubt or uncertainty."[45] Mancini was silent regarding the naturalization decree's specification that Nissim must conform to Article 10; presumably, if pressed, Mancini would have responded that the requirements of the naturalization decree had been written in error. What mattered was that Nissim had indeed recovered his Italian citizenship—to which he was entitled as an inheritance from his ancestors.

In pointing out the differences between a foreigner and an oriundo italiano, Mancini probed some of the most sensitive spots at the heart of modern legal belonging. In general, membership in a state came about in one of two ways: a person could be born a member—either through his parents who were members or by virtue of being born in the territory of a state. Or a person could elect to become a member by going through some form of naturalization. In other words, belonging was conferred by birth or choice.

In medieval Europe, jurists' conceptions of legal belonging tended to emphasize the role of birth and descent. They presumed that citizenship or subjecthood was based on emotional and cultural bonds that could not easily be changed. Jurists presumed that naturalization typically occurred only when a person had spent so much time in a place—and developed such thick social and identitarian bonds there—that it was as if he had been born a citizen.[46]

The French Revolution marked a short-lived turn toward conceiving of citizenship as a choice rather than a destiny. Early on, the revolutionary government styled itself as the epitome of elective citizenship; any person who believed in the ideals of the revolution could pledge loyalty to France and become a citizen. Subsequent French nationality law, however, stressed descent over elective affinity (or even being born in French territory). And French politicians' willingness to allow non-Europeans the status of full citizens was quite limited.[47] Nevertheless, metropolitan France remained a country in which outsiders were more easily assimilated than, say, in Germany.[48]

But the bright red line between choice and birth was constantly blurred, even by those who positioned themselves squarely on one side or the other. The influential work on nationality by Ernest Renan is a case in point. Shortly after Mancini wrote his briefs on the Shamama case, Renan—already among France's most celebrated scholars—published what remains one of the most famous articulations of the elective approach to citizenship. In "What Is a Nation" (*Qu'est-ce qu'une nation?)*, Renan warned against confusing "race" with "nation": "The truth is that there is no pure race and that to base politics upon ethnographic analysis is to base it on a chimera. The noblest countries, England, France, and Italy, are those where the blood is the most mixed."[49] Even the idea of a "pure Germanic country"—put forward by "the Germans, who have raised the banner of ethnography so high"—was, according to Renan, "an illusion."[50] Renan insisted that a modern nation was a combination of "the possession in common of a rich legacy of memories" and "present consent, the desire to live together." Without that desire—that *choice*—the "everyday plebiscite" that assures the nation's existence would be impossible.[51]

Yet through the center of Renan's voluntary nation ran a stubborn trickle of blood. Renan affirmed that Civilization with a capital C was universal and thus potentially shared by all humans. However, Renan eternally deferred opening the tent of Western Civilization to non-Europeans, like most of his European contemporaries. And despite his protestation that membership in a nation must not be confused with membership in a single racial, linguistic, or religious group, he nonetheless laid enormous import on the sense of shared ancestry: "The cult of ancestors is the most legitimate of all."[52] Could someone participate in that cult of ancestors without claiming those ancestors himself? Could, say, a French-educated Algerian Muslim truly become part of the French nation by having "suffered, rejoiced, and hoped together" with those native to the metropole? Could they recite "our ancestors the Gauls" with the *français de souche*?[53] Renan declined to answer this question directly in "What Is a Nation," but his other writings—particularly those devoted to Jews and Muslims—suggest deep skepticism on this point.[54]

Mancini's understanding of the nation closely aligned with the ideas professed by Renan. The Italian jurist believed that such elements as race, religion, and language were important in the construction of a nation. They were not, however, sufficient; one needed the "consciousness of a nationality" to breathe life into the "inert matter" that was race.[55] Mancini's focus on national consciousness—the "spiritual element" of nationality—is echoed in Renan's insistence that "a nation is a soul, a spiritual principle."[56] And like Renan, Mancini could not get away from descent. He insisted on the existence of an Italian race that could be traced to Roman times and "certainly must inform the national spirit."[57] A shared language was, for Mancini—like for so many other European nationalists of the nineteenth century—the "strongest of the bonds of national unity. . . . In language, the filiation of race is reflected."[58] As much as nationality required its members to be conscious of their belonging, it relied on the existence of racial and linguistic characteristics that were far from voluntary or easily adopted.

The importance of race and language to the construction of the nation was not an academic question for a jurist like Mancini. In early 1865, the Chamber of Deputies was busy debating the precise nature of Italy's nationality law about to be enshrined in the Civil Code. Mancini argued for the importance of assigning citizenship according to blood—a principle that was just becoming known by its neo-Roman term jus sanguinis; he insisted that "man is born [a] member of a family and, since the nation is an aggregate of families, man is a citizen of the nation to which belongs his father, his family."[59] Mancini succeeded in ensuring that children born to Italian fathers would still be considered Italian, whether or not they were born in Italy. This vision of Italian nationality as persisting wherever Italians might go dovetailed nicely with the nationalist principles that undergirded the newly unified state.

The special provisions in the Civil Code for *oriundi italiani* rested on the same foundation of nationalist ideology. In the early years of the Risorgimento, many of these oriundi italiani—also called *italiani non regnicoli,* or "nonresident Italians"—were political exiles who had been forced to leave the peninsula on account of their pro-Risorgimento activity. Like Garibaldi, they had spent years or even decades in places like Tunisia or Latin America. During and after unification, these exiles were welcomed back with open arms—and the law facilitated their acquisition of Italian citizenship.[60] Immigrants to Italy who could claim *Italianità*—Italianness—were to be distinguished from true foreigners.

Irredentism also played a role in the special nationality laws for oriundi italiani. Well into the twentieth century, Italian nationalists believed that large chunks of the Mediterranean under foreign rule rightfully belonged to Italy; when Mancini was working on the Civil Code, nationalists were particularly concerned about the Veneto (annexed in 1866) and Rome (where papal rule ended in 1870). Even after the Papal States were reduced to the walls of Vatican City, nationalists continued to hope for the annexation of Trieste, Trento, Fiume, and even Nice—sacrificed to France in 1860, but made up of Italian speakers considered to be italiani non regnicoli. Italian politicians and jurists held out hope that these regions would one day fulfill their true destiny by joining Italy. Lawmakers like Mancini designed Italian nationality law to further their irredentist convictions. Mancini defended this policy by explaining that "citizenship did not necessarily follow the political borders of the state but could go well beyond them."[61] The many Italians living in regions outside unified Italy justified generous provisions for their easy naturalization. By fast-tracking citizenship for oriundi italiani, Italy would send a message to all of Europe that Italians everywhere deserved to be united in a single state.[62]

Mancini built his argument for Nissim's Italian citizenship on the distinction between oriundi italiani and true foreigners. If one acknowledged that Nissim descended from Italian stock—that his father, or perhaps his father's father, had come to Tunis from Livorno, like so many other members of the Grana community—then the qā'id had never truly been a foreigner, a *straniero*. Like Italian speakers from the Fiume or other members of the Italian diaspora in Tunisia (both Jewish and Catholic), Nissim had not *acquired* Italian citizenship but rather *recovered* it. Mancini seamlessly inserted Nissim into the vision of a greater, unified Italy in which all Italians, wherever they might be, should be welcome.

The approach to nationality law taken by Mancini and his associates was steeped in nationalism. The nationalist movements of the 1830s and 1840s maintained that states should match the nationality of the people in them. In fact, it mattered little whether one placed emphasis on race and language, as the Germans tended to; or on citizens' "consciousness" of nationality forged by their common past, as Renan would have it. Either way, nationalism could not escape heritage. The double meaning of nationality captures this overlap perfectly. When "nationality" became commonplace in the vocabulary of all European languages, it did so with two meanings. Nationality was both a synonym for citizenship, a way to describe legal belonging to a state; and a way to describe one's identity, a marker of membership in a group that existed independently of political borders—roughly overlapping with what we call "ethnicity" today.

Mancini's take on Nissim's nationality rested on this double meaning of the word. For Mancini, Nissim was a member of the Italian nation in the ethnocultural sense, having descended from Livornese Jews settled in Tunisia. Nissim's Italian blood also meant that he was an Italian national in the legal sense, having recovered his Italian citizenship according to rules designed to offer oriundi italiani their rightful place in the Italian nation-state.

The brilliant audacity of his nationalist-infused logic notwithstanding, Mancini recognized the holes in his own case. He knew it was impossible to conclusively prove Nissim's Livornese origins. No documents recording Nissim's birth survived and "nothing is known for certain" about his family.[63] Nissim was hardly the only one whose birth was undocumented by paperwork. Complete and reliable birth records were absent in most of the world. Even decades after France's revolutionary government instituted the *état civil*—a nationwide registry of births, marriages, and deaths—it was common for there to be gaps in the records. Italy had only implemented its own statewide record system after unification; previously, Italian city-states mainly relied on religious communities to track births, deaths, and marriages.

In the fall of 1873, Moses, Joseph, and Nathan asked to consult the registers of the Jewish community of Livorno, which kept records of births, deaths, and marriages. Moses hoped to prove Nissim's Italian lineage through the communal archives, while Joseph and Nathan hoped to show that the family had no connection to Livorno. Moses was disappointed; he could find no one with the name Shamama (or any of its variant spellings, including Samama, Semama, and Scemama).[64] There was no prospect of finding anything equivalent in Tunis; neither the Twansa nor the Grana kept records of births or deaths. And though the Grana did keep communal registers that included copies of marriage contracts (*ketubbot*), this would not help with tracking down Nissim's origins.[65] Everyone took for granted that record keeping on both sides of the Mediterranean was spotty when Nissim was born; the absence of a written record of his birth was entirely unremarkable. Given the vociferous claims from Nissim's nephews that he had always been a member of the Twansa, it was hard to tell what the Italian judges would make of the man.

The uncertainty surrounding Nissim's heritage prompted Mancini to formulate a second line of attack—one that would hold in case the judges of the court of appeal were unconvinced of Nissim's Livornese origins. Regardless of Nissim's failure to register his naturalization decree, Mancini pointed out that the qā'id had acted in good faith—and thus that his naturalization had legal effect.[66] Acting in good faith meant two things: first, that Nissim's reasonable efforts to follow the law and his belief in his own naturalization were probative. And second, that Nissim's reputation as an Italian citizen constituted evidence that he *had* become Italian.

According to Mancini, Nissim's "consciousness of having undoubtedly become and died an *Italian citizen*" amounted to proof that Nissim intended no subterfuge; any failure to follow minor regulations should not delegitimize his naturalization.[67] Mancini pointed to Nissim's correspondence as evidence that the qā'id believed he was Italian. In multiple letters to friends and colleagues, Nissim described himself as a "naturalized Italian" and "Italian citizen."[68] This was evidence that Nissim acted in "good faith."[69] According to Mancini, Nissim had every intention of following Italian law. If he had failed to do so—if he had failed to fulfill the requirements of Article 10—it was not out of laziness or malice but instead due to "his ignorance of a law that was foreign to him."[70] This ignorance should be all the more excusable given that "Italian commentators and jurists" themselves were divided on these points.[71] Nor was the procedure for naturalization decrees fixed at the time in question; like a good historian, Mancini noted that the Italian Ministry of Foreign Affairs only issued instructions to its consulates regarding the registration of naturalization decrees in 1868—two years after Nissim was admitted to Italian citizenship by King Vittorio Emanuele II.[72] Given the confusion among jurists and bureaucrats alike, it was reasonable for Nissim, who had spent most of life in Tunis, to fall afoul of the finer points of Italian nationality law.

In Mancini's deft hands, Nissim's reputation amounted to further evidence of his citizenship. Everyone agreed that Nissim was widely accepted as an Italian citizen at the time of his death. The opposing side of the case contended this was simply a mistake. But Mancini argued that the public perception of Nissim as Italian was a legally meaningful fact. The famous lawyer pointed to Nissim's membership in the Italian Charitable Society of Paris (Società di Beneficenza Italiana), which he joined shortly after receiving his naturalization decree. This type of charitable society existed all over the Italian diaspora—wherever Italians had gone abroad in search of better opportunities. Some bore patriotic names, like 20th September (the date Rome was captured by unified Italian forces in 1870) in Buenos Aires or the Garibaldi Legions in New York City; all performed the double role of social hub—a way to affirm italianità outside Italy—and providing aid to Italian emigrants who had fallen on hard times.[73] The Italian Charitable Society, "composed only and exclusively of *Italian citizens*," allowed Nissim to "exercise his generosity in favor of his co-nationals."[74] According to Mancini, Nissim's participation demonstrated that everyone considered him an Italian citizen.

Mancini was not concerned with whether the charity had vetted Nissim's citizenship credentials; indeed, it seems highly unlikely that anyone in the organization asked to see his naturalization decree, and even less so that they checked whether he had complied with the requirements of Article 10. Needless to say, the ease with which Nissim assumed an Italian persona was related to his class; a non-Italian speaker from Tunisia with less funds at his disposal might have encountered considerable barriers to joining such a society. Presumably, the charity's directors were happy to have a member as wealthy as Nissim. Nissim's participation in the Società di Beneficenza was important not as proof of his citizenship but rather as evidence of his perceived legal belonging.

Just as crucial in Mancini's eyes was the "all-important fact" that every Italian official with whom Nissim came into contact took him at his word that he was a "naturalized" Italian. As Nissim was preparing to leave France in the midst of the Commune, the Italian consulate general in Paris issued him a passport. This document described him as "originally from Livorno and a *naturalized Italian*." When Nissim formally established his domicile in Livorno in 1871, the Livornese official recorded him as having been "naturalized in the Kingdom of Italy."[75] Again, Mancini's point was not that the passport or the registration of domicile proved Nissim's citizenship. It was common knowledge that passports were not issued as identity documents in the nineteenth century, even if they sometimes functioned as such.[76] What mattered to Mancini was that the consular authorities considered Nissim to be Italian; he had a reputation as an Italian, further demonstrated by his encounters with Italian officials.

Nissim's "certainty of having become an Italian citizen" and his reputation as such produced real "juridical effects."[77] Even if Nissim was not from Livorno, and even if he should have registered his naturalization decree and taken an oath of fealty within six months of its issuance, none of this could counteract the fact that Nissim *thought* he was obeying Italian law—as did everyone else. "There is no more secure legal principle," Mancini pointed out, than the precedent for considering a "putative quality" as equivalent to a "real" quality, just as "good faith" amounts to a "legal reality."[78] In support of this assertion, Mancini cited the maxim "common error makes law" (*Error communis facit Jus*).[79] The fact that Nissim believed himself to be Italian—and convinced so many others that this was the case—translated into legal reality.

The importance of self-perception and reputation was hardly limited to Mancini's side of the case. In trying to prove that Nissim died a Tunisian, Pierantoni and Galeotti similarly paid attention to the qā'id's "putative" nationality—though they argued that Nissim considered himself a subject of the bey until the day he died. Like Mancini, Pierantoni cited multiple details of Nissim's life; for instance, when Nissim was asked to serve as a judge in the World Fair in Paris in 1867, he first asked permission from the prime minister of Tunisia—precisely because as a government official, he could not accept such a role without his superior's consent.[80] Galeotti pointed to Nissim's correspondence as evidence of his self-perception as a Tunisian. Until the last months of his life, Nissim signed all of his letters to colleagues and friends with his Tunisian titles, including "Brigadier General" (*amīr liwā*), "Director of Finances" (*mudīr al-māl*), and "Receiver General" (*ra'īs al-qubbāḍ al-awwal*).[81] Both lawyers offered Nissim's divorce from Esther Lellouche in 1868 as further proof that he considered himself a Tunisian subject and hence bound by Jewish law for private matters. On the advice of his lawyer, who explained that as a Tunisian, Nissim had the right to divorce his wife according to Jewish law, Nissim sent Esther a get, a bill of divorce. This was nearly two years after King Vittorio Emanuele II's naturalization decree.[82] According to Pierantoni and Galeotti, Nissim could only have divorced with a Jewish legal document because he believed he was still a subject of the bey.

In trying to establish Nissim's reputation and self-perception as evidence of his nationality, the lawyers on both sides were building on centuries of judicial precedent concerning proof of citizenship. In seventeenth- and eighteenth-century Europe, citizenship was rarely conferred solely by decree, such as the one Nissim had obtained from King Vittorio Emanuele II. Instead, individuals became citizens by socially embedding themselves in their adopted home. Participation in the foundational institutions of a place, especially local charitable organizations; social connections with locals; and the ability to exercise rights associated with citizenship—these were the most common ways to prove belonging. Often, an immigrant first established his reputation as a citizen before he could obtain an official decree of naturalization.[83] Reputation and social embeddedness were similarly central to how questions of citizenship were determined in the Roman Empire.[84] By the nineteenth century, nationality law presumed that a comprehensive web of paperwork would make questions of self-perception and reputation irrelevant. And historians have generally taken these laws at their word by implicitly assuming the existence of such paperwork, which would have rendered questions of performance and reputation obsolete.[85]

The prominent lawyers working on the Shamama case were unanimous in attributing weight to how Nissim thought about himself. Unlike the jurists who wrote treatises on citizenship or the historians who rely on them, Mancini and Pierantoni both knew that ascribing a person's legal belonging was more complicated than producing the correct paperwork. In a world of imperfect archives and evolving legislation, intention and notoriety counted for quite a lot.

Yet Mancini reserved his most passionate prose for his central claim: Nissim was Italian by virtue of his Livornese descent. In arguing that Nissim's Italian ancestry gave him privileged access to Italian citizenship, Mancini's universalist tendencies bumped up against the exclusivist heart of nationalism. He believed in a version of Renan's "everyday plebiscite": nationality could not be reduced to the physiology of race. Nonetheless, his liberalist approach to nationality was inextricably bound up with blood, and he worked hard to ensure that Italian law reflected this. Mancini's arguments for Nissim's Italian nationality reflected a brilliant combination of old and new: an emphasis on reputation that reached back to the ancient world, set alongside the fashionably modern insistence on nationality as a biological fact.

In the Shamama case, Mancini used the essential nature of nationality to make an argument for the inclusion of a Jew like Nissim; because Nissim descended from Italians, he could claim Italian citizenship without the formalities imposed on true "foreigners." But many of his peers—including liberals—used this same logic to exclude Jews, who could not share the same ethnic makeup as "true" Italians (or French or Germans).[86] In an age of nationalism, fights over the legal belonging of individuals—whether dead or alive—became proxies for political agendas both right and left.

7

Qā'id Nissim the Tunisian

NOW IT WAS up to Pierantoni to disprove his teacher, partner, and father-in-law. The young jurist constructed a narrative about Nissim that diametrically opposed the one presented by Mancini. In Pierantoni's eyes, Nissim died a proud subject of the bey of Tunis; the Livornese court had thus "stripped the cadaver" of his true nationality.[1] Pierantoni set out to dismantle the Livornese court's ruling.

But before the ambitious young lawyer could demonstrate why Nissim died a Tunisian, he had to address a more basic question: whether a Jew like Nissim could even be a Tunisian national. The lower court had expressed doubt that it was possible for Jews to be members of the Tunisian polity since they lacked the civil and political rights allotted to Muslims. According to the Livornese justices, Jews were subjects, not nationals. In order to have Tunisian law applied as Nissim's national law, Pierantoni had to prove that Tunisian Jews were just as Tunisian as Muslims—which required him to weigh in on the relationship between rights and state membership.

Next Pierantoni turned to the question of expatriation. The Livornese court argued that Nissim had tacitly renounced his Tunisian nationality, invoking natural law theory granting the right to forsake state membership at will. Pierantoni denied the existence of such a universal right, arguing that Tunisian law proscribed voluntary expatriation. Even had Nissim wanted to shed his Tunisian nationality, Pierantoni maintained, he was not able to do so without the express consent of the bey. Yet the question of natural law and universal rights was made doubly tricky by the trans-Mediterranean nature of the case. It remained unclear whether these rights extended to Tunisia. Reaching outside the legal world of western Europe forced everyone involved to face questions that international law had largely left unspoken: How did states like Tunisia fit into the international legal order?

Mancini was able to ground his arguments for Nissim's Italian citizenship in the familiar soil of Italian and Roman jurisprudence. Pierantoni, however, had no choice but to build his case on Tunisian law. Needless to say, Pierantoni had not been trained in the law of the Islamic world. For this part of his reasoning, he leaned heavily on Husayn, who wrote three briefs helping prove the government's case.[2] At times, Pierantoni repeated Husayn's points almost verbatim—adding the weight of his stature as one of Italy's finest lawyers to the Muslim official's opinions.[3] On other points, though, Pierantoni maintained a studied silence about Husayn's views; the Italian lawyer simply could not bring himself to adopt certain claims about Islam that swam directly against the tide of received wisdom in Europe.

Husayn was not trained as a jurist. Nor was he an *ʿālim*, a scholar thoroughly versed in classical Islamic texts. Rather, he received a basic Islamic education alongside his studies at the Tunisian Military School (*maktab al-ʿulūm al-ḥarbīya)*, founded by Ahmad Bey on the model of the École Polytechnique in Paris.[4] It was precisely Husayn's background as a government official that gave him the necessary tools to articulate a sophisticated understanding of legal belonging in Tunisia. Husayn's arguments amounted to a kind of translation. He sought to render his understanding of legal belonging in a Muslim-ruled polity in the language of Western citizenship. "The laws of Islam," Husayn pointed out, "do not have the same basis as Roman legislation."[5] Rather, the legal belonging of Nissim was based first and foremost on Islamic law: "all subjects of a Muslim state, regardless of race or creed, are politically ruled by the dispositions of the shariʿa."[6] Tracing Husayn's reasoning offers a glimpse at how Muslims conceived of legal belonging in the Islamic world on their own terms—not as an imitation of European ideas about citizenship, but as an extension of Islamic legal principles.

Pierantoni faced an uphill battle in proving that Nissim died a Tunisian. Not only had the Livornese court declared that Nissim was stateless when he passed away; the judges had questioned whether a Jew like Nissim could even be a Tunisian national in the first place. The ruling acknowledged that Nissim had been "a *subject* of the regency of Tunisia." But was he also "a *citizen* of this regency—given that a subject is one who lives under the sovereignty of a given country, while one can only be a citizen or national if he is recognized as a member of a given society . . . and is able to exercise significant benefits therein?"[7] The court concluded that the nationality principle required determining in which state Nissim held citizenship; that is, in which state he was a full member with full rights.

The Livornese judges operated on the assumption—widespread in Italy at the time—that "citizen" and "national" were synonyms.[8] And they posited that Jews were barred from full state membership on the other side of the Mediterranean; Nissim "professed the Jewish religion, and as a Jew he was barred from civil life in a society regulated by the Quran." Betraying a teleological view of progress, the judges noted that Tunisia "had not yet accepted the great principles of liberty of conscience and absolute equality of all individuals before the law, regardless of religious faith." Because Jews were not legally emancipated in Tunisia—because they were not considered the civil and political equals of Muslims—they were mere subjects of the bey. Only Muslims could be considered citizens (or nationals) in a society "regulated by the Quran." Therefore a Jew like Nissim "never had Tunisian nationality and was never a citizen of this state."[9] The initial ruling called into question whether Nissim had ever been a Tunisian national in the first place.

This argument reflected genuine confusion surrounding the vocabulary of legal belonging in the late nineteenth century. The French Civil Code already implied a distinction between someone who was French—described as possessing the *qualité de français*, the "quality of being French"—and a citizen invested with full political rights.[10] And until the 1870s, French jurists employed "nationality" to connote both the stripped-down version of membership enjoyed by those who possessed the *qualité de français* and the full membership embodied by the *citoyen*. The terms "citizenship," "nationality," and "subjecthood" were used as synonyms by laypeople and jurists alike.[11]

This was starting to change right around the time that Mancini and Pierantoni were writing their legal briefs on the Shamama case. Jurists increasingly found it useful to distinguish between nationality, as a word to describe bare-bones legal belonging; and citizenship, reserved for full membership in a state. In 1879, George Cogordan published one of the first studies of nationality as a legal status. Though trained as a jurist, Cogordan made a career as a French diplomat; his approach to legal belonging must have emerged at least in part from the reams of correspondence exchanged between the Quai d'Orsay and France's web of consulates. Cogordan began his book by defining a citizen as "a national invested with full rights." A national, on the other hand, was a member of the state, but did not enjoy the full range of political and civil rights reserved for citizens. According to Cogordan's scheme, women and Algerian

Muslims (of both sexes) lacked political rights in France; they were not citizens. But women and Algerian Muslims were nonetheless French nationals.[12] Eventually Cogordan's distinction became widely accepted among jurists of international law, but this consensus had not yet emerged when the Livornese court issued its initial ruling.[13]

The precise timing of the evolution of the terms "national" and "citizen" is crucial to understanding this part of the Shamama case. The Livornese judges made a similar distinction to Cogordan's, but used the terms differently. In the lower court's ruling, bare-bones membership was referred to as subjecthood, while full membership was described interchangeably as nationality and citizenship. The Livornese judges' "subject" was equivalent to Cogordan's "national": both designated an individual who was merely under the sovereignty of a given state, but who was barred from political rights—such as women, colonial subjects, and in the eyes of the court, Jews in Tunisia. And the Livornese judges' "national" was equivalent to Cogordan's "citizen": by this scheme, Muslims were the only ones with Tunisian nationality since they alone enjoyed full civil and political rights.

Pierantoni interpreted the terms differently from both the Livornese judges and Cogordan. Rather than parse the precise valences of citizen, national, and subject, Pierantoni insisted, the court must decide to which state Nissim had legally belonged. The only meaningful difference between "subject" and "national" had to do with the nature of the state in question: "the citizen is a man who is a member of a free fatherland, with a constitutional or republican government."[14] Subjecthood, on the other hand, was associated with absolutist states. Yet citizens, nationals, and subjects were all members of the state in question. Before emancipation, Jews in the various states of the Italian Peninsula had lacked citizenship, yet they were unquestionably subjects of the sovereign.[15] What mattered was not whether Nissim had full rights—and thus whether he should be called a subject, national, or citizen of Tunisia; all that counted was that he legally belonged to the Tunisian state.

If the distinctions between subject, national, and citizen were murky in European languages, they were even more so in Arabic and Ottoman. The Ottoman decree regulating legal belonging from 1869 used the term *tabiiyet* to describe membership in the Ottoman state; though often translated as "nationality," it is lexically closer to "subjecthood" since *tabi* derives from the Arabic for "follower" or "servant" (*tābiʿ*).[16] Husayn himself used various terms to describe legal belonging. Perhaps his most common designation was *raʿāyā* (s. *raʿīya*; Ottoman, *reaya*)—translated as subjects or citizens, from the Arabic root meaning to pasture animals.[17] He also employed *jinsīya,* from the Arabic word *jins,* originally meaning genus, and eventually coming to denote race or ethnicity—usually translated as "nationality" in European languages.[18] In some cases, Husayn used *ahālin,* the plural of *ahl*—typically translated as "people," as in *ahl al-dhimma,* but in this case meaning the inhabitants of Tunisia. Although Husayn may well have trod carefully in his own terminology, he claimed to find the whole discussion a bit exasperating: "I fail to understand how one makes this distinction"—that is, between subjects and citizens. "It can only be a difference of words."[19]

In arguing against the distinction between "subject," on the one hand, and "citizen" or "national," on the other, Pierantoni and Husayn made claims similar to the one I outlined in the introduction: that the question at the heart of the Shamama case concerned not the niceties of nationality or citizenship but rather the more abstract category of legal belonging (though they did not name it as such). They pushed back against the Livornese judges, who insisted that the nationality principle compelled the question of civil and political rights—what we think of today as substantive citizenship. One wonders whether the court would have been so quick to dismiss the nationality of a Jew from a place like Germany, where Jews similarly lacked full civil and political rights. The perception of the Islamic world as a hotbed of religious fanaticism—a place "regulated by the Quran," where Muslims oppressed Jews and Christians as a matter of course—was undoubtedly behind the Livornese court's decision to bring the question of Jewish equality into the mix.

Husayn was keenly attuned to the ways in which stereotypes about the Islamic world seeped into the Italian jurists' arguments. He flatly denied the accusation at the heart of the Livornese court's claim about the status of Jews as less-than-full members of the Tunisian polity. "In fact," Husayn contended, "citizens [*al-ra'āyā*] and subjects [*al-ahālī*] both refer to one thing: is there not just one shepherd [the bey of Tunis] and his flock [his subjects]? And Islam has given dhimmīs under Islamic rule the same rights and duties as Muslims."[20]

The Islamic legal tradition provided the basis for Jews' status as full members of the Tunisian state. "In Islamic law, nationality [*al-jinsīyatu*] is based on religion for Muslim subjects, and on the pact of dhimma for non-Muslim subjects [*lil-ra'āyā ghayri muslimīna*]."[21] In other words, Muslims owed religious allegiance to the sovereign, while the allegiance of non-Muslims was based on their status as dhimmīs. "The pact of dhimma," Husayn explained, "means that non-Muslims obligate themselves to come under the rule of Islam, and in so doing they are classified as members of the Islamic state, both in terms of rights and duties."[22]

Pierantoni had neatly sidestepped the substantive question behind the Livornese court's claim; whether or not Jews were full members of the Tunisian polity was irrelevant, he asserted. But Husayn aimed the thrust of his reasoning at the heart of the Livornese judges' prejudice, arguing at length that Jews were full members of the Tunisian state, with "the same rights" as Muslims. In this line of thinking, he was joined by Elmilik, the Algerian Jew working as Husayn's fixer for all matters rabbinic. As the legal representative for some of Nissim's more distant relatives, Elmilik now had formal standing to argue the case. And as a Jew himself, his assertion of Jews' equal rights provided powerful amplification of Husayn's claims.

In presuming that Jews could not be full and equal members of the Tunisian state, the Livornese court divided the world into two kinds of states: those in which Jews were citizens—that is, where Jews had been "emancipated"—and those in which Jews were excluded from full membership. In the judges' worldview—shared by many liberal jurists across Europe—"modern" states like Italy and France had emancipated their Jews, while "backward" states like Tunisia had not.[23] The reality of Jews' legal belonging, though, was far murkier than this binary admitted. In early modern Europe, where no state granted absolute equality to Jews, jurists still argued over the nature of Jews' legal belonging. In eighteenth-century England, jurists maintained that Jews could never be naturalized as full members of the state—a privilege open only to Christians. Similarly, in German lands, Jews could only be *incolae*—Latin for "resident," and best translated into English as "denizens"—but never full citizens.[24] On the other hand, Jean Bodin, a sixteenth-century French jurist, envisioned citizenship as a status that could accommodate hierarchy, including different laws for different "religions" (like Jews) and "nations."[25] Even while the discourse of emancipation gathered steam in the nineteenth century, jurists continued to produce a range of answers to the question of whether Jews could become full and equal members of the state. The French and Italian model of absolute emancipation are best understood as exceptions; the rule was enormous variation in just what rights Jews were granted and to what extent they were considered citizens.[26]

Husayn knew well the wide scope of positions on Jewish emancipation within Europe. He had invoked this very diversity when, in 1860, he defended his decision to exclude Jews from the newly constituted Supreme Council (*majlis al-'āla*), a judicial and administrative body instituted as part of the reforms sparked by the 'Ahd al-Amān. Another government official had argued that European states would use the exclusion of Jews from the Supreme Council to accuse Tunisia of religious discrimination. Husayn asked in turn,

> Who is the foreigner who might complain that we are not admitting a Jew to this Council . . . ? Is it Spain, where no one knows if Jews are allowed to enter its territory? Is it Italy, where, to our knowledge, there is not a single Jew who exercises public office? . . . Is it the States of Germany, where until yesterday, Jews had to wear yellow hats? Is it England, where for the past fifty years the House of Commons has been debating whether they should admit a Jew to the High Chamber?[27]

Only France, Husayn argued, could boast of admitting Jews to full and equal rights. Tunisia was hardly behind most of Europe when it came to religious tolerance; on the contrary, since the 'Ahd al-Amān had declared Jews and Muslims equal before the law, Tunisia was ahead of many European states. Husayn insisted that his reticence to admit Jews to the Supreme Council was not about prejudice but rather about the phase of Tunisian Jews' evolution; they simply were not properly prepared to serve in such a role. And when compared to European governments, Husayn pointed out, the beys of Tunis proved far more willing to elevate Jews to positions of power. Nissim's career offered vivid proof that Sadiq Bey had been happy to "favor and put his faith in his subject whose religion differed from his own." "How," Husayn demanded, "could you accuse us of fanaticism?"[28]

The shortcomings of Europe aside, Husayn's point in the Shamama case was that Jews in Tunisia undoubtedly enjoyed full membership in the state. "Islam accords dhimmīs and Muslims the same rights and the same obligations."[29] This was a position Husayn knew would be hard for the Italian judges to swallow. There was general consensus in Europe that Muslims oppressed non-Muslims, who were at the mercy of their fanatic sovereigns. For this reason, Husayn instructed Elmilik to secure the corroboration of the English consul in Tunis. Momentarily triumphant, Elmilik reported that he had obtained a document in which the consul affirmed the "equality of Jews before the law."[30]

Elmilik further reinforced Husayn's assertions in his own legal brief, printed in 1878 in Hebrew, French, and Italian. Like Husayn, Elmilik asserted that "Jews and Muslims were equal before the law."[31] One might dismiss Elmilik's statement as pure opportunism—an example of dhimmī Stockholm syndrome. But Elmilik's claim of equality between Jews and Muslims was part of his broader agenda to defend the Tunisian government as a guarantor of Jews' rights. And Elmilik was in good company; he joined other Jews across North Africa and the Middle East who expressed confidence in their Muslim sovereign's ability to ensure equal treatment—European presumptions about Islamic oppression notwithstanding.[32]

Husayn's insistence that Jews in Tunisia had "the same rights and the same obligations" as Muslims sat uneasily beside his invocation of the dhimma as the basis of Jews' membership in the state. The Pact of ʿUmar clearly distinguished between the rights and responsibilities of Muslims and those of non-Muslims; Christians and Jews were required to wear distinctive clothing as well as "show deference to the Muslims." They were prohibited from building new churches or synagogues, riding on horses, or possessing weapons.[33] The ahl al-dhimma paid a special head tax called the jizya (one of the few regulations regarding dhimmīs mentioned in the Quran). Because they could not own weapons, non-Muslims were generally excluded from the military.[34] Although the details of dhimmī status varied widely across time and place, Jews in Tunisia were subject to a number of restrictions enacted in the spirit of the Pact of ʿUmar. Jews did not perform military service. Until the 1850s, they had been required to wear a black shāshīya; the bright red ones were reserved for Muslims. And in recent years, new restrictions were being added, including the prohibition against Jewish musicians playing at Muslim weddings, enacted by Khayraddin in 1876.[35] Being a dhimmī necessarily implied *not* being equal to Muslims; their distinct rights and responsibilities were at the very heart of what made them dhimmīs.

As contradictory as this may seem, Husayn was hardly alone in asserting that a kind of equality could coexist with dhimmī status. The ʿAhd al-Amān of 1857 did just that; it decreed "equality between Muslims and non-Muslims of the province in claiming their rights," while continuing to refer to Jews as dhimmīs.[36] Husayn had made the link between dhimmīs' right to equality and the ʿAhd al-Amān explicit, noting that Jews and Muslims in Tunisia can claim the same rights "according to the rule of equality proclaimed in the ʿAhd al-Amān."[37] Husayn's understanding of dhimma aligned with that of other North African reform-minded Muslims, who argued that dhimmīs were equal before the law—meaning that the sharīʿa guaranteed justice to both Jews and Muslims.[38] Even if Jews claimed a distinct set of rights from Muslims, this did not exclude them from the basic prerogative to seek justice before the law.

Husayn was not content with painting Tunisia as equivalent to western European states when it came to religious equality. He went a step further, arguing that Tunisia's form of tolerance—in which Jews were allotted significant legal autonomy—was superior to the kind practiced in France. How could the Tunisian bey be called "fanatic and intolerant" when he appointed Jewish judges to adjudicate among his Jewish subjects—all "according to the recommendations of the rabbis"? Husayn contrasted the autonomy of Tunisian Jews with the restrictions on religion in France, where the state kept a tight rein on religious personnel. "According to your logic," Husayn explained, "France is a hundred times more fanatic and intolerant—France, where the king, emperor, or president of the republic nominates the bishops and archbishops by decree! Tunisian Jews," he concluded, "live in our country with greater liberty than anywhere else."[39]

In this seemingly far-fetched claim—Jews in Tunisia had more freedom than their coreligionists in Europe!—Elmilik once again echoed Husayn. Elmilik emphasized Jews' access to a range of judicial options; they could choose a Jewish judge who applied Jewish law, a Muslim judge who ruled "according to the Quran," or a court presided over by a Muslim state official. Could Jews in Italy claim "greater liberty than this?"[40] Like Husayn, Elmilik invoked a distinct model of tolerance from the one pioneered in the wake of Napoléon's Sanhedrin, where to be equal meant to have exactly the same rights as everyone else. Instead, Husayn and Elmilik insisted that true equality meant the right to have different rights according to one's religion.[41] They refused Europe's exclusive claim to equality, countering with an alternative vision that they saw as rooted in Islamic law and culture.

Whereas Pierantoni hewed carefully to so many of Husayn's other arguments, in this instance the Italian jurist openly differed from his employer.[42] Pierantoni had a reputation to uphold; he could not advance arguments that risked making him out to be ridiculous. It seems safe to presume that Pierantoni found Husayn's claim that Tunisian Jews enjoyed "greater liberty than anywhere else" simply preposterous. Instead, Pierantoni followed a different line of reasoning: Jews in the Islamic world did have a distinct legal status from Muslims—and thus were not "perfectly equal," as they were in Italy.[43] Jews' legal autonomy did not, however, exclude them from membership in the state. On the contrary, many Western states had different laws for different territories, including Switzerland, Germany, the United States, Britain, and even France. In Italy itself, Jews had only recently been emancipated; before that—when they were denied full equality on most of the peninsula—Jews were nonetheless considered members of their respective states.[44] In Pierantoni's logic, Jewish subjects of the bey were inferior to Muslims. They nonetheless possessed Tunisian nationality.[45]

Husayn was fighting a losing battle in his efforts to defend the model of religious tolerance practiced in Tunisia. Religious liberty in Europe had become synonymous with radical equality—a single law for all. And as Europe became the unquestionable bastion of this kind of freedom, the Islamic world came to stand for its antithesis. Little wonder that Pierantoni was unwilling to take up Husayn's line of reasoning. As historians, though, we ought to take note of the alternate ways to order difference articulated by North Africans involved in the lawsuit.

Of course, proving that Jews like Nissim were members of the Tunisian state was only the first step. Pierantoni still had to demonstrate that Nissim was a Tunisian national the day he died. The Livornese court had ruled that even if Nissim had been a Tunisian national, he tacitly renounced his Tunisian nationality after leaving Tunis in 1864. Because expatriation was a basic liberty accorded to all human beings, Nissim had been free to shake off any allegiance he owed the bey. In engaging this argument, lawyers on both sides waded into the murky waters where international law met a more universalist discourse based on natural law.

Although the Livornese court ruled that expatriation was a basic right accorded to all humans, this proved a bone of contention. Mancini maintained that natural law gave everyone the liberty to expatriate themselves at will. Pierantoni, on the other hand, asserted that expatriation was subject to the laws of a particular country. Both stances reflected ongoing tensions among international law scholars, who debated between positivism and universalism—between a concept of law as stemming solely from the edicts of a state, and a natural law that guides and sometimes opposes the laws of states. In Anglo-American legal circles, this dispute would have its most famous echoes in the positions of Herbert Hart and Lon Fuller.[46] Hart took a positivist position, arguing that law consists of the rules enacted by states, even if those rules went against some sort of higher morality. Fuller, on the other hand, echoed a natural law approach in asserting that law exists independently of what states do. Mancini and Pierantoni's disagreement boiled down to a similar debate over the essence of law.

Natural law constituted the implicit foundation of Mancini's argument: that Nissim had the right to renounce his Tunisian nationality.[47] In this he followed the Livornese court, which had determined that Nissim's right to expatriate himself existed irrespective of Tunisian law. According to the ruling, "even the least civilized nations" recognized that individuals are always free to renounce their citizenship.[48] Mancini could not have agreed more: "The liberty of emigration and expatriation is one of the universal principles of human rights."[49] A bit carried away by his passionate convictions, he made the dubious claim that all legal theorists—from Roman jurists to the giants of international law such as Hugo Grotius and Samuel von Pufendorf—recognized the right of expatriation. Mancini's only concession was to acknowledge that until recently, a few "civilized" countries like the United States and Great Britain had nonetheless limited their subjects' right to expatriate themselves. Such regressive legislation, however, had been an error, now happily corrected. In 1868 and 1870 respectively, these states "reestablished the unrestrained right to expatriation and naturalization abroad."[50] As a human, Nissim was free to forego his Tunisian nationality.

Mancini believed that international law rested on a foundation more profound than mere legislation. In this he was in good company; his colleague Johann Caspar Bluntschli, one of the eleven jurists present alongside Mancini and Pierantoni at the founding of the Institute of International Law in 1873, saw things the same way. Bluntschli was committed to the idea that law was universal rather than built on the will of states or sovereigns. Natural law endowed people with rights such as the universal freedom of expatriation, for which Bluntschli argued in his writing on the Bauffremont Affair. Adjudicated just a few years earlier, the case concerned whether the Countess de Bauffremont was free to expatriate herself and marry a new husband after a judicial separation in France. Her marriage to a French count had made the countess French. After her judicial separation, however, the countess argued that she had the right to naturalize as a German and remarry in Germany. The countess's nationality became something of a cause célèbre. Had she become German or must she remain French? Bluntschli contended that any attempt to tether the countess to her French nationality curtailed her personal liberty: "Contemporary international law permits each person to choose another nationality."[51] Mancini's position on expatriation aligned perfectly with Bluntschli's opinion in the Bauffremont Affair. Both jurists maintained that certain universal principles guided international law—the right to expatriation among them. As Bluntschli wrote about the Countess de

Bauffremont, "It is not up to the arbitrary will of the State to follow or reject international law."[52]

Mancini portrayed his invocation of the universal right of expatriation as self-evident. Yet scholars of international law were sharply divided about whether there was a universal, moral core to their science. In opposing Mancini's claim that a universal right to expatriation undergirded international law, Pierantoni staked out an opposing position popular with many of the leading scholars of international law at the time. Pierantoni quoted Georg Friedrich von Martens, a German jurist whose treatise on the law of nations, published in 1789, marked a turn away from natural law. As Martens put it, "A universal, positive law of nations does not exist for all nations of the universe."[53] Pierantoni's position was echoed by his Belgian colleague François Laurent, another prominent figure in international law. Laurent recognized that it would be desirable for "science" to articulate a uniform international law that all states would sign onto.[54] But this was aspirational; in the meantime, jurists remained "slaves of law." Laurent, too, weighed in on the Bauffremont Affair; he conceded that Bluntschli's invocation of the countess's personal liberty was "morally" correct. Bluntschli's conclusion nevertheless went against the positive law of France and thus was unsound. Laurent explained that "only the legislator has the power to deliver a married woman from the chains that he imposed on her."[55] Jurists had to follow the positive laws enacted by politicians, whether they agreed with them or not.

Pierantoni explained that because law came from states—and not from abstract, moral principles—different polities often came to conflicting conclusions about what nationality law should look like. Thus in some Western states, expatriation was illegal without the approval of the government; this was still the case in Russia, and had been so until only recently in the United States and Great Britain.[56] The Ottoman Empire and Tunisia similarly prevented their subjects from expatriating themselves without express permission. International law required jurists to respect each state's laws of legal belonging, not to impose some universal standard that existed only in the minds of scholars.

Pierantoni dwelled a bit on the serious problems that these conflicting approaches to nationality law could produce—problems that testified to the predominance of state legislation over natural law. Perhaps a tad too gleefully, Pierantoni proved his point using Mancini's own words. He quoted his father-in-law's address to the Institute of International Law in 1874, when Mancini had lamented the position of Italian women who married Englishmen. These brides were considered to have acquired the nationality of their English spouses by Italian law. English law, however, did not automatically accord such women English nationality—leaving them stateless.[57] Similarly, a person might be considered to have more than one nationality; this occurred in the Bauffremont Affair, as French courts considered the Countess de Bauffremont to be French, while German courts considered her German. Clearly, then, there existed no single international law regulating nationality. It was hypocritical to invoke a universal right to expatriation in the Shamama case, when Mancini knew full well that the reality of international law produced countless instances in which positive laws clashed—sometimes with tragic results.

Husayn had little interest in the debate over positivism and universalism that so concerned Pierantoni and Mancini. Nonetheless, he was thoroughly familiar with the problems produced by clashing nationality laws. A Tunisian Jew, for instance, might naturalize as a French citizen in neighboring Algeria. But, Husayn explained, the bey's administration "does not recognize" the naturalization of its subjects abroad, as the Qānūn al-Dawla made explicit; when the newly minted French citizen returned to Tunisia, "Tunisian law is simply applied to him."[58] Husayn left his commentary at this, implying that the bey had solved this problem with his legislation of 1861.

The reality, of course, was otherwise. Husayn remained strategically silent about the many times Tunisian authorities had proved unable to enforce their own laws of legal belonging.[59] In the hypothetical of a Tunisian Jew who naturalized as a French citizen in Algeria, French authorities would stand by the Jew's naturalization back in Tunis. In fact, there were countless instances of Tunisians obtaining foreign nationality or protection, and the bey's government being forced to defer to the consuls of Western states. Joseph and Nathan's departure from Tunis is a case in point; neither Joseph nor Nathan could lay any formal claim to Italian protection, but Pinna gave them refuge in the sanctuary of his consulate. In making demands on their behalf, Pinna invoked universal principles of rights—with the threat of Italian aggression hovering in the background. Legal belonging was a contest, a fraught negotiation of the highly fragmented sovereignty that characterized the Mediterranean.[60]

These sorts of conflicts over nationality in Tunisia made the debate between positivism and universalism seem a bit quaint. There was a crucial difference between the Bauffremont Affair and the bey's attempts to prevent expatriation. When it came to the Countess de Bauffremont, the states that laid claim to her—Germany and France—were considered roughly equal on the international playing field. There was little question that both were admitted to the "family of nations" to which principles of international law applied.

But whether these principles also applied to states like Tunisia remained an open question—one that exposed significant gaps in jurists' ability to extend their understanding of international law to the non-Western world.

It was this uncertain status of Tunisia that gave Pierantoni a second reason to argue that Nissim never lost his Tunisian nationality. Even if Pierantoni had accepted the existence of a universal right to expatriation, he maintained that it would not apply to a state like Tunisia. A polity administered by the bey, who ruled according to Islamic law, lay outside the boundaries of "the law of nations of Europe." Moreover, the specifically European law of nations had an explicitly religious foundation; "Europe" was equivalent to Christendom.[61] The debate over the application of natural law principles to the Middle East and North Africa forced a reckoning with the edges of international law.

According to Pierantoni, the judge in Livorno had committed a "grave error" in pretending that there were "principles of international law concerning the loss of nationality that are common to all states." By including Tunisia in this presumption, the Livornese court had ignored "the legal relations among Christian and Eastern, Islamic states." It is "elementary" that Islamic states were long excluded from European international law; "the Ottoman world was only recently admitted to the law of nations of Europe" (by the Treaty of Paris in 1856). Tunisia, however, continued to be treated as an independent state in European international law—and thus did not benefit from the admission of the Ottoman Empire to the family of nations. Moreover, everyone knew that the Ottoman Empire's admission had been only "partial, and that great differences still exist in international relations between the East and the West."[62]

Again, Pierantoni quoted his opponent's own words for effect. As Mancini had said when addressing Parliament concerning Italian consular jurisdiction in Egypt, "The law of nations is not a natural law that regulates the relations for all the people of the earth. . . . rather, it is a particular, circumscribed law that applies only to Christian nations, which is why it tends to be called the law of nations of Europe or Christendom."[63] The Shamama case forced jurists like Pierantoni and Mancini to face an assumption about international law that they rarely had to articulate: its presumed subject was the Christian world. When jurists did consider non-Christian states in light of international law, it was usually in the context of colonization: did a particular Western state have the right to colonize a people or not? (Unsurprisingly, the answer usually turned out to be yes.)[64]

Most of the time, experts in the budding field of international law were only concerned with the status of Muslim-ruled states like Tunisia when discussing the extraterritorial privileges of foreign nationals. Pierantoni smugly pointed out that the "existence of consular jurisdiction is the best proof of the legal difference that distinguishes Europe from Tunisia."[65] European states insisted on extraterritorial privileges for their subjects precisely because they claimed that states ruled by Muslims were not civilized enough to effectively guarantee justice. On this the members of the Institute of International Law were nearly unanimous; all save one agreed that extraterritoriality remained absolutely necessary given the state of justice in countries deemed uncivilized.[66] The jurists expansively declared that "non-Christian nations will be granted the same rights and responsibilities as Occidental nations." But in the same breath, they dialed back any recognition of full sovereignty "until a more complete assimilation of the judicial institutions of Oriental and Occidental nations is achieved."[67] Until that point, nationals of Western states would retain the extraterritorial privileges they currently enjoyed.[68] "Oriental" states were ultimately relegated to an eternal liminality, neither in nor out of the community of nations subject to international law.

Both Pierantoni and Mancini were attempting to impose clarity where none existed. Either one admitted that a state like Tunisia was bound by the universalist principles underlying international law, as Mancini claimed. Or one recognized that a Muslim state like Tunisia was outside the boundaries of the "civilized" world of Christendom, as Pierantoni maintained. But the institute's approach belied this precision, keeping states like Tunisia both in and out of the international legal order.

Only after Pierantoni and Mancini ceased their work on the Shamama case did jurists name the liminal sovereignty ascribed to places like Tunisia. In 1883, James Lorimer proposed a solution. Another founding member of the Institute of International Law—to which he dedicated his book on the law of nations—Lorimer offered a beguiling dose of clarity by dividing humanity into three groups: one comprised "civilized humanity," including Europe and the Americas, whose states deserved "plenary" or complete recognition; another was made up of "savage humanity," whose nations were unquestionably outside the boundaries of the international legal order and could not be recognized as members of the family of nations; and in between was "barbarous humanity," states like the Ottoman Empire, China, and Japan, whose polities were only somewhat civilized and thus deserved only "partial" recognition.[69] Lorimer's schema caught on among his peers; it became standard practice to categorize places like the Ottoman Empire and Tunisia as "semicivilized"—civilized enough to make treaties with, but not civilized enough to forego extraterritorial privileges for Westerners.[70]

But Lorimer's ideas had not yet been published when Pierantoni and Mancini articulated their positions concerning the application of universal legal principles to Tunisia. There was simply no consensus on how Tunisia fit into the emerging science of international law. Nonetheless, both father-in-law and son-in-law agreed that Tunisia was fundamentally different from Europe. Pierantoni made this clear in excluding a non-Christian state like Tunisia from the family of nations. And even Mancini—who implicitly included Tunisia within the boundaries of the international—was quick to denounce the nation's backwardness. He painted Tunisia as a land without rule of law, governed by an "irritated despot" who failed to guarantee his subjects the most basic of rights.[71]

Husayn made plain his frustration at this openly prejudicial attitude. He concluded his brief with an implicit challenge to the exclusion of Tunisia from the rights accorded to European states: "At this time, when civilized nations are animated by the same feelings of sovereign tolerance; when justice is distributed equally, without distinction of nationality; we remain completely convinced that our rights—so respectable and so justified—will be consecrated and protected by the ruling for which we confidently wait."[72] Husayn's plea touched at the core of the principles animating international jurists like Pierantoni, Mancini, and their colleagues. The founders of the institute believed that international law had the power to pacify and civilize relations among states, replacing violence with mutual respect for the rule of law.[73] Yet the discussion about where Tunisia fit in the international order belies their beatific vision. The mutual respect they championed petered out somewhere in the waters of the Mediterranean.

Pierantoni's case against a universal right of expatriation was just the first part of his argument. In part two, he had to prove that Tunisian law explicitly forbade voluntary expatriation. Once again, Pierantoni's understanding of Tunisian legislation came from Husayn. Together, the Italian lawyer and the mamlūk maintained that the bey of Tunis forbade his subjects to expatriate themselves at will.

As Husayn had done in arguing for Jews' full membership in the Tunisian state, his account of Tunisia's approach to expatriation grounded contemporary law in the shariʿa: "the loss of nationality does not exist in Islamic law."[74] He explained that the bond between sovereign and subject is based on "religion"; Muslim subjects are tied to their sovereign by virtue of their faith, while non-Muslims are tied to their sovereign through the pact of dhimma. This "religious law forbids non-Muslims to violate the pact of dhimma, just as it forbids Muslims to apostatize."[75] Muslims and non-Muslims are free to travel as they like, but both must remain "subject to the bonds of religion and refrain from exceeding the limits set by the Quran."[76] Otherwise, Islamic law prescribes punishment—of Muslims as apostates and dhimmīs as violators of the pact of dhimma. Husayn pointed to a case from the court of appeal of the mixed courts in Egypt, which in 1876 ruled that Islamic law required perpetual allegiance to the sovereign.[77] Pierantoni was careful to echo Husayn, quoting the French translation of his brief at some length.[78] The Italian lawyer also cited the Ottoman proclamation of 1869 regulating legal belonging (*tabiiyet-i osmaniye kanunnamesi*). The Ottoman decree similarly prevented subjects of the sultan from changing nationality without permission. According to Pierantoni, this was evidence that Islamic states enforced perpetual allegiance—not because Tunisia was bound by Ottoman law, but because the Ottomans, like the bey of Tunis, followed the prescriptions of the shariʿa regarding indelible allegiance.[79]

In speaking about Islamic law, Husayn transposed the language of indelible allegiance to Islamic legal concepts originally formulated for other contexts. There is little question that Islamic jurisprudence (*fiqh*) prescribes severe punishment for a Muslim who apostatizes—in most cases, the death penalty.[80] But this law has little to do with allegiance to a particular Muslim sovereign. Indeed, Muslim jurists were generally silent on the subject of a Muslim who switches his allegiance from one Muslim sovereign to another. Muslims were required to follow Islamic law, but this was relatively easy as long as a Muslim remained within the *dār al-islām*, the abode of Islam. Problems only arose when a Muslim found himself under the sovereignty of non-Muslims, such as during the Reconquista in Spain or in Algeria following the French conquest; many jurists prescribed emigration in both cases.[81] Muslim jurists also had little to say about status of dhimmīs who switched allegiance from one sovereign to another—and even less about those who left the Islamic world altogether. As Husayn noted, dhimmīs were prohibited from contravening the pact of protection. Those who did could be exiled, plundered, enslaved, or even killed—in short, had no legal right to life, liberty, or property under a Muslim sovereign.[82] What Husayn neglected to point out, however, was that Muslim jurists were concerned with the status of those dhimmīs who contravened the pact of dhimma, not those who were no longer the subjects of a Muslim sovereign.

Husayn was well aware of the gaps between the concerns of Muslim jurists and the approach to legal belonging in Italian courts. He felt he needed some corroboration of his assertions. In order to prove that Islamic law did not permit dhimmīs to break their bond of allegiance with their Muslim sovereign, Husayn solicited an expert opinion from Tunisia's *shaykh al-islām,* the country's highest religious authority.[83] In this fatwā, the shaykh al-islām attested that a Tunisian subject (whether Muslim or non-Muslim) who requested naturalization abroad did not cease to be a subject of his sovereign. This is exactly the sort of question a mufti might face all the time—a legal case that required a new interpretation of old texts. Given that classical Islamic jurisprudence did not address questions of expatriation, Husayn's instinct to solicit a fatwā made perfect sense.

Yet his strategy was not as successful as he had hoped. Whereas Husayn saw the fatwā as a helpful explanation of Islamic law for nonexperts, Mancini dismissed it as "vague and equivocal" statements, made by functionaries who are "subject to the unrestrained arbitrariness of a despotic governor."[84] In discrediting this important evidence, Mancini dealt a serious blow to the Tunisian government's case. With his typical indignation, Husayn refused to stand for what he saw as Mancini's "ignorance." He protested that the Italian jurist had dismissed the fatwā because he erroneously presumed that Tunisian "jurists are functionaries of the government"—an error that was "very widespread in Europe." In reality, jurisprudence in Tunisia "is a religious matter written in books. . . . And the government does not, nor has it ever, disturbed the freedom of muftis."[85] Husayn bolstered his case with a document signed by the consuls of England, Spain, and Italy, affirming the judiciary's autonomy in Tunisia.[86] Far from being suspect or "vague," the fatwā clearly explained the law of expatriation in the Islamic world. This time, Pierantoni was more than happy to repeat Husayn's arguments.[87]

Should any doubt remain about the prohibition on expatriation in Islamic law, Husayn and Pierantoni pointed to legislation in the Qānūn al-Dawla as confirmation. Article 92 of the 1861 law specified that "every Tunisian [*al-tūnisī*] who moves to a different state—for whatever reason, whether his absence is long or short, and whether he is counted among the people of the state or not—becomes a Tunisian subject again on reentering Tunisia."[88] In other words, a Tunisian who went abroad and then returned to Tunisia remained a Tunisian subject—even if he was naturalized elsewhere. According to Husayn and Pierantoni, Article 92 demonstrated that Tunisia had explicitly legislated the principle of indelible allegiance.[89]

But even the relatively straightforward text of Article 92 proved open to attack. The problem was that this law only outlined what happened to a Tunisian who left Tunisia and then returned; the decree was silent regarding the status of a Tunisian who went abroad and remained there, as Nissim had.[90] Mancini objected that this law had nothing to do with expatriation. Rather, Article 92 was aimed at the "frequent abuses by indigenous Tunisian subjects" who naturalized abroad to take advantage of extraterritorial privileges and thus escape the jurisdiction of the Tunisian government.[91]

Husayn readily conceded Mancini's point; the context for Article 92 was undoubtedly the abuses of extraterritorial privileges by Tunisians. Many subjects of the bey—especially his Jewish ones—acquired foreign nationality to access extraterritorial privileges.[92] In acknowledging Mancini's objection, Husayn articulated what was obvious to consular officials across the Islamic Mediterranean: extraterritoriality was the context for the development of law surrounding legal belonging.[93] But, Husayn insisted, the fact that Article 92 was silent regarding those who did not return to Tunisia "is no reason to suppose that the government renounces its bond with its subjects while they are abroad."[94] Instead, Article 92 must be read through the prism of Islamic law, which explicitly forbade subjects of Muslim sovereigns to voluntarily break their bond of belonging. It thus applied even to those Tunisians who remained abroad, preventing them from shedding their allegiance to the bey at will.

One might be tempted to dismiss Husayn's arguments as expedient attempts to make Islamic law fit his interpretation of the Shamama lawsuit. Classical *fiqh* was not particularly concerned with the question of expatriation, which suggests that Muslim states like Tunisia simply did not have rules about nationality until the Qānūn al-Dawla.[95] But we would do well to seriously consider Husayn's insistence that questions of sovereignty and allegiance—the bread and butter of state membership—were part and parcel of Islamic jurisprudence. Husayn's approach offers a way to think about legal belonging in the Islamic world on its own terms. His reasoning did not presume that nationality was predicated on religious membership, and hence that it transcended political boundaries. Instead, Husayn offered a theologically grounded understanding of legal belonging based on the sovereignty exercised by the bey.

While Husayn was busy writing his briefs to demonstrate that Nissim had died a Tunisian national, a close associate of his suggested another line of argumentation altogether. Carlo Gallian, the Ottoman consul general in Rome, was in regular touch with Husayn about the Shamama lawsuit. In February 1879, Gallian Effendi, as he was known to his Ottoman superiors, wrote an upbeat letter to Husayn explaining that "he had just found a way to put his hands on the Shamama inheritance."[96] The solution was to "consider Qā'id Shamama as an Ottoman subject." They would then argue that the treaty between the Sublime Porte and Italy should be applied, according to which "the liquidation of Turkish estates in Italy is reserved for Ottoman consuls."[97] If Nissim was declared to be an Ottoman subject when he died, Gallian conjectured, then he, the Ottoman consul, could ensure that Tunisian courts disbursed the estate.

Gallian was well aware of just how malleable legal belonging could be. A Greek Catholic, born to a Piedmontese family in Istanbul and educated in Athens, Gallian had navigated multiple affiliations across the Mediterranean.[98] Gallian also knew that his superiors in the Sublime Porte preferred to make a stronger claim to sovereignty over Tunisia—another way to hopefully avoid colonization by a European power. The Ottoman authorities regularly asserted that Tunisians in Ottoman cities like Tripoli, Smyrna, and Istanbul were subjects of the sultan. This mirrored their treatment of Egyptians, who were considered to be Ottoman subjects despite the great degree of autonomy afforded the governor of Egypt since the rule of Muhammad 'Ali.[99] Why could the sultan not claim the same for a Tunisian who had died in Italy?

Despite Gallian's confidence in the genius of his plan, Husayn maintained a studied silence; he had no interest in arguing that Nissim had died an Ottoman subject.[100] This opposition might have come from the lawyers working for Husayn; one imagines Pierantoni explaining that the Italian courts would insist on treating Tunisia as an independent state. In this the lawyers and courts followed the imperial interests of Italy, which had its sights set on colonizing Tunisia just as much as France did. This approach also conformed to the tradition of international relations dating to the early modern period, when Italian city-states began signing treaties directly with the bey of Tunis. Or perhaps Husayn himself refused to pursue Gallian's strategy, knowing it would do little to change the basic contours of the case. Even if the court of appeal in Lucca determined that Nissim was an Ottoman subject, the judges would still apply Jewish law—since Jews in the Ottoman Empire were subject to halakhah for matters of inheritance, just like their coreligionists in Tunisia. There was little to gain by putting energy into proving that Nissim belonged to the Ottoman Empire.

Tunisia was part of the Ottoman Empire, and the bey of Tunis was appointed by the Ottoman sultan; it seems commonsensical to presume that a Tunisian who died in Italy might be considered Ottoman. And this is exactly the argument that was made about Husayn after his death some years later.[101] But only Gallian hoped to make the case for Nissim's Ottoman nationality. Legal belonging was determined not by a series of logical deductions but rather by the interests of governments and individuals. One had to construct a narrative about belonging in order for it to become a legal reality. And no one directly involved in the case wished to tell a story in which Nissim belonged to the Ottoman Empire.

Husayn and Pierantoni's case boiled down to the following: Nissim had possessed Tunisian nationality as a subject of the bey; Tunisian law—grounded in the shari'a—did not permit subjects to abandon their allegiance at will; and thus Nissim could not have renounced his Tunisian nationality and must have died a Tunisian.

Had they been debating about a man born a citizen of France, Germany, or the United States, these arguments might have been relatively straightforward. But Tunisia was a place where, according to the majority of Europeans, Jews were denied full rights; Pierantoni and Husayn had to prove that a Jew could be considered a Tunisian national in the first place. The very question betrayed the fragmented nature of citizenship; belonging was not a simple binary but rather a spectrum of bonds between individuals and the state. Nor was it enough to simply determine whether international law accorded everyone the universal right to expatriation; even if this were the case, most believed that universalism extended only to the limits of the Christian world. Pierantoni was a skilled lawyer, and he made the strongest case possible for Nissim's Tunisian nationality. But even his considerable skills could not steer clear of the fault lines running through ideal types of citizenship.

8

Rav Nissim the Jew

FROM THE VERY first weeks after Nissim's death, all of those with a stake in the estate—potential heirs and Tunisian government officials alike—chose one of two sides: either they argued that Nissim died an Italian citizen or that he remained a subject of the bey of Tunis until his death. But as the lawsuit progressed, the team of lawyers working for the Tunisian government came up with yet a third possibility. There was unanimous agreement that Article 8 of the Italian Civil Code required the application of Nissim's national law to his estate; the difficult part was determining his nationality. The team working on Husayn's behalf suggested that as a Jew, Nissim's national law was none other than Jewish law. Because Jews constituted a distinct nation, Nissim's nationality was identical to his faith.

The Italian lawyers employed by the Tunisian government were divided on whether to argue that Nissim had died a Jewish national. Galeotti, the celebrated Tuscan lawyer who had been working on the case since shortly after Nissim's death, took up this line of reasoning. He contended that *halakhah* satisfied the requirements for a "national law," as outlined in Article 8 of the Italian Civil Code. Should the judges reject the claim that Tunisian law prohibited voluntary expatriation, perhaps they would accept the idea that Jewish law followed even stateless Jews across the Mediterranean. Pierantoni, however, could not bring himself to assert that Jews constituted a distinct nationality; he maintained a studied silence on this aspect of his colleague's reasoning.

For others working on the Tunisian government's behalf, the argument in favor of Judaism as a nationality became the centerpiece of their case. The greatest proponent of this approach was Elmilik, the Algerian Jew whom Husayn hired to help wrangle rabbis and potential heirs. Though not a jurist, Elmilik was the only one with any expertise in matters Jewish among the "Livorno mission"—the group of Tunisian government officials charged with overseeing the Shamama lawsuit. Elmilik made a forceful argument that Nissim could have no nationality other than Judaism. In his eyes, allegiance to states like Italy and Tunisia was subsidiary to his true affiliation and true national law, which could only be halakhah.

Elmilik's insistence that Judaism was a nationality posed a particular challenge for Mancini. The great jurist had no choice but to reject the assertion, which went against his claim that Italian law must be applied to the estate. But for the father of the nationality principle, rejecting the claim that Judaism amounted to a nationality was no simple matter. He ultimately offered two reasons why Jewish law could not be Nissim's national law: first, Jews' distinctiveness did not amount to a separate nationality. Second, Jewish law was not a proper legal system but rather a confused jumble of customs and usages—and thus could not properly be considered a national law. Mancini had never written extensively about how Jews fit into the mosaic of European nations. He now found himself confronted with the gaps in his own vision of nationality as the foundation of both public and private international law.

The argument that Jewish law constituted the national law of Jews like Nissim exposed the slippage between nationality as a form of legal belonging and nationality as a form of identity. On the one hand, Jews and non-Jews in Europe ubiquitously referred to the Jewish people as a nation. There was little question that Judaism was *both* a religion and a nationality, in the ethnocultural sense of the term. Jews in the Ottoman Empire came to be referred to as a *millet*, which described the autonomous administration of religious communities, while also connoting ethnocultural nationality. But the entire structure of the Ottoman Empire was premised on an aggregate of multiple ethnicities, languages, and religions; the fact that Jews constituted yet another millet, yet another "nation," made them neither remarkable nor threatening.[1]

It was precisely the national dimension of Judaism that caused Jews so many problems during the age of nationalism. Long before Zionism or the establishment of the state of Israel, the perceived ethnocultural nationality of Jews opened them up to accusations of dual loyalty. If Jews constituted their own nationality, then they could never be fully French, British, or Italian. The specter of dual loyalty reared its ugly head in Italy just months after Nissim died, when Francesco Pasqualigo, a member of the Camera dei Deputati, opposed the nomination of Isacco Pesaro Maurogonato, a Jew from Venice, as minister of finance. Pasqualigo's opposition was all the more striking because he was a staunch liberal, not a clericalist on the Right—whence the usual suspects for rabid antisemitism came. Pasqualigo nonetheless argued that it was precisely the "dual nationality" (*doppia nazionalità*) of all Jews—who constituted a "state within the state"—that made Maurogonato unfit for such a high office. Maurogonato declined the appointment in any case, but Pasqualigo's opposition ignited a wide-ranging debate over whether Jews in Italy could ever be fully Italian.[2]

Even opponents of Pasqualigo—those who vociferously proclaimed Italian Jews as full members of the state—were tripped up by the question of Jews' status as a distinct nation. Marco Mortara, a rabbi in Mantua, Italy, published a refutation of Pasqualigo's logic in which he grappled with the status of Judaism as both a religion and an ethnicity. Mortara distinguished between "race" (*stirpe*) and "nation" (*nazione*). Jews undoubtedly constituted a race, as they shared a common lineage—a typical attitude among Jews and non-Jews, who followed racial scientists' distinction between the Jewish race and those of the peoples among whom they lived. But Mortara insisted that Jews did not constitute a nation, which was defined by "the union of men born in a region, speaking the same language—a union of people linked by civil, moral, and intellectual traditions."[3] Jews had originally come up with the idea of loyalty to a common nation. But their "Palestinian" patriotism had given way to the "love of the various homelands" in which they lived.[4]

Yet as Mancini's theories demonstrate, race and nation were not entirely indistinguishable—even for Italian liberals; race played a role in Mancini's concept of the nation, despite his resistance to reducing nationality to race.[5] And Mortara had to admit that Jews were distinctive, whether one named them a race, religion, or nationality. Nobody familiar with nationalism could fail to recognize the intimate connection between language and nation. Jews' use of Hebrew—their peculiar tongue that bound them together across polities—made them an obvious candidate for constituting their own nationality. The push to revive Hebrew among *maskilim*, Jewish thinkers influenced by the Enlightenment, only reinforced this sense of Jewish linguistic particularity.

The status of Jews as a distinctive nationality is usually associated with the history of Jewish nationalism: Zionism first and foremost, and to a lesser extent Bundism. These movements formally began in the last years of the 1890s; the first Zionist Congress and the formation of the General Jewish Labor Bund both took place in 1897. Neither movement, however, initiated the debate about Judaism as a nationality; on the contrary, both offered answers to a long-standing question. Theodor Herzl's pamphlet "The Jewish State," which launched him as the leader of the budding Zionist movement, presumed the "distinctive nationality of the Jews." The only question in Herzl's mind was whether this distinctive nationality would eventually die out through assimilation. He believed the extinction of Jewish nationality was not only undesirable but also impossible; "external enemies consolidate" Jews' separate nationality, whether they liked it or not. Given the reality of antisemitism, Jews would never be able to assimilate. The answer, then, was to constitute their own state, something other nations had managed despite being "poorer, less educated, and consequently weaker than ourselves."[6]

Historians have lavished attention on the history of Jewish nationalism. Yet they have made far less space for the history of Jewish nationality, especially as it intersected with state membership.[7] The Shamama case suggests that the debates around citizenship in the late nineteenth century included unanswered questions about the status of "nations" like the Jews—dispersed across states and empires, but undeniably members of a distinct ethnocultural group. Jews did not fit easily into nationalists' vision of the world, thus raising tricky questions about how linguistic, ethnic, racial, and religious nationality translated into legal nationality.

Elmilik was no stranger to the power of belonging. As an Algerian, he had long benefited from the right to French protection in Tunisia. During the early years of his work on the Shamama case, he mounted a campaign to secure French protection for his fellow Algerian Jews in Tunisia.[8] And since the Crémieux Decree granted Algerian Jews citizenship in 1870, Elmilik was a full citizen of France, with the same rights as any Frenchman born in Paris. Elmilik was clearly proud of being French; he was a founding member of La Persévérance, a Masonic lodge under the Grand Orient of France. Despite the avowed universalism of freemasonry, the lodge's members included only European Christians (mostly French and Italian) and Jews (overwhelmingly from the Grana community).[9] Once resident in Livorno, Elmilik made a point of sending his sons to study in France rather than offering them a much cheaper education locally. Perhaps as an apology for his Algerian origins, Elmilik aggressively adopted the trappings of European culture—hiring fine carriages for rides around town and buying tickets for his family to attend the theater.[10]

Yet in the context of the Shamama lawsuit, Elmilik was the in-house expert on all matters Jewish—emphasizing not his French citizenship, but his intimate knowledge of Judaism in North Africa. Faced with the task of arguing why Jewish law should apply to Shamama's estate, Elmilik explained that Jews had always considered themselves a nation. To prove this, Elmilik reached back into Jewish liturgy; Jews had referred to themselves as a nation (*'am* in Hebrew) since biblical times: "We call ourselves by the name 'the nation [*'am*] of God,' as is shown in our daily prayers, such as 'And what one nation in the earth is like thy people Israel?'" (1 Chronicles 17:21).[11] Elmilik also evoked Jewish history: "In Europe before Jews' emancipation, they called us 'the nation of Israel' [*'am yisrael*]. And the decrees of the Grand Duke of Tuscany concerning the Jews called us a nation. Even today, the gate of the Jewish cemetery in Livorno reads 'Cemetery of the Nation of the Jews' [*'am ha-yehudim*]."[12] For Elmilik, the antiquity of the term 'am (as in "the nation of Israel," *'am yisrael*) demonstrated that Jews and non-Jews had always considered the Jewish people to be a nation.

Much like his employer Husayn, Elmilik engaged in a process of translation—not just between Hebrew and Italian, but between old conceptions of what it meant to be Jewish, and new ways of thinking about nationhood and nationality. The literal translation of 'am as "nation" was hundreds of years old; the King James Bible, from 1611, generally translated 'am as "people," though in a few instances it was rendered as "nation."[13] But the early modern term "nation" and the nineteenth-century meaning of "nationality" were quite distinct. Needless to say, the author of First Chronicles did not have the nationality principle in mind when he wrote about Jews constituting an 'am. Nor did the translators of the King James Bible. The ways in which Jews thought of themselves as a collective was (and is) always evolving. For Elmilik's purposes, however, it was far more effective to draw a straight line from the Hebrew Bible to the meaning of nation in the 1870s.[14]

Elmilik was on somewhat firmer ground in arguing that non-Jews considered Jews to be a nation, at least during the ancien régime. He invoked Grand Duke Ferdinando di Medici, who issued the Livornine allowing Jews to settle in Livorno in the late sixteenth century. The Livornine did indeed refer to Jews as a nation, promising all members of the "Hebrew nation" that they would be free in Livorno. Other groups, including "Turks and Moors," were also designated as nations and similarly welcomed in Livorno.[15]

Yet Elmilik elided the differences between early modern understandings of "nations" and those of the late nineteenth century. In early modern Europe, "nation" generally referred to any group of foreigners that state authorities recognized as constituting a distinct and semiautonomous group.[16] The Jewish community in Livorno used the term "nation" (*nazione*) to refer to its self-government even as late as the early nineteenth century; a broadside printed in 1815 explains that the "national tax" (*diritto nazionale*) must be paid by Jews living in Livorno and by "foreign nationals" (*nazionali forestieri*), which in this case meant Jews who were "not domiciled" in Livorno.[17]

The meaning of nationality relevant to the Shamama case—as a term describing a legal bond between an individual and a state—only became widespread in the early nineteenth century.[18] Even so, Elmilik's collapse of "nation" as it appeared in the Livornine and nationality as it related to the Shamama case was not altogether outlandish. At least the "nation" of the Livornine was etymologically connected to the nationality referred to in Article 8 of the Italian Civil Code. And as we have seen, Jews were very much perceived as forming their own nationality in Europe—a distinctiveness that had premodern roots.

Elmilik grounded his argument for Jewish nationality in the legal autonomy historically afforded to Jews. He asserted that Judaism was a nationality precisely because Jews had almost always lived under the jurisdiction of Jewish law. This was why the national law of a Jew like Nissim was *halakhah*. Only recently had some Jews in Europe renounced "their original laws in submitting themselves to those of the country in which they reside." Today, Jews in France and Italy lived in "constitutional countries," as the French translation put it, where they had traded Jewish law for full civil equality. In Tunisia, however, Jews "still conserve their laws and traditions, and consider themselves a nation."[19] For a Jew living under Islamic rule, "his laws are those of Moses, which it is fitting to call the laws of the Nation of Israel [*'am yisrael*]. And thus the national law of Nissim Shamama is the law of the Nation of Israel [*mishpatei 'am yisrael*] since he and his ancestors are of African origin."[20] In distinguishing between constitutional and nonconstitutional states, Elmilik drew a bright red line across the Mediterranean. His division was not based on lineage or custom, which had long differentiated Ashkenazi from Sephardi Jews. What separated Jews in Europe from those in North Africa was their legal status and the extent of their judicial autonomy. Because Jews in Tunisia lived in a world where they were still under the jurisdiction of the "laws of Moses," this was their national law.

Elmilik pushed his argument for indelible Jewish difference even further, in a way that might seem surprising for a Francophile Jew. Not only was Jewish law the national law of Jews like Nissim, Elmilik contended; such a Jew could never really be either Tunisian or Italian. As a Jew from Tunisia, Nissim could only be of "Jewish nationality"—*nationalité israélite*, as the French translation had it.[21] The variations between the Hebrew and French versions are instructive; modern Hebrew, still a work in progress, had not yet found a stable vocabulary for questions of legal belonging. Elmilik used a familial metaphor to describe Nissim's nationality. A literal translation of Elmilik's Hebrew text reads, "[Nissim] was neither one of the children of Tunis nor one of the children of Italy; rather, he was one of the children of the nation of the Jews." As a Jewish national, Jewish law was Nissim's national law—in Elmilik's flowery Hebrew, "the crown of the Torah of Moses was placed on his head."[22] Despite differences in nuance, both the Hebrew and French were clear: according to Elmilik, Judaism was a nationality, one that followed Jews no matter which sovereign they served or how many decrees of naturalization they received.

In asserting that Nissim was "one of the children of the nation of the Jews," Elmilik unwittingly echoed the antisemitic claims of figures like Pasqualigo—that Jews constituted their own nation and hence could never be fully Italian. The potentially antisemitic overtones of Elmilik's argument must have bothered Pierantoni. Despite the obvious advantages of maintaining that the court should consider Jewish law to be Nissim's national law, Pierantoni kept silent on this point.

Pierantoni's politics were undoubtedly behind his refusal to argue for Judaism as a nationality. Since 1874, he had served in the Camera dei Deputati as a representative of the Left. Pierantoni was virulently anticlerical. He had even managed to write a treatise on international law that so offended the Catholic church, it was placed on the Index of Prohibited Books.[23] For many liberals in Italy, as elsewhere in Europe, the belief that Jews should have full rights of citizenship was a kind of creed.[24] This does not mean that there was no antisemitism on the Left; Pasqualigo is a perfect example of a liberal who feared the specter of Jews' "double nationality" infiltrating the government. But it seems safe to presume that Pierantoni was committed to the emancipation of Jews as a dimension of progress. It would have been impossible to square his political commitments with the argument that Jews constituted a separate nationality, and thus that the Italian Civil Code required the application of Jewish law as their national law.

These qualms were not entirely shared by Galeotti, Pierantoni's colleague on the Tunisian government's legal team. Like Mancini, Galeotti was a hero of the Risorgimento. Yet the Tuscan lawyer positioned himself on the opposite side of the political spectrum from his more famous colleagues. Galeotti got his start in the political world of unified Italy as the spokesperson for Bettino Ricasoli, a leader of the conservative branch of Risorgimento politicians who advocated a gradualist approach to unification and favored compromise with the Catholic church.[25] Elected to Parliament in 1860, Galeotti served in the government for the rest of his career, first as a member of the Camera dei Deputati and then in the senate starting in 1874. In his legal work and political positions, Galeotti sought a middle ground between the anticlericalism of Pierantoni (and Mancini for that matter) and the pope's intransigence. He believed that the Catholic church—though in need of reform—was a guarantor of political and social stability. Galeotti did not have the same allergy to religion harbored by so many of his anticlericalist colleagues; he contended that religious groups should be guaranteed freedom of expression—a position that made him popular with evangelical Christians and Jews alike.[26] Though occupying opposite sides of the political spectrum, Galeotti and Mancini could agree on their love of Italian operas, those "perennial curative unctions for national wounds."[27]

Galeotti did not go quite as far as Elmilik in claiming that Nissim's nationality was his Jewishness; the Tuscan lawyer's primary assertion remained that Nissim had died a Tunisian national. Nonetheless, Galeotti explained that if Nissim had expatriated himself, the judges would be wrong to presume that he had no national law. On the contrary, as a Jew, "the deceased belonged to a nation."[28] Jews may not currently possess a state, Galeotti reasoned. Yet they had conserved

> their character, their language, their religion, their laws, their customs, their traditions—in sum, all that constitutes a nationality except for territory and political existence; to the extent that, until recently, this people remained separate from the other peoples and nations among whom they lived; they were treated and considered like a people of a distinct race.[29]

In listing the aspects of Jews' distinctiveness—character, language, religion, law, custom, and race—Galeotti checked nearly all the boxes that had come to define nationality. Indeed, this list might have been lifted from Mancini's criteria for a nation, outlined in his 1851 breakout book.[30] But Galeotti also seemed to collapse the distinction between race and nation, explaining that Jews were always separate from "the other peoples and nations among whom they lived" because they belonged to a "distinct race." Unlike Rabbi Mortara—whose response to Pasqualigo asserted that Jews were a distinct race, but still part of the Italian nation—Galeotti remained relatively vague on just where race ended and nation began.

Galeotti nevertheless acknowledged that Jews lacked a "political existence," meaning a state. Only a state could elevate Jews to the rank of a full-fledged nation. But the absence of a nation-state was hardly reason to deny Jews a distinctive nationality. As Mancini himself had advocated in 1851, nationality—and *not* states—should be the basis for international law. And as champions of the Risorgimento on both the Right and Left could agree, Italy was a single nation before it was a unified state. Galeotti allowed that Article 8 of the Italian Civil Code "used the word 'nation' or 'nationality' in a political sense, and thus in a sense synonymous with a state." Still, he maintained, "one cannot rationally question that this word . . . also includes historical nationality, which is found in the highest degree among Jews." Echoing Elmilik, Galeotti appealed to the way in which Italians generally spoke of Jews: "in common parlance, they have even conserved the quality and the name of 'nation.'"[31] Nissim's Jewish nationality was to a certain degree self-evident, regardless of whether Jews lacked the political independence that normally constituted a nation.

Galeotti doubled down on the fact that Jews unquestionably possessed their own system of law. Being "an essential part of the religion" and therefore incumbent on all Jews, their law was "the most personal law imaginable."[32] Galeotti seconded Elmilik in distinguishing between the countries in which Jews had equal rights and those in which they lived under regimes of toleration. Jewish law was incumbent on all Jews who had not yet been emancipated. In places like Tunisia, their religious law had jurisdiction over their personal status, just like in premodern Europe. Galeotti reached back to the Justinian Code to show that the Roman legal tradition required Jews to observe Jewish law. Halakhah retained its authority over Jews even under the *ius commune*—the combination of Roman and canon law that served as the basis for the common law of much of Europe through the early modern period. Galeotti cited Marquardus de Susannis, a sixteenth-century authority on the status of Jews in the Papal States, who wrote that "Mosaic law" (*lex mosaica*) applied to Jews for matters such as inheritance.[33]

Despite Galeotti's willingness to argue that Judaism was a nationality, there is no evidence that he shared the prejudices of Italians like Pasqualigo. On the contrary, Galeotti's earlier publications advocated for incorporating Jews into the body politic, following France's model of absolute equality. He called for abolishing a "distinction that is currently repugnant to law in general and the spirit of our century."[34] But the perception of Jews as constituting a discreet nationality was hardly a hallmark of antisemitism; on the contrary, as we have seen, Jews widely embraced the self-understanding of belonging to a nation—if not yet with the intention of founding their own nation-state.

Nonetheless, it seems fair to assume that Galeotti was willing to make the case for a Jewish nationality in part because it aligned with his political commitments. For Pierantoni—a staunch leftist and opponent of religion in general—such an argument would have reeked of opportunism and hypocrisy. Galeotti, on the other hand, was believable as someone who recognized the ways in which Jews' legal distinctiveness might persist, in keeping with "the spirit of our century."

———

The assertion that Jews constituted a distinctive nationality with their own national law posed a problem for Mancini. The father of the nationality principle built his reputation on the idea that international law should concern itself with relations among nations rather than among states. Yet Mancini predicated his understanding of nationality on the presumption that in an ideal world, states would follow national contours. When he wrote *Nationality as the Foundation for the Law of Nations* in 1851, Italy was still largely an ambition, endorsed by a small kingdom (Piedmont) and some ragtag revolutionaries in red shirts. Mancini argued that nationality should be respected regardless of whether it was (yet) embodied in a state—offering proponents of the Risorgimento a foundation for their politics in international law. His ideas formed an early precursor to the right of self-determination—a principle that undergirds many forms of nationalism, including Zionism, to this day.[35]

But Mancini's vision of nationality never properly accounted for Jews. He could not possibly have intended his ideas to form the basis of a Jewish nationalist movement. And while religion featured prominently in his understanding of what made a nation (if not quite as prominently as race or language), the religion that Mancini had in mind was much like that envisioned by French Republicans: a private affair that should be properly sequestered from public life.[36]

Jews, of course, stubbornly refused to conform to these categories. They were more than just a religion; they constituted a race with their own language and even their own legal tradition. Mancini admitted that Jews had conserved not only their faith but were conscious of belonging to a separate race too; they possessed a "physiognomy" that was distinct from their gentile neighbors. It was this isolation that produced the "hatred and religious intolerance" found in both Christianity and Islam, and caused Jews to be deprived of political and civil rights across the globe.[37] In Mancini's eyes, Jews' distinctiveness gave them the "full liberty to change domicile and nationality, qua Jews"—a polite way of saying "rootless cosmopolitans" avant la lettre.[38]

Yet Mancini wholly shared Pierantoni's convictions about the importance of incorporating Jews into unified Italy as full and equal citizens. If Italy was the paragon of the new nation-state—a state that matched the nationality of its inhabitants—then Italian Jews could not belong to a distinct nationality: they, too, must be fully Italian, just like Catholics and Protestants. And Mancini walked the walk when it came to defending Jews' rights. In 1871, he worked pro bono to defend a Jewish man accused of murdering his Christian servant in Florence. The defendant was Momolo Mortara, tragic father of Edgardo Mortara—a Jewish boy whose nursemaid claimed to have baptized him, and whom papal authorities sequestered from his family in 1858 and raised as a Catholic. Mancini argued for Momolo's innocence in large part by observing that his accusers harbored antisemitic prejudices; it was this antisemitism—not any actual evidence of Momolo's guilt—that fueled their unfounded suspicions. Mancini's powers of persuasion triumphed and Momolo was acquitted of the terrible charge.[39]

How, then, could Mancini remain true to his commitments regarding nationality while also denying the existence of a separate Jewish nation? The answer he produced drew a distinction between nationality in a general sense, and the legal meaning of the term. A group of people commonly thought of as a nation might nonetheless lack "a true nationality that is politically constituted and recognized, which allows them the protection of a personal law emanating from a national sovereign to whom they are subject." People coming from "the interior regions of Africa," or tribespeople from India or Oceanica, did not have a national law; this is simply because they were not "citizens of a foreign state that can cover them with the protective shadow of its law." Jews were in a similar position; although they possessed a state in antiquity, their political existence ended hundreds of years ago. Instead, "the Jewish people were dispersed among all the other nations of Europe, and ceased to form a political aggregate under a true and national sovereignty, from which a law to govern them would emanate." Jews only constituted an historical nation, not an extant one; "the Jewish nation, in the true sense of the term, ceased to exist centuries ago."[40]

In doubling down on the need for a state to constitute a true nationality—a state capable of promulgating a true national law—Mancini made something of an about-face from his earlier position on the link between state and nation. In 1851, he had argued that nationality should be respected regardless of whether it was already embodied in a state. In short, nationality, and not states, should constitute the "foundation for the law of nations." This was crucial for the Italian nationalist movement, predicated as it was on the existence of a nation not yet united into a single state. For Mancini, as for many of his contemporaries, the state was an "artificial and arbitrary subject," whereas the nation was "natural and necessary."[41]

Mancini's privileging of state over nation in the Shamama case should not be perceived as pure opportunism but rather as a reflection of the evolution of his theories. During a speech in the Camera dei Deputati in 1865, he admitted that a nation was "an aggregation of people formed in a state"; this was, it seems, a capitulation to those who said that nations were too vague a foundation on which to build the science of international law.[42] Mancini responded to his critics at greater length in his inaugural lecture at the University of Rome in 1872, conceding that states did not always match nations. The reality of international relations thus meant that a state often represented multiple nationalities. He nevertheless continued to insist that nationality existed at a more foundational level of law than did the state.[43] Mancini dedicated himself to the principle of nationality as an ideal that should pervade relations not only among states but also among all humanity. Yet he also lived in a world where nations struggled against empires and where regions were claimed by two nations at the same time—such as Nice, part of France but full of Italian speakers, or Alsace, recently annexed to Germany but still coveted by France. Even the great Mancini faced the limits of his own idealism.

In hindsight, the triumph of state over nation in international law seems foreordained. But the relationship between nation and state began to flip only in the 1870s; increasingly, jurists premised nationality on states. Critics of Mancini's 1851 views grew in number until they formed a chorus; both in Italy and elsewhere in Europe, scholars of international law pointed to the state as the only possible locus of rights.[44] The statists won a decisive victory; today, even the briefest of internet searches reveals the presumption that international law regulates interactions among existing states, not potential ones. But no one involved in the Shamama case could have known this at the time. Galeotti's argument was hardly preposterous; he and Mancini agreed that Jews had all the qualities of a true nation *except* a territorial state. The plausibility of considering Jews to be a nation was precisely what made the case so tricky for a nationalist like Mancini.

Mancini's opposition to applying Jewish law stemmed not only from his understanding of nationality; even were Jews a true nation, he claimed, Jewish law could not possibly fulfill the criteria implied by the Italian Civil Code. Mancini had helped to draft Article 8, which asked jurists to apply a person's "national law" in matters of inheritance; now he maintained that the Italian Civil Code made certain presumptions about what might constitute a national law. Jewish law fell short of a true "national law" due to its premodern nature: it lacked the rational organization of a modern legal system; Jewish courts' jurisdiction was not true sovereignty but rather a privilege granted at the whim of the sovereign; and as a religious law, halakhah threatened "public order" in Italy, a secular state. Demonstrating the nonmodernity of Jewish law gave Mancini a powerful argument in favor of his clients: if Jewish law did not fulfill the criteria required by the Italian Civil Code, then the court had no choice but to apply Italian law and thus uphold the will. Beyond the case at hand, Mancini's assertions about Jewish law demonstrated the extent to which Europeans had come to view law and religion as reflections of progress and civilization.[45]

In Mancini's eyes, Jewish law lacked the rationality and systematization that characterized any legal system worthy of the name. It was hard enough for Italian judges to be asked to apply foreign law to foreign nationals when those laws were "written and codified, and might be read, translated, and interpreted." But Jewish law, Mancini objected, was composed of contradictory "customs and opinions." "It seems quite obvious to us that nonwritten law, mere practices, and customary traditions, especially when they are not certain or recognized—indeed, when they provide fodder to vivid and irreconcilable controversies over centuries—cannot rationally form the object of Article 8."[46] Mancini explained that a bunch of rules could not be called law unless they were organized into a clear system; undoubtedly he had the model of the Napoleonic Code in mind—which Italy had emulated—as the highest ideal of rationalized law. The Talmud, for Mancini, was about as far from true law as one could get: a cacophony of opinions only rarely settled in the text itself, giving way to legal disputes that lasted "centuries."

According to Mancini, Jewish law was deficient because it had followed the same evolution as Jewish nationality; when Jews possessed their own sovereign state, their law was "civil and personal." Once Jews scattered across the Diaspora, however, their law was reduced to "religious obligations and relationships."[47] Drawing on triumphalist metaphors usually associated with Christianity's victory over Judaism, Mancini explained that "the mutilated vestiges [of Jewish law] no longer constitute a judicial institution, nor a systematic set of rules; they are the languid and distant echo of a remote past during which these existed, but that today . . . are an historical memory."[48] Jewish law had ceased to be a "judicial institution," one that necessarily evolved with the times. What remained of halakhah was a vestige of its former self—a shadow of law, not actual law. Only a few religious remnants of what had once been a full-fledged legal system persisted; these were "simple traditions and customs dependent on religious belief, and lacking the necessary characteristics of a true and proper law, even less those of a national law."[49] There was simply no way to apply halakhah as Nissim's national law.

The inherent deficiencies of Jewish law were compounded by the limitations on Jews' judicial autonomy. Mancini argued that Jews' ability to rule according to Jewish law had never exempted them from the laws of the states in which they lived. On the contrary, Jews in Europe had always been subject to ius commune, the common law applicable to all subjects of a state since Roman times. Mancini reached back to the Justinian Code, which described Jews as living "under the common Roman law" and required them to "appear in court according to the usual custom." Any jurisdiction that Jews exercised was merely a privilege (*privilegio*)—"precious or odious exceptions to the general law of a nation and a state"—which should not be confused with "national law."[50] These privileges did not amount to true "judicial autonomy." Sovereigns in Europe gave Jews special "indulgences" to apply their own laws in a limited number of areas, including inheritance, marriage, divorce, and personal status. Jews remained "subject to the common law, that is, the general, territorial law in which they are domiciled."[51] Mancini even reached beyond his area of expertise, contending that Muslim rulers similarly granted Jews only "privileges," not true autonomy. The privileges accorded to Tunisian Jews were outlined in the Qānūn al-Dawla, which specified that Muslim courts lacked jurisdiction over Jews regarding marriage, adoption, inheritance, wills, and other matters pertaining to their personal status.[52] Even the Ottoman *hatt-ı hümayun* of 1856—which allowed non-Muslims to continue adjudicating inheritance according to their religious laws—conceded this as a privilege.[53]

Mancini's classification of Jewish legal autonomy as a privilege was more than mere semantics. If the application of Jewish law was a favor granted by the sovereign, it could not transcend political borders like national law. Privileges granted to Jews were "strictly limited to the territory of the granting sovereign."[54] According to the nationality principle, national law should be applied to the private life of individuals wherever they may be. But the privilege to apply Jewish law was given at the whim of the sovereign and thus had force only within the sovereign's jurisdiction. Mancini dismissed the idea that Jewish law should have the same kind of transnational power as Italian law.

In arguing that Jews did not have true judicial autonomy and were always subject to ius commune, Mancini offered a simplified approach to a complex legal landscape. Some well-known jurists, including Bartolo da Sassoferrato (d. 1357) and de Susannis (d. 1578), author of *De iudaeis*, agreed that Jews were citizens and therefore under ius commune. Others, including Giovanni Battista de Luca (d. 1683), renowned jurist of the Roman court, took the opposite view.[55] The diversity among theorists was reflected in the distinct legal statuses imposed on Jews in different parts of the Italian Peninsula. Jews in the Papal States were increasingly subject to ius commune over the course of the seventeenth century. In 1621, the pope obligated Jews to bring all disputes—even intra-Jewish civil disputes—to state courts, where they would be adjudicated according to ius commune.[56] Yet in Tuscany, the Jews of Livorno had famously been granted considerable autonomy, which they conserved into the nineteenth century. Until unification, the Jewish court of the Massari—presided over by a group of laymen—had jurisdiction over all intra-Jewish civil cases; the Jewish communal authorities also had the power to grant Livornese citizenship to Jewish immigrants who moved to the port city.[57]

In equating the status of Jews in Tunisia to premodern Italy, Mancini similarly smoothed over significant differences in the judicial status of non-Muslims under Islamic rule. The Islamic world had no equivalent of ius commune, and Muslim jurists had never questioned the legitimacy of Jewish courts for intra-Jewish civil matters. The only point of contention concerned what to do if dhimmīs brought intracommunal cases to a shariʿa court. Jurists debated various responses: Should such litigants be sent back to their own communal courts? Should the qadi apply Islamic law or the dhimmīs' own law? But the presumption was that this question only mattered in instances in which non-Muslims chose Islamic law; otherwise, they were under the jurisdiction of their own courts for nearly all matters that did not involve Muslims—serious crimes being the only exception.[58] Nor did Muslim sovereigns allow Jews to administer their own courts and apply their own laws as a privilege; on the contrary, this was almost universally understood as part of the pact of dhimma. The right of dhimmīs to apply their own law sprang not from the generosity of the sovereign, as Mancini implied, but instead from the Islamic legal tradition.[59]

Ultimately, Mancini's objections to the application of Jewish law ran even deeper than the problematic nature of the law itself or the limitations on Jews' judicial autonomy. Mancini saw Jewish law as a threat to the very principles of religious freedom on which the Italian nation-state was built. Applying Jewish law to foreign Jews would force them to conform to Judaism, whether they wanted to or not; this was an attack on the "absolute liberty of conscience . . . which, in our civil and constitutional system, constitutes one of the fundamental principles of public order and morality."[60] Mancini made repeated references to the threat that Jewish law posed to "public order" in Italy, drawing on his broader conception of the limitations that should be placed on the nationality principle in private international law. The application of a foreigner's national law must always be tempered by the refusal to apply laws that would harm "public order and public morality"—a clause he inserted into the Italian Civil Code just after the ones regulating private international law.[61] In an article drafted for the Institute of International Law, Mancini explained that foreign laws permitting slavery or polygamy could not be tolerated. These abominations went against a universalized conception of morality, and Italian courts must not admit them under any circumstances.[62] Unsurprisingly, Mancini remained silent about Nissim's own polygamous marriages, including the fact that he was married to two women when he obtained his decree of naturalization in 1866. But Mancini's fears of applying Jewish law evoked the specter of immoral practices threatening to infiltrate Italy. Whether or not halakhah was a national law, then, it could not possibly be allowed to corrupt the moral foundation of Italian civil society.

In making the case for why halakhah could not be Nissim's national law, Mancini declared Jewish law to be a vestige of a bygone order—the prolongation of the premodern into modernity. His approach echoed a popular chronology of modernization in which western Europe invented ideas like equality, while more backward regions like the Middle East and North Africa remained stuck in the medieval, hierarchical past.[63] The states that accommodated the application of Jewish law among Jews adhered to a model superseded by the nation-state. Mancini's vision of Jews implicitly derided the kind of equality proposed in Tunisia and the Ottoman Empire, where Jews were declared "equal before the law," but nonetheless preserved considerable judicial autonomy. Like so many of his contemporaries in the West, Mancini insisted that the European model of modernity was the only proper way to organize the world—legally, religiously, and politically.

Mancini's claims forced his opponents to prove that Jewish law did meet the criteria of a modern legal system. For Elmilik, the status of halakhah as a proper law was so obvious, so undeniable, he did not even bother arguing for it. Husayn sidestepped Mancini's dismissal of halakhah as mere "customs." Instead, he doubled down on his vision of equality through difference: it would be wrong to say that Jewish law is not a national law because it does not apply to everyone in Tunisia. Plenty of European states had laws that regulated the lives of only one group of people; the military penal code of Italy, for instance, was a state law, despite only applying to soldiers. If the military penal code was a national law for Italian soldiers, then halakhah should be a national law for Tunisian Jews.[64]

It was up to Galeotti—the sole Italian lawyer willing to maintain that Judaism was a nationality—to convince the judges that Jewish law was indeed a national law. In so doing, Galeotti selectively addressed Mancini's arguments; he ignored his opponent's objections that Jewish law was just a bunch of customs rather than a real law. He said nothing about the potential hazard posed by Jewish law to Italian public morality. Instead, he limited his attacks to Mancini's assertion that Jewish legal autonomy was a privilege. Galeotti made the case that Jews' ability to administer their own courts, which applied their own laws, was a right in both Tunisia and Europe. As such, halakhah could travel across political borders just like any other national law.

In explaining the status of Jewish law in Tunisia, Galeotti pointed to the same article of the Qānūn al-Dawla as Mancini. But where Mancini found proof that Jewish law was granted as a privilege, Galeotti saw evidence of a right. "The use of religious law for Jews is not the effect of mere tolerance," he argued, "it is the effect of a positive legal disposition, which is Article 29 of the Qānūn."[65] In other words, clear legislation prescribed legal autonomy for Tunisian Jews. This had nothing to do with the bey's grace; it was as much of a right as those enshrined in Italy's constitution.

As for the ius commune, Galeotti cited the same passage by de Susannis that Mancini quoted; again he drew opposite conclusions. De Susannis asserted that Jews were considered "not only of the Roman people, but that they were called citizens of the place they lived."[66] For Mancini, this was proof that Jews were under ius commune and thus halakhah could not be considered a true law. For Galeotti, on the other hand, de Susannis's statement offered evidence that Jews were citizens—and hence not tolerated by the ruler but rather full members of the state. Because of their distinctive characteristics, Jews were allowed to live under the jurisdiction of their national law. This amounted to the kind of federalism that characterized the United States or Switzerland, where states had distinct laws for different groups of citizens.[67]

To demonstrate that modern, western states recognized the validity of Jewish law, Galeotti turned to France—that paragon of enlightenment liberalism. Even France admitted the applicability of Jewish law for its Algerian Jewish subjects before the Crémieux Decree—proof, according to Galeotti, that modern European states acknowledged the jurisdiction of Jewish law under certain circumstances. "Despite the unity of legislation for people of French origin," the government upheld "the personal laws [of] the new Muslim and Jewish citizens [*sic*] of Algeria."[68] In support of his position, Galeotti cited a somewhat obscure case regarding the estate of Abraham Senior (or Señor), an Algerian Jew who died in Jerusalem in 1849.[69] Much like the Shamama lawsuit, Senior's heirs contested his will. The French courts confirmed that the will must be adjudicated according to Jewish law and deemed it valid according to "the laws of the Jews in Jerusalem."[70] "The examination of Jewish law," Galeotti insisted, "is a true and proper question of law"—one the Italian courts could and indeed must undertake.[71]

Nonetheless, Galeotti glossed over the complexity of the status of Jewish law in Algeria. Before 1870, Jews remained under the jurisdiction of Jewish law for most private matters; the Senior case was one of a number that French courts of appeal heard concerning the application of Jewish law.[72] But since the Crémieux Decree turned them into citizens, Algerian Jews were under French law for all matters public and private. Galeotti's assertion that the French government recognized the "personal laws" of the "Jewish citizens of Algeria" was outdated, perhaps strategically so. Still, in evoking France, the epitome of liberalism on which Italy had modeled much of its legal and political establishment, Galeotti hoped to allay any doubts that an Italian court was justified in applying Jewish law.

Once again, Galeotti's political convictions undergirded his persuasion that Jewish law could be compatible with modernity. His personal belief in the central role that Catholicism was destined to play in modern Italy translated into a broader appreciation for the continued relevance of religion. This ostensibly conservative perspective allowed him to see Jewish law not as a vestige of premodernity but instead as a right that might be accorded to Jews even in the modern age.

The glare of hindsight makes it tempting to side with Mancini's objections. It seems self-evident that Article 8 presumed the existence of a state-sanctioned national law; Judaism, however, could not be a full-fledged nationality in the absence of a state. It is equally tempting to dismiss Elmilik and Galeotti's arguments that Judaism was a nationality as the opportunism of interested parties. Yet it is precisely the perspective of subsequent decades that we must avoid, lest we impose a consensus on the meaning of nationality where there was none.

The cacophony of voices in the Shamama case reflected the diversity of opinions on both sides of the Mediterranean in the late nineteenth century. Antisemites could use the label of nationality as a weapon—adding firepower to the argument that innate Jewish difference made emancipation foolish at best and dangerous at worst. But Judaism as a nationality could also justify a different model of tolerance, as Husayn contended. In his inimitable prose, Husayn maintained that only in places like Tunisia was true devotion to God's commandments possible for Jews. He explained that a Jew like Nissim, who was devoted "to the minutiae of religious practice," would never abandon "the Orient, where Jews live subject to the laws of Moses." Such a pious Jew could not permanently settle in Europe, "where the Talmud is relegated to the library, among old books and dusty scrolls."[73] In requiring the abandonment of religiosity, Husayn explained, European modernity was not superior; in fact, this sort of absolute equality denied Jews their religious rights.

There was no more consensus among Jews about whether Judaism should be considered a full-fledged nationality. Nor did the rise of Zionism settle matters. If anything, the growing Jewish nationalist movement was itself divided and often deliberately vague concerning just what shape the Jewish return to Palestine should take. A national homeland? A semiautonomous territory under the auspices of the Ottoman or later British Empire? A full-fledged state?[74] Not to mention Jewish critics of Zionism, who grew more vocal as the new movement gained strength: Bundists, who argued that Jewish nationalism should be secular, socialist, and rooted in the places Jews already lived; the leaders of the Alliance Israélite Universelle, assimilationists who believed in the possibility of homologizing Jews to European bourgeois culture and, eventually, citizenship; or Jewish Ottomanists, who contended that the Ottoman

Empire afforded Jews the most complete liberty and that Jews should thank their benefactors by dedicating themselves to patriotic pursuits.[75]

If Mancini had lived to read about the First Zionist Congress, one wonders what he would have thought about Zionism. Would he have recognized Zionism as a nationalist movement trying to rectify the historical anomaly of a nation without a state? Or would he have doubled down on his insistence that Jews did not constitute a true nationality—and thus did not merit a nation-state of their own? Either answer seems plausible—not because we lack a purchase on Mancini's ideas, but because Jews were the proverbial square peg that refused to fit into the round hole of nationality. Mancini was not the only one who struggled to understand Jews' belonging in an age of nationalism; Jews and Christians, antisemites and philosemites, conservatives and liberals, all agreed that Jews' distinctiveness sat uncomfortably with emerging understandings of nationality.

9

Lucca to Florence (1880–83)

IN THE FIRST DAYS of 1880, a steady trickle of lawyers, aspiring heirs, and government employees alighted on the quays of the train station in Lucca. They came for the hearings in *Shamama v. Shamama*, the appeal of the ruling handed down in Livorno two years earlier. Mancini and Pierantoni arrived from Rome—though instead of working together, they stood on opposite sides of the courtroom. No fewer than thirty-four lawyers joined them. So did Husayn, Elmilik, Joseph, Nathan, Qā'id Momo, and Shlomo Shamama, the nephew and heir of Nissim's widow Mas'uda. Only 'Aziza and Moses were absent; they preferred to stay holed up in the palazzo in Livorno, sending an agent in their stead. One imagines that after seven years of fighting over their uncle's estate, 'Aziza and Moses could not stand to face their contentious relatives once again.[1]

The hearings for *Shamama v. Shamama* began on January 7, with Pierantoni taking the floor first. He spoke for hours, only stopping when the judge, "seeing that the hour was late," adjourned the proceedings until the next morning. Pierantoni continued his oral arguments through the entire next day. Not to be outdone, Mancini spoke for two full days. With such an all-star cast of professors and lawyers—neither profession known for brevity—it took until January 16 for the oral arguments to wrap up.[2]

When the Luccan judges issue their ruling—months later, as was typical—they upheld the Livornese court's verdict, proclaiming that Nissim had died stateless and Italian law applied to his estate. Accordingly, his will was held to be valid. The judges determined that Nissim had renounced his Tunisian nationality, which he was permitted to do based on the "natural right" of expatriation. Yet Nissim had failed to fulfill the requirements of the royal naturalization decree. Rejecting Mancini's claim that Nissim was an oriundo italiano, the judges ruled that the late qā'id never acquired Italian citizenship.[3] They summarily dismissed the idea that Jewish law might be Nissim's national law; Article 8 intended "only the case of an individual holding political nationality, meaning someone belonging to a group of people forming a state."[4]

The Tunisian mission in Livorno received the news of the Lucca ruling with resignation. Husayn had predicted the verdict would validate the will since Carlo Cesarini, the president of the court of appeal of Lucca, was "against us."[5] He immediately wrote to Mustafa Ibn Isma'il, the bey's new prime minister; the two were hardly allies, but Husayn was committed to fulfilling his duty as the government's representative.[6] He asked Ibn Isma'il to write directly to the Italian minister of foreign affairs to complain that the Lucca court's sentence violated the treaties signed between Tunisia and Italy. Husayn also passed along a rumor that Cesarini "only obtained a majority in favor of his sentence by threatening some of his colleagues."[7] By this time, however, Husayn was already out of favor in the Bardo; his suggestions were ignored.

The Lucca ruling came as developments on both sides of the Mediterranean transformed the nature of the Shamama case. Shortly after the court of appeal's verdict, a number of key actors stepped down or were pushed out: Mancini and Pierantoni quit, and Husayn was replaced. New players took center stage, including the banker who had helped ruin Tunisia's finances, a Livornese Jew who grew up in Tunis, a professor of Jewish studies, and a rabbi known for his mystical inclinations. The legal questions that most preoccupied either side also shifted—from a laser focus on nationality to the status of Nissim's will under Jewish law. Exactly a year after the Luccan court of appeal's verdict, France occupied Tunisia and established a protectorate over the Ottoman province. By the time the court of appeal in Florence delivered the final ruling—a decade after Nissim died—the landscape of the lawsuit had become almost unrecognizable.

The news from Lucca undoubtedly pleased 'Aziza and Moses. Moses sent a telegram to Mancini that very day to "announce our victory in the case of the Shamama will."[8] He followed up with a letter full of thanks: "I am endlessly grateful for all you did for my case in Lucca. I am perfectly cognizant of the zeal and goodwill that you put into this case."[9]

Shortly after the good tidings arrived from Lucca, Mancini received another telegram of congratulations. "Very happy about result from Lucca: I renew our thanks: assurance of our best sentiments."[10] This missive was signed by none other than d'Erlanger, the French banker of German Jewish origin who had loaned millions to Tunisia back in 1863; the same banker with whom Nissim had negotiated for another loan when he arrived in Paris the following year. D'Erlanger sent a longer letter to Mancini ten days later: "I know that if right triumphed in Lucca, it was thanks to your tremendous work . . . thanks to the brilliant and solid eloquence that you put in service of the good cause."[11] D'Erlanger's notes of thanks reflected a new phase of the Shamama case—one that began behind closed doors long before the hearings in Lucca.

There is nothing like a large estate to cause family members to argue, and the Shamama heirs were no exception; they had been bickering about finances since shortly after Nissim's death. The cash flow problems only intensified as the months and then years dragged on. 'Aziza and Moses had lived off their uncle's largesse after leaving Tunis in 1864; they had no intention of switching to a more modest lifestyle once Nissim was dead—especially as they expected to inherit such a large sum. Though they had to share the palazzo with a growing number of relatives, they nonetheless kept up appearances.

Nathan and Joseph had dropped everything in Tunis to pursue their shares of the estate in Livorno. Though we know little about their financial situation before arriving in Tuscany, there is evidence that they adopted a rather lavish existence once settled in their new home. The year the Lucca verdict was issued, Joseph kept no less than two private carriages—one open and one closed; he employed four domestic servants—two men and two women.[12] Joseph announced his standing in the community through his participation in Livorno's synagogue; in 1876, he held the Torah scroll on Shemini Atzeret, and in 1878 he led the first *hakafah* (circumambulation) on Simḥat Torah—both honors reserved for those able to offer generous donations to the Jewish communal coffers.[13] Joseph's family was also growing; his wife, Daya, gave birth to their son Salvatore just a few months after settling in Italy. She became pregnant again almost immediately and gave birth to Elia the following year. Eventually, Joseph moved his wife and eight children out of the Shamama palazzo and into his own villa down the street, adding to his already considerable expenses.[14]

Nathan arrived in Livorno at the age of twenty, still a bachelor. Three years later—on January 5, 1876, which corresponded to the seventh of the Hebrew month of Tevet—Nathan married Corinna Coen Salmon, a local woman five years his junior. Corinna was a beauty and scion of Livorno's Jewish elite. Her father, Saul Coen Salmon, had moved to Livorno from Algeria, established himself as a banker, and married a local woman from the storied Cassuto family (from which some of the lawyers working on the Shamama case hailed).[15] Salmon retained his French nationality and hence his children were born French. But when Corinna married Nathan, Italian law dictated that she automatically took her husband's citizenship and thus became Tunisian—at which her portrait subtly hints in the coat of arms on the wall behind her featuring a crescent moon and star, and the crescent moon pin atop her voluminous hair. Corinna and Nathan's first child, Emily, was born in 1879; Inès and Leonetto followed soon thereafter. By 1880, Nathan also had quite the household to maintain; not to be outdone by his uncle Joseph, he kept four carriages and six servants.[16] Nathan, too, donated to the synagogue and was rewarded with ritual honors: holding the Torah scroll on Sukkot in 1877, and opening the ark on the seventh day of Passover in 1878.[17]

The rebuke that Livornese Jews used to chastise those putting on airs—"you are not a Shamama!"—might originally have referred to the millionaire Nissim. But his potential heirs were doing an excellent job of keeping up the family reputation for lavish living, whether or not they could afford it—which, of course, they could not.

The solution to their cash shortage appeared quite simple: find a way to get an advance on future shares of Nissim's estate. Nathan began borrowing against his expected inheritance immediately after his great-uncle's death. Just before leaving Tunis for Livorno, he asked Abraham Gozlan, Joseph's father-in-law, for a loan of 100,000 francs; this was guaranteed by his future share in the estate.[18] But as the lawsuit dragged on—and as the lawyers' fees added up considerably—Nathan ran out of money. He was the first to cede his rights to the estate. On June 7, 1876, five months after marrying Corinna, Nathan signed a contract with Husayn; he agreed to give up his share of the inheritance in exchange for a flat sum of 2 million francs, to be paid in installments of 50,000 francs twice a year.[19] In exchange, Nathan agreed to support the government's efforts to have the will nullified, although the contract specified that the government would pay him whichever way the courts ruled. Nonetheless, Nathan settled for far less than his expected share: even if he got only a quarter of the estate, estimates predicted he would inherit nearly 7 million francs. The newlywed paid dearly for cash when he needed it.

'Aziza and Moses were as desperate as Nathan. By 1877, 'Aziza had signed over nearly half her share of the inheritance to two bankers in France, Michel Zirio and Adolphe Peridon.[20] In exchange, she would receive a payment of 250,000 francs each semester, for a total of about 4 million francs, instead of the 6.75 million she would otherwise have received were the will declared valid. It was a better deal than Nathan's, but still a significant loss.

FIGURE 9.1. Corinna Shamama, née Salmon, by Vittorio Matteo Corcos, 1893

From the comfort of his lavish home in London, to which he had relocated in 1870, d'Erlanger smelled opportunity. He knew Nissim from Paris and must have witnessed the man's opulence firsthand. In the winter of 1878, d'Erlanger's representative came to Livorno to negotiate a contract with 'Aziza. D'Erlanger offered to pay all of 'Aziza's debts to Zirio and Peridon along with 5 percent interest on her share of the inheritance until the Shamama dispute was settled. 'Aziza would also receive a lump sum of 2.75 million francs—all in exchange for signing over her share of the inheritance to d'Erlanger.[21] The banker offered a nearly identical contract for the portion of the estate promised to 'Aziza's son, Nissim Jr.—now fourteen years old.[22] Having signed these contracts, d'Erlanger acquired a direct interest in proving that Nissim's will was valid.

Persuading 'Aziza and Moses to sign over most of their family's rights to the estate was only the first step of d'Erlanger's plan. In order to turn a real profit, the banker needed to convince the other potential heirs to do the same thing. Nathan was a lost cause; he had already signed his rights over to the Tunisian government. So d'Erlanger went after Joseph—the only testamentary heir who had so far held out and refused to sign away his future inheritance. D'Erlanger's powers of persuasion proved irresistible, and Joseph finally gave in. With his growing family to consider, Joseph negotiated for every advantage he could find. He demanded that he be allowed to continue to pursue the nullity of Nissim's will—in which case he would be awarded the difference between the fourth he was allotted in the testament and the third he would get according to the biblical laws of inheritance.[23]

By 1879, d'Erlanger had bought up three-fourths of the estate if Nissim's will were upheld. If the estate was distributed according to Jewish law, however, d'Erlanger would collect only one-third. Hence his elation when Mancini's legal team prevailed in Lucca; d'Erlanger had thrown his considerable resources behind proving the will's validity. The next step was to convince the Tunisian government to cede its interests in the estate—which would account for almost all the money at stake (Nathan's share; a quarter of Momo's share, should the will be invalidated; and any debts the government claimed it was owed by Nissim). The only one standing in d'Erlanger's way was Husayn.

D'Erlanger was a formidable businessman; he had vast reserves of ready cash, with which he persuaded the various Shamama heirs to sign away their rights. But try as he might, d'Erlanger failed to convince Husayn to cede the government's claims. Husayn could not stomach putting more gold in the coffers of the man whom he perceived as responsible for sending Tunisia down the road to bankruptcy. He simply refused to negotiate with the slick banker.

Husayn, however, held no principled objection to the idea of finding a buyer for the government's claims on the estate. On the contrary, by the time of the Lucca ruling, he had already been looking to sell the Tunisian government's claims on Nissim's wealth for some years. The obvious solution to the endless lawsuit and mounting legal costs was to find some banker willing to buy out the government—other than d'Erlanger, of course. Husayn began sounding out investors soon after the Livorno court's ruling in fall 1877; at this point, he was confident that the Lucca court would rule in the government's favor and was advised against settling for less than eight million francs.[24] By December 1878, Husayn was negotiating with a French bank based in Marseille, the Société Marseillaise de Crédit, which offered the Tunisian government six million francs.[25] The contract fell through when the bank suddenly "had doubts about the examination of the government's accounts" and therefore about just how much money it stood to make on the deal.[26] Husayn did not give up. In the summer of 1879, he convinced Mustafa to send him a mandate granting him the authority to cede the government's claims on Nissim's estate.[27]

In early November, Husayn boarded a train for Rome. Once there, he signed a contract with François Mayer, who ostensibly represented an international group of bankers. On the basis of the mandate sent to him over the summer, Husayn agreed to cede all the Tunisian government's claims on the Shamama estate in return for six million francs. The agreement, however, would remain secret and the Tunisian government would continue to "figure in the lawsuit" over the succession; similarly, the bey would continue to appoint an agent in Livorno "like the one currently responsible for the lawsuit." In other words, the contract made it clear that Husayn would act as if the government still intended to pursue its claims on the estate.[28] Three days later, Husayn wrote to Ibn Isma'il with the good news that he had signed away the government's rights. He reported that Mayer represented a group of six bankers, all of whom insisted on secrecy; "bankers who openly buy [shares in] disputed lawsuits are viewed by the public with disdain." Husayn sent his letter—along with a copy of the contract in the original Italian, "not having time to translate it into Arabic"—with Spezzafumo, the bey's legal counsel, who was on his way back to Tunis.[29]

But the prime minister read Husayn's triumphant missive with alarm. Ibn Isma'il wrote back to Husayn to say that he refused to approve the contract: it was a bad deal for the government; it was irregular to keep the contract secret;

there was no guarantee that the unnamed bankers would be solvent enough to fulfill the terms of the contract; and to top it all off, Husayn had failed to ask for the bey's permission. Ibn Isma'il instructed Husayn to cancel the contract immediately.[30]

Husayn ascribed his failure to obtain the bey's permission to a misunderstanding and undelivered letter.[31] A likelier explanation is that Husayn signed the contract with Mayer for his own enrichment. The group of anonymous bankers was, in fact, just one man: Count Giuseppe Telfener, a capitalist who had recently married into a rich US family, and was about to embark on the construction of a railroad connecting New York to Mexico City (of which only ninety-one miles in Texas were ever built). After Husayn's death, evidence emerged that Husayn and Telfener secretly agreed to deposit half the profits from the Shamama estate directly in Husayn's private account.[32]

Nothing in Ibn Isma'il's correspondence with Husayn suggests that he suspected foul play. Nonetheless, the prime minister's trust in the general faded as Husayn time and again postponed annulling his contract with Mayer. Husayn's first response to the prime minister—written six weeks after he signed the contract—explained that he would happily go to Rome to have it canceled, but given the Christmas holidays, it would be impossible to assemble all the investors (a brazen falsehood given that Telfener was the sole investor).[33] Just after the new year, Husayn wrote to say that he had fixed a meeting on January 19, after the hearings in Lucca were expected to finish.[34] But he delayed again, explaining that he was occupied in writing up urgent notes in response to Mancini's arguments.[35] Husayn only returned to Rome in early March, but immediately turned back for Livorno without meeting Mayer, claiming that the lawyers working for the government needed to meet with him urgently. When Husayn finally sat down with Mayer on March 11—three months after Ibn Isma'il instructed him to cancel their contract—Mayer "politely gave me to understand that he could not accede to [my] demand and there was no reason to claim that the contract was null."[36]

Ibn Isma'il never accused Husayn of fraud outright. Yet Husayn knew that his superiors in Tunis were suspicious. Excuses, justifications, and expressions of bewilderment filled his letters; he protested that "one makes so much out of a small and quite simple matter."[37] Husayn justified his delays in canceling the contract with Mayer by explaining that he was all alone in Livorno, with no one to help him keep up with his correspondence in Arabic.[38] Finally, Husayn became so desperate that he tried throwing a political wrench into the works. He claimed that the anonymous Italian bankers with whom he signed the contract had complained to the Italian minister of foreign affairs, asserting that the Tunisian government wanted to cancel the contract simply because they were Italian—a way of expressing favor for France in the great chess game of European imperialism. The Italian government would surely support them, Husayn noted, "and I would be truly sorry to see my work cause political complications that I have sought, with all my powers, to avoid."[39] Husayn must have been unaware that Spezzafumo, the bey's lawyer, had already revealed Telfener's identity to Ibn Isma'il. Yet another story about the invented group of bankers would surely have erased any doubts the prime minister still had about Husayn's guilt.[40]

Perhaps Husayn's slip was the last straw; perhaps it was the court of appeal of Lucca's ruling, which again went against the Tunisian government; or perhaps it was simply the fact that the case had dragged on for over seven years, with nothing to show but astronomical fees for lawyers, fixers, and the expenses of the Livorno "mission." Whatever his precise reasons, in late June 1880, Ibn Isma'il decided that Husayn could no longer be trusted with the management of the Shamama case. He wrote to inform Husayn that the bey had appointed Giacomo Guttieres as Tunisia's new representative for the lawsuit.[41] The prime minister did not officially dismiss Husayn from his post or instruct him to return to Tunisia. But the mamlūk lost all power. Even before Guttieres arrived in Livorno, Ibn Isma'il ceased his correspondence with Husayn.[42]

Guttieres landed in Livorno on Saturday, June 12.[43] His arrival was in fact a homecoming; he was a native of the city, born there in 1823. Guttieres came from a large Sephardic family, the eldest of eight children. His family moved to Tunis in the 1820s, part of the wave of Jews infusing the Grana community with a stronger connection to Italy.[44] Thanks to the agreement between the bey and the Tuscan authorities in 1846, Guttieres remained an Italian national. He put his foreign citizenship to good use; in 1869, he was elected as one of two Italian representatives to sit on the Inspection Committee (Comité de Contrôle) of the International Financial Commission.[45]

Once back in Livorno, Guttieres took over Husayn's role as the government's representative in the Shamama lawsuit. A week after arriving, Guttieres boarded the train for Florence; he needed to consult with Galeotti about annulling the Husayn-Mayer contract.[46] Guttieres corresponded regularly with the authorities in Tunis, particularly the prime minister—to whom he wrote in his native Italian—and Pierre-Marie Depienne, the vice president of the International Financial Commission still in control of Tunisia's finances—to whom he wrote in excellent French. Guttieres must have gotten to know Depienne, vice president of the commission, during his time serving on the Inspection Committee; the two even developed a degree of social intimacy.[47] Guttieres was something of an outsider in the Tunisian government; his position on the International Financial Commission made it unclear where his loyalties lay, and his lack of Arabic meant that his letters required translation. But Guttieres had many advantages that Husayn lacked, not least his willingness to cut a deal with d'Erlanger.

This task was complicated by the fact that Husayn and Elmilik remained in Livorno, neither having been formally dismissed from their posts. Guttieres was wary of Husayn, whom he considered irrationally determined against signing a contract with d'Erlanger. And he saw Elmilik as Husayn's crony.[48] Guttieres did everything he could to hide his negotiations with d'Erlanger from Husayn and Elmilik—even traveling fifteen miles north to Pisa to send telegrams in order to prevent wagging tongues from spreading rumors.[49] Under different circumstances, Guttieres and Elmilik might have been friends, both Jews from abroad who had settled in Tunis and frequented the same Europeanized social sphere. But whether because of their positions or personalities, the two distrusted each other almost instantly. Years later, Elmilik publicly accused Guttieres of fraud and corruption.[50]

Elmilik and Husayn's hostility hardly deterred Guttieres from his task. He already knew Albert Dubois, d'Erlanger's representative—another acquaintance from the Inspection Committee back in Tunis.[51] By February 1881, Guttieres sent a telegram to Tunis explaining that he had reached a preliminary deal with d'Erlanger.[52]

Ibn Isma'il, however, was occupied with more pressing matters. That same month, tensions among tribes on the border with Algeria erupted when Algerians killed a Tunisian man. More distressing still, the French resisted negotiations that would have peacefully settled the matter.[53] The future looked bleak, and the prime minister was absorbed in trying to manage the crisis. Guttieres would have to pursue negotiations with d'Erlanger on his own.

In the meantime, the lawsuit went to another round of appeals, this time to the court of cassation in Florence. This court could only uphold or strike down the lower court's ruling. On April 25, 1881—just under a year after the judges in Lucca declared the will valid—the court of cassation reversed the earlier decision, abruptly steering the case in a new direction.

The judges of the court of cassation—including Paolo Onorato Vigliani, president of the court, and Francesco Bicci, who wrote the decision—began by addressing what they considered to be the heart of the matter: Was there a natural right to expatriation? Vigliani and Bicci ruled out the application of Roman law in this context—not because Tunisia was outside the family of nations, a matter they simply did not take up, but because they deemed Roman law inconclusive when it came to the acquisition and loss of citizenship.[54] In the absence of clear Roman legal doctrine, the judges were not at liberty to substitute the opinion of "scientists," which "cannot assume the authority or character of positive law"—a point that was certainly meant as a jab at Mancini, the preeminent expert in international law. There was nothing to do, Vigliani and Bicci concluded, but "adjudicate according to the constitutional principles that each independent state is pleased to establish, according to its politics and interests."[55] In this light, they noted that Article 92 of the Qānūn al-Dawla prohibited expatriation without the express permission of the Tunisian government. Nissim could not have legally expatriated himself, and thus could not have died stateless. The case was remanded to a higher court, the court of appeal in Florence, which would issue a new ruling. But Vigliani and Bicci made clear that they thought Nissim must have died a Tunisian.

Suddenly, the question of whether Nissim's will was valid according to Jewish law took on new urgency. Those hoping to invalidate the will had long counted on the application of halakhah. This was in large part why Husayn hired Elmilik in the first place. Elmilik had spilled much ink arguing for the will's invalidity according to Jewish law in his own briefs. But Elmilik was no rabbi, nor did he have any formal legal training. (This hardly stopped him from posing as a legal expert, however. He signed his publications "defense lawyer," adding "official of the Order of Nīshān al-Iftikhār" for good measure—titles that recall the proverbial lady who protests too much.)[56]

Elmilik had also gone to great lengths to obtain rabbinic rulings from rabbis in Tunisia invalidating the will, for which Husayn had originally hired him. In this Elmilik was largely successful; a number of publications appeared in Hebrew and Judeo-Arabic arguing that the will was null according to halakhah.[57] Both Elmilik and Pierantoni maintained that Tunisian rabbis were authoritative concerning the application of Jewish law to Tunisian Jews. As Elmilik put it, "Qā'id Nissim was from Tunis, and according to equity, law, and the established rules, any questions arriving among the testamentary heirs and the legal heirs—who are also Tunisian—should be adjudicated by the rabbis of Tunis."[58] In so arguing, Elmilik implicitly dismissed the presumption that Jewish law was entirely unbound from the state. Jewish law may be Nissim's national law, following him across the Mediterranean. Yet the version of Jewish law that had jurisdiction over Nissim's life and death was a particularly Tunisian version, and thus his will should be adjudicated by the rabbis of Tunis.

But the publications of the Tunisian rabbis were in dense and technical Hebrew; even a skilled translation could not make them legible to Italian judges.[59] Husayn needed a recognized authority on Jewish law who was also a local—someone steeped in the Italian intellectual tradition who could both write in Italian and speak the language of Italian courts.

He found his expert in David Castelli, born and bred in Livorno. Although Castelli began his career intending to seek rabbinical ordination, he had abandoned the rabbinate during a crisis of faith. Instead, Castelli devoted himself to the "scientific" study of Judaism in the tradition of *Wissenschaft des Judentums* that originated in Germany in the first decades of the nineteenth century. In 1876, he was appointed professor at a new secular university, the Istituto di Studi Superiore in Florence. The following year, Husayn convinced the professor to write briefs explaining why Nissim's will was invalid according to Jewish law. Called the Renan of Italy by admirers and detractors alike, Castelli was perfectly positioned to make the intricacies of Jewish law legible to Italian judges.[60]

Castelli began his first brief by orienting readers to the sources of Jewish law. Then he delved into the particulars of halakhic wills: only Jews who were ill had the capacity to testate in the way Nissim had—that is, to change the biblical rules of succession. Nissim, however, was clearly in good health, as he himself declared in the will. If healthy testators wanted to make changes to the biblical rules of succession, they had to do so as a donation, not as a bequest for after their death. These donations required a ritual act of acquisition, known as a kinyan.[61] There was no kinyan mentioned in Nissim's will; it was thus invalid according to Jewish law. Castelli's prose simplified the labyrinthine landscape of halakhah, offering a concise and persuasive case for the nullity of Nissim's will. Over the next two years, Castelli authored six more briefs elaborating on his arguments and responding to his critics.[62]

Husayn was willing to pay handsomely for the kind of expertise in Jewish law that would be accessible to Italian judges. And Castelli was not shy in seeking remuneration for his work. He billed the Tunisian government for countless meetings with Husayn, Elmilik, and Galeotti. He produced translations into Italian to support the government's case, including the opinion of the rabbis of Tunis invalidating the will (from Hebrew, for four hundred lire), and thirty pages of Moses Mendelssohn's book on Jewish law (from German, for two hundred lire). Castelli was careful to request reimbursement for any expenses he incurred along the way—everything from forty cents for postal fees, to two hundred lire for printing a pamphlet on the Jewish law of inheritance.[63] He charged a whopping thousand lire for his attendance during all ten days of the hearings in Lucca, though he did not utter a word.[64] His final bill topped fourteen thousand lire, nearly three times a professor's annual salary.[65] For an academic—then, as now, hardly a lucrative profession—Castelli was truly raking in the cash.

The ruling issued by the court of cassation alarmed d'Erlanger, who had a financial stake in ensuring that the will was declared valid. Now that the court of cassation had ruled that Nissim did not die stateless, it suddenly seemed quite likely that Jewish law would be applied to the will. Years earlier—just months after Nissim's death—'Aziza and Moses had asked Abraham Ashkenazi, chief rabbi of Jerusalem, to write a responsum upholding the will. But Ashkenazi's teshuvah was in highly technical Hebrew and remained inaccessible to Italian judges.[66] D'Erlanger realized that his investment would only pay off if he could prove that Nissim's will was valid according to Jewish law.

The need to engage a halakhic expert was all the more pressing because Mancini had entirely neglected this aspect of the case during his work for 'Aziza. The great jurist's briefs were silent concerning what Jewish law might have to say about Nissim's will. Mancini only reversed course following the hearings in Lucca; perhaps it finally occurred to him that it would be prudent to argue for the validity of Nissim's will according to Jewish law. In great haste, his legal team raced to write a new brief. This time, Mancini took a back seat, instead appointing two junior lawyers, Raffaello Baquis and Dario Cassuto, to write the opinion.[67] Both were young men from Livorno's Jewish community, though it remains unclear how much they knew about Jewish law or to what extent they were practicing Jews. Cassuto obtained his law degree at the university in Pisa, where he certainly did not receive any training in halakhah.[68] Their brief was not entirely useless, but whether Baquis and Cassuto could command much authority regarding "Talmudic law" was doubtful at best.

If d'Erlanger wanted to win in court, he would need someone who could exceed Castelli's authority. He set his sights on Elia Benamozegh, another Livornese native and far more famous than Castelli.[69] Benamozegh had taught Castelli as a young man in Livorno's rabbinical college. Whereas Castelli had opted for a life of "complete intellectual liberty," unfettered by demands for the "veneration of tradition and practice," Benamozegh remained committed to observing Jewish law and ritual.[70] By 1881, he was widely known for his work combining philosophy with Jewish mysticism. Benamozegh also had the advantage of being familiar with the Shamama case. Starting in June 1873, he worked as a translator for the inventory of Nissim's estate. He secured this job as one of the relatively few Jews in Livorno capable of translating between Italian and Judeo-Arabic; Benamozegh's maternal uncle, Yehudah Coriat, hailed from Morocco and had educated the boy in his native tongue.[71]

Nonetheless, Benamozegh was an odd choice for an expert on Jewish law. He was renowned as a theologian, philosopher, and mystic, but hardly as an authority on halakhah. What seems to have been more important was Benamozegh's status as the most illustrious rabbi in Livorno and indeed all of Tuscany. He was known as a patriot; like the famous lawyers working on both sides of the case, he had thrown his support behind the Risorgimento. It is equally unclear why Benamozegh accepted the commission. Presumably he was not immune to the generous compensation he received, amounting to nearly eight thousand lire.[72] And he wrote to a friend that the Shamama case constituted a "most serious work of enormous responsibility."[73] Perhaps he accepted in part because the question of Nissim's will had become a cause célèbre among rabbis across the Mediterranean; here was a chance to weigh in on the ongoing debate and get paid in the process. Needless to say, Benamozegh also saw the Shamama affair as another opportunity to express his ideas—not just about Jewish law, but about religion, universalism, and modernity broadly conceived.[74]

Benamozegh might also have accepted in order to fight one more round with Castelli, his former student turned intellectual rival. The two Livornese Jews had chosen sharply divergent approaches to the study of Judaism. For years, their antagonism had played out in biting reviews of each other's work. When Castelli published *The Messiah According to the Jews* in 1874, Benamozegh wrote a damning assessment, accusing Castelli of relativism.[75] Castelli fumed as he waited for an opportunity to strike back; three years later, he savaged Benamozegh's latest book, deeming it confusing, misleading, and inaccurate.[76] Standing on opposite sides of the Shamama case gave the two scholars another battleground for their ongoing ideological war.

Benamozegh was hired to demonstrate that Nissim's will was valid according to Jewish law. Yet he could not help himself from following various tangents, including the question of what halakhah had to say about Nissim's legal belonging. Benamozegh's first brief began with an argument that according to halakhah, Nissim had lost his Tunisian nationality.[77] The rabbi explained that in Jewish law, a Jew forfeited his right of membership in his community of origin when he left that city for more than three years or left with no intention to return.[78] Nissim was away from Tunis for more than three years and had no plans to go back; he had therefore forfeited his membership in the Tunisian Jewish community. At the same time, Benamozegh continued, Nissim became a member of his new community in Livorno. He cited the Mishnah, which asks, "How long must a Jew reside in a city to be considered a citizen?" The answer is twelve months, or if he buys a house, "immediately."[79] The Mishnaic (and Talmudic) discussions concerning membership in a community focus on the responsibility to contribute to caring for the city's poor and the upkeep of communal infrastructure; those considered part of a community had certain responsibilities toward their fellow members. Benamozegh seamlessly translated this kind of belonging into "citizenship," despite the absence of state membership in the rabbinic texts.

Benamozegh's tangent about the halakhic view of Nissim's citizenship was destined to have little effect on the Florentine judges charged with deciding the case. Yet this hardly stopped Castelli from blasting Benamozegh's attempt to equate Talmudic citizenship with modern legal belonging. A direct translation was impossible, Castelli asserted, precisely because the relevant Talmudic texts were not talking about the state. "It is true that the Talmud speaks of the obligations and rights that devolve to the men of a city," Castelli wrote. "But it concerns *men of the city, and not citizens* in the meaning that this word has acquired for us."[80] Citizen, Castelli explained, designates the civil and political rights that emanate from a state. But "the Talmud does not speak of the state; it speaks only of the city." The question of citizenship in the Shamama case had nothing to do with the meaning of citizen as "one who actually belongs to a particular city. . . . The passages cited by Benamozegh," Castelli concluded, "say nothing about the duties and rights of the citizen."[81]

Having indulged his desire to discuss the Jewish law of citizenship—despite its irrelevance to the case at hand—Benamozegh turned to his main argument: convincing his readers that a proper understanding of halakhah required the application of Italian law to Nissim's will. The foundation of his claim was the Talmudic maxim "the law of the state is the law" (*dina de-malkhuta dina*).[82] In Benamozegh's hands, this principle expressed an essential aspect of Judaism as a particularist religion with a universalist message. Citing his own book *Israel and Humanity*, Benamozegh explained that Jews believed in a universal God. They were commanded to recognize that "the law of the state is the law" precisely because God ordained an infinite variety of laws to correspond to the infinite variety of humanity. "In his own eyes," Benamozegh maintained, "every Jew is a citizen of every country."[83] In other words, whether or not a state officially recognized Jews as citizens, Jewish law obliged them to act as if they were citizens. "An essential part of Jewish law is that it concedes authority in civil matters to the law of the state."[84] In the Shamama case, therefore, the Jewish law of wills *was* Italian law.

Benamozegh did not entirely neglect what he termed the "internal" criteria of Jewish law—that is, halakhic jurisprudence concerning last wills and testaments—though he insisted that this was of secondary import. He argued that a kinyan, the ritual acquisition deemed necessary for a will of a healthy person, was optional. Moreover, a healthy person had the power to change the biblical order of inheritance as long as the testator used the word "gift" instead of "inherit."[85] Castelli's understanding of the will as null stemmed from a misreading of the relevant texts; according to Benamozegh, Nissim had written a kosher testament.

Much of the disagreement between Castelli and Benamozegh over the will stemmed from opposing understandings of the nature of Jewish law. The Livornese mystic grounded his explanation of halakhah in a Hegelian approach to law—one that presumed a tight relationship between legal and historical development. According to Benamozegh, the Talmud was Jews' "true national law of all ages, all places, and all phases of the nation."[86] "Everything else," he wrote, "is nothing but commentary."[87] This was a radical statement; it challenged the majority of rabbinic opinion, which put immense weight on post-Talmudic legal writing. Benamozegh, however, insisted that because the Talmud was the last authoritative text on Jewish law, the entire system needed to be reinterpreted in every generation. "Every Jew is a rabbi unto himself, and can and should interpret the tradition as he best sees fit."[88] In asserting that Jewish law was a "living organism," Benamozegh adopted the views of his contemporaries among European jurists.[89] Most agreed that a religious law fixed in ancient texts—like Jewish or Islamic law—was inherently problematic; such a system could not reflect the natural and healthy evolution of society. Recall that this was precisely one of the objections Mancini raised to applying Jewish law in Italy.[90] While the text of the Talmud might be unchanging, Benamozegh reasoned, Jewish law itself continually evolved: "Put simply, it is an essential condition of Jewish national law that it be desired, made, interpreted, proclaimed by the nation that chose it"—that is, by Jews; "without this, it is not a national law."[91] Benamozegh's contention that Jewish law evolved over time echoed the thinking of a number of German Jews central to rethinking Judaism in an Enlightenment context.[92]

Castelli offered a diametrically opposed philosophy of law, albeit one similarly inspired by his non-Jewish contemporaries. The agnostic professor followed the positivist rage sweeping much of Europe's legal profession.[93] According to Castelli, Jewish law amounted to the normative injunctions outlined in its ancient texts. The Talmud's authority was filtered through "briefer, clearer, and more precise" compilations of Jewish law, culminating in the *Shulḥan 'Arukh* by Joseph Caro (d. 1575)—"a code about which all Jews agreed" (a statement that directly contradicted Benamozegh).[94] Experts like himself had no authority to update Jewish law in order to make it "similar to modern legislation." Rather, their task was to "explain it, as it is read in the texts that have been transmitted."[95] Neither rabbis, professors, nor Italian judges had the right to take liberties with the law, even if they found it went against their notions of rationality or justice. Castelli might well have agreed with scholars like François Laurent, who described jurists as "slaves of law."[96]

It did not take long for the disagreement over the nature of Jewish law to degenerate into theological mudslinging. For his part, Benamozegh attacked Castelli's avowed ungodliness. He compared Castelli to "certain degenerate Jewish professors in [ancient] Alexandria—who were the scholars of more-or-less-Jewish letters in the Florence of their age." These "Hellenized Jews" were "not genuine, orthodox Jews" and were prone to falsification.[97] An unbeliever like Castelli, Benamozegh warned, could not possibly be trusted. Meanwhile, Benamozegh's own positions caused outrage among his opponents in Tunis. Yehudah Jarmon, a rabbi who argued for the nullity of Nissim's will, declared Benamozegh an "apostate" (*apikoros*) and "rebellious elder" (*zaken mamre*)—rabbinic terms reserved for an educated Jew who rejects the tenets of his faith.[98] Jarmon was particularly furious that someone professing to be a rabbi would dismiss the authority of a text like the *Shulḥan 'Arukh*. The debate over Nissim's will proved inseparable from the disagreements separating traditionalists from modernizers, and believers from agnostics.

———

The court of cassation's ruling had turned 'Aziza and Moses's legal strategy on its head, forcing them to engage an Italian-speaking authority on Jewish law. One might expect the verdict to have had the opposite effect in the halls of the Bardo; presumably, Tunisian officials would have welcomed the news that an Italian court had at last showed a willingness to consider Nissim a subject of the bey. But when Guttieres's telegram arrived reporting on the verdict, the prime minister was facing far graver problems at home.[99]

The day before the Florence court ruled, tensions on the Tunisian-Algerian border erupted into an open declaration of war. French forces marched into Tunisian territory, ostensibly to pacify the tribes whose incursions on the Algerian side had threatened French interests. It soon became apparent that French forces were taking the first steps in a military conquest that the government had been considering for years—an attack green lighted by France's rival powers at the Congress of Berlin. Two days later, advancing French forces occupied Le Kef, the largest Tunisian city near the Algerian border, and French naval ships bombarded the port city of Tabarka.[100] On May 12, French officials forced the bey to sign the Treaty of Bardo, formally establishing a protectorate in Tunisia.

France's occupation of Tunisia had profound effects in Italy. The Italian government was furious; Italy had long set its sights on colonizing Tunisia, where Italians lived in greater numbers than any other foreign community. The fait accompli presented by the Treaty of Bardo triggered a crisis; Benedetto Cairoli, the minister of foreign affairs, resigned. None other than Mancini was called to replace him; the law professor returned to the Ministry of Foreign Affairs on May 29. In light of his new responsibilities, Mancini resigned from the Shamama case.[101] The same month, Pierantoni also ceased his work on the lawsuit.[102]

Guttieres nonetheless persisted in his attempts to strike a deal with d'Erlanger. Even after Sadiq Bey signed the Treaty of Bardo, Guttieres and Ibn Isma'il continued to strategize about a contract with d'Erlanger.[103] By September, Guttieres and d'Erlanger had reached a preliminary accord, which gave

72 percent of the estate to the French bank and 28 percent to the government.[104] The Tunisian government's interests became those of d'Erlanger.[105] Guttieres was tempted to throw the weight of the government's legal team behind upholding Nissim's will. But as two Tuscan lawyers advised him, it would be "undignified" for the government to suddenly reverse itself after decades of fighting to have the will thrown out. Instead, the lawyers suggested that the government simply claim that it was tired after such a long fight, and no longer wanted to pay for lawyers and court fees.[106] In February 1882—nine years after Nissim died—Guttieres officially withdrew the Tunisian government from *Shamama v. Shamama.*[107]

D'Erlanger now set his sights on the last holdout among the Shamama heirs; only Qā'id Momo had refused to cede the totality of his rights. Yet even stiff-necked Momo was no match for d'Erlanger's powers of persuasion. From his new home on the island of Corfu, recently absorbed by the Kingdom of Greece, Momo signed away all claims to Nissim's estate; in return, d'Erlanger paid him a lump sum of 1.5 million francs. Now d'Erlanger and the Tunisian government would split nearly every penny of Nissim's riches, regardless of his nationality or whether the will was deemed valid.[108]

By this point, however, the lawsuit had taken on a life of its own. Even after the Tunisian government bowed out of the case, and even after d'Erlanger bought up nearly every possible portion of the estate, there were a few stubborn holdouts who refused to back down. Joseph continued the fight; although he had signed away his rights to d'Erlanger, he still stood to inherit more if the will was declared invalid. Elmilik similarly could not let go; although his role as an intermediary for the government had effectively ended, he was still the legal representative of various heirs. And he was stubborn as a mule, determined to string the lawsuit out for as long as possible.[109] The case went to another round of appeal.

In July 1883, the court of appeal in Florence delivered its verdict—the final ruling in a lawsuit that had lasted ten years and six months. The president of the court, Baldassarre Paoli, was one of Italy's most respected jurists; he had helped write the penal code of 1866 and served as a senator since 1876.[110] His younger colleague Calcedonio Inghilleri, who authored the verdict, was also a respected magistrate and, since 1875, a representative in the Camera dei Deputati on the Right.[111]

Paoli, Inghilleri, and the other judges on the court of appeal had complete freedom to rule as they saw fit; although the court of cassation had overturned the lower courts' rulings, Paoli and Inghilleri started from scratch. They seemed to have relished the opportunity to spar with one of Italy's most famous jurists. Although Mancini was no longer actively working on the case, his theories echoed throughout Inghilleri's opinion—the work of an intellectual giant, which the Florentine judge now proceeded to tear down stone by stone.

Inghilleri began by rejecting one of Mancini's central claims: the view that all people enjoyed a universal right to expatriation. Inghilleri pointed out that many modern nations demanded perpetual allegiance, including, until quite recently, England and the United States, "the two most civilized and most advanced nations when it comes to liberty."[112] Following Husayn's argument, he noted that in both the Ottoman Empire and Tunisia, the religious foundation of law (El-Cheriat) demanded perpetual allegiance from all subjects, Muslim and non-Muslim alike.[113] This religious requirement was confirmed by Article 92 of the Qānūn al-Dawla. Husayn's attempts to translate Islamic jurisprudence into the language of modern citizenship had at last succeeded in an Italian court.

To everyone's surprise, Inghilleri even echoed Husayn's views about Jews' rights as equal subjects, thereby allaying any doubt that Jews could be considered full members of the Tunisian state. "The Tunisian Jew is not tolerated," Inghilleri explained; rather, "he is equal with the other subjects in rights and duties, and all—without distinction of religion—are equal before the law."[114] This must have been something of a shock to Pierantoni, who had refused to repeat this part of Husayn's argument; the idea that a Muslim-ruled country might offer Jews equality before the law turned out to be less outlandish than Pierantoni had thought.[115]

Having ruled that Nissim died a Tunisian national, Inghilleri still had to determine whether it was possible to apply Jewish law to the estate. The judge dismissed out of hand the claim that Jewish law was Nissim's national law. Jews lack political sovereignty, he observed, and thus are not "a true nation in the juridical sense of the word."[116] So much for Elmilik's attempts to translate Jewish peoplehood (*'am yisrael*) into the modern meaning of nationality. Inghilleri also rejected Mancini's view that Jewish law could not be applied as a national law according to the criteria of the Italian Civil Code. "The Civil Code does not distinguish between law that is written or oral, codified, statuary, or customary": all that mattered was that the sovereign state of Tunisia had given this body of law the force of jurisdiction.[117] Jewish law must determine the legitimacy of the will because Tunisian law required it.

At this point, Inghilleri diverged from the vision of the case promoted by Husayn and his legal team. In one of the most surprising twists of the decade-long legal battle, Inghilleri concluded that Nissim's will was valid according to Jewish law. And he did so not by following the claims of the great Benamozegh, whose briefs he failed to cite even once.[118] Instead, Inghilleri made an argument that closely followed the legal brief hastily written by the lawyers Baquis and Cassuto just after the oral arguments in Lucca. Citing the same passage of the *Shulḥan 'Arukh* that Baquis and Cassuto quoted at length, Inghilleri explained that a healthy person could testate as he wished.[119] A will made by a healthy testator could ignore the biblical laws of inheritance as long as it used the term "gift" instead of "inherit." Indeed, the testator only had to use the word "gift" once for his will to be valid. And according to an expert in Judeo-Arabic, Nissim had used the language "I give" (*nu'ṭī*) in describing the portion he allotted to 'Aziza and Nissim Jr.[120] This sort of gift—made *causa mortis,* in contemplation of one's impending death—did not require a ritual acquisition (kinyan).[121] There was nothing in Nissim's will that made it invalid according to Jewish law.

Inghilleri's ruling demonstrated a broad-mindedness rare among his peers. He accepted the Islamic foundations of legal belonging in Tunisia. And he put Tunisia's approach to perpetual allegiance on par with that of the "most civilized and most advanced nations." He not only defended Jewish law against Mancini's attacks but also offered a vision of halakhah as a modern legal system evolving with the times. "The assertion that Jewish law was and remains unchanged," Inghilleri observed, "is contradicted by the inevitable rule of historical evolution that governs all human things."[122] Husayn was no longer working on the case, and the ruling went against what he had worked so hard to prove. He nonetheless might have taken some satisfaction in seeing a court affirm his arguments about nationality law and the status of Jews in Tunisia. Perhaps he even would have allowed that despite the Orientalist prejudices so rampant in Europe at the time, the court had ensured that "justice is distributed equally, without distinction of nationality."[123]

But for Husayn, as for the other interested parties, Inghilleri's ruling came too late to make much of an impact. Neither the heirs nor the Tunisian government—now under the sovereignty of France—gave much thought to how Nissim's estate was distributed. Since d'Erlanger had succeeded in paying everyone off, the caustic debates about Nissim's nationality and the nature of Jewish law had become academic questions.

The lawsuit formally came to an end, yet the Florentine court's decision hardly settled the matter of Nissim's legal belonging. Confusion about Nissim's true nationality persisted long after the court in Florence ruled. Inghilleri dismissed the idea that Nissim was of Livornese ancestry, despite Mancini's having thrown his considerable authority behind this claim. Nonetheless, prominent Livornese Jews continued to believe that Nissim's ancestors hailed from Tuscany. Raffaello Ascoli, a native of Livorno, offered an image of Nissim quite different from Inghilleri's. In a book of verse written three years after the final ruling, Ascoli repeated the story that Nissim himself had told about his Livornese origins:

Qā'id Nissim decided
To abandon France,
And it occurred to him
That it would be good to come back
To beautiful Livorno
To which he happily returned
Right away, since word had it
That his ancestors from there
Had gone to Tunisia
Where, clever and brave,
And with exceptional success,
An immense fortune
They wisely made,
And maintained with rare prudence.[124]

Ascoli was an actuary, which accounts for the banality of his verse. But it is the very amateur nature of his observations that offer a window onto how Jews in Livorno continued to view the late count: as a Livornese Jew whose family, like so many others, had moved to Tunisia, and who had made his way back to his ancestral homeland. Mancini may have failed to convince the judges that Nissim was an oriundo italiano who had recovered his original citizenship. In the court of public opinion, though, Nissim remained a Livornese Jew.

Despite the "various courtrooms in the various courts" to which both sides brought their "bitter litigation," no ruling could conclusively settle the matter of Nissim's nationality.[125] Ascoli bitingly captured the tragedy of the storied lawsuit, which in the end, profited the lawyers and d'Erlanger's bank far more than any Shamamas:

> It has already been many years
> That lawyers and their assistants,
> Breathing easy, fattened up
> With enormous sums.[126]

Everyone else was left only with regrets—Husayn, Elmilik, 'Aziza and her family, and all the Shamama heirs who had moved to Livorno to pursue their slice of the estate. And questions of legal belonging continued to torment the North Africans whose lives had been consumed by the Shamama case, rubbing salt in their wounds long after the courts put the lawsuit to rest.

PART III

Afterlives

10

Descendants (1883–1945)

AFTER SO MANY years of fighting over Nissim's estate, not everyone found letting go so easy. Castelli had already written hundreds of pages in connection with the Shamama case, for which he had been handsomely compensated. And like any good academic, Castelli turned all of that research on wills into another scholarly publication to add to his résumé.[1] Nonetheless, when the court of appeal in Florence ruled directly against Castelli's numerous publications arguing that Nissim's will was halakhically invalid, the professor was distressed. He could not help but write yet another book on the subject. *Observations on the Sentence of the Court of Florence concerning the Validity of the Will of Nissim Shamama* was finished on September 20, 1883, a month and a half after the ruling. The book, he claimed, would assuage "my conscience and my dignity."[2] In fact, Castelli's hundred-page attack on the verdict reads more like one of his reviews of Benamozegh; he could barely contain his contempt for the judges' errors, mistakes, and confusions. The screed must have helped Castelli move on; he devoted the rest of his years to research and teaching, until his death in 1901—just under a year after Benamozegh passed away.

But the North Africans who had become entangled in *Shamama v. Shamama* found it difficult to leave the nasty business of the lawsuit behind. Many learned that the questions of belonging at the heart of the case simply would not leave them alone. For some, their own nationality became a subject of intense scrutiny only after their death. For others, uncertain citizenship posed problems during their lifetimes, in some cases with violent consequences. The specter of legal belonging haunted these Jews and Muslims like a vengeful spirit.

Several years before the court of appeal in Florence issued its final ruling in the Shamama case, another war over inheritance commenced across the waters of the Mediterranean. This time, the trigger was the death of Ibn 'Ayyad, Nissim's first patron who had absconded to Paris and with whom Nissim had an ongoing lawsuit at the time of his death. As with *Shamama v. Shamama*, the fight over Ibn 'Ayyad's wealth turned in part on questionable claims of citizenship. As Muslims who had settled in the Ottoman Empire, the Ibn 'Ayyads were claimed by the Ottoman Ministry of Foreign Affairs as Ottoman subjects. No one involved in the Shamama affair, however, had taken seriously the possibility that a Jew from Tunis might have died an Ottoman subject. Yet the same level of doubt prevailed about the nature of naturalization and expatriation. And the stakes of claiming one legal belonging or another were just as high.

Ibn 'Ayyad moved to Istanbul in the early 1860s, perhaps because he ran out of money to support his lavish lifestyle in the City of Lights. From the capital of the Ottoman Empire, Ibn 'Ayyad reinvented himself as Tunuslu Mahmut Paşa (Mahmud the Tunisian). He bought multiple properties in some of the most desirable neighborhoods of the city and installed himself in a compound overlooking the Bosphorus, on top of Çamlıca Hill on the Asian side—where a street and park still bear his name.[3] On February 18, 1880, Ibn 'Ayyad passed away. He left behind two sons, Ahmad and Tahir; four daughters, Hayriye, Jamila, Amina, and Subiha; his widow, 'Aziza Nourissen Ibn 'Ayyad; and three concubines, Zubayda, Ikbal, and Gülfem.[4] As the eldest, Ahmad took over the ongoing lawsuit against the Shamama estate, attempting to extract the money that Mahmud had claimed Nissim owed him.[5] Before long, however, Ahmad found himself mired in an inheritance battle of his own.[6]

The fight over Mahmud's estate was initially waged not among his direct descendants but instead between Mahmud's children and his nephews Hamida, 'Ali, and Hassuna. The nephews maintained that they were entitled to half of Mahmud's estate—a claim they pursued in various courts in Istanbul, including the shari'a court presided over by the *kazasker* (or *kadıasker*, the chief military judge of the empire) and the *nizamiye* court of first instance of Scutari (a new civil tribunal instituted in the 1860s as part of the Tanzimat reforms).[7] Among Mahmud's children, some protested that they were French nationals. As such, they were exempt from the jurisdiction of Ottoman courts.[8] To make things more complicated, two of the three nephews held British patents of protection; they did not hesitate to drag British diplomats into the quagmire.[9] These lawsuits required Ottoman, French, and British officials to determine who had jurisdiction over the estate; naturally it all boiled down to legal belonging.

It remained unclear whether any of the Ibn ʿAyyads were actually French—a matter that bureaucrats in the Ottoman Ministry of Foreign Affairs, French diplomats stationed in Istanbul, French judges in Paris, and of course the heirs themselves tried desperately to sort out. Ahmad and Tahir, Mahmud's sons, described themselves as "French citizens"—a claim the French ambassador in Istanbul, the Marquis de Noailles, defended energetically.[10] De Noailles was equally adamant that ʿAziza Nourissen, Mahmud's widow, was French "by virtue of her marriage in France with a French citizen" (that is, Ibn ʿAyyad).[11] But the weakness of this position soon became apparent: Tahir walked back his claim of French citizenship, alleging only that he was a "Tunisian by birth, domiciled in France by a decree of 18 January 1881, at 49 Rue Blanche in Paris."[12] The Ottoman authorities naturally refused to consider any of the Ibn ʿAyyads French. In the eyes of Ottoman law, they were all subjects of the sultan. Tunisians in Istanbul had long been considered Ottoman subjects. And the Ottoman nationality law of 1869 made it illegal to expatriate oneself without the express permission of the sultan.[13]

By 1885, one could already assemble a "library of rulings and notarized documents" from the Ibn ʿAyyad case.[14] And the dispute dragged on for decades; at the turn of the century, the question of Ahmad's nationality was still unsettled. The Ottoman Ministry of Foreign Affairs continued to insist that all the Ibn ʿAyyad heirs were registered as Ottoman subjects.[15] Eventually a bureaucrat in the French Ministry of Justice was convinced by the Ottoman position, explaining that Ahmad was already a legal adult when Mahmud naturalized as a French citizen; Ahmad thus did not automatically acquire his father's French citizenship.[16] Before the lawsuit was finally concluded, the feud over Mahmud's estate had poisoned relations among his children. Hayriye sued Ahmad, claiming that her brother had cheated her out of her fair share of the inheritance.

Hayriye proved not only a formidable opponent in court but also an outspoken feminist and strident critic of the reigning Ottoman sultan on the international stage. She moved to Europe, where she made a name for herself as a member of international feminist movements. British newspapers reported on her series of lectures intended to make "known the social condition of her countrywomen"; she was the first Ottoman woman to attend a convention of the International Council of Women, held in Berlin in 1904; and she published a book in German titled *The Turkish Woman: Her Social Life and the Harem.*[17] Unlike her brothers, Hayriye made no pretensions to being French. She even married a man who had given up his Swedish citizenship for Ottoman nationality. Her husband, 'Ali Nuri Bey—described by none other than Theodor Herzl as a "Viking in a frock-coat"—was born in Malmö as Knut Gustaf; he emigrated to Istanbul in 1879, converted to Islam, and naturalized as an Ottoman subject.[18] Belonging to the Ottoman Empire was useful to both members of the odd couple; it allowed 'Ali Nuri Bey to work in the Ministry of Foreign Affairs, and it gave Hayriye a platform from which to speak as an authority on Ottoman women and court intrigue. Like the rest of her family, Hayriye did not shrink from a fight. She was, however, one of the rare elite Tunisians abroad whose nationality did not become the object of bitter dispute.

Those who had devoted their lives to *Shamama v. Shamama* found themselves at a bit of a loss when the curtain finally closed on the decade-long legal drama. Elmilik had found a perfect outlet for his frustrated ambitions during his time working on the Shamama lawsuit. He could not readily accept that the years of labor had been for naught, nor that only d'Erlanger and the lawyers made off with a profit, leaving the heirs—and him—to stew. Grasping at straws, Elmilik submitted yet another appeal, arguing that the Florentine court had misinterpreted Jewish law.[19] His request went nowhere; the case was finally closed.

To make matters worse, Elmilik's caustic personality had soured his relationship with Husayn, his employer. Elmilik set about trying to pry the maximum amount of money out of Husayn, claiming that the former government official owed him hundreds of thousands of francs in unpaid fees and expenses. In 1884, Elmilik brought his case against Husayn to the civil court in Livorno.[20] Eventually the case moved to Tunisia, where Elmilik demanded that Islamic law be applied. He argued that because Husayn was Muslim, their dispute fell under the jurisdiction of shari'a courts. But the French judge saw through Elmilik's attempts to shop among different legal fora in search of a more favorable outcome; his demand to have the case adjudicated in a shari'a court "seems unbelievable when one remembers that Elmilik is French!"[21] As a French citizen, Elmilik was exclusively under the jurisdiction of French courts in colonial Tunisia. The judge refused to allow this Jew of Algerian origin to have his cake and eat it too.

Once back in Tunis, Elmilik reversed course and again embraced his French citizenship. Being a member of the colonial power put him at a distinct advantage over other North Africans. Yet his detractors turned Elmilik's French connection against him. He was attacked for insufficient devotion to the French nation. In a vicious letter to the colonial administration in Tunis, a former associate described Elmilik as a man whose "sad reputation is notorious in Tunis and in Livorno." Elmilik was a "French protégé"—a loose use of the term since Elmilik's Algerian origins in fact entitled him to French citizenship—but this "rascal" had the nerve to oppose the colonization of Tunisia and instead "pray for France's ruin" while "noble French blood flowed on Tunisian soil."[22] Even worse, Elmilik benefited from French protection while seeking Spanish nationality for his children, hoping to save them from the military service required of all French citizens in the colonies. Anyone could be accused of disloyalty, but such accusations were particularly damaging to North Africans whose claims to French citizenship were inherently tenuous.

Whether Elmilik in fact played fast and loose with his loyalty to France is hard to say for sure. Yet there is no doubt that he saw nationality as a tool rather than an immutable identity or sacred duty. He explored the possibility of obtaining Italian citizenship in 1881 while still working for Husayn in Livorno.[23] And it was Elmilik who concluded that Nissim had sought Italian nationality simply in order to improve his chances at forum shopping; "Qā'id Nissim at times needed to be considered Tunisian and thus to be judged according to Tunisian law—and at other times, he required Italian law and thus invoked his quality of an Italian citizen."[24] In Elmilik's eyes, this was nothing to be ashamed of; on the contrary, Elmilik praised Nissim for his "finesse and savoir faire" in using nationality to his advantage.[25] It is not hard to imagine that Elmilik saw his own attempts to switch nationality for his personal benefit as similarly savvy rather than disloyal or treacherous.

Elmilik never mustered the finesse and savoir faire required to capitalize on all the advantages legal belonging could offer. He spent the rest of his days fighting a losing battle with the Tunisian government. The lawsuit only concluded after he passed away in 1891; as it turned out, his son David was of a far more temperate disposition than his father, and was happy to settle. Elmilik was mercifully spared the grief of the untimely demise of his youngest son, Mas'ud Felix, at the age of fifteen.[26] Perhaps good fortune finally found this tragic figure in bringing death while Mas'ud was still alive.

Before giving up his European adventures and returning to Tunis, however, Elmilik managed to provoke another conflict over belonging: that of his erstwhile employer, Husayn.[27] The battle over Husayn's estate concerned not only who would inherit his property but also who had jurisdiction to distribute the deceased man's wealth. In this instance, the ensuing confusion turned on the rivalry between France and the Ottoman Empire, and their distinct visions of the nature of sovereignty.

After years of illness, Husayn passed away on June 27, 1887. The mamlūk died in his rented rooms in the Villa Sicard, perched on the hills above the southern banks of the Arno River just outside Florence. Three days later, his body was interred in the "Ottoman cemetery" in Livorno—undoubtedly the Turks' quadrant, where Muslims who passed away in the Tuscan port city had been buried for decades.[28] Various Livornese notables accompanied the funeral cortege, as did the Ottoman consul in Livorno.

When Elmilik got wind of Husayn's death, he rushed from Livorno to Florence to see the French consul, Mr. de Laigne. Elmilik informed the French diplomat that he was a creditor of Husayn's estate "for considerable sums" and formally requested that de Laigne apply seals to Husayn's possessions.[29] The day of Husayn's funeral, de Laigne made his way to the Villa Sicard flanked by two assistants. To his surprise, a guard refused him entry. As de Laigne later found out, the man had been stationed there by Vasilaki Musurus Ghikis, the Ottoman consul in Florence. De Laigne was reduced to placing seals on the gate outside the house. He then went back to the center of the city, where he also sealed the entrance to the small house that Husayn had inhabited at 40 Via Fra Bartolomeo, a few blocks from the Piazza Camillo Cavour (now the Piazza della Libertà) north of the city center.[30]

The application of French seals to the late Husayn's residences was no mere formality. The official seals staked a claim to the late general's nationality; they announced who was in charge of his estate. De Laigne's claim reflected French policy since 1881, when France asserted the right to protect Tunisians outside Tunisia. The Treaty of Bardo, which established the protectorate in Tunisia, declared that "French diplomatic and consular officials abroad will be charged with the protection of Tunisian interests and nationals of the regency."[31]

De Laigne asserted his prerogative to administer Husayn's estate because the deceased was a Tunisian and hence "a French protégé."[32] The French consul argued that even if Husayn had once been Ottoman—having been enslaved to the Ottoman sultan at a young age—he subsequently "lost his nationality by serving in the army of the bey of Tunis."[33] At the heart of de Laigne's reasoning lay not a little confusion about the precise nature of France's claim of sovereignty over Tunisians. The French consul asserted that everyone considered Husayn to be Tunisian and that he had even sought French protection. But de Laigne never said the words "Tunisian national." Nor did he claim Husayn as a French national. Rather, de Laigne used the terms "protégé" and "protection" to explain Husayn's legal bond with France. Indeed, the precise legal status of Tunisians under the French protectorate had yet to be defined. Tunisians were certainly not French within Tunisia; there, "native" (*indigène*) Jews and Muslims were subject to local jurisdiction, whereas French citizens (and other European nationals) came under the jurisdiction of French courts. On the other hand, immediately after the ink dried on the Treaty of Bardo, French consuls asserted the right to "protect" Tunisians in the Ottoman Empire; this implied that these Tunisians abroad were somehow French, like Algerians and other colonial subjects.[34] If de Laigne was at all troubled by the ambiguity of the status he was claiming for Husayn, he certainly concealed it well.

Ottoman authorities, however, had never accepted France's assertion to protect Tunisians in the Ottoman Empire. The sultan and his ministers refused to formally recognize French sovereignty over the former Ottoman province and all the more so over Tunisians outside Tunisia.[35] This is why Ghikis had laid his own claim to Husayn's Ottoman nationality in the first place. The day Husayn died, Ghikis placed seals on everything the late general owned—from his body to his horses. Ghikis justified his actions by explaining that "the Ottoman Empire has never recognized France's protectorate over Tunisians."[36] He pointed out the glaring irony of France's claim in this particular case; Husayn himself had always been an ardent opponent of French colonization in Tunisia. In fact, Husayn had remained in Florence after 1881 in order to avoid living under French rule back in Tunisia. Of all people, Husayn would be the last to want the French consul administering his estate.[37] Husayn had also been nominated to sit on the Ottoman sultan's Council of State shortly before his death; only his ill health had prevented him from moving to Istanbul and taking up his new post.[38] This was a man who began his career as a slave to the sultan, devoted his life to serving the governor of an Ottoman province, and died an Ottoman subject.

Despite fighting over Husayn's nationality for three full months, de Laigne and Ghikis made little progress. The French and Ottoman ministers of foreign affairs finally agreed that the two consuls should read through Husayn's papers together and produce a joint report on the deceased's nationality.

Husayn's personal archive revealed a man whose approach to nationality differed little from any of the other North Africans involved in the Shamama case. Like Nissim himself—and like Elmilik after him—Husayn explored various possibilities. At one point he considered seeking naturalization as a Prussian; among his papers was "a copy of a letter from the Prussian minister of foreign affairs, announcing to Husayn that . . . his naturalization in Prussia would be valid everywhere except in Tunisia." He also possessed both Tunisian and Ottoman passports—documents issued to facilitate his travel across the Mediterranean, yet potentially useful as evidence of his legal belonging.[39]

But none of Husayn's papers could offer conclusive proof of either French or Ottoman nationality; the dispute turned not on Husayn himself but rather on the nature of imperial sovereignty. In the end, only the intervention of Khayraddin settled the matter; the former prime minister, who had since moved to Istanbul, convinced the Ottomans to abandon their claim of jurisdiction and leave the matter to the French.[40] In so doing, he found a way for the sultan to save face in a losing battle. As with so many other fights over the status of Tunisians outside Tunisia, French diplomats had the military and political clout to successfully assert their authority. The Ottoman consul limited himself to bringing Husayn's remains to Istanbul, where they were reinterred in the mausoleum of Sultan Mahmud II.[41]

Ghikis had been set up to fail from the start. The fight over Husayn's nationality was in this sense distinct from the Shamama case. When it came to Nissim's estate, Italian courts had uncontested jurisdiction. It seems likely that the Florentine judges were willing to declare Nissim a Tunisian national in part because they would still get to decide how to distribute his estate. Husayn's case more closely resembled those of Tunisians living in the Ottoman Empire, where all jurisdiction was determined by the capitulations—and where French consuls jealously guarded their protection of Tunisians as a way to impose their authority in the sultan's domains. Ghikis was already depressed about being posted to a third-rate city like Florence.[42] One imagines he took cold comfort in ascribing another defeat to forces beyond his control.

Elmilik's enemies wielded legal belonging as a weapon against him, accusing the Algerian-born Jew of lacking patriotism for France. And the death of both Husayn and Ibn 'Ayyad triggered the need to determine nationality—that of the deceased in Husayn's case and the heirs in the Ibn 'Ayyad dispute. Yet no one found themselves more tormented by the shadow of legal belonging than

Nissim's relatives. For some of the Shamamas who had left Tunis for Livorno, nationality determined aspects of their private lives as foreigners. For others, it offered a generative subject of work and ideology. And for many more, legal belonging had tragic and violent consequences during a calamitous twentieth century that proved particularly dangerous for Jews.[43]

Perhaps no one emerged from the Shamama lawsuit more obsessed with nationality than Nissim Samama (as he spelled it), the son of ʻAziza and Moses. Nissim Jr. was just a few days old when his parents bundled him up and boarded a steamship bound for France.[44] While Nissim lived, Nissim Jr. was sheltered from the world in an abundance of bourgeois affluence. Nissim's death made Nissim Jr.'s comfortable existence suddenly precarious; his parents sank into debt while trying to secure their share of the estate. By the time the court of appeal in Florence ruled in 1883, Nissim Jr. was nineteen years old; he had already left Livorno behind—perhaps an attempt to shake free from the nightmare of the Shamama lawsuit.

Even if Nissim Jr.'s intention was to escape, he could not shed the questions of private international law and nationality that had consumed his family for so long. Little surprise, then, that he decided to become a lawyer. (Perhaps he had also learned one of the main lessons of *Shamama v. Shamama*: lawyers are the only ones guaranteed to make money in legal disputes.) Nissim Jr. enrolled in the faculty of law at the Université d'Aix-Marseille at the age of eighteen, a year before the final ruling in the Shamama case.[45] He defended his dissertation in 1890—a collection of three articles all dealing with the law of inheritance; parts 2 and 3 explored the validity of wills in private international law. What else would someone named Nissim Samama write about?

The substantive arguments of the lawsuit also made their mark on the budding lawyer. Nissim Jr. became a devotee of the nationality principle in private international law; his dissertation explained that "the capacity of the testator should be regulated . . . according to the moral, intellectual, and political state of the country to which he belongs."[46] The young jurist pointed out that the nationality principle was a "modern theory" that better fit a world in which people "frequently moved."[47] He quoted none other than Mancini, who, he explained, was central to ensuring that private international law accepted nationality as the basis of personal status. The thesis was dedicated to his parents, described as "my guardians and my sweet glory" in a Latin epigraph from Horace.[48]

Nissim Jr. remained in Marseille and opened a legal practice there. By 1890, ʻAziza and Moses had joined him; the three lived together on the Avenue du

Prado, an enormous tree-lined boulevard on the scale of the Champs-Élysées.[49] Like a good Maghribi Jewish boy, Nissim Jr. married a distant cousin, Emilie Scemama de Gialluly, daughter of Liahu, one of great-uncle Nissim's successors as qā'id al-yahūd.[50] As Nissim Jr.'s career advanced, he moved to Paris to become a lawyer at the court of appeal; he settled on the Rue de Phalsbourg near the tony Parc Monceau—just a mile from the apartment he lived in as a small child in the 1860s.

But making his career in the French legal system did not mean turning his back on Italy. On the contrary, Nissim Jr. became intensely involved in advocating for Italians in France. He took a leadership role in the Franco-Italian league, eventually becoming its vice president.[51] The league undertook various activities celebrating relations between the two countries and promoting Italian culture. Nissim Jr. helped mark the fiftieth anniversary of the Battle of Solferino, in which French and Sardinian forces had united against the Austro-Hungarian Empire and succeeded in annexing Lombardy to unified Italy. In the grand amphitheater of the Sorbonne, Nissim Jr. stood as an honor guard around the French and Italian flags while crowds thronged the surrounding streets.[52]

In all of his writing—both in Italian and French—Nissim Jr. identified himself with a presumed European audience. Notably absent was any hint of his Tunisian background. In an article about the naturalization of Tunisian Jews, Nissim Jr. argued against making them French citizens en masse, as the Crémieux Decree had done in Algeria. It would be inadvisable, he explained, to grant "citizenship to masses that have not yet been thoroughly penetrated by our modern ideas."[53] And in any case, the vast majority of Tunisian Jews had nothing in common with French people from the metropole; they dressed like Arabs, practiced polygamy, and were thoroughly under the sway of their backward religious beliefs.[54] In arguing against the collective naturalization of Tunisian Jews, Nissim Jr. opposed a group of prominent Tunisian Jewish lawyers who shared his alma mater. Writing in the pages of *La Justice*, many of the Tunisian Jewish graduates of the law faculty at the University of Aix-Marseille advocated for the "emancipation" of Tunisian Jews through collective naturalization as French citizens.[55] Nissim Jr., however, maintained that only the naturalization of a small number of Jewish elites would benefit France. These Jews' assimilation to French culture meant that they "had almost nothing in common with true natives [*les véritables indigènes*], neither in their ideas or culture." Nissim concluded emphatically, "No one should be forced to keep a nationality that does not suit him."[56]

Nissim Jr.'s thorough identification with Europe—and his public silence about any personal connection to Tunisia—made it clear that he thought of himself neither as Arab nor African. In his personal life, however, he resisted having to choose just one nationality. His father Moses was from Algeria, and thus benefited from French nationality and, after 1870, citizenship. Nissim Jr. would normally have inherited that status, but he nonetheless took the precaution of naturalizing as a French citizen in 1891. Undoubtedly, he had also come to appreciate the advantages of hedging one's bets when it came to nationality.[57]

Meanwhile, his commitment to Italy only grew. In 1908, he attended the Italian Colonial Institute's first Congress of Italians Abroad in Rome, where he lectured on questions of nationality and expatriation. The congress grew out of the Italian government's long-standing concern over the growing numbers of Italian emigrants, seen by some as sucking the lifeblood from the nation. The question of belonging was at the heart of concerns about emigration, as nationalists tried to keep Italians tied to their homeland through both the duties and benefits of citizenship.[58]

Nissim Jr. made it clear that he was dissatisfied with the options presented to émigrés—a choice between retaining Italian citizenship or naturalizing in their new home. "You cannot," he asserted, "demand that a foreigner renounce his nationality, his most sacred bond."[59] Striking out boldly against the prevailing headwinds of the time, Nissim Jr. made the case for accepting dual citizenship. His colleagues were largely unanimous in condemning membership in multiple states as an undesirable judicial anomaly.[60] But Nissim insisted that objections to dual nationality were outdated. Opposition to dual citizenship reflected a time long gone, when emigrants left their home and never expected to return. "Today," he wrote, "everyone is able to travel, and most emigrants nurture the hope to return to their fatherland one day, after having made their fortune." Why should Italy lose thousands of its citizens every year, when they in fact "still felt profoundly Italian"?[61] Nissim Jr.'s recommendations were largely ignored; the new Italian citizenship law of 1913 demanded emigrants' exclusive loyalty to Italy, precluding the possibility of multiple allegiances.[62]

Echoes of the arguments made in the Shamama case rang throughout Nissim Jr.'s plea on behalf of dual citizenship. Decades earlier, Husayn pointed out the de facto existence of dual citizenship in the context of the Shamama lawsuit. Husayn noted that states with the principle of indelible allegiance—like Tunisia and the Ottoman Empire—simply did not recognize the naturalization of their subjects abroad. A Tunisian who naturalized in France might be considered French there, but back in Tunisia he would be treated as a Tunisian.[63] Ottoman officials in the Nationality Bureau and judges in the Egyptian Mixed Court of Appeal made the same observation: the reality was that some individuals had two nationalities.[64] How carefully had Nissim Jr. pored over Husayn's briefs? Did he recognize the ways in which his argument pulled on strands woven through the Shamama lawsuit? Might Nissim Jr. have remembered that his uncle presented himself as an Italian count while finding every opportunity to mention his position as a Tunisian official?

Nissim Jr.'s public shedding of his Tunisian roots eventually caught up with his private life. He divorced his first wife, with whom he had never had children.[65] He then married Rose Itier, a woman twenty-five years his junior, born to a Catholic family in Pomeys, France. How Nissim Jr.'s parents felt about his intermarriage remains a family secret. On the whole, though, 'Aziza and Moses seemed willing to go along with their son's enthusiastic embrace of Europe. In an undated photo, 'Aziza sits in a classically French park, sporting the tailored dress, enormous hat, and parasol characteristic of bourgeois ladies at the turn of the century—quite the contrast from the photograph taken in Paris in the 1860s, when she still wore Tunisian attire. When Moses died in 1912, he was buried in the Montparnasse Cemetery; 'Aziza joined him there in 1919.[66] This quintessentially Parisian resting place already housed prominent French Jews, including Adolphe Crémieux (d. 1880), who had worked briefly as Nissim's lawyer. Perhaps by interring his parents in the Cimetière Montparnasse, Nissim Jr. hoped to finally assuage his anxieties about legal belonging.

Nissim Jr.'s entire career can be understood as a reaction to the lawsuit that consumed his family; instead of running away from his past, he devoted his life to answering many of the legal questions raised in *Shamama v. Shamama.* Most of his relatives tried the opposite approach: turning their backs on both law and legal belonging. But no matter how much they tried to move on, questions of citizenship and nationality hounded the family like a biblical curse—one visited on the heirs, their children, and their children's children.

Joseph Shamama did not want to remain Tunisian. In 1879, he applied to become an Italian citizen. But the Italian Ministry of the Interior declined Joseph's request for naturalization. The ostensible reason given was the indelible allegiance that Tunisia demanded of its subjects, although at the time,

FIGURE 10.1. ʿAziza Shamama, n.d.
(courtesy of Gilles Boulu)

Tuscan courts were busy debating the very existence of this principle in the Shamama case. Nonetheless, the interior ministry determined that Joseph would be considered Tunisian in Tunisia no matter what Italy did. This made him a poor candidate for naturalization as an Italian.[67] Joseph and his children remained foreigners, though most of them lived the rest of their lives in Italy.

Joseph's son Abramo Alberto (Abraham in Hebrew) arrived in Livorno at the age of eleven. Like his father, Abramo similarly sought to shed his Tunisian roots, albeit through marriage rather than naturalization. At the age of twenty-two, he fell hopelessly in love with Vittoria Ida Stracca, an actress from Bologna two years his senior. In April 1885, Abramo abandoned his studies at the Università di Pisa, where he was training to be a lawyer. Abramo and Vittoria eloped in the small seaside town of Viareggio.[68] Joseph was furious; not only was Vittoria a Catholic, but her career on the stage made her thoroughly disreputable. He succeeded in having the marriage annulled in the civil court in Lucca; Abramo was not yet twenty-five years old, so the young man required his parents' consent to marry. The star-crossed lovers were undeterred, however; they traveled to London, where English law considered them full adults, and married again on July 25. Having succeeded in wedding despite Joseph's opposition, the couple returned to Italy and settled in Genoa. Not long after, Abramo wrote to Joseph to ask his pardon and for a small allowance to sustain his new married life. Joseph reluctantly agreed to give him 300 Italian lire per month. Abramo's lifestyle as a married man was a significant step down from his youth in Livorno, with carriages and multiple servants. Nevertheless, Joseph's contributions allowed the couple to keep body and soul together.

The newlyweds soon had their first child, Daya, whom they named after Abramo's mother.[69] Yet their good fortune was not to last; Abramo fell ill with tuberculosis. Joseph increased their stipend to 450 lire per month, but money could not save his son. Vittoria was heavily pregnant with their second child when Abramo died at the age of twenty-seven—ten days before the birth of another girl, named Albertina after the father she would never know.[70] At this point, relations between Joseph and Vittoria deteriorated; Joseph reduced her stipend back to 300 lire. Vittoria—furious, desperate, or perhaps both—sued her father-in-law, requesting 40 lire per day in maintenance. Joseph's defiance flared again, and he refused to pay his daughter-in-law anything. He returned to the same argument he made when his son had first eloped with Vittoria: the marriage was null because his son had been a minor at the time.[71] After multiple appeals, the court of cassation in Florence finally ruled against Joseph in 1891; the judges noted that he had paid his son a monthly allowance during four years of marriage, amounting to a tacit recognition of the union.

At this point, Joseph's lawyers turned to a strategy familiar from the Shamama case: they contended that Abramo was a Tunisian national, and as such, was not subject to Italian law for personal matters like marriage. Rather, any marriage Abramo might or might not have entered into should be regulated by Jewish law, which had jurisdiction over the private lives of Tunisian Jews. And according to halakhah, no marriage between a Jew and a Catholic could be legitimate. Joseph thus owed Vittoria and her bastard children nothing. To support this claim, Joseph's legal team procured opinions from rabbis in Tunis, the Italian consul in Tunis, and a translation of an excerpt from the *Shulḥan 'Arukh*, along with a declaration that "this was the authentic text of Talmudic law."[72] Joseph even engaged some familiar faces from the Shamama lawsuit; Castelli wrote a brief supporting the nullity of Abramo and Vittoria's marriage.[73]

Vittoria was unphased at the invocation of the Talmud. The eminently resourceful widow procured Italian translations of all the evidence produced by Joseph. Her lawyers shot back that Joseph's evidence was inadequate. In what might have been a page from Benamozegh's opinion on Nissim's will, Vittoria's lawyers argued that only the Talmud was an authoritative source of Jewish law; the *Shulḥan 'Arukh* was merely "one among many books of rabbinic literature."[74] Having failed to produce the Talmudic text itself, the counsel pointed out, Joseph had not proven that Jewish law considered Vittoria's marriage to Abramo null. The civil court of Livorno agreed and upheld the marriage; the judges ordered Joseph to pay 300 lire per month in maintenance as well as all the court and lawyers' fees for both sides.[75]

When Vittoria and Abramo fell in love, they were fully aware of breaking multiple taboos: marrying across religious and class lines, and in open defiance of Abramo's parents. But it is hard to imagine that they thought about the jurisdictional boundaries their marriage crossed—or knew that Abramo's Tunisian nationality would determine the law that applied to their union even after his untimely death. Vittoria nonetheless managed to triumph over Joseph's attempts to use nationality against her.

The Shamama heirs who lived through World War II were not so lucky. Like all Jews, the Shamamas who remained in Europe in the 1930s and 1940s saw their lives upended. As the Nazis spread across the continent, they turned the question of Jews' belonging into a rallying cry of antisemitism: Jews were racially distinct from Aryan Germans and thus did not deserve to be citizens of Germany. The attacks against Jews' legal belonging began with the Nuremberg laws passed in 1935, which reduced German Jews from citizens (*Reichsbürger*) to nationals without political rights (*Staatsangehöriger*). In 1941, around the time the Nazi regime started to implement the Final Solution, German Jews who had left the country—including those who had been deported—were deprived of citizenship en masse.[76] Even in Italy and Vichy France—where most Jews were not stripped of their citizenship—legal belonging took on lethal dimensions as foreign Jews were often the first to be deported.[77]

When war broke out between France and Germany in 1939, Nissim Jr. was seventy-five years old, undoubtedly retired from a successful career as a lawyer in Paris. We know little of how he spent the war, except that he survived; he returned to the south of France, where he passed away in a small suburb of Cannes in August 1945, just months after the Allied victory on May 7.[78] But his life was not unaffected by the war; he lost at least five precious pieces of art to Nazi looting, including a marble sculpture of two half-dressed women titled *Les Marguerites* by the nineteenth-century French artist Joseph-Marius

Ramus.[79] One imagines that these deprivations paled in comparison to the trauma of living through the war.

Qā'id Momo's family was less fortunate. Before the end of the lawsuit, Momo had already left Livorno for Corfu, where seven children were born to him from his two wives; the youngest, Nathan Donat, came into the world in January 1891, just before violent anti-Jewish riots erupted on the island around an alleged blood libel.[80] Antisemitic agitators accused Corfu's Jews of being disloyal to Greece and unworthy of Greek citizenship because of their inherently traitorous nature. Like thousands of other Jews, Momo and his family left Corfu after the riots; like Nissim Jr., they, too, headed to France.[81] Momo settled in Montpellier, about 150 kilometers west of Marseille. When Momo died in 1899, Nissim Jr. was there to report his grandfather's death to the authorities.[82]

Momo named his second child born on Corfu Isaac Jacques. Once settled in France, Isaac Jacques became a doctor; he married Jeanne Bloch, a native of Montpellier and, based on her name, almost certainly an Ashkenazi Jew (possibly from Alsace). According to the French civil code, Jeanne would have automatically taken her husband's nationality. In the early years of the war, Isaac Jacques and Jeanne seem to have joined the wave of Jews trying to escape Vichy rule. They went to Nice, then under Italian control. But the Germans invaded Nice in September 1943: Isaac Jacques and Jeanne were deported to Auschwitz, where they were murdered on January 25, 1944, both sixty-three years old.[83]

It is impossible to know whether the couple would have survived had they remained in Vichy France; as Tunisian nationals, they would almost certainly have been classified as French protégés, subjects, or even citizens rather than as foreigners.[84] And while belonging to France was not enough to spare Jews deportation—thousands of French Jews were murdered in concentration camps—the majority of Jews with French citizenship survived. Jews who were foreign citizens suffered from the double punch of xenophobia and antisemitism.[85] Yet the technicalities of French claims to protect Tunisians outside Tunisia likely did little to assuage Isaac Jacques and Jeanne's fears. As North Africans lacking full French citizenship, the couple must have felt doubly exposed to the terror of deportations. In the end, legal belonging made no difference; Isaac Jacques and Jeanne's Jewishness was all that mattered in the eyes of their Nazi murderers.

Even before World War II threatened the lives of Jews in Italy, Joseph's descendants had been dogged by tragedy. Salvatore, Joseph's first child to be born in Livorno, came into the world just a few months after the family arrived in Tuscany.[86] He was the only member of the Shamama family to become enamored with anarchism; Salvatore rejected his parents' adopted home and moved to Tunis in 1909, probably to escape persecution from the authorities. He died there at the age of forty-four, still a wanted man for "crimes against property."[87] Salvatore's youngest brother, Carlo, born in Livorno in 1883, was arrested in Milan in 1936 on charges of pederasty. Although he came from a home with multiple carriages and servants in livery, Carlo was thoroughly ruined; he worked as a day laborer, and frequented "crooks and swindlers." He was caught enticing two young boys, aged fourteen and fifteen, to his home, promising to pay them to perform "libidinous acts on his person." The prefecture recommended that Carlo be arrested to prevent him from posing any further "social danger."[88]

Abramo and Vittoria's daughter Daya remained in Livorno; her mother's success in securing support from Joseph notwithstanding, the family was hardly wealthy. Like so many of Joseph's progeny, Daya married a Catholic, Alfonso Fiorentini; they had two children in quick succession, Leone and Giuliana. When their younger daughter was just a year old, Alfonso died while serving in World War I; Daya must have felt doomed to repeat her mother's experience of raising two young children as a widow. She nonetheless persevered and eventually her son Leone was able to support her. But tragedy struck again, and in 1943, Leone was also killed, while in command of an Italian submarine.[89] Daya then did what so many destitute Italians had done since the rise of fascism; she wrote directly to Benito Mussolini asking for aid. Before Il Duce's secretaries could accede to Daya's request, however, they had to determine whether the woman should be considered Jewish. They decided that as the product of a mixed marriage herself, Daya did not belong to the "Hebrew race." Four months after her son died, she was awarded a subvention of five thousand lire.[90]

Mussolini's antisemitic policies spared Daya. But they wreaked havoc with the family of Elia Samama, Joseph's second child to be born in Tuscany. Elia came into the world in 1874, a year after his family arrived in Livorno.[91] Though reared in his father's lavish home, Elia's formal education ended at age eleven—undoubtedly a sign that shortly after the Shamama lawsuit ended, the family had fallen on hard times.[92] Like his elder brother Abramo, he married a Catholic woman, Anita Montelativi.[93] The couple had four children; they named their eldest, born in 1904, Giuseppe (Italian for Joseph) after Elia's father and following to Sephardic custom, although the boy was not Jewish according to halakhah. Three girls followed: Annamaria, Iolanda, and Maria Giovanna, all born in Livorno.

As with Joseph's other sons, a shadow hung over Elia's family. Giuseppe joined the National Fascist Party and enlisted in the army in 1920 at the age of sixteen. (The National Fascist Party did not officially adopt an antisemitic platform until 1937, and before then significant numbers of Italian Jews joined.)[94] In 1922, Giuseppe participated in the March on Rome, the fascist demonstration that led to Mussolini's rise to power. But he was expelled from the armed forces three years later for bad conduct as well as his sister's "immorality"; Annamaria, two years his junior, worked as a prostitute. The National Fascist Party followed suit, expelling him in 1932—this time for his own (unspecified) "immorality." Giuseppe's second sister, Iolanda, worked as a maid. Only Elia's fourth child, Maria Giovanna, managed the respectability of marriage. Giuseppe and his father eked out a living together; most of the time Elia could afford the rent for a furnished room, but he occasionally had to spend the night in a shelter. By the time war broke out, Elia and all four of his children were living in "a miserable economic condition."[95]

In June 1940, the prefecture of Livorno wrote to the Ministry of the Interior; the subject line was "Semama, Elia, son of the late Giuseppe and Daya Gozlan, born in Livorno on September 10, 1874, now residing at 12 Via Serristori, second floor; French subject."[96] The letter did not explain why Elia was described as French; it merely referred to him as a "foreigner." Only subsequent correspondence made it clear that Elia's Tunisian parentage meant that he was considered French. Despite having lived his entire life in Italy, Elia had never applied for Italian citizenship. Back in 1887, France's assertion of jurisdiction over Tunisians outside Tunisia had undergirded de Laigne's claims on Husayn's estate; more than half a century later, the French protection of Tunisians put Elia in the category of French subject—and enemy alien.

As both a foreigner and member of "the Jewish race," Elia was deemed by the prefecture to be "capable of conducting defeatist activity." Because of his "advanced age"—Elia was sixty-six years old and in bad health—the official recommended that he be interned in a town where he might be "more easily watched."[97] Four days later, Elia was taken to Chiaromonte, a tiny hamlet in Basilicata, deep in the south of Italy. Elia lost little time in writing to the minister of internment. In an elegant hand that evoked a brighter childhood, Elia explained that he was gravely ill: "I feel that my life is short, even very short;

from one moment to the next I may die."[98] He begged to be brought back to Livorno to be nearer to his children. A month later he repeated this request, adding various anecdotes about his life that might prove his loyalty to Italy: his brother Umberto was a commander in the navy, his son participated in the March on Rome, and he had always "remained patriotic."[99] The minister, however, was unconvinced. Elia's request was refused.

Giuseppe, Elia's son, took up his father's plight. In his shaky hand and even shakier grammar—evidence of a less coddled youth than his father's—Giuseppe tried to convince the minister that Elia was in fact Italian. "You sent him away," Giuseppe explained, "because he is a Tunisian subject, but Excellence, he is completely Italian since birth, having been born in Livorno and having a son who is an old fascist." Giuseppe seemed not to grasp exactly why Elia would be deemed a foreigner; in his somewhat garbled words, he noted that his father "is only considered a French citizen because his old parents were Tunisian, and they [would have] made his citizenship, but he was always sick. Yet he is completely Italian!"[100] In Giuseppe's mind, naturalization was a detail that could easily be overlooked; he constructed a narrative about his father's nationality based on the fact that his father had lived his entire life in Italy. Not unlike the ways in which both Mancini and Pierantoni emphasized reputation and self-perception in the Shamama case, Giuseppe argued that his father had felt Italian all of his life. He begged the government not to leave this "completely Italian man . . . on a cold mountain far from us children."[101]

Elia's illness finally convinced the authorities to transfer him to an internment camp in Sassetta, a town just outside Livorno.[102] Yet he continued to suffer from the cold. Periodically he wrote to the minister in charge of internment to ask for more clothing, optimistically including his measurements each time. All of his requests were denied.[103] The sole silver lining was that Giuseppe was now allowed to visit his father occasionally.[104] In his last attempt to inspire the mercy of the Italian authorities, Elia wrote again to ask for clothing. "I am barefoot," he wrote in a hand notably less steady than that of his first letters. "I am trembling with cold." He asked the minister to grant his request as a "great act of charity."[105] At that point, he had been interned for nearly three years.

Then, in the winter of 1944—when the Allied forces were advancing on Rome—the police headquarters of Livorno sent a telegram to the national guard with instructions to arrest Giuseppe.[106] Elia's son was imprisoned in an internment center set up at the Villa La Selva in Bagno a Ripoli just outside Florence—a magnificent property requisitioned from its absent Jewish owner

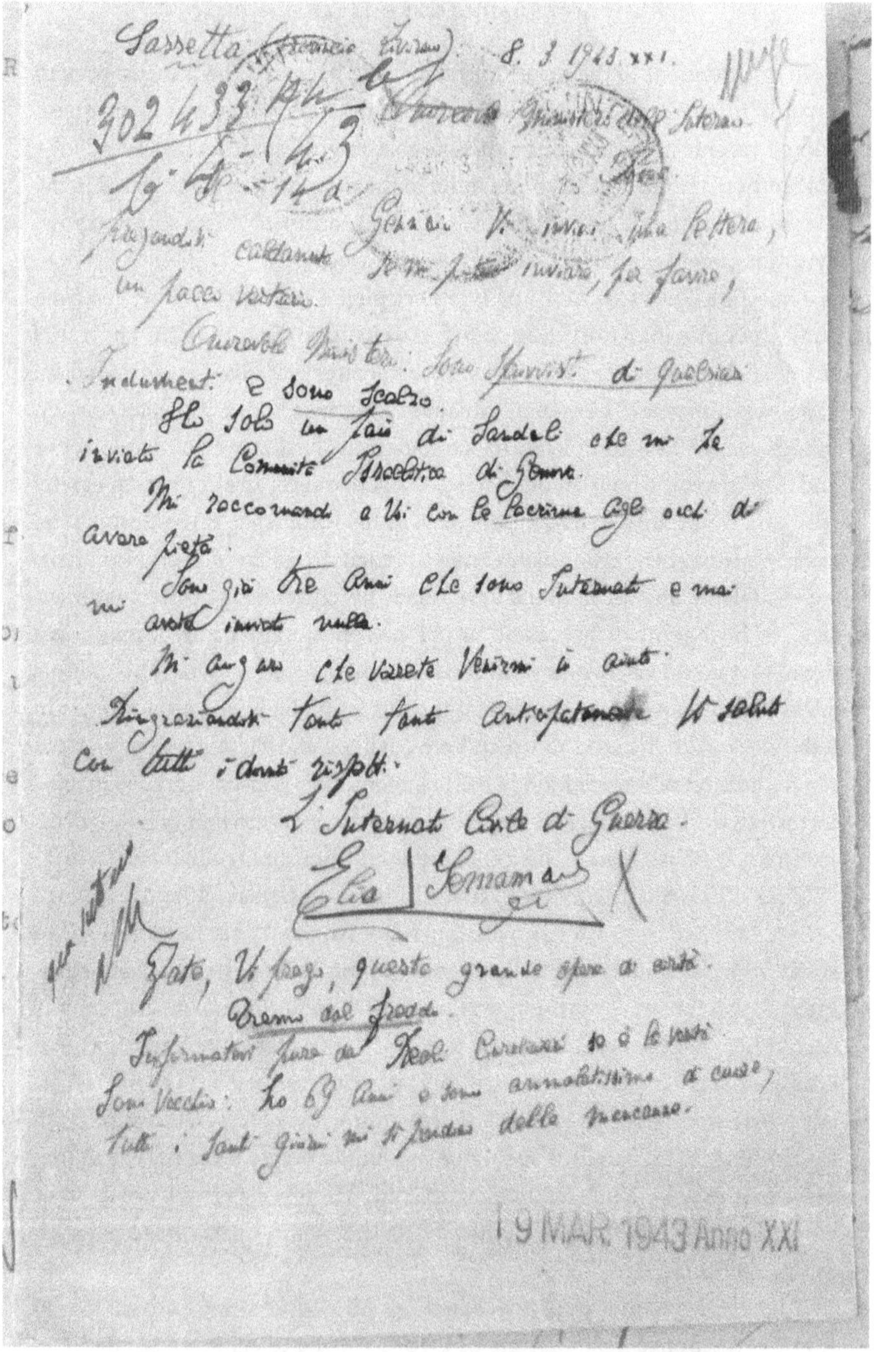

Sassetta (Francia Luisa) 8. 3. 1943 XXI.

302433

Eccellenza Ministro dell'Interno Roma

Onorevole Ministro: Sono sprovvisto di qualsiasi indumenti e sono scalzo.

Ho solo un paio di sandali che mi ha inviato la Comunità Israelitica di Genova.

Mi raccomando a Voi con le lacrime agli occhi di avere pietà.

Sono già tre anni che sono internato e mai mi avete inviato nulla.

Mi auguro che vorrete venirmi in aiuto.

Ringraziandovi tanto tanto anticipatamente vi saluto con tutti i dovuti rispetti.

L'Internato Civile di Guerra.

Elia Semama

Fate, Vi prego, questa grande opera di carità.

Tremo dal freddo.

Informatevi pure dai Reali Carabinieri se ciò che vi dico è vero.

Sono vecchio: ho 69 anni e sono ammalatissimo di cuore, tutti i santi giorni mi prendono delle ...

19 MAR 1943 Anno XXI

FIGURE 10.2. Letter from Elia Semama to the Ministry of the Interior, March 8, 1943 (Ministero dell'interno, direzione generale pubblica sicurezza, divisione affari generali e riservati, ufficio internati, A4 bis, internati stranieri e spionaggio, 1940–45, Busta 326, Samama, Elia fu Giuseppe, ACS)

Silvio Ottolenghi.[107] Giuseppe was far more fortunate than his father; shortly after his arrest, the police headquarters in Florence realized that he was from a "mixed family"—"a Jewish father and an Aryan mother"—and had been baptized at birth.[108] Giuseppe was allowed to leave Villa La Selva after three weeks. Still, his stay was long enough to have contracted tuberculosis. On release, he went straight to the hospital.[109]

Elia was only freed from his internment in Sassetta after the war ended in 1945. Back in Livorno, he lived at 25 Via San Jacopo in Acquaviva, less than a kilometer from Nissim's former palazzo. In 1947, Elia filed an application for aid with the International Refugee Organization. The person who interviewed him noted that he was "disabled"—suffering from heart disease and unable to work; he wanted "to remain in Italy with son and daughter." In addition to Italian, Elia spoke French fluently. One doubts that the interviewer bothered to ask him if he remembered any Arabic, the language in which his parents raised him.[110]

Elia may have survived, but he was nonetheless a victim of his legal belonging. Had his father, Joseph, succeeded in naturalizing as an Italian citizen in 1879, Elia would have most likely been spared internment. While some Jews with Italian citizenship were imprisoned or even deported, an elderly man like Elia with no political history and a son who was an "old fascist" would have made an unlikely target. As for so many Jews across Europe, Elia's nationality—a detail to which he ascribed little importance before the war—abruptly became a matter of life and death.

Nazi and Axis policies around citizenship during World War II took the logic of belonging to an extreme: groups deemed inherently "other" were stripped of their legal membership in a state. Hannah Arendt most famously articulated the danger of statelessness; having a nationality, she explained, amounted to "the right to have rights."[111] The plight of tens of thousands of Holocaust survivors in displaced persons camps who no longer had membership in any state proved her point. In 1948, the United Nations published the Universal Declaration of Human Rights; Article 15 declared that "everyone has the right to a nationality"—an attempt to avoid future plagues of statelessness like the one that swept through postwar Europe.[112] The stories of the Shamama descendants suggest that statelessness was just one way in which legal belonging could become a weapon. Having no nationality left one vulnerable—without the right to have rights. But having the wrong nationality—being Tunisian, and thus effectively French in wartime Italy—could prove equally dangerous.

As legal belonging became more and more entrenched in the lives of individuals across the Mediterranean, the power of nationality only grew. We continue to live in a world where the state to which one belongs determines nearly everything about one's life—from mobility to education to the ability to feed oneself and one's family.[113] And thousands die each year attempting to defy the constraints of their birthright: citizens of states in Africa, the Middle East, and South Asia who risk everything to cross the Mediterranean into a more prosperous Europe; and Central and South Americans who brave coyotes, walls, deserts, and detention centers to reach the United States.[114] The intense anxiety around mobility that characterizes twenty-first-century politics has only made belonging more crucial than ever before. For far too many, having the wrong nationality remains just as deadly.

EPILOGUE

Legal Belonging, Past and Present

WHEN NISSIM boarded a steamship in La Goulette and took leave of his native land, he was swimming against the migratory tide. Tunisia was not a sending country but rather a destination—for Maltese and Sicilians hoping to find prosperity; for Algerians seeking refuge from French rule or hoping to exploit extraterritorial privileges; for Livornese Jews escaping their city's sinking financial ship; and especially after colonization in 1881, for French adventurers chasing the advantages of empire. Nissim was not exactly alone among Tunisians who had settled on the other side of the Mediterranean. In Paris, he surrounded himself with the "Tunisian colony," many of whose members were his associates working for the bey. In Livorno, he lived in a Jewish community tightly bound up with the Grana of Tunis. Yet Nissim's trajectory was definitely unusual. It was in large part the oddity of a Maghribi Jew domiciled in Italy that made the Shamama case such a legal conundrum.

And while questions about legal belonging were by no means new in the nineteenth century, the age of nationalism and the territorialization of law made them more urgent than perhaps ever before. Nissim hardly posed the only thorny case of contested belonging; similar legal puzzles arose concerning Irish Americans who joined the Fenian Revolt, Franco-Americans who returned to the old country, Baghdadi Jews in China, and countless others whose stories have yet to be told.[1]

Yet it was hardly coincidental that the Shamama case spanned the Mediterranean—a sea that has served as both highway and barricade for centuries, alternatively connecting and separating people across divides of religion, culture, language, and politics. The Mediterranean and its Jews offer a preeminent platform from which to launch a new understanding of citizenship. North Africa and the Middle East have long been a foil to the West, just as Jews were the oldest Other in Christendom. Nissim's life and death forced Europeans and Maghribis to account for the gaps in their ideas about belonging. Likewise, the lawsuit over his estate compels historians to articulate an alternative account of citizenship—across the modern Mediterranean and beyond.[2]

To say that legal belonging existed along a spectrum is only novel because we have naturalized a binary notion of citizenship. The power of legislation, identity documents, and borders has so penetrated our worldview that it is hard to fathom a lawsuit in which a person's nationality was exceedingly difficult to pin down. It is even harder to imagine someone who might belong to various polities in different degrees. Today we tend to think of nationality like the colors on a map. We are used to seeing each country shaded in a single tone—all of France blue, all of Italy green, and all of Tunisia red. Likewise, we tend to think of people as belonging in a clear and uniform way—as if all French citizens could be shaded blue, all Italians green, all Tunisians red, and colorful stripes for those lucky enough to be dual citizens.[3]

Yet I strongly suspect that if we had the capacity to transport ourselves to the past—that superpower all historians most covet—we might find our instinctive grasp of legal belonging absent from the minds of all but theoreticians. Ordinary people would have accepted the fragmentation of legal belonging as normal and even natural. This was particularly so in a place like Tunisia, where everyone acknowledged multiple sources of authority. Sovereignty was divided between the bey in Tunis and the sultan in Istanbul. Sephardic Jews with roots in Livorno acquired first Tuscan, then Italian nationality—whether their family had lived in Tunis for a matter of years or centuries. Algerian Jews and Muslims might integrate seamlessly into Tunisian society, yet they could and did turn to the consulate of France to claim French nationality. Increasing numbers of Tunisians acquired foreign protection or naturalized abroad, though the extent to which their extraterritorial privileges were recognized varied from person to person.

Nissim and the other Shamamas navigated this world intuitively. And like most of his contemporaries, Nissim lived for decades without his questionable status posing a problem. It was typical that legal belonging came to matter in moments of crisis—in Nissim's case, after he died. Battles over inheritance forced administrative authorities or courts to pin down legal belonging, as we saw in the disputes triggered by the passing of both Ibn 'Ayyad and Husayn. It was Nissim's corpse that needed to be shaded a particular color. Only after his death could he no longer contain multiple hues, alternatively Tunisian or Italian according to the circumstances.

In trying to determine Nissim's nationality, Italian judges were tasked with imposing order and meaning on a life seemingly full of contradiction. A man who claimed Livornese ancestry and applied for Italian citizenship, yet who failed to follow the instructions of his naturalization decree. A devoted Jew who gave generously to Jewish charitable causes, yet who wrote a will that flouted the requirements of Jewish law. A government official who rose to the highest ranks of service in Tunisia and spoke only Arabic, yet who paid a hefty sum to become an Italian nobleman. A native of Tunis who spent the first half century of his life in his hometown and became one of the largest Jewish property owners in the country, yet who abruptly abandoned his native land, never to return.

Nissim was exceptional in many ways. He possessed a vast fortune. His wealth made him more mobile than most. And he moved from south to north at a time when most were crossing the Mediterranean in the other direction. But in other ways, Nissim's experience was entirely ordinary. Throughout North Africa, the Middle East, and Europe, individuals lived comfortably amid multiple layers of sovereignty. In those instances when they came up against the need for a single, uniform nationality, the strands of their lives often did not fit neatly into the mold of a single legal belonging. This was true both of affluent individuals like Nissim and ordinary folk like soldiers trying to avoid the draft.

Seeing belonging as fragmented should not be taken as an endorsement of the inequality implied in hierarchized regimes of state membership. Today differentiated degrees of belonging are usually associated with formal inequality and thus condemned. But projecting a twenty-first-century ideal of citizenship onto the past is, frankly, bad history.[4] The majority of people in the nineteenth century—both in Europe and the Middle East, and presumably elsewhere as well—believed that inequality and differentiated rights were inevitable, even necessary. Whether those distinctions emerged from taxonomies of race, gender, religion, or state membership, the idea that every single individual should have exactly the same rights and duties as everyone else could only be prescriptive or utopian, never descriptive of the world as it existed. To some extent, we continue to accept these kinds of distinctions; nobody—least of all parents of small children—proposes to give minors the same rights and duties as adults, even if some advocate changing the age of majority. And most implicitly affirm that citizens are entitled to different rights than foreigners, save a radical fringe who wish to abolish international borders altogether. This is the basic presumption that has created a global lottery based on birthright in which people born in rich nations have access to advantages unimaginable in most parts of the world.[5]

Understanding that our ideals of equality have always embraced hierarchy; that belonging so often fragmented along lines of race, religion, gender, and class; that state membership became inflected by ideologies like nationalism; in short, abstracting away from ideals of citizenship toward the historical reality of legal belonging—none of this negates a thirst for a more just world in which citizenship and nationality are no longer forces for exclusion. On the contrary, a clear-eyed view of the past can only help us better understand our present and reimagine our future.

What is perhaps harder to access for the historian is how people like Nissim felt about living their lives betwixt and between belongings. Did Nissim think of himself as first Tunisian and then Italian? Was he as strategic as Elmilik made him out to be—preferring at times to be adjudicated according to Tunisian law and thus appear Tunisian, and at other times opting for Italian jurisdiction and hence claiming Italian citizenship?[6] Or did he not think about it much at all—only confronting his own nationality when administrative officials required documentation, and otherwise finding himself spared such pesky questions? It seems a safe bet that Nissim was strategic in his approach to citizenship, as were so many in North Africa and the Middle East.[7] The best I can say is that Nissim's belonging was not singular or whole; it was fractured across the multiple strata of legal, political, and emotive experiences that together made up his life.

In some sense, legal belonging has always been fractured. Citizenship is a construct—a powerful one that comes with significant rights, but that nonetheless masks the contingencies of birth, experience, and affection that together make up the full expanse of what it means to belong. Does one ever truly feel entirely part of a given community, place, or state? Novelists have thought otherwise for decades, or at least the classics of modern literature collectively suggest that anyone whose inner state is worth investigating lacks a sense of absolute attachment, perfect ease, or unquestioning allegiance.[8] This may well be a modern phenomenon—an attribute of the "age of alienation" in which more and more people learned to question, and even rail against, their assigned station.[9] But I doubt that our fantasy time machine could ever bring us to a premodern idyll when everyone knew their place and felt entirely content with it. The fragmentation of legal belonging is in some sense an articulation of the human condition: never singular or simple, always multiple and complex.

However (or even whether) Nissim thought of himself, his life reminds us that we must denaturalize the overlap between ethnocultural and legal belonging that nationalism has so ingrained in us. Nationalist narratives make the coincidence of nationality as an identity and nationality as a legal status seem not only desirable but also inevitable. Yet this seductive wholeness masks the turbulent layering found in the hearts and minds of actual human beings. Why should a Jew born in Tunis not belong to both Tunisia and Italy? Nissim undoubtedly was shaped by his youth in sun-drenched North Africa. His mother tongue—as far as we know, the only language he spoke until the day he died—was a dialect of Arabic spoken only by Tunisian Jews. He elected Italy, though, for both his formal citizenship and final domicile. He even claimed an ancestral connection to Livorno—a genealogy no less notable for having probably been invented. Nissim could not erase his Tunisian roots, any more than others who have given up their homeland for somewhere new. Nor should he be reduced to his origins, as xenophobic nationalists might advocate.

Jews offer a particularly good lens onto the fragmentation of belonging. For most of their history, Jews remained religiously distinct from the peoples who ruled over them. Nissim was an Other on both sides of the Mediterranean. This perpetual state of difference became accentuated in the age of nationalism. While not all Jews had their nationality come under the intense scrutiny exercised in *Shamama v. Shamama*, Jews were particularly likely to find that they did not fit easily into modern categories of belonging. Despite those nationalists who took pains to include Jews in their vision of the nation, there was always a lingering question when it came to squaring Jews with modern regimes of citizenship. It was not until after World War II that Jews' access to equal rights became widely accepted in Europe and the Americas. And this was in no small measure a reaction against the horrors of the Holocaust, when being excluded from full citizenship counted among the least of the terrors visited on Europe's Jews.

Jews in North Africa and the Middle East had a somewhat different experience of inclusion and exclusion. In the nineteenth century, government officials in the Ottoman Empire, Tunisia, and Morocco articulated a vision of legal belonging that included Jews. Yet Jews were not expected to be exactly the same as their Muslim and Christian neighbors; even in those states that abolished the dhimma, Jews continued to live much of their lives under the jurisdiction of rabbinic law. This approach to equality differed from the model of emancipation in France and Italy. In places like Tunisia, religious communities might be equal before the law of the state without dissolving into a mass of legal homogeneity. Jews could belong without giving up their legal distinctiveness.

Historians long assumed that modern citizenship regimes—with the capacity to include religious minorities—emerged only in imitation of Europe. But the Shamama case points to the flaws in this narrative; when called on to articulate how Jews belonged to the Tunisian state, Husayn relied not on Western notions of equality but instead on Islamic principles of protection. Of course, not all statesmen in the Middle East and North Africa believed that Jews and Christians should be full members of the polities in which they lived; as in Europe, this was a matter of debate.[10] Yet to assume that a citizenship capable of including Jews had to be imported is to swallow whole the Eurocentric narrative by which Europeans appropriated "the language and the posture of modernity as their sole preserve."[11]

The dissolution of the Ottoman Empire left a political void that was filled in most places by colonization and then anticolonial nationalist movements. Nationalism in the Middle East and North Africa could not avoid the desire for an overlap between ethnocultural and legal belonging. Eventually, polities formed in which Jews struggled to find a place or found that they had no place at all. And once Zionism emerged as the preeminent state-based form of Jewish nationalism, Jews in the Islamic world became subject to a double exclusion—not only as non-Muslims, but as potential Zionists. A full elaboration of this history would require another book.[12] My point is that the Shamama case can help us recover a vision of belonging in the nineteenth-century Middle East and North Africa—one based neither on the exclusion of Jews as religious others nor on the rejection of Jews as being outside the bounds of the nation.

Jews continue to encounter trouble at the fuzzy borders between legal belonging and ethnocultural identity. Antisemitism has not disappeared, nor have accusations of dual loyalty—an updated version of *doppia nazionalità* (double nationality). While the question of Jews' distinctive nationality no longer has the same edge it once did, that time is not so distant in the past. When I was just beginning my work on the Shamama case, a dear mentor and friend recalled that as a child in the immediate postwar United States, she was often asked her "nationality"—code for asking if she was Jewish.[13]

But Nissim's Jewishness led not only to his exclusion. Wandering as a Jew made it possible for Nissim to belong intimately to Jewish communities wherever he went. He may have uprooted his entire life in leaving Tunis, but he never ceased his affiliation with synagogues and Jewish charitable associations in his adopted homes. He gave generously to poor Jews in Paris and Livorno, just as he had in Tunis. Like Jews all over the world, Nissim had the Jews of the Holy Land foremost in his mind when he wrote his will.[14] It is difficult to know with any certainty to what extent he felt Tunisian or Italian. But we can rest assured that being Jewish connected him to people and places across the Mediterranean.

Much has changed about citizenship since the nineteenth century. After World War I, legal belonging became increasingly associated with the right to benefit from the growing welfare state.[15] At the same time, borders only became harder to cross; by the late twentieth century, global mobility became largely limited to the privileged few from North America and Europe. As I write, political, economic, and ecological crises have driven more people from their homes than at any other point in recorded history. The stakes of belonging are higher than ever.

What does the life and afterlife of Nissim have to do with all of this? While history may not offer ready solutions to today's problems, it can remind us that the present is contingent. The overlap between citizenship and identity—between legal belonging and ethnocultural affiliation—is not some essential aspect of the way states work. It is a conflation that emerged at a particular time, and one that has always been contested. Like the lawyers, government officials, aspiring heirs, and rabbis involved in the lawsuit, Nissim lived in a world where the distinction between legal belonging and identity was more often than not taken for granted. Retrieving the Shamama case from the dustbin of history can change our perspective not only on belonging in the past but also on its present and future.

AFTERWORD

Writing Nissim Shamama

ON A GRAY DAY in Paris in fall 2017, I met a friend at the entrance to a building on the Boulevard Saint Germain, opposite the Odéon. It was the type of neighborhood that one scarcely believes real people live in—full of tourist traps and overpriced cafés—but there we were, about to visit a woman who had spent her entire adult life in Paris.

After navigating the tiniest elevator I have ever encountered, we entered the home of Nine Moati, a celebrated Tunisian Jewish writer. My friend had agreed to introduce me to Moati knowing I was working on a book about Nissim. Among Moati's best-known novels is a heavily fictionalized account of the Shamama family in which Nissim plays a small but crucial role.[1] When Moati opened the door, she ushered us into an Orientalist fantasy of an apartment; the walls were entirely covered with paintings, hangings, and tapestries. Colorful pillows lay scattered across low couches and chairs. Heavy, velvet curtains—mostly in shades of red—obscured most of the Parisian skyline. As my friend had promised, it was *le grand Orient*, "the great Orient."

When we were seated around a low table set with Tunisian almond cookies, we soon came around to the topic of our mutual interest. Moati explained that she became curious about Nissim because her mother was a Scemama (she insisted on this spelling), in some way related to the infamous qā'id.[2] She went on to describe herself as the product of a "mixed marriage": her father was a Livornese Jew, and her mother a "Tunisian." Moati, for one, was convinced that Nissim had been *twansī* and not descended from Grana Jews as some claimed. Since the Grana were always looking down their noses at the Twansa, her mother's family had been largely sidelined in her childhood. To make matters worse, the Scemama family "was always a little ashamed" of their notorious relative; according to Moati, Nissim had "made off with all the government's money" and was largely responsible for France's colonization of

Tunisia.[3] Hardly an ancestor to be proud of, but perfect for arousing the curiosity of a fiction-writing descendant.

By this time, I had learned that among those who knew about Nissim—mostly historically minded Tunisian Jews or historians of Tunisia—his reputation was associated not with thought-provoking debates over nationality but rather with corruption and greed.[4] When I first went to Tunis to conduct research in the archives, I made a pilgrimage of sorts to the last kosher restaurant in La Goulette. The owner, Jacob Lellouche, is a man of many talents and had also run for election to the constitutional assembly in 2011. He told me that Tunisian Jews in public life were still smeared with accusations of being descended from Nissim.[5] The general discomfort I encountered when discussing my research suggested that I had embarked on a far more nefarious topic than I had initially realized.

I admit that part of me wanted to see if my archival digging might clear Nissim's name for the historical record. Even microhistorians, it turns out, are in danger of falling in love with their subjects.[6] It soon became apparent that the financial accounts preserved in the Tunisian archives were just as partial and fragmentary as the versions I had already encountered in the secondary literature. And the correspondence among government officials in Livorno and Tunis showed that neither side was able to assemble conclusive proof of Nissim's guilt or innocence.

It seems highly unlikely that the man had been a saint; there is too much evidence against him to conclude that he had done absolutely nothing wrong. Yet I also became acutely aware that the popular image of Nissim—as a gold-hungry traitor who had profited from Tunisia's financial ruin—was shot through with antisemitic stereotypes. If I could not get to the bottom of Nissim's financial dealings, then at least I could excavate the narrative that had built up around him.

After Nissim's departure for France in 1864, Tunisian officials were not unanimous in denouncing him. Ibn Diyaf, a high-ranking official and the most famous of Tunisia's chroniclers, praised Nissim and remained convinced that the receiver general had settled all of his accounts with the bey before leaving Tunis.[7] It was only years later that an account developed in which Nissim was accused of corruption, enabling Tunisia's bankruptcy, and eventually its colonization. This narrative originated not with Tunisians but rather with Europeans deeply imbricated in the French imperial project.

Husayn knew the Shamama case better than anyone in Tunis, and he eventually numbered among Nissim's fiercest critics. But Husayn's gravest allegations against Nissim were made only after the qā'id's death. And it was only then that Husayn tinged his accusations with antisemitic stereotypes.[8] This is not to say that Husayn always saw Nissim as a saint; the general was clearly aware that Nissim had been involved in shady dealings during his tenure in the Ministry of Finance. In an 1869 letter to Khayraddin, who was about to assume his role as president of the International Financial Commission, Husayn described some of the fraudulent practices that had led to Tunisia's bankruptcy. His main target was Elias Mussalli, a Greek Melkite Catholic born in Cairo who worked in the bey's Foreign Ministry. According to Husayn, "Mussalli had millions of francs in his hands," which he had acquired by charging inflated fees on exchange rates. Nissim was similarly guilty of this type of scam; "I was with Qā'id Nissim once, and he charged ten thousand [francs?] for a hundred thousand. I said to him, 'This is too much, you should only charge five thousand!'"[9] But charging a 10 percent commission, instead of what Husayn viewed as the customary 5 percent, was hardly equivalent to committing fraud on a colossal scale. Nissim was no angel, but he did not figure as the main culprit in Husayn's early correspondence.[10]

The first to accuse Nissim of significant financial misconduct was Villet, the French president of the International Financial Commission. A year before Nissim died, Villet wrote a scathing report in which he gave his version of the crimes that had led Tunisia down the road to bankruptcy. The nearly eighty-page "note" began by making it crystal clear whom Villet blamed. The brunt of Villet's ire was directed squarely at Khaznadar, still prime minister when he wrote his report. "Khaznadar demonstrated a passion for gold and riches that only grew without ever being satisfied, and for which he sacrificed the country's fortune, its very population, and even the security of the sovereign to whom he owed everything."[11]

Yet Villet hardly spared Nissim. In Villet's account, Nissim lived in "very modest" circumstances until he became Khaznadar's new confidant following the departure of Ibn 'Ayyad. Together, Nissim and Khaznadar conspired to cheat the treasury out of millions of piasters—by conveniently "forgetting" to charge Nissim for export rights, pocketing commissions, and reducing the price of tax farms and monopolies for their own personal benefit.[12] With shocking speed, Nissim's wealth grew exponentially until he was rich enough to make the government a loan of 12 million francs. When he left in 1864, he took with him "25 to 30 million francs of *savings*" that he had skimmed from the treasury, with Khaznadar's full approval.[13]

In all likelihood, it was Villet's account of Nissim's fraud that framed the Tunisian government's claims on the estate. Khayraddin had been working closely with Villet since 1869; he was foreign minister when Nissim passed away, and was put in charge of various aspects of the Shamama case. Moreover, Khayraddin was at odds with Khaznadar and friendly with Villet; he surely welcomed the opportunity to go after some of the late qā'id's wealth. Khaznadar, for his part, must have been happy to direct attention away from accusations against himself and toward his former associate; like Khayraddin, Khaznadar supported Villet's account of Nissim's perfidy. So did Husayn, who was charged with locating evidence in the government's archives that could corroborate Nissim's guilt. As the Tunisian government's representative in *Shamama v. Shamama*, Husayn found numerous occasions to expound on Nissim's alleged debts to the treasury.[14] At the time of Nissim's death, all the high-ranking officials were primed to follow Villet's lead in indicting the qā'id for financial malfeasance.

Shortly after the colonization of Tunisia, the accusations against Nissim took a virulently antisemitic turn. Nissim's crimes grew exponentially in the hands of the anonymous author of *Tunis en France* (Tunis in France), signed by "a diplomat." The screed ostensibly responded to a lawsuit between Théodor Roustan, French consul general in Tunisia during the conquest, and Henri Rochefort, director of the newspaper *L'Intransigeant*. Roustan sued Rochefort for libel, following accusations that he had colonized Tunisia for his own personal profit. *Tunis en France* claimed to provide essential information on Tunisian finances before 1881; Roustan's misdeeds paled in comparison to those of Khaznadar, his "crony" Nissim, and the "badly Frenchified German" d'Erlanger.[15] Although hardly anyone emerged unscathed from the anonymous author's pen, Nissim was deemed "the soul of all the plots against the bey's money."[16] His description of Nissim as "the wandering Jew" had the dubious honor of being the least offensive moniker used for the former qā'id; Nissim was also called a "nabab stuffed with the fruits of his fatherland's misfortune" and, more succinctly, a "devil."[17]

Tunis en France turned the volume up considerably on Villet's narrative about Nissim. Where Villet simply claimed that Nissim had lived in "modest" circumstances when he entered government service, *Tunis en France* claimed he was "very poor" and "on the verge of bankruptcy."[18] Nissim's subsequent wealth was thus all the more suspect. Where Villet lay the blame for Tunisia's financial ruin squarely at Khaznadar's feet, *Tunis en France* constructed a diabolic triangle between Khaznadar, d'Erlanger, and Nissim, who together devoured the country's finances. And despite having been baptized a Catholic at birth, d'Erlanger was labeled as a "Jew" by the anonymous author—and a German Jew to boot.[19] The book's entire approach took its cue from antisemitic screeds like Edouard Drumont's *La France Juive*; all the "complicated" financial operations leading up to Tunisian bankruptcy were "nothing other than an immense swindle organized for the benefit of a secret organization," with the Jews Nissim and d'Erlanger at its helm.[20]

The raging antisemitism of *Tunis en France* might have been swallowed by the sands of time were it not for another distinctly antisemitic book—one whose influence on Tunisian history has stamped the field ever since. The respected historian Jean Ganiage was born in France; he spent a year teaching high school in Tunisia under French rule (from 1949 to 1950) and then set out to write a dissertation on the origins of the protectorate. The resulting work earned him recognition as France's leading scholar on Tunisian history; Ganiage replaced Charles-André Julien in the chair of the history of colonialism at the Sorbonne. First published in 1959, *Les origines du protectorat français en Tunisie* (The origins of the French protectorate in Tunisia) became an instant classic and remains one of the most widely cited books on the decades leading up to 1881.[21]

I simply do not know enough about Ganiage to say whether or not he harbored antisemitic beliefs. But even a cursory read of *Les origines* reveals a thread of antisemitic prejudice running through its pages. Though less openly antisemitic than the anonymous author of *Tunis en France*, Ganiage's work nonetheless ascribed much, if not most, of the financial and political ruin of Tunisia to a group of Jewish businessmen—Nissim foremost among them. Ganiage similarly identified d'Erlanger as Jewish; indeed, in his view, most of the "adventurers" who came to offer their services to the Tunisian government were "German Jews."[22] He relied exclusively on sources in European languages (mostly French); he leaned most heavily on the reports by Villet, whom he lionized, along with Khayraddin: "Without the support of Khayraddin, Villet would never have been able to triumph over the bad will of the Tunisian government, Khaznadar's intrigues, and the Jewish courtiers on the Inspection Committee."[23] Ganiage lamented that Villet's noble efforts were ultimately for naught; by 1878, the country "henceforth belonged to Livornese Jews."[24]

Ganiage's antisemitic bent by no means invalidates his entire oeuvre (and indeed I rely on him at times, though always with circumspection). But the biases in his source base—his exclusion of Arabic sources and uncritical reliance on Villet's "note"—call the book's legitimacy into question.[25] When combined with his tendency to blame "Jews" for Tunisia's downfall, it becomes hard to swallow anything Ganiage said about Nissim without a hefty dose of skepticism. Nonetheless, Ganiage is cited almost ubiquitously in subsequent historiography; this is undoubtedly in part because no one has yet to offer such a detailed account of the period. Yet it may also be the seductive simplicity of his narrative, which blamed greedy Jews, malevolent ministers, and rapacious bankers (also Jewish) for the colonization of Tunisia.[26]

We may be no closer to an historically sound account of Nissim's tenure in the Tunisian Ministry of Finance. And it is quite possible that Villet's version was entirely accurate: that Nissim had indeed skimmed from the treasury, successfully concealing his fraud until years after he had left the country. Nevertheless, a genealogy of Nissim's reputation says something about how European antisemitism has crept into the historiography of Jews in North Africa and the Middle East. The demonization of Nissim originated with a French functionary, was distorted by an anonymous French diplomat, and then amplified by a French historian—and still remains influential in how Nissim is remembered. The "shame" that Moati's family felt about being related to the infamous qā'id may not be solely attributable to a few Frenchmen's perceptions of Nissim. But it would be naive to ignore the influence of European antisemitism on the history and historiography of Jews in the Middle East—and on the way Nissim is remembered, when he is at all.[27]

CAST OF CHARACTERS

Ahmad Bey (1805–55) ruled as the bey of Tunis from 1837 until his death. He was an ambitious reformer who invested heavily in modernizing the military.

Adriano Bargellini served as the representative of Tunisia in Livorno from 1858 (when he took over the post from Pietro Tausch) until his death in 1875, when Bargellini's son Tommaso succeeded him in the role.

Hanna Bellaiche (d. 1859) was Nissim's first wife and widow of his cousin Moshe. Her daughter Esther married Momo, with whom she had a daughter, 'Aziza, who became like an adopted daughter to Nissim.

Mahmud Ibn 'Ayyad (~1810–80) came from a wealthy family in Djerba. His father, Muhammad, rose to power under Ahmad Bey, and Ibn 'Ayyad followed suit. After accumulating vast riches (probably illegally), Ibn 'Ayyad fled to Paris in 1852. He naturalized as a French citizen and invested in real estate. Despite being sued by the Tunisian government, Ibn 'Ayyad conserved his wealth. He moved to Istanbul in 1857, where he died.

Elia Benamozegh (1823–1900) was a Livornese rabbi widely known for his work on Jewish mysticism and philosophy. He was hired (probably by d'Erlanger) to prove that Nissim's will was valid according to Jewish law and wrote two books in Italian on the subject.

David Castelli (1836–1901) was born in Livorno and studied under Benamozegh. He subsequently left rabbinic studies for secular universities, eventually becoming a professor at the Istituto di Studi Superiori in Florence. He was hired by Husayn to prove that Nissim's will was invalid according to Jewish law and wrote multiple books in Italian on the subject.

Giacomo del Castelnuovo (1819–86) was born in Florence. He moved to Egypt and then to Tunisia, where he became a physician in the service of Ahmad Bey. He later lived between Tuscany and Tunis.

Castelnuovo bought an agricultural estate in Djedeida, over which he sued the Tunisian government for a large amount of money. Castelnuovo knew Nissim and supported his application for Italian citizenship.

Rushayd Dahdah (1814–89) was a Maronite Christian from the Ottoman province of Lebanon who moved to Paris in 1845. He became one of Khaznadar's allies and agents in 1863. Subsequently, Dahdah was central to the negotiations that produced the various loans from d'Erlanger to the Tunisian treasury.

Ibn Diyaf (Ahmad b. Abi al-Diyaf, 1802–74) served as private secretary to every bey from 1827 until he retired in the 1860s. His six-volume history of Tunisia is an indispensable source for this period.

Emile d'Erlanger (1832–1911) was born in Frankfort am Main into a banking family of Jewish origin (his father, Raphael, converted to Catholicism in 1829). In 1858, d'Erlanger moved to Paris, where he set up a branch of the family bank. He made his name in the banking world by investing in the Suez Canal and financing the Confederacy during the American Civil War. In 1863, he made the first of a series of ruinous loans to the Tunisian government, eventually leading to Tunisia's bankruptcy. After Nissim's death, d'Erlanger bought up the potential heirs' shares of the estate; in 1881, d'Erlanger signed a contract with the Tunisian government to divide the Shamama estate.

Leon Elmilik (also spelled Elmelich; Eliahu Almaliah in Hebrew, 1830–91) was born in Bône (Annaba), Algeria. He moved to Tunis and joined a Masonic lodge there in 1855. In 1873, Elmilik began working for Husayn on the Shamama case, mainly as a translator (he knew French, Judeo-Arabic, Arabic, and Hebrew) and an intermediary among the potential Shamama heirs, rabbis, and the Tunisian government. He eventually fell out with Husayn, which led to various lawsuits.

Leopoldo Galeotti (1813–84) was a lawyer and politician who made his career in Florence. He was a supporter of the conservative branch of Risorgimento activists. He represented the Tunisian government in the Djedeida affair before being hired for the Shamama case.

Giacomo Guttieres (1823–96/7) was born in Livorno and moved with his family to Tunis as a child. In 1869, he was elected as one of the Italian representatives for the Comité de Contrôle of the International Financial Commission. In June 1880, he moved to Livorno to take over from Husayn as the Tunisian government's representative in the Shamama case.

Husayn b. ʿAbdallah (General Husayn, 1820–87) was born in Circassia and enslaved at a young age. He entered the service of Ahmad Bey at a young age as a mamlūk. Husayn studied the Quran and attended the Bardo Military School. He later traveled to Florence to represent the Tunisian government in the Djedeida affair. In 1873, he was appointed as the bey's representative in the Shamama case—a position he held until June 1880. Husayn remained in Tuscany until his death.

Khayraddin (Hayreddin Pasha, Khayr al-Din, ~1822–90) was born in Circassia and grew up in Istanbul in an Ottoman notable's household, where he was educated in Ottoman and Arabic. Around age seventeen, Khayraddin was sold as a mamlūk and brought to Ahmad Bey's court. He attended the Bardo Military School and rapidly ascended the rungs of power, occupying various posts in the government (including minister of the navy and foreign minister). In 1873, Khayraddin took over from Khaznadar as prime minister—a post he occupied until his falling out with Sadiq Bey in 1877, when he resigned. Eventually Khayraddin moved to Istanbul, where he briefly served the Ottoman sultan as grand vizier (from December 1878 to July 1879).

Mustafa Khaznadar (1817–78) was born on the island of Chios, then part of the Ottoman Empire. He was enslaved during the Chios massacre and eventually sold as a mamlūk to the household of the Tunisian beys. Khaznadar began working in the Ministry of Finance in 1837 and eventually became prime minister. It was Khaznadar who elevated Nissim to the role of receiver general. He was driven out of power in October 1873 after being accused of grievous financial fraud and mismanagement.

Esther Lellouche was likely the daughter of Haim Lellouche, who worked as an agent for d'Erlanger. Esther was Nissim's third wife; they married before 1864, when she accompanied Nissim to Paris, and were divorced in 1868.

Jules de Lesseps (1809–87) was born in Pisa to the French diplomat Mathieu de Lesseps. In 1827, Mathieu took up a position as French consul in Tunis, where Jules learned Arabic. After Mathieu's death in 1832, the family remained in Tunisia and Jules took up a post as a French consular agent. In 1846, he was appointed Tunisian representative in Paris. His elder brother, Ferdinand, constructed the Suez Canal, which was partly financed by d'Erlanger.

Jacob (Giacomo) "Coco" Lumbroso was born in Tunis to a prominent Grana family. His father, Isaac Vita (1793–1871), was a rabbi, *dayyan*, and leader of the Grana community. Coco moved to Marseille, where he became a prominent businessman and the unofficial consul of Tunisia. His brother Abraham became a physician to the beys.

Pasquale Stanislao Mancini (1817–88) was born in Castel Boronia in Campania—then part of the Kingdom of the Two Sicilies. He became one of the most important jurists of international law and served as the inaugural president of the Institute of International Law, founded in 1873. Mancini occupied various academic and political positions in Italy. From 1879 to 1881, he worked on the Shamama lawsuit, representing 'Aziza and Nissim Jr.

Muhammad Bey (1811–59) ruled as the bey of Tunis from 1855 until his death. He inherited the throne from Ahmad Bey, his paternal cousin.

Augusto Francescopaolo Pierantoni (1840–1911) was born in Chieti, Abruzzo—then part of the Kingdom of the Two Sicilies. He studied law under Mancini and became a well-known scholar of international law in his own right. Pierantoni occupied various academic positions, including at the University of Rome. He was one of the founders of the Institute of International Law and was elected its president in 1881. Pierantoni was married to Mancini's daughter Grazia. From 1878 to 1881, he worked on the Shamama lawsuit, representing the Tunisian government.

Luigi Pinna (b. 1805) was a Sardinian diplomat who served in multiple posts in the Middle East and North Africa—first representing the Kingdom of Sardinia and then unified Italy. In 1864, he was appointed as the Italian consul in Tunisia, a post he occupied until his retirement in 1878.

Sadiq Bey (1813–82), whose full name was Muhammad al-Sadiq, ruled as the bey of Tunis from 1859 until his death. He inherited the throne from his elder brother, Muhammad Bey.

Nissim Samama (Nissim Jr., 1864–1945) was the son of 'Aziza and Moses Shamama. Named in honor of his great-great-uncle, Nissim Jr. and his parents accompanied the elder Nissim to Europe. Nissim left him a quarter of his estate in the will. At the age of eighteen, Nissim Jr. moved to Marseille, where he studied law and practiced as a lawyer. He later moved to Paris. Nissim Jr. was married twice, first to Emilie Scemama de Gialluly and then to Rose Itier.

'Aziza Shamama (d. 1919) was the daughter of Qā'id Momo (Shlomo Shamama). Estranged from her father at a young age, 'Aziza went to live with her great-uncle, Nissim. She married Moses Shamama, and the two had a boy whom they named Nissim. 'Aziza accompanied her great-uncle to Paris in 1864 and then Livorno in 1871. Nissim left her a quarter of his estate in his will.

Esther Shamama (1856–1942) was the sister of Nathan and the daughter of Judah, Nissim's nephew. In 1873, Momo tried to use his influence with Tunisian government officials to force Esther to marry him. By taking refuge in the Italian consulate, she was able to leave for Livorno with Joseph and Nathan, where she married Nissim Attal.

Joseph Shamama (1840–1910) was Nissim's nephew (the son of Nissim's brother, Nathan). He married Daya Gozlan, with whom he had at least nine children. In 1873, Joseph moved to Livorno to pursue his portion of Nissim's wealth. The will left Joseph a quarter of his estate; were biblical law applied, however, he would inherit a third of the estate.

Mas'uda Elmaya Shamama (d. 1876) was Nissim's second wife. She remained in Tunisia when Nissim left in 1864. At the time of his death, she was living in Sousse. She sent her nephew Shlomo to Livorno to represent her interests in the estate. If Nissim was determined to have died an Italian citizen, then Mas'uda stood to inherit a third of the usufruct on his estate, in addition to the 100,000 francs he left her in his will.

Moses Shamama (1839–1912) was born in 'Annaba (Bône), Algeria. He married 'Aziza Shamama, whom he accompanied to Europe. He was deeply involved in the lawsuit over Nissim's estate, working to represent the interests of his wife and their son, Nissim Jr.

Nathan Shamama (1853–1912) was Nissim's great-nephew (the son of Nissim's nephew Judah and the grandson of Nissim's brother Nathan). In 1873, Nathan moved to Livorno to pursue his portion of Nissim's estate. The will left Nathan a quarter of the inheritance, though he stood to inherit a third according to biblical law. In 1876, Nathan married Corinna Salmon, with whom he had three children.

Nissim Shamama (also spelled Samama, Semama, Scemama, 1805–73), known as Qā'id Nissim, was born in Tunis. He became a prominent government official in the 1840s and 1850s, first under the patronage of Ibn 'Ayyad and then that of Khaznadar. He left Tunis in 1864, first for Paris and then for Livorno, where he died. His will, written in

Judeo-Arabic in 1868, was contested after his death. A decade-long lawsuit ensued, requiring the Italian courts to determine Nissim's nationality in order to decide which law applied to his estate.

Shlomo Shamama was the nephew of Mas'uda, Nissim's widow. Shlomo was appointed as Mas'uda's legal agent shortly after Nissim's death and traveled to Livorno to represent his aunt's interests in the estate. After Mas'uda's death, Shlomo became her heir.

Solomon "Momo" Shamama (1830–99), known as Qā'id Momo, was Nissim's nephew (the son of his brother, Nathan, and brother to Joseph). Momo was the father of 'Aziza, though he divorced 'Aziza's mother before she was born and the young child went to live with Nissim. Momo received only twenty-five thousand francs in Nissim's will, though he stood to inherit a third of the estate according to the biblical laws of inheritance. In 1873, he moved to Livorno to pursue his share of the inheritance. He later moved to Corfu and then finally Montpellier, where he died.

Domenico Spezzafumo was born in Tunis in 1820 to an Italian family and baptized in the Catholic parish of Saint Croix. Spezzafumo worked as the head legal counsel (*primo avvocato*) for the bey and was sent to Livorno shortly after Nissim's death in 1873.

ACKNOWLEDGMENTS

ONE OF THE GREATEST pleasures of putting a book out into the world is the chance to thank all the people and institutions that helped to make it possible. The funding for research was provided by the University of Southern California (including through a Zumberge Individual Research Award), the American Academy in Rome (through a National Endowment for the Humanities postdoctoral Rome Prize), and the Institut d'Études Avancées de Paris.

Across the Mediterranean, a number of archivists went out of their way to help me in my research. I particularly want to thank Hedi Jallab, director of the Archives Nationales de Tunisie; Cristina Francioli at the Archivio di Stato di Livorno; Paola Conti and Orsola Gori at the Archivio di Stato di Firenze; Gisèle Levi at the library of the Unione delle Comunità Ebraiche Italiana in Rome; Jean-Claude Kuperminc at the Bibliothèque de l'Alliance Israélite Universelle in Paris; and Shulamith Berger at the Yeshiva University Library.

My first trips to Tunisia were made infinitely more rewarding by the inimitable Karima Dirèche, whose generosity knows no bounds. Karima also introduced me to Sami Bargaoui, Fatma Ben Slimane, and Habib Kazdaghli, who welcomed me with open arms to the world of Tunisian history.

I will be eternally grateful to Liana Funaro, whose kindness has been without limits. She welcomed me to Livorno when Nissim was just a twinkle in my eye, and has been a constant source of knowledge about Livorno and its Jewish community since. I was fortunate to benefit from the exceptional resources (intellectual, culinary, and aesthetic) of the American Academy in Rome, where Giulia Barra, Gianpaolo Battaglia, and Kim Bowes were especially helpful. It was there I met Mauro Canali; he unlocked the treasures of the Archivio Centrale dello Stato for me in an act of supreme generosity that I will never forget.

Giuliana Moreno welcomed me into her home and shared her family's history and circle of friends from Tunisia, both Grana and Twansa. Giuliana also introduced me to Renato Ben Sasson, whose research on his familial roots was immensely helpful. Gilles Boulu selflessly shared his published and unpublished work on the Shamamas as well as family photographs; my knowledge of the Shamama family tree comes chiefly from his meticulous research. The Institut d'Études Avancées de Paris was an exceptional (and exceptionally beautiful) place to work; I am particularly grateful to Simon Luck, Geneviève Marmin, and Gretty Mirdal. Guillaume Calafat helped publish and translated one of my first articles on the Shamama case, and was characteristically gracious in connecting me to the working group PROCIT: Citoyenneté et Propriété au nord et au sud de la Méditerranée (XVIe–XIXe siècle). Simona Cerutti, Isabelle Grangaud, and the other participants provided an invigorating intellectual community from which I learned an immense amount.

I am not sure if the saying "a good research assistant is better than gold" exists, but it should—if only to describe Semih Çelik, who shared his mastery of the Başbakanlık Archives in Istanbul and his passion for Ottoman history. Kevin Smith spent a summer wading through Italian legal briefs before I was familiar with the genre. Roberto Zucchi was kind enough to take beautiful photographs of Nissim's tomb in Livorno.

There are so many people who have bestowed their expertise and wisdom on me over the course of working on this book that I fear I will inevitably fail to thank them all. That said, I am especially grateful to Alessandro Buono, Nancy Green, Yuval Haruvi, David Kertzer, Mary Lewis, David Myers, M'hamed Oualdi, Clyde Spillenger, Corey Tazzara, and Yaron Tsur. Ridha Moumni was immensely helpful in educating me about the visual world of nineteenth-century Tunisia and with locating images. Susan Gilson Miller has been a source of sage advice and unending support since I was an undergraduate; it is thanks to her that I embarked on the study of Jews in North Africa, and I could not have wished for a better mentor. I will ever be in debt to my professors at Princeton, especially Mark Cohen, Michael Cook, and Molly Greene.

I have shared portions of this project in many venues, and want to particularly thank those who invited me to speak or share work in progress, and whose feedback was immensely helpful at various stages of my thinking: Sami Bargaoui, Jay Berkovitz, Susanna Blumenthal, Aomar Boum, Francesca Bregoli, Simona Cerutti, Thomas Duve, Michaël Gasperoni, Matt Goldish, Camilo Gómez-Rivas, Isabelle Grangaud, Cyril Grange, Lital Levy, Orit Ouaknine-Yekutieli, François Pouillon, Tamar Rudovsky, Pierre Savy, David Schorr, Daniel Schroeter, Suzanne Last Stone, Corey Tazzara, and Lucette Valensi.

I am blessed with colleagues and friends who have been generous enough to read part or all of this book. Naor Ben-Yehoyada and Daniel Hershenzon brought their good humor and their Mediterranean expertise to bear on some very early drafts. Lia Brozgal, Olivia Harrison, and Neetu Khanna have improved my prose and my ideas during many delightful meetings of our writing group. Sam Erman—who has been especially generous with his expertise in citizenship—Ariela Gross, Hilary Schor, and Nomi Stolzenberg as well as the community of scholars who make up the Center for Law, History and Culture at USC have all shaped my approach to legal history; I am grateful to them for never failing to make the intellectual sparks fly. Youssef Ben Ismail and Joshua Picard not only shared their brilliant dissertations with me before they were finished, but carefully read drafts of my book. Tamar Herzog, Matthias Lehmann, Christine Philliou, and Sarah Stein agreed to read the entire manuscript; I am at a loss for words to thank them for their sharp eyes and invaluable comments. And I could not have asked for more ideal reviewers than Derek Penslar and Julia Clancy-Smith, whose reports were generous and constructive in equal measure.

Fred Appel at Princeton University Press has been enthusiastic about this project for many years. I deeply appreciate his steady hand and willingness to bet that readers might just be interested in an obscure Jew from Tunis. My thanks go to Cindy Milstein for the attentive copyediting, Fred Kameny for the skillful index, and Kate Blackmer for the stunning maps and family tree.

I cannot do justice to all the friends who made the writing of this book possible in so many ways. But I would be remiss if I did not thank my fellow surfing academics for being at my side through good waves and rough waters: Cavan Concannon, Sarah Emanuel, Sarah Stein, and more recently, Mark Letteney. I also have a special well of gratitude for the Deutchmans, our epidemiological (i.e., pod) family during the depths of the pandemic. Without Michelle, Jeremy, Caleb, and Yael, I do not think I—or anyone else in our household—would have stayed sane. Kyle McCarthy has been at my side literally and figuratively throughout this project, including tagging along on a research trip to Livorno. She has since read the entire manuscript, lavishing me with her insights from the far more stylistically attuned world of fiction.

Deborah Rosenthal and Jed Perl, my in-laws, not only gave me invaluable feedback on the manuscript but also excellent advice throughout the publishing process. Their belief in beautiful prose served as challenge and inspiration throughout the writing and rewriting of this book.

Suzanne Perl-Marglin accompanied us to Italy and then France, braving new schools and languages with an open and curious mind. Emmanuelle Marglin-Rosenthal was born while I was doing research for this book in Rome;

her fierce spirit has brought a little of the Mediterranean back to California. Suzanne and Emmanuelle's infectious enthusiasm and joie de vivre are a gift every single day, for which I cannot thank them enough.

Without Nathan Perl-Rosenthal, none of this would have been possible. He facilitated research trips to various Mediterranean cities, fellowships in Rome and Paris, and hours of locking myself in the office to write as COVID turned the world upside down. And he shared his consummate brilliance in editing the manuscript itself. He is an exceptional partner in every way; I could never adequately sing his praises.

My mother, Frédérique Apffel-Marglin, and my father, Steve Marglin, have modeled the possibility of academic pursuits as vocation and passion. They are my first teachers and remain my chief inspiration. To say that each of them read the entire manuscript and offered invaluable insights does not begin to express how they have contributed to its final form—for they have shaped all I do. I dedicate this book to them, with love, deep gratitude, and admiration.

NOTES

Archives

Italy:

ACL	Archivio Comunale di Livorno
ACS	Archivio Centrale dello Stato, Rome
ASF	Archivio di Stato di Firenze, Florence
AS Lucca	Archivio di Stato di Lucca
ASCEL	Archivio Storico della Comunità Ebraica di Livorno
ASL	Archivio di Stato di Livorno
ASMAE	Archivio Storico del Ministero degli Affari Esteri, Rome
ISR	Archivio Storico del Istituto per la Storia del Risorgimento Italiano, Rome

France:

AIU	Archives de l'Alliance Israélite Universelle, Paris
AP	Archives de Paris
BNF	Bibliothèque Nationale de France, Paris
CADN	Centre des Archives Diplomatiques de Nantes
MAE Courneuve	Archives du Ministère des Affaires Etrangères, La Courneuve

Tunisia:

ANT	Les Archives Nationales de Tunisie (*al-arshīf al-waṭanī al-tūnisī*), Tunis

Turkey:

BOA	Başbakanlık Osmanlı Arşivi, Istanbul

Israel:

CAHJP	Central Archives for the History of the Jewish People, Jerusalem

Prologue. Death in Livorno

1. Atto di morte for Semama, Nissim Kaid, no. 180, January 24, 1873, Ufficio dello stato civile di Livorno. The doctors were Cesare Nissim and Eugenio Vitali. Shamama was also spelled Samama, Semama, and Scemama. I use Shamama throughout because I believe it most accurately reflects the pronunciation of the name in Judeo-Arabic, except in cases where a person had a publication record in a European language and used an alternate spelling (such as Nissim Jr., who spelled his surname Samama).

2. A French Jewish newspaper guessed that his fortune was worth thirty million francs. *Archives israélites* 34, no. 4 (February 15, 1873): 118. Rothschild died in 1868, and his estate amounted to nearly seventy million francs. I am grateful to Cyril Grange for sharing his personal data on the Rothschild estate with me. On the milieu of the Rothschilds more broadly, see Grange, *Une élite parisienne*.

3. Sapir, *'Edut be-Yehosef*, 4.

4. Bargellini to Khaznadar, January 24, 1873, SH.C249.D670.221, ANT. Bargellini was recognized as an official consul before Tuscany joined unified Italy in 1861; after this, Ottoman diplomats urged Italian authorities not to recognize Tunisian diplomats as consuls in order to avoid undermining the sultan's claims to sovereignty over Tunisia. On this conflict, see Ben Ismail, "Sovereignty across Empires," chap. 3.

5. On this practice, see, for example, Foreign Office, *British and Foreign State Papers, 1869–70*, 492; Heyking, *Practical Guide for Russian Consular Officials*, 102–3.

6. Bargellini to Khaznadar, January 24, 1873, SH.C249.D670.223, ANT. On Rignano, see Funaro, "Rignano."

7. Bargellini to Khaznadar, January 24, 1873, SH.C249.D670.223, ANT.

8. *Archives israélites* 34, no. 4 (February 15, 1873): 118.

9. Minute 33, n.p., 99, ASCEL. In Florence, weekly board for a man averaged about 20 lire per day and about 15 lire for a woman. *State of Labor in Europe: 1878*, 287.

10. Bargellini to Khaznadar and Nushir Basha Bey, January 31, 1873, SH.C249.D670.219, ANT.

11. Bargellini to Khaznadar and Nushir Basha Bey, January 31, 1873, SH.C249.D670.219, ANT. Mas'uda also appointed another Livornese lawyer named Coriat, a member of the local Jewish community, as her representative.

12. For the original Judeo-Arabic and a Hebrew translation, see Jarmon, *Naḥalat Avot*, 1a–3b. For the French translation, see Attal, *Le Caïd Nissim Samama*, 27–31.

13. These smaller sums were deducted from each of the four portions into which the estate was divided.

14. "*Jamī'a hād al-mutawaḍīn (līgātīr) khaṣūṣīn mā yanjamū yimshī ḥaqqahim kān fawq a-sāhama mata'a wirthī hiyya mu'ayyina lahum wa-laysa fawq a-sāhamāt li-wakhrīn al-ladī hūmān mumatawwiqīn [sic] bil-qaṣd*" (Jarmon, *Naḥalat Avot*, 3a).

15. They also met with Ferdinando Andreucci—a senator and Risorgimento activist like Galeotti—and Odoardo Luchini, Andreucci's son-in-law, himself an up-and-coming member of the legal profession with political ambitions. See http://www.treccani.it/enciclopedia/ferdinando-andreucci_%28Dizionario-Biografico%29/.

16. Bargellini to Khayraddin, February 21, 1873, SH.C249.D670.236, ANT. This is specified in Article 8 of the *Codice civile* (vi).

17. "Le défunt M. Samama n'aie pas accompli l'obligation de faire enregistrer à la légation Italienne à Paris le décret royal qui lui accordait le droit d'être sujet italien, régistration qui en son fermeté de la loi doit être faite dans l'espace des six mois de la date du décret" (Bargellini to Khaznadar, January 31, 1873, SH.C249.D670.230, ANT).

18. "Avocats disent que sans avoir rempli formalités décret naturalisation devient nul" (Bargellini to Khayraddin, February 21, 1873, SH.C249.D670.236, ANT).

Introduction. Legal Belonging across the Mediterranean

1. Vanel, "La notion de nationalité," 5.

2. I argue elsewhere that legal belonging should be seen as a spectrum. See Marglin, "Citizenship and Nationality"; Marglin, "Extraterritoriality and Legal Belonging." In this, I build on the work of Sarah Abrevaya Stein. See Stein, *Extraterritorial Dreams*, 9. See also Isin and Turner, "Citizenship Studies," 2, 4.

3. Or a shared nomos, in Robert M. Cover's terminology. Cover, "Nomos and Narrative." Historians of Jews in the nineteenth century have been singularly preoccupied with the history of emancipation—which in the context of Jewish history means the expansion of civil and political rights to Jews. Long before the uptick in citizenship studies, then, historians of Jews in Europe privileged the question of how and to what extent European Jews were made citizens. The bibliography on Jewish emancipation is vast, but see esp. Katz, *Out of the Ghetto*; Birnbaum and Katznelson, *Paths of Emancipation*; Sorkin, *Jewish Emancipation*. For a long time, historians of Jews in the Middle East were beholden to a version of a "first in Europe" narrative—presenting the emancipation of Jews in the Islamic world as a result of European pressure or colonial reforms. See Schroeter, "A Different Road to Modernity." For examples of this older historiography, see Chouraqui, *Les juifs d'Afrique du Nord*; Bensimon-Donath, *Evolution du judaïsme marocain*. For studies that have sought to avoid this Eurocentric approach, see esp. Stein, *Making Jews Modern*; Cohen, *Becoming Ottomans*; Schreier, *The Merchants of Oran*; Danon, *The Jews of Ottoman Izmir*.

4. See esp. Rozenblit, *Reconstructing a National Identity*, intro, chap. 1; Rozenblit, "From Habsburg Jews to Austrian Jews"; Yerushalmi, "Servants of Kings."

5. See, for example, Drumont, *La France juive*, 1:189–90; Brustein, *Roots of Hate*, 59.

6. See discussion in chapter 8. Such accusations were not exceptions to western European liberalism but rather part of its core—for nationalism and liberalism went hand-in-hand; recent work has broken down the opposition between antisemitism and liberalism, revealing that the very doctrine of equality was premised on a set of exclusions. See esp. Green and Levis Sullam, *Jews, Liberalism, Antisemitism*. The entanglement of liberalism and racism was particularly apparent in the context of empire. See esp. Wilder, "Colonial Ethnology"; Wilder, *The French Imperial Nation-State*; McKeown, *Melancholy Order*.

7. This was particularly true of Mancini's understanding of nationality. See Ancel, *Eléments d'histoire du droit international privé*, 454.

8. See chapter 8.

9. I use "Islamic" here to invoke the ways in which Europeans perceived the states of North Africa and the Middle East, not to evoke an essentially Islamic quality of these polities. On the widespread presumptions about the oppression of non-Muslims in the Ottoman Empire as a

rallying cry for Western states, see esp. Mahmood, "Religious Freedom." European jurists' most potent argument in favor of preserving the capitulations—despite the proliferation of abuses they engendered—was the inequalities to which non-Muslims were subject since Islam "dominates all aspects of the legal system" (Pélissié du Rausas, *Le régime des capitulations dans l'empire Ottoman*, 1:121). On the capitulations, see the discussion in chapter 2.

10. For recent work on the history of Jews in the twentieth-century Middle East and North Africa, see esp. Bashkin, *New Babylonians*; Boum, *Memories of Absence*; Sternfeld, *Between Iran and Zion*; Heckman, *The Sultan's Communists*.

11. On marginality and feminist critique, see the work of bell hooks, especially "Choosing the Margin." (I am grateful to Frédérique Apffel-Marglin for steering me to hooks's theory of marginality.) For the approach of using the history of non-Muslims to illuminate broader trends in Middle Eastern history, see esp. Philliou, *Biography of an Empire*; Boum, *Memories of Absence*.

12. On entanglement—sometimes called *histoire croisée* or connected history—see esp. Werner and Zimmermann, "Beyond Comparison." On the concept in global legal history, see Duve, *Entanglements in Legal History*.

13. Engin Isin argues that citizenship has become an emblem of how modernity was invented in Europe and how Western concepts such as citizenship migrated to the non-West. See Isin, "Citizenship after Orientalism." As Dipesh Chakrabarty explains in more general terms, "political modernity" is unthinkable without being attached to the "intellectual and even theological traditions of Europe." And he puts citizenship first in long list of concepts that "bear the burden of European thought and history" (Chakrabarty, *Provincializing Europe*, 4).

14. "It was enough to be Muslim in order to possess all public or private rights" (Belkeziz, *La nationalité dans les états arabes*, 13).

15. Mezghani, *Droit international privé*, 42; Hallaq, *An Introduction to Islamic Law*, 7–8; Augusti, *Questioni d'oriente*, 10. Although not focused on citizenship, Franz Rosenthal ("The Stranger in Medieval Islam," 35–36) sums up this view: "Within the community of believers and wherever Muslims were in political control, there was, in theory, no such distinct category as a 'stranger.'"

16. Goitein, *A Mediterranean Society*, 1:66–70; Schroeter, "A Different Road to Modernity," 151. Scholars do consistently acknowledge relatively minor variations among different Sunni schools of law (*madhāhib*) or in Shiʿite-dominated states like Persia, but the general emphasis on the personality of law persists.

17. As Ariel Salzmann ("Citizens in Search of a State," 38) explains, "Citizenship-like rights in the Ottoman Empire—that is, claims premised on a direct relation between state and individual—date only to the middle decades of the nineteenth century." See also Parolin, *Citizenship in the Arab World*; Kern, *Imperial Citizen*, 89.

18. The invention of Ottoman citizenship is understood as part of the Tanzimat, a series of reforms undertaken between 1839 and 1876 during which Ottoman officials moved toward a gradual embrace of equality that transcended differences of religion across the empire. The Rescript of the Rose Garden in 1839 first referred to all the sultan's subjects as belonging to a single category, "a significant first step toward the transformation of hitherto Muslim, Christian, and Jewish subjects into Ottomans" (Hanioğlu, *A Brief History of the Late Ottoman Empire*, 74). See also Sharkey, *A History of Muslims, Christians, and Jews*, 116. The Ottoman Nationality Law

of 1869 was the first legislation of Ottoman subjecthood that was empire-wide and independent of religion. On this law, see esp. Hanley, "What Ottoman Nationality Was and Was Not." Modernizing officials in Tunisia—and the influence of the Ottoman Tanzimat—are similarly considered to be the originators of Tunisian citizenship. Scholars point to Tunisian reformist decrees, promulgated at the urging of European officials, as the starting point of citizenship in Tunisia: the 'Ahd al-Amān of 1857 and Qānūn al-Dawla of 1861, which first used the language of "Tunisian" in much the same way the Rescript of the Rose Garden used the language of "Ottoman." See Mezghani, *Droit international privé*, 49; Ben Slimane, "Entre deux empires," 112. For other examples of citizenship as a Western or colonial invention, see Beaugrand, "Émergence de la 'nationalité' et institutionnalisation des clivages sociaux"; Banko, *The Invention of Palestinian Citizenship*. In an extreme version of this narrative, the Westernization of citizenship was necessarily incomplete because the hyperreligious environment of the Islamic world did not permit true secularization: Middle Eastern citizenship was not only derivative, then, but also destined to founder on the rocks of sectarianism. See Karpat, "Millets and Nationality"; Karpat, "Nation and Nationalism." Even the brief periods of transcommunal civic and political engagement, such as in the immediate aftermath of the Young Turk Revolution of 1908, are understood to have ceded to ethnonationalist particularism during and after World War I. See, for example, Campos, *Ottoman Brothers*. As Will Hanley ("When Did Egyptians Stop Being Ottomans?," 108–9) has observed, a focus on "political" citizenship "condemns analysis of Middle East citizenship to pathologies of a body that is either immature or broken." The presumption that the Islamic world was incapable of secularization is linked to the perception that Muslims lacked an autonomous political sphere separate from religion. See Grangaud, "Le bayt al-mâl," §29.

19. See chapter 7.

20. The work of Sami Bargaoui, Simona Cerutti, and Isabelle Grangaud is important in moving away from both a Eurocentric approach to citizenship and a diffusionist model of law. See esp. Bargaoui, Cerutti, and Grangaud, *Appartenance locale*; Grangaud, "Le bayt al-mâl"; Cerutti and Grangaud, "Sources and Contextualizations." For a similar rethinking of the modernization of Islamic law, see Ayoub, "The Mecelle, Sharia, and the Ottoman State." In challenging a Eurocentric understanding of citizenship, my goal is similar to that of Isin. But whereas Isin attempts to change the meaning of "citizenship," I propose a new appellation that is, I believe, more neutral. I nonetheless share with him the impulse to avoid importing European categories into law in the Islamic Mediterranean. See Isin, "Citizenship after Orientalism."

21. Baldwin, *Islamic Law and Empire in Ottoman Cairo*; Marglin, *Across Legal Lines*, chap. 2. Islamic law itself was a highly state-based endeavor in the early modern Ottoman Empire. Starting in the fifteenth century, Ottoman officials increasingly developed a particularly Ottoman form of the Hanafi school of law. See Burak, *The Second Formation*; Burak, "Dynasty, Law, and the Imperial Provincial Madrasa." Although Haim Gerber overstates the role of the shari'a in the landscape of Ottoman law, his work stresses the importance of the state in the legal history of the Ottoman Empire. Gerber, *State, Society, and Law*, chap. 2. See the more detailed discussion below in chapter 1.

22. On the importance of European imperialism in the Middle East to periodization and the nature of modernity, see Ze'evi, "Back to Napoleon?" On the impact of increased European trade, see, for example, Brown, *People of Salé*; Quataert, *Ottoman Manufacturing*; Ennaji, *Expansion européenne*. This is discussed further in chapter 2.

23. Moreover, as global legal historians have insisted, Western law was rarely imposed on the non-West fully formed; rather, law in metropole and colony transformed over the course of the interaction between the two. See, for example, Benton, *Law and Colonial Cultures*; Hajjat, *Les frontières de l'"identité nationale"*; Herzog, "Did European Law Turn American?"; Greer, *Property and Dispossession*; Duve, "Global Legal History." On the entanglement between metropole and colony more broadly, see Stoler and Cooper, "Between Metropole and Colony."

24. On those who were excluded from formal citizenship, see Herzog, *Defining Nations*, chap. 6; Cerutti, "Justice et citoyenneté"; Prak, *Citizens without Nations*, 36–38; Sorkin, *Jewish Emancipation*, 7–8.

25. I avoid the term "white" here simply because it was far less salient in the Mediterranean than in the United States. There is abundant evidence that the promise of equality in the American Revolution was mainly limited to white men at the time. See, for example, David Ramsay's (*A Dissertation*, 3) 1789 treatise, in which he distinguishes between a US citizen and resident "negroes," who are "inhabitants, but not citizens." See also *Dred Scott v. Sandford, 60 U.S. 393 (1856)*. On the restriction of citizenship in the United States to free white men, see, for example, Gross, *What Blood Won't Tell*, 7–8.

26. Only in France and Italy were Jews emancipated fully without any restrictions on their civil or political rights. Everywhere else in Europe, the emancipation of Jews was not as clear-cut. In Prussia, the Habsburg Empire, and the Italian city-states, emancipation was piecemeal and partial, and "restrictions on population and residential rights were the basic holdover from the ancien régime" (Sorkin, *Jewish Emancipation*, 161). Even after the unification of Germany, German states like Prussia continued to exclude Jews from full rights—often in defiance of federal laws on equality. In England, Jews could not be members of Parliament until 1858. Sorkin, *Jewish Emancipation*, 175–83, 210–12. On the emancipation of Jews in Italy, see Segre, "The Emancipation of Jews in Italy."

27. See, for example, Erman, *Almost Citizens*; Immerwahr, *How to Hide an Empire*. Individuals of Puerto Rican descent who have relocated stateside can vote in all elections, and Puerto Ricans on the island elect representatives who can speak but not vote in Congress.

28. Much of the historiography of citizenship is weighted toward intellectual history. See, for example, Costa, *Civitas*. Among those who propose breaking free from the constraints of formal state membership, Willem Maas proposes the idea of "multilevel" citizenship. Maas, *Multilevel Citizenship*; Maas, "Multilevel Citizenship." Along similar lines, Isin has noted that individuals can perform "acts of citizenship" irrespective of their formal legal status as citizen or alien. Isin, "Theorizing Acts of Citizenship"; Isin and Turner, "Citizenship Studies." On the explosion of scholarship in citizenship studies, see Shachar et al., "Introduction," 3–4.

29. Bosniak, *The Citizen and the Alien*, 8–9; Shachar, *The Birthright Lottery*, 14. Hanley points out the focus on substantive citizenship in the context of Middle Eastern historiography. Hanley, *Identifying with Nationality*, 19–20. On this, see also Okan, "Coping with Transitions," 85–86.

30. In fact, even the universal presumption of identity documentation today proves far from the reality—especially for poor immigrants in the Americas, many of whom are unable to produce documentation of their birth and thus are rendered effectively stateless. See esp. Price, "Jus Soli and Statelessness."

31. Torpey, *The Invention of the Passport*; Caplan and Torpey, *Documenting Individual Identity*; Hanley, "Papers for Going."

32. This point has largely been ignored in the literature on nationality law. Instead, legal historians have privileged the evolution of legislation and jurisprudence, and the ideological debates that informed these changes. See esp. Weil, *Qu'est-ce qu'un français?*; Donati, *A Political History*; Légier, *Histoire du droit de la nationalité française.*

33. Rappresentanza italiana in Francia (1861–1950), Busta 7: pratiche private, 1866, ASMAE.

34. Bernardi, "Belli v. Consiglio di Levà"; Merello, "Volpinari"; Bandi, "Prefetto di Verona c. Vincentini"; Rosadi, "Prefetto di Lucca c. Malfanti"; Pacifici, "Prefetto di Roma v. Keller." See also Rappresentanza italiana in Francia (1861–1950), Busta 7: pratiche private, 1866, January 2, 1866, January 18, 1866, July 7, 1866, Ministero della guerra, direzione generale delle Leve, bassa-forza e matricola, to Ministero degli affari esteri, ASMAE.

35. On attempts to avoid the Ottoman draft, see, for example, Nationality of Constantin Moscodi (1884), HR.HK.384/2, BOA; Nationality of Yusufaki Franko (1885), HR.HK.348/8, BOA. On attempts to avoid the Romanian draft, see Nationality of Thomas Dmitri Zographos Hadulis (1892), HR.HK.96/5, BOA; Nationality of Moiz and İshak İsraeloviç (1893), HR.HK.96/15, BOA; Nationality of Yakof and Samuel Naftali (1895), HR.HK.97/11, BOA; Nationality of Mayer Matatia Coen (1896), HR.HK.97/20, BOA; Nationality of Asias Benjamin Goldenberg (1892), HR.HK.96/4, BOA; Nationality of Avram Youdas Alagem (1888), HR.HK.94/16, BOA; Nationality of Mihalicli Haci Bosinini (1888), HR.HK.96/21, BOA; Nationality of Menahim Merkado Athias and Ishak Brazianinin (1891), HR.HK.95/22, BOA; Nationality of Marco Kraentzler (1890), HR.HK.95/15, BOA; Nationality of Migirdic Toma Apraham (1888), HR.HK.94/18, BOA; Nationality of Maurice Ghedalia Waisse (1887), HR.HK.94/14, BOA. These sorts of questions persisted after World War I. See Okan, "Coping with Transitions," chap. 2. And of course these competing claims of belonging were not limited to the Ottoman Empire; see, for example, Salyer, *Under the Starry Flag.*

36. Hanley, "When Did Egyptians Stop Being Ottomans?" 102–3; Stein, "Protected Persons?"

37. In this sense, the Shamama case is an example of what Giovanni Levi calls an "extreme case" (*cas extrême* or *cas limite*): an unusual story that can shed light on the social contexts in which it was produced. Levi, "Les usages de la biographie," 1331–32. In my approach to microhistory, I am particularly inspired by Philliou, *Biography of an Empire*; Davis, *The Return of Martin Guerre;* Ginzburg, *The Cheese and the Worms.*

38. Scholars interested in the history of migration control and regimes of identification before the nineteenth century tend not to have to deal with questions of state belonging. On this literature, see esp. Moatti, *La mobilité des personnes*; Moatti and Kaiser, *Gens de passage en Méditerranée.* Beginning in the early twentieth century, legal belonging became central to questions of mobility, as migration control became more tightly linked to nationality. See, for example, McKeown, *Melancholy Order*; Mays, *Forging Ties.* If anything, nineteenth-century states attempted to control exit—and thus restrict the ability of their own subjects to leave. Yet even these efforts were hardly effective enough to prevent mobility in the age of mass migration. Only in the 1880s did European settler nations begin to restrict entry for Asians. See McKeown, *Melancholy Order.* The Ottoman government had made efforts to restrict internal mobility since the early modern period, and in 1841, issued a new set of empire-wide restrictions that demanded internal passports (*mürur tezkeresi*) for all who left their place of residence as well as exit permits to go abroad. See Gutman, "Armenian Migration to North America," 178; Yılmaz, "Governing the Armenian Question," 392. Yet it is clear that these measures were not

particularly effective. See Akarli, "Ottoman Attitudes towards Lebanese Emigration," 114–19. Most states only started to systematically restrict entry to nonnationals after World War I; in the nineteenth century, western Europe and North America "were opened to relatively untrammeled free movement" (Caplan and Torpey, "Introduction," 10).

39. Dickens, *Bleak House*; Trollope, *Orley Farm*.

40. Cover, "Nomos and Narrative," 10. Needless to say, Cover's understanding of the power of narrative in creating a legal world—what he calls a nomos—goes far beyond evidence of legal belonging. On the force of narrative in jurisprudence, see also Dworkin, "Law as Interpretation."

41. For a study that demonstrates the extent to which paperwork is difficult to come by for many today, see Price, "Jus Soli and Statelessness." Moreover, the complexity of proving belonging despite the existence of paperwork is evident in the lawsuit over the estate of Jean-Phillippe Léo Smet (d. 2017)—better known by his stage name Johnny Hallyday—still in progress as this book goes to press. The future of his fortune turns on whether Smet was domiciled in California or France. Though not exactly about legal belonging (Smet was a dual citizen), the elements of the case concern similar questions about the narrativization of Smet's life. See, for example, https://www.liberation.fr/debats/2020/07/07/le-cas-johnny-hallyday-d-une-justice-combative-a-participative_1793592.

42. See chapter 6.

43. On citizenship in the early modern period, see esp. Herzog, *Defining Nations*; Cerutti, *Étrangers*. On citizenship in the Roman Empire, see Ando, "Fact, Fiction and Social Reality," 302–5, 314–19. On medieval Italy, see Riesenberg, "Citizenship and Equality," 430. Scholars of race and slavery have similarly noted the extent to which categories such as whiteness/blackness and freedom/slavery were based on social performance, not just biology or documentation. See Ando, "Race and Citizenship"; Gross, *What Blood Won't Tell*; Scott, "Paper Thin."

44. Historians of modern nationality law have tended to emphasize the evolution of legislation, suggesting that it was just a matter applying the law correctly to know whether someone was Italian or Tunisian. See, for example, Weil, *Qu'est-ce qu'un français?*; Fahrmeir, *Citizenship*; Donati, *A Political History*; Légier, *Histoire du droit de la nationalité française*; Parolin, *Citizenship in the Arab World*.

45. I am grateful to Simona Cerutti for suggesting this metaphor.

46. Only the Ottoman consul in Rome, Carlo Gallian, suggested that Nissim might be considered an Ottoman subject. See chapter 7.

Chapter 1. Tunis (1805–59)

1. "Le kaïdnessin porte sur sa checchia un échantillon de toutes les pièces de monnaie qui ont cours dans la Régence" (de Flaux, *La régence de Tunis*, 71). On de Flaux, see Rocca, *À propos d'un livre récent sur la Tunisie*. On peaceful penetration, see Burke, *Prelude to Protectorate*, chap. 4.

2. "Aujourd'hui que les actes iniques et violents ne peuvent plus être accomplis, toutes les qualités mercantiles, innées chez les juifs, vont se développer rapidement avec l'audace que donne la sécurité, et je ne doute pas qu'ils n'aient en quelques années accaparé toute la fortune publique"(de Flaux, *La régence de Tunis*, 71).

3. Ben Rajeb, *Yahūd al-bilāṭ*, 91; Parks, *Medical Imperialism*, 81.

4. Darling, *A History of Social Justice*.

5. The canonical text outlining the rights and responsibilities of dhimmīs was the Pact of 'Umar (*'ahd 'Umar*), traditionally attributed to the third caliph 'Umar (d. 644), but more likely from the ninth century. See esp. Cohen, "What Was the Pact of 'Umar?" For an introduction to the status of *ahl al-dhimma*, see Cohen, *Under Crescent and Cross*, chap. 4.

6. Sebag, *Histoire des juifs de Tunisie*, 117; Ben Rajeb, *Yahūd al-bilāṭ*, 87–90.

7. Quran 9:29. The extent to which the jizya was onerous varied across space and time. On the jizya in Tunisia, see Ben Rajeb, *Yahūd al-bilāṭ*, 93–98. More generally, see Fattal, *Le statut légal*, chap. 7.

8. Hammuda Pasha reigned from 1782 to 1814, and Ibn Diyaf notes that he enacted this prohibition at the beginning of his reign. Ibn Diyaf, *Itḥāf*, 4:287. On this rule and its circumvention, see Hénia, *Propriété et stratégies sociales*, 311–18. See also Larguèche, "La communauté juive de Tunisie," 169.

9. Ben Rajeb, *Yahūd al-bilāṭ*, 160–78. On taxation in the eighteenth and nineteenth century, see Valensi, *Tunisian Peasants*, chap. 8.

10. Pellissier de Reynaud, *Description*, 319–23; de Flaux, *La régence de Tunis*, 183; Brunschvig, "Justice religieuse et justice laïque dans la Tunisie," 39, 63–64; Brown, *The Tunisia of Ahmed Bey*, 112–27.

11. De Flaux, *La régence de Tunis*, 177–83; Brunschvig, "Justice religieuse et justice laïque dans la Tunisie," 39–40, 55–56; Brown, *The Tunisia of Ahmed Bey*, 36; Clancy-Smith, *Mediterraneans*, 202–4. This was the Tunisian equivalent of the Divan-ı Hümayun, the Ottoman sultan's Imperial Council. See Wittmann, "Before Qadi and Vizier"; Ben-Bassat, "In Search of Justice"; Ben-Bassat, "'Al ṭelegraf ve-tzedeq."

12. Brown, *The Tunisia of Ahmed Bey*, 127–35.

13. Relatively little scholarship on the legal history of Jews in nineteenth-century Tunisia exists, but for evidence of Jews appealing to shari'a courts, see, for example, Elmelich, *Megilah 'Amukot*, 16. On Morocco, see Marglin, *Across Legal Lines*. On Jews appealing to shari'a courts in the Ottoman Empire more broadly, see Jennings, "Zimmis (Non-Muslims) in Early 17th Century Ottoman Judicial Records"; Gerber, "Arkhiyon beit ha-din ha-shara'i shel Bursah"; Al-Qattan, "Dhimmis in the Muslim Court."

14. Brunschvig, "Justice religieuse et justice laïque dans la Tunisie," 41. This was also true of Jews in the Ottoman heartlands and precolonial Morocco. See Wittmann, "Before Qadi and Vizier"; Marglin, *Across Legal Lines*, chap. 4.

15. Brown, *The Tunisia of Ahmed Bey*, 107. For the most promising account of the relationship between the central Ottoman administration and the beys of Tunis in the nineteenth century, see Ben Ismail, "Sovereignty across Empires," chap. 1. There is growing interest in tying Tunisian history more closely to the Ottoman Empire. See esp. Moalla, *The Regency of Tunis*; Ben Slimane, "Entre deux empires"; Kallander, *Women*; Oualdi, *A Slave between Empires*.

16. Brown, *The Tunisia of Ahmed Bey*, 29–30, 46–47. For the description of sovereignty as "divided," see Lewis, *Divided Rule*.

17. Ben Ismail, "Sovereignty across Empires," chap. 1. See also Brown, *The Tunisia of Ahmed Bey*, 238–40.

18. Ben Ismail, "Sovereignty across Empires," 118–32; Jerad, "Les agents des beys de Tunis," §7.

19. Smida, *Consuls et consulats*, 51, 67–68; Ben Ismail, "Sovereignty across Empires," 134–35.

20. Smida, *Consuls et consulats*, 76; Ben Ismail, "Sovereignty across Empires," 137–38.

21. "*usul-u mer'iyye-i düveliyye-ye mütevakif*" (29 Zilkade [or Zilhicce] 1272 / August 1 [or 31], 1856, A.AMD.71.21, BOA). See also Jerad, "Les agents des beys de Tunis," §8; Ben Ismail, "Sovereignty across Empires," 138, 148.

22. Smida, *Consuls et consulats*, 51–53, 112; Ben Ismail, "Sovereignty across Empires," 138–39.

23. Brown, *The Tunisia of Ahmed Bey*, 53–65. For the definitive treatment of mamlūks in modern Tunisia, see Oualdi, *Esclaves et maîtres*. Note that both kulughlis and mamlūks married local, Arabic-speaking wives.

24. Tunger-Zanetti, *La communication entre Tunis et Istanbul*, 43; Ben Ismail, "Sovereignty across Empires," 226–33. Similarly, when North African Jews traveled to Palestine—either on pilgrimage or to settle—they, too, integrated into local Jewish communities. This changed once French forces invaded Algeria and Algerian Jews began to claim French protection. See, for example, Cohen, "Les juifs '*moghrabi*' en Palestine."

25. On the ḥāra as a multireligious space, see Ben Rajeb, *Yahūd al-bilāṭ*, 90–93; Parks, *Medical Imperialism*, 81, 91. Jewish quarters were frequently known as the red-light districts of North Africa given that they were often the only places in which to procure alcohol. Prostitution tended to flourish in these neighborhoods as well. See Gottreich, *The Mellah of Marrakesh*, 75; Znaien, "Les raisins de la domination," 56–57; Clancy-Smith, *Mediterraneans*, 182–89. Regarding language, Jews had a distinct way of pronouncing Arabic dialects throughout the modern Middle East and North Africa, leading many linguists to call Jewish dialects "Judeo-Arabic." They were, however, mutually intelligible with dialects spoken by Muslims. On Judeo-Arabic, see esp. Kosansky, "When Jews Speak Arabic." For a wonderful description of a North African household—albeit many decades after the events portrayed here—see Bahloul, *The Architecture of Memory*. For an evocation of such households in Tunis, see Moati, *Les belles de Tunis*.

26. Shamama, *Shoresh Yishai*. The book includes long commentaries on the tractates *Bekhorot*, *Kiddushin*, and *Eruvin*, shorter commentaries on other tractates, and some halakhic and exegetical pieces. Samuel Shamama, born in the early eighteenth century, wrote a kabbalistic commentary titled *Keren ha-Tzvi* (horn of the gazelle). Samuel's son Shlomo (different from Nissim's father, also named Shlomo Shamama) followed in his father's footsteps and wrote various books, including *Bigdei shesh*, which was published posthumously by Samuel's grandsons Yitzhaq and Shlomo.

27. In his introduction to *Shoresh Yishai*, Isaac Hai gives Shlomo's death date as 2 Tamuz 5566 / June 18, 1806. Some Shamamas moved to Marseille in the early nineteenth century, though it is not clear how they were related to Nissim. See Planel, *Du comptoir à la colonie*, 43–44, 762–63.

28. For instance, the Ladino speakers of Anatolia and the Balkans used Hebrew letters to write their dialect of Spanish, as did the Yiddish speakers of eastern and central Europe.

29. Sebag, *Histoire des juifs de Tunisie*, 121–22. For an example of a Tunisian Jew literate in Arabic, see Valensi, *Mardochée Naggiar*. It was far more common for Jews to read and write in Arabic in the medieval period; by the nineteenth century, Arabic literacy became rare among Jews.

30. Larguèche, *Les ombres de la ville*, 364–70; Ben Rajeb, *Yahūd al-bilāṭ*. In some ways, the extent to which elite Jews in Husaynī Tunisia served as tax farmers, physicians, and financial officers at the bey's court mirrors the trajectory of Phanariots in the rest of the Ottoman Empire. See Philliou, *Biography of an Empire*, chap. 1.

31. Brown, *The Tunisia of Ahmed Bey*, 83–85, 87–90, 336–37, 340. *Khaznadār* comes from the verb *khazana*, which means "to store," and is the root of the word *Makhzan*, which literally means "storehouse," and that denoted the central government in Tunisia (as well as Morocco).

32. Jean Ganiage claims that Nissim began his career as a textile merchant and then entered Ibn 'Ayyad's service as a domestic servant to eventually became his accountant (*caissier*). See Ganiage, *Les origines*, 600. But Ganiage does not cite sources for this information, and in general is a highly unreliable source when it comes to the history of Jews in Tunisia and Nissim in particular (see the afterword).

33. Ben Rajeb, *Yahūd al-bilāṭ*, 161–71. On Jews' involvement in the tax farm on leather, see Ben Rajeb, *Yahūd al-bilāṭ*, 179–218. On "court Jews" in the Islamic world, see esp. Schroeter, *The Sultans' Jew*; Tsur, *Gevirim ve-yehudim aḥerim*. Needless to say, this was not a phenomenon limited to the Middle East.

34. Rashid to Muhammad, 13 Ṣafar 1295 / February 16, 1878, SH.C100.D223.3, ANT; Brown, *The Tunisia of Ahmed Bey*, 337.

35. Ben Rajeb, *Yahūd al-bilāṭ*, 166. See also Kraîem, *La Tunisie précoloniale*, 1:146.

36. Nissim was awarded the medal on 25 Dhū al-Qa'da 1264 / October 23, 1848. Galeotti, *Reale Corte d'Appello di Lucca*, 61. On the Nīshān al-Iftikhār, see Hugon, *Les emblèmes des beys de Tunis*, chap. 7.

37. Ben Rajeb, *Yahūd al-bilāṭ*, 485–86.

38. Aksan, "War and Peace"; McDougall, *A History of Algeria*, chap. 2.

39. On military reform in Tunisia, see Brown, *The Tunisia of Ahmed Bey*, 263–65. In Egypt, see Fahmy, *All the Pasha's Men*. In the Ottoman Empire, see Shaw, "The Origins of Ottoman Military Reform"; Zürcher, "The Ottoman Conscription System," 80–82; Hanioğlu, *A Brief History of the Late Ottoman Empire*, 58–60. For a particularly helpful rethinking of this period, see esp. Philliou, *Biography of an Empire*, chap. 2, 5. On mass conscription in Europe, see Prak, *Citizens without Nations*, 304–5; Forrest, *Conscripts and Deserters*.

40. Brown, *The Tunisia of Ahmed Bey*, 214–15, 264–65. On French involvement in the Tunisian military, see Planel, *Du comptoir à la colonie*, 109–30.

41. Ben Ismail, "Sovereignty across Empires," 31–44.

42. Brown, *The Tunisia of Ahmed Bey*, 270, 278–80. While most European states instituted a census in order to more effectively conscript the largest number of people, Ahmad Bey refrained from taking this step. He did so in large part because during his father Mustafa Bey's brief reign (1835–37), an attempt to institute a census had met with immediate resistance in Tunis; a growing group of protesters gathered at the mosque of Sidi Mahrez, the same place from which the medieval scholar supposedly determined the boundaries of the ḥāra. Ahmad Bey instead chose to send out recruiters among the peasantry with orders to conscript enough men to fill the regiments. Generally, these recruiters took one man from each family between the ages of fifteen and forty—avoiding Tunis and other cities where they were likely to encounter organized opposition.

43. See, for example, Ferguson, "The Rise of the Rothschilds," 5–8.

44. Comte d'Avigdor, "Note lue au comité qui s'était formé pour entendre les propositions de l'Emprunt de 30 millions de fr," December 6, 1846, HR.SYS.2933/54, BOA. See also 1 Ṣafar 1263 / January 19, 1847, I.HR.38.1805, BOA.

45. Brown, *The Tunisia of Ahmed Bey*, 341–42.

46. Ibn Diyaf, *Itḥāf*, 4:160–66; Brown, *The Tunisia of Ahmed Bey*, 346–47.

47. Brown, *The Tunisia of Ahmed Bey*, 347; Gharbi, "Mahmoud Ben Ayyed," 23. He also bought a house on the Rue de la Ville-Lévêque, steps from the Madeleine in the eighth arrondissement—then, as now, one of the most elegant neighborhoods of the city. Gharbi, "Mahmoud Ben Ayyed," 23. Ibn 'Ayyad had already traveled to Europe on official government business; Ottoman authorities even reported that he went to Paris to spy on Ahmad Bey's behalf. It is probable that he used these opportunities to spirit his wealth out of the country. 1266 / 1850, A.MKT.UM.18–38, BOA. Ibn Diyaf (*Itḥāf*, 4: 95) reports that Ibn 'Ayyad bought a house in Paris in 1845.

48. Dalloz, *Recueil critique de jurisprudence*, 343.

49. Great naturalization was granted to only twenty-two foreigners between the law's promulgation in 1815 and 1848. Weil, *How to Be French*, 225–26.

50. Ben Rajeb, *Yahūd al-bilāṭ*, 489. According to Ibn 'Ayyad, he had appointed Nissim to oversee his properties in Tunisia after his departure, but Nissim betrayed his former patron and handed over Ibn 'Ayyad's papers to Khaznadar. Moreover, Nissim and two other officials divided Ibn 'Ayyad's tax farms among themselves for their personal gain. Ganiage, *Les origines*, 123.

51. Cheramy, *Tribunal de la Seine*, 5; Ben Rajeb, *Yahūd al-bilāṭ*, 492–93.

52. Rashid to Muhammad, 13 Ṣafar 1295 / February 16, 1878, SH.C100.D223.3, ANT; Ben Rajeb, *Yahūd al-bilāṭ*, 486–87. A Jacob Bishi Shamama served in the government starting in 1841, though it is not clear exactly how Jacob was related to Nissim and whether Nissim was responsible for getting him hired. Ben Rajeb, *Yahūd al-bilāṭ*, 484.

53. Moumni, *L'éveil d'une nation*, 239.

54. For an English translation, see: http://www.anayasa.gen.tr/reform.htm. For the French original, see Koçunyan, *Negotiating the Ottoman Constitution*, 313.

55. Articles 7, 8, 9, 15.

56. Özsu, "The Ottoman Empire," 127.

57. Koçunyan, *Negotiating the Ottoman Constitution*, 316.

58. Zürcher, "The Ottoman Conscription System," 88–89; Aytürk, "Bedel-i Askeri." Egypt was an exception in the Islamic world in that the khedive, 'Abbas I, began to conscript Copts around 1850, albeit at first in a somewhat haphazard way. Toledano, *State and Society*, 187. 'Abbas's successor, Sa'īd Pasha, formally abolished the jizya in 1855, two months before the Ottomans did so; the following month, Sa'īd started issuing an order that Copts would now regularly be conscripted to the military. Afifi, "The State and the Church," 281–82. Jews, however, seem to have been exempt from military service. Landau, *Jews in Nineteenth-Century Egypt*, 16.

59. See esp. Cohen, *Becoming Ottomans*. On Jews in the Ottoman military, see Cohen, *Becoming Ottomans*, 30–41; Penslar, *Jews and the Military*, 67–68. The *bedel-i askeri* was abolished following the Young Turk Revolution of 1908. Campos, *Ottoman Brothers*, 150–58.

60. My understanding of the Sfez trial is particularly indebted to the excellent scholarship by Joshua Picard, who was kind enough to share chapters of his forthcoming dissertation with me. Picard, "The Bathou Sfez Affair," chap. 2. For the account of Nissim's intervention, see Véhel, "Le martyre de Bathou"; Bel'ish, "Ha-'Kaid' Nissim Shamamah." (Picard has noted that the first account of Nissim throwing coins to distract the mob from claiming Sfez's body only appeared decades after the events, and thus is most likely an embellishment; I am grateful to him for sharing the Véhel source.) Haim Zeev Hirschberg also claims that a delegation was sent to the

French consul. Hirschberg, *A History of the Jews in North Africa*, 112. For more standard accounts, see Ibn Diyaf, *Itḥāf*, 4:259–66; Brunschvig, "Justice religieuse et justice laïque dans la Tunisie," 68–69; van Krieken, *Khayr al-Dîn*, 3–4; Sebag, *Histoire des juifs de Tunisie*, 117–18; Tsur, "'Ahd al-Amān"; Allagui, *Juifs et musulmans en Tunisie*, 44.

61. Van Krieken, *Khayr al-Dîn*, 5–8; Stillman, *The Jews of Arab Lands in Modern Times*, 183–85. The first article opened by promising "security to all our subjects and the inhabitants of our province" (*Ta'kīdu al-amāni li-sā'iri ra'yatinā wa-sukkāni iyālatinā)*. Ibn Diyaf, *Itḥāf*, 4:267–71. For a French translation, see https://www.justice.gov.tn/fileadmin/medias/ministere/musee/repertoire_musee/Pacte_fondamental_1857_fr.pdf.

62. Historians have tended to see the abolition of the dhimma as accomplished single-handedly with the 'Ahd al-Amān. See, for example, Brunschvig, "Justice religieuse et justice laïque dans la Tunisie," 60; Sebag, *Histoire des juifs de Tunisie*, 119; Larguèche, "La communauté juive de Tunisie," 166; Allagui, *Juifs et Musulmans en Tunisie*, 43. Following Fatma Ben Slimane, I argue that the process unfolded more gradually in the subsequent years. Ben Slimane, "La régence de Tunis à l'ère des réformes."

63. "*Al-taswīyatu bayna al-muslimi wa-ghayrihi min sukkāni al-iyālati fī istiḥqāqi al-inṣāfi*." The French translation reads, "Les Musulmans et les autres habitants du pays seront égaux devant la loi."

64. "*Al-nās kulluhum 'indanā fil-ḥaqqi sawā'*" (al-Nasiri, *Kitāb al-istiqṣā*, 8:129). For an English translation, see Stillman, *The Jews of Arab Lands*, 371–73.

65. "*Inna al-dhimmī min ra'yatinā lā yajburu 'alā tabdīl dīnihi . . . li-anna dhimmatahu taqtaḍā anna lahum mā lanā wa-'alayhim mā 'alaynā*" (Ibn Diyaf, *Itḥāf*, 4:269). For an earlier use of the phrase "*anna lahum mā lanā wa-'alayhim mā 'alaynā*," see, for example, Ibn Qayim al-Jawziya, *Aḥkām ahl al-dhimma*, 1:256.

66. "Each sect, in localities where there are no other religious denominations, shall be free from every species of restraint as regards the public exercise of its religion" (http://www.anayasa.gen.tr/reform.htm).

67. "*Lā yumni'u min ijrā'i mā yalzimu diyānatuhu*" (Article 4). The Ottoman decree also gave non-Muslims wide latitude to both repair their houses of worship and build new ones—privileges that directly contradicted restrictions outlined in the Pact of 'Umar; the 'Ahd al-Amān said nothing about the building or repair of synagogues.

68. Ibn Diyaf, *Itḥāf*, 4:275; Slimane, "La régence de Tunis à l'ère des réformes," 508–11. Ibn Diyaf dubbed the commentary the council was to produce a *tafsīr*. Ibn Diyaf, *Itḥāf*, 4:273.

69. Notes from the council meeting (*majlis*), 21 Jumādā II 1274 / February 6, 1858, SH.C118.D403.18333, ANT; discussed in Slimane, "La régence de Tunis à l'ère des réformes," 514. I am supremely grateful to Fatma Ben Slimane for sharing a copy of this document with me.

70. "*Wa-difā'an li-mā yatawaqqa'ūnahu min al-ḥayfi*" (Article 6).

71. This was on 5 Ṣafar 1275 / September 14, 1858. Ibn Diyaf, *Itḥāf*, 4: 287; Hénia, *Propriété et stratégies sociales*, 316; Larguèche, "La communauté juive de Tunisie," 169.

72. On the permission to wear the red *shāshīya*, see Larguèche, "La communauté juive de Tunisie," 175. Ibn Diyaf notes that a decree in fall 1859 permitted Jews to live in the area known as Ḥawmat al-Jirāba (the quarter of the sacks), outside the ḥāra. Ibn Diyaf, *Itḥāf*, 5: 17–18

73. Oualdi, *A Slave between Empires*, 31.

74. Ammar, *Tunis*, 169–70.

75. On Sadiq Bey, see Moumni, "Une réforme de l'art pictoral?," 66–71.

76. On 28 Rabīʿ I 1276, which corresponded to October 25, 1859 or 27 Tishrei 5620—that is, the end of the major Jewish holidays. Galeotti, *Reale Corte d'Appello di Lucca*, 62. See also Ben Rajeb, *Yahūd al-bilāṭ*, 486.

77. Ralfon (El Kef) to Shamama (Bardo), telegram, April 8, 1861, SH.C100.D224.24, ANT.

78. Unfortunately we do not know if Nissim adjudicated such a court. On the qāʾid al-yahūd in Tunisia, see Sebag, *Histoire des juifs de Tunisie*, 95–97; Larguèche, *Les ombres de la ville*, 355. Normally the qāʾid al-yahūd was responsible for ensuring that all Jews paid the jizya, which in Tunis was remitted communally—though the ʿAhd al-Amān had abolished special taxes for dhimmīs, so this was no longer relevant. The position of qāʾid al-yahūd existed in Jewish communities throughout the Islamic world. On Morocco, see Gerber, *Jewish Society in Fez*, 86–94; Deshen, *The Mellah Society*, 53–61. On the medieval period, see Cohen, *Jewish Self-Government.*

79. This decree was dated 1 Shawwāl 1276, corresponding to April 22, 1860. Galeotti, *Reale Corte d'Appello di Lucca*, 62. Ben Rajeb gives the year as 1859, but does not give the Hijri date. Ben Rajeb, *Yahūd al-bilāṭ*, 486.

80. Sebag, *Histoire des juifs de Tunisie*, 88–89; Larguèche, *Les ombres de la ville*, 369; Ben Rajeb, *Yahūd al-bilāṭ*.

81. Binyamin ha-sheni, "Ḥadashot Kelaliyot"; Ashkenazi, *La chronique*, 18–19.

82. Binyamin ha-sheni, "Ḥadashot Kelaliyot."

83. Attal, *Le Caïd Nissim Samama*; advertisement by Yisrael Bak, printer in Palestine, for a new edition of texts by the Ari (Ḥayim Vital) funded by Nissim Shamama, *Ḥavatzelet*, November 26, 1863, 4.

84. "Munificence pieuse à Tunis"; Ben Rajeb, *Yahūd al-bilāṭ*, 495.

85. Ashkenazi, *La chronique*, 18. On Jewish notables and philanthropy in the Ottoman Empire, see Ben-Naeh, "Ottoman Jewish Courtiers."

86. Revault, *Palais et demeures de Tunis*, 393. In the 1880s, the street did not have a name. See "Reconnaissance des biens de la succession du Caïd Nessim Samama," properties #1, 3, 5, 6, 9–14, n.d., SH.C101.D231.335, ANT. By 1890, it was called the Rue du Caid-Nessim. Advertisement for sale of property on March 22, 1890, SH.C101.D231.164, ANT. *Mishnaqa* means gibbet; the street was eventually renamed for the gallows it housed as late as the 1840s. In French, it is referred to as the Rue El-Mechnaka.

87. On private synagogues in nineteenth-century Algeria, Schreier, *Arabs of the Jewish Faith*, 15–16; Assan, "Les synagogues," 71–72.

88. "Reconnaissance des biens de la succession du Caïd Nessim Samama," building #3, n.d., SH.C101.D231.335, ANT; Revault, *Palais et demeures de Tunis*, 394–95.

89. This information is from Gilles Boulu's genealogical work on the Shamamas. I am grateful to him for sharing his research.

90. "*Va-ye'ehav ha-kayid et ha-yaldah va-tehi lo ke-bat. . . . [V]a-ya'as ha-kayid kol asher otah, ve-kol ḥafetzah hishlim*" (Costa, *Yada' ma be-ḥashukha*, 12). Israel Costa does not, however, mention ʿAziza's mother's name, nor does he specify which of Nissim's wives was ʿAziza's grandmother; that information I have from Gilles Boulu, who interviewed descendants of Momo.

Chapter 2. Financial Trouble (1859–64)

1. Nissim's house was located between the Rue Kairouan and the Rue César. "Reconnaissance des biens de la succession du Caïd Nessim Samama," n.d., SH.C101.D231.335, ANT. On European migrants, see esp. Clancy-Smith, *Mediterraneans.*

2. The Kingdom of the Two Sicilies joined unified Italy in 1860; before that, the bey of Tunis signed treaties directly with the kingdom. See, for example, "Treaty of Commerce between the King of the Two Sicilies and the Bey of Tunis, November 17, 1833," in Foreign Office, *British and Foreign State Papers, 1834–1835,* 1034–41.

3. Marglin, "Extraterritoriality and Legal Belonging."

4. Salmieri, "La communauté italienne de Tunisie," 278. The Funduq des Français, which served as both the consulate and living quarters for French merchants and the diplomatic staff, also had a chapel (la chapelle Saint-Louis). Planel, *Du comptoir à la colonie,* 456–60.

5. Anne Mezin, "Etats Français Barbarie," inventory in preparation for the Archives Nationales de France. I am grateful to Dr. Mezin for sharing this with me.

6. Pellissier de Reynaud, *Description,* 51–52.

7. Price, *Malta and the Maltese,* esp. 59–60, 88–90; Clancy-Smith, *Mediterraneans,* 56, 75–80.

8. Pellissier de Reynaud, *Description,* 51, 56.

9. See, for example, Bendana, "The Avenue Bourguiba."

10. Salmieri, "La communauté italienne de Tunisie," 273–74.

11. Ammar, *Tunis,* 171. The consulate was inaugurated on December 31, 1860. Planel, *Du comptoir à la colonie,* 574.

12. These, in turn, continued a tradition begun by previous Muslim-ruled states, including the Ilkhanids, Fatimids, and Mamluks, dating at least to the twelfth century. Zarinebaf, *Mediterranean Encounters,* 94–96.

13. Lafon, "Les capitulations."

14. De Testa, *Recueil des traités,* 94, Articles 9, 11, 12.

15. "Donner ordre pour l'avenir que les capitulations et traités d'amitié et alliance faits entre les rois de France et les grands-seigneurs, empereurs des Turcs . . . soient gardés, suivis et observés comme ils doivent être" (De Testa, *Recueil des traités,* 321). On Tunisian beys' largely autonomous foreign relations, see Clancy-Smith, *Mediterraneans,* 205; Ben Ismail, "Sovereignty across Empires," 27, esp. 27n10.

16. De Testa, *Recueil des traités,* 327. In fact, this treaty refers to the dey, not the bey; before the eighteenth century, there was significant conflict between the deys and beys for authority in Tunisia, with the deys often holding the reins of power. See Moalla, *The Regency of Tunis,* 27–30. The position of a dey, however, did not differ markedly from that of a bey; they were simply rival factions.

17. Jerad, "Le premier traité de paix."

18. Clancy-Smith, *Mediterraneans,* 209–10.

19. Marglin, "Citizenship and Nationality." There was much ambiguity within the category of protection, especially for colonial subjects. On this, see esp. Can, "The Protection Question"; Can, *Spiritual Subjects*; Ahmed, "Contested Subjects."

20. Van Den Boogert, *The Capitulations,* 90.

21. On extraterritoriality in nineteenth-century Tunisia, see esp. Clancy-Smith, *Mediterraneans*, chap. 6. On the question of sovereignty, see Pélissié du Rausas, *Le régime des capitulations dans l'empire Ottoman*, 2:42.

22. For the claim that the consulate was French, see Brunschvig, "Justice religieuse et justice laïque dans la Tunisie," 61. Ibn Diyaf recorded that the consulate was British. Ibn Diyaf, *Itḥāf*, 4:131–33.

23. Quoted in Terem, "Al-Mahdī al-Wazzānī," 449. See also Brown, *The Tunisia of Ahmed Bey*, 257; Ben Slimane, "Une 'dhimma inversée'?," 352–53. On consulates as sanctuaries, see Clancy-Smith, *Mediterraneans*, 211–13. In the early twentieth century, most Muslim scholars came to believe that foreign naturalization amounted to apostasy. Kateb, *Européens, "indigènes" et juifs en Algérie*, 194; Parolin, *Citizenship in the Arab World*, 94; Lewis, *Divided Rule*, chap. 5.

24. 1266 / 1850, A.MKT.UM.18–38, BOA; Ibn Diyaf, *Itḥāf*, 4:130–31. See also Brown, *The Tunisia of Ahmed Bey*, 253–54. On other officials who sought foreign protection, see Brown, *The Tunisia of Ahmed Bey*, 255–59.

25. Ben Rajeb, *Yahūd al-bilāṭ*, 433–43.

26. On Livorno, see Tazzara, *The Free Port of Livorno*; Tazzara, "Religious Boundaries in Italy"; Filippini, *Il porto di Livorno*. Unlike other Jewish communities in Italy, the Jews of Livorno were almost all Sephardi.

27. On conflict over dress, see Masi, "Fixation du statut des sujets toscans israélites," 175–76; Ben Rajeb, *Yahūd al-bilāṭ*, 88–89. On language, see esp. Avrahami, *Pinkas ha-Kehilah*. The earliest entry in the pinkasim (mostly takkanot, or communal ordinances) is in Judeo-Arabic from 1710 (Avrahami, *Pinkas ha-Kehilah*, 3–21); others in Judeo-Arabic include entries from 1795 (73–75), 1806 (84–86, 86–89), 1811 (92–93), 1821 (103–6), and 1833 (117–21). The first entry in Spanish is from 1726 and concerns sumptuary laws (22–27); others in Spanish are from 1736 (27–31), 1748 (33–34), 1753 (35–39), 1759 (39–45), 1773 (47–55), 1789 (61–64), and 1800 (79–82). For Hebrew documents—which are numerous—see, for example, those from 1784 (56–60), 1790, and 1793 (64–73). On the Grana in general, see Lévy, *La nation juive portugaise*.

28. Bregoli, "A Father's Consolation."

29. The three sons born in Tunis arrived between 1833 and 1845. Ganiage, *Les origines*, 164, 586. According to family lore, the Guttieres family had originally moved from Iberia to Amsterdam and settled in Livorno after the Livornine were issued. Interview with Litza Guttieres, February 8, 2018. On the new wave of Livornese Jews, see Sebag, *Histoire des juifs de Tunisie*, 111–12; Avrahami, *Pinkas ha-Kehilah*, 15–16.

30. Salmieri, "La communauté italienne de Tunisie," 278.

31. "Les juifs, dits Grana, ou Livournais, établis depuis longtemps ou depuis plusieurs années à Tunis, seront toujours regardés et considérés comme sujets du Pays" (quoted in Masi, "Fixation du statut des sujets toscans israélites," 173). The Grana had traded under the French flag (*pavillon*), but did not, it seems, have recourse to consular courts. Masi, "Fixation du statut des sujets toscans israélites," 160–61.

32. Masi, "Fixation du statut des sujets toscans israélites," 179, 341. Nyssen's renewed efforts to secure permanent extraterritorial status for Tuscan Jews was sparked by an incident in which a Livornese Jewish man named Scialom was accused of theft by Tunisian authorities; because Scialom was born in Tunis—to Livornese parents—the bey insisted on treating him as a Tuscan

subject. Despite the stipulations of the 1822 treaty, Nyssen did his best to have Scialom put under his jurisdiction. Masi, "Fixation du statut des sujets toscans israélites," 335–38.

33. The precise mechanisms by which Grana Jews who had lived in Tunisia for generations managed to acquire Tuscan (or later Italian) nationality remain unclear, as does the number of Grana Jews who did. But we do know that there was not insignificant migration from Tunisia back to Livorno. See, for instance, Reiman, "Claiming Livorno," 81, 117.

34. By 1844, Grana made up eighteen out of forty-six Jewish merchants doing business with Europe; another fourteen were either protégés or foreigners. Filippini, *Il porto di Livorno*, 452.

35. Torpey, *The Invention of the Passport*, chap. 3; Caplan and Torpey, introduction, 10. The Ottoman Empire did, however, attempt to limit the exit of its own subjects as well as internal displacement. Gutman, "Armenian Migration to North America," 178; Yılmaz, "Governing the Armenian Question," 392.

36. Chapter 12, Article 6, https://www.justice.gov.tn/fileadmin/medias/ministere/musee/constitution_1861_ar.pdf. For a French translation, see https://mjp.univ-perp.fr/constit/tn1861.htm.

37. "*'alā muqtaḍā al-qawānīni al-maj'ūlati lahum*" (Chapter 3, Article 9 [Article 27 in the French translation]).

38. "*Al-majlis al-akbar huwwa al-muḥāfiẓu 'alā al-'uhūdi wal-qawānīni wal-ḥāmī li-ḥuqūqi jamī'i al-sukkāni*" (Chapter 7, Article 1 [Article 60 in the French translation]).

39. Bercher, "En marge du Pacte 'Fondamental.'" There was, however, a Christian member of the council, Count Joseph Raffo, who served as the bey's minister of foreign affairs. Bercher, "En marge du Pacte 'Fondamental,'" 244.

40. "*Al-tūnisī idhā intaqala li-waṭanin ākhirin 'alā ay wajhin wa-bi-ay sababin ṭālat muddatu mughībihi aw qaṣarat ḥasaba min ahli al-waṭani al-muntaqili ilayhi aw lam yaḥsab thumma raja'a li-mamlakati Tūnis yaḥsabu min ra'āyāhā kamā kāna*" (Chapter 12, Article 7 [Article 92 in the French version]).

41. "*Ghayru al-muslimi min ra'yatinā idhā intaqala li-dīn lā yakhrijuhu tanaqquluhu min al-ḥimāyati al-tūnisīyati wa-ra'āyatihā*" (Chapter 12, Article 9).

42. The London Society for Promoting Christianity among the Jews established a mission in Tunis in 1834 and reported some success converting Jews in Tunisia. Gidney, *History of the London Society*, 190–95. On missionaries in Tunis, see Clancy-Smith, *Mediterraneans*, chap. 7.

43. This is the standard claim in Tunisian historiography. See Mezghani, *Droit international privé*, 49; Ben Slimane, "Entre deux empires," 112.

44. Article 5, "Tabiiyet-i osmaniye kanunnamesi," *Düstur* 1289 (1872–73): 16–18. For an English translation, see Kern, *Imperial Citizen*, 157–58. On this law, see esp. Hanley, "What Ottoman Nationality Was and Was Not," 284–85; Marglin, "Extraterritoriality and Legal Belonging." See also Belkeziz, *La nationalité dans les états arabes*, 8–9; Parolin, *Citizenship in the Arab World*, 73.

45. Nissim to Khaznadar, 10 Rabī' II 1278, SH.C100.D219.4, ANT; Nissim to Khaznadar, 2 Jumādā I 1278, SH.C100.D219.3, ANT.

46. Vassel, *La littérature populaire*, 18–19. I am grateful to Noam Sienna for alerting me to the existence of this book and sharing a digital copy.

47. Sienna, "Making Jewish Books," 176–80.

48. "*Maktūb bi-lisān al-'arabī al-ṣaḥīḥ . . . al-ladhī ṣa'ïb fī fahāmatu*" (Shamama, *Kitāb qānūn al-dawla al-tūnisīya*, 2a).

49. "*Bāsh jamī' al-anna [sic] al-yahūd ḥafaḍahum Allāh yakūnū yafḥamū wa-ya'arifū hād al-qawā'id*" (Shamama, *Kitāb qānūn al-dawla al-tūnisīya*, 2a).

50. "*Al-amīr liwā Nissim Shamama ra'īs al-yahūd al-mudaraqanī [?] taḥta jināḥū Rabbī yaḥfuḍū wa-yabqīhi bil-'azz al-dā'im wal-sa'd al-qā'im amīn*" (Shamama, *Kitāb qānūn al-dawla al-tūnisīya*, 2b). While the introduction does not say explicitly that Nissim financed the publication, this seems extremely likely. Besides being thanked profusely by its author, Nissim was a loyal government official, the head of the Jewish community, and a wealthy patron of Hebrew printing—the obvious choice to pay for such an endeavor.

51. Binyamin ha-sheni, "Ḥadashot Kelaliyot."

52. Ammar, *Tunis*, 170. Eliézer Ashkenazi reported that it took 1.5 hours to reach La Goulette from Tunis. Ashkenazi, *La chronique*, 39.

53. "Semha aujourd'hui se trouve mieux, nous lui avons donné du lait d'anesse. Le docteur lui a fait prendre des glaces que lui ont fait beaucoup de bien il lui en faut encore aujourd'hui" (SH.C100.D224.14, ANT; SH.C100.D224.7, ANT).

54. February 20, 1861, SH.C100.D224.19, ANT.

55. On the loan from Lellouche, see the series of accounts relating to Shamama, n.d., SH.C102.D239.21, ANT. Lellouche was d'Erlanger's agent (d'Erlanger discussed below). De Flaux, a Frenchman who visited Tunis in 1861, reported that Nissim was awaiting a new wife coming from Paris. De Flaux, *La régence de Tunis*, 70–71. De Flaux assumed the wife was French, though it is much more likely that the woman was Esther. On the marriage, see Galeotti, *Reale Corte d'Appello di Lucca*, 128.

56. The date of 'Aziza and Moses's marriage is from Gilles Boulu.

57. Valensi, *Tunisian Peasants*, 104; Hénia, *Propriété et stratégies sociales*, 218–38. For a detailed account of Nissim's property in Tunisia, see "Reconnaissance des biens de la succession du Caïd Nessim Samama," n.d., SH.C101.D231.335, ANT. See also Ben Rajeb, *Yahūd al-bilāṭ*, 495.

58. The Funduq des Français occupied two adjacent buildings. The one closer to the Bab al-Bahr served as the consulate and the consul's residence; this was the one bought by Nissim. The second building was known as the Funduq des Négociants and still housed French merchants in 1860. Planel, *Du comptoir à la colonie*, 64–67, 358–69. According to a plaque on the outside of the former British consulate, Britain only moved its consulate from this location in 2004.

59. This building no longer exists; it is currently a park, between the Avenue Franklin Roosevelt (previously the Rue de Carthage) and the Avenue de la République, and between the Rue Al-Quds (previously the Rue de Jérusalem) and the Rue de Korbous (or Corbus).

60. We lack information on the precise property holdings of other wealthy Jews at this time. But given that the restrictions on acquiring real estate were lifted only seven years before Nissim left, it seems safe to presume that few Jews managed to acquire more property than him in such a short time.

61. Ammar, *Tunis*, 170; Jamoussi, "Le quartier franc de Tunis," 213.

62. One source says the government went into debt to the tune of eleven million piasters. Historique des faits se rattachant à la situation actuelle de la Dette Intérieur et Extérieure de la Régence de Tunis, n.d., MD, Tunisie, 12, MAE Courneuve. Victor Villet, president of the International Financial Commission instituted in 1869, records that Caillat was paid 150,000 francs

per year—plus, presumably, the cost of materials and labor. Note de Victor Villet, May 19, 1872, MD, Tunisie, 12, MAE Courneuve.

63. Historique des faits se rattachant à la situation actuelle de la Dette Intérieur et Extérieure de la Régence de Tunis, n.d., MD, Tunisie, 12, MAE Courneuve.

64. On the triennials, see Memoire des Commissaires des différentes conversions de la dette flottante, March 2, 1868, MD, Tunisie, 12, MAE Courneuve. On Nissim's investment, see Général Heussein, *Le Caïd Nessim*, 77. Villet claimed that Nissim lent the state twelve million piasters in 1862 at a rate of 12 percent interest, though I have found no other evidence of this loan—and given that Villet's report is extremely biased against Nissim, it seems unwise to accept this assertion without corroborating evidence. Note de Victor Villet, May 18, 1872, MD, Tunisie, 12, MAE Courneuve; Ganiage, *Les origines*, 178.

65. Ganiage, *Les origines*, 172–75.

66. Landes, *Bankers and Pashas*, 14–15.

67. Owen, *The Middle East in the World Economy*, 100–101; Aşçi, "Türkiye'nin 150 yıllık borç serüveni," 31.

68. Landes, *Bankers and Pashas*, 107–8.

69. Comte d'Avigdor, "Note lue au comité qui s'était formé pour entendre les propositions de l'Emprunt de 30 millions de fr," June 12, 1846, HR.SYS.2933.54, BOA; 1 Şafar 1263, Irade, I.HR.38.1805, BOA. See the discussion in chapter 1.

70. Nissim to Khaznadar, 27 Dhū al-Qaʿda 1277 / June 6, 1861, SH.C100.D219.2, ANT; Nissim to Khaznadar, 2 Dhū al-Ḥijja 1277 / June 6, 1861, SH.C100.D219.1, ANT.

71. Musurus to Aali Pacha, April 10, 1862, HR.SYS.1613.6, BOA.

72. Note de Victor Villet, May 19, 1872, MAE Courneuve.

73. For an extreme, antisemitic example, see Drumont, *La France juive*, 1:ix–xiv.

74. Stoskopf, *Les patrons du second empire*, 162–63.

75. Landes, *Bankers and Pashas*, 117.

76. Gentry, "A Confederate Success in Europe"; Stoskopf, *Les patrons du second empire*, 162–63.

77. Villet gives 5,075,000 francs as the total commission (14.5 percent of the loan). Note de Victor Villet, May 19, 1872, MD, Tunisie, 12, MAE Courneuve. Another report puts the figure at 6 million. Mémoire des Commissaires des différentes conversions de la dette flottante, March 2, 1868, MD, Tunisie, 12, MAE Courneuve.

78. Mémoire des Commissaires des différentes conversions de la dette flottante, March 2, 1868, MD, Tunisie, 12, MAE Courneuve. The majba had been reinstituted in 1856. Valensi, *Tunisian Peasants*, 237–38.

79. Aartin Effendi (ambassador in Paris) to Aali Pacha (telegram), May 28, 1863, HR.SYS.1613.6.6, BOA.

80. Relevé des titres et valeurs dépendant de la Succession du Caid Nissim Samama, December 31, 1877, SH.C102.D239, ANT.

81. N.d., SH.C102.D239.21, ANT. D'Erlanger's agent in Tunis at the time was named Cernuschi.

82. Aartin Effendi (ambassador in Paris) to Aali Pacha (telegram), May 28, 1863, HR.SYS.1613.6.6, BOA.

83. Aali Pacha to Ottoman embassies in Paris and London (telegram), n.d., HR.SYS.1613.6.5, BOA.

84. "Nous ne pouvons déranger aux habitudes traditionnelles qui ont été suivies en France à l'égard de ce pays, et en particulier pendant le règne précédent. Il nous est par conséquent impossible de retirer l'autorisation que le Gouvernement de l'Empereur a accordée pour l'émission et la cote de cet emprunt. L'administration Tunisienne a tout aussi le droit de contracter cet emprunt que celui de faire des routes, des canaux et autres améliorations" (Djemil Pacha [Paris] to Aali Pacha, July 3, 1863, HR.SYS.1613.6.14, BOA).

85. "Du moment que l'administration dépend d'un souverain territoire elle est en conséquence obligée d'avoir recours à son autorisation pour conclure son emprunt" (Djemil Pacha [Paris] to Aali Pacha, July 3, 1863, HR.SYS.1613.6.14, BOA).

86. Djemil Pacha to Aali Pacha, July 31, 1863, HR.SYS.1613/6.17, BOA; Djemil Pacha to Aali Pacha, September 4, 1863, HR.SYS.1613/6.19, BOA.

87. Mémoire des Commissaires des différentes conversions de la dette flottante, March 2, 1868, MD, Tunisie, 12, MAE Courneuve; Note de Victor Villet, May 19, 1872, MD, Tunisie, 12, MAE Courneuve.

88. On the financial difficulties of this period, see Sraieb, "Elite et société," §13.

89. Slama, *L'insurrection de 1864*, 8. Thirty-two piasters were the equivalent of about 21 francs, while 72 piasters were worth about 42 francs.

90. "*Wa-ḥāluhā ka-ḥāli al-baqarati idhā ḥuliba ḍar'uhā ḥattā kharaja al-damm*" (Ibn Diyaf, *Itḥāf*, 5:129).

91. Slama, *L'insurrection de 1864*, 23; Valensi, *Tunisian Peasants*, 238–40. A new majba had been instituted in 1856 to replace a slew of taxes from the previous decades, but it was regressive in that its burden fell heavily on the poor, whereas previous taxes had been levied on olive trees, livestock, and other forms of property.

92. Slama, *L'insurrection de 1864*, 24–32, 55–59; Oualdi, *Esclaves et maîtres*, 325–38.

93. The sultan sent money in August 1864, though the reported sum varies from 50,000 Ottoman sovereigns, to 500,000 francs, to 1.6 million Tunisian piasters. Slama, *L'insurrection de 1864*, 101. See also Slama, *L'insurrection de 1864*, 59–60, 87–88.

94. Slama, *L'insurrection de 1864*, 89, 94.

95. On the reversal of hierarchies enforced by the dhimma in Morocco, see Abdellah Laroui, *Les origines*, 310–17. On the tendency to blame Jewish advisers for the bad decisions of sovereigns, see Dakhlia, *L'empire des passions*, 104–15.

96. "*Wa-balaghahu anna ba'ḍa al-ra'ā'i min akhlāṭi zawāwati yatawa"adūna al-hujūma 'alā dārihi li-qatlihi, wa-akhdhi mā yujidūnahu min mālihi*" (Ibn Diyaf, *Itḥāf*, 5:190).

97. Meyan, *Annuaire des diplômés 1890*, 477. North African Jews did not share the custom that remains widespread among Ashkenazi Jews, who avoid naming a child after anyone living.

Chapter 3. Tunis to Paris (1864–68)

1. On Esther's accompanying Nissim to Paris and Mas'uda remaining in Tunisia, see Galeotti, *Reale Corte d'Appello di Lucca*, 128.

2. 4 Muḥarram 1281, SH.C100, D223.1, ANT. The date on this document is confusing; the Hijri date correlates to June 9, but the European date given on the decree is May 27. It is likely that one (if not both) of the dates was inaccurate.

3. Ashkenazi, *La chronique*, 24.

4. Sadiq Bey to Italian consul (Pinna), 2 Muḥarram 1281, SH.C100.D228.1, ANT.

5. "*Al-rajul min khuddāmi al-dawlati . . . wa-lahu fī khidmatihā al-yaddu al-bayḍā'*" (Ibn Diyaf, *Itḥāf*, 5:189). See also Chérif, "Ben Dhyâf et les juifs tunisiens," 94. On the date of Ibn Diyaf's chronicle, see Brown, *The Tunisia of Ahmed Bey*, 12–13.

6. Quran 3:75; Ibn Diyaf, *Itḥāf*, 5:190.

7. "*Ana khadīmuka wa-khadīmu ābā'ika wa-ibnu khuddāmika, wa-akhlāṭu al-'āmmati yata'adhdhuru al-iḥtifāẓa bihim, wa-innī ikhshā al-mawta min al-juz'. Aṭlubu anna tabqī 'ala ramaqī bi-tasrīḥī lil-ṣafar*" (Ibn Diyaf, *Itḥāf*, 5:190). See also Ben Rajeb, *Yahūd al-bilāṭ*, 496–97.

8. Abraham Beïda to Nissim Shamama, 10 Rabi I 1283 / July 23, 1866, in Heussein, *Le Caïd Nessim*, 27.

9. *Ha-Magid*, June 29, 1864, 1–2. See also Shemla, "Afrika"; *Ha-Magid*, January 27, 1874, 9–10.

10. Note de Victor Villet, May 19, 1872, MD, Tunisie, 12, MAE Courneuve; Note de Victor Villet, January 1874, MD, Tunisie, 12, MAE Courneuve.

11. See especially Husayn's denunciation of Nissim in the Arabic version of his first brief—which interestingly, was not included in the French translation. Husayn, "Al-qusṭās," 272–76.

12. "*Zuhd fī ḥubbi al-waṭani*" (Ibn Diyaf, *Itḥāf*, 5:190). See also Chérif, "Ben Dhyâf et les juifs tunisiens," 94.

13. "*Fa-sāfara li-farānsā salīman min al-tabā'ati, naqīya al-'arḍi min danasi al-khayānati, 'alā anna yarja'a li-masqaṭi ra'sihi al-ladhī huwwa a'azzu al-biqā'i 'indahu*" (Ibn Diyaf, *Itḥāf*, 5:190). Moreover, Ibn Diyaf uses the verb *sāfara* for "travel," which connotes a temporary trip rather than a permanent move. I am grateful to Youssef Ben Ismail for this observation. Note that the editor of this edition of Ibn Diyaf's chronicle interprets Nissim's birthplace as Livorno, which I believe is a misinterpretation of the text.

14. Letters to Khaznadar and Muhammad al-'Aziz bu 'Atur, 5 Muḥarram 1281, SH.C100.D219.7 and SH.C100.D219.8, ANT; Nissim to Khaznadar, 23 Muḥarram 1281, SH.C100.D219 (no number), ANT; Nissim to Muhammad al-'Aziz bu 'Atur, 23 Muḥarram 1281, SH.C100.D219.24, ANT. Muhammad b. 'Aziz Bu 'Atur was another high-ranking official in the ministry of finance.

15. Nissim to Muhammad al-'Aziz Bu 'Atur, 13 Ṣafar 1281, SH.C100.D219.40, ANT.

16. See, for example, Brann, *Power in the Portrayal*, chaps. 1–2; Dakhlia, *L'empire des passions*, 104–15.

17. See the afterword.

18. In his will, Nissim left twenty-five thousand francs each to Ya'aqov b. Avraham Shamama and Yosef b. Natan Bessis, both of whom served as his private secretaries. Jarmon, *Naḥalat Avot*, 2a–2b. I know almost nothing about these secretaries, who undoubtedly must have had enormous personal knowledge about Nissim's finances; such are the limitations of the archives.

19. Shamama to Khaznadar, 5 Muḥarram 1281, SH.C100.D219.7, ANT. The same day, Nissim sent a nearly identical letter to Muhammad al-'Aziz bu 'Atur. Shamama to Muhammad al-'Aziz bu 'Atur, 5 Muḥarram 1281, SH.C100.D219.8, ANT. For the letters Nissim exchanged with Khaznadar, see Dossiers 219, 220, 221, SH.C100, ANT.

20. Shamama to Khaznadar and Muhammad al-'Aziz bu 'Atur, 5 Muḥarram 1281, SH.C100.D219.7 and SH.C100.D219.8, ANT; Shamama to Khaznadar and Muhammad al-'Aziz bu 'Atur, 8 Muḥarram 1281, SH.C100.D219.9 and SH.C100.D219.10, ANT.

21. Shamama to Khaznadar, 8 Muḥarram 1281, SH.C100.D219.9, ANT.

22. Letters to Khaznadar and Muhammad al-'Aziz bu 'Atur, 16 Muḥarram 1281, SH.C100.D219.15 and SH.C100.D219.16, ANT.

23. Corcos and Grande, "Lumbroso." Khaznadar had asked Nissim to advance Coco money—probably his salary as a representative of the bey. Nissim, however, claimed he did not have access to funds, assuring Coco that Khaznadar would send bills of exchange soon. Shamama to Khaznadar, 16 Muḥarram 1281, SH.C100.D219.15, ANT.

24. Ganiage, *Les origines*, 590; Corcos and Grande, "Lumbroso"; Planel, *Du comptoir à la colonie*, 447, 741.

25. "Gazette des tribunaux," *Le Figaro*, June 15, 1867, 2. The newspaper reported that Joseph's father was Nissim's brother, but in fact it seems he was Nissim's first cousin, Moshe. Again, I am grateful to Gilles Boulu for the genealogical details of the family tree.

26. Shamama to Khaznadar, 16 Muḥarram 1281, SH.C100.D219.17, ANT.

27. On Guillaume-Jules-Prosper de Lesseps (1809–87), see Smida, *Consuls et consulats*, 76–78; Planel, *Du comptoir à la colonie*, 174, 738–39; Ben Ismail, "Sovereignty across Empires," 40–42. Mathieu Maximilien Prosper de Lesseps (1774–1832) served as a French diplomat in Morocco, Egypt, Livorno, and Aleppo, with a brief stint in the United States; his tombstone is still displayed in the garden of the Cathedral of Saint-Louis in Carthage.

28. Smida, *Consuls et consulats*, 96. In the late 1870s and 1880s, he was also involved in the construction of the Panama Canal.

29. For instance, the US vice-consul in Mogador (Essaouira, Morocco) in the 1860s was a local Jew named Abraham Corcos. See James de Lang to Abraham Corcos, Rg. 84, vol. 001, January 1, 1862, United States National Archives at College Park, MD.

30. Empire français, *Annuaire diplomatique*, 67; République française, *Annuaire diplomatique*, 69; Stoskopf, *Les patrons du second empire*, 162, 165.

31. As a member of the Grana community, it is quite likely that Lumbroso was an Italian national, however I have not been able to find confirmation of this.

32. Nissim to Muhammad al-'Aziz bu 'Atur, 19 Muḥarram 1281, SH.C100.D219.19, ANT; Nissim to Khaznadar, June 18, 1864, SH.C100.D224.28, ANT.

33. Zola, *La Curée*, 82–83.

34. Nissim to Khaznadar, 19 Muḥarram 1281, SH.C100.D219.18, ANT; Nissim to Khaznadar, 20 Muḥarram 1281, SH.C100.D219.20, ANT; Nissim to Khaznadar and Muhammad al-'Aziz bu 'Atur, 20 Muḥarram 1281, SH.C100.D219.21 and SH.C100.D219.22, ANT; Nissim to Khaznadar, 23 Muḥarram 1281, SH.C100.D219.23, ANT.

35. *La Petite Presse*, May 10, 1889; Ganiage, *Les origines*, 578–79; Naaman, *Histoire des orientaux de France*, 289–90; Planel, *Du comptoir à la colonie*, 271. The next day, Nissim wrote to say that Muhammad al-Bakush, another government official, had also arrived. Nissim to Muhammad al-'Aziz bu 'Atur, 20 Muḥarram 1281, SH.C100.D219.22, ANT.

36. Postscript on letter from Nissim to Khaznadar (dated 18 Muḥarram 1281), 16 Muḥarram 1281, SH.C100.D219.17, ANT.

37. Nissim to Khaznadar, 20 Muḥarram 1281, SH.C100.D219.21, ANT.

38. The same day, he wrote to tell Khaznadar that his new address was 47 Rue Faubourg Saint Honoré. Nissim to Khaznadar, 23 Muḥarram 1281, SH.C100.D219 (no number), ANT.

39. This may be the Morpurgo loan of July 1864, reported in note de Victor Villet, May 19, 1872 and January 1874, MD, Tunisie, 12, MAE Courneuve.

40. "*Anā ʿumrī [sic] mā khadamtu fī al-būlītīk . . . sīdī al-sulṭān al-mutawallī yuḥābū [sic] al-farānsīs katīr [sic] . . . wa-nuḥibuka asyāda tāʿṭīnī likā idhni bash natassalafa . . . qālī shūf dawlat farānsa qadāsh tuḥibbu dawlat tūnis? Tuḥibā fī thalātha ḥawāʾij, awwal tuḥibā a-takūn dawlat tūnis ḥabība yāsir li-dawlat farānsa; wal-thānī tuḥibā dawlat a-takūnīhā dawla wāḥida mā min taḥta aḥad; wal-thālith tuḥibā mabsūṭa; wa-uʿṭānī lahā idhan mushāfāt [?] fī ʿamal a-salaf*" (Nissim to Khaznadar, 23 Muḥarram 1281, SH.C100.D219 [no number], ANT).

41. Nissim to Khaznadar, 23 Muḥarram 1281, SH.C100.D219 (no number), ANT; Nissim to Muhammad al-ʿAziz bu ʿAtur, 26 Muḥarram 1281, SH.C100.D219.28, ANT.

42. Postscript on letter from Nissim to Khaznadar (dated 18 Muḥarram 1281), 16 Muḥarram 1281, SH.C100.D219.17, ANT.

43. Ganiage, *Les origines*, 172–75.

44. Nissim to Khaznadar, 1 Ṣafar 1281, SH.C100.D219.30, ANT.

45. Nissim to Khaznadar, 4 Ṣafar 1281, SH.C100.D219.33, ANT.

46. On August 16, Khaznadar sent a telegraph to Nissim saying he had found a better loan. Nissim to Khaznadar, 13 Rabīʿ I 1281, SH.C100.D219.57, ANT.

47. See various letters in SH.C100.D219, ANT.

48. Nissim's building was originally conceived of as an investment by Emile Pereire, one of Paris's most famous bankers. Pereire was also Jewish—originally from a Sephardi family settled for centuries in Bordeaux. In 1863, Pereire sold the property—with its old, outdated house now demolished—to the architect Joseph-Michel-Anne Le Soufaché, who completed a new building that same year (the inscription on the facade with the date 1863 is still there). Dugast and Parizet, *Dictionnaire par noms d'architectes*, 3:66; DQ18.138, AP; DQ18.557, AP; DQ18.1339, AP.

49. Smida, *Consuls et consulats*, 96.

50. Series of accounts relating to Shamama, n.d. SH.C102.D239.21, ANT. Esther's father was Haim, and this document refers to the Lellouche in question as Hai, but it seems safe to presume that they were one and the same.

51. D1.P4.416, AP.

52. Ashkenazi, *La chronique*, 19.

53. This Rabbinic Bible (or Mikraot Gedolot) was published by Moses ben Simeon Frankfurter in Amsterdam between 1724 and 1728. See https://blogs.yu.edu/library/2018/12/27/musings-on-moses/. I am grateful to Shulamith Berger, librarian at Yeshiva University, where the set is on loan by Richard and Debra Parkoff.

54. Ashkenazi, *La chronique*, 25.

55. "*Tukhāf bālik innā namuddu yaday fī al-dirāhim wa-Allāh al-ʿaẓīm law naʿrif Allāh lā naqdur. . . . Mā namdīdī wa-law frank wāḥid illā bi-idhni al-sayādati wa-ana ʿarraftu al-sayādata bi-kulli ḥājati wal-ladhī yaḍharu al-sayādatu asdad [sic] wa-aṣlaḥ*" (Nissim to Khaznadar, 27 Ṣafar 1281, SH.C100.D219.46, ANT.

56. Nissim to Khaznadar, 27 Rabīʿ II 1281, SH.C100.D219.80, ANT. The Morpurgo loan went through in July. Ganiage, *Les origines*, 243. For Morpurgo's first name, see Nissim to Khaznadar, 26 Rajab 1281, SH.C100.D219.112, ANT.

57. Nissim to Muhammad al-ʿAziz bu ʿAtur, 12 Jumādā I 1281, SH.C100.D219.84, ANT; Nissim to Khaznadar, 17 Jumādā I 1281, SH.C100.D219.87, ANT; Nissim to Khaznadar, 18 Jumādā I 1281, SH.C100.D219.34, ANT; Nissim to Khaznadar, 25 Jumādā I 1281, SH.C100.D219.90, ANT; Nissim to Khaznadar, 10 Jumādā II 1281, SH.C100.D219.97, ANT; Nissim to Khaznadar, 23 Jumādā

II 1281, SH.C100.D219.104, ANT. In these letters, Nissim also asked for the details of the Morpurgo loan.

58. Nissim to Khaznadar, 17 Rabīʿ II 1281, SH.C100.D219.75, ANT. See also Boulu, "Les Caïds Scemama," 7–8.

59. Ganiage, *Les origines*, 244. For the conditions of the original contract that Nissim negotiated, see Nissim to Khaznadar, 27 Ṣafar 1281, SH.C100.D219.46, ANT.

60. Nissim to Khaznadar, 23 Jumādā II 1281, SH.C100.D219.104, ANT.

61. See, for example, Nissim to Muhammad al-ʿAziz bu ʿAtur, 13 Rabīʿ II, SH.C100.D219.72, ANT; Nissim to Khaznadar, 17 Rabīʿ II 1281, SH.C100.D219.75, ANT.

62. Nissim to Khaznadar, 17 Jumādā I 1281, SH.C100.D219.87, ANT.

63. See, for example, Nissim to Khaznadar, 12 Ramaḍān 1281, SH.C100.D219.120, ANT; Nissim to Khaznadar, 26 Ramaḍān 1281, SH.C100.D219.121, ANT; Nissim to Khaznadar (and other letters in this series), 17 Shawwāl 1281, SH.C100.D219.125, ANT.

64. The first such letter is from August 3, in which Nissim reported to Khaznadar that his children were all well. Nissim to Khaznadar, 29 Ṣafar 1281, SH.C100.D219.51, ANT.

65. "*Wajadtu al-asʿad sīdī Muḥammad qadāma jamīʿ taṣwīrati mulūk frānsa wa-jamīʿ assakka [sic] munāʿihim min awwalihim lil-yawm wa-kutub bayna yadayhi*" (Nissim to Khaznadar, 26 Rajab 1281, SH.C100.D219.112, ANT). On Muhammad Khaznadar, see Moumni, "Archaeology and Cultural Policy" (Nissim's visit is mentioned on 269).

66. Nissim to Khaznadar, 18 Dhū al-Ḥijja 1282, SH.C100.D219.192, ANT.

67. "*Wa-naṭlubu min karīm faḍli al-sayādati lam talkhaṣ ʿalaynā*" (Nissim to Khaznadar, 28 Ṣafar 1283, SH.C100.D220.12, ANT).

68. Nissim to Khaznadar, 6 Rabīʿ I 1283, SH.C100.D220.13, ANT.

69. Nissim to Khaznadar, 11 Jumādā I 1283, SH.C100.D220.24, ANT; Nissim to Khaznadar, 13–14 Jumādā I 1283, SH.C100.D220.25, ANT; Nissim to Khaznadar, 24 Jumādā I 1283, SH.C100.D220.28, ANT.

70. De Grouchy, *Meudon*, 95; Biver, *Histoire du château de Bellevue*, 94–95. Nissim must have been brought to Bellevue by de Lesseps, who owned property there. Two years later, de Lesseps brought another bit of Tunis to Sèvres; he was in charge of the Tunisian Pavilion at the World's Fair in Paris in 1867 and had the magnificent Moorish-style mansion built for the exhibition moved to Bellevue. Much like the palaces of Tunis, not a single window penetrated the imposing facade; instead, all the rooms gave onto a central courtyard. *Le Figaro*, July 15, 1877, 2; "The Tunisian Scandal and Its Authors," *Pall Mall Budget*, October 7, 1881, 10–11.

71. D1P4 416, 47 Rue du Faubourg Saint Honoré, 2ème étage, AP.

72. In the fall of 1865, he went to Lyon, where he stayed in the opulent Hôtel de Provence et des Ambassadeurs. *Le Constitutionel*, October 23, 1865, 2. Zagdun, Fellous, Ashkenazi, and Sitruk were all given money in Nissim's will, as were Jacob Shamama and Bessis (named in the will as first and second secretaries).

73. "Abbandonata alle lucertole e ai cani" (journal of Fortunée Coriat, a member of the Grana community born in Tunis in 1842, summer 1865; my thanks to Liana Funaro for providing this reference). On Coriat, see Scardozzi, "Una storia di famiglia," 725.

74. Ben Rajeb, *Yahūd al-bilāṭ*, 428–67.

75. Khayraddin in particular turned against Nissim, but he was more focused on his opposition to Khaznadar. Van Krieken, *Khayr al-Dîn*, chap. 4. Discussed further in the afterword.

76. Elmelich, *Observations*, 19.

77. Weil, *Qu'est-ce qu'un français?*, 37–38, 67.

78. "Il generale commendatore Nissim del fu Salomone Semama native di Tunisi ma di famiglia originaria Livornese, fino da qualche giorno umiliò domanda al R. Trono onde gli venisse concessa la naturalità italiana, nel desiderio di tornare a domiciliarsi come cittadino nella terra degli avi suoi" (presidenza del consiglio dei ministri, consulta araldica, fascicoli nobiliari e araldici delle singole famiglie, Busta 9, Semama, Nissim e Moise, June 1, 1866, Cempini to Vittorio Emanuele II, ACS). It was not uncommon in Europe to essentially buy noble titles, though nobility and nationality did not necessarily go hand in hand. Nissim's lawyer was Leopoldo Cempini, a native of Florence who had served as a deputy in the Tuscan Assembly since 1859. See http://www.montesca.eu/dbm/cempini-leopoldo/.

79. In 1879, Messaouda de Moïse Samama married Isaac de Daniel Forti; in 1881, Sara de Rabbi Jacob Samama married Salomon de Isaac Bensimon. Boulu and Nedjar, *La communauté juive portugaise de Tunis*, 196, 211.

80. Lumbroso, "Le Baron Giacomo del Castelnuovo"; Lévy, *La nation juive portugaise*, 99–101.

81. Ministero per gli affari dell'interno to Sig. Avv. Leopoldo Cempini, June 13, 1866, Presidenza del consiglio dei ministri, consulta araldica, fascicoli nobiliari e araldici delle singole famiglie, Busta 9, Semama, Nissim e Moise, ACS.

82. June 18, 1866, no. 71, Consulta Araldica, Decreti Reali, ACS.

83. Gabinetto particolare di S. M. to Ministro dell'interno, June 2, 1866, Presidenza del consiglio dei ministri, consulta araldica, fascicoli nobiliari e araldici delle singole famiglie, Busta 9, Semama, Nissim e Moise, ACS.

84. Franchi-Vemey to Ministero dell'Interno, November 9, 1866, Presidenza del consiglio dei ministri, consulta araldica, fascicoli nobiliari e araldici delle singole famiglie, Busta 9, Semama, Nissim e Moise, ACS.

85. November 22, 1866, no. 73, Consulta Araldica, Decreti Reali, ACS.

86. Debbasche, *Memorie, appunti, e note rettificative*, 55.

87. *Codice Civile*, 1–5; Donati, *A Political History*; chap. 3.

88. Mancini, *Corte di Appello di Lucca*, 255.

89. See, for example, *Ha-Magid*, March 5, 1873, 4; "Ḥadashot le-beit Yisrael," *Ḥavatzelet*, August 3, 1883, 6; "Ḥadashot be-Yisrael," *Ha-Yom*, August 19, 1886, 3.

90. Nissim to Khaznadar, 26 Rajab 1281, SH.C100.D219.112, ANT; Nissim to Khaznadar, 13 Shaʿbān 1281, SH.C100.D219.113, ANT; Nissim to Khaznadar, 27 Shaʿbān 1281, SH.C100.D219.117, ANT.

91. Nissim later reported to Khaznadar that the Empress Eugénie, Napoléon III's wife, had visited the Tunisian pavilion and was pleased by the replica of the Bardo constructed on the Champ de Mars. Nissim to Khaznadar, 13 Dhū al-Qaʿda 1283, SH.C100.D220.51, ANT; Nissim to Khaznadar, 20 Dhū al-Qaʿda, SH.C100.D220.52, ANT; Nissim to Khaznadar, 12 Dhū al-Ḥijja 1283, SH.C100.D220.50, ANT.

92. "Mudīr al-māl wa-raʾīs al-qubbāḍ."

93. Pierantoni, *Corte di Appello di Lucca*, 179; Galeotti, *Reale Corte d'Appello di Lucca*, 128–33. The letter from Le Roy advising Nissim that his divorce could only be regulated by Jewish law was dated April 30, 1866.

94. For the standard biography, see Posener, *Adolphe Crémieux*. On the Crémieux Decree, see Steven Uran, "Crémieux Decree."

95. "Un tribunal français, pour ces orientaux, c'est la justice même. . . . Le caïd a trois femmes. (on rit)" ("Gazette des tribunaux," *Le Figaro*, June 15, 1867, 2).

96. "Gazette des tribunaux," *Le Figaro*, June 15, 1867, 2. The newspaper reported that Joseph's father was Nissim's brother, but in fact it seems he was Nissim's first cousin, Moshe.

97. "Quel contour charmant! quell artiste, en un mot!" ("Gazette des tribunaux," *Le Figaro*, June 15, 1867, 1).

98. Ibn 'Ayyad moved to Istanbul in 1857. Gharbi, "Mahmoud Ben Ayyed." On his properties in Istanbul, see HR.H 432–1/32, BOA.

99. Nissim to Khaznadar, 21 Sha'bān 1284, SH.C100.D220.111, ANT. He used the term *kawāghiz*, meaning "archives." Nissim also requested documents concerning the lawsuit between the bey and Ibn 'Ayyad in France following his departure from Tunis in 1852.

100. "*Wal-ān lam wajadnā al-taqyīda al-madhkūra wa-māzalnā [sic] jufattishū 'alayhi . . . yumkinu ḍā'ū fī al-ṭarīq qa'adū fī Tūnis*" (Nissim to Khaznadar, 22 Ramaḍān 1284, SH.C100.D220.116, ANT).

101. Nissim to Khaznadar, 5 Dhū al-Qa'da 1284, SH.C100.D220.125, ANT.

102. Nissim to Khaznadar, 28 Muḥarram 1285, SH.C100.D220.147, ANT.

103. Khaznadar to Crémieux, 8 Ṣafar 1285, SH.C100.D220.125, ANT.

104. "*Wa-lamā naẓara lahum Masyū Krīmīyū al-abuqāt ghaḍaba 'alaynā kathīr akhadha fī khāṭirihi min al-sayāda li-ajli qāla anna hādhihi al-nusakhi lā yaṣluḥū bihi li-annahum mutasawwakhīn min nusakhin lā min al-aṣli*" (Nissim to Khaznadar, 25 Rabī' I 1285, SH.C100.D220.165, ANT).

105. Nissim to Khaznadar, 6 Ṣafar 1286, SH.C100.D221.5, ANT.

106. The last such letters are Nissim to Khaznadar, 28 Muḥarram 1284, SH.C100.D221.76, ANT; Nissim to Khaznadar, 16 Rabī' I 1287, SH.C100.D221.47, ANT.

107. Nissim to Khaznadar, 8 Ṣafar 1285, SH.C100.D220.125, ANT; Nissim to Khaznadar, 1 Shawwāl 1285, SH.C100.D220.190, ANT.

108. Nissim to Khaznadar, 8 Dhū al-Qa'da 1286, SH.C100.D221.40, ANT.

109. Nissim to Khaznadar, 5 Muḥarram 1287, SH.C100.D221.46, ANT.

110. Nissim to Khaznadar, 5 Muḥarram 1287, SH.C100.D221.46, ANT.

Chapter 4. Paris to Livorno (1868–73)

1. "*Faḍl li-rabbī wa-muṭāwi'a li-gharḍī . . . ākhir gharḍī . . . wa-ana mu'āmir bi-siḥḥat khidnī*" (Jarmon, *Naḥalat Avot*, 1a). A more literal translation of *ākhir gharḍī* is "last intention."

2. Lehmann, *Emissaries*.

3. "*Jamī'a hād al-mutawaḍīn (līgātīr) khaṣūṣīn mā yanjamū yimshī ḥaqqahim kān fawq a-sāhama mata'a wirthī hiyya mu'ayyina lahum wa-laysa fawq a-sāhamāt li-wakhrīn al-ladī hūmān mumatawwiqīn [sic] bil-qaṣd*" (Jarmon, *Naḥalat Avot*, 3a–b).

4. Le Roy to Nissim, November 14 and 18, 1866, transcribed in Elmelich, *Observations*, 11–13.

5. Elon, *Jewish Law*, 4:1681–82.

6. Nissim to Khaznadar, 23 Ṣafar 1286 / June 4, 1869, SH.C100.D221.8, ANT.

7. By November, however, Nissim returned to using ordinary paper for his correspondence with Khaznadar; perhaps he felt the Tunisian prime minister no longer merited special stationery given the deterioration of their relationship. Nissim to Khaznadar, 20 Sha'bān 1286 / November 25, 1869, SH.C100.D221.29, ANT.

8. Nissim also bought another country house in Beaumont-sur-Oise, about forty-five kilometers north of Paris. See accounts relating to Nissim Shamama, n.d., SH.C102.D239.21, ANT.

9. *Le Gaulois*, January 20, 1869.

10. *Recueil des dépèches télégraphiques*, 251. See further correspondence from Sauveur Samama and Zéza Samama in Marseille to Nessim Samama, Chaillot 105, between December 1, 1870 and January 31, 1871. *Recueil des dépèches télégraphiques*, 366, 403, 536.

11. February 23, 1871, quoted in Mancini, *Corte di Appello di Lucca*, 256.

12. Merriman, *Massacre*, 49–53.

13. République française, *Annuaire diplomatique*, 71.

14. "Monsieur le Comte Semama Nissim, General de Cavalerie, natif de Tunis, originaire de Livorno, naturalisé italien; partant de Paris, allant en Italie, accompagné de son secretaire [*sic*]. . . . Agé de 64. Profession: Rentier. Dernier domicile : Paris" (Debbasche, *Memorie, appunti, e note rettificative*, 56).

15. Torpey, *The Invention of the Passport*, 114, 130, 141, esp. 76–77, 111–12. By the 1860s, passports were starting to resemble identification documents issued only by an individual's home state, but this was by no means true everywhere (Torpey, *The Invention of the Passport*, 101). On early modern passports, see also Ulbert, "Identifier pour contrôler."

16. Filippini, "La ballotazione"; Frattarelli Fischer, *Vivere fuori dal ghetto*; Trivellato, *The Familiarity of Strangers*; Bregoli, *Mediterranean Enlightenment*; Calafat, "L'indice de la franchise"; Tazzara, "Religious Boundaries in Italy." On other non-Catholic communities in Livorno, see also Grenet, *La fabrique communautaire*; Calafat and Santus, "Les avatars du 'turc.'"

17. Lévy, *La nation juive portugaise*; Reiman, "Claiming Livorno"; Viscomi, "Out of Time." For records of departures from Livorno—including many recognizably Jewish families—see Registro de immigrazione ed emigrazione, dal 1866 al 1900, ACL.

18. Sonnino, *Storia della tipografia ebraica in Livorno*; Bregoli, "Hebrew Printing in Eighteenth-Century Livorno," esp. 172. The railway connecting Livorno to Rome was completed in 1867.

19. Mancini, *Corte di Appello di Lucca*, 8.

20. Today the urban fabric has changed significantly and a sports center has been built behind the palazzo. For architectural drawings of the buildings and an account of the renovation, see Tomassi, *Architettura come colore*, 126–29.

21. Minute 32, May 31, 1871, 98, ASCEL.

22. "Non sei un Samama!" (interview with Liana Funaro, June 10, 2014).

23. "Enfin toutes les sommes restant libres sur les impôts affectés à titre de garantie à l'Emprunt de 1863" (advertisement for buying shares of the loan in *Journal général de l'instruction publique; revue hebdomadaire politique* 37, no. 19 [May 8, 1867]: 289).

24. Gehring, *Les relations entre la Tunisie et l'Allemagne*, 43. Gehring cites a letter from Bismarck to the bey dated December 1867, SH.C110.D286, ANT. See also Ganiage, *Les origines*, 258.

25. Djemil Pacha to Fuad Pacha, May 14, 1868, HR.SYS.1613/6.36, BOA. On Ottoman officials' concerns about Tunisian debt, see the rest of this dossier for the correspondence

between Naoum Effendi (Ottoman consul in Malta), Djemil Pasha (Ottoman ambassador in Paris), and Fuad Pasha (Ottoman minister of foreign affairs), April 1868 to May 1869.

26. "S'adresser aux soi-disants banquiers qui n'ont aucune espèce de crédit sur les marchés de l'Europe et qui sont capables de lui créer des difficultés" (Djemil Pacha [Paris] to Fuad Pacha, May 22, 1868, HR.SYS.1613.6.46, BOA).

27. Naoum Effendi (Malta) to Aali Pacha (Ottoman minister of foreign affairs), May 18, 1869, HR.SYS.1609.34.2–3, BOA. This dossier includes a cutting from a newspaper with news from Tunis.

28. Van Krieken, *Khayr al-Dîn*, 151–54. See also Ganiage, *Les origines*, 306–7, 606. For the French text of the decree, see Sadiq Bey, "Décret de S. A. le Bey instituant la Commission financière."

29. *Aqwam al-Masālik fī Ma'rifat Aḥwāl al-Mamālik*. For a translation of the introduction, see Khayraddin, *The Surest Path*. On Khayraddin, see van Krieken, *Khayr al-Dîn*; Clancy-Smith, *Mediterraneans*, 315–41.

30. Van Krieken, *Khayr al-Dîn*, 150–51.

31. Stigall, *The Santillana Codes*, 57–58. On dragomen, see, for example, Dursteler, *Venetians in Constantinople*; Rothman, *Brokering Empire*.

32. Ganiage, *Les origines*, 583, 586, 589–90.

33. Bonfils was the agent of Alphonse Pinard, then head of the Comptoir d'Escompte, which had underwritten one of Tunisia's more recent loans, and Albert Dubois was d'Erlanger's agent in Tunisia at the time. Ganiage, *Les origines*, 313.

34. On the extent to which many "foreigners" in North Africa and the Middle East were, in fact, more local than foreign, see Hanley, *Identifying with Nationality*.

35. Brown, *The Tunisia of Ahmed Bey*, 220–22.

36. "Dilapidation et des opérations financières insensées qui se sont succédées surtout depuis 10 à 12 ans . . . que tant que Sidi Mustapha conserva le pouvoir il n'aura jamais et ne pourrait même avoir autre préoccupation que celle . . . de la satisfaction de la cupidité à laquelle il n'a jamais hésité et n'hésitera jamais à sacrifier le Pays et le Souverain qui l'a adopté" (Note de Victor Villet, 79, May 19, 1872, MD Tunisie 12, MAE Courneuve).

37. Note de Victor Villet, 14, 18, May 19, 1872, MD Tunisie 12, MAE Courneuve.

38. Note de Victor Villet, 4, January 1874, MD Tunisie 12, MAE Courneuve.

39. Gehring, *Tunisie et l'Allemagne*, 43–45. Tulin himself has a fascinating biography. He was born in Tunis in 1837 to a Swedish father and US mother. His father was the consul of Sweden and Norway, and sent him to Sweden to be educated. In 1857, Tulin was named vice-consul of Sweden and Norway in Tunis. In 1864, he published *Le royaume tunisien et les représentants des puissances étrangères à Tunis*. Tulin succeeded his father as representative of Sweden, Norway, and Prussia in 1865. In 1860, he married Laure Costa, daughter of the Genoese doctor Domenico Costa and Thérèse Gay, cousin of Oscar Gay, employed at the ministry of foreign affairs. Tulin was appointed German consul in Tunisia in 1871. See Gehring, *Tunisie et l'Allemagne*, 31, 30–38.

40. Wali of Tunis to Sublime Porte, 15 Jama'a I 1289 / July 21, 1872, HR.TO.456.34, BOA. See also Gehring, *Tunisie et l'Allemagne*, 47; Ganiage, *Les origines*, 326–27.

41. Mancini, *Corte di Appello di Lucca*, 9; Bargellini to Khaznadar and Nushir Basha Bey, February 7, 1873, SH.C249.D670.230, ANT.

42. Nissim to Khaznadar, September 16, 1871, SH.C100.D221.55, ANT.

43. Nissim to Khaznadar, November 7, 1871, SH.C100.D221.48, ANT; Nissim to Khaznadar, 22 Ramaḍān 1288 / December 5, 1871, SH.C100.D221.49, ANT. On French concerns about Khayraddin's trip to Istanbul and the *firman*, see HR.SYS.1614.3, BOA.

44. The following February, Nissim wrote to Khayraddin himself, wishing him a happy 'Īd al-kabīr. Nissim to Khayraddin, 7 Dhū al-Ḥijja 1288/ February 17, 1872, SH.C100.D221.52, ANT.

45. Nissim to Khaznadar, November 29, 1872, SH.C100.D221.57, ANT.

Chapter 5. Heirs Apparent (1873)

1. Hesiod, *Works and Days*, in Cooke, Goknar, and Parker, *Mediterranean Passages*, 31.

2. *Archives israélites* 34, no. 4 (February 15, 1873): 118. See also Bargellini to Khaznadar, January 31, 1871, SH.C249.D670.219, ANT.

3. The palazzo was valued at a hundred thousand francs in 1877. "Relevé des titres et valeurs dépendant de la Succession du Caïd Nissim Samama," December 31, 1877, SH.C102.D239, ANT.

4. *L'educatore israelita*, February 1873, 84; *Archives israélites* 34, no. 4 (February 15, 1873): 118.

5. "Relevé des titres et valeurs dépendant de la Succession du Caïd Nissim Samama," December 31, 1877, SH.C102.D239, ANT.

6. See Piketty, Postel-Vinay, and Rosenthal, "Wealth Concentration"; relevant data appendix, http://piketty.pse.ens.fr/rentiersociety/PPVR2011DataAppendix.pdf, esp. table B8. On the Rothschilds, see, for example, Grange, *Une élite parisienne.*

7. Young, *Labor in Europe and America*, 444; *State of Labor in Europe: 1878*, 90–91, 293. For the exchange rate used between the franc and US dollar in the 1879 report, see *State of Labor in Europe: 1878*, 79. I am grateful to Stephen Marglin for suggesting theses sources.

8. *Archives israélites* 34, no. 4 (February 15, 1873): 118.

9. "*Al-wuratha [sic] lil-qā'id Nisīm al-qā'id Mūmū wa-akhīhi wa-ibn akhīhi wa-hum twānsa wa-qāṭinīn al-ān bi-Tūnis*" (Khayraddin to Bargellini, Dhū al-Qa'da 1289, SH.C100.D228.9, ANT).

10. It seems that Momo was subsequently forced out of this position, but reappointed in 1869. Boulu, "Les Caïds Scemama," 7–8.

11. See, for example, Al-Hadif, Ha-Cohen-Ganunah, and Ben 'Attar, *Zekhut Yosef*, 1b.

12. "*Gam im efshar she-dodi ha-sar 'asah 'imakhem ra'ah, anokhi ehyeh 'imakhem be-kesher amitz ve-ḥazak . . . Akh im ereh ki he'evarti mi-naḥalat dodi asher eleha takiti [sic] kol yemei hayay, lo anoaḥ ve-lo eshkot lavo be-'akifin ule-hit'olel 'alilot be-resha'* [Psalms 141:4]" (Al-Hadif, Ha-Cohen-Ganunah, and Ben 'Attar, *Zekhut Yosef*, 2b). This account appears in *Zekhut Yosef* (The Merit of Joseph), a highly partisan text written six months later by three rabbis: Aharon Al-Hadif (an emissary from Tiberias in Ottoman Palestine), Mordekhai Ha-Cohen-Ganunah (from Tunis), and Yehudah Ben 'Attar (another emissary from Palestine). *Zekhut Yosef* was written to disprove Momo's claims about the arrangements he made with Joseph and Nathan. Nonetheless, in almost every instance in which the account in *Zekhut Yosef* is corroborated by evidence from archival sources, it proves mostly (if not entirely) accurate. It does mix up the sequence of events immediately following Nissim's death as it claims that Khaznadar told Momo he was cut out of the will before Momo forced Joseph to sign an agreement that they would split the inheritance evenly three ways; this agreement was signed on Saturday, January 24—two days

before the public reading of the will (which took place the following Monday). Al-Hadif, Ha-Cohen-Ganunah, and Ben 'Attar, *Zekhut Yosef*, 2b. On this source, see Haruvi, "Ha-elitah ha-toranit," 79–80.

13. Contract between Momo and Joseph, 27 Tevet 5633, SH.C106.D266.26, ANT. A few days later, Momo had the contract signed by the chief rabbi of the Twansa (Nathan Bouzgel), two rabbis of the Grana community (Abraham Boccara and Abraham Lumbroso), and sixteen other rabbis.

14. It is possible that Momo wanted to marry Esther in order to get his hands on a portion of Nathan's inheritance. Perhaps Nathan, as Esther's legal guardian since the passing of their father, would be expected to pay her dowry. After inheriting the millions from Nissim, Nathan might have been required to provide a handsome dowry indeed. See Pinna to Venosta, March 4, 1873, Ministero Affari Esteri Regno d'Italia (Moscati VI), 1440, ASMAE; Haruvi, "Ha-elitah ha-toranit," 88–89.

15. For this description of Attal, see Al-Hadif, Ha-Cohen-Ganunah, and Ben 'Attar, *Zekhut Yosef*, 5b.

16. Document prepared in the French consulate, March 3, 1873, SH.C100.D228.10, ANT. The witnesses were Yosef Zaytoun and Rafael Jawi.

17. Document prepared in the French consulate, March 3, 1873, SH.C100.D228.10, ANT.

18. 29 Dhū al-Ḥijja 1289, SH.C102.D239.19, ANT; 29 Dhū al-Ḥijja 1289, SH.C104.D246.55, ANT. Although date converters give 29 Dhū al-Ḥijja 1289 as February 27, that day fell on a Thursday, and the contract specifies that it was written on a Wednesday. Moreover, other sources confirm that the contract was signed on February 26. Elmelich, *Tribunale Civile di Livorno*, 7. Momo also asked that the bey give his word that Nissim's estate would be adjudicated "by the intercession of our rabbis, according to the laws and customs of our religion" ("par l'entremise de nos rabbins selon les lois et coutumes de notre religion")—something the Tunisian authorities were clearly hoping for in any case.

19. Document prepared in the French consulate, March 3, 1873, SH.C100.D228.10, ANT.

20. Bargellini wrote that he expected Joseph and Nathan to arrive in Livorno in mid-February. Bargellini to Khaznadar, 14 February 1873, SH.C249.D670.234, ANT.

21. "*Taqtaḍā al-muḥāfiẓa 'alā al-ḥurrīya al-shakhṣīya*" (3 Muḥarram 1290, SH.C102.D239.27–32, ANT). Spezzafumo was born in Tunis in 1820. Planel, *Du comptoir à la colonie*, 765.

22. 3 Muḥarram 1290, SH.C102.D239.27–32, ANT.

23. "Défendue par la loi religieuse" (1 Muḥarram 1290, SH.C102.D239.17, ANT).

24. 1 Muḥarram 1290, SH.C102.D239.17, ANT; 3 Muḥarram 1290, SH.C102.D239.27–32, ANT.

25. Pinna was appointed in 1865. Perry, *Carthage and Tunis*, 553.

26. "L'ajuto e la protezione della bandiera italiana per essere liberati dalle oppressioni . . . del Governo locale" (Pinna to Venosta, March 4, 1873, Ministero Affari Esteri Regno d'Italia [Moscati VI], 1440, ASMAE). The archival record does not specify who did the talking, but given descriptions of other such meetings, it seems safe to hypothesize that Joseph again acted as spokesperson.

27. The tradition of asylum had deep roots in the Islamic world; saints' shrines were generally considered places where anyone could take asylum and remain beyond the reach of the authorities (*ḥurm*). See esp. Westermarck, *Ritual and Belief*, 64–65, 560–61. By the late nineteenth century, foreign consulates had also become sites of asylum, not just in Tunis, but beyond; for

instance, in 1906, twelve thousand people reportedly took refuge in the British consulate in Tehran to demand that the shah promulgate a constitution. Savory, "Bast." On consulates as sanctuaries in Tunisia, see Clancy-Smith, *Mediterraneans*, 211–13.

28. See, for example, Kenbib, *Les protégés*; Clancy-Smith, *Mediterraneans*, chap. 6; Hanley, *Identifying with Nationality*; Todd, "Beneath Sovereignty."

29. "Il permesso di recarsi a Livorno ove sono chiamati per curare gl'interessi della successione che loro lasciava il Zio?" (Pinna to Venosta, March 4, 1873, Ministero Affari Esteri Regno d'Italia [Moscati VI], 1440, ASMAE).

30. Pinna to Venosta, March 4, 1873, Ministero Affari Esteri Regno d'Italia (Moscati VI), 1440, ASMAE.

31. Sadiq Bey to Pinna, 3 Muḥarram 1290 / March 3, 1873, SH.C100.D228.2, ANT; Pinna to Venosta, March 4, 1873, Ministero Affari Esteri Regno d'Italia (Moscati VI), 1440, ASMAE.

32. "Un sentimento di umanità" (Pinna to Venosta, April 8, 1873, Ministero Affari Esteri Regno d'Italia [Moscati VI], 1440, ASMAE).

33. This was not yet a full-blown discourse of human rights, though it constituted an important precursor that has been underexplored. See, for example, Mahmood, "Religious Freedom"; Marglin, *Across Legal Lines*, 124. This is also related to the concept of the "responsibility to protect," which already influenced foreign policy in the nineteenth century. Glanville, *Sovereignty and the Responsibility to Protect*.

34. "Furono seguite da tutta la colonia europea, e più particolarmente dagli ebrei indigeni col massimo interesse, e che da ogni parte, compresivi i miei colleghi di Francia e d'Inghilterra, mi sono stati fatti e mi fanno dei complimenti" (Pinna to Venosta, March 4, 1873, Ministero Affari Esteri Regno d'Italia [Moscati VI], 1440, ASMAE).

35. "PS Mi viene all'istante la notizia che il Caid Salomone Scemama di cui è stato il caso di parlare più volte nel presente rapporto, si è da parte sua rifugiato nel Consolato di Francia, senza che però me ne siasi saputo dire il motivo" (Pinna to Venosta, March 4, 1873, Ministero Affari Esteri Regno d'Italia [Moscati VI], 1440, ASMAE).

36. Declaration by Caid Momo prepared in the French consulate, March 3, 1873, SH.C100.D228.10, ANT.

37. Declaration by Caid Momo prepared in the French consulate, March 3, 1873, SH.C100.D228.10, ANT.

38. See Registro de immigrazione ed emigrazione, dal 1866 al 1900 (no. 9), under Semama, ACL. Salvatore Semama was born in Livorno on June 18, 1873. Consolato Generale d'Italia in Tunis to Prefetto di Livorno, March 25, 1930, Ministero dell'interno, direzione generale pubblica sicurezza, divisione affari generali e riservati, Casellario Politico Centrale, Busta 4556, ACS).

39. Minute 33, n.p. 9, March 27, 1873, ASCEL; Nedjar et al., *Registres de ketubbot*, 491.

40. Tribunale di Livorno, b. 30, no. 60, February 19, 1873, ASL.

41. "Les relations entre les héritiers commencent à se troubler" (Bargellini to Khayraddin, July 11, 1873, SH.C249.D670.300, ANT).

42. "Les héritiers on [*sic*] toujours des discussions entr'eux pour la moindre des choses, ils sont des gens sans aucune respectabilité, et de mauvaise foi, et qui se font entr'eux des dépits comme les petits enfants" (Bargellini to Khayraddin, January 23, 1874, SH.C249.D670.6, ANT).

43. *Codice Civile*, vii.

44. "De plus le Gouvernement de Tunis allegue [*sic*] en général l'Intérêt que chaque gouvernement a / intérêt pas matériel, politique / de faire déclarer la *sudditanza* d'un cytoien [*sic*] qui etant [*sic*] allé à l'étranger ne devint pas cytoyen [*sic*] de l'Etat dans lequel il se rende [*sic*]" (Bargellini to Khayraddin, February 21, 1873, SH.C249.D670.236, ANT).

45. "Da alcuni pretendenti vuolsi porre seriamente in dubbio la qualità di Italiano nel Defunto Conte Generale Semama . . . e ciò sull'asserto fondamento di non avere il Generale adempiute le formalità volute dalla Legge per conservare la qualità concessagli dopo le pratiche come sopra fatte dal defunto Generale, non solo non è permesso di dubitare della sua intenzione di voler godere di una grazia da esso tanto favorosamente implorata. . . . Se vera fasse la omissione della formalità, non a lui, ma alla Legazione Italiana di Parigi prima, ed al Sindaco di Livorno poi, ai quali fu esibito dal Generale personalmente il Decreto Reale, dovrebbe imputare la omissione medesima" (Moses Shamama to Vittorio Emanuele II, May 2, 1873, real casa, casa civile del re, Gabinetto particolare di Vittorio Emanuele II, b. 124, ACS).

46. "Non si è trascurato di far eseguire delle ricerche per mezzo della R. Legazione a Parigi e del Prefesso di Livorno affine di sapere se mai altrove il fu Nissim Scemama avesse adempito alle prescrizione del Codice Civile, ma è risultato che egli si limitò ad eleggere domicilio in Livorno con atto ricevuta dall'uffizioale dello stato civile il 9 Novembre 1871, cioè cinque anni dopo il termine di sei mesi stabilito a pena di nullità per l'adempimento delle prescrizioni suaccennate" (Ministero del'interno to Capo del Gabinetto particolare di S. M., June 28, 1873, real casa, casa civile del re, Gabinetto particolare di Vittorio Emanuele II, b. 124, ACS).

47. Jews from Algeria were made citizens by virtue of the Crémieux Decree of 1870; although it was not always clear whether Algerian Jews outside Algeria could benefit from the decree's collective naturalization, there is extensive evidence that many successfully claimed French citizenship (see the discussion in chapter 2). I did not find a direct discussion of Moses's nationality; and his son Nissim Jr. naturalized in France after settling there (see chapter 10). It nonetheless seems highly likely that Moses would have claimed French citizenship by virtue of his Algerian origins.

48. Gabinetto Particolare to Prefetto di Livorno, March 1874, real casa, casa civile del re, Gabinetto particolare di Vittorio Emanuele II, b. 124, ACS. It seems that Moshe asked for the title around the same time that he requested a declaration concerning Nissim's citizenship. See Prefetto di Livorno to Gabinetto particolare di S. M. Vittorio Emanuele II, June 23, 1873, real casa, casa civile del re, Gabinetto particolare di Vittorio Emanuele II, b. 124, ACS.

49. The secretary wrote to the municipal authorities of Livorno, and they responded that such an honor "would not contribute to the prestige of the Ordine della Corona d'Italia" ("verosimilmente questa onorificenza non contribuirebbe a dar pregio all'ordine della Corona d'Italia") (Prefetto di Livorno to Gabinetto particolare di S. M. Vittorio Emanuele II, June 23, 1873, real casa, casa civile del re, Gabinetto particolare di Vittorio Emanuele II, b. 124, ACS).

50. "Una paralisi al lato sinistro della faccia . . . pensando che la causa civile di successione in che egli travasi, non tocca punto la di lui onorabilità, sulla quale io garantisco" (Castelnuovo to N. Aghemo, capo del gabinetto particolare di S. M., December 31, 1873, real casa, casa civile del re, Gabinetto particolare di Vittorio Emanuele II, b. 124, ACS).

51. Lehmann, *Emissaries.*

52. I am resorting to some conjecture here, as the source—a later polemic by Léon Elmilik—is highly biased and not entirely trustworthy. Elmelich, *Megilah 'Amukot.* Yuval Haruvi

has found evidence that Yasha (an acronym) Bracha and Shalom Moshe Hai Gagin were the emissaries sent from Jerusalem, and that they met with 'Aziza and Moses in Livorno after Nissim's death. He, too, hypothesizes that the two emissaries were the link between the aspiring Shamama heirs in Livorno and Ashkenazi in Jerusalem. Haruvi, "Ha-elitah ha-toranit," 109. For another inheritance dispute—this one over the estate of a wealthy Jew from Aden—in which the heirs engaged rabbis from Palestine, see Brown and Radzyner, "Tzeva'ah goralit."

53. See Singer and Rosenthal, "Ashkenazi, Abraham"; "Ashkenazi, Abraham ben Jacob"; Levy, "Haham Başı (Chief Rabbi)."

54. In other words, the testator is the owner of the usufruct (*pri*), but the heirs own the property itself (*guf*). On this, see Elon, *Jewish Law*, 4:1681–82. See also *Shulḥan 'Arukh*, Ḥoshen Mishpat, 250.

55. *"Wa-ana mu'āmir bi-siḥḥat khidnī"* (Jarmon, *Naḥalat Avot*, 1a). This is translated as *ve-ani bari' ve-ḥazak* in the Hebrew.

56. On this, see also Haruvi, "Ha-elitah ha-toranit," 104–9.

57. Even though Nissim's will also lacked this formula, Ashkenazi argued that Nissim's description of what should happen "after my death" was functionally equivalent to the phrase "from this day and after my death" (Ashkenazi, *Kuntres yismaḥ Moshe*, 3b).

58. *"Zakhar asher kevar 'asah ve-ratzah litanam be-matanat shekhiv me-ra'"* (Ashkenazi, *Kuntres yismaḥ Moshe*, 12a).

59. *"Yadu'a u-mefursam haskamat kol ha-poskim z[ikhronam]'l[i-vracha] be-khol safek ha-nofel be-dinei mamonot be-khol . . . matanot tzevaot . . . asher minhag ha-medinah hu ha-soḥrim hu ha-'ikar lalekhet aḥarav"* (Ashkenazi, *Kuntres yismaḥ Moshe*, 8a).

60. He cited the maxim *minhag mevatel halakhah*. Ashkenazi, *Kuntres yismaḥ Moshe*, 9b. Ashkenazi further noted that Jewish law valued honoring the intentions of a testator; the will should thus be upheld even though certain formulas might be missing. Ashkenazi, *Kuntres yismaḥ Moshe*, 7b.

61. Ashkenazi, *Kuntres yismaḥ Moshe*, 14a.

62. On the use of haskamot across the Mediterranean, see Marglin, "Mediterranean Modernity."

63. The rabbis in Russia were Moshe Kahane from Choslowitz, Mordekhai b. Aryeh Lev of Mogilev (now in Belarus), and Ya'akov b. Moshe from Volochys'k (now in Ukraine). See the catalog information of the National Library of Israel, https://www.nli.org.il/en/books/NNL_ALEPH001839171/NLI.

64. Bargellini to Khaznadar, February 14, 1873, SH.C249.D670.234, ANT. This assertion was confirmed by Ibn Diyaf, *Itḥāf*, 5:190.

65. For the definitive biography of Husayn, see Oualdi, *A Slave between Empires*.

66. Husayn handed the report to Khaznadar on March 13. Accounting, March 13, 1873, SH.C102.D239.14, ANT; wazīr al-mubāshir [Khaznadar] to Husayn, 15 Rabī' II 1290, SH.C102.D239.3, ANT.

67. Spezzafumo arrived on February 8, 1873. Bargellini to Khaznadar, February 7, 1873, SH.C249.D670.230, ANT. On his role as representative of the government's claims on the estate, see Bargellini to Khayraddin, March 14, 1873, SH.C249.D670.244, ANT.

68. Bargellini to Khaznadar, March 21, 1873, SH.C249.D670.250, ANT.

69. See, for example, Bargellini to Khaznadar, May 23, 1873, SH.C249.D670.288, ANT; Bargellini to Khaznadar, May 30, 1873, SH.C249.D670.289, ANT; Bargellini to Khaznadar, June 7, 1873, SH.C249.D670.290, ANT.

70. Bargellini to Mustafa (Khaznadar) and Nushir Basha Bey, May 30, 1873, SH.C249.D670.289, ANT; Husayn, *Rasā'il*, 1:194. The procuration was dated June 7. Sadiq Bey to Husayn, 10 Rabīʿ II 1290, SH.C108.D275.20, ANT. For an Italian translation, see 15 Rabīʿ II 1290, SH.C104.D254, ANT.

71. Particularly Galeotti. See Bargellini to Khaznadar, May 23, 1873, SH.C249.D670.288, ANT. On the Djedeida affair, see Ganiage, *Les origines*, 333–42.

72. "Il serait très important de savoir avec précision si dans sa qualité de Tunisien se trouvant à l'Etranger le Caid Nissim pouvait faire un testament olographe, et si ce testament serait considéré comme valide par les lois Tunisiennes et Mosaïques" (Bargellini to Khayraddin, March 14, 1873, SH.C249.D670.241, ANT). See also the letter in which Bargellini asks Khayraddin to ask Momo to "gather all possible documents relative to the validity of a holographic will made by the Qā'id Nissim Shamama, once it is demonstrated that he died a Tunisian" ("recueille tous les documents possibles relativement à la validité qui peut avoir un testament olographe fait par le Caid Nissim Samama quand il sera demontré qu'il est mort Tunisien") (Bargellini to Khayraddin, March 7, 1873, SH.C249.D670.241, ANT).

73. Husayn was present as the rabbis tried to decide whether a *kiddushin* between Momo and Esther had taken place, and then was sharing a carriage with Momo when a messenger told them that the rabbis finally decided that Esther was not in fact married to Momo. Document prepared in the French consulate, March 3, 1873, SH.C100.D228.10, ANT.

74. On Elmilik, see Marglin, "Jews, Rights, and Belonging in Tunisia." Elmilik acquired the grade of apprentice in a Masonic lodge in Tunis (the Loge les enfants choisis de Carthage et Utique) in August 1854. Constitution, April 8, 1861, FM2.865, BNF; requêtes des diplômes qui constatent leur qualité de maçons réguliers au grade de Maître, May 26, 1861, FM2.865, BNF.

75. For instance, he made a plea in a courtroom in Tunis asking for equal treatment for one of his coreligionists who was imprisoned. SH.C131.D454.7699, ANT. I am grateful to Fatma Ben Slimane for this reference.

76. See Marglin, "The Two Lives of Masʿud Amoyal"; Marglin, "Crémieux Decree."

77. "Il est notoire que leurs origines leur donne [*sic*] droit à la protection française" (Elmilik to AIU president, September 17, 1874, Tunsisie I B 011 b, #103–4, AIU). See also *L'univers israélite* 21, no. 3 (November 1865): 141–45.

78. Elmilik later claimed that he had initially signed a contract with Momo in February 1873 in which Momo pledged to give him 2 percent of his share of the inheritance in return for his services as an intermediary. Elmilik, *Arbitrage Léon Elmilik contre le gouvernement tunisien*, 27, 35; Gueydan and Santillana, *Arbitrage*, 33. Elmilik came to Livorno with Momo in early April. Bargellini to Khaznadar, April 11, 1873, SH.C249.D670.267, ANT. Elmilik's relationship with Momo seems to have petered out relatively swiftly, however; starting in June, Elmilik was already working for Husayn. Wazīr al-mubāshir (Khaznadar) to Husayn, 15 Rabīʿ II 1290, SH.C102.D239.3, ANT. In August, Momo wrote a bitter letter to Khaznadar complaining that Elmilik was poisoning his relationship with Khaznadar and the other potential heirs. Telegram from Momo in Livorno to Khaznadar in La Goulette, August 2, 1873, SH.C104.D246.13, ANT.

79. *"Fa-innahu yabdhilu jahadahu fī iʿānatihā, limā lahu min al-maʿarafati bil-lughāt"* (wazīr al-mubāshir [Khaznadar] to Husayn, 15 Rabīʿ II 1290, SH.C102.D239.3, ANT). See also Husayn, *Rasāʾil*, 1:195.

80. Elmilik to Husayn, 15 Jumādā II 1290, SH.C108.D275.11, ANT.

81. See, for example, Elmilik to Husayn, 14 Ramaḍān 1290, SH.C108.D275.18, ANT; Elmilik to Husayn, 27 Ṣafar 1291, SH.C108.D275.14, ANT; accounts prepared by Leon Elmilik, SH.C108.D276.19, ANT; Husayn, *Rasāʾil*, 1:197,

82. Pinna to Venosta, October 22, 1873, Ministero Affari Esteri Regno d'Italia (Moscati VI), 1440, ASMAE. See also Oualdi, "Le retrait après la disgrâce." On Khayraddin's efforts at reform during his tenure as prime minister, see Sraieb, "Elite et société," §91–107.

83. *"Al-latī hiyya ilā ḥusni idāratikum aḥwaja"* (Husayn, *Rasāʾil*, 1:216).

84. Elmilik, *Affaire Heussein et Elmilik*, 24.

85. Elmilik was the representative of Hai and Mordekhai Bellais (or Bellaich), the children of the late Masʿuda (née Shamama—not to be confused with Masʿuda, Nissim's widow) and Joseph Bellais; Masʿuda was Nissim's niece as well as the sister of Momo and Joseph, and Nissim's will allocated twenty-five thousand francs to her. In the fall of 1876, Husayn convinced the Bellais heirs—through Elmilik, no doubt—to sign a contract with the Tunisian government agreeing to fight for the annulment of the will and cede their portion of the estate in exchange for a lump sum payment from the Tunisian government. Samama v. Heussein v. Samama, June 8, 1880, Sentenze no. 77, AS Lucca; contracts dated 25 Rabīʿ I 1294 and 4 Dhū al-Ḥijja 1294, SH.C104.D253, ANT. For Nissim's original gift to Masʿuda's children, see Jarmon, *Naḥalat Avot*, 2b.

86. Salvatore Semama (b. June 18, 1873), Ministero dell'interno, direzione generale pubblica sicurezza, divisione affari generali e riservati, Casellario Politico Centrale, Busta 4556, ACS; Salvatore Semama (b. June 18, 1873), Ministero dell'interno, direzione generale pubblica sicurezza, divisione affari generali e riservati, ufficio internati, A4 bis, internati stranieri e spionaggio, 1940–45, Busta 326, ACS.

87. She died on December 15, 1876. Legal document, February 18, 1884, SH.C104.D245, ANT.

88. See, for example, Samama v. Heussein v. Samama, June 8, 1880, Sentenze no. 77, AS Lucca.

89. Cappelleti and Perillo, *Civil Procedure in Italy*, 69–73.

90. The ruling was issued on December 28; the president of the court was Agosto Bandini. I have not found a copy of the ruling itself, as the archives for the Tribunale di Livorno are incomplete. Nonetheless, the ruling is discussed extensively in various works. See, for example, Cesarini, "Samama v. Samama," 226. On Bandini, see *Gazzetta ufficiale del regno d'Italia*, 1013.

91. "Che non può invocarsi, a riguardo della sua successione, l'art. 8 delle disposizioni preliminari al Codice civile, per la semplicissima ragione, che egli, sebbene straniero all'Italia, non apparteneva ad alcuna nazione, e non aveva nè poteva avere quella legge nazionale di cui è parola nell'articolo suddetto" (Galeotti, *Reale Corte d'Appello di Lucca*, 7).

92. Pierantoni, *Corte di Appello di Lucca*, 183.

93. Cesarini, "Samama v. Samama," 243. The provision for stateless individuals in the Italian Civil Code represented a recent trend in European jurisprudence; before the mid-nineteenth century, statelessness was quite simply not addressed. Siegelberg, *Statelessness*, 27.

94. Siegelberg, *Statelessness*, chap. 1. On statelessness as a legal anomaly, see Siegelberg, *Statelessness*, esp. 39. Siegelberg argues that statelessness went largely untheorized until after

World War I, when the millions of people rendered stateless by the breakup of the Ottoman, Austro-Hungarian, and Russian Empires forced the issue.

95. Cogordan, *La nationalité*, 10. See also Siegelberg, *Statelessness*, 35.

96. Here I rely on the legal arguments made by the Corte d'Appello di Lucca, which confirmed the lower court's sentence. Cesarini, "Samama v. Samama," 237–38.

97. Cesarini, "Samama v. Samama," 239.

98. See esp. Slezkine, *The Jewish Century*.

Chapter 6. Conte Shamama the Italian

1. "*Wa-yakūn Nisīm laysa huwwa bi-Iṭāliyānī, wa-lākin kharaja min al-jinsīyati al-tūnisīyati. Wa-ḥaythu baqiya bi-lā jinsīyatin, fal-ḥukhu al-ṭaliyānīyu yajrī ʿalayhi . . . bi-ḥawli Allāh ana [sic] narbaḥu fī majlisi abāl [appel]*" (Husayn *Rasāʾil*,2:151, letter dated 1 Muḥarram 1295 / January 5, 1878). Just months after Nissim died, Bargellini wrote to Khaznadar explaining that eventually the case would end up in the Court of Cassation in Florence. Bargellini to Mustafa (Khaznadar) and Nushir Basha Bey, April 18, 1873, SH.C249.D670.272, ANT.

2. On Galeotti, see Funaro, "La barca cammina."

3. See http://www.treccani.it/enciclopedia/augusto-francescopaolo-pierantoni_%28Dizionario-Biografico%29/.

4. Malaspina, "Toil of the Noble World," 5. See also Vidari, "Un secolo e mezzo fa," 273–74.

5. In January 1851, Mancini gave his inaugural lecture, titled "On Nationality as the Foundation of the Law of Nations." It was published later that year as *Della nazionalità come fondamento del diritto delle genti; Prelezione al corso di diritto internazionale e marittimo pronunziata nella R. Università di Torino*. See also Vidari, "Un secolo e mezzo fa." On Mancini's biography, see Rosi, "Pasquale Stansilao Mancini"; Halpérin, *Entre nationalisme juridique*, 67–85; http://www.treccani.it/enciclopedia/pasquale-stanislao-mancini_(Dizionario-Biografico)/.

6. Martti Koskenniemi has argued that international law did not emerge until the 1870s, in large part with the founding of the Institute of International Law. Koskenniemi, "International Law and *Raison d'État*," 298; Koskenniemi, *The Gentle Civilizer of Nations*, chap. 1. Jean-Louis Halpérin similarly contends that "a true doctrine of 'private international law,' dealing with both the status of foreigners and conflicts of law affecting individuals," dates to the 1830s or 1840s. Halpérin, *Entre nationalisme juridique*, 35.

7. In this, he was part of a broader movement that Halpérin has dubbed "legal nationalism." Halpérin, *Entre nationalisme juridique*. See also Casey, *Nationals Abroad*, 58–61.

8. Mancini, *Della nazionalità*, 9, 11–12. For a precursor to this in the French Revolution, see Castellanos-Jankiewicz, "Nationality," 8.

9. Floriana Colao argues that Mancini's view of the nation was somewhere between the racial, essentialist version that was dominant in Germany and the purely elective one characteristic of France. Colao, "L'idea di nazione," 270–71.

10. Mancini, *Della nazionalità*, 63.

11. Malaspina, "Toil of the Noble World," 16. See also Nuzzo, *Origini di una scienza*, 93–94.

12. Piccoli, "La famiglia di P. S. Mancini," 125; http://www.treccani.it/enciclopedia/grazia-mancini_(Dizionario-Biografico)/.

13. "La nazionalità, o signori, non è un'astratta creazione della mente dell'uomo, ma una verità oggettiva ed una base necessaria dell'ordine certo del mondo" (Pierantoni, *Il progresso del diritto pubblico*, 8).

14. "La traduzione del principio di nazionalità nella fratellevole comunione degli Stati va fermando il nuovo giure internazionale sul diritto certo e naturale dei popoli e non su quello astioso ed innaturale dei principi" (Pierantoni, *Il progresso del diritto pubblico*, 136).

15. "Figlio del mio affetto e della mia scientifica adozione" (Mancini to Pierantoni, July 6, 1871, b. 732 63.2, ISR).

16. See, for example, Mancini to Pierantoni, July 3, 1880, b. 775, no. 1.4, ISR; Mancini to Pierantoni, June 4, 1880, b. 775, no. 2.6, ISR; Mancini to Pierantoni, August 1879, b. 880, 24.6, ISR; Mancini to Pierantoni, n.d., b. 880, 8.24, ISR. For a particularly evocative account of Mancini's travel schedule, see Mancini to Pierantoni, July 6, 1871, b. 732 63.2, ISR.

17. See esp. Koskenniemi, *The Gentle Civilizer of Nations*, chap. 1.

18. He assumed the chair on December 13, 1878. See http://www.treccani.it/enciclopedia/augusto-francescopaolo-pierantoni_%28Dizionario-Biografico%29/.

19. "Della dottrina del Giure Internazionale" (Pierantoni to Primo Presidente [Cesarini] of the Court of Appeal in Lucca, January 9, 1883, SH.C105.D259.7, ANT). Husayn also promised to allow Pierantoni "complete liberty to request doctrinal opinions . . . on rabbinic jurisprudence from the greatest Orientalists and the most illustrious jurists of every part of Europe" ("gli die amplissima libertà di richiedere di pareri dottrinali e di indicazioni di giurisprudenza rabinica i maggiori orientalisti ed i più illustri guiristi [*sic*] di ogni parte di Europa").

20. Pierantoni to Primo Presidente (Cesarini) of the Court of Appeal in Lucca, January 9, 1883, SH.C105.D259.7, ANT). Husayn paid him a deposit of 1,000 lire that month, another 3,000 in May, and another 10,000 in July. Account book, b. 985, no. 10, ISR. Between 1879 and 1888, Pierantoni's highest annual income was 73,385 lire (in 1887); his average salary over this period was 44,824 lire per year—including 69,800 lire paid to him for his work on the Shamama case. Account book, b. 985, no. 10, ISR. In the end, Pierantoni settled for less than half of the 150,000 lire he claimed were promised to him, after Italian courts ruled that the Tunisian government had to pay him 50,000 lire plus expenses. Sentence in Pierantoni v. Guttieres, July 20, 1886, SH.C105.D259.21, ANT).

21. Though in and out of public service for much of his adult life, Mancini was between government positions when he agreed to work for 'Aziza and Moses in 1879; he had just stepped down from serving as minister of justice, and did not take up another government post until he became foreign minister in 1881. Jayme, *Pasquale Stanislao Mancini*, 41.

22. "Per non soffrire l'affanno morale di lottare contro persona, a un'è legato da affetto e reverenza" (Pierantoni to Primo Presidente [Cesarini] of the Court of Appeal in Lucca, January 9, 1883, SH.C105.D259.7, ANT).

23. Pierantoni, *Corte di Appello di Lucca*, 42–49, 211; Mancini, *Corte di Appello di Lucca*, 57, 108–9, 355–56.

24. On the history of private international law, see esp. Halpérin, *Entre nationalisme juridique*; Ancel, *Histoire du droit international privé*; Banu, *Nineteenth-Century Perspectives on Private International Law*.

25. Jean-Jacques Gaspard Foelix was one of the first jurists to argue for a kind of protonationality principle in private international law. Foelix, *Traité de droit international privé* (1st ed.). On

Foelix, see Halpérin, *Entre nationalisme juridique*, 38–41. Mancini might also have been influenced by Antoine Mailher de Chassat, who published one of the earliest French books on international private law. Mailher de Chassat contended that foreigners should be ruled by their national laws when it came to private matters—particularly marriage, divorce, and inheritance. Ultimately the importance of an individual's national law would vie with the sanctity of sovereignty over a particular territory. But for Mailher de Chassat, this compromise of a state's sovereignty was necessary in order to respect the rights of foreigners. He concluded that "reciprocity"—what jurists typically called "comitas," whereby states mutually agreed to allow foreigners to be ruled by their national laws in matters of private law—was the only way to balance these desires. Mailher de Chassat, *Traité des statuts*, 186. On Mailher de Chassat's influence on Mancini, see also Halpérin, *Entre nationalisme juridique*, 69. Note that historians of international private law often argue that the nationality principle was introduced in the Napoleonic Code. Yet as Halpérin points out, that code regulated only the application of French law to French people abroad. Its silence regarding the status of foreigners in France and lawmakers' preoccupation with preventing French nationals from escaping French law by leaving the country (rather than with the essential importance of national law) are evidence that the regulations concerning private international law in the Napoleonic Code "left jurists considerable latitude to accentuate, or not, the [code's] tendency towards legal nationalism" (Halpérin, *Entre nationalisme juridique*, 27).

26. See, for example, Mancini, *Della nazionalità*, 52. On the new use of the term "nationality principle," see Esperson, *Il principio di nazionalità*. I use male pronouns in this chapter deliberately; international private law was distinct for women, as it presumed that on marriage, a woman would automatically take her husband's nationality. See, for example, Cott, "Marriage and Women's Citizenship"; Green, *The Limits of Transnationalism*, esp. 71–75.

27. Mancini, "De l'utilité," 231. See also Esperson, *Il principio di nazionalità*, 29.

28. Halpérin, *Nationalisme juridique*, 14. Mancini's approach differed from that of the other giant of private international law, Friedrich Carl von Savigny, who refused "d'imposer aux États l'admission de la loi étrangère au nom d'un strict devoir de justice" (Halpérin, *Entre nationalisme juridique*, 61).

29. In the 1860s, Mancini tried to achieve this through diplomacy, but largely failed. Eyffinger, *T. M. C. Asser*, 1:553–54. He took up the cause again at the Institut du Droit International. See esp. Mancini, "De l'utilité." On Mancini's nationality principle, see Nadelmann, "Mancini's Nationality Rule"; Jayme, *Pasquale Stanislao Mancini*, 17–26; Mills, "The Private History of International Law," 39–41; Ancel, *Histoire du droit international privé*, 439–56.

30. Nadelmann, "Mancini's Nationality Rule," 52. On the influence of the nationality principle in private international law, see also Castellanos-Jankiewicz, "Nationality."

31. See "Disposizioni sulla pubblicazione, interpretazione ed applicazione delle leggi in generale," esp. Articles 4 and 8, in *Codice Civile*, vi–vii.

32. "L'uomo ha molto vissuto, ha molto amato ed ha sempre apprezzato la buona cucina ed i sereni piaceri della vita" (*Budapester Taglatt*, June 28, 1885, quoted in Jayme, *Pasquale Stanislao Mancini*, 42).

33. On Mancini's failure to write a thesis, see Pierantoni Mancini, *Alcune lettere di P. S. Mancini*, 314; Jayme, *Pasquale Stanislao Mancini*, 55; Vidari, "Un secolo e mezzo fa," 283. On Mancini's delays, see Eyffinger, *T. M. C. Asser*, 1:551–53.

34. On Mancini's involvement in the Shamama case, see Nadelmann, "Mancini's Nationality Rule," 63–67; Halpérin, *Entre nationalisme juridique*, 82–85. Mancini's most important contribution to the Shamama case was written in the form of a legal memo, dated January 1879, but not printed until 1880. Mancini, *Corte di Appello di Lucca.*

35. Mancini himself does not use "blood," but it is a central concept for Ernest Renan (discussed further below). See, for example, Renan, "What Is a Nation?," 255–58.

36. "Due forme perpetue dell'associazione umana, la famiglia e la nazione" (Mancini, *Della nazionalità*, 30). "Particolare intimità di rapporti . . . impossibile ad esistere tra individui di nazioni diverse" (Mancini, *Della nazionalità*, 32).

37. Halpérin, *Entre nationalisme juridique*, 68. Mancini's position contrasted with that of Savigny, who favored domicile over nationality as the organizing principle of private international law—in large part because people could more easily choose their domicile. Halpérin, *Entre nationalisme juridique*, 62–63.

38. This was particularly true in the extraterritorial context of the Islamic Mediterranean. See, for example, Marglin, "The Two Lives of Mas'ud Amoyal"; Noureddine Amara, "1830, l'improbable frontière," 92, 98–99.

39. One was a document signed by five rabbis and Jewish notaries (*sofrim*) from Sousse attesting that Nissim was a member of the Grana community; the other was an act of notoriety attesting that Nissim's father was an "oriundo Toscano." Mancini, *Corte di Appello di Lucca*, 252–53.

40. *Codice Civile*, 3.

41. Mancini, *Corte di Appello di Lucca*, 260.

42. "Oriundo" is a Latin term from Roman law, "regularly used in the sense of an indissoluble legal bond with the city" ("régulièrement employé dans le sens d'un lien juridique indissoluble avec la cité") (Thomas, "Le droit d'origine," 279).

43. The full text of Article 6 is as follows: "Il figlio nato in paese estero da padre che ha perduto la cittadinanza prima del suo Nascimento, è reputato straniero. Egli può tuttavia eleggere la qualità di Cittadino, purchè ne facia la dichiarazione a norma dell'articolo precedente e fissi nel regno il suo domicilio entro l'anno dalla fatta dichiarazione" (*Codice Civile*, 2). Mancini also pointed to Article 13, which concerned an Italian who had lost his citizenship and wished to recover it. This article specified that such a person must return to Italy with special permission of the government, renounce foreign citizenship, and declare before state officials the fixing of his domicile within a year. *Codice Civile*, 4–5.

44. Mancini, *Corte di Appello di Lucca*, 261.

45. "Per sottrarsi all'obbligo ed alle difficoltà di apprestare copiosi documenti e prove dell'originaria cittadinanza. . . . Il Decreto di naturalità fu chiesto a cautela, a sovrabbondanza, a rimzione di ogni dubbio ed incertezza" (Mancini, *Corte di Appello di Lucca*, 261–62).

46. See, for example, Kirshner, "Between Nature and Culture." The jurist Bartolo da Sassoferrato (d. 1357), however, emphasized that citizenship was created by the city-state, and thus that the category included both natural-born and naturalized citizens—even if each of these categories implied a different status. Nonetheless, Peter Riesenberg argues that many medieval jurists increasingly stressed the possibility of choosing one's city and therefore one's citizenship—especially in contrast to the ancient world. Riesenberg, *Citizenship*, 131–34. Peter Sahlins identifies a "tension" in the petitions for naturalization in prerevolutionary France

"between a voluntary affiliation to the king and kingdom, and a 'natural' condition" (Sahlins, *Unnaturally French*, 130). On the immutability of origin and thus original citizenship (*origo*) in the ancient world, see Thomas, "Le droit d'origine." I am grateful to Tamar Herzog for sharing her work on this subject with me.

47. Rapport, *Nationality and Citizenship*, chap. 2; Verwilghen, *Conflits de nationalités*, 59. On French nationality law in general, see Weil, *Qu'est-ce qu'un français?*; Légier, *Histoire du droit de la nationalité française*.

48. For the classic study comparing France and Germany, though widely critiqued (often with good reason), see Brubaker, *Citizenship and Nationhood*.

49. Renan, "What Is a Nation?," 247, 255. On Mancini as a precursor to Renan, see Vidari, "Un secolo e mezzo fa."

50. Renan, "What Is a Nation?," 255, 257. Renan further argued that neither language nor religion were sufficient bases on which to establish modern nationality.

51. Renan, "What Is a Nation?," 261–62.

52. Wilder, "Colonial Ethnology," 261.

53. Renan, "What Is a Nation?," 261. "Nos ancêtres les Gaulois" was a phrase taught to French schoolchildren in the nineteenth and twentieth centuries—and often also to children attending French schools who were not at all French, including in colonial and postcolonial settings.

54. See, for example, Almog, "The Racial Motif"; Le Cour Grandmaison, *Ennemis mortels*, 48–59. In his placing of race at the center of even a voluntarist view of the nation, Renan was fairly typical of his time. For an excellent account of the entanglement of race and nation in European thought in the eighteenth and nineteenth centuries, see Weitz, *A Century of Genocide*, chap. 1.

55. Mancini, *Della nazionalità*, 38–39. On the role of race in Mancini's understanding of nationality and his affinity with Renan, see Colao, "L'idea di nazione," 270–71, 276.

56. Mancini, *Della nazionalità*, 39; Renan, "What Is a Nation?," 261.

57. "Che di certo informar debbono lo spirito nazionale" (Mancini, *Della nazionalità*, 36).

58. "Ma di tutt' i vincoli di nazionale unità nessuno è più forte della comunanza del linguaggio. . . . Nelle lingue si riflette pure la filiazione delle razze" (Mancini, *Della nazionalità*, 37). On language and nationalism, see, for example, Anderson, *Imagined Communities*, chap. 5.

59. Discussion in Camera dei Deputati, February 17, 1865, quoted in Donati, *A Political History*, 27. On jus sanguinis, see Perl-Rosenthal and Erman, "Inventing the Rules of Blood and of Soil."

60. Donati, *A Political History*, 70–71. For instance, whereas foreigners who naturalized only enjoyed "small naturalization," which limited their political rights—barring the rare cases in which an act of parliament granted "great naturalization"—italiani non regnicoli automatically enjoyed full naturalization with full political rights. Donati, *A Political History*, 76. Donati translates italiani non regnicoli as "immigrants of Italian nationality," which presumes that the *regnicoli* (subjects or citizens, equivalent to the French *régnicole*) in question immigrated to Italy; while this is what the provisions of the Italian Civil Code had in mind, clearly the term itself is broader.

61. Donati, *A Political History*, 79. In 1899, Pierantoni himself made the case that those from Trieste and Trento should be considered italiani non regnicoli (Donati, *A Political History*, 73). Donati argues that the discourse around the citizenship of oriundi italiani was particularly forceful in the 1860s during the drafting of the Civil Code and became more moderate after the annexation of Rome (Donati, *A Political History*, 77).

62. See his remarks in Camera dei Deputati, March 25, 1863, quoted in Donati, *A Political History*, 80.

63. Mancini, *Corte di Appello di Lucca*, 250.

64. Serie Minute 33, n.p. 99, November 16, 1873, ASCEL. In fact, there is a *ketubah* (marriage contract) preserved in the archives of the Jewish Community of Livorno, between Salvadore Yeoshua de Biniamin Semama and Meriam de Josef Arez, who married in Livorno on April 1, 1825. Nedjar et al., *Registres de ketubbot*, 354. There is, however, no indication that Salvadore was a direct ancestor of Nissim's; it is possible that Moses did not mention this record because Salvadore was unrelated to Nissim, or it is possible that he simply did not find the relevant documentation.

65. See Attal and Aviv, *Pinkas ha-ketubot*; Avrahami, *Pinkas ha-Kehilah*.

66. Good faith (*buona fede* in Italian, and *bono fides* in Latin) is a legal principle taken from Roman law that is particularly important in contracts, but has implications in a number of areas—including, of course, nationality law. It is "an abstract and comprehensive term that encompasses a sincere belief or motive without any malice or the desire to defraud others" ("Good Faith," 122). On good faith, see esp. Garofalo and Burdese, *Il ruolo della buona fede*. For an example of the use of good faith in nationality law, see, Act of May 9, 1918, Sec. 2 (40-Stat. 546–47), which legislated that aliens in the United States who had lived in the country for five years, "and who during or prior to that time, because of misinformation regarding his citizenship status erroneously exercised the rights and performed the duties of a citizen by the United States in good faith" may nonetheless naturalize, despite having failed to make the required declaration of intention. For an example of the importance of intention in determining the jurisdiction of an inheritance dispute, see Green, *The Limits of Transnationalism*, 72.

67. "Ma ben anche la di lui piena sicurezza e coscienza di essere ormai indubitatamente divenuto e di morire *Cittadino italiano*" (Mancini, *Corte di Appello di Lucca*, 255).

68. Mancini, *Corte di Appello di Lucca*, 256–57.

69. "Buona fede" (Mancini, *Corte di Appello di Lucca*, 264).

70. "Sia che ignorando una Legge per lui straniera" (Mancini, *Corte di Appello di Lucca*, 258).

71. Mancini, *Corte di Appello di Lucca*, 264.

72. Mancini, *Corte di Appello di Lucca*, 258.

73. See, for example, Ministero per gli affari esteri, *Annuario diplomatico*, 270–81. For a parallel among Jewish immigrants from eastern Europe, for whom charitable giving was also constitutive of their communal identity, see Kobrin, *Jewish Bialystok*, chap. 3.

74. "Composta unicamente ed esclusivamente di *cittadini italiani*, esercitando largamente in essa la sua generosità a favore dei proprj connazionali" (Mancini, *Corte di Appello di Lucca*, 255).

75. "Il fatto gravissimo . . . la qualità di originario di Livorno e *naturalizzato italiano* . . . ammesso alla *naturalità del Regno italiano*" (Mancini, *Corte di Appello di Lucca*, 255).

76. On the history of the passport, see esp. Torpey, *The Invention of the Passport*. On their nearly accidental functioning as identity documents, see, for example, Hanley, *Identifying with Nationality*, 76–80.

77. "Effetti giuridici abbia prodotto la perfettissima *buona fede*, la certezza della coscienza del Nissim Samama di esser divenuto cittadino italiano" (Mancini, *Corte di Appello di Lucca*, 264).

78. "Or non v'ha più sicuro principio di diritto, che quello della equivalenza di una qualità putativa alla reale, e del possesso di buona fede alla realtà del diritto" (Mancini, *Corte di Appello di Lucca,* 265).

79. This maxim was associated with the case of Barbarius Phillipus, a Roman slave who escaped and was subsequently elevated to a praetor. Although Phillipus should have been ineligible to act as a praetor because of his enslaved status, jurists deemed his actions valid because everyone presumed he was freeborn. Mancini, *Corte di Appello di Lucca,* 265.

80. Pierantoni, *Corte di Appello di Lucca,* 173. See also Galeotti, *Reale Corte d'Appello di Lucca,* 127–28.

81. Galeotti, *Reale Corte d'Appello di Lucca,* 140. See also Heussein, *Lettre de Général Heussein au collège de la défense,* 31. For Shamama's use of these titles in his correspondence, see, for example, Shamama to Khaznadar, 2 Dhū al-Hijja 1277 / June 11, 1861, SH.C100.D219.1, ANT.

82. Pierantoni, *Corte di Appello di Lucca,* 177–80; Galeotti, *Reale Corte d'Appello di Lucca,* 128–32. Unlike French Jews—who were bound by the French prohibition on divorce after 1816—Nissim had only to deliver a get, a Jewish writ of divorce. On his divorce, see "Samama *utrinque* et gouvernement de Tunis," 556.

83. On the importance of social embeddedness to early modern citizenship, see esp. Herzog, *Defining Nations;* Cerutti, *Étrangers.* See also Prak, *Citizens without Nations.* On performance and reputation as evidence of race and the status of free or enslaved, see Gross, *What Blood Won't Tell;* Scott, "Paper Thin."

84. See esp. Ando, "Race and Citizenship."

85. See, for example, Fahrmeir, *Citizenship;* Weil, *Qu'est-ce qu'un français?;* Donati, *A Political History;* Légier, *Histoire du droit de la nationalité française.*

86. This is explored at greater length in chapter 8.

Chapter 7. Qā'id Nissim the Tunisian

1. "Facendo un processo ad un morto per togliere al cadavere la qualità, che ebbe in vita" (Pierantoni, *Corte di Appello di Lucca,* 211).

2. Husayn wrote in Arabic, and then printed translations in French and Italian. The first (and most important for my purposes) is Husayn, "Al-qusṭās." It was printed in French as Heussein, *Lettre de Général Heussein au collège de la défense,* and in Italian as Heussein, *Lettera del Generale Heussein.* The second is Heussein, *Le Caïd Nessim.* The third is Husséïn, *Lettera del Generale Husséïn.* The original Arabic versions of the second and third treatises have yet to be published, and I have not been able to locate them in the Tunisian archives.

3. See, for example, the discussion of the fatwā from Sousse in Heussein, *Lettre de Général Heussein au collège de la défense,* 23; Pierantoni, *Corte di Appello di Lucca,* 141.

4. Oualdi, *A Slave between Empires,* 27–28.

5. "*Anna aḥkāmu al-islāmi ghayru mubanīyatin 'alā aḥkāmi al-rūmān*" (Husayn, "Al-qusṭās," 237).

6. "*Fa-ra'āyā al-islāmi 'alā ikhtilāfi ajnāsihim wa-millihim munāqadūnu li-aḥkāmi sharī'ati al-islāmi*" (Husayn, "Al-qusṭās," 236).

7. "Se il fu Conte Caid Nissim Samama oltre ad essere suddito della Reggenza di Tunisi avesse anche la qualità di Cittadino di quella Reggenza, imperocchè se suddito è colui che vive soggetto alla sovranità d'un dato paese, Cittadino o Nazionale può chiamarsi soltanto colui, che

viene riconosciuto come membro di una data socièta o consorzio politico ed è ammesso al godimento almeno dei maggiori benefizi" (Pierantoni, *Corte di Appello di Lucca,* 7).

8. Galeotti explained that in Italy, the two terms were synonymous, while in France they were distinguished; one could lose one's French citizenship without losing one's "quality of Frenchness" (*qualité de français*). Galeotti, *Reale Corte d'Appello di Lucca,* 24.

9. "Potrebbe ben sostenersi che il fu Conte Caid Nissim Samama sebbene fosse suddito per nascita e per origine del Regno di Tunisi, non ha avuto mai la nazionalità Tunisina e non è stato mai il cittadino di quello Stato, poiché egli professava la religione Israelitica e come israelita non ha potuto essere ammesso al godimento della vita civile in una società, ch'è regolata dal Corano e non ha per ora accolti i grandi principî della piena libertà di coscienza e della assoluta egua-glianza di tutti i sudditi di fronte alla legge, qualunque sia la loro fede religiosa" (Pierantoni, *Corte di Appello di Lucca,* 8).

10. See, for example, *Code civil des français,* Articles 7–16.

11. See, for example, Foelix, *Traité de droit international privé* (2nd ed.); Foelix and Demangeat, *Traité de droit international privé.* See also the US Supreme Court's definition of citizenship as "membership of a nation, and nothing more" in *Minor v. Happersett,* 88 Waite, Morrison Remick 162 (US Supreme Court, 1875). "Nationality" as a way to describe state membership was a new term at the beginning of the nineteenth century. Noiriel, "Socio-histoire d'un concept"; Gosewinkel, "Citizenship, Subjecthood, Nationality." The emergence of the term qualité de français to some extent reflects the concept of "population" suggested by Michel Foucault, who noted that this term arose in the eighteenth century as a way to describe all individuals under the sovereignty of a state—though not necessarily those who joined together to form any sort of social contract. See Foucault, *Security, Territory, Population.*

12. Cogordan, *La nationalité,* 6. On Cogordan, see Hajjat, *Les frontières de l'"identité nationale,"* 76. In fact, it was not until relatively late that Algerians were deemed to possess French nationality (first in the courts, through the Enos case, and then in the Sénatus-Consulte of July 14, 1865). See Rabinovitch, "The Quality of Being French"; Marglin, "Citizenship and Nationality." For a precursor to Cogordan (though without as crystal clear of a distinction between nationality and citizenship), see Bluntschli, *The Theory of the State,* 180–83.

13. For this distinction, see Weis, *Nationality and Statelessness,* 3; Koessler, "'Subject,' 'Citizen,' 'National,' and 'Permanent Allegiance'"; Boll, *Multiple Nationality,* 58. For historians who make use of this distinction, see, for example, Hanley, *Identifying with Nationality,* 5–7; Manby, *Citizenship in Africa,* chap. 1.

14. "Il Cittadino è l'uomo membro della patria libere, retta da governi costituzionali, o repubblicani" (Pierantoni, *Corte di Appello di Lucca,* 11).

15. Pierantoni, *Corte di Appello di Lucca,* 8, 10–11. See also Galeotti, *Reale Corte d'Appello di Lucca,* 166.

16. See Lane, *An Arabic-English Lexicon,* 1:295–96; Redhouse, *A Turkish and English Lexicon,* 471.

17. Lane, *An Arabic-English Lexicon,* 1:1109; Redhouse, *A Turkish and English Lexicon,* 979

18. Lane, *An Arabic-English Lexicon,* 1:470; Wehr, *A Dictionary of Modern Arabic,* 167.

19. "*Annā lam nafham murādahu bil-farq fī ghayri Nisīm, fa-inna al-ra'āyā wal-ahālī wa-inna ikhtalafan lafẓan madlūluhumā wāḥidun*" (Husayn, "Al-qusṭās," 276–77). For the French, see Heussein, *Lettre de Général Heussein au collège de la défense,* 35. Ben Ismail argues that Husayn

was well aware of the distinct valences of *jins*, which denoted the legal meaning of nationality and was associated with full state sovereignty (and thus, if used to describe legal belonging in Tunisia, might well have upset the Ottomans). Husayn was careful to distinguish *jins* from either *ra'āyā* or *ahālin*, which merely connoted administrative jurisdiction. Ben Ismail, "Sovereignty across Empires," 201–26.

20. "*Fa-inna al-ra'āyā wal-ahālī wa-inna ikhtalafan lafẓan madlūluhumā wāḥidun idh laysa hunāka illā rā'un wa-ra'īyatun, wal-diyānatu al-islāmīyatu ja'alat li-ahli dhimmati al-islāmi mā lil-muslimīna wa-'alayhim mā 'alayhim*" (Husayn, "Al-qusṭās," 277). The French translation reads, "Citoyens ou sujets sont tous à nos yeux des Tunisiens ayant la même patrie, les mêmes droits et la même sanction" (Heussein, *Lettre de Général Heussein au collège de la défense*, 35).

21. "*Thumma lammā kānat al-jinsīyatu fī sharī'ati al-islāmi manūṭatu bil-dīni bil-nisbati lil-muslimi, wa-bi-'ahdi al-dhimmati bil-nisbati lil-ra'āyā ghayri al-muslimīna*" (Husayn, "Al-qusṭās," 252).

22. "*Wa-innamā 'aqdu al-dhimmati 'ibāratun 'an kawni ghayri al-muslimīna yaltazimūna bil-dukhūli taḥta aḥkāmi al-islām, wa-bi-dhālika yaḥṣalūna 'alā al-intiẓāmi fī silki al-islāmi fīmā lahum wa-'alayhim*" (Husayn, "Al-qusṭās," 254). The French translation reads, "Le pacte de sujétion constate que des individus non musulmans consentent à devenir sujets d'une puissance musulmane et à se soumettre à la loi islamique" (Heussein, *Lettre de Général Heussein au collège de la défense*, 21).

23. See, for example, Pélissié du Rausas, *Le régime des capitulations dans l'empire Ottoman*, 1:107.

24. Stow, *Anna and Tranquillo*, 107; Sorkin, *Jewish Emancipation*, 32, 44–45.

25. Lee, "Citizenship, Subjection, and Civil Law," 118–20. See also Wells, *Law and Citizenship in Early Modern France*, chap. 3. Similarly, Jews were made citizens in medieval Florence. Riesenberg, "Citizenship and Equality," 436.

26. Sorkin, *Jewish Emancipation*. For an example of debates over Jews' citizenship in Romania, see Picot, "La question des israélites roumains."

27. "Je demanderai seulement à Votre Excellence quel est l'Etat étranger qui pourrait nous faire grief de ne point admettre un Juif à ce Conseil, et qui concevrait, à notre égard, une antipathie accrue ? Est-ce l'Espagne dont nous ne savons encore si elle a admis ou non l'entrée des Juifs sur son territoire ? Est-ce l'Italie où, à notre connaissance, il ne se trouve jusqu'ici aucun Juif pourvu d'une charge publique ? . . . Sont-ce les Etats d'Allemagne où, hier encore, les Juifs se distinguaient par le port de bonnets jaunes ? Est-ce l'Angleterre où les membres de la Chambre des Communes sont, depuis plus de cinquante ans, divisés sur le point de savoir s'ils admettront un Juif au sein de la Chambre Haute ?" (Bercher, "En marge du Pacte 'Fondamental,'" 259).

28. "E accusate noi di *fanatismo*? . . . Curiosa accusa in verità, quando è scagliata contro un Sovrano al quale, nel caso presente, una sola colpa si potrebbe onestamente rimproverare: quella di avere accordato la sua fiducia e la sua grazia ad un suddito di religione diversa dalla sua" (Husséïn, *Lettera del Generale Husséïn*, 15). Although Husayn did not mention this, Nissim was hardly the only Jew to be appointed to a high government position. See esp. Ben Rajeb, *Yahūd al-bilāṭ*.

29. "*Wal-diyānatu al-islāmiyatu ja'alat li-ahli dhimmati al-islāmi mā lil-muslimīna wa-'alayhim mā 'alayhim*" (Husayn, "Al-qusṭās," 277).

30. "*Istiwā al-yahūd laday al-ḥukm*" (Elmilik to Husayn, 15 Sha'bān 1295, SH.D108.D275.96, ANT).

31. *"Ha-yehudim shavim heimah lifnei ha-mishpat 'im ha-yishma'elim"* (Elmelich, *Megilah 'Amukot*, 16). It is not entirely clear in which language Elmilik first wrote; I quote the Hebrew in part because I have a hunch that he originally wrote in this language and in part because the word choice is generally more interesting.

32. Marglin, "Léon Elmilik." Historians have traditionally paid much more attention to the way new discourses of equality emanating from Europe caused Jews to appeal to foreigners to protect their rights. But recent research has emphasized a different kind of discourse among Jews—one in which Jews appealed to the Muslim-ruled state in which they lived to secure their sense of belonging and their rights. See esp. Cohen, *Becoming Ottomans*; Marglin, *Across Legal Lines*, chap. 5.

33. Stillman, *The Jews of Arab Lands*, 157–58.

34. There were a few notable exceptions to this rule in medieval Spain and North Africa, in which Christians did bear arms in Muslim states. Fancy, *The Mercenary Mediterranean*, 86–94.

35. Pinna to Melegari, Ministero Affari Esteri Regno d'Italia (Moscati VI), 1440, ASMAE.

36. *"Al-taswīya bayna al-muslimi wa-ghayrihi min sukkān al-iyālati fī istiḥqāqi al-inṣāf"* (Article 3, http://www.e-justice.tn/fileadmin/images/repertoire_musee/husseinite_avant_protec/Pacte_fondamental_1857_ar.pdf).

37. This was in the context of a debate he had with Ibn Diyaf concerning whether Jews should sit on the Supreme Council (the *majlis al-'āla*). Bercher, "En marge du Pacte 'Fondamental,'" 250.

38. Marglin, "A New Language of Equality." The idea that equality before the law could coexist with differentiated rights and duties was common in medieval Italian city-states, where citizenship conferred legal equality, without presuming either political or civil equality. Riesenberg, "Citizenship and Equality."

39. "Fanatico e intollerante il Sovrano che sulla proposta dei collegii rabbinici nomina i giusdicenti ad amministrare la giustizia para i sudditi isdraeliti [*sic*]? . . . Cento volte più fanatica e più intollerante sarebbe, secondo voi, la Francia: dove il re, l'imperatore, o il presidente della repubblica, nomina con suo decreto i vescovi e gli arcivescovi. . . . Gli isdraeliti [*sic*] tunisini vivono nel nostro paese con larghezza di libertà propria maggiore che per tutto altrove" (Heusséïn, *Lettera del Generale Heusséïn*, 20).

40. *"Ha-yesh lekha Rav Yosef Costa ḥofshit yoter gedolah mi-zot"* (Elmelich, *Megilah 'Amukot*, 16). On the range of legal options available to Jews in Morocco, see Marglin, *Across Legal Lines*.

41. This is similar to other arguments made for equality through difference, such as by advocates of national cultural autonomy in the Austro-Hungarian Empire. See esp. Renner, "State and Nation." The question of whether religious minorities deserve their own religious law or civil equality remains a live issue, especially in inheritance cases. See, for example, *Molla Sali v. Greece*, European Court of Human Rights, 2018 and 2020, https://hudoc.echr.coe.int/eng#{%22itemid%22:[%22001-188985%22]} and https://hudoc.echr.coe.int/eng#{%22appno%22:[%2220452/14%22],%22itemid%22:[%22001-203370%22]}.

42. The only exception is a brief mention of Jews *requesting* equal rights in commerce, residence, and real estate—though Pierantoni does not say whether they were granted this. Pierantoni, *Corte di Appello di Lucca*, 20.

43. Unlike in Piedmont, where Jews had been admitted to "perfetta eguaglianza di diritto" in 1854. Pierantoni, *Corte di Appello di Lucca*, 15.

44. Pierantoni, *Corte di Appello di Lucca,* 8.

45. Pierantoni, *Corte di Appello di Lucca,* 25. Galeotti similarly refrained from echoing Husayn, making arguments quite like those of Pierantoni. Galeotti, *Reale Corte d'Appello di Lucca,* 165–69.

46. Koskenniemi, *The Gentle Civilizer of Nations,* 19–24; Hart, "Positivism"; Lon Fuller, "Positivism and Fidelity to Law." See also Hart, *The Concept of Law.* Ronald Dworkin similarly had a debate with Hart, in which Dworkin argued for the importance of founding principles that existed independently of legislation and influenced judges. See, for example, Dworkin, *Taking Rights Seriously.*

47. Mancini had dismissed the evidence that Tunisia required perpetual allegiance from its subjects; he concluded that "no express prohibition" against expatriation existed in Tunisian law ("non esisteva alcuna espressa disposizione proibitiva") (Mancini, *Corte di Appello di Lucca,* 269). On the articulation of expatriation as a natural right in the US context, see Green, "Expatriation"; Green, *The Limits of Transnationalism,* 67. In the broader context of Western law, see Casey, *Nationals Abroad,* chap. 2. On natural law and concepts of citizenship in the early modern period, see Riesenberg, *Citizenship,* 237–42. See also Ibbetson, "Natural Law."

48. "Che i nuovi criterii oggi accolti comunemente dalle nazioni anche le meno civili" (Pierantoni, *Corte di Appello di Lucca,* 41). For more on the ruling, see Pierantoni, *Corte di Appello di Lucca,* 39–42.

49. "Che sia nei principia universale del Diritto delle Genti la *Libertà di Emigrazione ed Espatriazione*" (Mancini, *Corte di Appello di Lucca,* 268).

50. "Ristabilito il libero diritto di *Espatriazione* e di *Naturalizzazione all'estero*" (Mancini, *Corte di Appello di Lucca,* 273). See also Mancini, *Corte di Appello di Lucca,* 272, 274.

51. "Le droit international actuel établit la faculté pour chacun de choisir une autre nationalité" (Bluntschli, *De la naturalisation en Allemagne,* 13).

52. In *Das moderne Völkerecht,* quoted in Koskenniemi, *The Gentle Civilizer of Nations,* 50. Bluntschli shared this view with other founding members of the institute, including John Westlake and Gustave Rolin-Jaequemyns. Koskenniemi, *The Gentle Civilizer of Nations,* 42–51.

53. "Il n'existe point un droit des gens *positif universel pour toutes les nations de l'univers*" (de Martens, *Précis du droit des gens,* 13, quoted in Pierantoni, *Corte di Appello di Lucca,* 57). On de Martens, see Augusti, *Questioni d'Oriente,* 100–101; Koskenniemi and Kari, "A More Elevated Patriotism," 980.

54. Laurent, "Etudes sur le droit international privé," 318. On Laurent, see Jessurun d'Oliveira, "Principe de nationalité"; Jessurun d'Oliveira, "Once Again," 26–28; Tarazona, "Writing International Legal History," 105–6.

55. "Bluntschli a certainement pour lui le sens moral, mais il oublie qu'il s'adresse à l'interprète, qui lui aussi est esclave de la loi; le législateur seul a le pouvoir de délivrer la femme mariée des chaines qu'il lui a imposées" (Laurent, "Etudes sur le droit international privé," 317). On Laurent's belief that all states *should* allow the freedom of emigration and naturalization elsewhere, see Jessurun d'Oliveira, "Principe de nationalité," 829–30.

56. On the prohibition against expatriation (and even emigration) in the Russian Empire, see Lohr, *Russian Citizenship,* chap. 4.

57. Pierantoni, *Corte di Appello di Lucca,* 48.

58. "*Anna al-tūnisī idhā intaqala li-waṭani ākhiri wa-faraḍna annahu akhadha jinsīyata al-waṭani al-muntaqili ilayhi fa-inna al-dawlatu al-tūnisīyatu lā ta'tabiru tilka al-jinsīyata jinsīyatan ḥaqīqīyatan . . . idhā raja'a lil-mamlakati al-tūnisīyati tajrī 'alayhi aḥkāmihā kamā kāna bidūn iḥtiyāji li-tajdīdi al-dukhūli fī al-jinsīyati al-tūnisīyati wa-aḥrā idhā lam yatamm akhdha al-jinsīyati al-ajnabīyati kamā fī nāzilatinā*" (Husayn, "Al-qusṭās," 239). It was, in fact, common for Tunisian and Moroccan Jews to naturalize as French citizens in Algeria after 1870. See Blévis, "En marge du décret Crémieux."

59. The Ibn 'Ayyad lawsuit of the 1850s is a case in point. Whether or not Ahmad Bey wanted to acknowledge Ibn 'Ayyad's French naturalization, his administration had to pursue the lawsuit in France, where Ibn 'Ayyad was recognized as a French citizen.

60. See chapters 2 and 5. The Ottoman archives similarly preserve a number of cases in which an individual was claimed by two states at once. See, for example, HR.HK.380/11 (Antoine Zelitz), BOA; HR.HK.378/11 (Sabino Cosulich), BOA; HR.HK.211/4 (Nicho Pavlovich), BOA; HR.HK.318/3 (Joseph Simon Alacaci), BOA. See also *Osman Khaleb Bey c. Gouvernement Egyptién*, April 10, 1876, in *Jurisprudence des tribunaux de la réforme en Egypte*, 69–70. There were also numerous other cases in which Ottoman authorities competed with another state over the nationality of an individual—though in these instances, naturalization was not the legal matter under consideration but rather the origins of the individual in question. See, for example, HR.HK.384/22 (Antoine Parissi), BOA; HR.HK.97/20 (Mayer Matatia Coën), BOA; HR.HK..96/15 (Moise Israelovitch), BOA; HR.HK.96/4 (Asias Benjamin Goldenberg), BOA; HR.HK.94/16 (Avram Youdas Alagem), BOA.

61. Pierantoni, *Corte di Appello di Lucca,* 147. On this argument, see Augusti, *Questioni d'Oriente,* 99–106. Husayn did not address the question of whether Tunisia participated in a universal international legal system. Yet his observation that Tunisian law did not have Roman law as its base (as did Italian law) might have been a subtle reference to this question. Husayn, "Al-qusṭās," 237.

62. "Prestando fede all'impero di principi di diritto internazionale sopra la Perdita della nazionalità comuni a tutti gli stati, ha creduto che essi fossero osservati dagli Stati maomettani. . . . Altra è invece la condizione giuridica delle relazioni tra gli Stati cristiani e gli Stati Orientali Maomettani . . . recente è l'epoca, in cui il mondo ottomano fu ammesso al diritto delle genti d'Europa . . . tuttora esistono grandi differenze nelle relazioni internazionali tra l'oriente e l'occidente" (Pierantoni, *Corte di Appello di Lucca,* 145–46). On the admittance of the Ottoman Empire to the family of nations, see Özsu, "The Ottoman Empire," 127.

63. "Il diritto delle Genti non già come la legge naturale di giustizia regolatrice dei rapporti per tutti i popoli della terra e le varie famiglie nazionali, che compongono l'umanità, ma come una legge particolare e circoscritta nel suo impero alle sole nazioni cristiane, per modo che venne in uso di appellarla il Diritto delle Genti di Europa o della Cristianità" (Pierantoni, *Corte di Appello di Lucca,* 146–47).

64. On this, see esp. Anghie, *Imperialism*; Koskenniemi, "Expanding Histories"; Koskenniemi, "Introduction"; Koskenniemi, *To the Uttermost Parts of the Earth.*

65. "L'esistenza della giurisdizione consolare è la prova migliore della differenza di diritto, che distingue il popolo europeo dal popolo tunisino" (Pierantoni, *Corte di Appello di Lucca,* 150).

66. See esp. Ruskola, *Legal Orientalism*; Augusti, *Questioni d'Oriente,* 125–26. The exception among members of the institute was Joseph Hornung (1822–84), a jurist from Geneva. On

Hornung, see *Annuaire de l'Institut de droit international* 8 (1886): 45–53. Hornung argued that extraterritoriality was Eurocentric and unjust. See *Annuaire de l'Institut de droit international* 4, no. 1 (1879–80): 305–37.

67. "Les nations orientales ou, pour parler d'une manière plus précise, les nations non-chrétiennes seront admises à la jouissance de tous les droits, et soumises à tous les devoirs des nations de l'Occident . . . avec cette seule exception: Jusqu'à ce qu'il se soit réalisé une assimilation plus complète des institutions judiciaires des nations orientales et occidentales, il sera établi des tribunaux mixtes et une procédure spéciale pour le jugement de toutes contestations, d'intérêt public ou privé, où des Américains et des Européens seront partis" (*Annuaire de l'Institut de droit international* 4, no. 1 (1879–1880): 300). For another example of this argument, see *Ross v. McIntyre*, 140 U.S. 453 (1891).

68. In so doing, the institute had done little more than repeat the doublespeak of the Treaty of Paris, which admitted the Ottoman Empire to the family of nations of Europe, yet failed to abolish the capitulations that fundamentally undermined Ottoman sovereignty. Özsu, "The Ottoman Empire," 437–38. See also Hanley, "International Lawyers," 100; Koskenniemi and Kari, "A More Elevated Patriotism," 987–88. On early nineteenth-century debates on this question, see esp. Pitts, *Boundaries of the International*, chaps. 5–6. On the question of Jews, extraterritoriality, and the different standards to which Christian and Muslim states were held, see esp. Green, "From Protection."

69. Lorimer, *Institutes of the Law of Nations*, 1:101. On Lorimer, see Özsu, "The Ottoman Empire," 133. On the association between "civilization" and Christianity, see Augusti, *Questioni d'Oriente*, 111–18.

70. On the subsequent development of the "standard of civilization," as it came to be known, see Gong, *The Standard of "Civilization"*; Horowitz, "International Law and State Transformation"; Rodogno, "European Legal Doctrines."

71. Mancini, *Corte di Appello di Lucca*, 299. See also p. 284.

72. "A cette heure où les nations civilisées sont animées des mêmes sentiments de souveraine tolérance, où la justice est distribuée équitablement sans distinction de nationalité pour les justiciables, nous demeurons dans la croyance la plus absolue que nos droits si respectables et si justifiés seront consacrés et protégés par l'arrêt que nous attendons en toute confidence" (Heussein, *Lettre de Général Heussein au collège de la défense*, 35).

73. See esp. Koskenniemi, *The Gentle Civilizer of Nations*, chap. 1.

74. "*Wa-ḍiyā'u al-jinsīyati lā aṣla lahu fī sharī'ati al-islām*" (Husayn, "Al-qusṭās," 237).

75. "*Al-dīn lā yubīḥu naqḍa al-'ahdi min al-dhimmī kamā lā yubīḥu al-raddata min al-islām*" (Husayn, "Al-qusṭās," 236).

76. "*Wa-lahum al-ḥurrīyatu al-tāmmatu yamshūna fī manākib al-arḍi, wa-yaqṭa'ūnahā bil-ṭūli wal-'arḍi wa-yuskinūna ḥaythu shā'ū 'alā sharṭi al-taqayyudi bi-rusūmi al-dīn wa-'adami al-khurūji 'an ḥudūdi al-qur'ān al-latī min jumlatihā al-wafā'i bil-'uhūd*" (Husayn, "Al-qusṭās," 237). The French translation turns "the bonds of religion" into the "lois fondamentales de leur patrie" (Heussein, *Lettre de Général Heussein au collège de la défense*, 7).

77. Husayn to Ibn Isma'il [French translation], 1 Muḥarram 1298 / December 4, 1880, SH.C12.D109.8090, ANT; Husayn to Ibn Isma'il [French translation], 1 Muḥarram 1298 / December 4, 1880, SH.C12.D109.8091, ANT. For a copy of the ruling, see *Osman Khaleb Bey c. Gouvernement Egyptién*, April 10, 1876, in *Jurisprudence des tribunaux de la réforme en Egypte*, 69–70.

78. Pierantoni, *Corte di Appello di Lucca,* 155–56.

79. Pierantoni, *Corte di Appello di Lucca,* 151. The original law was published in *Düstür* (1869): 16–17. For a translation, see Kern, *Imperial Citizen,* 157–58. On this law, see Hanley, "What Ottoman Nationality Was and Was Not." Husayn, on the other hand, was silent about the Ottoman nationality law, perhaps from a desire to emphasize Tunisia's autonomy.

80. Heffening, "Murtadd."

81. Verksin, *Islamic Law and the Reconquista.*

82. See, for example, Fattal, *Statut légal,* chap. 1; Hunwick, "Al-Mahîlî." See also the lengthy discussion among scholars in response to the Moroccan sultan Mawlay Hasan's question concerning the rules of the dhimma from 1883, in which the Pact of 'Umar was reaffirmed as the foundational text outlining the rights and restrictions applying to Jews. Mawlay Hasan to Muhammad b. 'Abd al-Rahman, 6 Rabī' II 1300; Ahmad b. Muhammad b. al-Hajj to Mawlay Hasan, 10 Jumādā I 1300, Fez, Direction des Archives Royales (Rabat, Morocco).

83. This must have been Ahmad II b. Muhammad Ibn Khuja, who was appointed *shaykh al-islām* in 1875. Green, *The Tunisian Ulama,* 252–53.

84. "Più o meno vaghi ed equivoci . . . soggetti all'effrenato arbitrio di un Governo dispotico" (Mancini, *Corte di Appello di Lucca,* 284).

85. "*Anna mafātī al-muslimīna min nū'i a'ḍā' al-dawlati al-islāmīyati wa-hādhā al-ghulṭu waqa'a li-kathīr min al-ūrubāwiyīn. . . . Bal al-tashrī'i amrun dīnīyun mudawwinun fī kutubihi . . . wal-dawlatu lam tu'aṭṭilu ḥurrīyata al-muftiyīna fī waqtin min al-awqāti*" (Husayn, "Al-qusṭās," 251). I translate *a'ḍā'* as "functionaries" even though its literal meaning is "member," in part because the French translation makes it clear that Husayn's intention was to convey that most Europeans believed muftis were "dependent on the government" (Heussein, *Lettre de Général Heussein au collège de la défense,* 18). The Livornese jurists' objection to the form was similarly born of ignorance since "the custom of Islamic fatwās was that the person who asks the question is not named" (*al-'ādatu al-jārīyatu fil-fatāwā al-islāmīyati anna al-sā'ila lā yudhkaru ismahu fī su'ālihi*) (Husayn, "Al-qusṭās," 250).

86. Husayn to Muhammad Khaznadar, 20 Rajab 1295, SH.C108.D275.95, ANT.

87. Pierantoni, *Corte di Appello di Lucca,* 122–24.

88. "*Al-tūnisī idhā intaqala li-waṭanin ākhirin 'alā ayy wajhin wa-bi-ayy sababin ṭālat muddatu mughayyabihi [sic] aw qaṣarat ḥasaba min ahli al-waṭani al-muntaqili ilayhi aw lam yaḥsab thumma raja'a li-mamlakati tūnis yaḥsabu min ra'āyāhā kamā kāna*" (Chapter 12, Article 7, http://www.legislation.tn/sites/default/files/constitution/Pdf/constitution_1861_ar.pdf). For a French translation, in which this is Article 92, see http://mjp.univ-perp.fr/constit/tn1861.htm#12. The second article invoked by various lawyers ruled that "a non-Muslim subject [of Tunisia] who changes his religion does not escape Tunisian protection or sovereignty" (*ghayru al-muslimu min ra'īyatinā idhā intaqala li-dīni lā yukharrijuhu tanaqquluhu min al-ḥimāyati al-tūnisīyati wa-ri'āyatihā*) (Chapter 12, Article 9). I translate *ri'āyatihā* as "sovereignty," given the connection to "subject" (*ra'īya*), even though Hans Wehr (*Dictionary of Modern Arabic,* 401) translates it as "custody" or "patronage, auspices."

89. Heussein, *Lettre de Général Heussein au collège de la défense,* 9; Pierantoni, *Corte di Appello di Lucca,* 153–54.

90. Pierantoni, *Corte di Appello di Lucca,* 159. Moreover, there were some questions raised about whether the 'Ahd al-Amān and Qānūn al-Dawla had been abrogated in 1864 during the

great revolt that had caused Nissim to abandon his homeland; Husayn, though, insisted that both were still in force. Heussein, *Lettre de Général Heussein au collège de la défense*, 15.

91. The Livornese court interpreted Article 92 narrowly, insisting that it only regulated the reacquisition of Tunisian nationality on return to Tunisia. Mancini, *Corte di Appello di Lucca*, 280. Both Pierantoni and Mancini were familiar with the jurisprudence of extraterritoriality, and each pronounced a discourse in the Chamber of Deputies on the subject as it affected Italians in Egypt. Mancini, "Sulla modificazione della giurisdizione consolare in egitto." Pierantoni quotes his own remarks from February 1, 1879, in Pierantoni, *Corte di Appello di Lucca*, 18–21.

92. Heussein, *Lettre de Général Heussein au collège de la défense*, 11–12.

93. Marglin, "Extraterritoriality and Legal Belonging."

94. "*Wa-ḥīna'idhin fa-lā yakūnu sukūta al-faṣli 'an ṣūrati 'admi al-rujū'i mūhimā [sic] anna al-dawlata tasallama fī 'ilāqatihim bihā mā dāmū khārijīn 'an waṭanihā*" (Husayn, "Al-qusṭās," 244). Pierantoni similarly acknowledged the extraterritorial context of the Ottoman nationality law of 1869. Pierantoni, *Corte di Appello di Lucca*, 152.

95. See esp. Ben Slimane, "Définir ce qu'est être Tunisien." I fear I myself have succumbed to this interpretation in previous writing. Marglin, "La nationalité en procès."

96. Procès Verbal, letter dated February 9, 1879, from Gallian Effendi to Husayn, August 21, 1887, HR.H.171/13.29, BOA.

97. Procès Verbal, letter dated February 12, 1879, from Gallian Effendi to Husayn, August 21, 1887, HR.H.171/13.29, BOA.

98. Soetens, *Le congrès eucharistique*, 52.

99. Ben Ismail, "Sovereignty across Empires," 226–33; Hanley, "When Did Egyptians Stop Being Ottomans?" According to Ben Ismail, the Ottoman nationality of Tunisians who were in the Ottoman Empire (but outside the borders of Tunisia) was largely implicit before the establishment of the French protectorate in 1881. After that, the status of Tunisians as Ottomans became a point of considerable tension between Ottoman and French authorities. Ben Ismail, "Sovereignty across Empires," chap. 3. See also Çaycı, *La question tunisienne et la politique ottomane*, 78–85, 160–65; Hanley, *Identifying with Nationality*, 179, 251; Oualdi, *A Slave between Empires*, 90–92. And see the discussion of Husayn's estate in chapter 10.

100. Procès Verbal, letter dated May 2, 1879, from Gallian Effendi to Husayn, August 21, 1887, HR.H.171/13.29, BOA.

101. This is discussed further in chapter 10.

Chapter 8. Rav Nissim the Jew

1. See, for example, Braude and Lewis, "Introduction." Indeed, starting in the late nineteenth century, Ottoman Jewish leaders strived to portray Jews as the "model millet," the loyal Ottoman subjects par excellence. Cohen, "A Model *Millet*?"

2. Canepa, "Emancipazione"; Molinari, *Ebrei in Italia*, 37–38; Facchini, *David Castelli*, 90–92; Schächter, *The Jews of Italy*, 110. Maurogonato declined the position in large part because he did not think it appropriate for a Jewish minister to be in charge of instituting anticlerical measures. Canepa, "Emancipazione," 176–77. On antisemitism in unified Italy more broadly, see Schächter, *The Jews of Italy*, chap. 4.

3. "Unione di uomini nati in una regione, parlanti la lingua medesima—un'unione di genti in vincolo di tradizioni civili, morali e intellettuali" (Mortara, *Della nazionalità*, 10, quoted in Facchini, *David Castelli*, 91). See also Molinari, *Ebrei in Italia*, 37. On Jews as a distinct race, see, for example, Efron, *Defenders of the Race*.

4. Mortara, *Della nazionalità*, 12, quoted in Facchini, *David Castelli*, 91.

5. Mancini, *Della nazionalità*, 34–37.

6. Herzl, "The Jewish State," 211, 220.

7. For an exception, see Pianko, *Jewish Peoplehood*.

8. See Elmilik to AIU President, September 17, 1874, Tunsisie I B 011 b, #103–4, AIU; *L'univers israélite* 21, no. 3 (November 1865): 141–45; AIU Committee in Tunis to AIU Central Committee, November 3, 1876, Tunsisie I B 011 b, #818–21, AIU.

9. See FM2.865, BNF. The lodge was created in 1861 by Solomon Garsin, a Livornese Jew who obtained French nationality in 1849. It was dissolved in 1866. On Masonic lodges in the Middle East, see Campos, "Freemasonry in Ottoman Palestine"; Sommer, *Freemasonry in the Ottoman Empire*.

10. Elmilik, *Affaire Heussein et Elmilik*, 24.

11. "*Kor'im u-mekhanim et 'atzmeinu ba-shem 'am Hashem, ke-nisdar be-tefiloteinu yom yom ve-ka'amur umi ke-'amkha Yisrael goy ekhad ba-aretz*" (Elmelich, *Megilah 'Amikta*, 31). The translation of the biblical verse is from the King James Bible.

12. "*Ve-gam be-'arei Eropa kodem et ḥofshit le-yehudim kor'im hayu lanu 'am yisrael. Ve-ka'asher yir'e ha-kore' na'im be-ma'amarot ha-dukus ha-gadol shel 'arei Toskana asher be-peh male' kara' lanu 'am yisrael. Ve-'od ha-yom gadol sham timtzeh katuv 'al pitḥei beit he-ḥayim shel ha-yehudim ba-'ir Livorno zot hi' beit he-ḥayim shel 'am ha-yehudim*" (Elmelich, *Megilah 'Amikta*, 31). In French, it reads: "On le voit, du reste, par leurs prières journalières, où ils s'intitulent : 'd'une nation.' Les décrets de l'ex-grand duc de Toscane, concernant les Israélites de son pays, les traitaient de nation. Encore aujourd'hui, on voit à Livourne, à la porte d'un cimitière : 'Cimitière de la nation israélite'" (Elmelich, *Observations*, 28).

13. 'Am is translated as "nation" in, for example, 1 Chronicles 16:20, 1 Chronicles 17:21, and 2 Chronicles 7:20. It is translated as "people" in, for example, Genesis 11:6 and Genesis 17:14. "Goy" was generally translated as "nation," such as in Genesis 10:5 and Genesis 12:2.

14. For a discussion of changing notions of Jewish collectivity, see Pianko, *Jewish Peoplehood*, esp. chap. 1.

15. For a full text of the Livornine, see https://leghornmerchants.wordpress.com/home/laws-documents/the-livornine-1593-it/. On Jews in the Livornine, see Tazzara, "Religious Boundaries in Italy."

16. Trivellato, *The Familiarity of Strangers*, 43–44.

17. Estrato della delibarzione del governo della Nazione Ebrea di Livorno riguardante le imposte stabilite . . . "diritto nazionale" (26 January 1815), IT-Li 11, CAHJP.

18. According to the *Oxford English Dictionary*, "nationality" is attested in English for the first time in 1691 to mean "national quality or character," but historians generally agree that it became widespread as a legal term equivalent to citizenship only in the early nineteenth century. See Noiriel, "Socio-histoire d'un concept"; Gosewinkel, "Citizenship, Subjecthood, Nationality."

19. "*Rak ele ha-tzon ha-nefutzim be-aḥat 'ayarei Eropa asher dror kar'u lamo ke-yehudi ke-notzri bli shum hefresh hukhraḥo la'azov brit avotam u-leḥabek datei u-ḥukei ha-medina. Lo ken*

ha-yehudim ha-nimtza'im be-she'ar ha-mamlakhot... be-'arei ha-mizraḥ ve-ha-ma'arav ve-afrika ve-khulei asher ḥofshit lo natan lahem 'odnam maḥzikim be-vritam" (Elmelich, *Megilah 'Amikta,* 31). The French translation is fairly different and thus worth quoting: "Seulement, dans les pays constitutionnels, c'est-à-dire ceux où le gouvernement reconnaît le droit de citoyen, ils ont pour ainsi dire renoncé à leurs lois originaires en se soumettant à celles du pays où ils résident; mais ceux qui habitant les pays non-constitutionnels, tels que le Maroc, l'Afrique, les régions orientales et autres, conservent toujours leurs lois et leurs traditions, et se considèrent comme une nation" (Elmelich, *Observations,* 28–29).

20. *"Ha-yotzei mi-kol ha-amur she-datei ve-ḥukei u-mishpatei kol ish yehudi asher lo me-'arei dror hu ve-asher datot u-minhagim nokhriyot lo ḥabak datei u-mishpatei u-ḥukei M[oshe] R[abeinu] 'a[lav] ha[-shalom] heimah. Ve-ye'otah lanu lomar mishpatei 'am yisrael. Ve-i[m] k[en] mishpatei 'am ha-sar ha-n[izkar] le[-ma'lah] mishpatei 'am yisrael heimah—lihyot hu ve-avotav ve-avot avotav me-'arei Afrikah hema ka'amur."* (Elmelich, *Megilah 'Amikta,* 31).

21. Elmelich, *Observations,* 29

22. *"Lo mi-yaldei Tunis ve-lo mi-yaldei Italiyah hu. Mi-yaldei 'am ha-yehudim hu ve-keter torat M[oshe] R[abeinu] 'a[lav] ha[-shalom] munaḥ 'al rosho"* (Elmelich, *Megilah 'Amikta,* 31).

23. The book in question was the first volume of *Trattato di diritto internazionale,* which was put on the index in 1888. Pierantoni never published the planned subsequent three volumes. See http://www.treccani.it/enciclopedia/augusto-francescopaolo-pierantoni_%28Dizionario-Biografico%29/.

24. For a long time, historians emphasized the complete absence of a "Jewish question" in liberal Italy; even if this is a stretch, there is little doubt that many Italians on the Left were supporters of emancipation. On this historiography, see Schächter, *The Jews of Italy,* 97–99.

25. Ricasoli was the statesperson after whom the street in Livorno on which Nissim's palazzo stood was named. On Ricasoli, see https://www.treccani.it/enciclopedia/bettino-ricasoli_%28Dizionario-Biografico%29/.

26. Galeotti, *La storia del concilio di Trento,* 43; Funaro, "La barca cammina," 21–22. See also Funaro, "Rignano." On Galeotti's biography, see http://www.treccani.it/enciclopedia/leopoldo-galeotti_(Dizionario-Biografico).

27. Galeotti was particularly fond of Antonio Rossini, like Mancini, as well as Giuseppe Verdi. Funaro, "La barca cammina," 11–12. The quotation is from Giuseppe Di Lampedusa, *The Leopard,* 172.

28. "Il defunto appartenga ad una nazione" (Galeotti, *Reale Corte d'Appello di Lucca,* 29).

29. "Il suo tipo, la sua lingua, la sua religione, le sue leggi, le sue consuetudini, le sue tradizioni, tutto quello in somma che costituisce la nazionalità, infuori del territorio, e della esistenza politica, talchè questo popolo fino agli ultimi tempi rimase separato dagli altri popoli e nazioni, in mezzo alle quali viveva, come un popolo di razza diversa, come tale trattato e considerate" (Galeotti, *Reale Corte d'Appello di Lucca,* 30).

30. Mancini's (*Della nazionalità,* 31) list included "region, race, language, customs, history, law, and religion."

31. "Anche concesso che i detti articoli 6 e 8 delle disposizioni generali usino le parole, *nazione* e *nazionalità,* in senso politico, e così nel senso sinonimo di *stato,* non può ragionevolmente impugnarsi, che, per somiglianze e per analogia, dette parole possano anche comprendere la *nazionalità istorica,* che ricorre in sommo grado negli Ebrei... questo popolo... come tale

trattato e considerato, conservando perfino, nel linguaggio comune, la qualità e il nome di *nazione*" (Galeotti, *Reale Corte d'Appello di Lucca,* 30).

32. "E quindi la legislazione ebraica, faciente parte essenziale della religione, è la legge più personale che mai si possa immaginare" (Galeotti, *Reale Corte d'Appello di Lucca,* 31).

33. Galeotti, *Reale Corte d'Appello di Lucca,* 34–37. On de Susannis, see esp. Stow, *Catholic Thought,* part II. On *ius commune,* see, for example, Gordley, *The Jurists,* chap. 2.

34. Galeotti, *Della riforma municipale,* 18.

35. Fisch, *A History of the Self-Determination of Peoples,* 105–8.

36. Mancini, *Della nazionalità,* 37–38.

37. Mancini, *Corte di Appello di Lucca,* 65–66.

38. "Pienissima libertà di mutare sede e paese come Israelita" (Mancini, *Corte di Appello di Lucca,* 289). On "rootless cosmopolitanism," see, for example, Gelbin and Gilman, *Cosmopolitanisms and the Jews,* chap. 6.

39. Tribunale di Firenze, atti in materia penale, rito: processi d'assise, 1871, pezzo 29, April 29, 1871, ASF; Kertzer, *The Kidnapping of Edgardo Mortara,* chap. 26. See also "Appunti riguardanti gli israeliti e i Valdesi, 1871," b. 629, no. 12, ISR.

40. "Una vera *nazionalità* politicamente costituita e riconosciuta, cioè efficace a ricoprirle della protezione di una Legge personale emanante dalla *Sovranità Nazionale* a cui siano soggette. . . . In essi il legislatore trova soltanto la natura dell'uomo col suo carattere cosmopolitico, non la veste politica del cittadino di un estero Stato che possa ricoprirlo con l'ombra protettrice delle sue Leggi. . . . Il popolo Giudaico fu disperso in mezzo a tutte le altre nazioni di Europa, e cessò di formare un aggregato politico sottoposto ad una propria e nazionale Sovranità, donde emanassero le Leggi per governarlo . . . Una nazione Ebraica nel vero senso della parola ha cessato da secoli di esistere" (Mancini, *Corte di Appello di Lucca,* 64–66). Mancini might also have doubled down on the absence of a single territory associated with the Jewish nation. On the centrality of territory to nationality, see, for example, Jessurun d'Oliveira, "Principe de nationalité," 823–24.

41. Mancini, *Della nazionalità,* 50. Other prominent jurists who similarly proposed the supremacy of nation over state included Ludovico Casanovo and Luigi Palma. Casanova, *Corso di diritto costituzionale ed internazionale*; Palma, *Del principio di nazionalità.* See also Colao, "L'idea di nazione," 268–74, 279–80.

42. Quoted in Jayme, *Pasquale Stanislao Mancini,* 59.

43. Mancini, *Diritto internazionale,* 196–97.

44. Colao, "L'idea di nazione," 260, 276.

45. See esp. Asad, *Formations of the Secular*; Ruskola, *Legal Orientalism.*

46. "Allorchè sono scritte e codificate, e quindi possono esser lette tradotte ed interpretate. . . . A noi sembra evidentissimo che il *gus non scriptum,* le semplici *pratiche e tradizioni consuetudinarie,* specialmente dove non siano certe e riconosciute, ma porgano alimento da secoli a controversie vivaci ed inconciliabili, non abbiano menomamente formato, nè ragionevolmente potuto formare oggetto della disposizione dell'art. 8" (Mancini, *Corte di Appello di Lucca,* 93).

47. Mancini, *Corte di Appello di Lucca,* 74.

48. "Le sue mutilate vestigia non costituiscono più un istituto giuridico, nè un ordinamento sistematico; sono l'eco languida e lontana di un passato che in tempi ben remoti ebbe esistenza, ma che oggi . . . è un ricordo storico" (Mancini, *Corte di Appello di Lucca,* 74).

49. "Che semplici Tradizioni e Consuetudini dipendenti da credenze religiose non hanno i necessari caratteri di una vera e propria LEGGE, e tanto meno di una LEGGE NAZIONALE" (Mancini, *Corte di Appello di Lucca,* 92).

50. "'Judaei communi *Romano Jure* viventes in his causis, quae tam ad superstitionem eorum quam ad forum et leges et jura pertinent, adeant solemni more judicia, omnesque *Romanis Legibus* CONFERANT ET EXCIPIANT actiones.' . . . Per la loro natura ed origine non erano che Privilegi, non già Leggi Nazionali, ma preziose o odiose eccezioni e deroghe alla Legge generale della Nazione e dello Stato" (Mancini, *Corte di Appello di Lucca,* 76–77). For the English text of the Justinian Code (1.9.8), see Scott, *The Civil Law,* 12. The law was promulgated in 398 and is also attested in the Theodosian Code (2.1.10). I am grateful to Mark Letteney for alerting me to this as well as for his assistance with the Latin.

51. "È propria e naturale condizione giuridica degli Israeliti di esser soggetti al DIRITTO COMUNE, cioè alla LEGGE GENERALE TERRITORIALE de' paesi ove hanno il loro DOMICILIO" (Mancini, *Corte di Appello di Lucca,* 89). Mancini further argued that even the US Supreme Court agreed with this view; its justices had ruled on numerous instances that the customs and traditions of religious groups did not constitute law in the true sense of the word. Indigenous people were similarly subject to US common law. Even if the United States tolerated the limited recognition of religious or tribal law, this never amounted to the "same rank and dignity of national law" ("al grado ed alla dignità di LEGGE NAZIONALE") (Mancini, *Corte di Appello di Lucca,* 103).

52. Mancini, *Corte di Appello di Lucca,* 91–92.

53. Mancini mistakenly called this the *Hatti-Scherif di Gulhianè.* Mancini, *Corte di Appello di Lucca,* 94n1.

54. "Strettamente limitato ai con fini del territorio della Sovranità concedente" (Mancini, *Corte di Appello di Lucca,* 89).

55. Colorni, *Gli ebrei,* 15–16.

56. Stow, *Anna and Tranquillo,* 114–18, 123. To further reduce Jews' judicial privileges, the pope banned all Jewish notaries in 1640.

57. Trivellato, *The Familiarity of Strangers,* 77. See also Oliel-Grausz, "Modalité d'accueil." On the nature of Jewish judicial autonomy in other parts of early modern Europe, see Fram, *A Window on Their World*; Berkovitz, *Protocols of Justice*; Berkovitz, *Law's Dominion.*

58. Fattal, *Le statut légal,* 352–58; Libson, "Otonomiyah."

59. Fattal, *Le statut légal,* chap. 8.

60. "L'assoluta libertà di coscienza . . . costituisce nel nostro ordinamento Civile e Costituzionale uno dei principii fondamentali di ORDINE PUBBLICO e di ALTA MORALITA" (Mancini, *Corte di Appello di Lucca,* 86). Foreigners in Italy were afforded civil rights equal to those of citizens—an innovation that began with the Napoleonic Code in 1804. But if Jewish law was applied to foreign Jews in Italy, then a foreign Jew would be denied the right to a civil marriage—a right afforded all those in Italian territory. Mancini, *Corte di Appello di Lucca,* 100.

61. Article 12, in *Codice Civile,* viii.

62. Mancini, "De l'utilité," 297. On the specter of polygamy in the construction of French law—particularly law in colonial Algeria—see Surkis, *Sex, Law, and Sovereignty.*

63. See, for example, Fabian, *Time and the Other.*

64. Heussein, *Lettera del Generale Heussein*, 18–19. Elmilik printed his briefs before Mancini's; it is hard to know how he might have responded had he penned a rebuttal.

65. "Non è effetto di una *mera tolleranza* . . . ma è effetto di UNA DISPOSIZIONE POSITIVA DI LEGGE, cioè dell'articolo 29 del *Canun*" (Galeotti, *Reale Corte d'Appello di Lucca*, 165).

66. "Adde quod non solum dicuntur Judaei de populo Romano, sed etiam dicuntur de eodem corpore CIVITATIS UBI HABITANT" (de Susannis, *De Judaeis*, part II, chap. 2, n. 1, quoted in Galeotti, *Reale Corte d'Appello di Lucca*, 162–63; Mancini, *Corte di Appello di Lucca*, 69).

67. Galeotti, *Reale Corte d'Appello di Lucca*, 168–69.

68. "Come in Francia, malgrado la unità delle legislazioni per gli originarii francesi, furono per prudenza politica mantenute in osservanza, rispetto ai nuovi cittadini maomettani ed ebrei dell'Algeria, le respettive loro leggi personali" (Galeotti, *Reale Corte d'Appello di Lucca*, 169). Note Galeotti's use of "citizen" here to describe Algerian Muslims; clearly he meant "citizen" in the sense of a member of the French state rather than in the sense of full and equal members endowed with civil and political rights. His language was just as imprecise regarding Algerian Jews since during the period of the cases he cites, Jews were not yet naturalized en masse as French citizens.

69. Galeotti, *Reale Corte d'Appello di Lucca*, 367–74. On this case, see Algérie, Oran, 3U/1, Archives Nationales d'Outre Mer, (Aix-en-Provence, France); ruling from the Court of Cassation of Paris, August 19, 1858, in *Journal du Palais de Paris* 70 (1859): 64–65.

70. *Journal du Palais de Paris* 70 (1859): 64.

71. "L'esame della legge ebraica costituisce . . . una vera e propria questione di diritto" (Galeotti, *Reale Corte d'Appello di Lucca*, 373–74). Mancini ignored Galeotti's arguments about the application of Jewish law for Jews in Algeria; his only mention of Algerian Jews was in the context of citing Casimir Frégier's *Les juifs algériens* as evidence that Jews no longer constituted a nation. Mancini, *Corte di Appello di Lucca*, 66–67.

72. See, for example, Femme Edjerah c. Zerafa, Cour d'appel d'Alger, January 23, 1855, in *Journal du Palais de Paris* (1855): 365–67; Ben-Chimol c. Cohen et autres, Cour de Cassation, March 14, 1877, in *Journal du Palais de Paris* (1878): 38–42; Séror c. Tabet, Cour de Cassation, November 12, 1878, in *Journal du Palais de Paris* (1879): 259–61. Starting in the 1840s, though, the Jewish community of the metropole made concerted efforts to convince its coreligionists in French Algeria to opt for French civil law. Many Algerian Jews thus found themselves under a hybrid system—not knowing whether their divorces in Jewish courts were considered binding by the French state.

73. "E così devota a tutte le quisquilie delle pratiche religiose, potesse allignare l'idea di abbandonare l'Oriente, dove l'israelita vive soggetto alla legge di Mosè, per fermare la sua dimora negli stati d'Europa dove il Talmud è relegato in biblioteca fra i libri vecchi e le pergamene polverose" (Heusséïn, *Lettera del Generale Heusséïn* 18).

74. Myers, *Between Jew and Arab*; Pianko, *Zionism and the Roads Not Taken*; Shumsky, *Beyond the Nation-State*.

75. On Bundism, see, for example, Mendelsohn, *Class Struggle in the Pale*; Zimmerman, *Poles, Jews, and the Politics of Nationality*. On the Alliance Israélite Universelle, see esp. Rodrigue, *French Jews, Turkish Jews*; Rodrigue, *Images of Sephardi and Eastern Jewries*; Leff, *Sacred Bonds*, chap. 4. On Ottomanism, see esp. Cohen, *Becoming Ottomans*; Campos, *Ottoman Brothers*.

Chapter 9. Lucca to Florence (1880–83)

1. Samama v. Heussein v. Samama, June 8, 1880, Sentenze no. 77, AS Lucca. Ferdinando Andreucci, Galeotti's associate, came from Florence, as did Adriano Mari, another prominent Florentine lawyer—now working on the opposite side of the case from Andreucci, his former boss. See http://www.treccani.it/enciclopedia/adriano-mari_(Dizionario-Biografico. On Mancini and Pierantoni's joint work on other lawsuits, see Pierantoni to Mancini, 1879, b. 691, no. 7.1, ISR; Mancini to Pierantoni, August 1879, b. 880, no. 24.6, ISR; Mancini to Pierantoni, n.d., b. 880, no. 24.8, ISR; Mancini to Pierantoni, July 3, 1880, b. 775, no. 2.4, ISR.

2. Samama v. Heussein v. Samama, June 8, 1889, Sentenze no. 77, AS Lucca.

3. Cesarini, "Samama v. Samama," 218, 231, 239.

4. "Unicamente il caso di individui rivestiti di politica nazionalità, che è quanto dire appartenenti ad un aggregato di persone formate a Stato" (Cesarini, "Samama v. Samama," 241).

5. Husayn, *Rasāʾil*, 3:84.

6. Khayraddin was pushed out in the summer of 1877, replaced by Khaznadar. On August 24, 1878, Ibn Ismaʿil became prime minister. Ganiage, *Les origines*, 594. Husayn opposed Ibn Ismaʿil's appointment as prime minister. See, for example, Husayn, *Rasāʾil*, 3:71–73.

7. "*Lam yaḥṣal raʾīsuhu ʿalā al-aktharīyati illā bi-tahaddudi baʿḍi al-iʿḍāʾ kamā qīla*" (Husayn to Ibn Ismaʿil, 9 Rajab 1297, SH.C12.D109.8045, ANT).

8. Moses Shamama to Mancini, June 8, 1880, b. 856, no. 13, ISR.

9. "Je vous remercie infiniment de tout ce que vous avez fait pour mon affaire à Lucques. Je reconnais parfaitement le zèle et la volonté que vous avez mis dans cette affaire" (Moses Shamama to Mancini, June 22, 1880, b. 856, no. 13, ISR).

10. "Tres [*sic*] heureux du resultat [*sic*] de Lucques je vous renouvelle avec nos rémérciéments [*sic*] l'assurance de nos meilleurs sentiments: Baron Erlanger" (d'Erlanger to Mancini, June 14, 1880, b. 856, no. 13, ISR).

11. "Je sais que si à Lucques le bon droit a triomphé c'est grâce à votre immense travail . . . grâce à la brillante et solide éloquence que vous avez muni au service de la bonne cause" (d'Erlanger to Mancini, b. 871, no. 9.1, June 24, 1880, ISR).

12. Comunità di Livorno, serie no. 4, Affari Finanziari, Prestito Comunale, Inv. 55, Imposta sulle Vetture e Domestici, 1881–82, entry for Samama, Giuseppe di Natan, ASL.

13. Serie Minute, 33, n.p. 99, entries for October 9, 1876, and October 20, 1878, ASCEL.

14. The villa was on the Via della Barriera Maremmana. For the first mention of it, see contract between Joseph Shamama and Albert Dubois, December 29, 1878, SH, C106, D266.4, ANT.

15. Gini, "Salmon v. Manetti"; Nedjar et al., *Registres de ketubbot*, 495.

16. Four men and two women, two of them in livery. Comunità di Livorno, serie no. 4, Affari Finanziari, Prestito Comunale, Inv. 55, Impuesta sulla Vetture e Domestici, 1881–82, entry for Samama, Natan, ASL.

17. Serie Minute 33, n.p. 99, entries for September 22–23, 1877, and April 18–19, 1878, ASCEL.

18. Tribunale di Livorno, May 15, 1880, b. 42, no. 145, ASL. Nathan agreed to repay within thirty days, after he had arrived in Livorno and obtained his share of the inheritance. Whether Gozlan believed that Nathan would have secured his share of the inheritance in less than a month is hard to say, although it certainly seems naive in retrospect.

19. Husayn to Nathan Shamama, August 17, 1876, SH.C105.D263, ANT; Nathan Shamama to Husayn, July 10, 1876, SH.C106.266.2, ANT. See also Elmelich, *Tribunale Civile di Livorno*, 4. The date of the contract is given variously as June 7 or June 9.

20. Contract between d'Erlanger, Peridon, and Zirio, October 25, 1877, SH.C106.D266.15, ANT. Zirio lived in Marseille, while Peridon lived in Paris.

21. 'Aziza's full payment depended on the will being upheld by the Italian courts. In fact, d'Erlanger negotiated two contracts: in the first, he would still receive four-ninths of 'Aziza's portion of the estate—and d'Erlanger would pay 'Aziza the interest on her expected portion twice yearly, for a sum total of 38,194.45 francs. Private contract between Giuseppe Nissim (agent of 'Aziza Samama) and Albert Dubois (agent of d'Erlanger), December 11, 1878, SH.C106.D266.2, ANT. The second—signed less than two weeks later—followed the conditions outlined above. Tribunale civile di Livorno, contract between Moses Shamama (representative of his son Nissim Samama) and Albert Dubois (representative of d'Erlanger), December 24, 1878, SH.C106.D266.14, ANT. D'Erlanger first learned about 'Aziza's deal with the French bankers; in October 1877, he approached Zirio and Peridon about splitting the cost of their contract with 'Aziza. Contract between d'Erlanger, Peridon, and Zirio, October 25, 1877, SH.C106.D266.15, ANT.

22. Private contract between Giuseppe Nissim (agent of Nissim Samama) and Albert Dubois (agent of d'Erlanger), December 11, 1878, SH.C106.D266.3, ANT; tribunale civile di Livorno, contract between Moses Shamama (representative of his son Nissim Samama) and d'Erlanger, December 24, 1878, SH.C106.D266.14, ANT.

23. Contract between Joseph Shamama and Albert Dubois (representative of d'Erlanger), December 29, 1878, SH, C106, D266.4, ANT.

24. Husayn to Muhammad Khaznadar, n.d. (written between November 29, 1877, and August 24, 1878), SH.C12.D109.7989, ANT.

25. Contract between unnamed bankers and Husayn, 10 Dhū al-Ḥijja 1295, SH.C12.D109.7979, ANT.

26. "*Bi-mā dakhalahum min al-wahmi min kalāmi al-murajji'īni fī ḥisābāti al-dawlati*" (Husayn to Ibn Isma'il, 29 Dhū al-Qa'da 1296, SH.C12.D109.7998, ANT.

27. Decree by Sadiq Bey in favor of Husayn, 19 Rajab 1296, SH.C12.D109.7986, ANT. See also Oualdi, *A Slave between Empires*, 77.

28. Contract between Husayn and F. Mayer, November 7, 1879, SH.C12.D109.7992, ANT. The contract also specified that Mayer and his associates would cover the payment of two million francs to Nathan Shamama, based on the agreement from 1876, and that the government's current lawyer—Spezzafumo—would remain in his current position.

29. "*Al-bankīrāt al-ladhīna yataẓāhirūna bi-akhdhi al-nawāzili al-mutanāzi'i fīhā tanẓuru al-nāsu ilayhim bi-'ayni al-izdirā' . . . wa-lam yas'unā al-waqtu li-tarjimatihā ilā al-'arabīyati*" (Husayn to Ibn Isma'il, 29 Dhū al-Qa'da 1296, SH.C12.D109.7998, ANT).

30. Ibn Isma'il to Husayn, 18 Dhū al-Ḥijja 1296, SH.C12.D109.7998, ANT.

31. For these explanations, see Husayn to Ibn Isma'il, 28 Dhū al-Ḥijja 1296, SH.C12.D109.8047, ANT.

32. "Succession Samama" (report almost certainly authored by the d'Erlanger bank), December 10, 1889, SH.C12.D109.8329, ANT. On Telfener, see Rayburn, "Count Joseph Telfener."

33. Husayn to Ibn Isma'il, 28 Dhū al-Ḥijja / December 19, 1879, SH.C12.D109.8047, ANT.

34. Husayn to Ibn Isma'il, 20 Muḥarram 1297, SH.C12.D109.8017, ANT.

35. Husayn to Ibn Isma'il, 17 Rabī' I 1297, SH.C12.D109.8022, ANT.

36. "*Lākin masyū Mayir ma'a iẓhārihi . . . wal-mulāṭifi afhamanā bi-lisāni al-ḥāli wal-maqālu annahu lā haḥsubā [sic] ilā hādhā al-maṭlabi wa-lā hunāka sababan yad'ū ilā faskhi 'aqadati al-ijālati*" (Husayn to Ibn Isma'il, 1 Rabī' II 1297, SH.C12.D109.8025, ANT). Husayn continued to try to convince Ibn Isma'il to delay canceling the contract. Husayn to Ibn Isma'il, 28 Jumādā I 1297 / May 8, 1880, SH.C12.D109.8199, ANT.

37. "Je ne comprends plus l'énormité du crime qu'on m'impute, ni pourquoi on grossit une petite affaire bien simple" (Husayn to Ibn Isma'il [French translation], 28 Dhū al-Ḥijja 1296 / December 19, 1879, SH.C12.D109.8047, ANT).

38. Husayn to Ibn Isma'il, 17 Rabī' I 1297, SH.C12.D109.8022, ANT.

39. "Et je serais vraiment désolé de voir mon ouvre [*sic*] aboutir à des complications politiques que je cherche par tous mes moyens à écarter" (Husayn to Ibn Isma'il [French translation], 28 Jumādā I 1297 / May 8, 1880, SH.C12.D109.8199, ANT).

40. Spezzafumo to Ibn Isma'il, April 16, 1880, SH.C12.D109.8037, ANT.

41. Ibn Isma'il to Husayn and Spezzafumo (French translation), 12 Rajab 1297 / June 19, 1880, SH.C12.D109.8046, ANT.

42. Ibn Isma'il to Guttieres (French translation), 16 Ṣafar 1298 / January 17, 1881, SH.C12.D109.8204, ANT; Husayn, *Rasā'il*, 3:85, dated 30 Jumādā II 1297 / June 9, 1880, in which Husayn complains to Khayraddin that "for weeks the government has not answered my letters" (*wa-mundhu asābī'in 'adīdatin lam yujībūnī 'an makātībī al-sābiqati min Tūnis*).

43. Husayn, *Rasā'il*, 3:85.

44. Giacomo was born in 1823, and then Angelo in 1824; Cesare (b. 1833) was born in Tunis, as was Abramo (1843) and Guglielmo (1845). Ganiage, *Les origines*, 164, 586. Giacomo also had three sisters, Messodi, Eva, and Judica, whose names were given to me by Litza Guttieres-Green, the great-granddaughter of both Guglielmo (her paternal grandfather's father) and Angelo (her paternal grandmother's father). Interview with Litza Guttieres-Green, February 8, 2018.

45. Ganiage, *Les origines*, 310.

46. Guttieres to Ibn Isma'il, July 2, 1880, SH.C12.D109.8049, ANT.

47. P. D., "Depienne, Pierre-Marie." In one of his letters, Guttieres sent Depienne regards from his wife and daughters. Guttieres to Depienne, SH.C12.D109.8066, August 20, 1880, ANT.

48. Guttieres to Ibn Isma'il, ANT, January 7, 1881, SH.C12.D109.8203, ANT; Guttieres to Ibn Isma'il, May 13, 1881, SH.C12.D109.8217, ANT.

49. Guttieres to Elia Shamama, February 3, 1881, SH.C12.D109.8204, ANT; Guttieres to Elia Shamama, February 3, 1881, SH.C12.D109.8206, ANT. See also Elmilik, *Arbitrage Léon Elmilik contre le gouvernement tunisien*, 41.

50. Elmilik, *Arbitrage Léon Elmilik contre le gouvernement tunisien*, 2–11. Guttieres's brother Cesare had even belonged to the same Masonic lodge as Elmilik. Tableau des FF. Composant la R. L., sous le titre distinctif de La Persévérance à l'Orient de Tunis, April 5, 1862, FM2, 865, BNF.

51. Dubois was elected along with Guttieres in 1869—which many immediately denounced as corrupt given that the role of the commission was largely to manage Tunisia's debt to d'Erlanger. The *Moniteur des Fonds publics*, a financial newspaper founded in 1869 that defended small capitalists, denounced the French election of representatives as thoroughly corrupt; it

accused Alphonse Pinard, a French financier who served as the second director of the Comptoir d'Escompte, which had issued Tunisia its second loan in 1865, of rigging the elections. Ganiage, *Les origines*, 312–13.

52. D'Erlanger would take three-fourths of the estate, and the Tunisian government would get one-fourth; in return, the government would cede all of its rights to d'Erlanger. The costs would henceforth be split in equal proportions, with d'Erlanger paying 75 percent and the Tunisian government 25 percent. And d'Erlanger would take care of whatever settlement was eventually reached with Telfener concerning the secret contract signed by Mayer and Husayn. Guttieres to Elia Shamama, February 2, 1881, SH.C12.D109.8204, ANT.

53. Perkins, *A History of Modern Tunisia*, 15.

54. The opinion explained that for Roman jurists, citizenship was a matter of relations among cities, not among states. Bicci, "Samama v. Samama, Cassation, Florence," 309. Although the ruling is quite laconic on this point, it seems likely that Vigliani and Bicci were referring to the fact that citizenship in premodern Europe usually defined an attachment to a city rather than to a state. On this, see esp. Prak, *Citizens without Nations*.

55. "Non possono assumere l'autorità e il carattere di diritto positivo . . . non può altrimenti giudicarsi che alla stregua dei principii costituzionali che a ciascuno stato independente piace di stabilire, secondo la sua politica, e d'accordo co'suoi interessi" (Bicci, "Samama v. Samama, Cassation, Florence," 309).

56. Elmilik, *Il rivelatore*, 175.

57. Jarmon, *Naḥalat Avot*; Jarmon, *Kuntres nosaf 'al naḥalat*; Bismuth et al., *Mishpat ha-Yerushah*; Bel'ish and Jarmon, *Yisrael lo yada'*.

58. "Sachant que le caid Nissim était de Tunis, et que, d'après l'équité, le droit et les règles établies, les questions pouvant survenir entre les héritiers testamentaires et les héritiers légaux, qui sont aussi Tunisiens, devaient être jugées par les rabbins de Tunis" (Elmelich, *Observations*, 8). See also Pierantoni, *Corte di Appello di Lucca*, 117, 128.

59. This is largely my surmise based on the fact that Elmilik sought out opinions from Tunisian rabbis beginning just months after Nissim had died. The Italian judges who issued the final ruling did not cite any of these opinions, suggesting that they were not influential (see below).

60. Facchini, *David Castelli*.

61. Castelli, *Parere*.

62. Castelli, *Secondo parere*; Castelli, *Terzo parere*; Castelli, *Confutazione del parere firmato*; Castelli, *Il diritto di testare*; Castelli, *Osservazioni sul parere*; Castelli, *Replica ai pareri del Rabbino J. Costa*.

63. Accounts from David Castelli for February 1878 to February 1879, SH.C108.D276.23, ANT. The pamphlet in question is Castelli, *Il diritto di testare*.

64. Accounts from David Castelli for February 1879 to February 1880, SH.C108.D276.22, ANT.

65. Castelli to Guttieres, June 13, 1890, SH.C108.D276.24, ANT. Professor's salaries were three thousand lire for *secondo ordine* and five thousand lire for *primo ordine* in 1889. Martello, "Il professore d'università in Italia e all'estero," 119.

66. Ashkenazi, *Kuntres yismaḥ Moshe*. The exceptions were haskamot (approbations) published in the second edition of Ashkenazi's *teshuvah*, some of which were translated into Italian. See the "Parere" in Ashkenazi, *Kuntres yismaḥ Moshe*, 1–5. See also the French haskamot in Ashkenazi, *Kuntres yismaḥ Moshe*, 5–16. The only other full-length *teshuvah* that validated the

will was by the Italian rabbi Israel Costa, but he, too, published in Hebrew. Costa, *Yada' ma be-ḥasukhah.*

67. Baquis and Cassuto, *Note dopo la discussione*. The brief is dated January 24, 1880; the hearings in Lucca ended on January 16.

68. Cassuto (1850–1920) was born in Livorno and later became a member of the Camera dei Deputati. See https://storia.camera.it/deputato/dario-cassuto-18500619/interventi#nav. On his education, see https://siusa.archivi.beniculturali.it/cgi-bin/pagina.pl?TipoPag=prodpersona&Chiave=292. Baquis descended from a Moroccan family by way of Gibraltar. Filippini, *Il porto di Livorno*, 150. His mother, Elena, née Nissim, was the daughter of the lawyer Raffael Nissim (Nedjar et al., *Registres de ketubbot*, 406).

69. In fact, it is not clear whether d'Erlanger or Moses Shamama hired Benamozegh; a statement from 1890 attests that Benamozegh was paid by Moses. Statement by Elia Benamozegh, June 1890, SH.C108.D276.25, ANT. It is possible, however, that the two worked together given that by 1881, d'Erlanger had bought out 'Aziza's interests in the estate and was financially responsible for the lawsuit.

70. Orvieto, "Di David Castelli," 37.

71. On Benamozegh, see Boulouque, *Another Modernity*. On his biography, see also Benamozegh, "Autobiografia"; Guetta, *Philosophy and Kabbalah*, 3–5. On his work on the Shamama inventory, see Benamozegh, *Delle fonti del diritto ebraico*, 1:1; Bargellini to Mustafa (Khaznadar) and Nushir Basha Bey, June 20, 1873, SH.C249.D670.295, ANT; Funaro, *Un tempio nuovo*, 77. Benamozegh had also been asked to write an opinion on a lawsuit against the estate by Mustafa El Morali, who claimed that Nissim had owed him a debt of five hundred thousand francs; Benamozegh wrote a long analysis of the Judeo-Arabic document that El Morali presented as evidence for the debt, finally concluding that it was forged. See Elia Benamozegh, "Perizia Causa El Morali, Mustafa-Nissim Samama," January 21, 1879, ASCEL.

72. Benamozegh himself was vague on just how much he made working on the Shamama case; in a statement from June 1890, he declared that Moses paid him between seven and eight thousand lire for his work. SH.C108.D276.25, ANT.

73. Elia Benamozegh to Eugenio Falcucci, June 1, 1882, ms. 880, Biblioteca Universitaria, Pisa, cited in Funaro, *Un tempio nuovo*, 77.

74. Which he did throughout his briefs. See, for example, his discussion of the tension between rationalism and revelation in Benamozegh, *Delle fonti del diritto ebraico*, 1:204–6.

75. Castelli, *Il Messia secondo gli Ebrei*; Benamozegh, "Recensione di David Castelli." Benamozegh claimed that in trying to discover a supposedly scientific "truth" about Judaism, Castelli had sapped the religion of its deeper truth, thereby committing the same sin of which Renan and other so-called scientists were guilty. For another critique of Castelli's work, see Morais, *Italian Hebrew Literature*, 217–21.

76. Castelli, "Recensione di *Teologia dogmatica*."

77. Benamozegh realized that his reasoning would lead to the conclusion that Jewish law was not applicable to Nissim's estate, thus rendering the rest of his brief inconsequential; nonetheless, he seems to have felt compelled to say something on the subject. Benamozegh, *Delle fonti del diritto ebraico*, 1:8.

78. Benamozegh cites the gloss by Moshe Isserles on the *Shulḥan 'Arukh, Ḥoshen Mishpat*, 156, which discusses the criteria for membership in a city. Benamozegh, *Delle fonti del diritto ebraico*, 1:8–9.

79. "Si domanda quanto tempo un Israelita dovrà abitare in una città per esservi considerato cittadino" (Benamozegh, *Delle fonti del diritto ebraico*, 1:9). He cites Mishnah Bava Batra 1:5, which concerns the responsibility to contribute to the building of a wall for the town; a man is considered responsible for contributing if he has lived in the town for twelve months or has bought a residence (*beit dirah*) there.

80. "È vero che il Talmud parla degli obblighi e dei diritti che spettano agli uomini della città; ma si noti bene *uomini della città, e non cittadini* nel senso che ha acquistato presso di noi quest'ultima parola" (Castelli, *Nullita*, 15). This text—written after the Tunisian government recused itself from the lawsuit—was commissioned by Joseph Shamama, who still had an interest in the will being pronounced null. See contract between Joseph Shamama and Albert Dubois (representative of d'Erlanger), December 29, 1878, SH, C106, D266.4, ANT.

81. "Il Talmud non parla dello Stato, parla soltanto della città. . . . S'intende la parola Cittadino nel suo ristretto significato etimologico di *chi appartiene di fatto ad una data città* . . . nei passi citati dal Benamozegh, non si parla punto dei doveri e diritti del cittadino" (Castelli, *Nullita*, 16–17). Castelli explained that Benamozegh's assertion that Jewish law considers a person who has been absent for more than three years to have forfeited his membership in a community was similarly irrelevant; the membership in question concerned the state, and states generally did not give Jewish communities the power to admit or refuse citizenship. Castelli, *Nullita*, 13.

82. On this maxim, see Shilo, *Dina de-malkhuta dina*; Shilo and Elon, "Dina de-Malkhuta Dina."

83. "L'Israelita agli occhi propri Cittadino di ogni paese" (Benamozegh, *Delle fonti del diritto ebraico*, 1:96).

84. "Parte essenzialissima del diritto ebraico è l'autorità conceduta in materia civile alla legge dello stato" (Benamozegh, *Delle fonti del diritto ebraico*, 2:89).

85. Benamozegh, *Delle fonti del diritto ebraico*, 2:3–26, 2:60–69. Ashkenazi made a similar argument. Ashkenazi, *Kuntres yismaḥ Moshe*, 6a. Curiously, Benamozegh neglected to say whether Nissim indeed used the word "gift." Benamozegh also suggested that Nissim had in fact performed a kinyan, even if this was not recorded in the will. While Benamozegh recognized that he could not prove this hypothesis, he contended that faced with two possibilities that were equally unknown—that Nissim had performed a kinyan and that he had not—it was "infinitely less absurd" to presume that he had indeed executed the "highly valid" ritual acquisition. Benamozegh, *Delle fonti del diritto ebraico*, 2:28–29.

86. "La vera legge Nazionale di tutti i secoli, di tutti i luoghi, di tutte le fasi della Nazione" (Benamozegh, *Delle fonti del diritto ebraico*, 1 :72).

87. "Il resto non ne è che il commento" (Benamozegh, *Delle fonti del diritto ebraico*, 1:64); "la legge dei tempi di esilio e di decadenza" (Benamozegh, *Delle fonti del diritto ebraico*, 1:6).

88. "Ogni Israelita è dottore a sè stesso, e può e deve interpretare la tradizione come meglio gli sembri dicevole" (Benamozegh, *Delle fonti del diritto ebraico*, 1:78).

89. "La legge era dunque un organismo vivente in pieno esercizio delle sue funzioni, sempre desta, sempre in moto" (Benamozegh, *Delle fonti del diritto ebraico*, 1:80).

90. Mancini, *Corte di Appello di Lucca*, 74. This approach crystallized with Friedrich Carl von Savigny. See Beiser, *The German Historicist Tradition*, chap. 5.

91. "In una parola, è requisito essenziale della legge nazionale isrealitica di essere voluta, fatta, interpretata, proclamata, dalla nazione in quanto ha di più eletto, senza di che non è legge nazionale" (Benamozegh, *Delle fonti del diritto ebraico*, 1:80).

92. Particularly Moses Mendelssohn (d. 1786), father of the Haskalah; Abraham Geiger (d. 1874), founder of the Reform movement; and Heinrich Graetz (d. 1891), the first modern scholar to write a comprehensive history of the Jews. Batnitzky, *How Judaism Became a Religion*, chaps. 1–2.

93. Legal positivism in the nineteenth century was mainly influenced by the thought of John Austin. See Murphy, *The Philosophy of Positive Law*, chap. 4. For a more recent positivist position, see Hart, "Positivism." On positivism in nineteenth-century thought more generally, see Pickering, "Positivism."

94. "Codice da tutti gli ebrei consentita" (Castelli, *Parere*, 5).

95. "Sentiamo il coscienzioso dovere non di abbellirla, né di renderla filosofica, né di farla eguale alla legislazioni moderne, ma di spiegarla, quale la leggiamo negli scritti in cui ci fu tramandata" (Castelli, *Replica ai pareri del Rabbino J. Costa*, 13).

96. Laurent, "Etudes sur le droit international privé," 318.

97. "Certi degeneri ebreini Professori, anche loro di lettere più o meno ebraiche nella Firenze di quell'epoca nel Museo di Alessandria, che si chiamano gli Ebrei Ellenisti; non dei veri e ortodossi ebrei" (Benamozegh, *Controreplica*, 4).

98. Jarmon, *Kuntres nosaf 'al naḥalat*, 10–11. I am grateful to Yuval Haruvi for pointing me to this source. This was not the first time Benamozegh had been declared an apostate. See Harel, "Ha'alat Em la-Mikra 'al ha-moked"; Boulouque, *Another Modernity*, chap. 3.

99. Guttieres to Ibn Isma'il, April 29, 1881, SH.C12.D109.8219, ANT.

100. Perkins, *A History of Modern Tunisia*, 15.

101. Mancini, B. 613, no. 1 (4), ISR.

102. It remains unclear whether Pierantoni was influenced by his father-in-law or simply wanted to move on to other matters. Pierantoni to Primo Presidente (Cesarini) of the Court of Appeal in Lucca, January 9, 1883, SH.C105.D259.7, ANT.

103. Guttieres to Ibn Isma'il, May 13, 1881, SH.C12.D109.8217, ANT; Guttieres to Ibn Isma'il, May 22, 1881, SH.C12.D109.8220, ANT; Guttieres to Ibn Isma'il, June 5, 1881, SH.C12.D109.8223, ANT. This correspondence refers to two letters from Ibn Isma'il to Guttieres, written on 19 Jumādā II 1298 / May 18, 1881, and 4 Rajab 1298 / June 1, 1881. On the Treaty of Bardo, see Perkins, *A History of Modern Tunisia*, 15–17.

104. Draft of a contract between Guttieres and Dubois, September 8, 1881, SH.C12.D109.8225, ANT. In November, Guttieres and Dubois finally signed. Contract between Guttieres and Dubois, November 10, 1881, SH.C12.D109.8232, ANT. This was even more favorable than the arrangement proposed back in February.

105. If the will was declared valid, the government's 28 percent share would be taken from a larger pool of money since Momo, the last holdout, would inherit nothing. And it was unquestionably in d'Erlanger's interest to have the will upheld.

106. "Avis" by Adriano Mari and Edoardo Maggiorani, February 3, 1882, SH.C105.D257.38, ANT.

107. Muhammad Khaznadar (prime minister since September 12, 1881) to Guttieres, February 13, 1882, SH.C105.D257.43, ANT.

108. Italian translation of a Greek notarial document written in Corfu, November 10, 1882, SH.C106.D266.17, ANT. The first archival trace of Momo in Corfu dates from the beginning of 1882. Caid Momo to Muhammad Khaznadar, January 30, 1882, SH.C104.D46.95, ANT. The only

part of the estate that d'Erlanger had not acquired was the 8 percent that Joseph would keep if the will was declared invalid.

109. Sentenza di Corte Civile di Livorno, February 4, 1882, SH.C107.D271, ANT. The heirs for whom Elmilik became the legal representative had forfeited the minor sums allotted them in Nissim's will in exchange for supporting the Tunisian government's original position—that is, that the will was invalid. It is not clear what motivated Elmilik to continue the legal battle, though; I found no evidence that he would profit materially from a decision one way or another. Given what we know about his personality, it is quite possible that Elmilik kept up the fight purely out of spite.

110. See http://www.treccani.it/enciclopedia/baldassarre-paoli_(Dizionario-Biografico).

111. Inghilleri also became a senator in 1889. See http://notes9.senato.it/Web/senregno.NSF/e56bbbe8d7e9c734c125703d002f2a0c/1b00efd2c67e30724125646f005c9254?OpenDocument.

112. "Le due nazioni più civili e più avanzate in opera di libertà" (Inghilleri, "Samama v. Samama," 388). He also noted that Roman law required perpetual allegiance, thus disagreeing with the court of cassation, which had ruled that Roman law was indeterminate when it came to the loss of citizenship.

113. Inghilleri cited the ruling of the Egyptian Mixed Court of Appeal concerning the case of Osman Khaleb Bey that Husayn had written to the Tunisian prime minister about (though erroneously citing the date of the ruling as November 22, 1880). Inghilleri, "Samama v. Samama," 389–90. Again, Inghilleri did not refer to the Ottoman Empire because Ottoman law was directly binding on Tunisia; according to Inghilleri, Tunisia was for all intents and purposes an "autonomous state." Rather, Inghilleri cited Ottoman law as further evidence of how Islamic law in general approached legal belonging.

114. "L'israelita tunisino non è tollerato; esso nei diritti e nei doveri è pareggiato agli altri sudditi che tutti, senza distinzione di religione, sono eguali dinanzi alla legge" (Inghilleri, "Samama v. Samama," 396).

115. Inghilleri further argued that Nissim showed no desire to expatriate himself; Nissim displayed an "animus redundi" (intention to return) to Tunisia; and the qā'id continued to think of himself as a Tunisian until the day he died. Inghilleri, "Samama v. Samama," 392.

116. "Vera nazionalità nel senso giuridico della parola" (Inghilleri, "Samama v. Samama," 395).

117. "Perchè il codice civile non fa distinzione tra la legge scritta od orale, codificata, o statutaria, o consuetudinaria, quando la sovranità di uno Stato agli statute, alle consuetudini, alle tradizioni attribuisce efficacia e forza di legge" (Inghilleri, "Samama v. Samama," 396).

118. Inghilleri did, however, cite Castelli twice, despite the fact that he disagreed with the professor. Inghilleri, "Samama v. Samama," 381, 401. Moreover, Inghilleri summarily dismissed Benamozegh's contention that the Jewish legal maxim "the law of the state is the law" (*dina de-malkhuta dina*) required that Italian law be applied to the estate; the judge noted that the Talmud only required Jews to apply the law of the state to certain matters, such as commerce or transactions with non-Jews. On the contrary, "è loro debito seguire la propria legge nelle relazioni giuridiche nate tra loro" (Inghilleri, "Samama v. Samama," 397). Inghilleri also ignored Benamozegh's long discussion of the principle *shuda de-dayana* (*sciudà de dajanè*), which he explained was the halakhic equivalent of "equity," allowing a judge to decide a case according to his own opinion if there was no way of resolving contradictory evidence. Benamozegh, *Delle*

fonti del diritto ebraico, 1:203–51. On this ruling, see Marglin, "Jewish Law across the Mediterranean."

119. *Shulḥan 'Arukh*, Ḥoshen Mishpat, 281:7; Baquis and Cassuto, *Note dopo la discussione*, 46–58. Benamozegh did cite this chapter, but quite briefly compared to the length at which Baquis and Cassuto cited it; this passage of the *Shulḥan 'Arukh* was of less relative importance for Benamozegh, who generally downplayed the significance of Caro's compendium. Benamozegh, *Delle fonti del diritto ebraico*, 2:66–69. Note that Inghilleri did not cite Baquis and Cassuto explicitly because memos produced by lawyers were not typically cited in rulings (though expert opinions, such as those of Benamozegh and Castelli, were).

120. The expert in question was Professor Fausto Lasinio, who determined that for 'Aziza and Nissim Jr.'s portion of the estate, Nissim used "la parola, *nàti* [*nu'ṭī*, from *'ṭw III*, to give], che veramente significa *do* o *dono* o *cedo*, e per gli altri due eredi la parola *nuassi* [*wṣw*, II or IV, to bequeath], lascio per testamento" (Inghilleri, "Samama v. Samama," 405).

121. Inghilleri, "Samama v. Samama," 407. Baquis and Cassuto similarly argued that a kinyan was unnecessary—just a "precautionary measure" (*cautela*), rather than an action necessary for the act to be valid. Baquis and Cassuto, *Note dopo la discussione*, 60. Although Benamozegh claimed that a kinyan was not necessary, he did so on the basis of different texts and for different reasons. Benamozegh, *Delle fonti del diritto ebraico*, 2:3–26.

122. "L'assunto, che la legislazione ebraica immutabile fosse, e immutata rimanesse, è contradetto dalla legge fatale della evoluzione storica che governa tutte le cose umane" (Inghilleri, "Samama v. Samama," 399). Baquis and Cassuto devoted many pages to proving that "law always changes, and is in a state of continual transformation" ("il diritto muta sempre, è in istato di continua trasformazione") (Baquis and Cassuto, *Note dopo la discussione*, 6). Benamozegh similarly argued for the ever-evolving nature of Jewish law, though given Inghilleri's general aversion to following Benamozegh's arguments, it seems safe to conclude that in this he was inspired more by Baquis and Cassuto.

123. Heussein, *Lettre au collège de la défense*, 35.

124. "Caid Nissim decide / La Francia abbandonare, / Nella sua mente vide / Ch'è bene ritornare / Nella bella Livorno / A cui lieto ritorno / Subito fa, poichè dice la fama / Che già di quà i suoi avi / A Tunisi n'andaro / E là da destri e bravi / E con successo raro, / Una grande ricchezza / Fecero con saviezza, / E la mantenner con rara prudenza" (Ascoli, *Gli ebrei venuti a Livorno*, 97). On Ascoli, see Funaro, "Massoneria e minoranze religiose," 394–96. I am immensely grateful to Liana Funaro for having sent me the relevant pages of this exceedingly rare book, about which I would have been entirely ignorant were it not for her.

125. "E nelle varie sedi / Di tribunali varj / Liti e contrasti amari" (Ascoli, *Gli ebrei venuti a Livorno*, 97).

126. "Talché son giá molti anni / Che dai redditi ingenti / Impinguan senz'affanni / Legali ed assistenti" (Ascoli, *Gli ebrei venuti a Livorno*, 97–98).

Chapter 10. Descendants (1883–1945)

1. Castelli, *Il diritto di testare*. Castelli also published a book on Jewish law, which might well have grown out of his research on the Shamama case. Castelli, *La legge del popolo ebreo*.

2. "La nostra coscienza e per il nostro decoro" (Castelli, *Osservazioni di David Castelli*, 96).

3. See esp. the dossier HR.H.432.1, BOA.

4. See, for example, Ottoman Ministry of Foreign Affairs, Chambre des conseillers légistes, October 18, 1883, HR.H.432.1.13, BOA; 'Aziza Ibn 'Ayyad to Marquis de Noailles, November 17, 1883, HR.H.432.1.53, BOA.

5. See, for example, ruling by the Cour d'appel de Paris, Ahmed Ben Aïad v. Nathan Sạmama, Joseph Samama, Aziza and Moïse Samama, and the bey of Tunis, May 2, 1882, SH.C105.D262.12, ANT.

6. The story of the Ibn 'Ayyad family awaits its own book. The National Archives of Tunisia holds dozens of dossiers relating to the Ibn 'Ayyads, particularly Mahmud, and the Başbakanlık Archive in Istanbul holds hundreds of documents related to Mahmud and his descendants.

7. On Hamida, 'Ali, and Hassuna's claims, see esp. Cruppi, *Conclusions*. On the courts in which they pursued the claims, see Ottoman Ministry of Foreign Affairs, Chambre des conseillers légistes, October 18, 1883, HR.H.432.1.13, BOA. On the nizamiye courts, see Rubin, *Ottoman Nizamiye Courts*.

8. Ambassade de France près la Porte Ottomane to Assim Pacha, August 25, 1881, HR.H.432.1.12, BOA.

9. Ottoman Ministry of Foreign Affairs, Chambre des conseillers légistes, October 18, 1883, HR.H.432.1.13, BOA.

10. Ambassade de France près la Porte Ottomane to Assim Pacha, August 25, 1881, HR.H.432.1.12, BOA.

11. Marquis de Noailles to Aarifi Pacha, November 20, 1883, HR.H.432.1.52, BOA.

12. "Tunisien de naissance, admis à domicile en France par décret du 18 janvier 1881, domicilié à Paris, 49 rue Blanche" (Tahir Ibn 'Ayyad to Marquis de Noailles, September 18, 1882, HR.H.432.1.29, BOA).

13. On Tunisians in the Ottoman heartlands, see Ben Ismail, "Sovereignty across Empires," 226–33. Mahmud Ibn 'Ayyad was, needless to say, an exception; the Ottomans considered him to be a French national. Ben Ismail, "Sovereignty across Empires," 229–30. On the Ottoman nationality law, see Hanley, "What Ottoman Nationality Was and Was Not." Moreover, the fact that the case was pending before a French court had no impact on its denouement in Istanbul since Ottoman judges did not recognize the authority of a foreign judicial institution. Ottoman Ministry of Foreign Affairs, Chambre des conseillers légistes, October 18, 1883, HR.H.432.1.13, BOA.

14. Cruppi, *Conclusions*, 38.

15. Ottoman Ministry of Foreign Affairs, Note Verbale à l'ambassade de France, September 11, 1900, HR.H.139.9.5, BOA.

16. La Borde (directeur des affaires civile et du Sceau au Ministère de la Justice Français) to Georges Barbier (lawyer in Paris), August 7, 1900, HR.H.139.9.9, BOA.

17. Ben-Aïad, *Die türkische Frau*. Hayriye became a vocal critic of Sultan Abdulhamid and his absolutist rule. See, for example, "The Sultan's Spy System: A Woman's View from the Inside," *Los Angeles Times*, April 20, 1902, part 4, 1. On Hayriye generally, see "The Newsletter: London Week by Week," *Sphere*, August 31, 1901, 238; Van Os, "Ottoman Muslim and Turkish Women," 464. See also Baktıaya, "Hayriye Hanım"; Baktıaya, *Bir Osmanlı Kadınının Feminizm Macerası*.

18. Soysal, "Yüzyıl Sonlarında Türk Ulusal Kütüphanesi'ni Kurma Girişimi," 12; Flemming, "Romantic Emigrants," 190–91. The Herzl quote is from *Theodor Herzl Tagebüche 1895–1904, III* (Berlin 1923), 571, cited in Flemming, "Romantic Emigrants," 201.

19. This he did in his capacity as the representative of some distant relatives who had been allotted small sums in Nissim's will and years ago had agreed to cede their rights to the estate in exchange for taking the Tunisian government's side in the lawsuit. Corte di appello di Firenze, November 14, 1883, SH.C107.D271.10, ANT. These heirs included Aron Hai and Mordekhai Bellais, Esther Taib, and Israel Shamama.

20. Elmilik, *Arbitrage Léon Elmilik contre le gouvernement tunisien*, 42. On Elmilik's lawsuits against Husayn, see also Oualdi, *A Slave between Empires*, 122–23.

21. "Ceci parait invraisemblable quand on songe que Elmilik est français!" (Pontois, *Jugement*, 10). See also Elmilik, *Affaire Heussein et Elmilik*, 29–30.

22. "La réputation triste de cet homme est bien notoire à Tunis comme à Livourne . . . pendant que le noble sang français coulait sur le sol de la Tunisie, cet infâme a eu la lâcheté d'écrire des lettres en maudissant la République française et en priant Dieu pour sa ruine" (Eugène Rosa to Eugène Regnault, November 19, 1886, SH.C104.D254.63, ANT). In 1886, Elmilik was named as one of the seven Jewish notables charged with distributing the 150,000 francs that Nissim had bequeathed to the community of Tunis. But Eugène Cohen Rosa (also known as Salomon) objected to Elmilik's appointment, denouncing him as disloyal. Rosa had also worked for Husayn in Livorno, though like Elmilik he had a falling out with the general and ended up suing him for unpaid wages. Oualdi, *A Slave between Empires*, 79–80, 122–23.

23. Elmilik to Husayn, April 21, 1881, cited in Gueydan and Santillana, *Arbitrage*, 105.

24. "Le caïd Nissim avait besoin quelquefois, dans l'intérêt de ses affaires, d'être déclaré Tunisien, et, par conséquent, être jugé par les lois tunisiennes, et, dans d'autres cas, les lois italiennes lui étant encore nécessaires, il invoquait alors sa qualité de citoyen italien" (Elmelich, *Observations*, 19)

25. Elmelich, *Observations*, 20.

26. On the settlement, see contract between David b. Liah Elmelik and Sidi Mohamed El Aziz Benattar, n.d., SH.C108.D275.26, ANT. On the death of Mas'ud Felix in 1901, see the tombstone in the Borgel Cemetery in Tunis (visited June 15, 2021). Elmilik had remarried a woman named Rachel, daughter of Mas'ud Saadoun; Felix must have been born around 1886 (he is mentioned as still being a minor at his father's death).

27. For an account of the dispute over Husayn's nationality, see Oualdi, *A Slave between Empires*, chap. 4.

28. Eram (Ottoman consul in Livorno) to Said Pacha (Ottoman minister of foreign affairs in Istanbul), July 2, 1887, HR.H.171/13.17, BOA. Oualdi incorrectly reads de Laigne as "de Laigue." See, for example, Despagnet, *La diplomatie*, 244.

29. "Sur réquisition formelle du Sieur Elmelik, tunisien, habitant Livourne et créancier de somme considérable" (de Laigne to V. Musurus Ghikis, n.d. [although before July 2, 1887], HR.H.171/13.20, BOA).

30. De Laigne to V. Musurus Ghikis, n.d. [although before July 2, 1887], HR.H.171/13.20, BOA; V. Musurus Ghikis to de Laigne, July 2, 1887, HR.H.171/13.20, BOA. Ghikis was a Phanariot, elite Greek Orthodox Christians who were overrepresented among the ranks of Ottoman diplomatic posts; he was the grandson of Stephanos Vogorides. For more on Vogorides, see Philliou, *Biography of an Empire*. I am grateful to Christine Philliou for this biographical information on Ghikis.

31. "Les Agents diplomatiques et consulaires de la France en pays étrangers seront chargés de la protection des intérêts tunisiens et des nationaux de la Régence" (Article 6, http://mjp.univ-perp.fr/constit/tn1881.htm).

32. Photiades Pacha to Said Pacha, July 5, 1887, HR.H.171/13.2, BOA. In all of these arguments, de Laigne was supported by his boss, Émile Flourens, the minister of foreign affairs in Paris.

33. "Le défunt avait perdu sa nationalité en prenant du service dans l'armée du Bey de Tunis" (de Laigne to V. Musurus Ghikis, n.d. [although before July 2, 1887], HR.H.171/13.20, BOA).

34. Even before the ratification of the treaty, Laurent-Charles Féraud, the French consul general in Tripoli (Libya), informed the local Ottoman governor that henceforth, Tunisians in that Ottoman province would be considered French protégés; the governor's protests against this infringement on the sultan's sovereignty were mostly ignored. See Çaycı, *La question tunisienne et la politique ottomane*, 78–80.

35. Ben Ismail, "Sovereignty across Empires," chap. 5. Only in the last days of 1913 did the Sublime Porte sign an accord with France whereby Tunisians in the Ottoman Empire would be considered French protégés. Çaycı, *La question tunisienne et la politique ottomane*, 163–64. The same went for Moroccans (Morocco became a French protectorate in 1912). Ottoman authorities officially recognized Algerians as French protégés in 1910.

36. Said Pacha to Photiades Pacha, July 6, 1887, HR.H.171/13.1, BOA.

37. Said Pacha to Essad Pacha, July 6, 1887, HR.H.171/13.4, BOA; Rapport de la Chambre des Conseillers Légistes de la Ministère des Affaires Etrangères de la Sublime Porte, September 12, 1887, HR.H.171/13.24, BOA.

38. At a salary of five thousand piasters per month. Photiades Pacha to Said Pacha, July 6, 1887, HR.H.171/13.19, BOA; "Procès Verbal," signed by de Laigne and Musurus-Guikès, August 21, 1887, HR.H.171/13.29, BOA.

39. "Une copie de lettre du Ministère des Affaires Etrangères de 'Prusse' annonçant à Husseïn Pacha que, d'après les informations fournies par l'Agent d'Allemagne à Tunis, sa naturalisation en Prusse serait valable par tout ailleurs qu'en Tunisie." The Ottoman passport was issued after his appointment to the Council of State to allow his travel to Istanbul (which he never undertook because of health problems). "Procès Verbal," signed by de Laigne and Musurus-Guikès, August 21, 1887, HR.H.171/13.29, BOA.

40. Khayraddin requested that as a manumitted slave of the bey of Tunis, Husayn's estate be allowed to revert to his former master, as stipulated in the shari'a. Photiades Pacha to Said Pacha, September 24, 1887, HR.H.171/13.33, BOA; Oualdi, *A Slave between Empires*, 97.

41. Said Pacha to Photiades Pacha, November 5, 1887, HR.H.171/13.34, BOA; Oualdi, *A Slave between Empires*, 97–102.

42. Oualdi, *A Slave between Empires*, 86.

43. Stein, *Extraterritorial Dreams*, 118–26.

44. Nissim Jr. was born in La Goulette on June 2, 1864, and Qā'id Nissim boarded a steamship bound for Cagliari on June 7. Meyan, *Annuaire des diplômés 1890*, 477; Sadiq bey to Pinna, 2 Muḥarram 1281, SH.C100.D228.1, ANT.

45. Meyan, *Annuaire des diplômés 1890*, 477; Derobert-Ratel, "La faculté de droit d'Aix-en-Provence," 88.

46. "La capacité du disposant doit se trouver réglée . . . d'après l'état moral, intellectuel, politique du pays auquel appartient le testateur"(Samama, *De l'indivision*, 202). The first section of the thesis concerned the Roman law of indivision—the sharing in property rights of an estate.

47. "De nos jours, où l'on change souvent de résidence. . . . Nous préférons adopter la théorie moderne d'après laquelle il faut appliquer en cette matière la loi nationale" (Samama, *De l'indivision*, 212–13).

48. "O et praesidium et dulce decus meum" (Horace, Odes, 1.1, referring to the ancestors of Maecenas). Nissim Jr. also cited a resolution of the institute of international law (which he called the "Institut de droit international privé")—passed at its meeting in Oxford in 1880—to recognize the nationality principle. Samama, *De l'indivision*, 213–14.

49. Ruling by the Tribunal de Tunis, December 21, 1889, SH.C101.D231.162, ANT; *Indicateur marseillais*, 457.

50. "Gazette des tribunaux," *Le Figaro*, March 8, 1918, 2; Boulu, "Les Caïds Scemama," 9–10.

51. He was vice president at some point before 1917. *Paris-Midi*, March 29, 1917, 2.

52. *Le Figaro*, June 28, 1909, 2.

53. "La qualité de citoyens français à des masses non encore bien pénétrées de nos idées modernes" (Samama, "De la naturalisation française," 359).

54. Samama, "De la naturalisation française," 361. On the centrality of polygamy to debates about Algerian Jews' potential for assimilation, see Schreier, *Arabs of the Jewish Faith*, chap. 5; Surkis, *Sex, Law, and Sovereignty*, 75–82.

55. Derobert-Ratel, "La faculté de droit d'Aix-en-Provence," 95–96; Allagui, "L'état colonial et les juifs de Tunisie," 36–37.

56. "Qui n'ont Presque plus rien de commun avec les véritables indigènes, ni dans les idées ni dans les moeurs. . . . Nul ne doit être, d'ailleurs, forcé de garder une nationalité qui ne lui convient pas" (Samama, "De la naturalisation française," 360). Moreover, he argued, if France refused these elite Jews its citizenship, they would simply turn elsewhere; Spain, Italy, Switzerland, and a host of other nations would be more than happy to accept them, thus ultimately harming French sovereignty.

57. Boulu, "Recherches sur les Scemama ou Samama de Tunis," 40.

58. Samama, *Contributo allo studio della doppia cittadinanza*, iii, 72. On this congress, see Gabbacia, Hoerder, and Walaszek, "Emigration and Nation Building," 73–74. On Italian emigration and citizenship, see also Choate, *Emigrant Nation*, 204–7. On concerns about emigration in general, see Douki, "The Liberal Italian State."

59. "Vous ne pouvez pas exiger de l'étranger qu'il renonce à son lien le plus sacré, celui de sa nationalité" ("Bulletin de la société internationale pour l'étude des questions d'assistance, séance du 25 octobre 1911," *La Revue philanthropique* 15, no. 30 (1911): 85).

60. Following the 1908 congress in Rome, Vittorio Scialoia, Italian minister of justice, requested that Nissim Jr. write a study of "dual citizenship," following up on a presentation by Giulio Cesare Buzzati, a professor of international law at the Università di Pavia. Samama, *Contributo allo studio della doppia cittadinanza*, iii–iv. But Nissim Jr.'s arguments were squarely opposed to the consensus among jurists. Alfred Boll argues that there was a general distaste for dual nationality before the turn of the century and that in the early twentieth century most jurists agreed "that multiple nationality was undesirable" (Boll, *Multiple Nationality*,

192). Spain was an exception in allowing dual nationality with its former colonies in Latin America. Boll, *Multiple Nationality*, 187–90. Nonetheless, many jurists on both sides of the Atlantic recognized that dual nationality was at times the reality. See, for example, *Lynch v. Clarke*, in which the US Supreme Court recognized the existence of "double allegiance, which exists in the tens of thousands of instances of our naturalized citizens, who were once subjects of the crown of Great Britain. We recognize its existence, because we adopt them as citizens, with full knowledge that by the law of their native country, they never can put off the allegiance which they owe to its government" (Lynch v. Clarke, 1 Sand. Ch. 583 U.S. 659 [1844]). See also Cockburn, *Nationality*, 183–98. I am grateful to Nathan Perl-Rosenthal for these last two references.

61. "Ora a tutti è dato viaggiare, e la maggior parte degli emigrati nutre Speranza di ritornare un giorno, dopo fatto fortuna, in patria . . . [sono] profondamente italiano di sentimento" (Samama, *Contributo allo studio della doppia cittadinanza*, 10). Moreover, whether jurists liked it or not, thousands of emigrants had dual citizenship de facto. Since most states in the Americas awarded citizenship based on jus soli, the children of Italians born in Brazil, Argentina, Mexico, and the United States were considered citizens of their adopted homes. But Italian law recognized jus sanguinis, which meant that Italy considered these children to be Italian citizens. Samama, *Contributo allo studio della doppia cittadinanza*, 16–17.

62. Green, "The Politics of Exit," 277–78; Choate, *Emigrant Nation*, 207.

63. Husayn, "Al-qusṭās," 239.

64. HR.HK.380/11 (Antoine Zelitz), BOA; HR.HK.378/11 (Sabino Cosulich), BOA; HR.HK.211/4 (Nicho Pavlovich), BOA; HR.HK.318/3 (Joseph Simon Alacaci), BOA; *Osman Khaleb Bey c. Gouvernment Egyptién*, April 10, 1876, in *Jurisprudence des tribnuax de la réforme en Egypte*, 69–70.

65. Emilie née Scemama de Gialluly demanded sixty-three thousand francs per year in maintenance; the court awarded her thirty thousand (reduced to fifteen thousand during wartime). "Gazette des tribunaux," *Le Figaro*, March 8, 1918, 2.

66. *Le Figaro*, June 4, 1912, 7; *Le Matin*, August 26, 1919, 2.

67. Joseph's request was refused on August 19, 1879. Inghilleri, "Samama v. Samama 1883," 391.

68. Scipione Becchini, *Sentenza 2–5 maggio 1894*, 4–6.

69. Joseph's wife was Daya Gozlan; her granddaughter Daya was born in 1886.

70. Alberto died on May 21, 1889. Becchini, *Sentenza 2–5 maggio 1894*, 6.

71. Becchini, *Sentenza 2–5 maggio 1894*, 7–8.

72. "Con dichiarazione che esso è il testo autentico della legge Talmudica" (Becchini, *Sentenza 2–5 maggio 1894*, 10).

73. Becchini, *Sentenza 2–5 maggio 1894*, 14–15. Joseph turned to additional familiar faces from the Shamama lawsuit, hiring Dario Cassuto and Isacco Rignano—both lawyers who had worked for ʿAziza and Moses in their attempts to have the will upheld. See Rignano, *Parere dell'avv. Isacco Rignano.*

74. "È uno fra i tanti libri di letteratura rabbinica" (Becchini, *Sentenza 2–5 maggio 1894*, 11).

75. Becchini, *Sentenza 2–5 maggio 1894*, 33–35.

76. Caldwell, "The Citizen and the Republic," 54; Arendt, *The Origins of Totalitarianism*, 280.

77. The exception is Algerian Jews, whose French citizenship was revoked in 1940. Schroeter, "Between Metropole and French North Africa."

78. Nissim Jr. died in Le Cannet on August 14, 1945. I am grateful to Gilles Boulu for this information.

79. These also included two still lifes by Jacques Callot, a landscape by Camille Corot, and a bronze sculpture of a lion by Antoine Barye. Commandement en chef français en Allemagne, service des réparations et restitutions, bureau central des restitutions, Répertoire des biens spoliés en France durant la guerre 1939–1945, troisième supplément aux tomes II, III, IV, et VII: objets d'art et livres rares.

80. Nathan Donat enlisted in the French army's medical corps and died in Marrakesh in 1917 of an "illness contracted during service." See http://www.agam-06.com/actes2/acte_bans.php?xid=5245&xct=6450..

81. Two to three thousand Jews are reported to have abandoned Corfu after the spring of 1891. Gekas, "The Port Jews of Corfu," 186–88.

82. AM-34000 Montpellier/D—10 février 1899 acte n°215. I am grateful to Gilles Boulu for sharing this document with me.

83. See https://www.ushmm.org/online/hsv/person_view.php?PersonId=4322650. See also http://niceoccupation.free.fr/arrestations-et-deportations-liste-de-2876-noms.html.

84. Ryan, *The Holocaust and the Jews of Marseille*, 184; Lalloum, "Persécutions et déportations," 18.

85. Ryan, *The Holocaust and the Jews of Marseille*, chap. 4.

86. Consolato Generale d'Italia in Tunis to Prefetto di Livorno, March 25, 1930, Ministero dell'interno, direzione generale pubblica sicurezza, divisione affari generali e riservati, Casellario Politico Centrale, Busta 4556, "Salvatore Semama," ACS.

87. Prefetto di Livorno to Consul General of Italy in Tunisia, February 26, 1930, Ministero dell'interno, direzione generale pubblica sicurezza, divisione affari generali e riservati, Casellario Politico Centrale, Busta 4556, "Salvatore Semama," ACS.

88. "Ed associandosi alle imprese di truffatori e lestofanti . . . inducendoli ad atti di libidine sulla sua persona" (Prefettura di Milano to Ministero dell'Interno, August 27, 1936, direzione generale della Pubblica Sicurezza, Ministero Interno, P.S., Cat. A1, Semana Carlo di Giuseppe, n. Livorno 19.12.1883, PS A1–1936-B45, ACS).

89. Maria [*sic*] Semama to Mussolini, April 7, 1943, Segreteria particolare del duce, carteggio ordinario, f. 553.878, Maria Samama, vedova Fiorentini, Livorno, ACS. Alfonso died in 1918.

90. Prefettura di Livorno to Segretaria particolare del Duce, May 22, 1943, Segreteria particolare del duce, carteggio ordinario, f. 553.878, Maria Samama, vedova Fiorentini, Livorno, ACS.

91. He was born on September 10, 1874. Prefettura di Livorno to Ministero dell'Interno, June 14, 1940, Ministero dell'interno, direzione generale pubblica sicurezza, divisione affari generali e riservati, ufficio internati, A4 bis, internati stranieri e spionaggio, 1940–45, Busta 326, Samama Elia fu Giuseppe, ACS.

92. Arolsen Archives, Registrations and Files of Displaced Persons, Children and Missing Persons, Relief Programs of Various Organizations, International Refugee Organization "Care and Maintenance" Program, Application for Assistance (CM/1), ITS no. S-1753, https://collections.arolsen-archives.org/en/archive/80493459/?p=1&doc_id=80493460.

93. Questura di Firenze to Prefettura di Firenze, December 26, 1944, Ministero dell'interno, direzione generale pubblica sicurezza, divisione servizi informativie e speciali, SIS, 1946–9, Sezione prima, internati, categoria A5G/32, Busta 132, Semama, Giuseppe, ACS.

94. Sarfatti, "Italy's Fascist Jews." See also other articles in this special issue of *Quest*.

95. Prefettura di Livorno to Ministero dell'Interno, August 22, 1940, Ministero dell'interno, direzione generale pubblica sicurezza, divisione affari generali e riservati, ufficio internati, A4 bis, internati stranieri e spionaggio, 1940–45, Busta 326, Samama Elia fu Giuseppe, ACS.

96. "Oggetto: Semama Elia, fu Giuseppe, e fu Gozlan Daya, nato a Livorno il 10/9/1874, ivi residente via Serristori no. 12 p[iano] 2, suddito francese" (Prefettura di Livorno to Ministero dell'Interno, June 14, 1940, Ministero dell'interno, direzione generale pubblica sicurezza, divisione affari generali e riservati, ufficio internati, A4 bis, internati stranieri e spionaggio, 1940–45, Busta 326, Samama Elia fu Giuseppe, ACS).

97. "È ritenuto capace di svolgere attività disfattista . . . ove potrebbe essere più agevolmente sorvegliato" (Prefettura di Livorno to Ministero dell'Interno, June 14, 1940, Ministero dell'interno, direzione generale pubblica sicurezza, divisione affari generali e riservati, ufficio internati, A4 bis, internati stranieri e spionaggio, 1940–45, Busta 326, Samama Elia fu Giuseppe, ACS).

98. "Sento che la mia vita è corta, anzi cortissima; che da un momento al altro posso morire" (Elia Semama to Ministero degli Interni, July 8, 1940, Ministero dell'interno, direzione generale pubblica sicurezza, divisione affari generali e riservati, ufficio internati, A4 bis, internati stranieri e spionaggio, 1940–45, Busta 326, Samama Elia fu Giuseppe, ACS).

99. "Rimaste patriottica" (Elia Semama to Ministero degli Interni, August 9, 1940, Ministero dell'interno, direzione generale pubblica sicurezza, divisione affari generali e riservati, ufficio internati, A4 bis, internati stranieri e spionaggio, 1940–45, Busta 326, Samama Elia fu Giuseppe, ACS). On petitions for exemption from the racial laws in France, which often employed similar language about patriotism, see Asquer, "Rivendicare l'appartenenza."

100. "Poi lui fù mandato via perchè è suddito Tunisino, ma Eccelenza lui è puro Italiano fino dalla nascita essendo nato a Livorno ed avendo ciò figlio vecchio fascista e squadista del 1920 con Diploma della Marcia su Roma. . . . Ed è per ciò che un uomo vecchio come lui sia considerate cittadino francese quando puficamente [?] Tunisino erano i suoi vecchi genitori egli fecero prendere la sua sudditanza perché [*sic*] è sempre stato ammalato. Ma lui è puro Italiano" (Giuseppe Semama to Ministero degli Interni, October 21, 1940, Ministero dell'interno, direzione generale pubblica sicurezza, divisione affari generali e riservati, ufficio internati, A4 bis, internati stranieri e spionaggio, 1940–45, Busta 326, Samama Elia fu Giuseppe, ACS).

101. "Lontano da noi figli ed in una montagna che cì fà assai freddo" (Giuseppe Semama to Ministero degli Interni, October 21, 1940, Ministero dell'interno, direzione generale pubblica sicurezza, divisione affari generali e riservati, ufficio internati, A4 bis, internati stranieri e spionaggio, 1940–45, Busta 326, Samama Elia fu Giuseppe, ACS).

102. Elia's last letter from Chiaromonte was dated January 26, 1941.

103. See, for example, Elia Semama to Ministro degli Interni, September 5, 1940, Ministero dell'interno, direzione generale pubblica sicurezza, divisione affari generali e riservati, ufficio internati, A4 bis, internati stranieri e spionaggio, 1940–45, Busta 326, Samama Elia fu Giuseppe, ACS.

104. Though these visits were approved only after applying to the prefecture of Livorno and only for short periods. See, for example, Questura di Livorno to Ministero dell'Interno, December 7, 1941, Ministero dell'interno, direzione generale pubblica sicurezza, divisione affari generali e riservati, ufficio internati, A4 bis, internati stranieri e spionaggio, 1940–45, Busta 326, Samama

Elia fu Giuseppe, ACS; Prefettura di Livorno to Ministero dell'Interno, August 17, 1942, Ministero dell'interno, direzione generale pubblica sicurezza, divisione affari generali e riservati, ufficio internati, A4 bis, internati stranieri e spionaggio, 1940–45, Busta 326, Samama Elia fu Giuseppe, ACS; Prefettura di Livorno to Ministero dell'Interno, March 15, 1943, Ministero dell'interno, direzione generale pubblica sicurezza, divisione affari generali e riservati, ufficio internati, A4 bis, internati stranieri e spionaggio, 1940–45, Busta 326, Samama Elia fu Giuseppe, ACS.

105. Elia Semama to Ministero dell'Interno, March 8, 1943, Ministero dell'interno, direzione generale pubblica sicurezza, divisione affari generali e riservati, ufficio internati, A4 bis, internati stranieri e spionaggio, 1940–45, Busta 326, Samama Elia fu Giuseppe, ACS.

106. Guardia nazionale repubblicana to Questura di Livorno, March 6, 1944, Ministero dell'interno, direzione generale pubblica sicurezza, divisione servizi informativi e speciali, SIS, 1946–49, Sezione prima, internati, categoria A5G/32, Busta 132, Semama, Giuseppe, ACS.

107. Ottolenghi had emigrated to Palestine. See https://www.bathontheriver.it/it/it/storie/18735-villa-la-selva-un-lager-dell-italia-fascista-a-bagno-a-ripoli.html.

108. Questura di Firenze to Questura di Livorno, March 10, 1944, Ministero dell'interno, direzione generale pubblica sicurezza, divisione servizi informativi e speciali, SIS, 1946–49, Sezione prima, internati, categoria A5G/32, Busta 132, Semama, Giuseppe, ACS. On Italian policies concerning the classification of children of mixed marriages as Aryan or Jewish, see De Grand, *Fascist Italy*, 73.

109. Questura di Firenze to Prefettura di Firenze, December 26, 1944, Ministero dell'interno, direzione generale pubblica sicurezza, divisione servizi informativi e speciali, SIS, 1946–49, Sezione prima, internati, categoria A5G/32, Busta 132, Semama, Giuseppe, ACS.

110. He is listed as living in Livorno on December 27, 1945; it is quite possible he left Sassetta before then, however. Arolsen Archives, Registrations and Files of Displaced Persons, Children and Missing Persons, Relief Programs of Various Organizations, International Refugee Organization "Care and Maintenance" Program, Application for Assistance (CM/1), ITS no. S-1753, https://collections.arolsen-archives.org/en/archive/80493459/?p=1&doc_id=80493460.

111. Arendt, "The Rights of Man," 30.

112. See https://www.un.org/en/universal-declaration-human-rights/. On the deliberations over Article 15 and the committee's hope that it would address the problem of statelessness, see Morsink, *The Universal Declaration of Human Rights*, 80–83.

113. Shachar, *The Birthright Lottery*.

114. On the death toll on the southern border of the United States, see James Verini, "How U.S. Policy Has Turned the Sonoran Desert into a Graveyard for Migrants," *New York Times Magazine,* August 18, 2020.

Epilogue. Legal Belonging, Past and Present

1. On territorialization, see Maier, "Consigning the Twentieth Century to History"; Marglin, "Extraterritoriality and Legal Belonging." On Irish immigrants to the United States, see Salyer, *Under the Starry Flag*. On the Franco-American case, see Green, *The Limits of Transnationalism*, chap. 1. On Baghdadi Jews in China, see Stein, "Protected Persons?"

2. Henri Pirenne, the scholar usually considered the founder of Mediterranean studies, saw the sea as a dividing line between Christendom and the Islamic world. Pirenne, *Mahomet et*

Charlemagne. Fernand Braudel (*The Mediterranean*, 1:14), on the other hand, argued for the "unity and coherence of the Mediterranean region." More recently, Peregrine Horden and Nicholas Purcell have presented a theory of the Mediterranean based on connectivity across diverse microregions. Horden and Purcell, *The Corrupting Sea*. On the Islamic world as the ultimate Other for Europeans, see Said, *Orientalism*. On Jews as the ultimate Other in Christianity, see Nirenberg, *Anti-Judaism*.

3. Since the second half of the twentieth century, dual citizenship has become increasingly common. Yet even though dual citizens might have stripes—red and blue for those with both Tunisian and French nationality—the colors do not fade or mix. One has French nationality or one lacks it. The possibility of dual nationality does not erase the idea of citizenship as a binary.

4. I admit I have little sympathy for the Whiggish approach to legal history, though I recognize it serves a certain purpose in the realm of politics and activism.

5. Shachar, *The Birthright Lottery*.

6. Elmelich, *Observations*, 19.

7. Sarah Abrevaya Stein makes this argument regarding Ottoman Jews in the decades following the collapse of the Empire. Stein, *Extraterritorial Dreams*.

8. There are too many examples of alienation or fragmentation in literature to cite all of them. The works that immediately come to my mind include James Joyce's *Ulysses*, Fyodor Dostoyevsky's *Crime and Punishment*, and Leo Tolstoy's *Anna Karenina*.

9. Slezkine, *The Jewish Century*, 1.

10. See, for example, Cohen and Stein, *Sephardi Lives*, 120–21; Sharkey, *A History of Muslims, Christians, and Jews*, 142–53.

11. McDougall, "Modernity in 'Antique Lands,'" 15.

12. On nationalism and religious diversity in the twentieth-century Middle East and North Africa, see, for example, Beinin, *The Dispersion of Egyptian Jewry*; Bashkin, *New Babylonians*; Boum, *Memories of Absence*; Wyrtzen, *Making Morocco*; Heckman, *The Sultan's Communists*.

13. Conversation with Susan Gilson Miller, October 2016.

14. See esp. Lehmann, *Emissaries*.

15. Marshall, "Citizenship and Social Class."

Afterword. Writing Nissim Shamama

1. Moati, *Les belles de Tunis*.

2. Moati noted that different branches of the Shamama family had adopted distinct orthographies.

3. "On a toujours eu un peu honte . . . il est parti avec toute la caisse du gouvernement" (interview with Nine Moati, November 13, 2017).

4. The few exceptions were scholars interested in the Shamama case as a way to study the history of Tunisian nationality, including Fatma Ben Slimane and M'hamed Oualdi.

5. Interview with Jacob Lellouche, La Goulette, Tunis, July 30, 2015. On the restaurant, which Lellouche named Mamie Lily in honor of his mother (and in true Mediterranean fashion), and which has since closed, see https://www.nouvelobs.com/rue89/rue89-tunisie-libre/20120401.RUE4905/jacob-lellouche-tunisien-arabo-andalou-et-juif.html. On Lellouche's candidacy,

which failed, see https://identitejuive.com/elections-en-tunisie-un-unique-candidat-juif-gilles-jacob-lellouche/.

6. Lepore, "Historians Who Love Too Much."

7. Ibn Diyaf, *Itḥāf*, 5:189–90. See also chapter 3.

8. On Husayn's antisemitic views, see Oualdi, *A Slave between Empires*, 38–40.

9. "*Fa-ʿaraḍa ʿalayhi miʾat alfin bi-ʿasharati ālāfin. Fa-qultu lahu: hādhā al-mablaghu kathīrun, lā tadfaʿu ilā khamsata ālāf!*" (Husayn to Khayraddin, 2 Jumādā I 1286 / August 10, 1869, in Husayn, *Rasāʾil*, 1:99). On Khayraddin's appointment to the International Financial Commission, see van Krieken, *Khayr al-Dîn*, 150–51.

10. Moreover, an anonymous treatise written in 1877 explains that the Tunisian government did not realize that Nissim owed twenty million francs until after his death. Mzali and Pignon, *Kheredine*, 169.

11. "Sidi Mustapha laissa voir, pour l'or et les richesses, une passion qui n'a fait que grandir sans avoir jamais pu être assouvie et à la satisfaction de laquelle il a fini par sacrifier la fortune du pays, sa population elle-même et jusqu'à la sécurité du souverain auquel il doit tout" (MD, Tunisie 12, May 19, 1872, Note de Victor Villet, 1–2, MAE Courneuve).

12. For instance, Nissim bought the right to export oil from Sousse. He then claimed that there was no oil in Sousse to export, but in Sfax, Mahdia, Monastir, and Tunis there was. His right to export the oil from Sousse was replaced with the rights to export oil from these four other cities—at no extra charge and without having to give up the rights to the oil from Sousse. Naturally, Nissim then found oil in Sousse to export—just as he exported oil from the other ports, and Khaznadar conveniently "forgot" to ask him to give up the rights he had not paid for. Note de Victor Villet, 15–18, May 19, 1872, MD, Tunisie 12, MAE Courneuve.

13. Note de Victor Villet, 14, 18, May 19, 1872, MD, Tunisie 12, MAE Courneuve.

14. Later in life, Husayn became enamored with European antisemitic ideas and sent a copy of Edouard Drumont's *La France juive* to Khayraddin. Oualdi, *A Slave between Empires*, 39–40.

15. "Âme damnée" (anonymous, *Tunis en France*, 34–35); "ces allemands mal francisés" (anonymous, *Tunis en France*, 110).

16. "L'âme de tous les complots qui se tramaient contre l'argent du Bey" (anonymous, *Tunis en France*, 94).

17. "Nabab gorgé du fruit des malheurs de la patrie" (anonymous, *Tunis en France*, 93); "diable" (anonymous, *Tunis en France*, 93, 99).

18. "Où il avait été très-pauvre dans son enfance et dans sa jeunesse, et se trouvait dans l'imminence d'une faillite à la fin de l'année 1854" (anonymous, *Tunis en France*, 99).

19. Anonymous, *Tunis en France*, 184. The book always uses *juif* to refer to Jews, never the more polite *israélite*.

20. "N'étaient autre chose qu'une immense escroquerie organisée au bénéfice d'une association secrète" (anonymous, *Tunis en France*, 57).

21. Ganiage, *Les origines*. On Ganiage, see Martin, "Jean Ganiage 1923–2012."

22. "Nombreux étaient les aventuriers de la finance qui venaient offrir leurs services aux gouvernements locaux. C'étaient des Juifs allemands pour la plupart" (Ganiage, *Les origines*, 175).

23. "Sans l'appui de Khérédine, Villet n'aurait sans doute pu triompher de la mauvaise volonté du gouvernement tunisien, des intrigues du Khaznadar et des courtiers juifs du Comité du Contrôle" (Ganiage, *Les origines*, 310).

24. "Appartenait désormais aux Juifs livournais" (Ganiage, *Les origines*, 400).

25. As far as I can tell, Ganiage never cites *Tunis en France*. His main sources for this period are Villet's reports as well as correspondence among French diplomats stationed in Tunisia and occasionally the Ottoman Empire.

26. Ganiage is cited concerning Nissim with particular frequency, for the most part uncritically. See, for example, van Krieken, *Khayr al-Dîn*, 26; Jamoussi, *Juifs et chrétiens en Tunisie*, 282–83; Haruvi, "Ha-elitah ha-toranit," 175. Azzedine Guellouz, Abdelkader Masmoudi, and Mongi Smida do not cite their sources, but their account of Nissim hews closely to that of Ganiage. Guellouz, Masmoudi, and Smida, *Histoire générale de la Tunisie*, 406. The same goes for Avrahami, *Pinkas ha-Kehilah*, 24. A few Tunisian historians have conducted extensive research on Nissim in the Tunisian National Archives. Abdelhamid Larguèche and M'hamed Oualdi both cite Ganiage, though with a more nuanced approach to the story. Larguèche, *Les ombres de la ville*, 369–70; Oualdi, *A Slave between Empires*, 70–73. Fatma Ben Slimane does not cite Ganiage. Ben Slimane, "Définir ce qu'est être Tunisien." Ridha Ben Rajeb generally avoids citing Ganiage except to correct him. See, for example, Ben Rajeb, *Yahūd al-bilāṭ*, 486. For a critique of Ganiage unrelated to the question of antisemitism, see Brown, *The Tunisia of Ahmed Bey*, 389–90. For an example of a nonacademic interpretation of Nissim's role in the downfall of Tunisia, see https://tunisiastrategicreport.wordpress.com/2018/01/14/history-repeats-itself-in-post-revolution-tunisia-looting-and-destroying-the-country-after-the-revolution-of-2011-was-inspired-from-the-19-century-tunisian-beys-regimes/.

27. On the impact of European antisemitism on Jewish-Muslim relations, see esp. Cohen, "Modern Myths of Muslim Anti-Semitism"; Schreier, "A Jewish Riot," 762–63; Schroeter, "Islamic Anti-Semitism"; Schroeter, "Between Metropole and French North Africa"; Cole, *Lethal Provocation*; Heckman, *The Sultan's Communists*, chaps. 1–2.

BIBLIOGRAPHY

Afifi, Muhammad. "The State and the Church in Nineteenth-Century Egypt." *Die Welt des Islams* 39, no. 3 (1999): 273–88.

Ahmed, Faiz. "Contested Subjects: Ottoman and British Jurisdictional Quarrels *in re* Afghans and Indian Muslims." *Journal of the Ottoman and Turkish Studies Association* 3, no. 2 (2016): 325–46.

Akarli, Engin Deniz. "Ottoman Attitudes towards Lebanese Emigration, 1885–1910." In *The Lebanese in the World: A Century of Emigration*, edited by Albert Hourani and Nadim Shehadi, 109–38. London: I. B. Tauris, 2002.

Aksan, Virginia. "War and Peace." In *The Cambridge History of Turkey, Volume 3: The Later Ottoman Empire, 1603–1839*, edited by Suraiya Faroqhi, 81–117. Cambridge: Cambridge University Press, 2008.

Al-Hadif, Aharon, Mordekhai Ha-Cohen-Ganunah, and Yehudah Ben 'Attar. *Zekhut Yosef.* Livorno, 1873.

al-Nasiri, Ahmad b. Khalid. *Kitāb al-istiqṣā li-akhbār duwal al-maghrib al-aqṣā*. 8 vols. Casablanca: Manshūrāt wizārat al-thaqāfa wal-ittisāl, 2001.

Al-Qattan, Najwa. "Dhimmis in the Muslim Court: Legal Autonomy and Religious Discrimination." *International Journal of Middle Eastern Studies* 31, no. 3 (1999): 429–44.

Allagui, Abdelkrim. "L'état colonial et les juifs de Tunisie de 1881 à 1914." *Archives juives* 32, no. 1 (1999): 32–39.

———. *Juifs et Musulmans en Tunisie: Des origines à nos jours.* Paris: Tallandier / Projet Aladin, 2016.

Almog, Shmuel. "The Racial Motif in Renan's Attitude to Jews and Judaism." Translated by Nathan H. Reisner. In *Antisemitism through the Ages*, edited by Shmuel Almog, 255–78. Oxford: Pergamon Press, 1988.

Amara, Noureddine. "1830, l'improbable frontière: les écritures précaires de la possession française d'Alger; Le Djérid à l'épreuve de la nationalité algérienne." In *Penser le national au Maghreb et ailleurs*, edited by Fatma Ben Slimane and Hichem Abdessamad, 89–105. Tunis: Diraset-Etudes maghrébines, 2012.

Ammar, Leïla. *Tunis d'une ville à l'autre: Cartographie et histoire urbaine.* Tunis: Editions Nirvana, 2010.

Ancel, Bertrand. *Eléments d'histoire du droit international privé.* Paris: Panthéon-Assas Paris II, 2017.

Anderson, Benedict. *Imagined Communities: Reflections on the Origin and Spread of Nationalism.* London: Verso, 1983.

Ando, Clifford. "Fact, Fiction and Social Reality in Roman Law." In *Legal Fictions in Theory and Practice*, edited by Maksymilian del Mar and William Twining, 295–323. Boston: Springer, 2015.

———. "Race and Citizenship in Roman Law and Administration." In *Xenofobia y racismo en el mundo antiguo*, edited by Francisco Marco Simón, Francisco Pina Polo, and J. Remesal Rodríguez, 175–88. Barcelona: Edicions de la Universitat de Barcelona, 2019.

Anghie, Antony. *Imperialism, Sovereignty and the Making of International Law.* Cambridge: Cambridge University Press, 2005.

Anonymous. *Tunis en France: Questions politiques contemporaines par un diplomate.* Geneva: Charles Perrottel, Éditeur, 1882.

Arendt, Hannah. "The Rights of Man: What Are They?" *Modern Review* (Summer 1949): 24–37.

———. *The Origins of Totalitarianism.* 2nd ed. Orlando, FL: Harvest Book, 1968.

Asad, Talal. *Formations of the Secular: Christianity, Islam, Modernity.* Stanford, CA: Stanford University Press, 2003.

Aşçi, Hatice Bahar. "Türkiye'nin 150 Yıllık Borç Serüveni (1855–2005)." PhD diss., Başkent Üniversitesi Sosyal Bilimler Enstitüsü, 2007.

Ascoli, Raffaelo. *Gli ebrei venuti a Livorno.* Livorno: Israel Costa, 1886.

Ashkenazi, Avraham. *Kuntres Yismaḥ Moshe.* Jerusalem, 1873.

Ashkenazi, Eliézer. *La chronique d'Eliézer Ashkenazi sur les juifs de Tunis (1865–1870).* Edited by Robert Attal. Paris: Société d'Histoire des Juifs de Tunisie, 2006.

"Ashkenazi, Abraham ben Jacob." In *Encyclopaedia Judaica*, edited by Michael Berenbaum and Fred Skolnik, 571–72. 2nd ed. Detroit: Macmillan Reference, 2007.

Asquer, Enrica. "Rivendicare l'appartenenza: Suppliche e domande di deroga allo statut des juifs nella Francia di Vichy." *Quaderni Storici* 160, 54, no. 1 (2019): 225–58.

Assan, Valérie. "Les synagogues dans l'Algérie coloniale du XIXe siècle." *Archives juives* 37, no. 1 (2004): 70–85.

Attal, Avraham. *Le Caïd Nissim Samama de Tunis, mécène du livre hébraïque.* Jerusalem, 1995.

Attal, Avraham, and Yosef Aviv. *Pinkas ha-ketubot shel ha-kehilah ha-porṭugalit he-Tunis be-me'ot ha-18–19: Reshimat ha-peratim.* Jerusalem: Makhon Ben Zvi, 1992.

Augusti, Eliana. *Questioni d'oriente: Europa e Impero Ottomano nel diritto internazionale dell'ottocento.* Naples: Edizioni Scientifiche Italiane, 2013.

Avrahami, Itshaq. *Pinkas ha-kehilah ha-yehudit ha-portugezit be-Tunis: 1710–1944.* Lod: Orot Yahadut ha-Magreb, 1997.

Ayoub, Samy. "The Mecelle, Sharia, and the Ottoman State: Fashioning and Refashioning of Islamic Law in the Nineteenth and Twentieth Centuries." In *Law and Legality in the Ottoman Empire and Republic of Turkey*, edited by Kent F. Schull, M. Safa Saraçoğlu, and Robert Zens, 129–55. Bloomington: Indiana University Press, 2016.

Aytürk, İlker. "Bedel-i Askeri." In *Encyclopedia of Jews in the Islamic World*, edited by Norman Stillman, 360–61. Leiden: Brill, 2010.

Bahloul, Joëlle. *The Architecture of Memory: A Jewish-Muslim Household in Colonial Algeria, 1937–1962.* Cambridge: Cambridge University Press, 1996.

Baktıaya, Adil. "Hayriye Hanım Avrupa ve Amerika'da. Gönüllerin prensesi." *Toplumsal Tarih* 237 (2013): 88–94.

———. *Bir osmanlı kadınının feminizm macerası*. Istanbul: H_2O Kitap, 2016.

Baldwin, James E. *Islamic Law and Empire in Ottoman Cairo*. Edinburgh: Edinburgh University Press, 2017.

Bandi. "Prefetto di Verona c. Vincentini." *Annali della giurisprudenza* 13, no. 1 (1879): 139–40.

Banko, Lauren. *The Invention of Palestinian Citizenship, 1918–1947*. Edinburgh: Edinburgh University Press, 2016.

Banu, Roxana. *Nineteenth-Century Perspectives on Private International Law*. Oxford: Oxford University Press, 2018.

Baquis, Raffaello, and Dario Cassuto. *Note dopo la discussione per la Signora Aziza Samama e il Signor Cav. Nissim Samama contro il governo di Tunisi e altri sopra la validità del testamento del defunto Conte Caid Nissim Samama a termini del diritto talmudico*. Livorno: Tip. A. B. Zecchini, 1880.

Bargaoui, Sami, Simona Cerutti, and Isabelle Grangaud, eds. *Appartenance locale et propriété au nord et au sud de la Méditerranée*. Aix-en-Provence: Institut de recherches et d'études sur les mondes arabes et musulmans, 2015.

Bashkin, Orit. *New Babylonians: A History of Jews in Modern Iraq*. Stanford, CA: Stanford University Press, 2012.

Batnitzky, Leora. *How Judaism Became a Religion: An Introduction to Modern Jewish Thought*. Princeton, NJ: Princeton University Press, 2011.

Beaugrand, Claire. "Émergence de la 'nationalité' et institutionnalisation des clivages sociaux au Koweït et au Bahreïn." *Chroniques yéménites* 14 (2007): 89–107.

Becchini, Scipione. *Sentenza 2–5 maggio 1894 a relazione del giudice Avv. Scipione Becchini in causa Vittoria Stracca ved. Semama contro Cav. Giuseppe Semama*. Livorno: Tipografia Elzeviriana, 1894.

Beinin, Joel. *The Dispersion of Egyptian Jewry: Culture, Politics, and the Formation of a Modern Diaspora*. Berkeley: University of California Press, 1998.

Beiser, Frederick C. *The German Historicist Tradition*. Oxford: Oxford University Press, 2011.

Bel'ish, Aharon, and Yehudah Jarmon. *Yisrael Lo Yada'*. Livorno, 1878.

Bel'ish, Yosef. "Ha-'Kaid' Nissim Shamamah Zal, Sar Be-Yisrael." *Hod ha-Mizraḥ*, January 14, 1944, 8–9.

Belkeziz, Abdelouahed. *La nationalité dans les états arabes*. Rabat, Morocco: Editions "La Porte," 1963.

Ben Ismail, Youssef. "Sovereignty across Empires: France, the Ottoman Empire, and the Imperial Struggle over Tunis (ca. 1830–1920)." PhD diss., Harvard University, 2021.

Ben Rajeb, Ridha. *Yahūd al-bilāṭ wa-yahūd al-māl fī Tūnis al-'uthmānīya*. Beirut: Dār al-mudār al-islāmī, 2010.

Ben Slimane, Fatma. "Entre deux empires: l'élaboration de la nationalité tunisienne." In *Maghreb et Sciences Sociales*, 107–18. Tunis: L'Harmattan-IRMC, 2012.

———. "Une 'dhimma inversée'? La question des protections dans la régence ottomane de Tunis." In *Les musulmans dans l'histoire de l'Europe II: Passages et contacts en Méditerranée*, edited by Jocelyne Dakhlia and Wolfgang Kaiser, 345–69. Paris: Albin Michel, 2013.

———. "Définir ce qu'est être tunisien: litiges autour de la nationalité de Nessim Scemama (1873–1881)." *Revue des mondes musulmans et de la Méditerranée* 137 (May 2015): 31–48.

———. "La régence de Tunis à l'ère des réformes (XIXe siècle); le référent religieux et ses usages." In *Tunisie 2040, le renouvellement du projet moderniste Tunisie*, 487–519. Tunis: Sud Edition, 2016.

Ben-Aïad, Haïrié. *Die türkische Frau: Ihr soziales Leben und der Harem*. Vienna: Georg Szelinski, 1904.

Ben-Bassat, Yuval. "In Search of Justice: Petitions Sent from Palestine to Istanbul from the 1870's Onwards." *Turcica* 41 (2009): 89–114.

———. "'Al ṭelegraf ve-tzedeq: Ha-petitziot shel toshavei Yafo ve-'Azah le-vazir ha-gadol be-Istanbul." *Ha-mizraḥ he-ḥadash* 49 (2010): 30–52.

Ben-Naeh, Yaron. "Ottoman Jewish Courtiers: An Oriental Type of the Court Jew." *Jewish Culture and History* 19, no. 1 (2018): 56–70.

Benamozegh, Elia. "Recensione di David Castelli, *Il messia secondo gli ebrei*." *Giornale napoletano di filosofia e lettere, scienze morali e politiche* 1 (1875): 329–49.

———. *Delle fonti del diritto ebraico e del testamento del fu Conte Caid Nissim Samama, considerado rispetto a ciascuna di esse*. 2 vols. Livorno: Tip. A. B. Zecchini, 1882.

———. *Controreplica del Prof. Elia Benamozegh alla replica del Prof. David Castelli sul testamento del fu Caid Nissim Samama*. Livorno: Tipografia di Franc. Vigo, 1883.

———. "Autobiografia." In *Scritti Scelti*, edited by Alfredo S. Toaff, 17–23. Rome: La Rassegna Mensile d'Israel, 1955.

Bendana, Kmar. "The Avenue Bourguiba, Never to Be Forgotten Again." *Hypotheses*, September 8, 2014.

Bensimon-Donath, Doris. *Evolution du judaïsme marocain sous le protectorat français, 1912–1956*. Paris: Mouton and Co., 1968.

Benton, Lauren. *Law and Colonial Cultures: Legal Regimes in World History, 1400–1900*. Cambridge: Cambridge University Press, 2002.

Bercher, Léon. "En marge du Pacte 'Fondamental': un document inédit." *Les cahiers de Tunisie* 79–80 (1972): 243–60.

Berkovitz, Jay R. *Protocols of Justice: The Pinkas of the Metz Rabbinic Court 1771–1789*. Leiden: Brill, 2014.

———. *Law's Dominion: Jewish Community, Religion, and Family in Early Modern Metz*. Leiden: Brill, 2019.

Bernardi. "Belli v. Consiglio di Levà." *Annali della giurisprudenza* 6, no. 2 (1872): 446–48.

Bicci, Francesco. "Samama v. Samama, Court of Cassation, Florence." *Annali della giurisprudenza* 17, no. 1 (1883): 306–10.

Binyamin ha-sheni, Yisrael ben Yosef. "Ḥadashot Kelaliyot, Deutchland." *Ha-magid*, June 14, 1859, 3.

Birnbaum, Pierre, and Ira Katznelson, eds. *Paths of Emancipation: Jews, States and Citizenship*. Princeton, NJ: Princeton University Press, 1995.

Bismuth, Yitzḥak, et al. *Mishpat ha-yerushah*. Livorno: Mordekhai Finzi, 1878.

Biver, Comte Paul. *Histoire du château de Bellevue*. Paris: Libraire Gabriel Enault, 1933.

Blévis, Laure. "En marge du décret Crémieux; les juifs naturalisés français en Algérie (1865–1919)." *Archives juives* 45, no. 2 (2012): 47–67.

Bluntschli, Johann Caspar. *De la naturalisation en Allemagne d'une femme séparée de corps en France et des effets de cette naturalisation*. Paris: A. Marescq Ainé, 1876.

———. *The Theory of the State.* Kitchener, ON: Batoche Books, 2000.

Boll, Alfred M. *Multiple Nationality and International Law.* Leiden: Martinus Nijhoff Publishers, 2007.

Bosniak, Linda. *The Citizen and the Alien: Dilemmas of Contemporary Membership.* Princeton, NJ: Princeton University Press, 2006.

Boulouque, Clémence. *Another Modernity: Elia Benamozegh's Jewish Universalism.* Stanford, CA: Stanford University Press, 2020.

Boulu, Gilles. "Les Caïds Scemama ou Samama: Une dynastie des personnalités de la régence de Tunis." *Etsi—Revue de Généalogie et d'Histoire Séfarades* 24 (2004): 3–11.

———. "Recherches sur les Scemama ou Samama de Tunis; Une dynastie de personnalites et de hauts-fonctionnaires de la regence de Tunis." 2005. https://harissa.com/images/SCEMAMA.pdf.

Boulu, Gilles, and Alain Nedjar. *La communauté juive portugaise de Tunis, dite livournaise ou grana: registres matrimoniaux, 1812–1844 et 1872–1881 (avec notices généalogiques).* Paris: Cercle de Généalogie Juive, 2015.

Boum, Aomar. *Memories of Absence: How Muslims Remember Jews in Morocco.* Stanford, CA: Stanford University Press, 2013.

Brann, Ross. *Power in the Portrayal: Representations of Jews and Muslims in Eleventh- and Twelfth-Century Islamic Spain.* Princeton, NJ: Princeton University Press, 2002.

Braude, Benjamin, and Bernard Lewis. "Introduction." In *Christians and Jews in the Ottoman Empire: The Functioning of a Plural Society.* Two vols, edited by Benjamin Braude and Bernard Lewis, 1:1–34. New York: Holmes and Meier Publishers, 1982.

Braudel, Fernand. *The Mediterranean and the Mediterranean World in the Age of Philip II.* 2 vols. New York: Harper Colophon Books, 1972.

Bregoli, Francesca. "Hebrew Printing in Eighteenth-Century Livorno: From Government Control to a Free Market." In *The Hebrew Book in Early Modern Italy,* edited by Joseph Hacker and Adam Shear, 171–95. Philadelphia: University of Pennsylvania Press, 2011.

———. *Mediterranean Enlightenment: Livornese Jews, Tuscan Culture, and Eighteenth-Century Reform.* Stanford, CA: Stanford University Press, 2014.

———. "A Father's Consolation: Intra-Cultural Ties and Religion in a Trans-Mediterranean Jewish Commercial Network." In *Jews and the Mediterranean,* edited by Matthias Lehmann and Jessica M. Marglin, 129–48. Bloomington: Indiana University Press, 2020.

Brown, Kenneth. *People of Salé: Tradition and Change in a Moroccan City, 1830–1930.* Manchester: Manchester University Press, 1976.

Brown, L. Carl. *The Tunisia of Ahmed Bey, 1837–1855.* Princeton, NJ: Princeton University Press, 1974.

Brown, Nathan, and Amihai Radzyner. "Tzeva'ah goralit: Ha-ma'avakim 'al ha-yerushah shel 'ha-Rotshild me-'Aden.'" *Ha-'Umah* 200 (2015): 162–78.

Brubaker, Rogers. *Citizenship and Nationhood in France and Germany.* Cambridge, MA: Harvard University Press, 1992.

Brunschvig, Robert. "Justice religieuse et justice laïque dans la Tunisie des deys et des beys: jusqu'au milieu du XIXe siècle." *Studia Islamica* 23 (1965): 27–70.

Brustein, William I. *Roots of Hate: Anti-Semitism in Europe before the Holocaust.* Cambridge: Cambridge University Press, 2003.

Burak, Guy. "Dynasty, Law, and the Imperial Provincial Madrasa: The Case of al-Madrasa al-'Uthmaniyya in Ottoman Jerusalem." *International Journal of Middle East Studies* 45, no. 1 (2013): 111–25.

———. *The Second Formation of Islamic Law: The Hanafi School in the Early Modern Ottoman Empire.* Cambridge: Cambridge University Press, 2015.

Burke, Edmund. *Prelude to Protectorate in Morocco: Precolonial Protest and Resistance, 1860–1912.* Chicago: University of Chicago Press, 1976.

Calafat, Guillaume. "L'indice de la franchise: politique économique, concurrence des ports francs et condition des juifs en Méditerranée à l'époque moderne." *Revue Historique* 686 (2018): 275–320.

Calafat, Guillaume, and Cesare Santus. "Les avatars du 'turc'; Esclaves et commerçants musulmans à Livourne (1600–1750)." In *Les musulmans dans l'histoire de l'Europe I; Une intégration invisible,* edited by Jocelyne Dakhlia and Bernard Vincent, 471–522. Paris: Albin Michel, 2011.

Caldwell, Peter C. "The Citizen and the Republic in Germany, 1918–1935." In *Citizenship and National Identity in Twentieth-Century Germany,* edited by Geoff Eley and Jan Palmowski 40–56. Stanford, CA: Stanford University Press, 2008.

Campos, Michelle U. "Freemasonry in Ottoman Palestine." *Jerusalem Quarterly File* 22–23 (2005): 37–62.

———. *Ottoman Brothers: Muslims, Christians, and Jews in Early 20th Century Palestine.* Stanford, CA: Stanford University Press, 2010.

Can, Lâle. "The Protection Question: Central Asians and Extraterritoriality in the Late Ottoman Empire." *International Journal of Middle East Studies* 48 (2016): 679–99.

———. *Spiritual Subjects: Central Asian Pilgrims and the Ottoman Hajj at the End of Empire.* Stanford, CA: Stanford University Press, 2020.

Canepa, Andrew M. "Emancipazione, integrazione e antisemitismo liberale: Il caso Pasqualigo." *Comunità* 29, no. 174 (1975): 166–203.

Caplan, Jane, and John Torpey, eds. *Documenting Individual Identity: The Development of State Practices in the Modern World.* Princeton, NJ: Princeton University Press, 2001.

———. "Introduction." In *Documenting Individual Identity: The Development of State Practices in the Modern World,* edited by Jane Caplan and John Torpey, 1–12. Princeton, NJ: Princeton University Press, 2001.

Cappelleti, Mauro, and Joseph M. Perillo. *Civil Procedure in Italy.* Dordrecht: Springer-Science+Business Media, 1965.

Casanova, Ludovico. *Corso di diritto costituzionale ed internazionale.* Genoa: C. Cabella, 1858.

Casey, Christopher. *Nationals Abroad: Globalization, Individual Rights, and the Making of Modern International Law.* Cambridge: Cambridge University Press, 2020.

Castellanos-Jankiewicz, León. "Nationality, Alienage and Early International Rights." Paper presented at the Legal Histories beyond the State seminar, Lauterpacht Centre for International Law, Finley Library, Cambridge, UK, May 9, 2018.

Castelli, David. *Il messia secondo gli ebrei.* Florence: Le Monnier, 1874.

———. "Recensione di *Teologia dogmatica e apologetica* per Elia Benamozegh, volume primo, Dio." *La rivista europea* 8, no. 4 (1877): 169–81.

———. *Parere.* Florence: Tipografia di Luigi Niccolai, 1877.

———. *Secondo parere sulla validità secondo la legge ebraica del testamento de fu Caid Nissim Samama*. Florence, 1877.

———. *Terzo parere sulla validità del testament de fu Caid Nissim Samama*. Florence, 1877.

———. *Confutazione del parere firmato dal Sig. Rabbino Roberto Funaro ed esame del libro Hiccarè Addat*. Florence, 1877.

———. *Il diritto di testare nella legislazione ebraica*. Florence: Successori Le Monnier, 1878.

———. *Osservazioni sul parere dei Professori de Benedetti e Serafini sulla validità del testamento del Sig. Conte Caid Nissim Samama, secondo il diritto ebraico*. Florence, 1878.

———. *Replica ai pareri del Rabbino J. Costa e di altri rabbini sulla validità del testamento del fu Conte Caid Nissim Samama*. Florence, 1879.

———. *Nullità secondo la legge ebraica del testamento del fu Caid Nissim Samama; Replica di David Castelli, consultato dal Cav. Giusepe Samama*. Florence: Tipografia di Luigi Niccolai, 1882.

———. *Osservazioni di David Castelli sulla sentenza della regia Corte di Appello di Firenze intorno alla validità del testament del Caid Nissim Samama*. Florence: Tipografia di Luigi Niccolai, 1883.

———. *La legge del popolo ebreo*. Florence: G. C. Sansoni, Editore, 1884.

Çaycı, Abdurrahman. *La question tunisienne et la politique ottomane (1881–1913)*. Istanbul: Baha Matbaasi, 1963.

Cerutti, Simona. "Justice et citoyenneté à Turin à l'époque moderne." In *Lois, justice, coutume. Amérique et Europe latines (16e–19e siècles)*, edited by Juan Carlos Garavaglia and Jean-Frédéric Schaub, 57–91. Paris: Editions de l'EHESS, 2005.

———. *Étrangers; Étude d'une condition d'incertitude dans une société d'ancien régime*. Montrouge, France: Bayard, 2012.

Cerutti, Simona, and Isabelle Grangaud. "Sources and Contextualizations: Comparing Eighteenth-Century North African and Western European Institutions." *Comparative Studies in Society and History* 59, no. 1 (2017): 5–33.

Cesarini, Carlo. "Samama v. Samama, Court of Appeal, Lucca." *Annali della giurisprudenza* 14, no. 3 (1880): 216–51.

Chakrabarty, Dipesh. *Provincializing Europe: Postcolonial Thought and Historical Difference*. Princeton, NJ: Princeton University Press, 2000.

Cheramy, P.-A. *Tribunal de la Seine; mémoire en défense pour 1. M. le Comandeur Moïse Samama, 2. Mme Ziza Samama, 3. M. Joseph Samama, 4. M. Nathan Samama contre M. le Général Mahmoud-Ben-Aiad*. Paris: Renou, Maulde et Cock, 1874.

Chérif, Mohamed-Hédi. "Ben Dhyâf et les juifs tunisiens." *Confluences Méditerranée* 10 (1994): 89–96.

Choate, Mark I. *Emigrant Nation: The Making of Italy Abroad*. Cambridge, MA: Harvard University Press, 2008.

Chouraqui, André. *Les juifs d'Afrique du nord: marche vers l'occident*. Paris: Presses universitaires de France, 1952.

Clancy-Smith, Julia. *Mediterraneans: North Africa and Europe in an Age of Migration, c. 1800–1900*. Berkeley: University of California Press, 2011.

Cockburn, Sir Alexander James Edmund. *Nationality: Or, the Law Relating to Subjects and Aliens, Considered with a View to Future Legislation*. London: William Ridgway, 1869.

Code civil des français. Paris: L'imprimerie de la République, 1804.

Codice civile del Regno d'Italia. Turin: Stamperia Reale, 1865.

Cogordan, George. *La nationalité au point de vue des rapports internationaux*. Paris: L. Larose, 1879.

Cohen, Julia Phillips. *Becoming Ottomans: Sephardi Jews and Imperial Citizenship in the Modern Era*. Oxford: Oxford University Press, 2014.

———. "A Model *Millet*? Ottoman Jewish Citizenship at the End of Empire." In *Jews, Liberalism, Antisemitism: A Global History*, edited by Abigail Green and Simon Levis Sullam, 209–32. London: Palgrave Macmillan, 2020.

Cohen, Julia Philips, and Sarah Abrevaya Stein, eds. *Sephardi Lives: A Documentary History, 1700–1950*. Stanford, CA: Stanford University Press, 2014.

Cohen, Mark R. *Jewish Self-Government in Medieval Egypt: The Origins of the Office of Head of the Jews, ca. 1056–1126*. Princeton, NJ: Princeton University Press, 1980.

———. *Under Crescent and Cross: The Jews in the Middle Ages*. Princeton, NJ: Princeton University Press, 1994.

———. "What Was the Pact of 'Umar? A Literary-Historical Study." *Jerusalem Studies in Arabic and Islam* 23 (1999): 100–157.

———. "Modern Myths of Muslim Anti-Semitism (in Hebrew)." *Politikah* 19 (Spring 2009): 121–40.

Cohen, Rina. "Les juifs '*moghrabi*' en Palestine (1830–1903): Les enjeux de la protection française." *Archives Juives* 38, no. 2 (2005): 28–46.

Colao, Floriana. "'L'idea di nazione' nei giuristi italiani tra ottocento e novecento." *Quaderni Fiorentini per la storia del pensiero giuridico moderno* 30, no. 1 (2001): 255–360.

Cole, Joshua. *Lethal Provocation: The Constantine Murders and the Politics of French Algeria*. Ithaca, NY: Cornell University Press, 2019.

Colorni, Vittore. *Gli ebrei nel sistema del diritto comune fino alla prima emancipazione*. Milan: Dott. A Giuffrè, Editore, 1956.

Cooke, Miriam, Erdag Goknar, and Grant Parker, eds. *Mediterranean Passages: Readings from Dido to Derrida*. Chapel Hill: University of North Carolina Press, 2008.

Corcos, David, and Frank D. Grande. "Lumbroso." In *Encyclopaedia Judaica*, edited by Michael Berenbaum and Fred Skolnik, 256. 2nd ed. New York: Macmillan Reference USA, 2007.

Costa, Israel. *Yada' ma be-ḥasukhah, ve-hu perush ve-hasagot le-sefer Megillah 'amikta*. Livorno: Israel Costa and Associates, 1878.

Costa, Pietro. *Civitas: Storia della cittadinanza in Europa*. 4 vols. Rome: Editori Laterza, 2001.

Cott, Nancy F. "Marriage and Women's Citizenship in the United States, 1830–1934." *American Historical Review* 103, no. 5 (1998): 1440–74.

Cover, Robert M. "Foreword: *Nomos* and Narrative." *Harvard Law Review* 97, no. 4 (1983): 4–68.

Cruppi. *Conclusions du procureur de la république, M. Cruppi, et jugement de la 1ère chambre du tribunal civil de la Seine, rendu le 18 juillet 1885 en faveur de la succession du Général Mahmoud Ben-Aïad contre Hamida Ben-Aïad et consorts*. Paris: Imprimerie L. Guérin et Cie., 1885.

D., P. "Depienne, Pierre-Marie." In *Dictionnaire illustré de la Tunisie; Choses et gens de Tunisie*, edited by Paul Lambert, 153–54. Tunis: C. Saliba Ainé, Éditeur, 1912.

Dakhlia, Jocelyne. *L'empire des passions; L'arbitraire politique en islam*. Paris: Aubier, 2005.

Dalloz. *Recueil critique de jurisprudence et de législation*. Paris: Bureau de la jurisprudence, 1904.

Danon, Dina. *The Jews of Ottoman Izmir: A Modern History.* Stanford, CA: Stanford University Press, 2019.

Darling, Linda T. *A History of Social Justice and Political Power in the Middle East: The Circle of Justice from Mesopotamia to Globalization.* London: Routledge, 2013.

Davis, Natalie Zemon. *The Return of Martin Guerre.* Cambridge, MA: Harvard University Press, 1984.

de Flaux, Armand. *La régence de Tunis au dix-neuvième siècle.* Paris: Challamel aîné, 1865.

De Grand, Alexander J. *Fascist Italy and Nazi Germany: The "Fascist" Style of Rule.* New York: Routledge, 2004.

de Grouchy, Emmanuel-Henri. *Meudon, Bellevue et Chaville.* Paris: Société de l'histoire de Paris, 1893.

de Martens, Georg Friedrich. *Précis du droit des gens moderne de l'Europe fondé sur les traités et l'usage.* 2nd ed. Gottingen: Libraire du Dieterich, 1801.

De Testa, Ignaz. *Recueil des traités de la porte ottomane avec les puissances étrangères.* Vol. 1. Paris: Amyot, 1864.

Debbasche, Giuseppe. *Memorie, appunti, e note rettificative in replica all'avversario scritto del 7 maggio 1875 del Cavaliere Giuseppe Debbasche contro gli eredi testamentari del Caid Nissim Samama.* Lucca, Italy: Tipografia Benedini, 1875.

Derobert-Ratel, Christiane. "La faculté de droit d'Aix-en-Provence, creuset d'une élite juive nord-africaine sous la troisième république." *Archives juives* 45, no. 1 (2012): 87–100.

Deshen, Shlomo A. *The Mellah Society: Jewish Community Life in Sherifian Morocco.* Chicago: University of Chicago Press, 1989.

Despagnet, Frantz. *La diplomatie de la troisième république et le droit des gens.* Paris: L. Larose, 1904.

Di Lampedusa, Giuseppe. *The Leopard.* Translated by Archibald Colquhoun. New York: Pantheon Books, 2007.

Dickens, Charles. *Bleak House.* New York: Macmillan, 2006.

Donati, Sabina. *A Political History of National Citizenship and Identity in Italy, 1861–1950.* Stanford, CA: Stanford University Press, 2013.

Douki, Caroline. "The Liberal Italian State and Mass Emigration, 1860–1914." In *Citizenship and Those Who Leave: The Politics of Emigration and Expatriation,* edited by Nancy L. Green and François Weil, 91–113. Urbana: University of Illinois Press, 2007.

Drumont, Edouard Adolphe. *La France juive: Essai d'histoire contemporaine.* Paris: C. Marpon and E. Flammarion, 1886.

Dugast, Anne, and Isabelle Parizet, eds. *Dictionnaire par noms d'architectes des construction élevées à Paris aux XIXe et XXe siècles, période 1876–1899.* 4 vols. Paris: Service des travaux historiques, 1990.

Dursteler, Eric R. *Venetians in Constantinople: Nation, Identity, and Coexistence in the Early Modern Mediterranean.* Baltimore: Johns Hopkins University Press, 2006.

Duve, Thomas, ed. *Entanglements in Legal History: Conceptual Approaches.* Frankfurt am Main: Max Planck Institute for European Legal History, 2014.

———. "Global Legal History: Setting Europe in Perspective." In *The Oxford Handbook of European Legal History,* edited by Heikki Pihlajamäki, Markus D. Dubber, and Mark Godfrey, 114–39. Oxford: Oxford University Press, 2018.

Dworkin, Ronald. *Taking Rights Seriously.* Cambridge, MA: Harvard University Press, 1977.

———. "Law as Interpretation." *Critical Inquiry* 9, no. 1 (1982): 179–200.

Efron, John M. *Defenders of the Race: Jewish Doctors and Race Science in Fin-de-Siècle Europe.* New Haven, CT: Yale Unversity Press, 1994.

Elmelich, Leon. *Megilah 'Amikta.* Livorno: Israel Costa and Associates, 1877.

———. *Megilah 'Amukot Minei Hoshekh.* Livorno: Shelomoh Belforte, 1878.

———. *Observations relatives au testament de feu le General Comte Nissim Samama de Tunis et présenté à messieurs les juges européenes et aux rabbins israélites.* Bône: Imprimerie de J. Dagand, M. Nicolas, Successeur, 1878.

———. *Tribunale Civile di Livorno: Note defensionali del Cav. Leone Elmilik contro il Signor Comm. Giacomo Guttieres N. N.* Livorno: B. Ortalli, 1886.

Elmilik, Léon. *Affaire Heussein et Elmilik; Heussein et Haim Bismut Maliah; Haim Bismut Maliah et Heussein; Notes sur le jugement rendu par le Tribunal Civil de 1ere Instance de Tunis, Le 18 Juin 1885.* Tunis: Imprimerie V. Finzi, 1885.

———. *Arbitrage Léon Elmilik contre le gouvernement tunisien: conclusions de M. Elmilik déposées aux arbitres, Messieurs Auguste Ventre et Raymond Valensi, le 12 et 24 juin 1890, en réplique aux conclusions du gouvernement déposées le 10 juin 1889.* Tunis: Imprimerie Internationale, 1890.

Elmilik, Leone. *Il rivelatore dei misteri dalle tenebre; ovvero stringente confutazione degli argomenti recati dal Signor Rabbino Israele Costa nel suo opuscoletto di poca entità, e di niun pregio che porta il titolo: conosce ciò che è nelle tenebre.* Livorno: Tip. di B. Ortalli, 1879.

Elon, Menachem. *Jewish Law: History, Sources, Principles (Ha-Mishpat Ha-Ivri).* Translated by Bernard Auerbach and Melvin J. Sykes. 4 vols. Philadelphia: Jewish Publication Society, 1994.

Empire français. *Annuaire diplomatique de l'empire français.* Paris: Veuve Berger-Levrault et Fils, 1868.

Ennaji, Mohammed. *Expansion européenne et changement social au Maroc: (XVIe–XIXe siècles).* Collection Etudes. Casablanca: Editions Eddif, 1996.

Erman, Sam. *Almost Citizens: Puerto Rico, the U.S. Constitution, and Empire.* Cambridge: Cambridge University Press, 2018.

Esperson, Pietro. *Il principio di nazionalità applicato alle relazioni civili internazionali e riscontro di esso colle norme di diritto internazionale privato sancite dalla legislazione del regno d'Italia.* Pavia, Italy: Tipografia dei fratelli Fusi, 1868.

Eyffinger, Arthur. *T. M. C. Asser (1838–1913): 'In Quest of Liberty, Justice, and Peace.'* 2 vols. Leiden: Brill Nijhoff, 2019.

Fabian, Johannes. *Time and the Other: How Anthropology Makes Its Object.* New York: Columbia University Press, 2014.

Facchini, Christiana. *David Castelli: Ebraismo e scienze delle religioni tra otto e novocento.* Brescia, Italy: Morcelliana, 2005.

Fahmy, Khaled. *All the Pasha's Men: Mehmed Ali, His Army and the Making of Modern Egypt.* Cairo: American University in Cairo Press, 1997.

Fahrmeir, Andreas. *Citizenship: The Rise and Fall of a Modern Concept.* New Haven, CT: Yale University Press, 2006.

Fancy, Hussein. *The Mercenary Mediterranean: Sovereignty, Religion, and Violence in the Medieval Crown of Aragon.* Chicago: University of Chicago Press, 2016.

Fattal, Antoine. *Le statut légal des non-musulmans en pays d'islam*. Beirut: Imprimerie Catholique, 1958.

Ferguson, Niall. "The Rise of the Rothschilds: The Family Firm as Multinational." In *The World of Private Banking*, edited by Youssef Cassis and Philip Cottrell, 1–30. Surrey, UK: Ashgate, 2009.

Filippini, Jean Pierre. "La ballotazione a Livorno nel settecento." *La Rassegna Mensile di Israel* 49, no. 1-2-3-4 (1983): 199–268.

———. *Il porto di Livorno e la Toscana (1676–1814)*. 3 vols. Naples: Edizioni Scientifiche Italiane, 1998.

Fisch, Jörg. *A History of the Self-Determination of Peoples: The Domestication of an Illusion*. Cambridge: Cambridge University Press, 2015.

Flemming, Barbara. "Romantic Emigrants in the Empire of Abdülhamid." In *Essays on Turkish Literature and History*, 190–202. Leiden: Brill, 2017.

Foelix, Jean-Jacques Gaspard. *Traité de droit international privé, ou du conflit des lois de différentes nations en matière de droit privé*. 1st ed. Paris: Joubert, 1843.

———. *Traité de droit international privé*. 2nd ed. Paris: Joubert, 1847.

Foelix, Jean-Jacques Gaspard, and Charles Demangeat. *Traité de droit international privé*. 3rd ed. 2 vols. Paris: Marescq et Dujardin, 1856.

Foreign Office, ed. *British and Foreign State Papers, 1834–1835*. Vol. 23. London: James Ridgway and Sons, 1852.

———, ed. *British and Foreign State Papers, 1869–70*. London: William Ridgway, 1876.

Forrest, Alan. *Conscripts and Deserters: The Army and French Society during the Revolution and Empire*. New York: Oxford University Press, 1989.

Foucault, Michel. *Security, Territory, Population: Lectures at the Collège De France, 1977–78*. Translated by Graham Burchell. Edited by Michel Senellart. New York: Palgrave Macmillan, 2007.

Fram, Edward. *A Window on Their World: The Court Diary of Rabbi Hayyim Gundersheim, Frankfurt Am Main 1773–1794*. Cincinnati: Hebrew Union College Press, 2012.

Frattarelli Fischer, Lucia. *Vivere fuori dal ghetto: ebrei a Pisa e Livorno (secoli XVI–XVIII)*. Turin: Silvio Zamorani, 2008.

Frégier, Casimir. *Les juifs algériens: leur passé, leur présent et leur avenir juridique*. Paris: M. Lévy Frères, 1865.

Fuller, Lon. "Positivism and Fidelity to Law—a Reply to Professor Hart." *Harvard Law Review* 71, no. 4 (1958): 630–72.

Funaro, Liana. "Massoneria e minoranze religiose nel secolo XIX." In *La Massoneria a Livorno: del Settecento alla Repubblica*, 343–416. Bologna: Il Mulino, 2006.

———. *Un tempio nuovo per una fede antica: a cinquant'anni dall'inaugurazione del tempio ebraico di Livorno*. Livorno: Salomone Belforte and C., 2012.

———. "Una duplice qualità: Isacco Rignano israelite e avvocato." *Le Carte e la Storia* 18, no. 1 (2012): 82–102.

———. "'La barca cammina.' per un nuovo epistolario di Leopoldo Galeotti." *Annali Sismondi* 2 (2016): 1–28.

Gabbacia, Donna R., Dirk Hoerder, and Adam Walaszek. "Emigration and Nation Building during the Mass Migrations from Europe." In *Citizenship and Those Who Leave: The Politics of Emigration and Expatriation*, edited by Nancy L. Green and François Weil, 63–90. Urbana: University of Illinois Press, 2007.

Galeotti, Leopoldo. *Della riforma municipale; pensieri e proposte.* Florence: Gabinetto Scientifico-Letterario, 1847.

———. *La storia del concilio di trento di Fra Paolo Sarpi non era soggetta alla preventiva censura episcopale; memoria del'avvocato Leopoldo Galeotti a favore del Signor G. Barbèra accusato di trasgressione all'art. 83 della legge sulla stampa del 7 maggio 1848.* Florence: Barbèra, Bianchi e Comp., 1858.

———. *Reale Corte d'Appello di Lucca; Memoria in causa governo di Tunisi e Samama; Applicazione della legge ebraica, legge nazionale del defunto—nullità di testamento secondo la legge ebraica.* Florence: Tipografia di L. Niccolai, 1879.

Ganiage, Jean. *Les origines du protectorat français en Tunisie (1861–1881).* 2nd ed. Tunis: Maison Tunisienne de l'Edition, 1968.

Garofalo, Luigi, and Alberto Burdese, eds. *Il ruolo della buona fede oggettiva nell'esperienza giuridica storica e contemporanea: atti del convegno internazionale di studi in onore di Alberto Burdese, Padova, Venezia, Treviso, 14-15-16, giugno 2001.* 4 vols. Padua: CEDAM, 2003.

Gazzetta ufficiale del regno d'Italia. Rome, 1878.

Gehring, Gilbert. *Les relations entre la Tunisie et l'Allemagne avant le protectorat français.* Tunis: Publications de l'Université de Tunis, 1971.

Gekas, Sakis. "The Port Jews of Corfu and the 'Blood Libel' of 1891: A Tale of Many Centuries and of One Event." *Jewish Culture and History* 7, no. 1–2 (2012): 171–96.

Gelbin, Cathy, and Sander Gilman. *Cosmopolitanisms and the Jews.* Ann Arbor: University of Michigan Press, 2017.

Gentry, Judith Fenner. "A Confederate Success in Europe: The Erlanger Loan." *Journal of Southern History* 36, no. 2 (1970): 157–88.

Gerber, Haim. "Arkhiyon beit ha-din ha-shara'i shel Bursah ke-mekor histori le-toldot yehudei ha-'ir." *Mi-kedem u-mi-yam* 1 (1981): 31–37.

———. *State, Society, and Law in Islam: Ottoman Law in Comparative Perspective.* Albany: State University of New York Press, 1994.

Gerber, Jane S. *Jewish Society in Fez, 1450–1700: Studies in Communal and Economic Life.* Leiden: Brill, 1980.

Gharbi, Mohamed Lazhar. "Mahmoud Ben Ayyed: Le parcour transméditerranéen d'un homme d'affaires tunisien du milieu du XIXe siècle." *Méditerranée* 124 (2015): 21–27.

Gidney, William Thomas. *The History of the London Society for Promoting Christianity amongst the Jews, from 1809 to 1908.* London: London Society for Promoting Christianity amongst the Jews, 1908.

Gini, Ciro. "Salmon v. Manetti." *Annali della giurisprudenza* 34, no. 3 (1900): 385–91.

Ginzburg, Carlo. *The Cheese and the Worms.* Baltimore: Johns Hopkins University Press, 1980.

Glanville, Luke. *Sovereignty and the Responsibility to Protect: A New History.* Chicago: University of Chicago Press, 2014.

Goitein, Shlomo Dov. *A Mediterranean Society.* 5 vols. Berkeley: University of California Press, 1967–88.

Gong, Gerrit W. *The Standard of 'Civilization' in International Society.* Oxford: Clarendon Press, 1984.

"Good Faith." In *Gale Encyclopedia of American Law*, edited by Donna Batten, 122–23. Detroit: Gale, 2011.

Gordley, James. *The Jurists: A Critical History.* Oxford: Oxford University Press, 2013.

Gosewinkel, Dieter. "Citizenship, Subjecthood, Nationality: Concepts of Belonging in the Age of Modern Nation States." In *European Citizenship: Between National Legacies and Postnational Projects,* edited by Klaus Eder and Bernhard Giesen, 17–35. Oxford: Oxford University Press, 2003.

Gottreich, Emily. *The Mellah of Marrakesh: Jewish and Muslim Space in Morocco's Red City.* Bloomington: Indiana University Press, 2007.

Grangaud, Isabelle. "Le bayt al-mâl, les héritiers et les étrangers. Droits de succession et droits d'appartenance à Alger à l'époque moderne." In *Appartenance locale et propriété au nord et au sud de la Méditerranée,* edited by Sami Bargaoui, Simona Cerutti, and Isabelle Grangaud. Aix-en-Provence: Institut de recherches et d'études sur les mondes arabes et musulmans, 2015.

Grange, Cyril. *Une élite Parisienne; les familles de la grande bourgeoisie juive (1870–1939).* Paris: CNRS Éditions, 2015.

Green, Abigail. "From Protection to Humanitarian Intervention? Enforcing Jewish Rights in Romania and Morocco around 1880." In *The Emergence of Humanitarian Intervention: Ideas and Practice from the Nineteenth Century to the Present,* edited by Fabian Klose, 142–61. Cambridge: Cambridge University Press, 2015.

Green, Abigail, and Simon Levis Sullam, eds. *Jews, Liberalism, Antisemitism: A Global History.* London: Palgrave Macmillan, 2020.

Green, Arnold. *The Tunisian Ulama, 1873–1915: Social Structure and Response to Ideological Currents.* Leiden: Brill, 1978.

Green, Nancy L. "The Politics of Exit: Reversing the Immigrant Paradigm." *Journal of Modern History* 77, no. 2 (2005): 263–89.

———. "Expatriation, Expatriates, and Expats: The American Transformation of a Concept." *American Historical Review* 114, no. 2 (2009): 307–28.

———. *The Limits of Transnationalism.* Chicago: University of Chicago Press, 2019.

Greer, Allan. *Property and Dispossession: Natives, Empires and Land in Early Modern North America.* Cambridge: Cambridge University Press, 2017.

Grenet, Mathieu. *La fabrique Communautaire: les grecs à Venise, Livourne et Marseille 1770–1840.* Rome: Ecole française de Rome, 2016.

Gross, Ariela. *What Blood Won't Tell: A History of Race on Trial in America.* Cambridge, MA: Harvard University Press, 2008.

Guellouz, Azzedine, Abdelkader Masmoudi, and Mongi Smida. *Histoire générale de la Tunisie: Tome 3, les temps modernes (941–1247 H/1534–1881 CE).* Tunis: Sud éditions, 2007.

Guetta, Alessandro. *Philosophy and Kabbalah: Elijah Benamozegh and the Reconciliation of Western Thought and Jewish Esotericism.* Albany: SUNY Press, 2009.

Gueydan, A., and David Santillana. *Arbitrage: Réclamations du sieur Liaou Elmilik contre le gouvernement tunisien: mémoire pour le gouvernement tunisien.* Tunis: Imprimerie française B. Borrel, 1890.

Gutman, David. "Armenian Migration to North America, State Power, and Local Politics in the Late Ottoman Empire." *Comparative Studies of South Asia, Africa and the Middle East* 34, no. 1 (2014): 176–90.

Hajjat, Abdellali. *Les frontières de l'"identité nationale"; l'injonction à l'assimilation en France métropolitaine et coloniale.* Paris: La Découverte, 2012.

Hallaq, Wael B. *An Introduction to Islamic Law.* Cambridge: Cambridge University Press, 2009.

Halpérin, Jean-Louis. *Entre nationalisme juridique et communauté de droit.* Paris: Presses Universitaires de France, 1999.

Hanioğlu, M. Şükrü. *A Brief History of the Late Ottoman Empire.* Princeton, NJ: Princeton University Press, 2008.

Hanley, Will. "When Did Egyptians Stop Being Ottomans? An Imperial Citizenship Case Study." In *Multilevel Citizenship,* edited by Willem Maas, 89–109. Philadelphia: University of Pennsylvania Press, 2013.

———. "Papers for Going, Papers for Staying: Identification and Subject Formation in the Eastern Mediterranean." In *A Global Middle East: Mobility, Materiality and Culture in the Modern Age, 1880–1940,* edited by Liat Kozma, Avner Wishnitzer, and Cyrus Schayegh, 177–200. London: I. B. Taurus, 2014.

———. "International Lawyers without Public International Law: The Case of Late Ottoman Egypt." *Journal of the History of International Law* 18 (2016): 98–119.

———. "What Ottoman Nationality Was and Was Not." *Journal of the Ottoman and Turkish Studies Association* 3, no. 2 (2016): 277–98.

———. *Identifying with Nationality: Europeans, Ottomans, and Egyptians in Alexandria.* New York: Columbia University Press, 2017.

Harel, Yaron. "Ha'alat em la-mikra 'al ha-moked: Ḥalab, 1865." *Hebrew Union College Annual* 64 (1993): 27–36.

Hart, Herbert Lionel Adolphus. "Positivism and the Separation of Law and Morals." *Harvard Law Review* 71, no. 4 (1958): 593–629.

———. *The Concept of Law.* London: Clarendon Press, 1961.

Haruvi, Yuval. "Ha-elitah ha-toranit shel ha-ʿir Tunis be-ʿidan ha-moderni, 1873–1921." PhD diss., Tel Aviv University, 2013.

Heckman, Alma. *The Sultan's Communists: Moroccan Jews and the Politics of Belonging.* Stanford, CA: Stanford University Press, 2020.

Heffening, W. "Murtadd." In *Encyclopedia of Islam, Second Edition,* edited by Peri J. Bearman, Thierry Bianquis, Clifford Edmund Bosworth, E. J. van Donzel, and Wolfhart Heinrichs. Leiden: Brill, 2003.

Hénia, Abdelhamid. *Propriété et stratégies sociales à Tunis à l'époque moderne (XVIe–XIXe siècles).* Tunis: Université Tunis I: Faculté des sciences humaines et sociales de Tunis, 1999.

Herzl, Theodor. "The Jewish State." In *The Zionist Idea,* edited by Arthur Hertzberg, 204–25. New York: Jewish Publication Society, 1997.

Herzog, Tamar. *Defining Nations: Immigrants and Citizens in Early Modern Spain and Spanish America.* New Haven, CT: Yale University Press, 2003.

———. "Did European Law Turn American? Territory, Property and Rights in an Atlantic World." In *New Horizons in Spanish Colonial Law: Contributions to Transnational Early Modern Legal History,* edited by Thomas Duve and Heikki Pihlajamäki, 75–96. Frankfurt am Main: Max Planck Institute for European Legal history, 2015.

Heussein, Général. *Lettre de Général Heussein au collège de la défense du gouvernement tunisien dans l'affaire du Caïd Nessim Samama; Traduction de l'arabe.* Paris: Typographie Ves Renou, Maulde et Cock, 1878.

———. *Le Caïd Nessim peint par lui-même; Traduction de l'arabe.* Paris: Renou, Maulde et Cock, 1879.

———. *Lettera del Generale Heussein agli onorevoli avvocati componenti il collegio della difesa del governo di Tunis.* Florence: Tipografia di M. Ricci, 1880.

Heusséïn, Generale. *Lettera del Generale Heusséïn all'onorevole Avvocato Comm. Adriano Mari.* Livorno: Tipografia di Francesco Vigo, 1880.

Heyking, Baron A. *A Practical Guide for Russian Consular Officials and Private Persons Having Relations with Russia.* London: Eyre and Spottiswoode, 1904.

Hirschberg, Haim Zeev. *A History of the Jews in North Africa, Volume II: From the Ottoman Conquests to the Present Time.* Leiden: Brill, 1981.

hooks, bell. "Choosing the Margin as a Space of Radical Openness." *Framework: The Journal of Cinema and Media* 36 (1989): 15–23.

Horden, Peregrine, and Nicholas Purcell. *The Corrupting Sea: A Study of Mediterranean History.* Oxford: Blackwell Publishers, 2000.

Horowitz, Richard S. "International Law and State Transformation in China, Siam, and the Ottoman Empire during the Nineteenth Century." *Journal of World History* 15, no. 4 (2005): 445–86.

Hugon, Henri. *Les emblèmes des beys de Tunis: étude sur les signes de l'autonomie husseinite.* Paris: E. Leroux, 1913.

Hunwick, John O. "Al-Mahîlî and the Jews of Tuwât: The Demise of a Community." *Studia Islamica* 61 (1985): 155–83.

Husayn b. ʿAbdallah. *Rasāʾil Ḥusayn ilā Khayr al-Dīn.* Edited by Ahmed Abdesselem. 3 vols. Tunis: Bayt al-Ḥikma, 1991.

———. "Al-qusṭās al-mustaqīm fī ẓuhūr ikhtilāl al-ḥukm bi-nafī jinsīyat al-Qāʾid Nisīm." In *Al-Ginirāl Ḥusayn: Ḥayātuhu wa-ātharuhu,* edited by Aḥmad al-Ṭawīlī, 231–78. Tunis, 1994.

Ibbetson, David. "Natural Law in Early Modern Legal Thought." In *The Oxford Handbook of European Legal History,* edited by Heikki Pihlajamäki, Markus D. Dubber, and Mark Godfrey, 566–82. Oxford: Oxford University Press, 2018.

Ibn Abi al-Diyaf, Ahmad. *Itḥāf ahl al-zamān bi-akhbār mulūk Tūnis wa-ʿahd al-amān.* Tunis: Al-Dār al-Tūnisīya lil-Nashr, 1989.

Ibn Qayim al-Jawziya, Muḥammad b. Abī Bakr. *Aḥkām ahl al-dhimma.* 2 vols. Beirut: Dār al-kutub al-ʿilmīya, 2002.

Immerwahr, Daniel. *How to Hide an Empire: A History of the Greater United States.* New York: Farrar, Straus and Giroux, 2019.

Indicateur marseillais: guide de l'administration et du commerce; annuaire du département des Bouches-du-Rhône pour l'année 1905. Marseille: G. Allard et Bertrand, 1905.

Inghilleri, Calcedonio. "Samama v. Samama." *Annali della giurisprudenza* 17, no. 3 (1883): 377–414.

Isin, Engin F. "Citizenship after Orientalism: Ottoman Citizenship." In *Citizenship in a Global World: European Questions and Turkish Experiences,* edited by E. Fuat Keyman and Ahmet İçduygu, 31–51. London: Routledge, 2005.

———. "Theorizing Acts of Citizenship." In *Acts of Citizenship,* edited by Engin F. Isin and Greg Nielsen, 15–43. London: Zed Books, 2008.

Isin, Engin F., and Bryan S. Turner. "Citizenship Studies: An Introduction." In *Handbook of Citizenship Studies*, edited by Engin F. Isin and Bryan S. Turner, 1–11. London: Sage Publications Ltd., 2002.

Jamoussi, Habib. "Le quartier franc de Tunis au XIXe siècle: dynamisme d'un espace socio-culturel de la Tunisie précoloniale." In *Les communautés méditerraneénes de Tunisie: Actes en hommage au doyen Mohamed Hédi Chérif*, 203–19. Tunis: Centre de Publication Universitaire, 2006.

———. *Juifs et chrétiens en Tunisie au 19e siècle; essai d'une étude socio-culturelle des communautés non-musulmanes, 1815–1881*. Sfax, Tunisia: Amal Editions, 2010.

Jarmon, Yehudah. *Naḥalat Avot*. Livorno: Mordekhai Finzi, 1877.

———. *Kuntres nosaf 'al naḥalat*. Livorno: Shlomo Belforte ve-ḥaverav, 1882.

Jayme, Erik. *Pasquale Stanislao Mancini: Il diritto internazionale privato tra risorgimento e attività forense*. Padua: Casa editrice Dott. Antonio Milani, 1988.

Jennings, Ronald C. "Zimmis (Non-Muslims) in Early 17th Century Ottoman Judicial Records: The Sharia Court of Anatolian Kayseri." *Journal of the Economic and Social History of the Orient* 21, no. 3 (1978): 225–93.

Jerad, Mehdi. "Le premier traité de paix et de commerce conclu entre la régence de Tunis et la couronne suédoise en 1736." *Cahiers de la Mediterranée* 89 (2014): 237–63.

———. "Les agents des beys de Tunis au xixe siècle: entre intérêts de pouvoir et enjeux marchands." *Cahiers de la Mediterranée* 98 (2019): 113–29.

Jessurun d'Oliveira, Hans Ulrich. "Principe de nationalité et droit de nationalité: notes de lecture au sujet du *droit civil international* de François Laurent." In *Liber memorialis François Laurent 1810–1887*, edited by Johan Erauw, Boudewijn Bouckaert, Hubert Bocken, Helmut Gaus, and Marcel Storme, 819–36. Brussels: E. Story-Scientia, 1989.

———. "Once Again: Plural Nationality." *Maastricht Journal of European and Comparative Law* 25, no. 1 (2018): 22–37.

Jurisprudence des tribunaux de la réforme en Egypte; Recueil officiel, première partie; arrêts de la cour d'appel d'Alexandrie (tome premier, année judiciaire 1875–76). Alexandria: Imprimerie de Commerce, 1876.

Kallander, Amy Aisen. *Women, Gender, and the Palace Households in Ottoman Tunisia*. Austin: University of Texas Press, 2013.

Karpat, Kemal. "Millets and Nationality: The Roots of the Incongruity of Nation and State in the Post-Ottoman Era." In *Christians and Jews in the Ottoman Empire: The Functioning of a Plural Society*, edited by Benjamin Braude and Bernard Lewis, 141–69. New York: Holmes and Meier, 1982.

———. "Nation and Nationalism in the Late Ottoman Empire." In *Studies on Ottoman Social and Political History: Selected Articles and Essays*, edited by Kemal Karpat, 544–55. Leiden: Brill, 2002.

Kateb, Kamel. *Européens, "indigènes" et juifs en Algérie (1830–1962); représentations et réalités des populations*. Paris: Insitut National d'Etudes Démographiques, 2001.

Katz, Jacob. *Out of the Ghetto: The Social Background of Jewish Emancipation, 1770–1870*. Cambridge, MA: Harvard University Press, 1973.

Kenbib, Mohammed. *Les protégés: contribution à l'histoire contemporaine du Maroc*. Rabat, Morocco: Faculté des lettres et des sciences humaines, 1996.

Kern, Karen. *Imperial Citizen: Marriage and Citizenship in the Ottoman Frontier Provinces of Iraq.* Syracuse, NY: Syracuse University Press, 2011.

Kertzer, David I. *The Kidnapping of Edgardo Mortara.* New York: Vintage Books, 1997.

Khayraddin. *The Surest Path; the Political Treatise of a Nineteenth-Century Muslim Statesman.* Translated by L. Carl Brown. Cambridge, MA: Harvard University Press, 1967.

Kirshner, Julius. "Between Nature and Culture: An Opinion of Baldus of Perugia on Venetian Citizenship as Second Nature." *Journal of Medieval and Renaissance Studies* 9, no. 2 (1979): 179–208.

Kobrin, Rebecca. *Jewish Bialystok and Its Diaspora.* Bloomington: Indiana University Press, 2010.

Koçunyan, Aylin. *Negotiating the Ottoman Constitution, 1839–1876.* Paris: Peeters, 2018.

Koessler, Maximilian. "'Subject,' 'Citizen,' 'National,' and 'Permanent Allegiance.'" *Yale Law Journal* 56, no. 1 (1946): 58–76.

Kosansky, Oren. "When Jews Speak Arabic: Dialectology and Difference in Colonial Morocco." *Comparative Studies in Society and History* 58, no. 1 (2016): 5–39.

Koskenniemi, Martti. *The Gentle Civilizer of Nations: The Rise and Fall of International Law 1870–1960.* Cambridge: Cambridge University Press, 2001.

———. "International Law and *Raison d'État*: Rethinking the Prehistory of International Law." In *The Roman Foundations of the Law of Nations: Alberico Gentili and the Justice of Empire,* edited by Benedict Kingsbury and Benjamin Straumann, 297–339. Oxford: Oxford University Press, 2010.

———. "Expanding Histories of International Law." *American Journal of Legal History* 56, no. 1 (2016): 104–12.

———. "Introduction: International Law and Empire; Aspects and Approaches." In *International Law and Empire: Historical Explorations,* edited by Martti Koskenniemi, Walter Rech, and Manuel Jiménez Fonseca, 1–18. Oxford: Oxford University Press, 2017.

———. *To the Uttermost Parts of the Earth: Legal Imagination and International Power, 1300–1870.* Cambridge: Cambridge University Press, 2021.

Koskenniemi, Martti, and Ville Kari. "A More Elevated Patriotism: The Emergence of International and Comparative Law (Nineteenth Century)." In *The Oxford Handbook of European Legal History,* edited by Heikki Pihlajamäki, Markus D. Dubber, and Mark Godfrey, 974–99. Oxford: Oxford University Press, 2018.

Kraîem, Mustapha. *La Tunisie précoloniale: Tome I, état, gouvernement, administration.* 2 vols. Tunis: Société Tunisienne de Diffusion, 1973.

Lafon, Jacques. "Les capitulations ottomanes: un droit paracolonial?" *Droits: Revue française de théorie, de philosophie et de cultures juridiques* 28 (1999): 155–80.

Lalloum, Jean. "Persécutions et déportations des juifs natifs d'Algérie présents en métropole dans les années noires." *La Revue des Tournelles* 25 (2016): 18–20.

Landau, Jacob M. *Jews in Nineteenth-Century Egypt.* London: Routledge, 1969.

Landes, David S. *Bankers and Pashas: International Finance and Economic Imperialism in Egypt.* London: Heinemann, 1958.

Lane, Edward. *An Arabic-English Lexicon.* 2 vols. London: Williams and Norgate, 1863.

Larguèche, Abdelhamid. "La communauté juive de Tunisie à l'epoque husseinite: unité, contrastes et relations inter-communautaires." In *Histoire communautaire, histoire plurielle: la communauté juive de Tunisie*, 165–80. Tunis: Université de Tunis I Faculté des lettres de la Manouba, 1999.

———. *Les ombres de la ville: Pauvres, marginaux et minoritaires à Tunis, XVIIIème et XIXème siècles*. Manouba, Tunisia: Centre de publication universitaire, Faculté des lettres de Manouba, 1999.

———. "Nasim Shammama; Un caïd face à lui-même et face aux autres." In *Juifs et musulmans en Tunisie: Fraternité et déchirements*, edited by Sonia Fellous, 143–57. Paris: Somogy éditions d'art, 2003.

Laroui, Abdellah. *Les origines sociales et culturelles du nationalisme marocain (1830–1912)*. Paris: François Maspero, 1977.

Laurent, François. "Etudes sur le droit international privé." *Journal du droit international privé* 5 (1878): 309–44, 421–46.

Le Cour Grandmaison, Olivier. *"Ennemis mortels": représentations de l'islam et politiques musulmanes en France à l'époque coloniale*. Paris: La Découverte, 2019.

Lee, Daniel. "Citizenship, Subjection, and Civil Law: Jean Bodin on Roman Citizenship and the Theory of Consensual Subjection." In *Citizenship and Empire in Europe 200–1900: The Antonine Constitution after 1800 Years*, edited by Clifford Ando, 113–34. Stuttgart: Franz Steiner Verlag, 2016.

Leff, Lisa Moses. *Sacred Bonds of Solidarity: The Rise of Jewish Internationalism in Nineteenth-Century France*. Stanford, CA: Stanford University Press, 2006.

Légier, Gérard. *Histoire du droit de la nationalité française des origines à la veille de la réforme de 1889*. 2 vols. Aix-en-Provence: Presses universitaires d'Aix-Marseille, 2014.

Lehmann, Matthias B. *Emissaries from the Holy Land: The Sephardic Diaspora and the Practice of Pan-Judaism in the Eighteenth Century*. Stanford, CA: Stanford University Press, 2014.

Lepore, Jill. "Historians Who Love Too Much: Reflections on Microhistory and Biography." *Journal of American History* 88, no. 1 (2001): 129–44.

Levi, Giovanni. "Les usages de la biographie." *Annales : Economies, sociétés, civilisations* 44, no. 6 (1989) : 1325–36.

Levy, Avigdor. "Haham Başı (Chief Rabbi)." In *Encyclopedia of Jews in the Islamic World*, edited by Norman A. Stillman. Leiden: Brill, 2010.

Lévy, Lionel. *La nation juive portugaise: Livourne, Amsterdam, Tunis, 1591–1951*. Paris: L'Harmattan, 1999.

Lewis, Mary Dewhurst. *Divided Rule: Sovereignty and Empire in French Tunisia, 1881–1938*. Berkeley: University of California Press, 2014.

Libson, Gideon. "Otonomiyah shippuṭit u-feniyah le-ʿarkaot mi-tzad bnei he-ḥasut ʿal pi mekorot muslimiyim be-tekufat ha-ge'onim." In *Ha-islam ve-ʿolamot ha-shezurim bo; Kovetz ma'marim le-zekharah shel Ḥavah Lazarus-Yafeh*, 334–92. Jerusalem: Makhon Ben Zvi, 2002.

Lohr, Eric. *Russian Citizenship: From Empire to Soviet Union*. Cambridge, MA: Harvard University Press, 2012.

Lorimer, James. *The Institutes of the Law of Nations: A Treatise of the Jural Relations of Separate Political Communities*. 2 vols. Edinburgh: W. Blackwood and Sons, 1883–84.

Lumbroso, Bruno. "Le Baron Giacomo del Castelnuovo: Médecin, explorateur, diplomate et homme politique juif italien du XIXe siècle." *Revue d'Histoire de la Méditerranée Hébraïque* 26, no. 102 (1973): 51–52.

Maas, Willem, ed. *Multilevel Citizenship*. Philadelphia: University of Pennsylvania Press, 2013.

———. "Multilevel Citizenship." In *The Oxford Handbook of Citizenship*, edited by Ayelet Shachar, Rainer Bauböck, Irene Bloemraad, and Maarten Vink, 645–68. Oxford: Oxford University Press, 2017.

Mahmood, Saba. "Religious Freedom, the Minority Question, and Geopolitics in the Middle East." *Comparative Studies in Society and History* 54, no. 2 (2012): 418–46.

Maier, Charles. "Consigning the Twentieth Century to History: Alternative Narratives for the Modern Era." *American Historical Review* 105, no. 3 (2000): 807–31.

Mailher de Chassat, Antoine. *Traité des statuts (lois personnelles, lois réelles) d'après le droit ancien et le droit modern, ou du droit international privé*. Paris: A. Durand, 1845.

Malaspina, Elisabetta Fiocchi. "'Toil of the Noble World': Pasquale Stanislao Mancini, Augusto Pierantoni and the International Legal Discourse of 19th Century Italy." *Clio Themis: Revue électronique d'histoire du droit* 18 (2020): 1–18.

Manby, Bronwen. *Citizenship in Africa: The Law of Belonging*. London: Hart Publishing, 2018.

Mancini, Pasquale Stanislao. *Della nazionalità come fondamento del diritto delle genti; prelezione al corso di diritto internazionale e marittimo pronunziata nella r. Università di Torino*. Turin: Tipografia Eredi Botta, 1851.

———. *Diritto internazionale: prelezioni, con un saggio sul Machiavelli*. Naples: Giuseppe Marghieri Editore, 1873.

———. "De l'utilité de rendre obligatoires pour tous les états, sous la forme d'un ou de plusieurs traités internationaux, un certain nombre de règles générales du droit international privé, pour assurer la décision uniforme des conflits entre les différentes législations civiles et criminelles." *Journal de droit international privé* 1, no. 4 (1874): 221–39, 285–304.

———. *Corte di Appello di Lucca; Per gli eredi testamentari del fu Conte Caid Nissim Samama contro i pretendenti alla sua eredità ab intestato; ricerca della legge regolatrice della successione del testatore*. Rome: Tipografia Fratelli Pallotta, 1880.

———. "Sulla modificazione della giurisdizione consolare in egitto." In *Discorsi parlamentari di Mancini raccolti e pubblicati per deliberazione della Camera Dei Deputati*, 535–683. Rome: Tipografia della Camera dei Deputati, 1895.

Marglin, Jessica M. "The Two Lives of Mas'ud Amoyal: Pseudo-Algerians in Morocco, 1830–1912." *International Journal of Middle East Studies* 44, no. 4 (2012): 651–70.

———. "Mediterranean Modernity through Jewish Eyes: The Transimperial Life of Abraham Ankawa." *Jewish Social Studies* 20, no. 2 (2014): 34–68.

———. *Across Legal Lines: Jews and Muslims in Modern Morocco*. New Haven, CT: Yale University Press, 2016.

———. "A New Language of Equality: Jews and the State in Nineteenth-Century Morocco." *British Journal of Middle Eastern Studies* 43, no. 2 (2016): 158–75.

———. "La nationalité en procès : droit international privé et monde Méditerranéen." *Annales. Histoire, Sciences Sociales* 73, no. 1 (2018): 83–118.

———. "Jews, Rights, and Belonging in Tunisia: Léon Elmilik, 1861–1881." *L'Année du Maghreb* 23 (2020): 167–84.

———. "Citizenship and Nationality in the French Colonial Maghreb." In *Routledge Handbook of Citizenship in the Middle East and North Africa*, edited by Roel Meijer, Zahra Babar, and James Sater, 45–60. London: Routledge, 2021.

———. "The Crémieux Decree Seen from Afar." *Journal of North African Studies* (2021): 1–23.
———. "Extraterritoriality and Legal Belonging in the Nineteenth-Century Mediterranean." *Law and History Review* 39, no. 4 (2021): 679–706.
Marshall, T. H. "Citizenship and Social Class." In *Citizenship and Social Class and Other Essays*, edited by T. H. Marshall, 1–85. Cambridge: Cambridge University Press, 1950.
Martello, Tullio. "Il professore d'università in Italia e all'estero." *L'Università* 3 (1889): 116–25.
Martin, Jean. "Jean Ganiage 1923–2012." *Outre-Mers. Revue d'histoire* 374–75 (2012): 375–77.
Masi, Corrado. "Fixation du statut des sujets toscans israélites dans la régence de Tunis (1822–1847)." *Revue tunisienne* 40 (1938): 155–86, 323–42.
Mays, Devi. *Forging Ties, Forging Passports: Migration and the Modern Sephardi Diaspora*. Stanford, CA: Stanford University Press, 2020.
McDougall, James. *A History of Algeria*. Cambridge: Cambridge University Press, 2017.
———. "Modernity in 'Antique Lands': Perspectives from the Western Mediterranean." *Journal of the Economic and Social History of the Orient* 60, no. 1–2 (2017): 1–17.
McKeown, Adam. *Melancholy Order: Asian Migration and the Globalization of Borders*. New York: Columbia University Press, 2008.
Mendelsohn, Ezra. *Class Struggle in the Pale: The Formative Years of the Jewish Workers' Movement in Tsarist Russia*. Cambridge: Cambridge University Press, 1970.
Merello. "Volpinari." *Annali della giurisprudenza* 10, no. 2 (1876): 8–9.
Merriman, John. *Massacre: The Life and Death of the Paris Commune*. New York: Basic Books, 2014.
Meyan, Paul. *Annuaire des diplômés 1890*. Paris: Société d'éditions scientifiques, 1891.
Mezghani, Ali. *Droit international privé: etats nouveaux et relations privées internationales; système de droit applicable et droit judiciaire international*. Tunis: Cérès Productions, 1991.
Mills, Alex. "The Private History of International Law." *International and Comparative Law Quarterly* 55 (2006): 1–49.
Ministero per gli affari esteri. *Annuario diplomatico del regno d'Italia per l'anno 1890*. Rome: Tipografia delle Mantellate, 1890.
Moalla, Asma. *The Regency of Tunis and the Ottoman Porte, 1777–1814*. London: RoutledgeCurzon, 2004.
Moati, Nine. *Les belles de Tunis*. Paris: Editions du Seuil, 1983.
Moatti, Claudia, ed. *La mobilité des personnes en Méditerranée, de l'antiquité à l'époque moderne; procédures de contrôle et documents d'identification*. Rome: Ecole française de Rome, 2004.
Moatti, Claudia, and Wolfgang Kaiser, eds. *Gens de passage en Méditerranée de l'antiquité à l'époque moderne: procédures de contrôle et d'identification*. Paris: Maisonneuve et Larose, 2007.
Molinari, Maurizio. *Ebrei in Italia: Un problema di identità (1870–1938)*. Florence: Editrice La Giuntina, 1991.
Morais, Sabato. *Italian Hebrew Literature*. New York: Jewish Theological Seminary, 1926.
Morsink, Johannes. *The Universal Declaration of Human Rights: Origins, Drafting, and Intent*. Philadelphia: University of Pennsylvania Press, 1999.
Mortara, Marco. *Della nazionalità e delle aspirazioni messianiche degli ebrei a proposito della questione sollevata dall'onor. deputato Pasqualigo*. Rome: Cotta e C., 1873.
Moumni, Ridha, ed. *L'éveil d'une nation*. Tunis: Officina Libraria, 2016.

———. "Une réforme de l'art pictoral? La nouvelle représentation du pouvoir tunisien." In *L'éveil d'une Nation*, edited by Ridha Moumni, 51–77. Tunis: Officina Libraria, 2016.

———. "Archaeology and Cultural Policy in Ottoman Tunisia, Part I: Muhammad Khaznadar (1865–70)." *Muqarnas* 37 (2020): 265–89.

"Munificence pieuse à Tunis." *Archives israélites* 21 (1860): 518–21.

Murphy, James Bernard. *The Philosophy of Positive Law: Foundations of Jurisprudence.* New Haven, CT: Yale University Press, 2005.

Myers, David N. *Between Jew and Arab: The Lost Voice of Simon Rawidowicz.* Waltham, MA: Brandeis University Press, 2008.

Mzali, Mohamed-Salah, and Jean Pignon. *Kheredine, homme d'état: documents historiques annotés.* Tunis: Maison Tunisienne de l'Edition, 1971.

Naaman, Abdallah. *Histoire des orientaux de France du Ière au XXème siècle.* Paris: Ellipses Édition, 2004.

Nadelmann, Kurt H. "Mancini's Nationality Rule and Non-Unified Legal Systems: Nationality versus Domicile." In *Conflicts of Law: International and Interstate*, edited by Kurt H. Nadelmann, 49–84. The Hague: Martinus Nijhoff, 1972.

Nedjar, Alain, Gilles Boulu, Liliane Nedjar, and Raphaël Attias, eds. *Registres de ketubbot de la nation juive de Livourne (1626–1890); généalogies et itinéraires familiaux.* 2 vols. Paris: Cercle de Généalogie Juive, 2020.

Nirenberg, David. *Anti-Judaism: The Western Tradition.* New York: W. W. Norton and Company, 2013.

Noiriel, Gérard. "Socio-histoire d'un concept; les usages du mot 'nationalité' au XIXe siècle." *Genèses: Sciences sociales et histoire* 20 (1995): 4–23.

Nuzzo, Luigi. *Origini di una scienza: diritto internazionale e colonialismo nel XIX secolo.* Frankfurt: Vittorio Klostermann, 2012.

Okan, Orçun Can. "Coping with Transitions: The Connected Construction of Turkey, Syria, Lebanon, and Iraq, 1918–1928." PhD diss., Columbia University, 2020.

Oliel-Grausz, Evelyne. "Modalité d'accueil et de contrôle des passants et migrants dans la diaspora séfarade d'occident (XVIIe–XVIIIe siècles)." In *Gens de passage en Méditerranée de l'antiquité à l'époque moderne: procédures de contrôle et d'identification*, edited by Claudia Moatti and Wolfgang Kaiser, 135–54. Paris: Maisonneuve et Larose, 2007.

Orvieto, Angiolo. "Di David Castelli e della sua opera." In *David Castelli, pubblicato in occasione del primo anniversario della morte di lui per cura del figlio Guido*, edited by Guido Castelli. Livorno: S. Belforte e C., 1901.

Oualdi, M'hamed. *Esclaves et maîtres; Les mamelouks des beys de Tunis du XVIIe siècle aux années 1880.* Paris: Publications de la Sorbonne, 2011.

———. "Le retrait après la disgrâce: les Khaznadār à Tunis dans la seconde moitié du XIXe siècle." *Cahiers de la Mediterranée* 82 (2011): 325–40.

———. *A Slave between Empires: A Transimperial History of North Africa.* New York: Columbia University Press, 2020.

Owen, Roger. *The Middle East in the World Economy.* London: I. B. Tauris, 2002.

Özsu, Umut. "The Ottoman Empire, the Origins of Extraterritoriality, and International Legal Theory." In *The Oxford Handbook of the Theory of International Law*, edited by Anne Orford and Florian Hoffman, 123–37. Oxford: Oxford University Press, 2016.

Pacifici. "Prefetto di Roma v. Keller." *Annali della giurisprudenza* 14, no. 1 (1880): 136–39.

Palma, Luigi. *Del principio di nazionalità nella moderna società europea.* Milan: Editori della Biblioteca utile, 1867.

Parks, Richard C. *Medical Imperialism in French North Africa: Regenerating the Jewish Community of Colonial Tunis.* Lincoln: University of Nebraska Press, 2017.

Parolin, Gianluca P. *Citizenship in the Arab World: Kin, Religion, and Nation-State.* Amsterdam: Amsterdam University Press, 2009.

Pélissié du Rausas, Gérard. *Le régime des capitulations dans l'empire Ottoman.* 2 vols. Paris: Arthur Rousseau, Editeur, 1902–5.

Pellissier de Reynaud, E. *Description de la régence de Tunis.* Exploration Scientifique de l'Algérie. Vol. 16. Paris: Imprimerie Impériale, 1853.

Penslar, Derek J. *Jews and the Military: A History.* Princeton, NJ: Princeton University Press, 2013.

Perkins, Kenneth J. *A History of Modern Tunisia.* Cambridge: Cambridge University Press, 2004.

Perl-Rosenthal, Nathan, and Sam Erman. "Inventing the Rules of Blood and of Soil: Nineteenth-Century Origins of Birthright Citizenship." Unpublished paper, 2021.

Perry, Amos. *Carthage and Tunis: Past and Present.* Providence, RI: Providence Press Company, 1869.

Philliou, Christine. *Biography of an Empire: Governing Ottomans in an Age of Revolution.* Berkeley: University of California Press, 2011.

Pianko, Noam. *Zionism and the Roads Not Taken: Rawidowicz, Kaplan, Kohn.* Bloomington: Indiana University Press, 2010.

———. *Jewish Peoplehood: An American Innovation.* New Brunswick, NJ: Rutgers University Press, 2015.

Picard, Joshua. "The Bathou Sfez Affair: A Microhistory of French Imperialism in North Africa." PhD. diss., Princeton University, Forthcoming.

Piccoli, Luigi Lauro. "La famiglia di P. S. Mancini." In *Pasquale Stanislao Mancini: Il diritto internazionale privato tra risorgimento e attività forense*, edited by Erik Jayme, 122–27. Padua: Casa editrice Dott. Antonio Milani, 1988.

Pickering, Mary. "Positivism in European Intellectual, Political, and Religious Life." In *The Cambridge History of Modern European Thought; Volume 1: The Nineteenth Century*, edited by Warren Breckman and Peter E. Gordon, 151–71. Cambridge: Cambridge University Press, 2019.

Picot, Emile. "La question des israélites roumains au point de vue du droit." *Revue historique de droit français et étranger* 14 (1868): 47–78.

Pierantoni, Augusto. *Il progresso del diritto pubblico e delle genti: introduzione allo studio del diritto costituzionale ed internazionale.* Modena, Italy: Tipi di Nicola Zanichelli e Soci, 1866.

———. *Corte di Appello di Lucca: Per il governo di S. A. il Bey di Tunisi nella successione Samama: parte prima: della nazionalità del testatore.* Rome: Tipografia Fratelli Pallotta, 1879.

Pierantoni Mancini, Grazia. *Alcune lettere di P. S. Mancini: estratto dalla nuova antologia, fascicolo 16 marzo 1900.* Rome: Direzione della Nuova Antologia, 1900.

Piketty, Thomas, Gilles Postel-Vinay, and Jean-Laurent Rosenthal. "Wealth Concentration in a Developing Economy: Paris and France, 1807–1994." *American Economic Review* 96, no. 1 (2006): 236–56.

Pirenne, Henri. *Mahomet et Charlemagne.* Paris: Félix Alcan, 1937.

Pitts, Jennifer. *Boundaries of the International: Law and Empire.* Cambridge, MA: Harvard University Press, 2018.

Planel, Anne-Marie. *Du comptoir à la colonie; histoire de la communauté française de Tunisie, 1814–1883.* Paris: Riveneuve éditions, 2015.

Pontois. *Jugement rendu par le tribunal civil de 1ère instance de Tunis dans l'affaire entre le Général Heussein Pacha et Léon Elmilik ex secrétaire administrateur et Haim Bismuth Maliach ex sous mandataire.* Livorno: A. B. Zecchini, 1885.

Posener, S. *Adolphe Crémieux: A Biography.* New York: Jewish Publication Society of Ameria, 1940.

Prak, Maarten. *Citizens without Nations: Urban Citizenship in Europe and the World, c. 1000–1789.* Cambridge: Cambridge University Press, 2018.

Price, Charles A. *Malta and the Maltese: A Study in Nineteenth Century Migration.* Melbourne: Georgian House, 1954.

Price, Polly J. "Jus Soli and Statelessness: A Comparative Perspective from the Americas." In *Citizenship in Question: Evidentiary Birthright and Statelessness,* edited by Benjamin N. Lawrance and Jacqueline Stevens, 28–42. Durham, NC: Duke University Press, 2017.

Quataert, Donald. *Ottoman Manufacturing in the Age of Industrial Revolution.* Cambridge: Cambridge University Press, 1993.

Rabinovitch, Simon J. "The Quality of Being French versus the Quality of Being Jewish: Defining the Israelite in French Courts in Algeria and the Metropole." *Law and History Review* 36, no. 4 (2018): 811–46.

Ramsay, David. *A Dissertation on the Manner of Acquiring the Character and Privileges of a Citizen of the United States.* 1789.

Rapport, Mike. *Nationality and Citizenship in Revolutionary France: The Treatment of Foreigners 1789–1799.* Oxford: Oxford University Press, 2000.

Rayburn, John C. "Count Joseph Telfener and the New York, Texas, and Mexican Railway Company." *Southwestern Historical Quarterly* 68, no. 1 (1964): 29–42.

Recueil des dépèches télégraphiques reproduites par la photographie et adressées à paris au moyen de pigeons-voyageurs pendant l'investissement de la capitale. Tours-Bordeaux, 1871.

Redhouse, James W. *A Turkish and English Lexicon Shewing in English the Significations for the Turkish Terms.* Constantinople: A. H. Boyajian, 1890.

Reiman, Alyssa. "Claiming Livorno: Commercial Networks, Foreign Status, and Culture in the Italian Jewish Diaspora, 1815–1914." PhD diss., University of Michigan, 2017.

Renan, Ernest. "What Is a Nation?" (Qu'est-ce qu'une nation?) (1882). In *What Is a Nation? And Other Political Writings,* edited by M. F. N. Giglioli, 247–63. New York: Columbia University Press, 2018.

Renner, Karl. "State and Nation." In *National Cultural Autonomy and Its Contemporary Critics,* edited by Ephraim Nimni, 14–47. London: Routledge, 2005.

République française. *Annuaire diplomatique de la république française pour 1872–1873.* Paris: Berger-Levrault et Cie, 1873.

Revault, Jacques. *Palais et demeures de Tunis, XVIIIe et XIXe siècles.* Paris: Editions du CNRS, 1971.

Riesenberg, Peter. "Citizenship and Equality in Late Medieval Italy." *Studia Gratiana* 15 (1972): 423–39.

———. *Citizenship in the Western Tradition: Plato to Rousseau.* Chapel Hill: University of North Carolina Press, 1992.

Rignano, Isacco. *Parere dell'avv. Isacco Rignano nella causa di pretesa nullità di matrimonio pendente davanti il tribunale civile di Livorno fra il Signor Giuseppe Semama e la Signora Ida Vittoria Stracca ved. Semama.* Livorno: Tipografia Francesco Vigo, 1894.

Rocca, Nonce. *À propos d'un livre récent sur la Tunisie: Observations.* Paris: F. Salmon, 1866.

Rodogno, Davide. "European Legal Doctrines on Intervention and the Status of the Ottoman Empire within the 'Family of Nations' throughout the Nineteenth Century." *Journal of the History of International Law* 18 (2016): 1–37.

Rodrigue, Aron. *French Jews, Turkish Jews: The Alliance Israélite Universelle and the Politics of Jewish Schooling in Turkey, 1860–1925.* Bloomington: Indiana University Press, 1990.

———. *Images of Sephardi and Eastern Jewries in Transition: The Teachers of the Alliance Israélite Universelle, 1860–1939.* Seattle: University of Washington Press, 1993.

Rosadi. "Prefetto di Lucca c. Malfanti." *Annali della giurisprudenza* 13, no. 3 (1879): 65–70.

Rosenthal, Franz. "The Stranger in Medieval Islam." *Arabica* 44, no. 1 (1997): 35–75.

Rosi, Michele. "Pasquale Stansilao Mancini." In *Dizionario del risorgimento nazionale; dalle origini a Roma capitale. Fatti e persone*, edited by Michele Rosi, 461–63. Milan: Casa editrice dottor Francesco Vallardi, 1933.

Rothman, E. Natalie. *Brokering Empire: Trans-Imperial Subjects between Venice and Istanbul.* Ithaca, NY: Cornell University Press, 2011.

Rozenblit, Marsha L. *Reconstructing a National Identity: The Jews of Habsburg Austria during World War I.* Oxford: Oxford University Press, 2001.

———. "From Habsburg Jews to Austrian Jews: The Jews of Vienna, 1918–1938." In *Jüdische Gemeinden: Kontinuitäten und Brüche*, edited by Eleonore Lappin, 105–30. Berlin: Philo, 2002.

Rubin, Avi. *Ottoman Nizamiye Courts: Law and Modernity.* New York: Palgrave Macmillan, 2011.

Ruskola, Teemu. *Legal Orientalism: China, the United States, and Modern Law.* Cambridge, MA: Harvard University Press, 2013.

Ryan, Donna F. *The Holocaust and the Jews of Marseille: The Enforcement of Anti-Semitic Policies in Vichy France.* Urbana: University of Illinois Press, 1996.

Sadiq Bey. "Décret de S. A. le Bey instituant la Commission Financière." *Archives Diplomatiques; recueil de diplomatie et d'histoire* 10 (1870): 134–36.

Sahlins, Peter. *Unnaturally French: Foreign Citizens in the Old Regime and After.* Ithaca, NY: Cornell University Press, 2004.

Said, Edward. *Orientalism.* New York: Vintage Books, 2003.

Salmieri, Adrien. "La communauté italienne de Tunisie (milieu du XIXe siècle-milieu du XXe siècle)." In *Les communautés méditerranéennes de Tunisie*, 271–84. Tunis: Centre de Publication Universitaire, 2006.

Salyer, Lucy. *Under the Starry Flag: How a Band of Irish Americans Joined the Fenian Revolt and Sparked a Crisis over Citizenship.* Cambridge, MA: Harvard University Press, 2018.

Salzmann, Ariel. "Citizens in Search of a State: The Limits of Political Participation in the Late Ottoman Empire." In *Extending Citizenship, Reconfiguring States*, edited by Michael Hanagan and Charles Tilly, 37–66. Lanham, MD: Rowman and Littlefield, 1999.

Samama, Nissim. *De l'indivision (communio incidens) des objets considérés individuellement: droit international privé; des conditions requises pour la validité des testaments.* Aix-en-Provence: J. Remondet-Aubin, 1890.

———. "De la naturalisation française des israélites tunisiens et accessoirement de l'extension de la juridiction des tribunaux français." In *Congrès de l'Afrique du Nord, tenu à Paris, du 6 à 10 octobre 1908: compte rendu des travaux, tome II: questions indigènes,* edited by Charles Depincé, 356–74. Paris: Au siège du comité d'organisation du congrès, 1909.

———. *Contributo allo studio della doppia cittadinanza nei riguardi dei movimento migratorio.* Florence: Tipografia Enrico Ariani, 1910.

"Samama *utrinque* et gouvernement de Tunis." *Journal de droit international privé* 8, no. 11–12 (1881): 552–57.

Sapir, Ya'akov. *'Edut be-Yehosef.* Mainz, 1874.

Sarfatti, Michele. "Italy's Fascist Jews: Insights on an Unusual Scenario." *Quest: Issues in Contemporary Jewish History* 11 (2017): i–xvii.

Savory, R. M. "Bast." In *Encyclopedia of Islam,* edited by P. Bearman, T. Bianquis, C. E. Bosworth, E. van Donzel, and W. P. Heinrichs. 2nd. Leiden: Brill, 2003.

Scardozzi, Mirella. "Una storia di famiglia: I Franchetti dalle coste del Mediterraneo all'Italia liberale." *Quaderni Storici* 38, no. 114 (2003): 697–740.

Schächter, Elizabeth. *The Jews of Italy 1848–1915: Between Tradition and Transformation.* London: Vallentine Mitchell, 2011.

Schreier, Joshua. *Arabs of the Jewish Faith: The Civilizing Mission in Colonial Algeria.* New Brunswick, NJ: Rutgers University Press, 2010.

———. "A Jewish Riot against Muslims: The Polemics of History in Late Colonial Algeria." *Comparative Studies in Society and History* 58, no. 3 (2016): 746–73.

———. *The Merchants of Oran: A Jewish Port at the Dawn of Empire.* Stanford, CA: Stanford University Press, 2017.

Schroeter, Daniel J. *The Sultan's Jew: Morocco and the Sephardi World.* Stanford, CA: Stanford University Press, 2002.

———. "A Different Road to Modernity: Jewish Identity in the Arab World." In *Diasporas and Exiles: Varieties of Jewish Identity,* edited by Howard Wettstein, 150–63. Berkeley: University of California Press, 2002.

———. "'Islamic Anti-Semitism' in Historical Discourse." *American Historical Review* 123, no. 4 (2018): 1172–89.

———. "Between Metropole and French North Africa: Vichy's Anti-Semitic Legislation and Colonialism's Racial Hierarchies." In *The Holocaust and North Africa,* edited by Aomar Boum and Sarah Abrevaya Stein, 19–49. Stanford, CA: Stanford University Press, 2019.

Scott, Rebecca J. "Paper Thin: Freedom and Re-Enslavement in the Diaspora of the Haitian Revolution." *Law and History Review* 29, no. 4 (2011): 1061–87.

Scott, S. P. *The Civil Law: The Enactments of Justinian; the Code.* Vol. 12. Cincinnati, 1932.

Sebag, Paul. *Histoire des juifs de Tunisie: Des origines à nos jours.* Paris: L'Harmattan, 1991.

Segre, Dan V. "The Emancipation of Jews in Italy." In *Paths of Emancipation: Jews, States and Citizenship,* edited by Pierre Birnbaum and Ira Katznelson, 206–37. Princeton, NJ: Princeton University Press, 1995.

Shachar, Ayelet. *The Birthright Lottery: Citizenship and Global Inequality.* Cambridge, MA: Harvard University Press, 2009.

Shachar, Ayelet, Rainer Bauböck, Irene Bloemraad, and Maarten Vink. "Introduction: Citizenship—*Quo Vadis*?" In *The Oxford Handbook of Citizenship*, edited by Ayelet Shachar, Rainer Bauböck, Irene Bloemraad, and Maarten Vink, 3–11. Oxford: Oxford University Press, 2017.

Shamama, Moshe b. Ya'akov. *Kitāb qānūn al-dawla al-tūnisīya.* Tunis: Maṭba'at Mīster Monṣ Fīlad al-Ingilīz, 1861.

Shamama, Shlomo. *Bigdei shesh.* Livorno: Eliyahu Benamozegh, 1866.

Shamama, Shlomo b. Yehudah. *Shoresh Yishai.* Livorno: Daniel ve-Shmuel Sa'adun, 1809.

Sharkey, Heather. *A History of Muslims, Christians, and Jews in the Middle East.* Cambridge: Cambridge University Press, 2017.

Shaw, Stanford J. "The Origins of Ottoman Military Reform: The Nizam-i Cedid Army of Sultan Selim III." *Journal of Modern History* 37, no. 3 (1965): 291–306.

Shemla, Abraham. "Afrika." *Ha-Magid*, March 1, 1865, 4.

Shilo, Shmuel. *Dina de-malkhuta dina.* Jerusalem: Hotza'at defus akademi be-Yerushalayim, 1974.

Shilo, Shmuel, and Menachem Elon. "Dina de-Malkhuta Dina." In *Encyclopedia Judaica*, edited by Michael Berenbaum and Fred Skolnik, 663–69. 2nd ed. Detroit: Macmillan Reference USA, 2007.

Shumsky, Dimitry. *Beyond the Nation-State: The Zionist Political Imagination from Pinsker to Ben-Gurion.* New Haven, CT: Yale University Press, 2019.

Siegelberg, Mira L. *Statelessness: A Modern History.* Cambridge, MA: Harvard University Press, 2020.

Sienna, Noam. "Making Jewish Books in North Africa, 1700–1900." PhD diss., University of Minnesota, 2020.

Singer, Isidore, and Herman Rosenthal. "Ashkenazi, Abraham." In *Jewish Encyclopedia*, edited by Isidore Singer, 193. New York: Funk and Wagnalls, 1906.

Slama, B. *L'insurrection de 1864 en Tunisie.* Tunis: Maison tunisienne de l'édition, 1967.

Slezkine, Yuri. *The Jewish Century.* Princeton, NJ: Princeton University Press, 2006.

Smida, Mongi. *Consuls et consulats de Tunisie au 19e siècle.* Tunis: Imprimerie de l'Orient, 1991.

Soetens, Claude. *Le congrès eucharistique international de Jérusalem (1893) dans le cadre de la politique orientale du Pape Léon XIII.* Recueil des travaux d'histoire et de philologie, 6ème série, fasc. 12. Louvain: Presses universitaires de Louvain, 1977.

Sommer, Dorothe. *Freemasonry in the Ottoman Empire: A History of the Fraternity and Its Influence in Syria and the Levant.* London: I. B. Tauris, 2015.

Sonnino, Guido. *Storia della tipografia ebraica in Livorno.* Turin: Tip. Giuseppe Lavagno, 1912.

Sorkin, David. *Jewish Emancipation: A History across Five Centuries.* Princeton, NJ: Princeton University Press, 2019.

Soysal, Özer. "Yüzyıl Sonlarında Türk Ulusal Kütüphanesi'ni Kurma Girişimi." *Türk Kütüphaneciliği* 1, no. 1 (1987): 9–16.

Sraieb, Noureddine. "Elite et société: l'invention de la Tunisie de l'état dynastie à la nation moderne." In *Tunisie au présent: une modernité au-dessus de tout soupçon?*, edited by Michel Camau, 65–96. Paris: Centre National de la Recherche Scientifique, 1987.

State of Labor in Europe: 1878; Reports from the United States Consuls in the Several Countries of Europe. Washington, DC: Government Printing Office, 1879.

Stein, Sarah Abrevaya. *Making Jews Modern: The Yiddish and Ladino Press in the Russian and Ottoman Empires.* Bloomington: Indiana University Press, 2004.

———. "Protected Persons? The Baghdadi Jewish Diaspora, the British State, and the Persistence of Empire." *American Historical Review* 116, no. 1 (2011): 80–108.

———. *Extraterritorial Dreams: Jews, Citizenship, and the Calamitous Twentieth Century.* Chicago: University of Chicago Press, 2016.

Sternfeld, Lior B. *Between Iran and Zion: Jewish Histories of Twentieth-Century Iran.* Stanford, CA: Stanford University Press, 2018.

Stigall, Dan E. *The Santillana Codes: The Civil Codes of Tunisia, Morocco, and Mauritania.* Lanham, MD: Lexington Books, 2017.

Stillman, Norman. *The Jews of Arab Lands: A History and Sourcebook.* Philadelphia: Jewish Publication Society, 1979.

———. *The Jews of Arab Lands in Modern Times.* Philadelphia: Jewish Publication Society, 1991.

Stoler, Ann Laura, and Frederick Cooper. "Between Metropole and Colony: Rethinking a Research Agenda." In *Tensions of Empire: Colonial Cultures in a Bourgeois World,* edited by Frederick Cooper and Ann Laura Stoler, 1–56. Berkeley: University of California Press, 1997.

Stoskopf, Nicolas. *Les patrons du second empire: banquiers et financiers parisiens.* Paris: Picard, 2002.

Stow, Kenneth. *Catholic Thought and Papal Jewry Policy, 1555–1593.* New York: Jewish Theological Seminary of America, 1977.

———. *Anna and Tranquillo: Catholic Anxiety and Jewish Protest in the Age of Revolutions.* New Haven, CT: Yale University Press, 2016.

Surkis, Judith. *Sex, Law, and Sovereignty in French Algeria, 1830–1930.* Ithaca, NY: Cornell University Press, 2019.

Tarazona, Liliana Obregón. "Writing International Legal History: An Overview." *Monde(s)* 1, no. 7 (2015): 95–112.

Tazzara, Corey. *The Free Port of Livorno and the Transformation of the Mediterranean World.* Oxford: Oxford University Press, 2017.

———. "Religious Boundaries in Italy during an Era of Free Trade, 1550–1750: The Case of Livorno." In *Jews and the Mediterranean,* edited by Matthias Lehmann and Jessica M. Marglin, 107–28. Bloomington: Indiana University Press, 2020.

Terem, Etty. "Al-Mahdī al-Wazzānī." In *Islamic Legal Thought: A Compendium of Muslim Jurists,* edited by Oussama Arabi, David S. Powers, and Susan Spectorsky, 435–56. Leiden: Brill, 2013.

Thomas, Yan. "Le droit d'origine à Rome: contribution à l'étude de la citoyenneté." *Revue critique de droit international privé* 84, no. 2 (1995): 253–90.

Todd, David. "Beneath Sovereignty: Extraterritoriality and Imperial Internationalism in Nineteenth-Century Egypt." *Law and History Review* 36, no. 1 (2018): 105–37.

Toledano, Ehud R. *State and Society in Mid-Nineteenth-Century Egypt.* Cambridge: Cambridge University Press, 1990.

Tomassi, Francesco. *Architettura come colore.* Venice: Arsenale, 1994.

Torpey, John. *The Invention of the Passport: Surveillance, Citizenship and the State.* Cambridge: Cambridge University Press, 2000.

Trivellato, Francesca. *The Familiarity of Strangers: The Sephardic Diaspora, Livorno, and Cross-Cultural Trade in the Early Modern Period.* New Haven, CT: Yale University Press, 2009.

Trollope, Anthony. *Orley Farm.* Oxford: Oxford University Press, 1985.

Tsur, Yaron. "'Ahd al-Amān." In *Encyclopedia of Jews in the Islamic World*, edited by Norman A. Stillman. Leiden: Brill, 2010.

———. *Gevirim ve-yehudim aḥerim be-Mizraḥ ha-Tikhon ha-'othmani, 1750–1830.* Jersualem: Mosad Bialik, 2016.

Tunger-Zanetti, Andreas. *La communication entre Tunis et Istanbul 1860–1913: province et métropole.* Paris: L'Harmattan, 1996.

Ulbert, Jörg. "Identifier pour contrôler." *Mélanges de la Casa de Velázquez* 51, no. 1 (March 2, 2021): §24–39.

Uran, Steven. "Crémieux Decree." In *Encyclopedia of Jews in the Islamic World*, edited by Norman Stillman, 688–90. Leiden: Brill, 2010.

Valensi, Lucette. *Tunisian Peasants in the Eighteenth and Nineteenth Centuries.* Translated by Beth Archer. Cambridge: Cambridge University Press, 1985.

———. *Mardochée Naggiar: Enquête sur un inconnu.* Paris: Stock, 2008.

Van Den Boogert, Maurits H. *The Capitulations and the Ottoman Legal System: Qadis, Consuls, and Beratlıs in the 18th Century.* Leiden: Brill, 2005.

van Krieken, G. S. *Khayr al-Dîn et la Tunisie, 1850–1881.* Leiden: Brill, 1976.

Van Os, Nicole A. N. M. "Ottoman Muslim and Turkish Women in an International Context." *European Review* 13, no. 3 (2005): 459–79.

Vanel, Marguerite. "La notion de nationalité: evolution historique en droit interne et en droit colonial comparé (droit français—droit britannique)." *Revue critique de droit international privé* 40 (1951): 3–39.

Vassel, Eusèbe. *La littérature populaire des israélites tunisiens.* Paris: Ernest Leroux, 1907.

Véhel, J. "Le martyre Bathou." In *Le Hara conte . . . : Folklore judéo-tunisien*, edited by J. Véhel, V. Danon, and Ryvel, 77–90. Paris: Les Éditions Ivrit, 1929.

Verksin, Alan. *Islamic Law and the Crisis of the Reconquista: The Debate on the Status of Muslim Communities in Christendom.* Leiden: Brill, 2015.

Verwilghen, Michel. *Conflits de nationalités: plurinationalité et apatride.* Recueil des Cours: Collected Courses of the Hague Academy of International Law. Vol. 277. The Hague: Martinus Nijhoff Publishers, 1999.

Vidari, Gian Savino Pene. "Un secolo e mezzo fa (22 gennaio 1851): la lezione torinese di Pasquale Stanislao Mancini sulla nazionalità." *Studi Piemontesi* 31, no. 2 (2002): 273–86.

Viscomi, Joseph. "Out of Time: History, Presence, and the Departure of the Italians of Egypt, 1933–Present." PhD diss., University of Michigan, 2016.

Wehr, Hans. *A Dictionary of Modern Written Arabic (Arabic-English).* 4th ed. Urbana, IL: Spoken Language Services Inc., 1994.

Weil, Patrick. *How to Be French: Nationality in the Making since 1789.* Durham, NC: Duke University Press, 2008.

———. *Qu'est-ce qu'un français? Histoire de la nationalité française depuis la révolution.* Paris: Gallimard, 2002.

Weis, Paul. *Nationality and Statelessness in International Law.* Westport, CT: Hyperion Press, Inc., 1956.

Weitz, Eric D. *A Century of Genocide: Utopias of Race and Nation.* 2nd ed. Princeton, NJ: Princeton University Press, 2013.

Wells, Charlotte Catherine. *Law and Citizenship in Early Modern France.* Baltimore: Johns Hopkins University Press, 1995.

Werner, Michael, and Bénédicte Zimmermann. "Beyond Comparison: Histoire Croisée and the Challenge of Reflexivity." *History and Theory* 45, no. 1 (2006): 30–50.

Westermarck, Edward. *Ritual and Belief in Morocco.* Vol. 1. New Hyde Park, NY: University Books, 1968.

Wilder, Gary. "Colonial Ethnology and Political Rationality in French West Africa." *History and Anthropology* 14, no. 3 (2003): 219–52.

———. *The French Imperial Nation-State: Negritude and Colonial Humanism between the Two World Wars.* Chicago: University of Chicago Press, 2005.

Wittmann, Richard. "Before Qadi and Vizier: Intra-Communal Dispute Resolution and Legal Transactions among Christians and Jews in the Plural Society of Seventeenth Century Istanbul." PhD diss., Harvard University, 2008.

Wyrtzen, Jonathan. *Making Morocco: Colonial Intervention and the Politics of Identity.* Ithaca, NY: Cornell University Press, 2015.

Yerushalmi, Yosef Hayim. "Servants of Kings and Not Servants of Servants: Some Aspects of the Political History of the Jews." In *The Faith of Fallen Jews: Yosef Hayim Yerushalmi and the Writing of Jewish History,* edited by David N. Myers and Alexander Kaye, 245–76. Waltham, MA: Brandeis University Press, 2013.

Yılmaz, İlkay. "Governing the Armenian Question through Passports in the Late Ottoman Empire (1876–1908)." *Journal of Historical Sociology* 32 (2019): 388–403.

Young, Edward. *Labor in Europe and America.* Philadelphia: S. A. George and Company, 1875.

Zarinebaf, Fariba. *Mediterranean Encounters: Trade and Pluralism in Early Modern Galata.* Berkeley: University of California Press, 2018.

Ze'evi, Dror. "Back to Napoleon? Thoughts on the Beginning of the Modern Era in the Middle East." *Mediterranean Historical Review* 19, no. 1 (2004): 73–94.

Zimmerman, Joshua D. *Poles, Jews, and the Politics of Nationality: The Bund and the Polish Socialist Party in Late Tsarist Russia, 1892–1914.* Madison: University of Wisconsin Press, 2004.

Znaien, Nessim. "Les raisins de la domination: histoire sociale de l'alcool en Tunisie à l'époque du protectorat (1881–1956)." PhD diss., Université Paris I Panthéon Sorbonne, 2017.

Zola, Émile. *La Curée.* Paris: Pocket, 1999.

Zürcher, Erik Jan. "The Ottoman Conscription System in Theory and Practice." In *Arming the State: Military Conscription in the Middle East and Central Asia, 1775–1925,* edited by Erik Jan Zürcher, 79–94. London: I. B. Tauris, 1999.

INDEX

Page numbers in *italics* refer to illustrations.

Aali Pasha, 55
Abdulmejid, Sultan, 27, 29, 31, 51
acts of notoriety, 127
Afas, M., 77
'Ahd al-Amān (1857), 30–32, 46, 48, 143, 144
Ahmad Bey, 43, 45, 52, 62, 71, 89, 98, 138, 239; during Crimean War, 27; Ibn 'Ayyad linked to, 20, 24; Khaznadar linked to, 25; Nissim sponsored by, 22; as reformer, 22, 23–24, 27, 50
Algeria, 14, 24; French conquest of, 5, 16–17, 22, 153, 195; Jewish law in, 175; migration from, 42, 46, 225
Al-Hadif, Aharon, 277–78n12
'Ali (nephew of Ibn 'Ayyad), 204
'Ali b. Ghadhahim, 56
'Ali Nuri Bey (Knut Gustaf), 206
Alliance Israélite Universelle, 75, 115, 176
al-Massih, Antun Yussuf 'Abd, 7
al-Riyahi, Ibrahim, 43
al-Wazzani, al-Mahdi, 43
Andreucci, Ferdinando, 250n15
'Annabi, Muhammad, 42–43
antisemitism, 160, 161, 164, 167, 168, 230, 234–38; under Nazism and Fascism, 217–20
Arendt, Hannah, 223
Arez, Meriam de Josef, 289n64
Ascoli, Raffaello, 199–200
Ashkenazi, Abraham, 111–13, 190
Ashkenazi, Meir, 69, 79
Ashkenazi Jews, 163
Attal, Nissim, 101, 103, 106, 243

Bandini, Agosto, 283n90
Baquis, Elena (Nissim), 308n66
Baquis, Raffaello, 190, 198
Barbarius Phillipus, 290n79
Bargellini, Adriano, xiv–xv, xvii–xviii, 100, 102, 108, 109, 113–14, 127, 239; official downgrading of, 18; Shamamas' bickering faulted by, 107
Bargellini, Tommaso, 239
Bartolo da Sassoferrato, 172, 287–88n46
Barye, Antoine, 318n79
Bash Agha, Mustafa, 328
Battle of Solferino (1859), 212
Bauffremont Affair (Countess de Bauffremont), 147–48, 149
Beida, Abraham, 59
Bekia (Mas'uda's sister), 48
Bellaiche, Hanna (wife), 35, 36, 48, 62, 239
Bellais, Hai, 283n85
Bellais, Joseph, 283n85
Bellais, Mordekhai, 283n85
Benamozegh, Elia, 191–94, 198, 203, 239
Ben 'Attar, Yehudah, 277–78n12
b. Maimon, Abraham, 65
b. Moshe, Ya'akov, 281n63
Bessis, Joseph, 69, 79, 269n18, 272
Bicci, Francesco, 188
Bismarck, Otto Eduard Leopoldo von, 88

Bloch, Jeanne, 218
Bluntschli, Johann Caspar, 147–48
Boccara, Abraham, 278n13
Bodin, Jean, 142
Boll, Alfred, 316–17n60
Bouzgel, Nathan, 278n13
Bracha, Yasha, 280–81n52
Braudel, Fernand, 320–21n2
Bundism, 160, 176
Buzzati, Giulio Cesare, 316–17n60

Cairoli, Benedetto, 195
Callot, Jacques, 318n79
capitulations, 37, 40–42, 46, 70, 106, 210
Carlo Alberto, king of Sardinia, 85–86
Caro, Joseph, 194
Cassuto, Dario, 190, 198, 317n73
Castelli, David, 189–94, 203, 216, 239
Castelnuovo, Giacomo del, 71–72, 110, 114, 239–40
Castelnuovo, Guglielmo, 114
Cerutti, Louis, 84
Cesarini, Carlo, 179
Chakrabarty, Dipesh, 252n13
China, 225
Christians, 14, 28; as slaves, 39
citizenship: as burden, 70–71; documentary proof of, 6–7, 84, 226; dual, 213–14; exclusions from, 6, 223, 229; in France after the Revolution, 128–29; in Germanic lands, 142; Islamic views of, 4; Italian reunification and, 45; in Jewish law, 166, 191–93; nationality compared with, 138–40; in Roman law, 136, 166, 172, 188; secularism linked to, 4, as tool, 62; during World War II, 223, 229. *See also* legal belonging; nationality
Civil War, U.S., 53, 240
Cogordan, George, 139–40
conflict of laws, 107–8, 112, 125
conscription, 32, 71, 144
Corcos, Abraham, 270n29
Coriat, Fortunée, 272n73
Coriat, Yehudah, 191
Corot, Camille, 318n79
Costa, Domenico, 276n39
Costa, Laure, 276n39
Cover, Robert, 8
Crémieux, Adolphe, 75, 76, 214
Crémieux Decree, 161, 175, 212
Crimean War, 27–28, 51
customs duties, 16, 20

Dahdah, Rushayd, 52, 63, 64, 68, 81, 240
d'Avigdor, Henri, 24
de Botmiliau, Adolphe-François, 105
Depienne, Pierre-Marie, 187
de Flaux, Armand, 13–14
De iudaeis (de Susannis), 172
de Laigne (French consul in Florence), 208–9, 220
de Lesseps, Ferdinand, 17, 62, 241
de Lesseps, Jules, xvii, 17, 62–64, 74, 81, 102, 241
de Lesseps, Mathieu, 62, 241
de Luca, Giovanni Battista, 172
d'Erlanger, Frederick Emile, 49, 52–56, 60, 62, 64, 67, 91, 200, 237, 240, 241; appellate decision praised by, 179–80; beneficiaries' shares pursued by, 181, 183–84; corruption accusations against, 90, 236–37; Gutierres's negotiations with, 187, 195–96; halakhic experts retained by, 190, 191; ruthlessness of, 53, 88, 90
d'Erlanger, Raphael, 53, 88, 240
de Susannis, Marquardus, 166, 172, 174–75
dhimmīs, 153–54; abolition of status of, 27–28, 30–32; choice of law among, 172–73; defined, 3; rights of, 4, 14–15, 16, 141–44; violations by, 153–54
Djemal Pasha, 55
Drouyn de Lhuys, Edouard, 55, 64
Drumont, Edouard, 237
Dubois, Albert, 187
Dworkin, Ronald, 294n46

Elmilik, David, 207
Elmilik, Léon (Eliyahu Almaliah), 48, 178, 190, 200, 228, 240; declining reputation of, 206–7, 210; expertise of, xviii, 114–16, 142, 158, 162, 187, 188; Francophilia of, 161; Guttieres's frictions with, 187; after Husayn's death, 208; Husayn's split with, 206, 207; Jewish nationality asserted by, 158–59, 162–64, 165, 174, 176, 197; persistence of, 196, 206; rabbinic rulings sought by, 188–89; Tunisian Jews' equality asserted by, 143–44, 145
Elmilik, Mas'ud Felix, 207
El Morali, Mustafa, 308n71
Enlightenment, 194
expatriation, 165, 204; as natural right, 137, 146–50, 152–55, 157, 178, 188, 197; Ottoman law of, 47, 148, 205; statelessness and, 117–19, 126, 138, 149, 158, 188, 190, 223; Tunisian law of, 46–47, 137, 148, 152–53, 158, 188

Fedriani, Gaetano, 89
Fellous, Shalom, 69, 79
Fenian Revolt (1867), 225
Féraud, Laurent-Charles, 315n34
Fiorentino, Alfonso, 219
Foelix, Jean-Jacques Gaspard, 285–86n25
Foucault, Michel, 291n11
France: Algeria occupied by, 5, 16–17, 22, 153, 195; extraterritorial jurisdiction of, 41–43, 45, 46, 48, 70, 115, 161, 206, 208–10, 213, 220, 226; on International Financial Commission, 59–60, 88–89, 187, 235; Jews' legal status in, 143, 145, 163, 175; nationality law of, 24–25, 63, 70–71, 72, 79, 117, 128–29, 142, 149, 161, 205, 207, 208–9, 213, 218; Tunisia occupied by, 179, 195, 198, 230–31; Vichy rule in, 217, 218
La France juive (Drumont), 237
Frégier, Casimir, 303n71
French Revolution, 27, 128–29, 132
Fuller, Lon, 146
Funduq des français, 38, 49, 263n4, 266n58

Galeotti, Leopoldo, xvii, 109, *120*, 135, 175, 186, 190, 240; Jewish nationhood asserted by, 158, 165–67, 169, 174, 176; Risorgimento supported by, 164–65
Gallian, Carlo, 124, 156
Ganiage, Jean, 237–38
Garibaldi, Giuseppe, 39, 89, 130
Garsin, Solomon, 299n9
Gay, Oscar, 276n39
Gay, Thérèse, 276n39
Geiger, Abraham, 310n92
General Jewish Labor Bund, 160–61
Ghikis, Vasilaki Musurus, 208, 209, 210
Gozlan, Abraham, 181
Graetz, Heinrich, 310n92
Grana Jews, 57, 58, 61, 70, 71, 132; as freemasons, 161; Italian citizenship of, 100; Tunisian settlement by, 43–45, 85, 186; Twansa Jews disdained by, 233
Great Britain, 41, 42, 46, 146
Greece, 5, 22
Grotius, Hugo, 147
Gülfem (concubine of Ibn 'Ayyad), 204
Gustaf, Knut ('Ali Nuri Bey), 206
Guttieres, Abramo, 44, 306n44
Guttieres, Angelo, 44, 306n44
Guttieres, Cesare, 44, 306n44, 306n50
Guttieres, Eva, 306n44
Guttieres, Giacomo, 44, 89, 186–87, 195–96, 240
Guttieres, Guglielmo, 44, 306n44
Guttieres, Judica, 306n44
Guttieres, Messodi, 306n44

Habsburg Empire, 41, 122, 254n26
Ha-Cohen-Ganunah, Mordekhai, 277–78n12
Hai Gagin, Shalom Moshe, 280–81n52
halakhah (Jewish law), 16, 112, 114; family law of, 36, 75, 79, 101, 135; funerary provisions of, 95; intermarriage banned

halakhah (Jewish law) (*continued*)
by, 216, 220; Italian secularism vs., 170, 173; as national law, 158, 159, 162, 163–64, 170–75, 179, 189, 197; as a non-territorial law, 4, 157, 158, 159, 163, 166, 188–89; testamentary provisions of, xvii, 80, 98, 107, 108, 110, 111, 156–57, 183, 190, 193
Hallyday, Johnny, 256n14
Halpérin, Jean-Louis, 284nn6–7
Hamida (nephew of Ibn 'Ayyad), 204
Hammuda Pasha, 15
ḥāra (Jewish quarter), 14, 19, 32, 35, 49
Hardoon, Silas Aaron, 7
Hart, Herbert, 146
Hasan I, sultan of Morocco, 31
Hassuna (nephew of Ibn 'Ayyad), 204
Haussmann, Georges-Eugène, baron, 40, 63
Herzl, Theodor, 161, 206
Hesiod, 95
Horace, 211
Horden, Peregrine, 320–21n2
Hornung, Joseph, 295–96n66
Husayn b. 'Ali, 16
Husayn Bey, 22, 23
Husayn ibn 'Abdallah (General Husayn), 56, 176, 178, 181, 200, 241; and antisemitism, 235; Castelli retained by, 189–90; as city councilor, 32; death of, 208–10, 220, 226; d'Erlanger rebuffed by, 183–84; dual citizenship viewed by, 213–14; Elmilik's expertise and, xviii, 114–16, 142, 158, 162, 187, 188; Elmilik's split with, 206, 207; European modernity criticized by, 176; experts retained by, 188, 189–90; Galeotti and, 120; Gallian's strategy avoided by, 156–57; government experience of, 138; Ibn Isma'il's split with, 184–87; Islamic law invoked by, 4–5, 138, 153–54, 197, 230; legal belonging viewed by, 136, 138, 140–42, 155, 198, 209–10; Lucca judge maligned by, 179; Nissim's debts to Tunisia inventoried by, 113, 236; Pierantoni retained by, 123–24, 138, 152; Qānūn al-Dawla invoked by, 149, 154–55; Tunisian antisemitism denied by, 143–46, 153, 176, 197; Tunisian estate claims ceded by, 183–86
Husaynid dynasty, 16, 20, 23

Ibn 'Ayyad, Ahmad, 204, 205
Ibn 'Ayyad, Amina, 204
Ibn 'Ayyad, 'Aziza Nourissen, 204
Ibn 'Ayyad, Hayriye, 204, 205–6
Ibn 'Ayyad, Jamila, 204
Ibn 'Ayyad, Mahmud (Tunuslu Mahmut Paşa), *21*, 235, 239, 243; death of, 204, 210; debts from Nissim alleged by, 70, 76, 91; dodgy practices of, 24–25, 60, 63; estate of, 204–5, 210, 226; French citizenship taken by, 70–71; as Nissim's patron, 19–20
Ibn 'Ayyad, Muhammad, 20, 43, 239
Ibn 'Ayyad, Subiha, 204
Ibn 'Ayyad, Tahir, 204, 205
Ibn Diyaf (Ahmad Ibn Abi al-Diyaf), 59–60, 234, 240
Ibn Isma'il, Mustafa, 179, 184–86, 187, 195
Ikbal (concubine of Ibn 'Ayyad), 204
Inghilleri, Calcedonio, 196–99
Institute of International Law, 123, 125, 126, 147, 148, 151, 152, 173
International Financial Commission, 59–60, 88–89, 90, 186–87, 235
international law, 28, 117, 120–25, 146–52, 164, 166–67, 169, 173
Israel and Humanity (Benamozegh), 193
Isserlis, Moshe, 308n78
Italy: extraterritorial jurisdiction of, 41; migration from, 45, 46, 74, 134, 213; nationality law of, 117, 119, 125–27, 130–33, 149–50, 158, 163, 166, 170, 176, 179, 181, 213; Tunisia coveted by, 156, 195; unification of, 17–18, 39, 45, 71–72, 85, 86, 108, 121, 130, 133–34, 165–67
Itier, Rose, 214, 242
ius commune, 166, 171, 172, 174–75

Jarmon, Yehudah, 194–95
Jewish law. See *halakhah*

"The Jewish State" (Herzl), 161
jizya (capitation tax), 15, 20, 28, 53, 144
Judeo-Arabic, 19
Julien, Charles-André, 237
jus sanguinis, 130, 288n59, 317n61
jus soli, 317n61
Justinian Code, 171

Kahane, Moshe, 281n63
Khayraddin (Hayreddin Pasha, Khayr al-Din), 92, 102, 103, 120, 144, 210, 235, 237; as foreign minister, 100, 236; Khaznadar vs., 113, 116, 236; Villet linked to, 89, 236
Khaznadar, al-Munji, 68
Khaznadar, Muhammad, *26*, 52, 68, 91
Khaznadar, Mustafa, xiv, xvii, xviii, 25, *26*, 31, 34, 35, 47, 89, 104, 105, 113, 240, 241, 243; accession as finance minister of, 20; corruption accusations against, 60, 90, 235, 237; government finances and, 52, 60, 65, 67, 88, 102; Khayraddin's discrediting of, 116; Nissim's letters from abroad to, 63, 64, 65, 67, 74, *82*, 91–92; Nissim's tensions with, 59, 67–68, 70, 76–77; promulgation of the Rescript of Reform backed by, 30; pursuit of alleged debts owed by Nissim's estate, 113–14
Kingdom of the Two Sicilies, 120–23
King James Bible, 162
Kinyan (ritual acquisition), 80, 111–12, 189, 193
kulughlis, 18
"Kulun," Monsieur, 47

Lasinio, Fausto, 312n120
Laurent, François, 148, 194
legal belonging, 1–2, 4; by birth vs. choice, 128–29; conventional views of, 5–6; extraterritoriality and, 13, 18, 37, 40, 44, 46, 70, 148, 149, 155; Husayn ibn 'Abdallah's view of, 136, 138, 140–42, 155, 198, 209–10; indeterminacy of, 6, 7, 106, 110, 139, 156, 199, 200, 203, 226–29; Jewish identity and, 3, 110, 142, 159, 192, 217, 229–30; in Muslim states, 138; narrative linked to, 8–9, 157; nationalism linked to, 3, 119, 136, 225, 229; official definitions of, 27, 29, 46, 47, 139–40, 153; welfare state and, 231. *See also* citizenship; nationality
legal positivism, 146, 148, 149
Lellouche, Esther (wife), 49, 58, 62, 65, 74, 79, 135, 241
Lellouche, Haim, 49, 65, 241
Lellouche, Jacob, 234
Le Roy (lawyer), 75, 79, 80
Le Soufaché, Joseph-Michel-Anne, 271n48
Lev, Mordekhai b. Aryeh, 281n63
Le Vacher, Jean, 39
Levy, Judah, 89
Levy, Moses, 89
Livornine, 162–63
Lorimer, James, 151–52
Louis XV, king of France, 68
Luchino, Odoardo, 250n15
Lumbroso, Abraham, xv, 62, 242, 278n13
Lumbroso, Giacomo "Coco," 61–65, 242
Lumbroso, Isaac Vita, 242

maḥalla, 16
Mahmud Bey, 45
Mahmud II, Sultan, 22, 23, 210
Mailher de Chassat, Antoine, 285–86n25
Maimonides, Moses, 65
Malta, 39–40, 42, 45, 46, 225
mamlūks, 18
Mancini, Grazia, 123, 242
Mancini, Pasquale Stanislao, 138, 149, 150, 152, 154, 180, 183, 185, 188, 199, 221; expatriation right viewed by, 146–48, 155; "good faith" argument of, 133; Jewish distinctiveness conceded by, 167–68, 169, 177; Jewish law dismissed by, 159, 167, 170–76, 190, 194, 197, 198; Jewish nationhood rejected by, 159, 168, 169–70, 176; nationality principle of, 119, 121–25, 126, 130, 131, 136, 159, 160, 165–73, 211; Nissim's Livornese ancestry asserted by, 127–28, 132, 199; as Pierantoni's mentor,

Mancini, Pasquale Stanislao (*continued*) 119, 121, 122–23; Renan linked to, 130; Risorgimento supported by, 121; in Shamama appeal, 178; Shamama work ceased by, 179, 195, 197
Martens, Georg Friedrich von, 148
Maurogonato, Isacco Pesaro, 159–60
Mawlay Hasan, 297n82
Mayer, François, 184–85
Medici, Ferdinando di, 162
Memmi, Albert, 49
Mendelssohn, Moses, 190, 310n92
The Messiah According to the Jews (Castelli), 191
Meyer, Maurice, 35
migration, 39–40, 42
Moati, Nine, 233–34
Montelativi, Anita, 219–20
Montesquieu, Charles de Secondat, Baron de, 125
Morocco, 31, 229, 315n35
Morpurgo, Carlo Marco, 44, 67
Mortara, Edgardo, 168
Mortara, Marco, 160, 165–66
Mortara, Momolo, 168
Muhammad (governor of A'rād), 32
Muhammad 'Ali (Mehmet 'Ali), governor of Egypt, 22, 156
Muhammad Bey, 62, 242; accession of, 27; 'Ahd al-Amān issued by, 30–32, 50; death of, 32; Rescript of Reform and, 29–30
Muratori, Pietro, 124
Mussalli, Elias, 67, 235
Mussolini, Benito, 219, 220

Napoleon Bonaparte, 22, 75, 145
Napoleonic Code, 285–86n25
Napoleon III, 63
Natan, Shim'on, 47
nationality: citizenship compared with, 138–40; documentary proof of, 6–7; ethnocultural form of, 3, 122, 131–32, 159; French law of, 24–25, 63, 70–71, 72, 79, 117, 128–29, 142, 149, 161, 205, 207, 208–9, 213, 218; importance of, 223, 224; Islamic law of, 141–42, 153; Italian law of, 117, 119, 125–27, 130–33, 149–50, 158, 163, 166, 170, 176, 179, 181, 213; Judaism as, 3, 158–61, 163–67, 168, 170–71, 174, 176–77, 230; Mancini's principle of, 119, 122–25, 126, 130, 131, 136, 159, 160, 165–73, 211; by marriage, 117, 147, 148–49, 218; "nation" distinguished from, 162–63; Ottoman law of, 47, 140–41, 148, 205; reputation and social embeddedness linked to, 135–36; statelessness and, 117–19, 126, 138, 149, 158, 188, 190, 223; Tunisian law of, 5. *See also* citizenship; legal belonging
Nationality as the Foundation for the Law of Nations (Mancini), 167, 169
natural law, 123, 137, 146–50, 152–55, 157, 178, 188, 197
Nazis, 217, 218, 223
Netherlands, 41
Nissim, Cesare, 250n1
Nissim, Raffael, 308n68
niẓāmī, 23, 24
Noailles, Emmanuel Henri Victurnien, marquis de, 205

Observations on the Sentence of the Court of Florence (Castelli), 203
Les origines du protectorat français en Tunisie (Ganiage), 237
oriundi italiani, 130–31, 132, 199
Osman Khaleb Bey, 311n113
Ottolenghi, Silvio, 223
Ottoman Empire, 5, 7, 24; capitulations in, 37, 40–42, 46, 70, 106, 210; expatriation law of, 47, 148, 205; French incursions into, 17; French subjects in, 41; indebtedness of, 51–52; internal mobility limited by, 255–56n38; Jewish loyalists in, 176–77; nationality law of, 47, 140–41, 148, 205; Orthodox rebels and, 22; Rescript of Reform in, 27–30, 31; Russian Empire vs., 27; Treaty of Paris and, 150

Pact of ʿUmar, 144, 257n5, 261n67, 297n82
Paoli, Baldassare, 196–97
Pasqualigo, Francesco, 159–60, 164, 166
passports, 7, 45, 84, 134
Pereire, Emile, 271n48
Peridon, Adolphe, 181, 183
Pierantoni, Augusto Francescopaolo, 135–42, 149, 151, 156, 168, 188, 221; anticlericalism of, 164, 165, 167; expatriation right disputed by, 137, 146, 148, 150, 152–55, 157; Husayn's retention of, 124; Institute of International Law cofounded by, 123, 125, 147; Jewish nationality rejected by, 158, 164; as Mancini's disciple, 119, 122, 123; Risorgimento supported by, 120–21, 123; in Shamama appeal, 178; Shamama work ceased by, 179, 195; Tunisian Jews' equality disputed by, 145–46, 197
Pinard, Alphonse, 306–7n51
Pinna, Luigi, 58, 103–6, 149, 242
Pirenne, Henri, 320–21n2
private international law, 119, 124–25, 173, 211
Pompadour, Jeanne Antoinette Poisson, marquise de, 68
polygamy, 173, 212
privateers, 39
Prussia, 254n26
Pufendorf, Samuel Freiherr von, 147
Purcell, Nicholas, 320–21n2

Qānūn al-Dawla (1861), 46–48, 149, 154–55, 156, 171, 174, 197
Qaramanli dynasty, 23
Quran, 15, 59, 139, 141, 144, 145, 153

rabbinic courts (*batei din*), 16, 28, 34, 43
Raffo, Joseph, 265n39
Ramel (plaintiff), 75
Remus, Joseph-Marius, 217–18
Renan, Ernest, 129–30, 131, 136, 189
Rescript of Reform (*hatt-i hümayun*), 27–30, 31
Ricasoli, Bettino, 86, 165
Rignano, Isacco, xiv, xv, 317n73
Rochefort, Henri, 236
Romania, 7
Roman law, 136, 166, 172, 188, 316n46
Rosa, Eugène Cohen, 314n22
Rosenthal, Franz, 252n15
Rossini, Gioachino, 126
Rothschild, James, Baron de, xiv
Roustan, Théodor, 236
Russia, 5, 22, 27, 148

Saadoun, Masʿud, 314n26
Saadoun, Rachel, 314n26
Sadiq Bey, 33, 48, 58, 62, 63, 89, 143, 195, 242; accession of, 32, 34; d'Erlanger's demands on, 91; economic realities facing, 50–51, 55–57, 88–89; extraterritoriality and, 45; *Qānūn al-Dawla* issued by, 46, 50
Saʿid Pasha, 51–52
Salmon, Corinna Coen, 180–81, *182*, 243
Salmon, Saul Coen, 180–81
Salzmann, Ariel, 252n17
Samama, Nissim (Nissim Jr.) (great-great-nephew), 57–58, 61, 62, 68, 81, 83, 119, 242, 243; death of, 217; legal career of, 211–13; as will beneficiary, xvi, 78, 183, 198
Santillana, Moses, 89
Savigny, Friedrich Carl von, 286n28, 287n37, 309n90
Scemama de Gialluly, Emilie, 212, 242, 317n65
Scemama de Gialluly, Liahu, 212
Selim II, Sultan, 41
Semama, Elia (great-nephew), 116, 180, 219–21, 223
Semama, Salvadore Yeoshua de Biniamin, 289n64
Senor (Señor), Abraham, 175
Sephardi Jews, 43–44, 163, 226
Sfez (Sfāz), Shmuel ("Bāṭū"), 29–30
Shamama, Abramo Alberto (Abraham) (great-nephew), 106, 215–17

Shamama, Albertina (great-great-niece), 216
Shamama, Annamaria, 220 (great-great-niece), 220
Shamama, ʿAziza (née Krief) (mother), 19
Shamama, ʿAziza "Zeza" (great-niece), xiii–xv, xviii, 36, 61, 62, 68, 81, *83*, 95, 98, 107, 178, 200, 211–12, 214, *215*, 239; marriage of, 49; rights to estate surrendered by, 181, 183; as will beneficiary, 78, 108, 110–11, 113, 119, 124, 179, 190, 195, 243
Shamama, Carlo (great-nephew), 219
Shamama, Daya (Gozlan; wife of nephew Joseph), 106, 116, 180, 220, 243
Shamama, Daya (great-great-niece), 216, 219
Shamama, Emily (great-great-niece), 181
Shamama, Esther (great-niece), 101–6, 243
Shamama, Esther (stepdaughter), 36, 239
Shamama, Giuliana (great-great-great-niece), 219
Shamama, Giuseppe (great-great- nephew), 220, 221, 223
Shamama, Iolanda (great-great-niece), 220
Shamama, Leone (great-great-great-nephew), 219
Shamama, Isaac Hai (uncle), 19
Shamama, Isaac Jacques (great-great-nephew), 218
Shamama, Jacob (Nissim's cousin and secretary), 69, 79, 269n18, 272n72
Shamama, Joseph (cousin in Marseille), 62, 75, 83
Shamama, Joseph (nephew), 149, 178, 181, 243; Abramo and family supported by, 216–17; inheritance relinquished by, 183; Italian citizenship sought by, 214–15, 233; Nissim's will contested by, xvii, xviii, 98, 102, 107, 108, 111, 180; as will beneficiary, xvi, 78, 100–101, 103–6, 132, 196, 309n80
Shamama, Judah (brother), 101
Shamama, Judah (nephew), 78
Shamama, Leonetto (great-nephew), 181
Shamama, Maria Giovanna (great-great-niece), 220
Shamama, Masʿuda (niece), 283n85
Shamama, Masʿuda Elmaya "Semha" (wife), xv, xvi, xviii, 36, 48, 58, 68, 74, 178; death of, 116; as will beneficiary, 78, 107, 243
Shamama, Moses (husband of ʿAziza), xiii, 49, 58, 61, 62, 68, 81, *83*, 95, 98, 107, 115, 178, 211–14, 243; as will beneficiary, 108, 109–11, 113, 119, 124, 132, 179, 181, 183, 190, 195
Shamama, Moshe (cousin), 35, 239
Shamama, Moshe Bishi b. Yaʿakov, 48
Shamama, Nathan (brother), 25, 67
Shamama, Nathan (great-nephew), 106, 147, 178; marriage of, 180–81; Nissim's will contested by, xvii, xviii, 98, 102, 107, 108, 111, 180; as will beneficiary, xvi, 78, 100–101, 103–6, 132, 243
Shamama, Nathan Donat (great-great-nephew), 218
Shamama, Nissim, 243–44; as bey's adviser, 25; birth of, 14; claims against estate of, 113; death of, xiii–xv, 95; extraterritoriality and, 47, 69–71; family tree of, *x–xi*; fraud accusations against, 90; government debt purchased by, 50–51, 52, 104; growing influence of, 25, 34; Italian citizenship claimed by, 44, 59, 72, 74, 91, 117–36; Jewish community led by, 34; Jewish "nationality" imputed to, 3, 158–61, 163–67, 170–71, 174, 176–77; lawsuits against, 75–76; Livornese ancestry claimed by, 45, 71–72, 126–28, 131–32, 136; in Livorno, 85–87, 91; marriages of, 35–36, 74; in Paris, 39, 58–59, 63–68, 83–85; as philanthropist, 34–35, 79, 227, 231; posthumous reputation of, 233–38; power as attraction for, 19–20; properties of, 35, 37, *38*, 49–50, *69*, 77, *80*, 81; reimbursements sought by, 68, 76–77; statelessness imputed to, 117–18, 120; as tax farmer, 20, 22, 25, 34, 60; tomb of, 95, *96–97*, 98; wealth of, 6, 99–100, 227; will drafting by, 78
Shamama, Nissim (great-nephew), 106

Shamama, Salvatore (great-nephew), 116, 180, 219
Shamama, Samuel, 258n26
Shamama, Shlomo (father), 19
Shamama, Shlomo (grandson of Samuel), 258n26
Shamama, Shlomo (nephew of Mas'uda), 107, 108, 116, 178, 244
Shamama, Solomon "Momo" (nephew), xvi–xvii, xviii, 36, 67, 68, 77, 178, 239, 243; death of, 218; family resentment toward, 107; mint headed by, 25; Nissim's will contested by, 98, 101–2, 108, 111; as will beneficiary, 78, 100–101, 103, 105–6, 196, 244
Shamama, Umberto (great-nephew), 221
Shamama, Yitzhaq, 258n26
shari'a, 4, 15, 42, 138, 144, 153, 157, 206
Shoresh Yishai (Shlomo Shamama), 19
Shulḥan 'Arukh (Caro), 194, 198, 216–17
Sicily, 37, 39, 42, 225
Sidi Mahriz, 14–15
Sitruk, Judah, 69, 79
Slidell, Marguerite Mathilde, 53
Società di Beneficenza Italiana, 74
Spain, 153
Spezzafumo, Domenico, 102, 114, 184, 186, 244
statelessness, 117–19, 126, 138, 149, 158, 188, 190, 223
Stracca, Vittoria Ida, 215–17
Suez Canal, 17, 62, 240, 241
sumptuary laws, 15, 32, 44, 144
The Surest Path to Knowledge (Khayraddin), 89
Sweden, 41
Tanzimat reforms, 204, 252–53n18
Tapia, Mordekhai, 48
Tausch, Giuseppe, 17
Tausch, Pietro, 18, 239
Telfener, Giuseppe, 185–86
Treaty of Bardo (1881), 18, 195, 208, 209
Treaty of Paris (1856), 27–28, 150
Tripolitania, 17, 23
Trollope, Anthony, 53
Tulin, Charles, 90–91
Tunis en France (anonymous), 236–37
Tunuslu Mahmut Paşa. *See* Mahmud Ibn 'Ayyad
Turco, Hamet Neyal, 98
The Turkish Woman (Hayriye Ibn 'Ayyad), 205
Tuscany, 44–45
Twansa Jews, 44, 71, 100, 132, 233

umma, 4
Universal Declaration of Human Rights, 223

Vigliani, Paolo Onorato, 188
Villet, Victor, 60, 89, 90, 91, 116, 235–38
Vita, Isaac, 61
Vitali, Eugenio, 250n1
vital records, 6–7, 127, 132
Vittorio Emanuele II, king of Italy, 71, 72, 109–10, 117, 133, 135
Vogorides, Stephanos, 314n30

The Way We Live Now (Trollope), 53

Zagdun, Shalom, 69, 79
Zionism, 160–61, 167, 176, 177, 230
Zirio, Michel, 181, 183
Zubayda (concubine of Ibn 'Ayyad), 204
Zwawa (tribespeople), 57

A NOTE ON THE TYPE

This book has been composed in Arno, an Old-style serif typeface in the classic Venetian tradition, designed by Robert Slimbach at Adobe.

GPSR Authorized Representative: Easy Access System Europe - Mustamäe tee 50, 10621 Tallinn, Estonia, gpsr.requests@easproject.com

www.ingramcontent.com/pod-product-compliance
Lightning Source LLC
Chambersburg PA
CBHW020828160426
43192CB00007B/561
* 9 7 8 0 6 9 1 2 3 7 1 3 8 *